Honoré M. Catudal
Nuclear Deterrence — Does it Deter?

Previous publications, Honoré (Marc) Catudal:

Steinstücken: A Study in Cold War Politics (New York: Vantage Press, 1971). Foreword by General Lucius D. Clay

The Exclave Problem of Western Europe (Alabama: University of Alabama Press, 1979). Foreword by Eleanor L. Dulles

The Diplomacy of the Quadripartite Agreement on Berlin (West Berlin: Berlin Verlag Arno Spitz, 1977). Foreword by Ambassador Kenneth Rush

A Balance Sheet of the Quadripartite Agreement on Berlin (West Berlin: Berlin Verlag Arno Spitz, 1978). Foreword by Ambassador Kenneth Rush

Kennedy and the Berlin Wall Crisis: A Case Study in U.S. Decision-Making (West Berlin: Berlin Verlag Arno Spitz, 1980). Foreword by Ambassador Martin J. Hillenbrand

Honoré M. Catudal

Nuclear Deterrence — Does it Deter?

Foreword by
Ambassador Martin J. Hillenbrand

HUMANITIES PRESS *INTERNATIONAL, INC.*
ATLANTIC HIGHLANDS, NEW JERSEY 07716

Originally published 1985 by Berlin Verlag

©1985 BERLIN VERLAG Arno Spitz

First published 1986 in the United States of America by
Humanities Press International, Inc., Atlantic Highlands, N.J. 07716

LIBRARY OF CONGRESS CATALOGING IN PUBLICATION DATA

Catudal, Honoré Marc, 1944 -
   Nuclear deterrence—does it deter?

   Bibliography: p.
   Includes index.
   1. Deterrence (Strategy)   2. Nuclear warfare.
3. United States—Military policy.   4. Soviet Union—
Military policy.   5. Strategic forces.   I. Title.
U162.6.C38   1986   355'.0217   85-30524
ISBN 0-391-03390-5
ISBN 0-391-03391-3 (pbk.)

All rights reserved.

MANUFACTURED IN THE UNITED STATES OF AMERICA

Read not to contradict nor to believe,
but to weigh and consider
>Francis Bacon
>*Essays* (1597)

To my daughter, Sandy

CONTENTS

Chart of Postwar U.S. Deterrent Strategies   14
Deployment of Nuclear Weapons — U.S./U.S.S.R.   21
List of Abbreviations   24
Preface   27
Acknowledgements   28
Foreword   31

I. INTRODUCTION: THE ILLUSION OF NUCLEAR SECURITY

    Deterrence as a Panacea   37
    The Danger of Nuclear War   39
    The Threat Posed by Large Stocks of Nuclear Weapons   40
    Summary   42

SECTION I
THE DOCTRINE AND STRATEGIES OF NUCLEAR DETERRENCE

II. DEADLY LOGIC

    Strategic Thinking and Public Reaction   47
    Three Types of Deterrence Strategies   50
    A Status Quo Doctrine   51
    Deterrence and Diplomacy   52
    Deterrence Old and New   52
    The Notion of Rationality   56
    Arguments For and Against Rationality   60
    The Role of Perception   62
    The Idea of Sufficiency   65
    The Notion of Fear   66
    The Notion of Credibility   66
    Ambiguity of Deterrence Doctrine   69

	Problem of Arms Promotion	70
	Game Theoretical Assumptions	70
	Problem of Empirical Verification	73
	Problem of Projecting a "Devil Image"	73
	Summary	75
III.	**THE ORIGINS OF U.S. NUCLEAR DETERRENCE POLICY**	
	U.S. Nuclear Supremacy	81
	The Containment Policy	83
	Conventional Imbalance in Europe	84
	Deterrence by Improvisation	86
	Impact of First Soviet Atomic Test	89
	Development of the H-Bomb	91
	NSC-68	92
	Reassessing the Soviet Threat	95
	Soviet Behavior in the Early Postwar Period	96
	Summary	97
IV.	**THE CHANGING DETERRENCE POSTURE**	
	Strategic Developments in the Early 1950s	102
	The "New Look"	103
	"Massive Retaliation"	105
	Strategic Vulnerability	108
	"Graduated Deterrence"	110
	"Flexible Response"	112
	NATO Implementation of "Flexible Response"	116
	A Critique of the Strategy	118
	Summary	120
V.	**FROM MAD TO NUTS**	
	The Impact of the "Missile Gap"	131
	The Development of the Triad	134
	The Single Integrated Operations Plan	140
	"No-Cities" Doctrine	141
	Assured Destruction	142
	Mutual Assured Destruction	144
	"Counterforce" Strategy	146
	Declaratory Versus Action Policy	149

From Superiority to Sufficiency 150
Sufficiency Versus Finite Deterrence 152
"Flexible Targeting" 156
A Return to "Counterforce" Strategy 160
Improving Delivery Systems and Warheads 161
Problems of Missile Accuracy in Wartime 161
Expanding U.S. "Nuclear War-Fighting" Capability — PD-59 163
Prevailing in a Nuclear War? 169
"Horizontal Escalation" 174
Capacity for a "Simultaneity" of Wars 177
Summary 179

VI. SOVIET VIEWS OF DETERRENCE 188

An American View of the Soviet Mind 189
Differing Conceptual Perceptions 190
The Abstract Nature of Western Military Doctrines 192
The Status Quo Nature of Deterrence Theory 193
The Self-Constrained Nature of Western Doctrines of War 195
The Correlation of Forces Versus the Balance of Power 198
Soviet Emphasis on Deterrence by Denial 201
The Notion of Mutuality 203
Soviet View of Pershing II and Cruise Missile Deployment 205
Summary 208

SECTION II
THE NUCLEAR DETERRENCE STRATEGIES OF NATO

VII. THE EVOLUTION OF NATO'S NUCLEAR DEFENSE

The Early Postwar Period 215
Implementation of "Massive Retaliation" 218
A Change to "Flexible Response" 219
A Joint NATO Nuclear Force? 221
The Question of Conventional Superiority 224
Quantity Versus Quality? 227
Soviet Military Weaknesses 230
The Nuclear Picture in Europe Today 234
Current Guidelines on NATO Nuclear Use 240

	Precision Guided Munitions	243
	Summary	244
VIII.	THE NO FIRST USE DEBATE	
	The "Foreign Affairs" Debate	247
	Haig and Jones Argue Against the No First Use Concept	248
	No First Use Pledge by the Soviet Union	249
	"Foreign Affairs" Debate Continues	250
	Reactions to McNamara's Nuclear Assessment	254
	Report by the Union of Concerned Scientists	254
	Henry Kissinger Joins the Debate	258
	A New Role for Europe	259
	Allied Reaction to Kissinger's Proposals	262
	Emphasis on European Responsibility	263
	Summary	265
IX.	THE EUROSTRATEGIC CONTROVERSY	273
	Eurostrategic Forces	274
	Characteristics of the Pershings and Cruise Missiles	276
	The SS-20 Threat	279
	The Politics of the Dual-Track Decision	284
	The INF Negotiations	287
	The Walk-in-the-Woods Agreement	291
	A New Soviet Proposal	293
	Allied Criticism	295
	A Crucial Election in Germany	298
	The Modified Zero Option Proposal	300
	A Test of NATO Unity?	302
	Shooting Down of the Korean Airliner	303
	The Soviet Walkout from the INF Talks	304
	The SS-20 Missile Threat Reconsidered	305
	Pershing IIs Versus Crisis Stability	306
	Launch on Warning Threat	308
	Does LRTNF Deter?	310
	Anti-Nuclear Missile Movements in Warsaw Pact Countries	311
	Summary	313

SECTION III
THE UBIQUITY OF NUCLEAR DETERRENCE

X. CHAIN OF COMMAND AND COMMUNICATION PROBLEMS

The Worldwide Military Command and Control System	325
The Chain of Command	329
Communications with Ballistic Missile Submarines	333
Strategic Air Command	338
Land-Based ICBMs	342
The Delegation of Presidential Authority	345
Launch on Warning	347
The Soviet Launching Set-up	350
Vulnerability of C^3I Systems	352
Summary	353
A Proposal to Ensure Central Command Authority	358

XI. DETERRENCE MOVES INTO SPACE

The ABM Controversy	360
The ABM Issue in Historical Perspective	361
The Implications of Reagan's Proposal	367
Background to Reagan's Decision	369
Scientific Recommendations	373
A Lesson from History	375
Antisatellite Weapons	376
Reagan's Decision	380
Deterrence, ABM Defense and Nuclear War-Fighting	382
Summary	384

XII. THE BOOMERANG EFFECT   392

Putting Things into Perspective	393
Overcoming Resistance	394
Long-Term Effects of Nuclear War	394
Some Policy Implications	396
The "Nuclear-Winter" Debate	398
The Soviet View	400
Studying the Effects of Nuclear Weapons	404
The EMP Effect	405
Ozone Depletion	408

The Uselessness of Nuclear Weapons	408
Summary	410

XIII. CIVIL DEFENSE

The Case for Civil Defense	412
The Case against Civil Defense	415
Experience with Civil Defense in the 1960s	417
Civil Defense in the Reagan Administration	419
CIA's Analysis of Soviet Civil Defense Efforts	424
Summary	428

SECTION IV
CASE STUDIES OF NUCLEAR DETERRENCE

XIV. THE FIRST ATOMIC BOMBING — 433

The A-Bomb as a Psychological Weapon	435
The Selection of Japan Rather Than Germany	438
Summary	439

XV. THE KOREAN WAR

Prelude: Game Theories	443
"Chicken"	443
Pascal's Wager: Purposeful Uncertainty	443
The Conflict Begins	445
China's Decision to Enter the Korean War	449
Atomic Bombs on Manchuria?	453
Eisenhower Threatens Use of A-Bombs to Gain a Truce	455
New Documents on 1953 Korean Atomic Policy	457
Summary	459

XVI. THE CUBAN MISSILE CRISIS — 462

Compellance Versus Deterrence	463
Background to the Crisis	464
The Time Element	466
The Human Factor	469
The Bureaucratic Factor	470
Asymmetry of Motivation	474

The Secret Compromise	475
Conventional Superiority	478
The Risk of War	479
Summary	481

XVII. THE BALANCE OF TERROR: AN APPRAISAL   485

SECTION V
APPENDICES

I.	Letter by Dean Rusk on the Korean War	493
II.	New Documents on U.S. Nuclear Policy in the Korean War	495
III.	What We Can Do: McNamara's Proposals	499

BIBLIOGRAPHY	504
INDEX	523

LIST OF ILLUSTRATIONS

1	B-1 Aircraft	53
2	Checking a Minuteman III intercontinental ballistic missile in its silo (Whiteman Air Force Base, Missouri)	137
3	Construction of a nuclear powered Trident submarine, the USS Michigan, at Croton, Connecticut	175
4	Launching of a Pershing II missile on a long-range flight from Cape Canaveral, Florida	207
5	Refueling of a U.S. Air Force B-1 prototype by a KC-135 tanker aircraft	261
6	Launching of a BGM-109 ground launched cruise missile (GLCM)	297
7	A Polaris submarine, the USS John Marshall	335

Chart of Postwar U.S. Deterrent Strategies[1]

U.S. Strategy	Implemented	Proclaimed Administration	Description	Reasons for Change	Comments
City busting	1947	1948 Truman	Deterrence of attack on U.S. vital interests rests on drastic threat of atomic destruction. Supported by plans to use SAC bombers to destroy largest Soviet urban-industrial centers.	Strategy developed in improvised fashion. Major advantage was it played to U.S. strength and Soviet weakness. Offered relatively cheap way (politically and economically) to maintain peace and freedom of Western Europe.	Until 1947, U.S. military planning was based on bombs and bombers that did not exist. Subsequently, what had been implicit assumption of some theorists became explicit principle of military planning.
Extended deterrence	1947	1948 (in Western Europe)	Use of nuclear power by U.S. to protect non-nuclear allies.	Developed to protect Western Europe against Soviet Union which was believed to possess overwhelming conventional superiority.	Soviet conventional superiority in Europe greatly exaggerated after World War II. 7,000 U.S. tactical nuclear warheads eventually stationed in Western Europe.

1 This chart distinguishes between the declaratory (i.e. publicly articulated) deterrent policies of the United States and its action policies (i.e. those actually reflected on the level of war plans). Frequently, a deterrent strategy was implemented by an administration before it was announced publicly. Also, just because a new strategy was publicly proclaimed did not necessarily mean that it was actually adopted, e.g. "assured destruction." Moreover, the adoption of a new strategy did not necessarily mean that the previous one was now obsolete.

Massive retaliation	1953	Eisenhower/ Dulles (1954)	Deterrence of different forms of possible aggression to be achieved by threat to launch all-out nuclear retaliation.	Fiscal considerations played major role in adoption. U.S. experience in Korean War also important.	U.S. now possessed large stockpile of atomic bombs. Credibility problem because efficacy of massive, undifferentiated nuclear threat not believable at least in influencing resolution of minor issues.
Graduated deterrence	...	...	Local aggression to be deterred by making it sufficiently costly to initiator so as not to be worthwhile. Aim to develop a form of limited nuclear war that would deter future Korean-size offensives.	Hotly debated in 1950s but never became official U.S. doctrine. Proponents hoped to develop form of limited nuclear war strategy to deter future Korean-size offensives.	Rested on U.S. nuclear superiority, especially in tactical nuclear weapons. Punishment should fit crime. Emphasis on military rather than civilian targets. Doctrine suffered because distinction between limited and general nuclear war not so clear cut.
Flexible response	early 1960s	1967 (by NATO) Johnson/ McNamara	Aggression to be deterred by capability to respond at all levels, including possible use of nuclear weapons.	Gave U.S. more options in conflict. Reduced reliance on nuclear weapons.	Rested on substantial increase in conventional forces. Suffered in Europe because necessary military buildup never took place.

U.S. Strategy	Implemented	Proclaimed Administration	Description	Reasons for Change	Comments
City avoidance (predicated on "damage limitation" or "counterforce" strategy)	1961	1962 Kennedy/ McNamara	Adversary to be deterred by threatened destruction of his military forces, not civilian population.	Gave U.S. more options in conflict, e.g., U.S. could respond to Soviet nuclear attack in Europe without necessarily initiating mutual exchange of attacks against cities. Said to provide more credible threat because USSR seen as placing higher value on its military forces.	Based on U.S. nuclear superiority. For first time portion of U.S. nuclear force to be held in reserve. Envisaged massive targeting of Soviet strategic forces and possibility that U.S. might launch first.
Assured destruction (formerly "assured retaliation")	...	1964 Kennedy/ McNamara	Deterrence rests on retaining capability to inflict "unacceptable damage" on adversary even after absorbing surprise nuclear attack.	Growing U.S. missile superiority. Allowed U.S. planners to establish quantitative criteria for determining size, characteristics and effectiveness of U.S. nuclear forces. Never incorporated by McNamara and successors as action policy.	Second-strike capability that could devastate USSR now officially part of deterrence policy. Unacceptable damage defined in various ways, e.g. 20-30% of Soviet population and 50-75% of industrial capacity.

Mutual assured destruction (MAD)	...	mid-1960s Johnson/ McNamara	Deterrence now rests on ability of both sides to destroy each other even after they have been attacked first.	Saved money because U.S. did not have to strive for nuclear superiority. Provided incentive for seeking arms limitations agreements.	Accepted Soviet parity with U.S. Populations held hostage while planners continued to develop other targeting options. Questionable whether USSR ever subscribed to.
Sufficiency	...	1969 Nixon/ Kissinger	Deterrence to be achieved by U.S. strategic power which would not be allowed to become inferior to that of Soviet Union.	Nixon administration inherited much larger nuclear force than needed to destroy USSR and China. Policy provided rationale for not having constantly to increase nuclear power. Created basis for mutual restraint.	Rough strategic parity of U.S.-USSR strategic forces now emphasized. Various targeting strategies pursued. Concept suffered greatly from its ambiguity.
Finite deterrence (also known as "minimum deterrence")	...	...	Deterrence to be achieved by maintaining only a minimum level of nuclear force which would inflict "unacceptable damage."	Never implemented.	Rejects all but a counter-city targeting strategy. Populations held hostage. Problem that sudden breakthrough in technology could jeopardize deterrent.

U.S. Strategy	Implemented	Proclaimed Administration	Description	Reasons for Change	Comments
Flexible targeting (or "selective options")	early 1970s	1974 Nixon/ Schlesinger	Deterrence to be achieved by developing wider range of strategic options against military targets.	Gave U.S. more options. Provided way in which U.S. surplus of warheads could be put to "good" use.	Represents revival of counterforce strategy. Assumes nuclear war can be kept limited.
Countervailing	late 1970s	1980 Carter/ Brown	Deterrence of any scale of nuclear attack to be achieved by emphasizing limited strike options against political and economic targets rather than exclusively against military targets.	Hoped to convince Soviets that no use of nuclear weapons of any scale and at any stage of conflict could lead to victory. New policy seen as more "moral" (people not to be directly targeted).	Nuclear war-fighting capability strengthened. First time armed forces required to be able to fight prolonged nuclear war. Decapitation strategy emphasized.
Intrawar deterrence	1970s	...	Deterrence to take place after outbreak of nuclear war. Through "escalation dominance" U.S. would seek to maintain margin of superiority at each rung of escalation ladder.	Developed in context of emphasis on nuclear war-fighting.	Presupposes ability to negotiate after limited nuclear exchange in order to control further escalation, preserving non-military targets. Soviets do not officially subscribe to it.

Prevailing counter-force	1981 Reagan/Weinberger	USSR to be deterred by U.S. capability to fight and "prevail" in protracted nuclear war.	Developed to counter alleged Soviet belief in their ability to win nuclear war. Consistent with quest of Reagan Administration for nuclear superiority.	U.S. nuclear war-fighting strategy enhanced. First time armed forces required to be able to "prevail" in protracted nuclear war. Based on U.S. obtaining and maintaining nuclear superiority. Development of survivable command and control system given heavy emphasis.
Nuclear utilization target selection (NUTS)	1980s	. . .	Unofficial name given to various targeting strategies developed in context of emphasis on deterrence through development of nuclear war-fighting capability.	Enhanced nuclear war-fighting capability.	Assumes that nuclear weapons can be used in certain circumstances without unleashing catastrophic series of consequences.

U.S. strategy	Implemented	Proclaimed Administration	Description	Reasons for Change	Comments
Horizontal escalation	early 1980s	1983 Reagan/ Weinberger	Soviet attacks against vulnerable U.S. military interests to be deterred by threatening to retaliate against equally important and vulnerable Soviet interests.	Grew out of frustration with previous policy which was said to be cast just to react to Soviet aggression. Reagan Administration wanted to be able to limit Soviet activities abroad.	Aims to put Soviet interests at risk on all fronts to to divert Soviet leaders from aggressive plans. Emphasis is on conventional means but nuclear use not ruled out. Grenada invasion is first application.
Simultaneity	early 1980s	1983 Reagan/ Weinberger	Soviet aggression to be deterred by capability to fight on all fronts.	Developed out of fear that in major conflict with Soviets U.S. might not have time to shift forces from one region to another.	Implies U.S. can force multi-front war on USSR. Worst-case scenario envisions U.S. fighting major wars against USSR in Europe, Persian Gulf and brushfire conflict against Soviet proxies in El Salvador.

Table compiled by the author

Table:
Deployment of Nuclear Weapons — U.S./U.S.S.R.

State	Delivery System	Date Deployed	Approximate Range (km)
Intercontinental Ballistic Missiles (ICBMs)			
U.S.	Titan II	1962	11,500
	Minuteman II	1966	9,000
	Minuteman III/MK-12	1970	9,000
	Minuteman III/MK-12A	1979	9,000
	Peacekeeper-MX (forthcoming)	1986 (?)	11,000
USSR	SS-11	1966	10,500
	SS-11 (Model 3)	1973	
	SS-13	1969	8,000
	SS-17 (Model 1)	1977	10,000
	SS-17 (Model 2)	1977	10,000
	SS-18 (Models 1 & 3)	1975/76	12,000
	SS-18 (Model 2)	1977	12,000
	SS-18 (Model 4)	1979	12,000
Submarine-launched Ballistic Missiles (SLBMs)			
U.S.	Poseidon C-3	1970	4,600
	Trident C-4	1979	7,500
	Trident D-5 (forthcoming)	1990s (?)	11,500
USSR	SS-N-5	1964	1,200
	SS-N-6 (Models 1 & 2)	1968	2,900
	SS-N-6 (Model 3)	1973	2,900
	SS-N-8	1973	7,900
	SS-NX-17	1979	n.a.
	SS-N-18	1978	7,500
	SS-NX-20	1981	7,500
Long-Range Sea-launched Cruise Missiles (SLBMs)			
U.S.	BGM-109 Tomahawk	1984	2,500
USSR	SS-N-3 Shaddock	1962	700

State	Delivery System	Date Deployed	Approximate Range (km)
Long Range Strategic Bombers			
U.S.	B-52 C/D/E/F	1956	18,500
	B-52 G/H	1959	20,000
	FB-111A	1970	n.a.
	B-1B	1987	n.a.
USSR	M-4 Bison	1955	10,000
	Tu-95 Bear	1956	12,500
Air-launched Strategic Weapons			
U.S.	Bombs	early 1950s	n.a.
	Hound Dog ALCM	1961	1,000
	Tomahawk ALCM (forthcoming)	late 1980s	2,500
	SRAM	1972	150
USSR	Bombs	1950s	n.a.
	AS-3 Kangaroo ALCM	1961	650
	AS-4 Kitchen ALCM	1962	700
	AS-5 Kingfish ALCM	1977	n.a.
Ballistic Missile Defenses (BMDs)			
USSR	ABM-1 Galosh	1967	300
Medium Range Bombers			
U.S.	FB-111 E/F	1970	6,000
USSR	Tu-16 Badger	1955	4,800
	Tu-22 Blinder	1961	2,250
	Tu-22M Backfire	1974	3,400
Long Range Theater Missiles			
U.S.	Pershing II	1983	1,800
	Tomahawk GLCM	1983	2,500
USSR	SS-4	1959	1,800
	SS-5	1961	3,500
	SS-20	1977	5,000

State	Delivery System	Date Deployed	Approximate Range (km)
Strike Aircraft			
U.S.	F-4	1962	1,100
	A-6E	1963	n.a.
	A-7E	1966	n.á.
	F-16	1979	n.a.
USSR	Su-17	1970	n.a.
	Su-24	1974	n.a.
	MiG 23/27	1971	n.a.
Short Range Theater Missiles			
U.S.	Lance	1972	1,900
	Pershing IA	1962	700
USSR	FROG-series	1965	30-70
	SS-1c—Scud B	1965	300
	SS-12 Scaleboard	1969	800
	SS-22	1979	900
Artillery			
U.S.	M-110 203mm howitzer	1962	15-30
	M-109 155mm howitzer	1964	15-30

List of Abbreviations

ABM	Antiballistic Missile
AEC	Atomic Energy Commission
ALCM	Air Launched Cruise Missile
ASAT	Antisatellite Weapons System
BMEWS	Ballistic Missile Early Warning System
$C^3 I$	C-cubed-I (Command, Control, Communications and Intelligence)
CD	Civil Defense
CENTAG	Central Army Group (NATO)
CEP	Circle Error Probable
CIA	Central Intelligence Agency
DEFCON	Defense Readiness Condition
DOD	Department of Defense
DSP	Defense Support Program
EAM	Emergency Action Message
EMP	Electromagnetic Pulse
FRG	Federal Republic of Germany
GLCM	Ground Launched Cruise Missile
HLG	High Level Group
ICBM	Intercontinental Ballistic Missile
INF	Intermediate Range Nuclear Forces
IONDS	Integrated Operational Nuclear Detection System
IRBM	Intermediate Range Ballistic Missile
JCS	Joint Chiefs of Staff
JSTPS	Joint Strategic Target Planning Staff
KT	Kiloton

LOW	Launch on Warning
LRINF	Long Range Intermediate Range Nuclear Forces
LRTNF	Long Range Theater Nuclear Forces
LUA	Launch under Attack
MAD	Mutual Assured Destruction
MARV	Maneuverable Re-entry Vehicle
MBFR	Mutual and Balanced Force Reductions
MILSTAR	Military Strategic and Tactical Relay System
MIRV	Multiple Independently Targetable Re-entry Vehicle
MRBM	Medium Range Ballistic Missile
MRV	Multiple Re-entry Vehicle
MLF	Multilateral Nuclear Force
MT	Megaton
MX	Missile Experimental
NATO	North Atlantic Treaty Organization
NCA	National Command Authority
NEACP	National Emergency Airborne Command Post
NIE	National Intelligence Estimate
NMCC	National Military Command Center
NORAD	North American Aerospace Defense Command
NPG	Nuclear Planning Group
NSC	National Security Council
NSDD	National Security Decision Directive
NUTS	Nuclear Utilization Target Selection
OTA	Office of Technology Assessment
PACOM	Pacific Command
PAL	Permissive Action Links
PD	Presidential Directive
PGM	Precision Guided Munitions
PRC	People's Republic of China
QRA	Quick Reaction Alert Force
RDF	Rapid Deployment Force
SAC	Strategic Air Command
SACEUR	Supreme Allied Commander Europe
SALT	Strategic Arms Limitation Talks

SDI	Strategic Defense Initiative
SIOP	Single Integrated Operations Plan
SLBM	Submarine Launched Ballistic Missile
SNF	Short Range Nuclear Forces
SRINF	Short Range Intermediate Range Nuclear Forces
START	Strategic Arms Reduction Talks
TACAMO	"Take Charge and Move Out"
TNF	Tactical Nuclear Forces
USAEUR	United States Army Europe
USCENTCOM	United States Central Command
UN	United Nations
WWMCCS	Worldwide Military Command and Control System

PREFACE

This study of nuclear deterrence is the first of two volumes. The second book, which will soon follow, is entitled *Soviet Nuclear Strategy*, and attempts to examine the nature of the Soviet nuclear threat and how it has evolved over the years.

Too often in the past, U.S. officials, in shaping and directing plans for American nuclear forces have tended to see Soviet military forces and strategy as a reflection of their own stance or simply to project the worst plausible case of Soviet intentions and capabilities. The result has been a distorted if not dangerous portrayal of the real threat.

The present investigation, while drawing on some of my most important findings in the second volume, is limited to a study of the concept of nuclear deterrence and its evolution over the years. Basically, it demythologizes the notion long held by strategic thinkers that "you can't test a negative," and concludes that there is a growing body of evidence which suggests that *nuclear deterrence does not deter — at least not as we think it does*. This thesis is startling in its conclusion, even to this writer who once subscribed to the core concept of deterrence. It necessarily needs the detailed analysis provided in this text, followed by several relevant case studies.

For reasons of space, this book contains a somewhat incomplete bibliography. My sources, which are extensive, can be found in the footnotes. A longer, comprehensive bibliography is planned for volume two.

Collegeville, Minn. *Honoré Marc Catudal*
January, 1985

Acknowledgements

This book is the product of the efforts of many people. I am especially indebted to the numerous middle-level officials in the Department of State, CIA, the Defense Department and the U.S. Arms Control and Disarmament Agency who screened my drafts for errors of fact. Many disagreed strongly with my conclusions but were willing to read copy if only to change my mind or tone down my argumentation.

Those individuals to whom I owe a special debt and who may be named include the following: Abbot Jerome Theisen, O.S.B., who took a personal interest in this project, contributing a rebuttal to the application of Pascal's Wager to the issue of nuclear deterrence;

President Hilary Thimmesh, O.S.B., St. John's University, who supported my research and provided extra secretarial assistance;

Dean Robert L. Spaeth, the author of an important book on nuclear weapons, who funded my extensive photocopying efforts, diligently scrutinized various draft chapters and warned me about my enthusiasms;

Professor Joe Farry, my department chairman, colleague and good friend, whose repeated kindness, perceptive advice and general guidance have been instrumental in my career;

My other colleagues at St. John's University, who read copy, engaged me in continual dialogue and brought much important material to my attention, especially Ernie Diedrich, Marty Andrews, Sy Theisen, Lee Blaske, Otmar Drekonja, Dan Finn, Joe Friedrich, Larry Waldman, Jane Opitz, Gabriele Winkler, Bob Joyce, Robert Jensen, Dave Pollick, Steve Antholt, Gerald Kimball and Helen Rolfson.

Theodore M. Hesburgh, C.S.C., President of the University of Notre Dame, who took an early interest in this manuscript and saw that draft chapters were subjected to extensive critique by noted authorities;

Ambassador Martin J. Hillenbrand, who critiqued several drafts of the text, astutely guiding me away from shoals and keeping me within the limits of the evidence at hand, and who, above all, contributed a valuable foreword;

Dean Rusk, for his detailed critique of the Korean War chapter and helpful comments on other work;

Robert McNamara, for his kind permission to publish as an appendix his detailed and very constructive proposals on what can be done in the area of nuclear weapons;

General Andrew Goodpaster, President of the Institute for Defense Analyses, for his detailed criticism of those chapters on the Soviet approach;

General Bruce C. Clarke, former Commander in Chief of the U.S. Army in Europe, who commented on the European chapters reminding me that "one knows more than one understands";

Hodding Carter, III, formerly State Department spokesman, who gave his enthusiastic support to this endeavor and criticized chapters;

Ray S. Cline, former Deputy Director of CIA and now Senior Associate at the Center for Strategic and International Studies, Georgetown University, for his incisive critique of some early draft chapters;

John C. Ausland, formerly Secretary to the American delegation in the SALT I negotiations, whose valuable advice and detailed comments saved me from many a pitfall and oversimplification;

William F. Buckley, Editor of the *National Review*, who thought this book was important and should be published;

Colonel Jonathan Alford, Deputy Director of the International Institute for Strategic Studies, for his insistence that young scholars seek out experts on their subject for advice;

John H. Herz, Emeritus Professor at the City University of New York, for his valuable suggestions and friendly encouragement;

Professor Elmer Plischke, Adjunct Scholar, American Enterprise Institute, for his careful review of draft chapters;

Professor Robert M. Slusser of Michigan State University, for his thorough review of the Soviet material and long-time scholarly advice and assistance;

Professor John J. Gilligan of the University of Notre Dame's Law School, for his detailed and perceptive comments on draft chapters;

Professor Alexander George whose award-winning study (with Richard Smoke) of nuclear deterrence laid the groundwork for this book and whose critical comments and suggestions on other work have proved highly instructive;

Professor Carl Anthon of American University, a long-time mentor who encouraged my best efforts at scholarship;

Michael Novak, noted author, currently at the American Enterprise Institute for Public Policy Research, who engaged me in valuable dialogue and took a special interest in my students;

Norbert Böttcher, who assisted me in numerous ways;

My right arm Shirley Zipoy, who selflessly typed the manuscript through numerous drafts with an energy and dedication that exceeded all bounds;

Toy Ward, who saw this manuscript through all its various drafts and put in many long hours editing the text;

Arno Spitz, my publisher and friend who went to considerable trouble and expense to edit and produce a book of high quality;

My assistants Sherman Marek and Jim Garry, who sacrificed many hours reading drafts, checking details, suggesting alternate language and challenging my arguments;

Finally, my students Paul Galatowitsch, Mark Gorham, Mike Goshey, Joe Guiney, Lynn Rausch, Julie Skram, Audrey Swartz, Jayme Trusty, Jim Ziegler, Wendi Varsoke and Sue Lawyer, who contributed many hours of their time tracking down materials, xeroxing draft chapters and otherwise providing me with important assistance and who showed once again the validity of the wisdom that "by one's students one will be taught."

For any merit in this study, these men and women deserve a large share of the credit. The errors are my own.

Foreword

"A confusion of voices" aptly describes the present condition of strategic thinking in the United States about nuclear weapons. We have seen a great proliferation of books and articles on the subject by a bevy of experts, but the citizen with an interest in such matters is likely to be both alarmed and bewildered by what he reads and hears. The problems presented by nuclear weaponry in the world today have come to the forefront of consciousness for an ever greater number of people as awareness of the awesome overkill capability of the two superpowers becomes more general. The growing concern is not, of course, confined to Americans. Many Europeans as well have developed a new sensitivity as a result of controversy over deployment of intermediate nuclear weapons in a number of NATO countries.

There is need, therefore, for a clear, insightful and well-researched discussion of the subject which displays both historical perspective and knowledge of the strategic debate as it is being conducted today. Professor Catudal in his book makes a real contribution to the ongoing debate. Anyone who reads it carefully will emerge with a better idea of what the issues were yesterday and are today. He will find a well-reasoned analysis of the development of strategic doctrines as well as arguments questioning the validity of some of the underlying assumptions of American weapons policy.

I should not want to imply that I agree with all the premises and conclusions of Professor Catudal. This is not surprising in an area where the conjectural and the hypothetical are bound to dominate. After all, strategic analysts must start with the reality that since 1945 no nuclear weapon has been fired in anger. Although one can cite defective logic or poor scholarship, it is impossible to prove beyond doubt on the basis of actual experience that strategies are clearly wrong or right. This is true as well of the basic concepts which underlie those strategies including that most basic concept of all — deterrence. Drawing on those facts which are available we can, however, so far as the human mind is able to reason, develop theories to help us understand how the process of decision-making in a nuclear context seems to operate.

I was glad to see Professor Catudal's reference to Pascal's Wager. Though developed for an entirely different purpose, it, in my view, suggests best the essential logic of deterrence between powers that have a multiplicity of strategic weapons and a leadership that is both rational and informed about what nuclear weapons can do. Pascal was, of course, a great mathematician with deep insight into the concept of infinity, and one does not expect our leaders to operate at that level of sophistication. But the principle that a risk should be avoided which verges on the unmeasurable and is clearly disproportionate to any possible gain, should be compelling logic to any rational leader.

It is perhaps difficult for those who have never been involved in the policy-making process to understand how strategic deterrence operates in the minds of those with responsibility to make recommendations for decisions, or those who actually have to make decisions, which might conceivably lead to a nuclear confrontation. In my own experience, I have never seen the kind of wild-man approach which some commentators imagine lurks in the bureaucratic jungle. If the two factors are present of rationality and understanding — understanding of the horrible potency of nuclear weapons — then deterrence is automatically also present. It is evident that as American nuclear superiority vanished into the mists of parity, equivalence, sufficiency or what have you, greater caution was bound to creep into contingency planning. Once massive retaliation as a strategy clearly made no sense, nuclear weapons were necessarily limited conceptually to a defensive or deterrent threat. One could in fact argue, on the basis of reasonably good evidence, that despite the heightened rhetoric both superpowers have become progressively more conservative in their crisis management with respect to each other.

It is, of course, possible to cite examples where deterrence has not worked in favor of the superpowers against non-nuclear powers. Some classical cases are Korea, Vietnam and Afghanistan. The superpowers deter each other, but the uninformed are willing to risk their wrath either not really understanding what might be at stake or relying on that moral restraint and peculiar inverted deterrence which has prevented the use of nuclear weapons since Hiroshima and Nagasaki even against opponents who have no counter nuclear threat.

Perhaps Professor Catudal expects too much of deterrence. In one sense the superpowers are helpless giants; they cannot prevent many things from happening contrary to their interests simply because of their massive strength in nuclear weaponry But in all discussions of the subject we must begin with the reality that nuclear weapons exist today. We cannot wish them away as much as we would like to do so. We can support policies and measures calculated to limit their role with the ultimate, and perhaps unrealistic, goal of eliminating them, or at least reducing their numbers to that minimum which the superpowers believe they must have to protect themselves against blackmail by third powers who possess or might come into possession of nuclear weapons. Meanwhile, we have no better alternative than to rely on the continuation of deterrence to preserve such mutual security as it provides. If deterrence fails between the superpowers, then everything fails.

All of this having been said, no one can be satisfied with the present state of affairs. A delicate balance of terror which rests on the persistence of human rationality involves unacceptable risks. Even rational leaders feel compelled to engage in a continuing arms race which not only distorts their economies but provides an ever greater capacity for mutual destruction. The arms control process has disappointed those who at one time had high hopes for its success, and there is a desperate need for new impulses in this field before galloping new technologies outrun all possibility for meaningful reductions or even for ceilings. The current debate about the nuclear winter which a strategic exchange of nuclear missiles might bring about has evoked considerations reminiscent of the 1960s' discussion of a so-called "Doomsday Machine."

Although the emotions behind large-scale demonstrations in Germany, the Netherlands, Great Britain and Italy during the autumn of 1983 against the proposed initial deployments of U.S. intermediate range nuclear weapons seem to have subsided somewhat, those demonstrations genuinely reflected widespread dissatisfaction with what was perceived to be a further heightening of the nuclear confrontation in Europe. The fact that the Soviets had begun the whole business with their massive deployment of SS-20s never seemed to carry the weight of argument which one might have expected. There was a detectable sense of unease even among defenders of the NATO decision to deploy over time 464 land-based cruise missiles and 108 Pershing II missiles, some of this deriving no doubt from a feeling that current NATO strategy did not seem quite to meet the needs of the 1980s. The debate over no-first use of nuclear weapons initiated, among others, by Mr. Robert McNamara — the conceptual father of the NATO strategy of flexible response — could not give much assurance to those troubled by the changing perspectives which technology and shifts in the strategic balance have brought about. Current plans for the modernization and expansion of the British and French nuclear forces add a further element of uncertainty as well as a growing complication for the arms control process.

We indeed live in a perilous world, and there is no case whatsoever for not attempting to come to grips with the reality of nuclear weapons. Fatalistic acceptance of their inevitable use contributes nothing to the avoidance of terminal destructiveness. We clearly need new initiatives which, while avoiding attempts at utopian solutions, will move us towards a more rational level of weaponry. An essential part of achieving this is an informed and engaged public aware of past controversies and present dilemmas. Professor Catudal's book can play a highly useful role in the necessary educative process.

Martin J. Hillenbrand

Titan missile launch from Vandenberg Air Force Base, Calif.

> I wonder if we could contrive ... some magnificent myth that would in itself carry conviction to our whole community
>
> *Plato, The Republic*

I. INTRODUCTION: THE ILLUSION OF NUCLEAR SECURITY

Deterrence as a Panacea

"If only nuclear weapons will deter aggression, then building and deploying American nuclear missiles becomes, in the view of many, a sure practical consequence of the moral mandate to defend the nation." So concludes Dean Robert Spaeth of Saint John's University in his recent book on the nuclear arms debate.[1] It is a notable fact that our deterrence policy continues to receive widespread public support despite the high cost of maintaining it and the claim by critics that it takes money away from other sectors of the economy.[2]

Deterrence refers to the policy of preventing or discouraging an action by confronting an opponent with risks he is unwilling to run. Thus, in the first instance, deterrence depends on psychological criteria. In the

---

[1] Robert L. Spaeth, *No Easy Answers: Christians Debate Nuclear Arms* (Minneapolis: Winston Press, 1983). On p. 46 a lay Catholic theologian is quoted: Nuclear deterrence policy is "the plainly expressed will of the American people, who have chosen to preserve their institutions through deterring both nuclear war and totalitarian might."

[2] Gordon Adams and his colleagues at the Council of Economic Priorities have calculated that President Reagan's plan to spend $ 1.6 trillion on military arms over five years comes out to about $ 20,000 per American household. This is "a considerable financial burden which sends 50 percent of every individual's tax dollar to the Department of Defense." A substantial portion of this money is going for weapons and work related to the American nuclear deterrent. See Gordon Adams, "The 'Iron Triangle' and the American Economy," in Congressman Ronald V. Dellums, *Defense Sense: The Search for a Rational Military Policy* (Cambridge: Ballinger, 1983), p. 171.

words of Henry Kissinger: "What the potential aggressor believes is more crucial than what is objectively true. *Deterrence occurs above all in the minds of men.*"[3] (Italics mine.)

As some advocates of nuclear deterrence argue, nuclear weapons may be used to fulfill a variety of deterrent purposes. These include deterring a nuclear or conventional attack on oneself or allies, client states and friendly neutrals.[4]

Today the "balance of terror" is usually justified on the basis that it has worked.[5] To quote one high-level U.S. government official: "our policy of deterrence is clearly desirable because, since it was implemented years ago, no nuclear weapon has been used in warfare."[6]

3 Henry A. Kissinger, *American Foreign Policy* (New York: W.W. Norton & Co., 1974), p. 15.

4 For details see Bruce M. Russett, *The Prisoners of Insecurity* (San Francisco, 1983). For some earlier studies of the different functions of nuclear doctrine see J. David Singer, "Threat Perception and National Decision-Makers," *Journal of Conflict Resolution* (1958), pp. 90-105; J. David Singer, *Deterrence, Arms Control and Disarmament* (Columbus: Ohio State University Press, 1962), and Thomas C. Schelling, *Arms and Influence* (New Haven: Yale University Press, 1966). Some proponents of deterrence see a "secondary purpose" in nuclear deterrence — deterring nuclear blackmail. Others view deterrence as a process of communication. Through deterrence, it is said, decisionmakers of one nation seek to communicate with their counterparts abroad. Glenn H. Snyder and others who subscribe to deterrence in general maintain that deterrence may operate *in* war as well as *before* war. See Snyder's *Deterrence and Defense: Toward a Theory of National Security* (Princeton, N.J.: Princeton University Press, 1961).

5 The seeds for the concept "balance of terror" were planted by that master phrasemaker Winston Churchill. Urging Britain's Labour government to negotiate with the Soviet Union in 1950, he stated: "Moralists may find it a melancholy thought that peace can find no nobler foundation than mutual terror but for my part I shall be content if these foundations are solid, because they will give us the extra time and the new breathing space for the supreme effort which has to be made for a world settlement." See his speech in the House of Commons, March 28, 1950. "Mutual terror" became the "balance" in a classic article by Albert Wohlstetter in 1959, entitled "The Delicate Balance of Terror," *Foreign Affairs*, Vol. 37, No. 2 (January, 1959), pp. 211-34.

6 Patrick M. Morgan, a distinguished deterrence theorist, outlines the following four criteria which together constitute a "pure deterrence situation":
(1) In a relationship between two hostile states the officials in at least one of them are seriously considering attacking the other or attacking some area of the world the other deems important.
(2) Key officials of the other state realize this.
(3) Realizing that an attack is a distinct possibility, the latter set of officials threaten the use of force in retaliation in an attempt to prevent the attack.
(4) Leaders of the state planning to attack decide to desist primarily because of the retaliatory threat(s).
According to Morgan, unless the first three of these conditions exist, one cannot

Actually, the situation is much more complicated than that. The happy "accident" that the world has survived the first 39 years of the nuclear age is inadequate evidence that we can avoid nuclear war in the coming era, as many proponents of nuclear deterrence assume.

The Danger of Nuclear War

According to Thomas J. Watson, Jr., former U.S. Ambassador to the Soviet Union, we have "deluded ourselves into believing that we could improve our own and our friends' security by building more and better [nuclear] weapons." In actuality, Ambassador Watson concludes: "at no time has our existence been as threatened as it is today."[7]

W. Averell Harriman, the former Ambassador to Moscow and the adviser of five presidents, explains in detail the nature of the threat: "Within a few years," he says, "both the United States and the Soviet Union will have in place intercontinental missiles interpreted each by the other as instruments of a massive first strike."[8] Within a span of months "both nations will put shorter-range nuclear missiles nearer each other's territory, missiles capable of striking critical command and control centers with flight times so short that caution may be the first casualty of some future crisis."[9]

As if this were not sufficient, "thousands of nuclear-armed cruise missiles will soon be stationed on American submarines, to be followed by thousands more carried on Soviet ships, or hidden,[10] in uncountable

---

say that deterrence is being attempted; without the fourth, one cannot say that deterrence is working. See his *Deterrence: A Conceptual Analysis* (Beverly Hills: Sage Publications, 1977), p. 36.

7 *The New York Times*, December 9, 1983.

8 "The U.S. already perceives the Soviets to have a 'first-strike' potential," states one American government official. "The claim of a similar U.S. capability is puzzling since they signed SALT II which permits the U.S. to build the weapons now in development." Actually, neither the United States nor the U.S.S.R. enjoys a first-strike capability. That is, neither side is able to launch a surprise nuclear attack against the other which would so overwhelm the defender that it would be unable to retaliate and inflict "unacceptable damage" on the aggressor.

9 Soviet submarines, of course, have been off U.S. coasts in small numbers for a decade or more. The estimated flight time of missiles sent from Soviet submarines thus deployed to land on Washington, D.C., is 5-10 minutes, according to one official in the U.S. Arms Control and Disarmament Agency.

10 "Soviet ships carried cruise missiles on them before U.S. plans for its cruise missiles ever reached engineering development stage, let alone production," says one U.S. official. "Yes," says one academic expert, "but the U.S. was the first to develop *intercontinental* cruise missiles."

numbers, in the vast expanse of the Soviet Union." These cruise missiles, Harriman says, "will vastly complicate the ability ever to achieve the nuclear reductions that American and Soviet leaders both say they seek."[11]

Perhaps the most tragic trend, because it is so avoidable, Harriman states, "is that the arms race is about to be launched into space. Anti-satellite weapons will be a continuing threat to early warning,[12] reconnaissance and communications satellites — all of which are critical to security and vital to preventing war by accident or miscalculation."

All of these developments greatly increase the likelihood of Soviet-American confrontations. They are being done (by the U.S. at least) under the guise of a strategic nuclear doctrine called deterrence, which is adhered to even though at best there is little evidence to show that it actually works in practice. *In fact, there is a growing body of evidence that would indicate that the doctrine of nuclear deterrence serves as a convenient rationalization for the development and deployment of the weapons made available by military technology.*

The Threat Posed by Large Stocks of Nuclear Weapons

Perhaps it is worth recalling the large danger inherent in our nuclear deterrence policy, which has been institutionalized and enshrined as the first principle of Soviet-American relations. This is that a single misinterpretation on the part of the Soviet Union (or the United States) could lead to a spiral of miscalculations, culminating in a nuclear war no one wanted and a conflict with no "real-world" foundation.[13]

The grave danger that exists at present may be stated in apocryphal terms. And here the legendary story of King Arthur's last battle springs to mind. This battle took place after a peace conference when the drawn sword of one of the knights about to kill a snake that had bitten him was misinterpreted as a sign that the battle had begun, whereupon the knights fell upon and virtually annihilated each other.

But one does not have to turn to the apocryphal to illustrate the very

11 *International Herald Tribune*, January 2, 1984.
12 According to U.S. intelligence officials, "present Soviet anti-satellite weapons cannot reach U.S. early-warning satellites, which are at geosynchronous orbit."
13 One critic argues here that "the danger of nuclear weapons lies in their use, rather than their existence. While high numbers may increase some statistical probability of use in an accidental or mechanical sense, and may encourage some exaggerated targeting plans by the military, they do not necessarily increase the probability that nuclear use would be initiated deliberately."

real danger today of an accidental nuclear war. Premier Khrushchev is reliably reported to have told Vice President Nixon about an "erratic" Soviet missile which was destroyed by a signal from the ground as it headed towards Alaska.[14] For its part, the United States is responsible for several close calls which nearly resulted in nuclear accidents.

There are various estimates of the number of accidents which have involved American nuclear weapons. In 1968, the Defense Department reported twelve accidents involving nuclear weapons carried on Air Force planes. However, in a study initiated by President John F. Kennedy, he was reportedly told that since the end of World War II there had been more than sixty accidents involving nuclear weapons — including two cases in which nuclear-tipped anti-aircraft missiles were inadvertently launched. Some knowledgeable authorities maintain that the total number of such accidents may actually be higher than the official estimate.

Whatever the true number, perhaps the single most important example in the published literature of an accident which nearly resulted in a nuclear catastrophe occurred in 1961 at Goldsboro in North Carolina. Dr. Ralph Lapp, formerly of the nuclear physics branch of the Office of Naval Research, has written the following about this episode:[15]

A B-52 bomber had to jettison a 24-megaton bomb over North Carolina. The bomb fell in a field without exploding. The Defense Department had adopted complex devices and strict rules to prevent the accidental arming or firing of nuclear weapons. In this case the 24-megaton warhead was equipped with six interlocking safety mechanisms, all of which had to be triggered in sequence to explode the bomb. When Air Force experts

14 The source of this story did not indicate whether this missile was an operational ICBM or just a test missile of another sort. Another reference, for which no corroboration has been found, states: "Helsinki — A tremendous explosion is reported to have blasted a Soviet ICBM base near Alakkrtti close to the Russian-Finnish border. Sources said they believed that blast was a nuclear explosion." See *Missiles and Rockets*, Vol. 6, No. 10 (March 7, 1960). In October 1960, an advanced Soviet missile engine exploded during a test launch, killing the first head of the Soviet Strategic Rocket Forces, Marshal Mitrofan Nedelin, and over 300 other observers. This tragedy was described by the Western spy who served in the General Staff, Colonel Oleg Penkovskiy. See *The Penkovskiy Papers* (New York: Doubleday, 1965). This book was published by the CIA through Doubleday and much of the material was compiled from CIA records.

15 For background see Subcommittee of the Committee on Government Operations, House of Representatives, *Failures of the North American Aerospace Defense Command's (NORAD) Attack Warning System* (Washington, D.C.: U.S. Government Printing Office, 1981).

16 Quoted in Marek Thee (ed.), *Armaments and Disarmament in the Nuclear Age* (Paris: UNESCO, 1981).

rushed to the North Carolina farm to examine the weapon after the accident, they found that five of the six interlocks had been set off by the fall! Only a single switch prevented the 24-megaton bomb from detonating and spreading fire and destruction over a wide area.

On thrêe more recent occasions — one in the fall of 1979 and the others in the spring of 1980 — U.S. Defense Department computers erroneously indicated that the Soviets had launched some of their nuclear missiles against the United States. On the first such occasion, a technician is said to have inadvertently run a test tape through the computer system which triggered the commencement of the retaliatory response. In June 1980, a malfunction in a computer was blamed. Then strategic bomber crews were ordered to man their planes (always on "quick-reaction" alert) and silo-based missiles were brought to a higher state of readiness after audio and visual signals showed that the Soviets had launched both submarine-based and land-based missiles. Some three minutes later the alert was called off.

A veil of secrecy still surrounds both incidents. In the aftermath of the last incident, Assistant Secretary of Defense Thomas B. Ross declared that "we weren't remotely close to World War III." But he declined to comment on the possibility that a similar malfunction might trigger a series of escalating responses in the United States and the Soviet Union that could get out of hand.

About the time U.S. technicians were removing the faulty computer in the June 1980 incident, David Jones, Chairman of the Joint Chiefs of Staff, was publicly admonishing the Soviets to take a lesson from the episode. "They had better know that we are ready and that we can respond in a very few minutes," he said.[16]

Summary

The danger of nuclear war in the 1980s is ever present. Rivalry and mutual suspicions by the U.S. and the U.S.S.R. have led to a buildup in nuclear weapons that is awesome. The two superpowers have acquired a potential for massive destruction that is unparalleled in history.

As a measure of comparison, we may recall that all the bombs dropped by the U.S. in World War II on Germany and Japan had a cumulative explosive power of two megatons (two million tons) of TNT. Today *one* large

---

17 For a review of these three incidents see Richard J. Barnet, *Real Security: Restoring American Power in a Dangerous Decade* (New York: Touchstone Books, 1981), pp. 30-31.

nuclear weapon in the arsenals of the United States and the Soviet Union surpasses that figure a number of times. Taken together, the approximately 50,000 nuclear warheads now in the hands of the superpowers have an explosive power exceeding a million times the yield of the Hiroshima bomb.

It is always easy for Americans to blame Soviet leaders for the current arms race. And no American — no matter how much he or she desires a safer world — should lose sight of the fact that Russian leaders do indeed bear a heavy burden of responsibility for where we are today. However, blaming the U.S.S.R., which seems to be so popular today in official government circles, is not a strategy or policy. It will not eliminate Winston Churchill's "iron curtain." Above all, it will not reduce the threat posed by large numbers of nuclear weapons.

The first nuclear weapons were made to win World War II. Some people in the United States have never given up the idea that a nuclear war could be fought and won under conditions comparable to those of 1941-45.

For some military men and strategic thinkers, nuclear weapons represent just another development in the evolution of human warfare. Indeed, the concepts by which these weapons of mass destruction were first understood were given validity by the speed with which the bomb's use in World War II was followed by the Japanese surrender.

However, as most military and civilian officials well understand, nuclear weapons have fundamentally changed the nature of conflict. In the past, there was always the possibility that wars could be fought between the armed forces of the state without including the people. This is far less likely today. For the first time in history nuclear weapons offer the possibility of destroying a country before one has defeated or destroyed its armed forces.

The existence of large stocks of nuclear weapons means that nuclear war would almost certainly not be protracted. Conventional wars used to go on for years, and some — like the war between Iraq and Iran — still do in different parts of the world. Nuclear war would probably be over in a matter of hours or days. In fact, it could be over before warnings of attack were discovered to be false alarms or statesmen had the chance to rethink their initial decisions and change their minds. Certainly, great destruction could be wreaked before leaders could reach each other and negotiate an end to the conflict. In short, nuclear war would be fundamentally different from any conventional war fought in the past.

Over the years, U.S. strategic doctrine and accompanying force structure have, to a large extent, been built around nuclear weapons, varying to meet what has been perceived as the principal threat. However, nuclear deterrence as a national strategy has remained unchanged in principle.[18]

18 "Deterrence is, strictly speaking, not a strategy," one U.S. arms control official observes. "Deterrence says nothing about the manner in which nuclear weapons

Lawrence Freedman, in a recent book that has been widely acclaimed by participants in the debate over the nuclear issue, suggests that nuclear strategizing has become so abstract and incestuous that it has only a tenuous connection with the real security problems of states.[19] One could take Freedman's arguments one step further by observing that until now, our primary reliance on nuclear deterrence has made it very difficult for many policymakers and others to consider seriously other approaches to our relationship with the Soviet Union. Before it is too late, we must apply our talents to the development of a new approach to the dangers that threaten the United States and the West. If we do not, neither the U.S. nor the U.S.S.R. may survive another forty years of the nuclear age.[20]

may be employed. It is, rather, a means to make their employment unnecessary. In this sense, it is the opposite of strategy."
A critic would disagree, contending that nuclear deterrence "is largely a function of specific targeting *strategies.*"

19 Lawrence Freedman, *The Evolution of Nuclear Strategy* (New York: St. Martin's Press, 1983).

20 In his State of the Union address in January, 1984, President Reagan said "restoration of economic growth and military deterrence" meant the "United States is safer, stronger and more secure in 1984 than before." But according to a Gallup Poll taken shortly thereafter Americans by three to one believe they live in a world that is less safe today than it was three years ago when Reagan took office. See *The Minneapolis Star and Tribune,* March 22, 1984.

SECTION I
THE DOCTRINE AND STRATEGIES OF NUCLEAR DETERRENCE

> If the only tool you have is a hammer, you tend to treat everything as if it were a nail.
>
> *Abraham Maslow*

II. DEADLY LOGIC

For almost forty years the threat of nuclear destruction has been inherent in the confrontations between the United States and the Soviet Union. During this period, some of the most active minds in the United States have labored hard to impose a coherent theory on this threat, which would render it understandable and manageable, thus providing a "foothold for sanity."[1] This effort has drawn heavily upon theoretical assumptions based on gaming and has produced a tenuous, very abstract set of doctrines.

Several American strategic thinkers have developed over the years a core logic underpinning nuclear weapons deployment. This logic revolves around the concept of deterrence. Other strategic thinkers, however, recognize nuclear deterrence theory as bald assumption, plagued with internal paradoxes and important unanswered questions. The simple fact of the matter is that there exists no body of evidence confirming that nuclear deterrence actually works.

This investigation seeks answers to the following two questions: (1) What are the basic assumptions underlying deterrence theory? and (2) Can we rely on national decision-makers armed with nuclear weapons to act in a rational (i.e., utility-maximizing) way?

Strategic Thinking And Public Reaction

"Symptomatic of the fundamental change from the conduct of war to the implementation of deterrence through exploitation of coercion," writes John Spanier, "is that all the seminal thinking on military force has been by civilian intellectuals."[2] The student interested in national security

---

1 John Steinbruner, "Beyond Rational Deterrence: The Struggle for New Conceptions," *World Politics* (January, 1976), pp. 223-245.
2 John Spanier, *Games Nations Play: Analyzing International Politics;* 4th ed. (New York: Holt, Rinehart and Winston, 1981), p. 180.

affairs does not usually go to the works written by generals and admirals. Rather, he or she turns often to the civilian experts, who are mostly academicians.

These political scientists, historians, mathematicians and physicists have concerned themselves largely with issues of strategy. Historically, the word "strategy" involved the use of battles to achieve the objectives of war. Now, however, it is usually applied to what Thomas C. Schelling, one of the foremost theoreticians of deterrence, calls the "manipulation of risk."[3]

There have been some benefits from this change. For example, by taking much of the mystery out of a subject thought by many civilians to be the domain of the professional soldiers, analysts like Schelling, Bernard Brodie and Henry Kissinger have transformed the interested layman into a qualified party, permitting him or her to question the judgment of soldiers about matters of strategy, force levels and weapons.

For the better part of the postwar period, the doctrine of nuclear deterrence has reigned supreme in official U.S. circles. During this time the public, for the most part, seemed to show only sporadic interest in nuclear matters, being content to hand the whole "dreadful business" over to the care of specialists.[4] However, towards the end of the 1970s, this wide consensus (consisting, on the one hand, of general doctrinal agreement among government officials — though less so than is commonly believed — and, on the other, of wide public acceptance of their stewardship) was unexpectedly shattered by two major upheavals. The first change was in the attitude of public opinion, which took the form of a new peace movement. The second was the change in government policy, which manifested itself in a subtle but profound and many-sided crisis in how the doctrine of nuclear deterrence was henceforth to be viewed.

---

3 Glenn Snyder details four factors a potential aggressor must consider in his *risk calculus*. "They are (1) his evaluation of his war objectives; (2) the cost which he expects to suffer as a result of various possible responses by the deterrer; (3) the probability of various responses, including 'no response'; and (4) the probability of winning the objectives with each possible response." See his *Deterrence and Defense* (Princeton, N.J.: Princeton University Press, 1961), p. 12.

4 The American public, until recently, was generally inattentive and uninformed on nuclear weapons and arms control issues. Several surveys during the 1960s and 1970s indicated that one-half to three-fourths of the adult population paid very little attention at all to such issues. For instance, in 1976 when the B-1 bomber program and the SALT negotiations were central preoccupations of U.S. policymakers, 71 percent of the public reported they had heard or read "nothing" or "very little" about the B-1 bomber, and 49 percent said they had not been "paying much attention at all" to SALT. Moreover, polls over the years have consistently shown that about half the population, even in major cities, did not expect their cities to be attacked in a nuclear war. See Thomas L. Brewer, *American Foreign Policy* (Englewood Cliffs, N.J.: Prentice-Hall, 1980), p. 208.

The resultant crisis in doctrine, which began to emerge under the Carter Administration, came into full public view under the Reagan Administration. Certain contradictions that had always underlain the doctrine (but had gone largely unnoticed by the public) began to receive more attention. For the most part, these contradictions had to do with the central unresolveable paradox of "defending" one's country by threatening to use weapons whose actual use would bring on one's own destruction.

Public involvement in the debate over deterrence intensified in 1981 when Pope John Paul II went to Hiroshima. In a talk at Peace Memorial Park, he repeated his theme four times — "To remember the past is to commit oneself to the future." "In the past," he stated, "it was possible to destroy a village, a town, a region, even a country. Now it is the whole planet that has come under threat. This fact should compel everyone to confront a basic moral consideration: From now on, it is only through a conscious choice and through a deliberate policy that humanity can survive. The moral and political choice that faces us is putting all the resources of mind, science and culture at the service of peace and building up a new society."[5]

The Pope's appeal, which was followed by a decision by the American bishops to study American nuclear policy, focused public attention on the basic moral problem posed by a deterrence policy. Stated by the most outspoken opponents, this moral principle warned: "A nation may never threaten what it may never do."

In May 1983, the bishops released their controversial Pastoral Letter on War and Peace. In this careful statement of guidance to Catholics, they declared that Catholics must give a clear "no" to the use of nuclear weapons.[6] However, they qualified what some theologians regarded as the logical extension of their moral position by reluctantly tolerating, however temporarily, the doctrine of deterrence or the threat to use nuclear weapons.[7]

---

5 Quoted in Jim Castelli: *The Bishops and the Bomb: Waging Peace in a Nuclear Age* (New York: Doubleday, 1983), p. 26.

6 It should be noted that the bishops letter reflects their teaching ministry in the Church. As the bishops state: " . . . not all statements in this letter have the same moral authority. At times we state universally binding moral principles found in the teaching of the Church; at other times the pastoral letter makes specific applications, observations and recommendations which allow for diversity of opinion on the part of those who assess the factual data of situations differently. However, we expect Catholics to give our moral judgments serious consideration when they are forming their own view on specific problems."

7 For the texts of the Pastoral Letters of the West German and French bishops on this subject see James V. Schall (ed.), *Out of Justice, Peace; Winning the Peace* (San Francisco: Ignatius Press, 1984).

In the fall of 1983, the explosive film "The Day After" became a major topic of conversation in homes and workplaces throughout the United States. The two-hour film portrayed Kansas after a "limited" nuclear attack and in effect repudiated the theory of deterrence. It drew one of the biggest nation-wide television audiences ever. Afterwards a panel of experts commented on the film and debated its policy ramifications. Generally, those who opposed deterrence saw the film as performing a public service by showing in graphic detail what catastrophic impact even a "small" nuclear strike would have. Those who saw the film as oversimplified and playing to the views of the peace movement criticized it on grounds of what they perceived to be a growing trend — in Henry Kissinger's words — of "scaring ourselves to death."

The debate over "The Day After" had hardly subsided when a group of American scientists led by Carl Sagan of Cornell University and Paul Ehrlich of Stanford University reported publicly their analysis of the projected long-term consequences of nuclear war. Their two-year study concluded that "the extinction of the human species was a distinct possibility in a nuclear war." This would be true even in the case — and this was most shocking of all — in which one of the superpowers was to launch but a fraction of its total nuclear arsenal and the other was to refrain entirely from retaliating (for more detail see Chapter XII).

Three Types of Deterrent Strategies

Briefly, nuclear deterrence relies on the premise that one side has sufficient nuclear capabilities to convince a potential adversary that it would not be worthwhile to attack.

Strategic theorists identify three basic types of deterrence:
(1) deterrence by denial;
(2) deterrence by punishment; and
(3) deterrence by defeat.

Under deterrence by denial (which comes close to describing how the Soviets view the situation), the side that might want to initiate a war will not do so because it is convinced that it cannot achieve its war objectives. Thus, it would have no reason to begin a war.

Under deterrence by punishment (which has been the American position), the side that might desire to start a war would not do so because it would believe that the side that is attacked could inflict "unacceptable damage" (i.e., punishment) on the attacking side. Theoretically, the higher the level of "cost tolerance" that an aggressor is willing to accept, the higher the level of damage that the victim must be capable of inflicting if deterrence by punishment is to work.

Under deterrence by defeat, the side that might want to initiate a war would not do so because of the certainty that it would be defeated.

The distinction between deterrence based on punishment, which involves threatening to destroy large portions of the civilian population and industry of an opponent, and deterrence based on denial, which requires convincing an opponent that it will not attain its objectives on the battlefield, has been developed at length by strategic thinkers in a rather abstract way. But former Secretary of State Dean Acheson expressed this distinction concretely when he stated "We mean that the only deterrent to the imposition of Russian will in Western Europe is the belief that from the outset of any such attempt American power would be employed in *stopping* it, and if necessary, would *inflict* on the Soviet Union *injury* which the Moscow regime would not wish to suffer."[8] (Italics mine.)

A Status Quo Doctrine

The doctrine of nuclear deterrence is complex and has been interpreted by different authorities in several different ways. However, from the viewpoint of successive American administrations, the doctrine generally assumes that the United States is a *status quo* power, a belief heartily challenged by revisionist historians and other dissenting observers. From this benign perspective, the United States government is not interested in acquiring new territories or areas of influence or in accepting great risks in order to rescue or reform those areas of the world which now have political systems radically different from our own. On the other hand, the U.S. — as a *status quo* power — is determined to hold on to what it has. And this *status quo* includes living in a world in which conflict is seen as the norm and states are encouraged to take measures to provide for their own defense. When viewed in this context, the minimum security objectives for the United States must include not only its own national independence but also that of other countries allied with the U.S. or dependent on it for the continued maintenance of their independence, especially those which possess democratic political institutions comparable to our own.[9] (The nuclear protection by nuclear powers of non-nuclear allies is called "extended deterrence.")

8 Quoted in John J. Mearsheimer, *Conventional Deterrence* (Ithaca: Cornell University Press, 1983), p. 15. "This statement by Acheson," one U.S. official observes, "was made before the Soviets had so many nuclear weapons."

9 Bernard Brodie, "The Anatomy of Deterrence," *World Politics*, Vol. II (1959), p. 173.

Deterrence and Diplomacy

It should be noted at the outset that deterrence is not primarily a military concept. The primary test for the soldier has always been what happens on the battlefield. Thus, his professional concern has been with weapons and the actual exercise of the use of force.

Deterrence is an aspect of diplomacy. Obviously, if it is to be successful, it must be based on weapons. But the litmus test is not in the use of violence but in successfully dissuading the enemy from attacking.[10] Thus, the purpose of deterrence is to influence the actions of the foe.

In the past, the ability to inflict great damage on one's adversary was often exploited diplomatically before the eruption of hostilities. In the view of Thomas C. Schelling, modern technology has enhanced the importance of "threats of war as techniques of influence, not of destruction; of coercion and deterrence, not of conquest and defense; of bargaining and intimidation."[11]

According to critics, the problem with this analysis in the nuclear age is that the threat to use nuclear weapons to influence the behavior of an adversary, also equipped with weapons of mass destruction, may appear to be a bluff — and a very dangerous one at that. Given the difficulty of limiting nuclear war, critics say, and given the extreme consequences even if the war is limited, almost any use of nuclear weapons is likely to be self-defeating and senseless. Nuclear deterrence is thus like a gun with two barrels: one points ahead; the other points back at the holder of the gun.

Deterrence Old and New

Deterrence as an element of national strategy is not a recent phenomenon. However, since the development of nuclear weapons, the term has acquired not only a special emphasis but also a distinctive connotation.

Strategic thinkers distinguish between "defense" and "deterrence."[12] The terms are sometimes confused, so it will be worthwhile to explain the differences. Defense is physical. It goes into operation when war breaks out. For instance, tanks move to the frontier in a conventional war, making

---

10 Thomas C. Schelling, *Strategy of Conflict* (New York: Oxford University Press, 1963), pp. 3-10.

11 Thomas C. Schelling, *Arms and Influence* (New Haven: Yale University Press, 1966), p. 33.

12 For a good discussion of the differences see Glenn H. Snyder, *Deterrence and Defense* (Princeton, N.J.: Princeton University Press, 1961).

Figure 1: *B-1 aircraft*

it difficult for the enemy to advance. Deterrence is psychological. Its primary use is *before* war breaks out. If it works, it keeps the foe from moving in the first place. Once war has broken out, deterrence has failed, and defense must take over.[13]

To put it another way: Being able to defend oneself implies that one is safe (or at least one can minimize his losses) *regardless* of what a potential enemy does with his military forces. On the other hand, deterrence through punishment rests on the assumption that one is secure not despite military attacks. Rather one is secure *only* if the adversary is dissuaded from attacking in the first place. In the nuclear age, perfect defense does not seem possible or likely. Consequently, the United States leadership has chosen to rest its security, in part, on the visions and decisions of the Soviet leadership. The Soviet approach, with its heavy emphasis on defense, is somewhat different.

Note that measures designed for defense can also deter. For example, the pitchfork that I wave over one of my possessions, although a physical measure, may well discourage someone from trying to steal it. In a similar way, states use fighter escorts for reconnaissance planes on intelligence-gathering missions, often making it unnecessary for them actually to defend the planes they are escorting.

This combination of defense and deterrence has been common throughout military history. Only recently have these two functions begun to separate. And this is what distinguishes in part the nuclear age from the pre-nuclear age. Today we invest huge sums of money in weapons that are designed for deterrence only; they have questionable value for actual employment. This condition is unlike anything we have experienced in the past.

David Ziegler, a professor of International Relations at Western Washington University, illustrates this important point.[14]

In the past a strong tank force might have had a deterrent effect, but if deterrence failed and an invasion began, that same tank force could defend the country. An ICBM force with nuclear warheads of megaton strength has only deterrent value; it can provide no defense. If war breaks out and an enemy attacks, will any American lives be saved if missiles are fired back? The answer is no. If war breaks out, deterrence has failed, and the sole reason for the existence of the missiles disappears.

---

13 Proponents of "intrawar" deterrence, of course, dispute this. As one Reagan Administration official told this writer: "Intra-war deterrence is not only possible, but a consummation is devoutly to be wished for."

14 David W. Ziegler, *War, Peace, and International Politics*, 2nd ed. (Boston: Little, Brown & Co., 1981), p. 227.

Actually, the matter is more complicated than the above explanation would suggest. If American missiles could in some way destroy enemy missiles on the ground *before* they were launched or in flight toward targets then that, of course, would be "defense"[15] (although one must acknowledge that the other side might regard such a capability as that of attack). Or if U.S. officials expected a war to last for several years, then the destruction of the industrial capacity of the enemy might physically impair the ability of the adversary to attack the United States. But generally, the type of war in which past administrations expected these missiles to be used is the kind that was expected to be over very quickly. The Reagan Administration would change all this with its emphasis on acquiring a nuclear "warfighting" capability.[16]

As soon as the capabilities and limitations of nuclear weapons were known, U.S. Defense Department officials began to consider new strategic policies which would provide a framework within which these weapons of mass destruction could be developed and employed. In the past, the task of military planners was straightforward. Weapons were developed to deter enemy aggression before war broke out, and they were used to defend against that aggression if deterrence failed. Today the situation is radically different, but that has not dissuaded American military thinkers from building new and more powerful nuclear weapons and devising plans for their justification under the guise of deterrence.[17]

It is worth noting that conventional deterrence has not always worked as military planners would have liked. In fact, as Bernard Brodie, one of the early theoreticians and proponents of nuclear deterrence, readily admits: "The very large number of wars that have occurred in modern times proves that the threat to use force, even what sometimes looked like superior force, has often failed to deter."[18]

Many Americans do not have to be told this. They witnessed it firsthand in World War II when the Japanese attacked Pearl Harbor. Apparently, the Japanese believed that a surprise attack and the samurai spirit would enable

---

15 For awhile, it appeared to a number of people outside the U.S. government that this capability was what President Reagan was hoping to develop with his controversial "Star-Wars" scheme of anchoring a missile defense system in space. But this is apparently not the case. As one U.S. official informed this writer, "Missiles would be attacked in their boost stage, in mid-course, and in their terminal phase."

16 In the words of one "insider" in the Reagan Administration, "Warfighting capability offers the possibility of intra-war deterrence and the possibility that full-scale escalation is not inevitable."

17 "The U.S. is modernizing its forces in line with the broad program permitted by SALT II," argues one U.S. Arms Control and Disarmament official.

18 Bernard Brodie, *opus cit.*, p. 175.

a country producing seven million tons of steel to overcome one with an annual *peacetime* production of 75 million. Even Bruce M. Russet of Yale University, himself a prominent advocate of deterrence, admits Pearl Harbor was "one of the most conspicuous and costly failures of deterrence in history..."[19]

The Notion of Rationality

The most basic notion underlying the present deterrent posture of the United States is that of "rationality." Leaders of states, much like individuals in the marketplace, are assumed to be utility-maximizing agents. Behavior is considered to flow from a set of objectives derived from national interests, and strategic policy is an attempt to obtain those objectives at minimal cost, given the environmental constraints bounding the options available to national decision-makers. As explicated by Graham T. Allison of Harvard University, one of the foremost students of decision-making theory, government heads are viewed in this context acting as if they were unitary "actors" faced with the relatively simple problem of devising the most cost-effective method of realizing the desired effect.[20]

19 There is still some debate about the reasons behind the decision by the Japanese leadership to attack the United States, a country which so obviously outmatched Japan in resources for undertaking a war. Most analysts seem to agree with Sir Winston Churchill, who stated that a "declaration of war by Japan could not be reconciled with reason..." See his *The Grand Alliance* (Boston: Houghton Mifflin, 1950), p. 603. Bruce Russet takes issue with this interpretation of the decision. He argues that in this case the "rationality-irrationality distinction" is not useful and suggests instead a detailed analysis of certain components of the decision and of the alternatives be considered. See "Pearl Harbor: Deterrence Theory and Decision Theory," *Journal of Peace Research*, No. 2 (1967), pp. 89-106. Alexander George and Richard Smoke in their classic treatise on deterrence classify Russet's foregoing argument as an attempt by some writers to "save the thesis by stretching the notion of 'miscalculation' to cover a broader range of incorrect assumptions and calculations that may lead a government to initiate war." The fact of the matter remains, however, "that the Japanese initiation of war flatly contradicted the theoretical assumption that a credible commitment by the defender is a necessary and sufficient condition for deterrence success." See their *Deterrence in American Foreign Policy* (New York: Columbia University Press, 1974), p. 524.
20 See Graham T. Allison, *Essence of Decision* (Boston: Little, Brown & Co., 1971). This book, which was summarized at the American Political Science Convention in September 1968, and in the lead article of the *American Political Science Review* in September 1969, sets forth three models of decision-making which are applied to the Cuban missile crisis. The main proposition articulated by Allison's path-breaking study is that "professional analysts of foreign affairs (as well as ordinary laymen) think about problems of foreign and military policy in terms of

The assumption of rationality is intuitively very appealing in strategic thinking. Indeed, some would even note that it is essential for defining the problems and opportunities facing adversary decision-makers. However, in the case of the theory of deterrence, critics argue, it is a marvel of circularity and paradox. For instance, to obtain the benefit of the policy, one must threaten to perform an irrational action. However, the benefit one seeks is precisely *not* to perform that action. Thus, one seeks to avoid performing an act by threatening to perform it.

John Steinbruner addresses this central problem in the following way: "The established strategy of rational deterrence has long been plagued by the paradox that if deterrence should fail and war should begin (a possibility which cannot be entirely eliminated), then it would not be rational actually to carry out the threat of massive retaliation upon which deterrence is based." Once attacked, "a rationally calulating player has nothing substantial to gain by massive retaliation. Even the inevitable desire for revenge must yield to more serious needs ... Though it is assumed that strategic forces, in order to deter, must have a real *capacity* to retaliate massively, such retaliation is not at all what the rational calculator would undertake in the actual event of war."[21]

Perhaps the main problem with the rational-actor model underlying deterrence is that it represents an ideal type. Some decision-makers come closer to others to fulfilling the requirements.[22] One would hope that the greatest rationality would prevail in those instances where the most important foreign policy decisions have to be made. However, this does not always seem to be the case, as Charles W. Kegley and Eugene R. Wittkopf note semi-facetiously in their college text on American foreign policy:[23]

It is tempting to speculate that the more important the decision, the less likely it is that the decision will be based on pure rationality... Notice how little effort is put into acquiring information, considering alternatives,

largely implicit conceptual models that have significant consequences for the content of their thought." Allison identifies his main task as making the most important of these models explicit. For a critique of Allison's decision-making analysis, see Ernest J. Yanarella, "'Reconstructed Logic' & 'Logic-in-use' in Decision-making Analysis: Graham Allison," *Policy*, Vol. 8, No. 1 (Fall, 1975), pp. 156-172.

21 John Steinbruner, *opus cit.*, p. 231.
22 Glenn H. Snyder, a distinguished student of nuclear deterrence strategy, writes that his book *Deterrence and Defense* "was motivated largely by the apparent lack of any definite agreed criteria for making rational decisions in national security policy."
23 Charles W. Kegley *et al., American Foreign Policy: Pattern and Process* (New York: St. Martin's Press, 1979), p. 337.

and making choices for the really big life decisions one makes, like choosing a career or a marriage partner. Here people seem to slide into the path of least resistance and to settle for the first available alternative, rather than conducting a thorough search and selecting that alternative which best fulfills one's basic values. More intellectual effort and rational behavior may typically be put into buying a car or a six-pack of beer, where at least people shop comparatively and gather some information. It is worth asking if the same pattern exists in the realm of foreign policy decisions, where it often appears more time, attention, and energy are given to choosing seating arrangements for a diplomatic reception than to . . . (considering) the effectiveness of the latest weapons system acquired by the Department of Defense.

The First World War is a classic example of how a major world war can start "irrationally."[24] In this case, one need only recall the extraordinary exchange between German Chancellor von Bülow and his successor, in the early hours of World War I. "How did it happen?," asked von Bülow. "Ah, if we only knew," was the reply.

One leading scholar sums up his analysis of the outbreak of World War I in the following way: "All the evidence goes to show that the beginning of the crisis . . . was one of those moments in history when events passed beyond man's control."[25] It is not true, as some historians assert, that the Kaiser wanted war.[26] As John G. Stoessinger writes: "The cliché of the saber-rattling Kaiser is misleading. What is closer to the truth is that he permitted others to rattle and ultimately use the saber for him."[27]

Numerous studies have been undertaken on the origins of conflict. While there is a great deal of disagreement about which elements should be emphasized as primary contributing factors to the outbreak of war, many

24 "The people of Europe *wanted* war," states one official in the Reagan Administration, "and their governments exercised the greatest rationality and realism in planning for it." The late Herman Kahn would disagree: "[T]he more historians examine World War I, the more it seems to be clear that this was a war none of the responsible governments wanted, a war set in motion by relatively trivial circumstances, a motion which given the state of the world, could not be stopped..." Quoted in Phillip Greene, *Deadly Logic: The Theory of Nuclear Deterrence* (Columbus: Ohio University Press, 1966), p. 206.

25 F.H. Hinsley, *Power and the Pursuit of Peace* (London: Cambridge University Press, 1963), p. 286.

26 On this point see the "Willy Nicky" telegrams between Kaiser Wilhelm II ("Willy") and his cousin Czar Nicholas II ("Nicky") in Karl Kautsky (ed.), *Die Deutschen Dokumente zum Kriegsausbruch* (Berlin: 1919). Also important here is Barbara Tuchman, *The Guns of August* (New York: Macmillan, 1962).

27 John G. Stoessinger, *Why Nations Go To War*, 3rd ed. (New York: St. Martin's Press, 1982), p. 5.

authors demonstrate how little supposedly "rational" concerns ultimately matter in the decision-making processes of inter-state behavior. History is often the scene of the irrational, not the rational. One scholar, commenting on the leaders involved in the major wars since 1910, concludes:[28]

About 60 percent turned out to be wrong — and that concerns the estimate of the capabilities and intentions of the other great powers at the time when the war began, as well as the assessment of the actual course of the war and its consequences. We know from many studies and simulations of the decision-making process that the number of misperceptions and mistakes tends to increase in crisis situations. Stress, threats, and time pressure reduce the capabilities for a rational processing and evaluation of information.

The classical example of an important leader who was not greatly influenced by purely rational calculations is Adolf Hitler. In fact, his career is a horrendous case in point, where the expression and perpetration of violence on an increasingly grandiose scale was an extension of his allegedly manic personality.[29] Was he merely an aberration, as some proponents of deterrence would have us believe? Perhaps not. Any confidence that Hitler was an isolated example must be tempered by the discovery by Jerome Frank that at least seventy-five chiefs of state in the last four centuries led their countries, actually or symbolically, for a total of several centuries while suffering from severe mental disturbances.

To illustrate the relevance of the above point to the contemporary nuclear era, it should be recalled that during the Cuban missile crisis of October 1962 U.S. leaders were quite worried about Khrushchev's mental stability at several points. They were particularly concerned about the possibility that he might react impulsively to threats.[30]

The rational-actor model of decision-making, for all its sophistication, coherence and utility, has always suffered from inherent implausibility.

---

28 For details, see Marek Thee (ed.), *Armaments, Arms Control and Disarmament* (Paris: UNESCO, 1981), p. 101. Hans Morgenthau would disagree. As he has commented more generally, "the assumption that the issues of international conflict, born as they are of misunderstandings, are but imaginary and that actually no issue worth fighting about stands between nation and nation" is wrong. Nothing could be farther from the truth. All the great wars which decided the course of history and changed the political face of the earth were fought for real stakes, not for imaginary ones. The issue in these great convulsions was invariably: who shall rule and who shall be ruled? Who shall be free, and who, slave? See Morgenthau's *Politics Among Nations* (New York: Alfred A. Knopf, 1966), p. 504.

29 See Jerome Frank, *Sanity and Survival: Psychological Aspects of War and Peace* (New York: Random House, 1967), pp. 45-47.

30 Albert and Wohlstetter maintain that neither side's concerns of this sort were borne out. See their "Controlling Risks in Cuba," in Robert Art *et al.* (eds.), *The Use of Force* (Boston: Little, Brown, 1971), pp. 234-73.

This is because, as John Steinbruner observes, the "calculations required of decision-makers in any extensive application of the theory are readily demonstrated to be impossibly burdensome."[31]

A classic example is the game of chess. There the most directly rational (but obviously not practical) solution requires an evaluation of the consequences of *all* possible moves and a selection of the best move at each point of choice. The problem is, however, that the number of theoretically possible move sequences is so enormous that, at best, decision-makers in real life can achieve only the faintest approximation of the requirements of the theory. And it is unikely that these persons do this without unusual effort.

Arguments For and Against Rationality

Theoretical attention shifted to limited war in the 1950s because it seemed the only answer to the following question: How can the United States employ military power as a rational instrument of foreign policy when the destructive potentialities of war exceed any rational purpose?[32]

Herman Kahn at first proposed retaining nuclear war as a "rational" instrument of foreign policy. However, in the end he saw it was impossible rationally to threaten nuclear war with the Soviet Union on behalf of our allies.[33] As Kahn wrote: "in most deterrence situations, once deterrence has failed, it is irrational to carry out the previously made warnings of threats of retaliation since that action will produce an absolute or net loss to the retaliation."[34]

Writings on deterrence strategy have made this point right down to the present. But if there is no rational basis for retaliation once deterrence has failed, then — as one student of deterrence has observed — there "is no disincentive to the opponent who is thinking of attacking."[35]

Some proponents of deterrence would respond that what seems "irrational" in one context may be "rational" in another. For instance, Thomas C. Schelling argues that some political leaders are people who either are, or feign to be, irrational, and in this respect they may be compared to some

---

31 John Steinbruner, *opus cit.*, pp. 234-35.
32 Robert Osgood, *Limited War: The Challenge to American Strategy* (Chicago: University of Chicago Press, 1957), p. 1.
33 Herman Kahn, *On Thermonuclear War* (Princeton, N.J.: Princeton University Press, 1960), p. 113.
34 Herman Kahn, *On Escalation* (New York: Praeger, 1965), pp. 57-58.
35 Pat M. Morgan, *Deterrence: A Conceptual Analysis* (Beverly Hills: Sage Publications, 1977), p. 94.

inmates of mental institutions. Schelling notes that the inmates "are either very crazy or very wise, or both [because they] make clear to the attendants that they may slit their own veins or light their clothes on fire if they don't have their way" — consequently, many have their way.

When this technique is used politically, it suggests that the "fire" will also burn those who are threatened. This can be seen when Arab terrorists, for example, hijack and threaten to blow up an airplane unless the pilot does what he is told. Surely, the proponents of deterrence say, this behavior is "irrational" in the sense that blowing up the plane will kill them too. But as fanatics, they are credible in their threats.[36]

The critics counter by saying that the threat to use nuclear weapons today is different from the above analogy. Moreover, they assert, the empirical observation that perfectly rational human beings sometimes do irrational things is a major weakness of deterrence through intimidation. In an environment where deterrence of nuclear war is based on intimidation there also is the very real danger that presumably rational acts in the short run become irrational acts in the long run. In the social sciences, this situation is called "phenomenon escalation"; one thing leads to another, each step just is a little more dangerous than the step before, until one side is fatally tempted to bluff with a nuclear weapon or use just one or two as a demonstration of will. The end result may be entanglement in a nuclear war not of one's choosing.

According to Robert S. McNamara, "There is less and less deterrent value to threatening to commit suicide."[37] However, if the threat of nuclear war is irrational, one might ask here why U.S. leaders go on making it, albeit in different forms? Why doesn't the absurdity of threatening what may well be mutual suicide lead to the collapse or abandonment of the policy?[38] This is an important question for which there is no simple answer. It may have to do with the harsh political reality that nuclear weapons exist in large numbers and U.S. officials believe they have to find a means for justifying their existence. But there is another more important consideration. This is the belief generally shared by policymakers that to affirm *not* to use them would put the United States at the mercy of its nuclear-armed foe who, allegedly, is guided by concerns that reflect a coldblooded, if not

---

36 For a further detailed analysis of the problems of "rationality" and deterrence, see Patrick M. Morgan, *Deterrence* (Beverly Hills: Sage, 1977) and John Steinbruner, "Beyond Rational Deterrence: The Struggle for New Concepts," *World Politics* (January, 1976), pp. 223-245.

37 *Newsweek*, December 5, 1983.

38 One White House adviser would add: "Because asymmetries at other levels of military force (e.g. INF, conventional forces) give the side possessing them an advantage. Strategic forces are minimum deterrents, not extended ones."

ruthless, assessment of the international situation. Rather than be put in this position, U.S. officials in the past preferred irrational threats — and hoped that they would never have to make good on them.[39]

The Role of Perception

"The importance of perceptions in the formulation of strategic policy cannot be underestimated," writes Gordon H. McCormick, the managing editor of *Orbis* and Coordinator of Military Studies at the Foreign Policy Research Institute.[40] For not only are perceptions the foundation upon which policy is based, but it is also clear that the accuracy of these perceptions is not insignificant for the policymaking process. It is not reality that determines the behavior of a nation's leaders but the image of reality. As Richards Heurer notes: "Perception is demonstrably an active rather than a passive process; it constructs rather than records reality."[41]

This observation has important ramifications for deterrence theory. Basically, it means that the actual circumstances which give credibility to deterrence from the perspective of U.S. policymakers may well have little influence on how the adversary chooses to respond. Given the fact that national leaders hold distinctive world views, they will thus respond often to what *seems* to be the same set of circumstances in very different ways. Such differences will occur despite the fact that each, from his own perspective, may well be operating in a purely "rational" fashion.

Deterrence, then, like all matters of human activity, is quite relative to time and place. Yet, the "cultural relativism" of strategic behavior is frequently lost on military analysts and observers. In focusing on the presumed "rationality" of enemy behavior, U.S. officials frequently fail to realize

---

39 A.F. Organski offers the following explanation: "Why all this talk of deterrence? ... The thought of nuclear war is intolerable and it is intolerable to believe that one's country is preparing to contribute to it. There are two ways to peace of mind: one is to change our national behavior; the other is to affirm that the behavior means the reverse of what it actually does. The latter course is obviously easier, and so we adopt it. Thus the American Air Force puts a sign on the gates of the Strategic Air Command ... saying 'Peace is our profession.' The American secretary of war is called the secretary of defense, and nuclear stockpiles are called a deterrent." A.F. Organski, *World Politics* (New York: Alfred A. Knopf, 1968), p. 336.

40 Gordon H. McCormick, "Surprise, Perceptions, and Military Style," *Orbis*, Vol. 26, No. 4 (Winter, 1983), p. 834.

41 Richards Heurer, "Cognitive Factors in Deception and Counterdeception," in Donald C. Daniel *et al.* (eds.), *Strategic Military Deception* (New York: Pergamon Press, 1982), p. 33.

that this behavior, while perhaps rational in its own terms, is rooted in perceptions of the world that are not themselves rational or universally shared. Thus, to the extent that nuclear deterrence is based on subjective assumptions, it cannot be approached in a purely objective light.

Let us take this rather abstract analysis and apply it to the very concrete American-Soviet strategic relationship. The fundamental assumption underlying U.S. deterrence theory is that decision-making in the Soviet Union involves a strictly "rational" process. This, in turn, is seen as reflecting similar considerations and weights which influence decision-making in the United States. Stanley Hoffman in his classic work *Gulliver's Troubles or the Setting of American Policy* has described fairly accurately the situation that characterizes U.S. war gamers: "Their calculations reveal clearly how they project their own mode of thought on the world and thus how they operate in a mental universe whose rationality is merely their own writ large — where opponents are supposed either to reason like Americans or to be in need of education bringing them up to this level."[42]

A case in point is the war in Vietnam. To a large degree, the perception of the threat there determined how U.S. policymakers decided to respond. Generally, American Presidents Harry Truman through Lyndon Johnson tended to view communism as monolithic even though the Sino-Soviet dispute showed that the communist world was not the monolith it was supposed to be.[43] Thus, all communist states were lumped together as evil and regarded as relentlessly hostile to the West. Given this distorted representation of the threat, containment of communism became the "logical" policy.

Today we know the "objective reality" of the situation in Asia was radically different from the perception of those U.S. policymakers, who thought of themselves as the leaders of the "free world" in the crusade against communism.[44] The reality was, as former Senator J. William

---

42 Two observers of U.S. practice relative to Soviet decision-making have noted: "It would be hard to exaggerate the influence of this (self) image on American thinking about the Soviet threat. It is perhaps safe to say that almost anything of consequence that has been written about Soviet military or foreign policy over the past decade or so has used this concept." See Matthew P. Gallagher *et al.*, *The Politics of Power: Soviet Decision Making for Defense* (Washington, D.C.: Institute for Defense Analysis, 1971), p. 774.

43 Roger Hilsman, Director of the Bureau of Intelligence and Research in the U.S. Department of State during the Kennedy Administration, maintains that "policy based on the assumption that [the communist world] was a monolith continued through the sheer inertia of the process [of policy development] itself." See his *The Politics of Policy Making in Defense and Foreign Affairs* (New York: Harper & Row, 1971), p. 128.

44 In his memoir, *A Soldier Reports* (New York: Doubleday, 1976), General William

Fulbright has argued, "a fragmented communist world in which some communist states were a threat while others did not pose a threat or very much of one."[45] If U.S. policy-makers had possessed at the time an accurate perception of the nature of different communist regimes, of the conflict among these regimes and the character of the war in Vietnam, the United States might well have avoided involvement in that disastrous struggle.[46]

Misperception, of course, is not unique to United States policymakers. Soviet Premier Nikita Khrushchev, as we know, badly miscalculated the reaction of President John Kennedy to the emplacement of Soviet nuclear missiles in Cuba in 1962.[47] As a result, the superpowers came uncomfortably close at that time to armed conflict which could have led to the use of nuclear weapons.[48]

What all this means for deterrence theory is that it does not take into account the differing styles of national behavior and thus suffers from being "culture bound." Rather than seeing our strategic relationship with the Soviet Union from the perspective of Soviet decision-makers, we have adopted a national strategy which is seen as "rational" in terms of our own view of the world. In short, U.S. officials tend to conceive of the enemy in their own image. The result may well be that our policymakers are simply taking into consideration what they would do if faced with what they believed to be a similar set of circumstances and choices. However, the Soviet leadership, which tends to view the international situation in terms of its own unique experience and worldview, can not be counted on to respond in the same way our leaders would.

C. Westmoreland, the overall commander of U.S. forces in Vietnam at the end, claims that U.S. officials realistically assessed the threat of communism in Vietnam. Our failure there was, in his view, due more than anything else to a failure of will.

45 J. William Fulbright, *Old Myths and New Realities* (New York: Vintage, 1964), pp. 3-46.
46 One must be careful here to avoid another pitfall of perception/misperception. Namely, that if only policymakers perceive each other correctly, there will be peace and harmony. See Robert Jervis, "Deterrence and Perception," *International Security*, Vol. 7 (Winter, 1982-83), pp. 3-14 and 19-30.
47 James L. Payne strongly disagrees. He says: "The Russians did not miscalculate in Cuba; they drew a reasonable conclusion from our behavior." See *The American Threat: The Fear of War as an Instrument of Foreign Policy* (Chicago: Markham Publishing Co., 1970), p. 47.
48 There is still some debate about how serious the crisis really was. President Kennedy, reviewing the thirteen days of the crisis, estimated that the probablity of disaster at the crucial point in the confrontation had been "between one out of three and even." See Theodore Sorensen, *Kennedy* (New York: Bantam Books, 1966), p. 705.

The Idea of Sufficiency

Applied to the nuclear age, effective deterrence depends on sufficient nuclear capability to frighten a possible aggressor. The potential aggressor must be convinced he is calling certain retaliatory destruction down on his head. Or, in the words of the U.S. Military Posture Statement for Fiscal Year 1983: "Deterrence depends upon the assured capability and manifest will to inflict damage on the Soviet Union disproportionate to any goals that rational Soviet leaders might hope to achieve."

But what is a "sufficient" nuclear capability? Not too long ago Navy Secretary John Lehman said: "You have to have a war-winning capability if you are to succeed." For his part, Secretary of Defense Caspar Weinberger stated: "You show me a Secretary of Defense who's planning not to prevail (in a war), and I'll show you a Secretary of Defense who ought to be impeached."[49] As the New York *Times*, after obtaining a "top secret" Administration planning document, reported: The document made clear that the United States should prepare to fight a "prolonged" nuclear war and be able to "prevail" in it and "force the Soviet Union to seek earliest termination of hostilities on terms favorable to the United States."[50]

The idea of some Reagan Administration officials that somehow we can "prevail" in a nuclear exchange, critics note, points up the dubious nature of the whole doctrine of deterrence. For, as it once was interpreted, deterrence doctrine seemed to call for rough equality in forces — not superiority. Should one side or the other ever obtain a so-called "first-strike" capability (that is, the ability to launch a nuclear strike against an enemy, so overwhelming him that he would not be able to retaliate and inflict "unacceptable damage" on the initiator) deterrence could seriously be upset. The theory of deterrence, as once applied, acknowledged the undesirability of an effective defense against a nuclear attack. But "prevailing" in a nuclear war now requires such a defense. Proponents of deterrence at one time sought stability, and deterrence was seen by some as consistent with arms control agreements based on rough equality.; but "prevailing," since it presupposes superiority, is inconsistent with such agreements. In short, the theory of deterrence is being turned on its head by the Reagan Ad-

---

49 "Unless a potential adversary believes your retaliation for his aggression is unacceptable," observes one U.S. official, "you do not have deterrence. Also planning to win does not guarantee you will. But not planning to win guarantees you will lose and cannot be the policy of any Administration."

50 This secret document was entitled "Fiscal Year 1984-1988 Defense Guidance," and provides general guidance over a five-year period for America's armed services. One U.S. official familiar with this document would add: "And, if we are not successful, we want to be certain we can sue for peace on the best terms possible."

ministration to justify plans that really are based on other more important (and in the eyes of most critics "more dangerous") assumptions, such as the idea that the U.S. can "prevail" in a nuclear war.

The Notion of Fear

How many or what kinds of nuclear weapons will create the precise degree of fear to promote the desired behavior in a potential aggressor? Which psychologist can define it? Which technician can measure it? All importantly, at what point will *too much* fear shatter rationality if it indeed prevails?

The concept of fear, which is crucial if deterrence is to work, tends to oversimplify motivation. There are more motives acting in favor of military restraint in the nuclear age than a simple fear of nuclear retaliation. But strict deterrence theory recognizes only this fear, disregarding all other factors.[51]

The Notion of Credibility

In the view of U.S. military strategists today deterrence can only work if our threat to use nuclear weapons is perceived as credible by the adversary. In other words, the Soviet leadership — if it is to be discouraged from aggression in areas vital to American interests (e.g., Western Europe) or using its nuclear missiles against the United States — must believe that the U.S. will use nuclear weapons against the U.S.S.R.[52]

51 One U.S. official would strongly disagree. As he sees it, "Deterrence is a state of mind which prevents a potential adversary from aggressive actions, not through fear, but through rational conclusions of the costs to him should he attack."

52 Professor John Herz of the City University of New York and the author of *International Politics in the Atomic Age* says here: "I think the role of purposeful uncertainty (will they or will they not — what the Germans call *Verrueckt-Spielen*) has to be emphasized. Leaving the opponent uncertain about retaliation may be the best way to deter him from first use . . ." Letter to this writer, April 6, 1984. Ambassador Martin J. Hillenbrand would emphasize in this regard: "Your discussion goes too far in saying that the view of U.S. military strategists today is that the Soviet leadership, if it is to be discouraged from committing aggression against an area in which we have a vital interest, must know with *complete* certainty that we will use nuclear weapons against the U.S.S.R. This does not allow for the fact that there is a great deal of dispute within the U.S. government as to what credibility means in practice. Here I come back to my point . . . about deterrence deriving essentially from lack of certainty that nuclear weapons will not be used rather than certainty that they will be used as the essence of deterrence. We have,

How is the opponent made to believe that this threat is credible? The principal answer given by strategic theorists is by means of a credible commitment. This answer has two major parts. In the first place, proponents of deterrence argue, credibility is an expression of the interests of a nation. According to this view, a nuclear state is most likely to go to war and risk enormous losses if its home territory is attacked. It is also said to be more willing to take this risk if more important allies are attacked than it is when lesser allies or friends in areas of secondary importance are threatened. Thus, Moscow's leaders must surely assume that an attack on the United States will lead to a retaliatory strike. From time to time there may be some question in the Kremlin whether or not U.S. officials would come to the defense of its NATO allies. However, the precedent of two interventions in two world wars would seem to make it clear that the United States does take its NATO obligations seriously.[53] However, proponents are willing to admit that in non-Western areas the American nuclear threat may be perceived as less credible and limited probes may be undertaken to test such resolve. In short, credibility from this perspective is largely the reflection of a nation's interests and the priorities among those interests.

Credibility can also be achieved by other means. These include staking one's reputation and making automatic commitments. The former technique consists of making a commitment that involves a state's national honor and/or prestige, its bargaining reputation and the confidence of its own

of course, always indulged in what I would call heavy rhetoric on the subject of defending our position in Berlin and in Europe against Soviet attack, and the recent debate about no-first-use is relevant in this context." Letter to the author, April 27, 1984.

53 It is sometimes argued that the introduction of nuclear weapons has greatly reduced the reliability of alliances. In the context of NATO, one West German official states: "There was no risk to the U.S. homeland during World War II; today there is." On its face, this hypothesis seems entirely plausible. Yet, according to one student of international affairs, A.F. Organski, "the evidence points the other way. "In the first twenty years of the nuclear era few countries have been abandoned by their allies. The United States defended Iran in 1946 and Turkey in 1947, and the Western powers have defended Berlin from 1948 to the present day..."

The behavior of France during the Cuban Missile Crisis is an interesting case in point. "Here was a confrontation between two nuclear giants where the danger of nuclear war was clear," writes Organski. "[H]ere too was a situation that endangered only American security. Yet when the United States decided to stand up to the Soviet Union, all her allies stood firmly by her." Even General de Gaulle of France, "by that time a bitter critic of American policy and intent on breaking up the Western bloc" (who had not even been consulted on the American decision beforehand) simply said when informed: "If there is a war, I will be with you." See Organski, *World Politics* New York: Alfred A. Knopf, 1968), p. 332.

citizens and allies. The idea is that once U.S. authorities make a threat involving these values in public, it will be difficult not to carry it out.

Staking one's reputation, then, is seen as the kind of commitment from which it is difficult to retreat (it is theoretically too costly not to honor such a pledge). On the other hand, an automatic commitment is one from which it is impossible to retreat. This type of pledge is likened to "burning one's bridges." For example, there is the ultimate but imaginary automatic commitment in Herman Kahn's famous "doomsday machine," which would blow up the whole world if the enemy fired its nuclear weapons — even if the defender were caught by surprise. In summary, then, the main point here is that the "power to bind oneself" is seen as the critical factor in any nuclear bargaining situation.[54]

Critics have stressed that the notion of credibility is one of the major weak points in the whole doctrine of nuclear deterrence. We have erred, they say, in taking a questionable military doctrine, applied traditionally in a conventional context, and injecting it (albeit with certain refinements) into a radically different international situation.

Moreover, these people would note that in real political life irrevocable commitments — the kind necessary under a nuclear deterrence policy — are rare if they exist at all.[55] The reason for this is that states seldom deliberately take inflexible stands from which they cannot retreat if their adversaries stand firm and hostilities appear to be both imminent and undesirable. Thus, threats are usually ambiguous and commitments somewhat looser.

The Vietnam War is a case in point. The United States had to fight that war, it was argued repeatedly in military and political circles in the 1960s, in order to demonstrate American will and determination in combating communism and publicly affirm the "credibility of U.S. power." But the Vietnam War, Robert J. Lifton argues, "demonstrated, if nothing else, the opposite — the *non*credibility of American power."[56]

The re-embrace of the concept of limited nuclear war, Lifton maintains, "is partly an effort to reassert the 'credibility' of that power by retaining

---

54 See Oran R. Young, *The Politics of Force: Bargaining during International Crisis* (Princeton: Princeton University Press, 1968), pp. 177-265.

55 For the argument that deterrent theorists have overemphasized the importance of resolve and paid insufficient attention to the interest of each side in the issue at stake see Robert Jervis, "Bargaining and Bargaining Tactics," in J. Roland Pennock et al. (eds.), *Nomos*, Vol 14: *Coercion* (Chicago: Aldine Atherton, 1972), pp. 281-83.

56 Robert J. Lifton, *Indefensible Weapons: The Political and Psychological Case Against Nuclearism* (New York: Basic Books, 1982), p. 32. One former U.S. official disagrees. "Vietnam demonstrated that we will fight, even though we did not win."

the nuclear option, together with the illusion of limit and control." Here the "unacceptable actuality that had to be denied at all cost was the self-image of the United States as the 'pitiful, helpless giant' so bitterly articulated by President Nixon." Precisely this struggle "around the persistent, never-realizable quest for nuclear weapons-based 'credibility' drove two presidents into states of something like madness and led to the near-ruin of our political system.'"

The fact that the Soviet Union now possesses its own formidable (and in some respects invulnerable) nuclear arsenal (with weapons so powerful as to be able to inflict on the United States much more death and destruction than mere "unacceptable damage") has seriously undermined the credibility of the U.S. nuclear threat, particularly the threat to use strategic forces to defend Western Europe. Critics point out here the military uselessness of these weapons of mass destruction. This awareness, they say, is now becoming more generally recognized thanks to the efforts of Robert McNamara, former Secretary of Defense, and Harland Cleveland, former U.S. Ambassador to NATO. (More on this later in Chapter XII, "The Boomerang Effect.")

In short, despite what U.S. government spokesmen say to the contrary, there will always be significant uncertainty in any deterrent posture. In the view of the critics, this uncertainty is a good thing, for it may be the only hope we have that such weapons of mass destruction will never be used, but it also represents a weakness in the logic of deterrence.

Ambiguity of Deterrence Doctrine

Opponents of the doctrine of nuclear deterrence maintain that another of its major weaknesses is its ambiguity. Often it is not clear just what kind of attack it is supposed to prevent.

Deterrence is often not credible because, even when the stakes are huge, carrying out the threat would be foolish both for threatener and threatened. The credibility of deterrence is dubious because the potential troublemaker realizes that his opponent's threatened retaliation may boomerang.

One could go farther than this. Not only the basic elements of the doctrine of deterrence, but also the "logic" of adding new, more dangerous weapons to one's arsenal of weapons would seem to work to multiply conflicts short of total war, but which could escalate into a nuclear exchange. Thus, the pendulum that swings from hope to panic comes frequently to rest on anxiety.

Problem of Arms Promotion

Another major problem with a nuclear deterrence strategy has to do with the dynamics of contemporary armaments. The main premise of deterrence is that an adversary can only be checked by the threat of nuclear destruction. The doctrine thus promotes a constant increase in armaments to enhance retaliatory power and inflict potentially ever greater damage on the enemy.[57] Presented to the general public as a formula to preserve peace, the policy of nuclear deterrence has, in fact, meant the constant perfection of the tools of mass destruction. In other words, as critics point out, the prevailing acceptance of the doctrine of deterrence is mainly responsible for the speeding up of technological innovations with a primarily military potential — and this has not always worked to promote international peace and security (which, proponents of deterrence say, a "balance of terror" hopes to ensure).

Both superpowers spend vast sums of money to make sure that a significant portion of their retaliatory forces is relatively invulnerable to enemy attack. They do this to ensure that whoever pre-empts will not escape unscathed. At the same time, both sides invest huge sums of money in the attempt to make each other's forces vulnerable. They do this in order to limit damage to themselves if deterrence fails and war begins. However, neither side feels comfortable with these efforts because in the end such a strategy still leaves the security of one side up to the "rational" decisions of the other. And neither the United States nor the Soviet Union wants to make itself dependent on the actions of the other.

Game Theoretical Assumptions

One of the major problems with nuclear deterrent strategies has to do with their game theoretical assumptions. Strategic thinkers in the West have been greatly influenced in their formulation of doctrine by game theory and its mathematical calculations. Game theorists base their models on the belief that decisions are derived from utility-maximizing choices which are objectively neutral. A noted example is the "prisoner's dilemma." It stresses interdependent choice in the combination of conflict and co-operation found in many social and political situations. The basic story of the dilemma is told by Bruce Russet and Harvey Starr:[58]

---

57 One U.S. official takes issue here. "The heart of the Administration's arms control policies is to seek mutual deterrence — but at much *lower* levels of armaments."

58 See Bruce Russet and Harvey Starr, *World Politics: The Menu for Choice* (San Francisco: W.H. Freeman & Co., 1981), pp. 337-38.

Two people are arrested on suspicion after an armed robbery and murder have been committed. They are kept in separate cells with no chance to communicate with each other. Each person "is presented with a pair of unattractive options, as each is questioned separately and given this choice by the police official: 'I'm pretty sure that you two were responsible for the killing, but I don't have quite enough evidence to prove it. If you will confess first and testify against the other prisoner, I will see that you are set free without any penalty, though he will be sentenced to life imprisonment. On the other hand, I am making the same proposal to him, so if he confesses first you will be the one to spend life in prison and he will go free. If you both confess on the same day we will have a little mercy, but you still will be badly off because you both will then be sentenced to 20 years in prison for armed robbery. Should you both be stubborn, we cannot convict you for a major crime, and I can only punish you for a small crime in your past life, carrying a one-year prison term. If you want to take a chance that your fellow prisoner will keep quiet, therefore, go ahead. But if he doesn't — and you know what sort of criminal he is — you will do very badly. Think it over.'"

What will the prisoners do? On the face of things, it seems that it would serve the interests of both prisoners to remain silent. However, there is a great deal of uncertainty. One prisoner worries that the other might feel compelled to talk, since it would be to his advantage to do so. If under such conditions Prisoner A does not talk, A serves a full jail sentence. Prisoner B is, of course, comtemplating similar thoughts about the possible actions of Prisoner A. Thus, both prisoners will talk and both will serve 20-year sentences, even though both would have been better off keeping quiet.

Importantly, according to game theory, both prisoners would be completely rational if they did talk. Both have to assume that the other prisoner will make his best move. Thus, each prisoner has to act in the way that would be best for himself *given the best move of the other prisoner.* This is the essence of game theory: Discover the best strategy of your adversary and act accordingly. While such a strategy may not obtain for you the maximum gain, it will prevent you from incurring the maximum loss.

The "prisoner's dilemma" turned out to be the perfect intellectual rationale for the "cold war." For instance, it was possible to apply the dilemma to the Soviet-American arms race. One only had to substitute "build more" for "talk" and "stop building" for "silence." It made sense for both sides to stop building, but neither superpower could have the confidence to agree to a treaty to stop building arms because it suspected that the other might cheat, build more and go on to victory. In this way, distrust and the fostering of international tensions could be elevated to the status of an intellectual exercise, a mathematical axiom.

One of the main problems with deterrent strategies based on such game-theoretical assumptions is that they presume simultaneous choice. Thus, game theory fails to capture the dynamic nature of international relations. World events do not simply occur in a historical vacuum. Rather, they take place in a highly complex context of action and reaction, much of which is difficult to explain without fuller information than often is initially the case.[59]

In this context, it may be useful to recall the warning offered by William H. Riker and Peter C. Ordeshook:[60]

Political scientists too often take examples (as well as the theorems of game theory) as fully operating models of real political processes. Thus, we read such sentences as "let China be the first decision maker with strategies a_1 and a_2, and let..." But it is absurd to believe that any complex process can be so simply modeled, just as it is absurd to suppose that the design of an efficient gas turbine resides somewhere as a deduction from the basic laws of thermodynamics.

This warning should not be misunderstood as a bar to inquiry based on mathematical theory. But one can not afford to overlook the very real and serious limitations of this theory when applied to real-life situations in international politics, particularly the crucial matter of nuclear deterrence.

No doubt, the major problem with trying to apply game theory to the field of nuclear deterrence is the growing body of literature which suggests that the Soviets are extremely skeptical of this approach. Perhaps one of the best studies of the Soviet views on the application of game-theoretic propositions to international relations is the investigation undertaken in the late 1960s by Thomas W. Robinson. He concludes that the Soviets generally view game theory with suspicion because of its Western origins.

---

59 Many deterrence theorists maintain that the exact relationship between game theory and deterrence theory is frequently misunderstood. Albert Wohlstetter, for instance, has managed at one and the same time to insist both that deterrence theorists have not, as charged, made much use of game theory, and that it has been very useful to them. His argument reminds one critic of the apocryphal defense attorney's opening address to the jury: "Ladies and Gentlemen of the jury, the defense will prove that my client never saw this woman before; that in any event he did not attack her but she consented; and that furthermore he was temporarily deranged while under the influence of alcohol and thus unable to tell right from wrong or know the nature and consequences of his acts." Phillip Greene, *Deadly Logic: The Theory of Nuclear Deterrence* (Columbus: Ohio State University, 1966), p. 93. Greene argues that misunderstanding has often been the fault of deterrence theorists rather than of their critics and the general public.

60 William H. Riker and Peter C. Ordeshook, *An Introduction to Positive Political Theory* (Englewood Cliffs, N.J.: Prentice-Hall, 1973), p. 239.

They also have trouble accepting the claim by Western strategic thinkers that this theory is "ideologically neutral."[61]

Problem of Empirical Verification

Proponents of deterrence generally like to treat their strategic theory as if it were scientific. To be sure, it tries, like science, to proceed by reasoning. However, it lacks an element that is crucial to science: empirical verification. In this respect, it is similar to theories in physics constructed without the benefit of experimentation or the formation of sociological theories without the benefit of a society to observe.

This is not an unimportant point, given the inherent danger with theory — namely, that it comes to supplant reality in the minds of theorists. In the nuclear age, this danger is especially acute. As Jonathan Schell put it in a recent article on nuclear weapons in *The New Yorker:* "Never, perhaps, has pure doctrine, uncorrected by empirical knowledge, been given freer rein or assigned a more important role in the regulation of human affairs."[62]

When experience is replaced by theory, the very real possibility always exists that the assumptions of the theory will be accepted as conclusions. And this seems to be the case with deterrence — even though there are some very good reasons not to do this. One especially dangerous assumption of this kind is that if our adversary gets the slightest opening to do his worst to us, he will do it.

One of the dire consequences of this assumption is that it introduces an extreme form of reductionism into policy. By emphasizing the importance of threatening to launch nuclear missiles against the Soviet Union, for instance, we downplay the significance of other influences on Soviet behavior such as diplomatic, economic and political measures. Our policy in a crucial area thus becomes primarily a military policy, and a dangerous one at that.

Problem of Projecting a "Devil Image"

Another pernicious result of this kind of reductionist thinking is the danger that it can become a self-fulfilling prophecy. Two countries, like the United States and the Soviet Union, by starting with the assumption of unmitigated enmity between them, and by proceeding on both sides to

---

61 Thomas W. Robinson, "Game Theory and Politics: Recent Soviet Views," *Studies in Soviet Thought,* Vol. 10 (1970), pp. 291-315.

62 Jonathan Schell, "The Abolition," *The New Yorker,* January 9, 1984.

build their nuclear forces accordingly, can soon discover that the unmitigated hostility has become real. Psychologists tell us that in a situation when one person threatens another with annihilation, this adversary relationship has emotional and psychological consequences independent of any prior, underlying enmity.[63]

A major assumption underlying U.S. foreign policy since the early postwar period has been the "devil image" of the Soviet Union, critics point out. Americans have assumed the Soviets to be diabolically aggressive and a malevolent force in the world. Generally, Americans have tended to see the U.S. role in the world as that of the good guys containing the bad guys, the protectors of Western civilization from the communist menace. They have more or less assumed that but for the powerful military forces in the U.S., the Soviet Union would have taken over the world through military conquest, since Soviet officials understand only brute military force. Many Americans have shared a profound distrust and even hatred of the Soviets. In their view, any temporary departure from this anti-Soviet stimulus has always been a brief aberration. President Reagan's re-articulation of the image of the Soviet Union as the "focus of evil in the modern world" may strike some people as crude. But the critics believe it accurately reflects certain popular and official attitudes.

A deterrence policy cannot be maintained unless one side manufactures greater and greater distrust of the other, they maintain. To prod Congress into voting larger and larger military budgets, the Soviet Union must be pictured in ever more lurid terms — thus making accommodation increasingly difficult. Utimately, our preoccupation with deterrence may lead us to become prisoners of our own fixations.[64] More concretely, the critics

63 Ray Cline, Senior Associate at the Center for Strategic and International Studies, Georgetown University, and a former high-level official in the CIA, would disagree here. He writes: "I agree with nearly everything you say in your chapter on deterrence, but the net thrust is to suggest that the policy is in error, which I do *not* believe. The key point is that Americans are not the source of the feeling of 'unmitigated enmity' with the USSR. They get euphoric over any contrary view! On the other hand, Russians have the concept of irreconcilable conflict between their socialist (Leninist) system of society and ours drummed into them from earliest school days. How do you deal with that?" Letter to this writer, February 29, 1984.

64 The great discrepancies between images of reality in the Soviet Union and the West have led some social scientists to imply that most cold-war conflicts were caused by incongruent images rather than by irreconcilable objectives. See, for example, Urie Bronfenbrenner, "Allowing for Soviet Perceptions," in *International Conflict and Behavioral Science*, ed. by Roger Fisher (New York: Basic Books, 1964), pp. 161-78; and the critical discussion by Ralph K. White, "Images in the Context of International Conflict: Soviet Perceptions of the U.S. and the U.S.S.R.," in *International Behavior*, ed., by Kelman, pp. 236-76.

argue, we may not be able to prevent a nuclear war or survive if we persist in a policy which promotes a devil image of the U.S.S.R.

To be sure, a rejection of the devil image of the Soviet Union would not convert Soviet leaders into angels or render them militarily harmless. To state the obvious, they are obsessed with national defense. But Soviet officials are not insane, and the Soviet people have no stomach for nuclear war.

In this view, it does us no good to continue to bewail the fact that Russian political traditions are less humane and more violent than ours. Our task is not to re-create the Russians in our own image but to deal with them as they are, practically and realistically. Despite our great ideological differences, we and the Russians must learn to live together on this planet or we will surely die together. In this context, the famous remark made by Henry Kissinger in 1976 still makes sense today: "We are doomed to coexist" with the Soviet Union.

Summary

Let us review briefly the conception of nuclear deterrence. It is often taken for granted that the possession of full nuclear power (i.e., a second-strike capability) will so instill fear in an adversary that it will be deterred from action that would provoke a major military attack. When two opposing nuclear powers confront each other in this way, a "balance of terror" is said to exist that will prevent nuclear war through mutual deterrence.

From the foregoing analysis, we can see that conceptually the idea of nuclear deterrence leaves much to be desired. It is a vague term that has been used in a number of different ways. For many officials, who talk about "prevailing" in a nuclear war, it is now apparently a slogan. However, the concept is useful for public relations purposes because it sounds good. But it has no real value as a guide to what we *should* do in our policy toward the Soviet Union.

Most of the theoretical problems with the idea of nuclear deterrence stem from vague notions and some questionable assumptions. These weaknesses have been highlighted by historians, diplomats and critical social scientists, although until now little systematic effort was made to combine their findings and make use of them.

To be sure, misgivings about the notion of nuclear deterrence do not stem from any doubt about the ability of the two superpowers to destroy each other in actual conflict. Nor do they stem from any doubt that the horror of nuclear war has inspired both American and Soviet leaders to reflect on this possibility. However, the evidence now available leaves serious doubts that the balance of terror has actually served to deter them in the manner often assumed by the proponents of nuclear deterrence.[65]

The first major problem with the concept of nuclear deterrence is the way in which it sprang up. Taken from the conventional context, it has radically been transplanted to apply with assured validity to the nuclear context. This was done without adequate thought being given to the fact that the conventional and nuclear situations are fundamentally dissimilar. In the past, conventional weapons were amassed to deter enemy aggression before actual war, and they were also used to defend against that aggression if deterrence failed (which was not infrequent). Today that practical utility of nuclear weapons, which can wreak havoc on an unprecedented scale, is highly questionable should deterrence fail.

The second serious problem with nuclear deterrence has to do with the notion of "rationality" which underpins the concept. Considerable evidence has been accumulated by social scientists and others, the net effect of which is to suggest that the rational-actor model does not prevail across the board in international politics. High-level decision-makers frequently do not act rationally, particularly under the stressful conditions inherent in a crisis situation when their tolerance for ambiguity is reduced. Moreover, as some scholars have noted, in stressing the alleged rational behavior of statesmen, strategic thinkers have tended to overlook the basically irrational component of the strategy when applied in the contemporary era. How rational is it for one side to threaten the other with massive destruction when the other side is capable of responding in kind?

Lawrence Freedman, head of policy studies at the Royal Institute of International Affairs, puts it this way in his 1982 article in *Foreign Policy:* "The United States would be irrational to commit suicide on behalf of Western Europe, but NATO has not found this fact a decisive flaw in its strategy."

65 The effect of nuclear weapons on international political behavior and misbehavior is the subject of hot debate. On the one hand, Michael Mandelbaum argues that to date at least nuclear-armed states have conducted their foreign relations regarding one another with a measure of caution that is unusual historically. See his *The Nuclear Revolution: International Politics Before and After Hiroshima* (New York: Cambridge University Press, 1981). This conclusion is contested by A.F. Organski. "A look at the prenuclear period before World War II reveals, to be sure," he says, "examples of recklessness by Nazi Germany and by Imperial Japan that may be without parallel in the nuclear age, but it also reveals examples of excessive caution. The Russians under Stalin were immensely cautious with Hitler, and who can forget Chamberlain and Daladier at Munich? One is tempted to be malicious and suggest that had Hitler possessed atomic bombs, an untold amount of scholarship would have been devoted to proving that they were the cause of Western caution." See his *World Politics* (New York: Alfred A. Knopf, 1958), p. 315.

Even if we assume for a moment that national decision-makers are rational, this would say virtually nothing about the accuracy of the information employed in rational calculations. Rationality refers only to the desire of maximizing certain specified values or preferences. It does not say anything about whether or not the information used is correct or incorrect. As a result, rational decision-makers may make grave errors in calculation that lead them to precipitate national destruction.

But one of the main problems with the theory of deterrence is that it fails to distinguish between the process of the strategy and the assumptions and perceptions from which the formulation of strategy proceeds. Where the former is a calculated act (and thus by definition a "rational" process), the latter are extremely subjective and, as a consequence, not easily reducible to rational explanation. As Ken Booth has observed in his insightful *Strategy and Ethnocentrism:* "Although strategy itself might be conceived as a universal preoccupation, (this) does not mean that it is conceived in universal terms."[66] Thus, while statesmen are often regarded as "utility maximizers," they are in fact both at the mercy of their assumptions and their perceptions of the world around them.

To put it more concretely, as the Harvard Nuclear Study Group observed in a recent report, "deterrence, like beauty, is in the eye of the beholder."[67] This, of course, is a cardinal weakness of the theory. And it is the main reason why our hopes for peace cannot be allowed to rest permanently upon it.

The general theory of deterrence assumes the same kind of rationality for all actors. However, we should not forget that the Soviet leadership operates on its own perceptions of reality — not ours. And these perceptions are derived from a set of circumstances quite different from our own. The Soviet view of the world and its security requirements is a view from the Kremlin; it is not a view from Washington where game theoretical assumptions have become enshrined in official U.S. strategic doctrine. In short, nuclear deterrence, as practised by the United States, assumes a symmetry of values. But, of course, this is not necessarily so. A status quo power will value peace more than leaders who feèl their country has been deprived of a "place in the sun."

Critics of nuclear deterrence maintain that nuclear war is, and ought to be, unthinkable. And it is true that the proponents of deterrence have not made the danger of nuclear war the central feature of their analysis. Indeed, as the Reagan Administration's emphasis on a nuclear war-fighting

---

66 Ken Booth, *Strategy and Ethnocentrism* (London: Croom, Helm, 1973), p. 20.
67 Albert Carnesale *et al., Living With Nuclear Weapons* (New York: Bantam Books, 1983), p. 33.

strategy suggests, there seems to be a wide-spread notion among U.S. military planners today that a "rational" government must plan to initiate nuclear war if only to deter. And if deterrence fails, the United States must be ready to "prevail" in a nuclear war. In this regard, one should note that deterrence must be the only public policy that is a total failure if it is successful only 99.9 percent of the time.

This situation brings us to the third major weakness in nuclear deterrence strategies — the problem of credibility. On the one hand, proponents of deterrence argue that the threat must be credible to work in the way it should (so that peace will be obtained). Yet how credible is the threat to commit mutual suicide? Henry Kissinger stated the case even more strongly in his jolting speech in Brussels in 1979. At that time he said: "It is absurd to base the strategy of the West on the credibility of the threat of mutual suicide."[68] The reality is that we know little about the psychology of credibility; yet deterrent theorists just assume it in their matrices.

Fourth, there is the great difficulty in operationalizing a concept which is inherently ambiguous. Who is being deterred? At what level? The lack of clarity in the concept turned general policy often creates situations in which the threat of retaliation is blurred and thus ineffective.[69]

A fifth significant weakness in nuclear deterrence strategy is that it rests to a large extent on game-theoretical assumptions. However, mathematical theory quite obviously falsifies the way in which many decisions are made in real world political contexts. Moreover, there is little evidence that the Soviet leadership subscribes to such thinking in international relations.

A sixth major problem with nuclear deterrence is the notion of sufficiency which underpins the theory. The development of new and more nuclear weapons systems is often justified by invoking the name of deterrence. Yet no strategic thinker can say with any degree of certainty how many — or what kinds — of weapons are sufficient for deterrence. The result is an upward spiral of the arms race which is frequently justified on the need to continue to deter the other side.

A seventh important conceptual problem with nuclear deterrence is its uni-dimensional character. Basically, the theory relies on instilling fear in an opponent to change his behavior. Thus, deterrence tends to disregard all other factors which may influence a foe's attitude. As a consequence, it leads to an imprudent militarization of foreign policy (in the attempt to

---

68 Speech of September 1, 1979, *Survival* (November-December, 1979), p. 266.

69 This recognition may have been what led Kissinger to declare in the fall of 1979 that "extended deterrence" — nuclear protection by nuclear powers of non-nuclear allies — is dead, although not everyone agrees, as NATO members continue to debate the role of nuclear deterrence in the defense of Western Europe.

back up the threat). Most importantly, the theory of deterrence as it is applied today tends to impede the consideration of developing *positive* inducements to modify the behavior of an adversary. For instance an over-reliance on deterrence stands in the way of implementing such traditional elements of state interaction as classical diplomacy and economic exchange which, at the very least, should supplement a strong defensive posture.[70]

Eighth, the policy of nuclear deterrence tends to promote and rely on a "devil image" of the adversary. Yet one can be considered a formidable opponent without at the same time being considered a "beast." Such an approach tends to perpetuate enmity and makes accomodation much more difficult. It also may turn into a self-fulfilling prophecy. As Ambassador George Kennan says: "If we insist on demonizing these Soviet leaders, on viewing them as total and incorrigible enemies . . ., that, in the end, is the way we shall assuredly have them."[71]

We know from a study of history that there is no such thing as a permanent enemy. This not unsubtle truth was reaffirmed in the 1970s when the "devil image" of Communist China to which important U.S. policymakers had subscribed for twenty years was replaced by a new image of Beijing as a limited adversary and, possibly, even a potential ally.

Finally, a policy which ensures an overreliance on threats in a relationship may actually be very dangerous. For as many psychologists tell us, people react differently to threats. While some may be induced to act more cautiously, others may actually be provoked to strike out in desperation. To be sure, much depends on the mindset of the adversary, but deterrence fails to take this important distinction into account; it tends to treat all opponents alike in their alleged susceptibility to threats. Paradoxically, then, the very weapons intended to deter nuclear war could well precipitate it, with consequences that are intolerable for civilization.

Peace and security require efforts not so much to respond to the hostility of an enemy as to make him less hostile. As Alexander L. George and Richard Smoke argue in their classic work *Deterrence in American Foreign*

---

[70] General Bruce C. Clarke, Commander-in-Chief of the U.S. Army in Europe between 1960 and 1962, would put things this way: "Weakness does not deter war. As Frederick the Great said: 'Diplomacy without the military is like an orchestra without instruments.' The Soviets believe in that and practice it." Letter to this writer, March 5, 1984. One critic would note here: "Does General Clarke know that Frederick the Great, who knew a lot about generals, also said: 'All generals are always on the stage.'"

[71] Speech at Dartmouth College on November 16, 1981. Here it may be worth recalling the warning issued by George Washington in his Farewell Address: "Observe good faith and justice towards all nations; cultivate peace and harmony with all ... The nation which indulges towards another an habitual hatred, or an habitual fondness, is in some degree a slave."

Policy, such efforts may be served less well by threats of punishment than by the prospect of rewards for willingness to compromise, by diplomacy rather than deterrence. However, this recognition will require willingness to modify our own objectives as well as inducing an adversary to modify his.[72]

These substantial analytical weaknesses of the theory of nuclear deterrence — a theory formulated out of expediency in the setting of the "cold war" — would seem to raise serious questions about the wisdom of relying heavily on such an idea in foreign policy. To be sure, more detailed treatment of the question needs to be carried out by scholars before a conclusive judgment can be rendered. But these findings should draw attention to the need to re-examine some of the basic assumptions we have seemed to take for granted when formulating American foreign policy.[73]

Should further study indicate the need to modify (or even replace) the doctrine of nuclear deterrence, we should not be overly optimistic about the prospects for effecting change of a policy in which there are so many important vested interests. As one four-star general said privately recently, "asking the military to relinquish nuclear deterrence is like asking unions to forego their right to strike or the clergy to renounce their doctrine of divine punishment."

---

72 Alexander L. George and Richard Smoke, *Deterrence in American Foreign Policy: Theory and Practice* (New York: Columbia University Press, 1974).

73 Ambassador Martin J. Hillenbrand argues here: "Whatever one may think about how deterrence has operated in the post-world war-II period, it is a fact that since we dropped our two fission bombs on Hiroshima and Nagasaki, no nuclear weapons have been used in anger for nearly 39 years. This is an overriding fact. Whether some rough sort of deterrence is primarily responsible, or other causal factors have been operative in a decisive sense, my own belief is that one cannot dismiss the reality of deterrence as an operating factor in the minds of decision-makers during times of crisis and confrontation." Letter to this writer, April 27, 1984.

It was assumed that we had a stockpile. We not only didn't have a pile; we didn't have a stock. *David Lilienthal*
former Chairman of the U.S. Atomic Energy Commission

III. THE ORIGINS OF U.S. NUCLEAR DETERRENCE POLICY

It is often said about nuclear deterrence that "You can't test a negative." This is not entirely true, as this book tries to show. On the one hand, one cannot know with certainty whether or not American deterrence has actually deterred until the appropriate government documents of U.S. adversaries are made available. However, one can subject the historical context in which nuclear deterrence was set to careful scrutiny to see how various American Administrations have tried to apply different deterrent theories. One can also study how these policies evolved and what U.S. policymakers really thought about them. Finally one can observe whether specific deterrence goals were met; and if not, speculate in an enlightened way why not. In short, no matter how limited our empirical observations are, the task of examining if nuclear deterrence has worked is by no means a hopeless endeavor.

U.S. Nuclear Supremacy

For a brief time after World War II, U.S. policy-makers enjoyed a dominant position that has never been equaled in history. The atomic bombs that ended the war contributed to making the United States temporarily supreme on the planet.

To be sure, the sense of supremacy that the U.S. enjoyed at the time did not prevent American officials from looking out at the world with a certain sense of foreboding. In particular, Stalin's determination to maintain an empire acquired by force in Eastern Europe disturbed them. At the same time, tensions between Soviet and American authorities in Germany were growing in intensity.[1] This convinced many officials in the Truman

---

1 In reviewing the early postwar period one must be careful, in Kurt Shell's words, not "to project the mood and insights of a later period into the first phase of postwar existence..." While the relationship between the United Stated and the

Administration that the Soviet Union was a political enemy whose ambitions were creating a state of Cold War.[2] Only the American monopoly of the atomic bomb prevented the U.S.S.R. from becoming an immediate military enemy as well. Or so it appeared to U.S. officials.[3]

    Soviet Union was by no means free of friction and increasing tensions during 1945 and 1946, both sides made genuine efforts at solving common problems. See Kurt L. Shell, "Berlin," in Walter Stahl (ed.), *The Politics of Postwar Germany* New York: Praeger, 1963), p. 87.

2 This is not the place to discuss in detail the many events, motives and perceptions that led to a hostile and fearful state of Cold War tension between Soviet and Western officials. The story is complicated and also somewhat controversial. The traditional accounts tend to put the blame for the Cold War on the Soviet Union, while "revisionist" interpretations argue that Soviet intentions were not aggressive at the time and that the Cold War was caused by unnecessary belligerence on the part of U.S. officials. More recent and balanced scholarship would suggest that the onset of hostilities in this period was due in large part to a tragedy of misperceptions on both sides.

    For some of the revisionist histories that place the responsibility for the Cold War on the U.S. see D.F. Fleming, *The Cold War and Its Origins* (2 Vols.; Garden City, N.Y.: Doubleday, 1961); Gar Alperovitz, *Atomic Diplomacy: Hiroshima and Potsdam* (New York: Vintage, 1967); William A. Williams, *The Tragedy of American Diplomacy* (Cleveland: World, 1959); Gabriel Kolko, *The Politics of War: The World and United States Foreign Policy, 1943-1946* (New York: Random House, 1968); and Thomas G. Paterson, *Soviet American Confrontation* (Baltimore: Johns Hopkins Press, 1973).

    For a critique of the revisionist approach see Arthur Schlesinger, Jr., "The Origins of the Cold War," *Foreign Affairs*, October, 1967, pp. 22-52; J.L. Richardson, "Cold War Revisionism: A Critique," *World Politics*, July 1972, pp. 579 ff.; and Robert J. Maddox, *The New Left and the Origins of the Cold War* (Princeton University Press, 1973).

3 Ambassador Martin J. Hillenbrand has this to say here: "I think you are wise to avoid falling into the morass of too much discussion of who is responsible for the Cold War. I have written a bit on the subject myself. It seems to me that one of the things lacking in revisionist treatments of the subject, and I have discussed this extensively with Professor Yergin, the author of *Shattered Peace*, which I regard as the best revisionist treatment, is that a true appreciation of the causal factors in the making of the Cold War can only come from those who were actually involved in those early post-war years. When General Clay went to Berlin in 1945 he was inclined to cooperate with the Soviet Union. However, Soviet bullying tactics in the Allied Control Council and elsewhere turned him around. It was not so much a question of what the Soviets actually were prepared to do in those days, and here I think there may have been a real misperception about their intentions. However, they did give the impression that they were prepared to use force in order to achieve their objectives in Germany and Central Europe, and there was real fear — whether misconceived or not — that a massive Soviet land invasion of Western Europe was possible and even likely. I was in Germany at the time and I can testify that the fear was real. Surprisingly enough, the nuclear factor did not play a very big role here . . ." Letter to this writer, date April 27, 1984.

The Containment Policy

In 1946 and 1947 the general perception by senior officials in the Administration of growing Soviet aggressiveness led to a debate on how to deal with the Soviet Union. In the main, this debate reflected two radically different conceptions of the U.S.S.R., which in turn led to opposed strategies for "taming" it. The first school of thought, emphasizing the military threat posed by the Kremlin, tended to rely for defense on the unspoken nuclear threat.[4] The second school generally saw the Soviet threat in a more subtle way; it viewed Stalin's Russia as posing primarily a political, economic and diplomatic challenge.[5] As things turned out, the first (or so-called "hard-line" school) prevailed in the early postwar period as Cold War tensions steadily mounted.

The first strategy for opposing Soviet ambitions that evolved was "containment," backed by an emphasis on deterrence.[6] The "containment" policy was developed by George Kennan. It grew out of his "long telegram," which was dispatched from Moscow in 1946, when he was serving in the U.S.S.R. as counselor of the embassy. This telegram, which had an alarming effect on some policymakers (it was not accepted by others), was later reworked into an article, "The Sources of Soviet Conduct," which appeared in the journal *Foreign Affairs* in 1947 under the pseudonym "Mr. X."

---

4 During this period of the Cold War, U.S. policy-makers, both senior political appointees and bureaucrats, tended to share a set of common perceptions of the Soviet Union, which was seen as expansionist and in direct conflict with the United States. Those individuals who did not fully share this set of perceptions and thus did not take a tough anti-Soviet stand were generally unable to influence policy to any great degree. A psychologist has explored this phenomenon and reached the following conclusion: Within the relatively small circle of leading officials, there was a great deal of peer pressure to conform to "groupthink"; "dovish" views were suppressed among this group whose members were trying to impress one another with their "toughness." See Irving Janis, *Victims of Groupthink* (Boston: Houghton Mifflin, 1972).

5 See John L. Gaddis, *Strategies of Containment: A Critical Appraisal of Postwar American National Security Policy* (New York: Oxford University Press, 1982).

6 The doctrine of preventing war by the threat of retaliation with atomic bombs — nuclear deterrence — remained ill defined in U.S. war plans during 1945 and early 1946. In this respect, its slow evolution in postwar strategy represented a subtle but portentous change from traditional American values. Emphasis was placed in this early period on preventing rather than fighting and winning a war. But there was the explicit provision for the first use of nuclear weapons against the civilian population of the adversary. By the summer of 1946 the atomic bomb began to assume a major role in U.S. war planning. As the Joint Chiefs of Staff wrote Barnard Baruch in June 1946, the bomb was "the one military weapon which may for the period until Russia obtains it exert a deterrent effect upon her will to expand."

In this article, Kennan advised the "containment of Russian expansive tendencies... by the adroit and vigilant application of counterforce at a series of constantly shifting geographical points..." Kennan's analysis seemed to dovetail with the strategic thinking that was developing in Washington, and his piece became influential very quickly. (Twenty years later an embarrassed Kennan wrote in his *Memoirs* that he regretted his failure not to make clear "that what I was talking about when I mentioned the containment of Soviet power was not the containment by military means of a military threat, but the political containment of a political threat.")[7] Kennan was skeptical of extending the policy of containment outside of democratic, industrialized Europe. However, with the outbreak of the Korean war in June 1950, the containment line was extended, first to the Far East and then later to the Middle East.

Conventional Imbalance in Europe

At the time the "containment" policy was being considered, the United States was at a distinctly inferior position *vis-a-vis* the Soviet Union in conventional strength in Central Europe. American, British and French occupation forces in Germany had been reduced to very low levels. Facing them across the demarcation line was an estimated force of some one hundred Red Army divisions.[8] America's wartime 12-million-man army was by then almost totally demobilized; in 1948, it had only approximately *two* divisions, which were stationed in the United States. (This tremendous disparity in conventional strength led some Germans at the time to comment that "all the Russians would need would be shoes" to march all the way to the Atlantic Ocean.)[9]

---

7 George F. Kennan, *Memoirs, 1925-1950* (Boston: Little, Brown, 1976).

8 Soviet conventional forces in Central Europe after 1945 were actually much smaller than Western estimates had them at the time. According to Khrushchev's report in 1950, the Soviet forces had been reduced after the war from 11 million men to 3 million. Western estimates in the late 1940s were 1 to 2 million men higher, exclusive of approximately half a million security troops. See Thomas W. Wolfe, *Soviet Power and Europe, 1945-1970* (Baltimore: Johns Hopkins Press, 1970), p. 10.

9 For official assessments of American and Soviet capabilities see CCS 092 U.S.S.R. (3-27-45) files for 1945-1950, Papers of the Joint Chiefs of Staff, RG 218 (National Archives). Of special importance are JWPC 416/1 Revised, January 8, 1946, section 3, and JCS 1924/2, December 16, 1948, section 34, *ibid*. See also JCS 1888/2, April 1, 1950, in CCS 370 (5-25-48), section 2, *ibid*.

Referring to this asymmetry of power in Europe, Kennan later recalled arguing[10]

We are like a man who has let himself into a walled garden and finds himself alone there with a dog with very big teeth. The dog, for the moment, shows no signs of aggressiveness. The best thing for us to do is surely to try to establish, as between the two of us, the assumption that the teeth have nothing whatsoever to do with our mutual relationship — that they are neither here nor there. If the dog shows no disposition to assume that it is otherwise, why should we raise the subject and invite attention to the disparity?

There is some debate among Cold War historians about the extent of the Soviet conventional threat to Western Europe at this time.[11] Traditional accounts highlight the sense of threat perceived by American officials in Washington, whereas more recent accounts stress the difference in how the Soviet threat was perceived in Western Europe. Professor Michael Howard of Oxford, for one, maintains that as late as the creation of NATO in 1949 "serious expectation of Soviet armed attack in Western Europe was . . . not very high." He notes it did rise dramatically for a few months in 1950 at the time of the Korean war "but even then the Europeans were less conscious of any imminent 'Soviet threat' than they were of their own weakness, disunity and inability to cope with such a threat if one emerged."[12] Of course, the view one takes of the Soviet threat depends to a large extent on where one is located. To many West Berliners situated in an "enclave," approximately 110 miles inside the Soviet occupation zone, the Berlin Blockade of 1948-49 was very real evidence of a Soviet threat.

During the Berlin crisis the U.S. government dispatched American bombers to bases in Europe within range of the U.S.S.R.[13] To be sure, this was more of a military ruse brought about by America's weakness in con-

---

10 Quoted in John L. Gaddis, *Strategies of Containment: A Critical Appraisal of Postwar American National Security Policy* (New York: Oxford University Press, 1982), p. 85.

11 The Soviet viewpoint has been analyzed very well by the Harvard Russian scholar Adam B. Ulam. He writes: "It was not until 1947 that the Soviets became convinced through a most amazing misunderstanding that the United States had an elaborate plan to undermine the Soviet empire." See Ulam, *The Rivals: America and Russia Since World War II* (New York: Penguin Books, 1980), p. 99.

12 Michael Howard, Reassurance and Deterrence: Western Defense in the 1980s," *Foreign Affairs*, (Winter, 1982/83) p. 310.

13 The two B-20 squadrons dispatched to Germany at this time were put on three-hour alert: the same was true for the B-29 group sent to the United Kingdom. See "Estimate of Berlin Situation," June 29, 1948, and "Urgent Message," Bradley to Clay, undated, "Hot File," Plans and Operations of Army General Staff, USJCS Records.

ventional strength rather than any change in strategy. Although U.S. government press releases described the B-29s flown overseas as "atomic-capable," the sixty planes sent to Britain and the small number sent to Germany had not yet been modified to carry the kind of atomic bomb that was then the centerpiece of the American nuclear arsenal.[14] But it did establish the practice of nuclear deterrence in advance of its theory for U.S. war planners.[15]

Deterrence by Improvisation

From the point of view of the Truman Administration, the most important thing during this early period was the United States' sole possession of the atomic bomb. If a war broke out, Russian cities and industrial areas would be vulnerable to atomic bombing by planes from the Strategic Air Command (SAC), the bombing division of the U.S. Air Force. As the Cold War developed, high-level U.S. officials made this threat more and more explicit.[16] (In December 1949, President Truman ordered the Strategic Air Command to include "retarding" nuclear attacks in its war planning. The purpose of such attacks would be to impede the advance of Soviet forces into territory along the borders of the Soviet Union.)[17]

The general strategy of U.S. officials at this point was to deter the outbreak of a new war by making what seemed like a drastic threat.[18] To be

14 It should be noted here that the Atomic Energy Commission had not yet granted custody of atomic bombs to the military.

15 Given the nature of Soviet espionage practices at the time, it is likely that the Russians were aware of the subtle deception being practiced in the skies over Europe. *Aviation Week* was one of the few American publications to observe that the B-29s were probably not outfitted with atomic bombs; it did report reassuringly, however, that the weapons themselves were but a day away on American territory and that the bomber crews were "ready for business."

16 See, for instance, Gregg Herke, *The Winning Weapon: The Atomic Bomb in the Cold War 1945-1950* (New York: Knopf, 1981).

17 The Strategic Air Command was the first U.S. nuclear delivery system. It was formed in March 1946, just seven months after the end of World War II, as a fleet of B-17 and B-29 medium bombers. In 1948, heavy, long-range B-36 bombers and B-50 medium bombers began to replace the World War II vintage bombers in the SAC. At the start of 1948 the U.S. Air Force had only thirty-three bombers capable of carrying atomic bombs.

18 The idea that the atomic bomb could be used in a strategy of deterring enemy attack was broached by the Joint Chiefs of Staff in their June, 1946, memorandum to Bernard Baruch. This document, which has now been declassified and can be found in the National Archives in Washington, D.C., reads in part: It is "remotely conceivable that the atomic bomb provides its own deterrent. . . . in that fear of

sure, the Soviets could not be physically prevented from seizing all of Europe (and this, in fact, was the counterthreat developed by Stalin). But the Soviet leadership would know that "Mother Russia" would be destroyed in the process if it did. Since U.S. officials believed Stalin would never risk this possibility, it was assumed that he would refrain from attacking Western Europe. Consequently, the drastic threat of nuclear destruction would never have to be carried out.[19]

In this improvised way, the strategy of nuclear deterrence sprang up. At this time, deterrence was straightforward and simple. The major advantage of the strategy was that it played to America's strength and Russia's weakness. Moreover, it seemed to offer a relatively cheap way (politically and economically speaking) to maintain the peace and freedom of Western Europe. Whether or not it would work, no one knew.[20]

A national policy of deterrence that required an emphasis on American possession of the atomic bomb was formally approved by the National Security Council in November 1948.[21] A short time later President Truman conceded to his top advisers that international control of atomic energy

> retaliation by atomic bombs against a violator who uses them will make the potential violator pause and consider before he decides to go ahead." Although the JCS entertained the notion of nuclear deterrence as "remotely conceivable" in their memo to Baruch in 1946, they later expressed concern with how such a strategy might backfire. The atomic bomb, they stated, might actually deter the United States from acting against Russian aggression. "A situation dangerous to our security could result from impressing on our own democratic peoples the horrors of future wars of mass destruction while the populations of the 'police' states remain unaware of the terrible implications."

19 In a document known as NSC-30 and entitled "Policy on Atomic Warfare," the official policy of the United States government became that of using atomic weapons in the event of war with the Soviet Union — even a war that the U.S. might initiate. This high-level policy paper, which was completed in September, 1948, noted that the atomic bomb "offers the present major counterbalance to the ever-present threat of . . . Soviet military power." This top secret document has now been declassified and can be read at the National Archives.

20 The "fragile hope" of nuclear deterrence was a dominant theme of Bernard Brodie's book, which was published in 1946 under the misleading title, *The Absolute Weapon: Atomic Power and World Order* (New York: Harcourt, Brace, 1946). Brodie, one of the earliest academic proponents of nuclear deterrence, challenged at this time some traditional military precepts such as the axiom that numerical superiority of forces makes victory more likely. But if this book foreshadowed America's reliance on nuclear deterrence, the concept of deterring rather than fighting and winning war was an idea whose time only came later in U.S. military doctrine.

21 See NSC 20/4, "Note by the Executive Secretary on U.S. Objectives with Respect to the USSR to Counter Soviet Threats to U.S. Security," November 23, 1948, U.S. Department of State, *Foreign Relations 1948*, Vol. I, pp. 662-69.

was impossible in the foreseeable future: "I am of the opinion we'll never obtain international control. Since we can't obtain international control we must be strongest in atomic weapons."[22]

If the strategy of nuclear deterrence seemed like a sound way to defend America's interests in an area where the U.S. lacked a large conventional force, it was virtually an "empty threat" in the early post-war period. For one of the most closely guarded secrets of this era was the fact that the United States had very few bombs with which to carry out its threat.[23] The technology of the day was such that atomic bombs were produced very slowly. The first atomic bombs of the 1940s were large, unwieldy and not very accurate. "By today's standards," one U.S. defense analyst observes, "they took a long time to assemble and transport."[24] After Hiroshima and Nagasaki, the U.S. reportedly had only one or two atomic bombs left in its nuclear arsenal.[25] And even as late as 1949 there were only about a hundred atomic bombs. (These were of very high yield, "city busters," and reserved for deterrence of attack on U.S. vital interests, including NATO.)[26] Since some of the SAC bombers carrying them over the Soviet

22 U.S. Department of State, *Foreign Relations of the United States: 1949*, Vol. I: *National Security Affairs, Foreign Economic Policy* (Washington, D.C.: Government Printing Office, 1976), pp. 481-82.

23 The secrecy of the number of atomic bombs in America's possession was so great that the figure was never written in reports but was always supplied verbally by the briefing officer, even to the President. According to a report by David Lilienthal, Chairman of the U.S. Atomic Energy Commission, the revelation of how few bombs were in the U.S. stockpile came as a great shock to President Truman when he was finally informed. See David E. Lilienthal, *The Journals of David E. Lilienthal*, Vol. II, *The Atomic Years, 1945-1950* (New York: 1964), pp. 580-634.

24 Michael Wormser, *U.S. Defense Policy*, 3rd ed. (Washington, D.C.: Congressional Quarterly, Inc., 1983), p. 51.

25 The number of atomic bombs in the U.S. nuclear stockpile during these early years remained a tightly held secret for a long time. General Carl Spaatz recalled later that there were only about a dozen during most of his tour as Commanding General of the Army-Air Force and Chief of Staff of the Air Force from February 1946 to April 1948. No military bomb assembly team was ready until December 1947 to replace the civilian teams that had disbanded in 1946. "This was at a time," writes David A Rosenberg, "when all bombs in the stockpile were unassembled, and it took twenty-four men nearly two days to prepare one weapon for combat." See his "American Atomic Strategy and the Hydrogen Bomb Decision," *Journal of American History* (June, 1979), p. 65.

26 In the words of Bernard Brodie, "For some time to come the primary targets for the atomic bomb will be cities. One does not shoot rabbits with elephant guns, especially if there are elephants available." Bernard Brodie, Atomic Age, quoted in Stuart Albert et al. (eds.), *On the Endings of Wars* (Port Washington, N.Y.: Kennikat Press, 1980), p. 33.

Union would presumably be shot down, every bomb that could be built was considered vitally important.[27]

U.S. bombing plans were such in the late 1940s that American planes were ordered to utilize a "bomb-as-you-go" system of attack. The few atomic bombs in the U.S. arsenal were targeted on the largest Soviet urban-industrial centers, a few large airfields and the largest Soviet ports. Should some bombs be left over in an attack, they were to be dropped on Moscow.

Impact of First Soviet Atomic Test

In the fall of 1949 two major events took place that gravely shocked the American people, making them anxious about their relative security. The first was the final victory of the communists in the Chinese civil war. The second — and most stunning — surprise was the first atomic test explosion by the Soviet Union.

The fall of China to Mao Zedong and the success of his People's Liberation Army were not a great surprise to those specialists in the government who had been following the struggle there. After all, ever since the Japanese had surrendered in 1945, the communists had been making steady progress against Chiang Kai-shek's Nationalist forces. However, the American people, who traditionally had felt a special, somewhat sentimental, attachment to China, were ill-informed about what was going on there. Thus, they were shocked when China was taken over by the communists, who were then allied with the Soviet Union.

The first atomic test explosion by the Soviet Union was an entirely different affair. The majority of U.S. officials felt that the Soviets, who did not even make good door bolts, would not be able to accomplish this for at least several more years.[28] Now, suddenly on September 23, 1949, U.S. authorities announced that it had already occurred. Hoping not to panic the American public, they cloaked this announcement with reassur-

---

27 Neither the President nor the Joint Chiefs of Staff (who had been given the job of coordinating American planning and strategy) knew how few bombs the U.S. had in its nuclear arsenal until April 1947. As Gregg Herke writes in his well-documented book: "U.S. military planning up to that date had been done in a vacuum; war plans had been based upon bombs and bombers that did not exist. By summer 1947, however, what had always been an implicit assumption of some theorists became an explicit principle of U.S. military planning when the bomb was recognized as the centerpiece of American security." See *The Winning Weapon*, p. 196.

28 A 1946 estimate by the CIA projected the first Soviet test between 1950 and 1953. See "Soviet Capabilities for Development and Production of Certain Types of Weapons and Equipment," October 31, 1946, "CIA Reports" Box, "Recently Declassified Documents," National Archives, Washington, D.C.

ance that the Soviet "device" was too large to be carried in an airplane and that real atomic bombs, even when designed, could not be manufactured in a short period of time.

The "loss" of China and the Soviet test, coming back to back, worried many Americans probably more than anything that had happened in the postwar period up to that point. While the danger was not immediate, the signs for the future were ominous. For together, the Soviet Union and "Red China" ruled over a fourth of the world's population and controlled most of the world's landmass. The question that many people had in 1949 was that if the communists had a nuclear capability, what aggressive action might they undertake next?

The reaction of the Truman Administration to these shocking developments was soon forthcoming. Basically, it was two-fold. First, the President ordered U.S. Defense Department officials to proceed with the development of a new and more terrible nuclear weapon, code named "Super."[29] (This was the hydrogen bomb or "H-bomb," as it is sometimes called.)[30] Second, Truman ordered a complete review of the world situation, with recommendations to be made for the formulation of a new national security policy.

29 There was considerable controversy in U.S. government circles over this decision. The Chairman of the Atomic Energy Commission, David E. Lilienthal, recommended against "development of the new bomb on the grounds that it was not consistent with this country's program for world peace or our own long term security." Lilienthal also questioned the deterrent effect of the H-bomb. Did the atomic bomb "provide a sense of security to us, or much elbow room?," he wrote. "What happened to the 'deterrent' — hadn't we seen how thin these arguments had proved in the past; why would it be different in the future?" We "are all giving far too high a value to atomic weapons, little, big, or biggest; and that just as the A-bomb obscured our view and gave a false sense of security, we are in danger of falling into the same error again in discussion of (the 'Super') — some cheap, easy way out."
See David Lilienthal, *The Journals of David E. Lilienthal*, Vol II, *The Atomic Energy Years, 1945-1950* (New York: 1964), pp. 581, 591.

30 On the basis of about seven minutes of Cabinet-level discussion, President Truman indicated his decision to develop the super-bomb (" . . . we have no other course") on January 31, 1950. There was little public expression of opposition. See David A. Rosenberg, "American Atomic Strategy and the Hydrogen Bomb Decision," *Journal of American History* (June, 1979), pp. 62-87).

Development of the H-Bomb

As things turned out, the Americans were the first to explode a hydrogen device — on a Pacific island in 1952. But it was the U.S.S.R. that was first to test an H-bomb, working partly on fusion, that was small enough to drop from an airplane. (This development was kept secret from the American public for many years.)[31]

The significance of this technological breakthrough was profound. Both the United States and the Soviet Union now possessed nuclear weapons that were enormously more destructive than the older fission bombs. Although there is an inherent upper limit to the explosive power of an A-bomb (termed "yield"), this is not true of the hydrogen bomb. The yield of fission weapons is measured generally by how many thousands of tons of the strongest chemical explosive (TNT) would be necessary to create a blast of equal size. The fission bomb dropped on the city of Hiroshima, for example, was equivalent to approximately fifteen thousand tons of TNT or fifteen "kilotons." However, hydrogen weapons are often measured in millions of tons of TNT or "megatons," though thousands of such weapons are in the kiloton range.

It is worth spending a minute to reflect on the oft-stated, but little comprehended, impact of this breakthrough. As a result of the discovery of the fusion bomb, a *single* modern strategic nuclear weapon could have a million times the yield of the high explosive strategic bombs of World War II or one hundred to a thousand times the yield of the atomic bombs that destroyed Hiroshima and Nagasaki, killing some 250,000 people.[32]

We get some idea of the awesomeness of this development when we consider the effect of a hypothetical Soviet drop of a single one-megaton weapon over the White House in Washington, D.C.[33]

(The blast alone) would destroy multistory concrete buildings out to a distance of about three miles (ten pounds per square inch overpressure with winds of 300 miles per hour) — a circle of almost complete destruction reaching the National Cathedral to the northwest, the Kennedy Stadium to the east, and across the National Airport to the south. Most people in this area would be killed immediately. The thermal radiation from the same weapon would cause spontaneous ignition of clothing and household

---

31 See Bernard Brodie et al., *From Crossbow to H-Bomb: The Evolution of Weapons and the Tactics of Warfare* (Bloomington: Indiana University Press, 1973).

32 Edwin O. Reischauer, *The United States and Japan* (Cambridge: Harvard University Press, 1957), p. 240.

33 Spurgeon M. Keeny, Jr. and Wolfgang K.H. Panofsky, "MAD Versus NUTS," *Foreign Affairs* (Winter, 1981/82), pp. 291-292.

combustibles to a distance of about five miles (25 calories per centimeter squared) — a circle of raging fires reaching out to the District line. Out to a distance of almost nine miles there would be severe damage to ordinary frame buildings and second-degree burns to exposed individuals. Beyond these immediate effects the innumerable separate fires that had been ignited would either merge into an outward-moving conflagration or more likely create a giant fire storm of the type Hamburg and Tokyo experienced on a much smaller scale in World War II. While the inrushing winds would tend to limit the spread of the fire storm, the area within five to six miles of the explosion would be totally burned out, killing most of the people who might have escaped initial injury in shelters.

Medical experts have recently made the point with great force that the vast numbers of injured who escaped death at the margin of the above holocaust could expect little medical help. Moreover, the resulting radioactive debris would produce fallout with lethal effects far beyond the site of the explosion.

Obviously, such a level of human and physical destruction is difficult for anyone, layman or specialist, to comprehend even for a single city — much less for an entire nation.

In short, with the development of hydrogen weapons the wholesale slaughter of a nation's people and the destruction of civilization became a distinct possibility.[34]

NSC — 68

President Truman's second initiative following the fall of China and the Soviet atomic test focused on the re-analysis of the challenge posed to American national security. It was carried out by a special task force drawn from several departments in the government. The document it produced was the subject of a great deal of controversy, but it soon became a landmark in the history of U.S. national security policy. For it created something that the United States government had never had before — a comprehensive national security policy and a general strategy.

This study, known as NSC-68 (that is, the 68th policy document prepared for the National Security Council), was submitted to the nation's highest foreign policy making body in April 1950. It began with what the military likes to call "The Definition of the Threat." In part, it read as follows:[35]

34 One U.S. official would observe here: "It was a possibility before; it just takes longer."

35 NSC-68 has been published in the *Naval War College Review*, Vol. 27, pp. 51-108.

... the Soviet Union, unlike previous aspirants to hegemony, is animated by a new fanatic faith, antithetical to our own, and seeks to impose its absolute authority over the rest of the world. Conflict has, therefore, become endemic ...

What made the present situation particularly dangerous was that the Soviet Union possessed atomic bombs and could be presumed to be working on hydrogen weapons. NSC-68 estimated that the Soviets could have some 200 fission bombs by 1954 and cautioned that its estimate might be low. Without a military build-up by the United States in Central Europe, the Soviets would be able to destroy enough of Western Europe to make any defense against the Red Army impossible. Should this occur, the Soviets would be in a good position to launch devastating attacks against the United States.

The relation of power and will to the use of force was set out explicitly in NSC-68. It was "cardinal" to U.S. policy that the United States "possess superior overall power."

Without superior aggregate military strength in being and readily mobilizable, a policy of 'containment' — which is in effect a policy of calculated and gradual coercion — is no more than a policy of bluff.

Because the Soviet Union was seen as possessing armed forces "far in excess of those [necessary] to defend its national territory," NSC-68 concluded that the Soviet Union was "developing the military capability to support its design for world domination." Clearly, in the eyes of U.S. officials, something had to be done.

Generally, NSC-68 called for taking dynamic steps to reduce the power and influence of the Kremlin inside the Soviet Union and other areas under its control. A few years later, in the era of John Foster Dulles, this policy would be termed "rollback," as opposed to "containment." Specifically, it recommended that the U.S. "provide an adequate defense against air attack on the United States." (Until this time, U.S. officials had not made serious efforts to protect American airspace.) This was one specific recommendation of NSC-68 that was carried out.[36]

> For one of the better historical accounts of the drafting of the document and the assessment of its political and military context see Samuel F. Wells, Jr., "Sounding the Tocsin: NSC-68 and the Soviet Threat," *International Security*, Vol. 4, pp. 116-158.
>
> 36 One of the most striking things about NSC-68 was its rhetorical flourish. "The idea of freedom is the most contagious idea in history ... Where the despot holds absolute power ... all other wills must be subjugated in an act of willing submission, a degradation willed by the individual upon himself under the compulsion of a perverted faith ... The system becomes God, and submission to the will of God becomes submission to the will of the system." This is not what an outsider would expect from a top secret document destined not to be made public until 1975.

A second step was to provide "an adequate defense against air and surface attack on the United Kingdom, Western Europe . . . and on the long lines of communication to these areas." Although NSC-68 did not say so explicitly, its assessment was such that the United States would have to commit a large number of U.S. troops to the defense of Western Europe. At the same time, the United States would have to make a significant commitment by its Air Force.

As a number of U.S. diplomatic historians have observed, the decision to defend Western Europe represented a major departure in American thinking. Until this time, it was assumed under the improvised strategy of deterrence that the Red Army was deterred from marching into Western Europe. Now a Soviet invasion of Europe would presumably mean all-out war, in which atomic attacks would be made against the Soviet Union. But since the Soviets would soon be in a position to counter by making atomic attacks on the U.S. and Western Europe, a new situation was in the making.

In this new situation, both American and Soviet officials would know that, if one side were to launch a nuclear strike against the other's cities, this would invite a counterstrike on its own. Thus, the nuclear forces of the two countries were now beginning to be seen as mutually deterring each other. U.S. strategic thinkers drew what they thought was the logical conclusion from this new situation, namely, that a nuclear stalemate would soon ensue, whereby neither side would dare risk launching an atomic attack on its adversary.

NSC-68 did not develop the argument explicitly. But the implication was there that U.S. officials would now have to find another way to protect their European allies. And the major alternative here was the stationing of conventional forces in Europe. But since they would not be sufficient in themselves, the NATO allies would have to contribute forces as well. The idea was that U.S. forces would serve a "tripwire" function. Not large enough themselves to match the Red Army man for man, they nevertheless would be substantial enough to give physical evidence of America's determination to defend Europe. Possibly, they would be large enough to make an invasion too costly for the Soviets to contemplate seriously. In other words, Western forces in Europe would serve to "deter" the Soviet Union, or at least that was the thinking behind the move.

"Implicit in NSC-68" writes Richard Smoke, "was a grim logic of deterrence and counter-deterrence on multiple levels."[37] This was a logic that was to become characteristic of national security problems in our contemporary period.

---

37 Richard Smoke, *National Security and the Nuclear Dilemma* (Reading, Ma.: Addison-Wesley Publishing Co., 1984), p. 62.

Throughout the spring of 1950, NSC-68 was studied and debated in the policymaking circles of our government. Before a consensus could be reached, however, the Korean War broke out. As a consequence, the approach to national security taken by the controversial paper was not approved by President Truman until September 30, 1950. By the time the Korean War was over three years later, a new Administration in Washington had decided on a different approach. Yet almost a decade later the philosophy of NSC-68 — under an entirely different name — would finally reemerge in American national security policy.

Reassessing the Soviet Threat

Whether the nuclear threat (implicit in the early years and explicit in later years) actually deterred the Soviet Union from military onslaught against Western Europe in the period 1945-1950 we cannot know for sure unless the Russians are one day as generous with access to their official documents as the United States has been. However, viewed with the benefit of hindsight, it seems likely that the Soviets were in no mind or position to attack Western Europe after World War II and risk war with the United States, even if the U.S. had possessed no nuclear weapons. As Henry Kissinger wrote recently: "Stalin's aggressiveness was real enough. But from the perspective of a generation, it is possible to argue that the West was too ready to attribute a military edge to an adversary only recently devastated by war and 20 million casualties..."[38]

Adam B. Ulam of Harvard University offers the following explanation for this grievous miscalculation. "Western statesmen, like the public in general, were overcompensating for a previous low opinion of Russia's fighting potential and of the cohesion of her political system. It was now secretly and shamefully recalled that when the Germans struck in June, 1941, the British and American general staffs had given the Red Army no chance of withstanding the German onslaught for more than a few months... Thus both remorse and an overreaction to an earlier slighting estimate of the Red Army's strength and fighting ability impelled Western statesmen to conjure up the Soviet armed forces as not only invincible but able to draw upon seemingly unlimited manpower." However, even more important

---

38 Henry A. Kissinger, "Strategy and the Atlantic Alliance," *Survival*, Vol. 24 (1982), p. 195. A CIA study of February 1950 already questioned the assertion that "only the existence of the U.S. atomic bomb prevented the USSR from carrying out an intention to continue its military advances to the Atlantic... *There is no reason to suppose... that the USSR had any such intention in 1945 or subsequently.*" (Italics mine.)

"was their conviction that the Soviets would be able to keep huge armies even after peace had been concluded, while in the West public opinion would force a very rapid pace of demobilization."[39]

As things turned out, the popular vision of multimillion-man Soviet armies ready to sweep to the English Channel at a moment's notice notwithstanding, by 1948 Soviet armed strength was reduced to 2.8 million. Given the extensive Soviet commitments in Eastern Europe and its garrison in Germany, this figure was hardly abnormally high.[40]

Soviet Behavior in the Early Postwar Period

Surprisingly, the behavior of the United States and the Soviet Union was not at all what one might have expected from the conception of nuclear deterrence. In 1948, for instance, it was the Kremlin which provided the provocation and behaved aggressively, whereas the U.S. was restrained and even timid. The suggestion by General Lucius D. Clay, U.S. Military Governor in Germany, that the United States push its way into West Berlin with military forces despite the Soviet blockade was rejected by President Truman. Instead, the expensive and difficult "Berlin Airlift" was undertaken. Even with the benefit of hindsight, it is still very hard to see what possible role the sole possession of atomic weapons by the U.S. played in the conflict over Berlin at this time.[41]

---

39 Adam B. Ulam, *The Rivals: America and Russia Since World War II* (New York: Penguin Books, 1980), pp. 7-8. We now know that at the time of the German capitulation, the U.S. had more men under arms than the U.S.S.R. Khrushchev gave the Soviet figure for May 1945 as 11 million (*Pravda*, January 15, 1960). The corresponding figure for the United States was 12 million (U.S. Department of State, *Documents on Disarmament 1945-1959* (Washington, D.C.: U.S. Government Printing Office, 1960), I, p. 682.

40 Adam B. Ulam, *opus cit.*, p. 8.

41 Some observers are disposed to regard the Berlin crisis of 1948-49 as an example of successful deterrence by the Western Powers. The Soviets, it is argued, confined themselves to the ground blockade and did not resort to stronger measures against the Western position in the isolated city. While it is true that stronger measures were certainly available to the Soviets for taking political control of West Berlin, it is difficult to speak, however, of the Soviets as being deterred — at least at the outset of the crisis. As Alexander George and Richard Smoke write in their study of the crisis from the point of view of deterrence, "the argument that this case is to be regarded as an example of successful deterrence would seem to rest on the dubious assumption that the Soviets were obliged to settle for the blockade because they felt deterred from using stronger options against West Berlin. Far from being a second-best strategy, however, the blockade may have been viewed by Stalin as a *preferred* option for pursuing his complex objectives. At the outset

American possession of the bomb, a weapon that separated the past from future as sharply as did man's discovery of fire, also had no noticeable effect on Stalin's policy in Eastern Europe. As Stephen E. Ambrose writes: Stalin and Molotov "continued to do as they pleased, refusing to hold elections or to allow Western observers to travel freely in East Europe. At Foreign Ministers' meetings the Russians continued to insist that the West had to recognize the puppet governments in East Europe before peace treaties could be written. [Secretary of State James] Byrnes's hope that the bomb would 'make Russia more manageable' proved abortive . . ."[42]

The Soviet Union simply did not comply with the simplistic American deterrent theory, which led to a poverty of theoretical and doctrinal development with respect to conflict below the strategic and bipolar level.[43] Instead of confronting the United States directly and frontally in the European theatre, the Soviets chose to probe, feign and challenge the U.S. and its allies in areas remote from Europe. Moreover, the Soviet challenge was initiated indirectly by proxies and allies. One might say, therefore, that in the ensuing Cold War period the "cowboy strategy" of nuclear deterrence came to confront a "commissar strategy," which rejected the core notion of the early American strategy of deterrence — either stable peace or nuclear incineration.[44]

Summary

The theory of nuclear deterrence is a uniquely American construct. It has been shaped by certain historical, political, institutional and other influences and circumstances of the post-World War II period. The theory,

> the Soviets had every reason to believe that the blockade would be effective and lead to a successful outcome of the crisis." See Alexander L. George and Richard Smoke, *Deterrence in American Foreign Policy* (New York: Columbia University Press, 1974), p. 135.

42 Stephen E. Ambrose, *Rise to Globalism: American Foreign Policy, 1938-1980* (New York: Penguin Books, 1980), p. 114.

43 Stalin *publicly* disparaged American possession of the atomic bomb in these early years as "a weapon to frighten the weak." In a recent book on Soviet-American relations, two Russian history professors assert that the "[m]onopoly of atomic arms did not nullify traditional foreign policy." See Nikolai V. Sivachev and Nikolai N. Yakovlev, *Russia and the United States: U.S.-Soviet Relations from the Soviet Point of View* (Chicago, 1979). These Soviet statements should not, of course, be taken at face value without consideration of other evidence.

44 The author is indebted here to Roman Kolkowicz. See his "U.S. and Soviet Approaches to Military Strategy: Theory vs Experience," *Orbis* (Summer, 1981), pp. 320-21.

which was not immediately endorsed unanimously within the U.S. government,[45] was conceived in the modern sense when it became possible to threaten vast damage and pain while leaving opposing military forces intact. Thus, the atomic bomb that ended the Second World War and the bipolar international system that emerged after the war provided the conditions for modern deterrence theory. In the words of two students of the early post-war period: "the former made deterrence necessary and the later made it possible."[46]

Contrary to popular belief, President Truman's initial response to the problems and opportunities posed by the atomic bomb after World War II was not decisive, but hesitant and even vacillating. As Adam Ulam writes: "As a matter of fact, what *is* astounding is that *no* attempt was made by the United States to exploit politically the monopoly of this weapon of unique destructiveness when it came to the peace settlement in Europe or Asia. *Even Soviet sources*, while freely accusing the United States of practicing atomic diplomacy during the Cold War, and assailing the atomic bombing of Hiroshima and Nagasaki as both unnecessary and barbarous, do not accuse the United States of threatening the Soviet Union in 1945..."[47]

Less by strategy than by necessity, the atomic bomb began to assume a major role in U.S. war planning by the summer of 1946. In the following years, U.S. war planners came to rely more and more on the bomb as an effective counter balance to the conventional strength of the Soviet Union. The wholesale destruction of cities at the beginning of a war envisioned by this planning — even though neither the President nor the Joint Chiefs of Staff knew how few bombs the U.S. had — was perhaps a culmination of the logic that had led to the terror bombings of World War II (which the *Strategic Bombing Survey*, published after the war, seriously questioned).

The modern doctrine of nuclear deterrence, which stressed the prevention of war by the threat of retaliation by atomic and later hydrogen bombs, developed from a strategy which integrated air power with atomic weapons.[48] Yet this "air-atomic" strategy was surprisingly slow to gain

---

45 For background see M.S. Blackett, *Fear, War, and the Bomb* (New York: Whittlesey House, 1948), pp. 229-236. Also important is the article "War Department Thinking on the Atom Bomb," *Bulletin of the Atomic Scientists*, Vol. 3 (1947), pp. 150-55, 168.

46 Alexander George et al., *Deterrence in American Foreign Policy* (New York: Columbia University Press, 1974), p. 20.

47 Adam Ulam, *opus cit.*, p. 82. This is an important point to take into account, especially in view of the allegations by revisionist historians that Soviet-American relations in 1945 were dominated by the possession by the U.S. of the atomic bomb.

48 Perhaps not surprisingly this strategy was opposed by the U.S. Navy. With the

acceptance by U.S. military planners. It was only in the late 1940s that the atomic bomb and America's atomic monopoly became integral to U.S. war plans and to the Administration's strategy for containing Soviet expansion. But even then the surprisingly small number of bombs in the American arsenal and the continuing lag in adopting military doctrine to the nuclear age meant that the nuclear deterrent doctrine of the U.S. remained a hollow threat during the years when only the United States had the bomb. (There were even doubts in the Administration, as late as 1949, as to whether all of the atomic bombs in the American arsenal would be sufficient to compel Moscow's capitulation *in the event of a full-scale war with the Soviet Union.*) It is probable that the Russians, who gained detailed knowledge of the atomic bomb through their spies,[49] knew well through espionage the deficiencies of America's nuclear threat.[50]

The Soviet attitude towards the American possession of the atomic bomb during this period was perhaps best expressed by Stalin in an interview with a United Press correspondent on October 23, 1946. At that time the Soviet dictator was asked what he thought of the atom bomb (i.e. "Aren't your people really scared?"). Stalin referred in an unruffled manner to a dictum uttered on another occasion, when he said: "Atom bombs are designed to scare those with weak nerves, but they cannot decide wars because there are not enough of them..."[51] Stalin's answer may well

> departure of Secretary of Defense James V. Forrestal in 1949, the Navy was losing its competition with the Air Force over the future direction of strategy. Initially, it professed skepticism about the effectiveness of the atomic bomb in war. Then, it appeared to embrace the bomb willingly, hoping that the geographic difficulties of intercontinental bombing would guarantee it a wartime role. With the scuttling of its first supercarrier and a loss of appropriations, the Navy retreated to a modified version of its first argument. This was that the bomb was not only militarily ineffective but ethically insupportable. This led one Air Force officer to remark sarcastically that to the Navy an immoral weapon was one it was unable to use.

49 Edward Shils argues in his study of the period *The Torment of Secrecy: The Background and Consequences of American Security Policies* that "The [atomic] secret ... became the central issue, equated directly with "security" and "national survival." The U.S.S.R.'s designation as the stealer of the secret became inseparable from the threat it posed.

50 Gregg Herke, *The Winning Weapon: The Atomic Bomb in the Cold War 1945-1950* (New York: Alfred A. Knopf, 1980). A recent controversial book on Soviet espionage by British journalist Andrew Boyle maintains that Soviet spies had access to an "impressive array of detailed and carefully selected material on the nuclear thinking, planning and stockpiling of the Americans and their allies," including the number of bombs in the U.S. atomic arsenal. So far little evidence has emerged to support this claim. See Andrew Boyle, *The Fourth Man* (New York, 1979), p. 295.

51 See J.V. Stalin, *Works* (in Russian) (Stanford: 1967), Vol. III, p. 56, pp. 567-68.

have been "excellent casuistry reflecting his early theological training — answers well designed to reassure the Russians and baffle the Westerners," as Adam Ulam states. But Stalin's response may well have revealed his realization that the Americans had few atomic bombs at this time to back up the nuclear threat.

Washington's early nuclear deterrent strategy was based on a policy of atomic monopoly. The idea was that the United States could retain such weapons exclusively and in "trust" for possibly as long as a generation. The folly of such an expectation, and a policy based on American atomic hegemony, was demonstrated in 1949 when the Soviets tested their first atomic bomb. This seminal event shattered the American nuclear monopoly a number of years before it was generally expected in the United States. At the same time, it revealed the much-heralded atomic secret to have been largely a myth rooted in certain misconceptions and much wishful thinking. "This is now a different world," Senator Vandenberg painfully recorded.[52]

Rather than reverse course, President Truman chose in early 1950 to proceed with a comprehensive rearmament plan, which included the development of the hydrogen bomb. In essence, this decision represented a continuation of the policies of secrecy, monopoly and exclusion. In retrospect, the H-bomb decision is decisive because it showed that despite the danger of nuclear war the statist imperative of staying ahead, or seeming to, was deeply ingrained.

"There was no decision to make on the H-bomb," Truman told his staff several days following his momentous decision. "[W]e had . . . to do it — make the bomb — though no one wants to use it. But . . . we have got to have it if only for bargaining purposes with the Russians."[53]

But here, too, U.S. government officials miscalculated. For the premature end of America's atomic monopoly had already demonstrated that these policies were founded on dangerous illusions. On the one hand, this was that the H-bomb would be of decisive advantage to the United States in war or peace.[54] On the other, this was that America could retain a uni-

---

52 See Arthur H. Vandenberg, Jr. (ed.), *The Private Papers of Senator Vandenberg* (Boston: 1952).

53 Quoted in John L. Gaddis, *Strategies of Containment: A Critical Appraisal of Postwar American National Security Policy* (New York: Oxford University Press, 1982), p. 82.

54 It is important to note here that the development of the H-bomb as a stockpile weapon took quite some time. Even though thermonuclear principles were first tested on May 8, 1951, and a true thermonuclear explosion was achieved on October 31, 1952, an air-deliverable hydrogen bomb was apparently not tested until March 1954. And it was not actually dropped from an aircraft until May, 1956. See Herbert F. York, *The Advisors: Oppenheimer, Teller, and the Superbomb* (San Francisco: 1976), pp. 77-85.

lateral advantage until her objectives in diplomacy were realized. Here was a device so frightfully destructive, it was thought, that the mere threat of its use would serve to dissuade would-be aggressors from carrying out their designs.

In retrospect, we can see clearly that the U.S. nuclear threat during this "neither war nor peace" period did not create the secure Pax Atomice that some had hoped for. U.S. security was not measurably enhanced. Indeed, one could argue that possession of the atomic bomb had in fact a debilitating effect on U.S. foreign policy *vis-a-vis* the Soviet Union. For a dictatorship, a special advantage in military technology may well be a spur to action; for a democracy, it became a convenient rationalization for inaction. In short, it encouraged a Maginot Line psychology. "Like a miser with a treasure," writes Adam Ulam, "so America hugged the evanescent atom monopoly to its bosom, equally unable to exploit it or to exchange it for something useful."[55]

U.S. influence would never be as great as American power. Over the next two decades U.S. policymakers and the American people would be forced to learn that bitter lesson, as U.S. generals began to order nuclear weapons "like mess kits and rifles" to use the words of David Lilienthal. While U.S. power remained for some time greater than that of anyone else, in many cases it was not usable power. Thus, it could not be translated into diplomatic victory.

Our current security dilemma is thus clearly linked with the decision of the post-war American leadership (and its successors) to base security largely on technology — to compensate for an assumed Soviet superiority in manpower and conventional weapons by reliance on our nuclear arsenal and a dubious strategy of nuclear deterrence. In this respect, we would do well to remember the warning given in 1948 by Secretary of Defense Forrestal: "It has long been one of my strongly held beliefs that the word 'security' ought to be stricken from the language and the word 'risk' substituted... The great danger in any country is for people to believe that there is anything absolute about security. Air power, atomic bombs, wealth — by itself none of these can give any security."[56]

---

55 Adam B. Ulam, *opus cit.*, p. 105.
56 Letter of early January 1948 to *The New York Times*, quoted in Gregg Herken, *opus cit.* "You overlook the real irony," states one critic. "While the U.S. managed to avoid armed conflict with the Soviet Union, the consequences of such a war grew with each passing year." John C. Ausland, letter to this writer, dated July 31, 1984.

> It is absurd to base the strategy of the West on the credibility of the threat of mutual suicide.
>
> *Henry Kissinger*

IV. THE CHANGING DETERRENCE POSTURE

A central assumption of nuclear deterrence is that it must be credible. Proponents of nuclear deterrence often argue that an adversary faced with the serious possibility of nuclear retaliation will change his mind about committing aggression against a nation with nuclear weapons or one of its allies. This proposition is widely and firmly believed. Moreover, it serves as a point of departure for justification of nuclear weapons programs.

The 1950s saw several strategies of deterrence come and go. What were these policies? Why did the United States change them? This chapter examines the historical background of these policies, what they hoped to achieve and what particular faults they had. If these policies were not credible, if they could not be operationalized, then it stands to reason that the theory of nuclear deterrence needs to be seriously reconsidered. The emperor may have no clothes.

Strategic Developments in the Early 1950s

By the time Dwight D. Eisenhower became President in 1953, some of the specific recommendations of NSC-68 were being implemented. Particularly important was the building of a large air defense system, including radar stations across America's large neighbor to the north, Canada. Moreover, jet interceptors, a ground-launched anti-aircraft missile (the "Nike") and a variety of radars were being developed. At the same time, officials were expanding America's offensive capability. SAC was now receiving the B-47 medium bomber, which could transport an atomic bomb to the U.S.S.R. much more quickly than the dated propeller-driven B-36 heavy-bombers. The B-47 was also far less vulnerable to Russian air defenses. A larger, more advanced jet bomber (the B-52), which could carry up to six nuclear bombs, was on the drawing board.

Perhaps most significantly, the Defense Department now possessed an ample stockpile of atomic bombs. Nuclear technology had a speed-up in production, so by the early 1950s more A-bombs were available than planners originally expected.[1] Despite the "surplus" of A-bombs, the more devastating hydrogen bombs would be entering America's nuclear arsenal before long.[2]

For their part, the Soviets appeared in the early 1950s to be lagging behind. Contrary to U.S. intelligence predictions in 1949 (after the U.S.S.R. surprised people by exploding an atomic device several years earlier than had been expected), the CIA was now reporting that the Russians had produced only a few atomic bombs.[3] More importantly, the Soviets possessed only a small number of medium range propeller-driven aircraft with which to deliver them. The Soviet air defense system was such that U.S. jet bombers could penetrate it relatively easily. Furthermore, Soviet propeller bombers would soon be no match for jet interceptors in the U.S. air defense system.

The "New Look"

Dwight Eisenhower entered office with the United States riding high on a great and growing degree of strategic superiority — even more than most people outside the government were aware. Given this favorable atomic position, it is not surprising that officials in the Administration came to stress technology over manpower (the Red Army still loomed ominously over NATO forces in Europe). The "New Look," as it was called, would play to America's strength while saving money. The Eisenhower Administration was very concerned at this time that excessive military spending

---

1 "The stockpile of nuclear bombs took a gigantic leap during Eisenhower's first term," writes one noted authority. "The 1953-54 figure of approximately 1,000 bombs had doubled by the beginning of 1956." Peter Pringle *et al.*, *SIOP: The Secret U.S. Plan for Nuclear War* (New York: W.W. Norton, 1983), p. 112.

2 Within six months after taking office, President Eisenhower — who as a military man believed that it was too cumbersome for the military not to have custody of its own nuclear weapons — transferred to it a sizable number of complete nuclear weapons. By 1961 over ninety percent of the U.S. nuclear stockpile was put under military control. (For some time, the fissionable material of the weapons — the uranium and plutonium — was kept apart from the bomb casings. But this was now no longer the case.)

3 U.S. intelligence estimates prepared after the Soviet test projected that the U.S.S.R. would not acquire a large enough stockpile or the necessary delivery systems to threaten the United States before 1951 at the earliest, and more probably 1953 or even 1955. See David A. Rosenberg, "American Atomic Strategy and the Hydrogen Bomb Decision," *Journal of American History* (June, 1979), p. 80.

would damage the economy. With this kind of defense posture, U.S. officials found it less expensive to fully develop its jet bombers, its arsenal of nuclear weapons and its air defenses, than to keep great numbers of men in uniform.[4]

With some modification, the "New Look" strategic emphasis served to guide Eisenhower's decisions in the area of defense during his two terms in office.[5] Contrary to the wishes of Army leaders U.S. combat troop strength was kept severely limited (although the role of the Army in air defense was strengthened). For its part, the U.S. Navy was adequately funded, especially its growing fleet of aircraft carriers, which was seen as a main support to America's rapidly expanding network of overseas alliances. (By the time Eisenhower left office in 1961, the U.S. was joined with over fifty countries in military alliances that were formed to serve as a powerful caution to feared Soviet expansionist tendencies.)

During this period, SAC, the Air Defense Command and America's growing nuclear weapons program received top priority.[6] Largely as a result of fears of a Soviet "bomber gap" (which later turned out to be unfounded), Administration officials greatly expanded the fleet of B-52s. By the end of the decade, the U.S. possessed more than 600 of these large intercontinental bombers.

Many of these long-range bombers were stationed in the United Kingdom and at other overseas bases. From these "forward bases," as they were called, SAC planes could launch a devastating nuclear attack on the Soviet

---

4   Jerome H. Kahan, *Security in the Nuclear Age: Developing U.S. Strategic Arms Policy* (Washington, D.C.: The Brookings Institution, 1975).

5   See Glenn H. Snyder, "The New Look of 1953," in Warner Schilling et al. (eds.), *Strategy, Politics, and Defense Budgets* (New York: Columbia University Press, 1962).

6   The decision to accelerate the American nuclear weapons program was influenced in part by the Soviet explosion of their first hydrogen bomb on August 8, 1953, which caused quite a stir in the intelligence community. Fred Kaplan tells the story: "It seemed that this Soviet bomb bore little resemblance to the American H-bomb. For one thing it was less powerful, something of a relief. But there was also something ominous. The H-bomb that the United States had set off was not really a practical bomb; it was more like a 'device.' It required a huge refrigeration system to keep it cool, something that could not be sent up on a rocket, or even, very easily, on a bomber. Yet analysis of fallout samples from the Soviet explosion indicated the presence of lithium, a chemical that made refrigeration unnecessary. "The implication was sensational. It meant that the Soviets could conceivably build an ICBM with an H-bomb on board much earlier than the United States. (Consequently the) Atlas project had to be pushed along at a much faster clip." See Kaplan, *The Wizards of Armageddon* (New York: Simon and Schuster, 1983), pp. 112-13.

Union. For their part, the Soviets had no comparable "forward bases," and their more primitive planes took much longer to reach the United States.

As part of this strategic build-up, all three armed services began receiving "tactical" nuclear weapons for delivery over medium to short ranges. These included special shells for the U.S. Army's largest nuclear artillery and nuclear bombs for U.S. Air Force and Navy tactical aircraft. (Here, too, the Soviet Union was lagging behind; from the mid-1950s through perhaps the early 1960s the U.S. was greatly superior in terms of tactical nuclear weapons.)[7]

The growing superiority of American strategic and tactical nuclear power led many U.S. war planners in this period to believe that, in the event of a war with the Soviet Union, the U.S. could "prevail."[8] Few Administration officials were prepared to speak publicly of "victory" in such a terrible war, but the general feeling in high-level government circles was somewhat optimistic.

"Massive Retaliation"

During the eight years of the Eisenhower Administration, U.S. officials proposed a number of policies of deterrence.[9] But the one to which the Korean experience seemed to contribute most directly came to be known as "massive retaliation." This policy was primarily associated with Secretary of State John Foster Dulles, although he did not use the exact words massive retaliation himself. The Dulles policy prevailed because the United States still retained nuclear superiority. This edge was essential to Eisenhower's strategy.

Dulles proclaimed the "massive retaliation" policy to the general public on January 12, 1954 in an address delivered to the Council of Foreign Re-

---

7 According to one U.S. insider, the Joint Chiefs of Staff did a study in 1954 suggesting "deliberately precipitating war with the U.S.S.R. in the near future" before the Soviet H-bomb became a "real menace." The President reportedly rejected this idea. In an updated National Security Policy guidance statement, it was proclaimed that "the United States and its allies must reject the concept of preventive war or acts intended to provoke war."

8 See Richard Smoke, *National Security and the Nuclear Dilemma: An Introduction to the American Experience* (Massachusetts: Addison-Wesley Publishing Co., 1984), p. 71. Here Smoke writes: "No one wanted to speak, at least publicly or casually, of 'victory' in such a terrible war, but administration spokesmen did say (in a phrase that became famous for a while) that should such a war come, 'we would prevail.'"

9 See Samuel F. Wells, "The Origins of Massive Retaliation," *Political Science Quarterly*, Vol. 96 (Spring, 1981), pp. 31-52.

lations in New York.[10] The Secretary of State began his speech by observing that American policy hitherto had represented nothing more than a succession of responses to emergencies created by Russian initiative. He referred to the need to avoid military expenditures so vast that they would lead to "practical bankruptcy," adding: "This can be done by placing more reliance on deterrent power and less dependence on local defensive power." Referring to the inadequacy of policy and planning under the previous Administration, he proclaimed that the new Administration had to make "some basic policy decisions." This, Dulles said, "had been done. The basic decision was to depend primarily upon a great capacity to retaliate, instantly, by means and at places of our choosing."[11]

This last remark immediately aroused a storm of alarm and indignation throughout the Atlantic community. Dulles' observations were generally taken to mean that the United States government was prepared to turn every local conflict into a worldwide nuclear war in which its allies could be destroyed. The use of the term "instantly" was generally interpreted by America's allies as meaning that U.S. officials would not take the time to consult them before acting to transform a local conflict into Armageddon. As one "insider" recalled later, "Within hours of delivering the address the Secretary of State was a severely embarrassed man." The very next day the President felt compelled to deny that any new "basic decision" on defense policy had been taken at all.[12]

10 Dulles' idea of massive retaliation did not originate with his speech of January 1954. For a number of years before, Dulles had accepted the use of nuclear weapons in war as an almost foregone conclusion. For details see Fred Kaplan, *The Wizards of Armageddon* (New York: Simon & Schuster, 1983), pp. 178-79.

11 John Foster Dulles, "The Evolution of Foreign Policy," *Department of State Bulletin*, 30 (January 25, 1954), pp. 107-10. The main paragraph reads: "The total cost of our security efforts... could not be continued long without grave budgetary, economic, and social consequences. But before military planning could be changed the President and his advisers... had to make some basic policy decisions. This has been done. The basic decision has to depend primarily upon a greater [nuclear] capacity to retaliate instantly by means and at places of our own choosing. As a result it is now possible to get and to share more basic security at less cost."

12 Eisenhower's reservations about Dulles' theory of asymmetrical strategic deterrence are contained in declassified government documents now available at the Eisenhower Library. "I... was as deeply impressed as ever with the directness and simplicity of your approach to such complex problems," the President wrote in an internal document. "There is only one point that bothered me... It is this: What should we do if Soviet *political* aggression, as in Czechoslovakia, successively chips away exposed positions of the free world? So far as our resulting economic situation is concerned, such an eventuality would be just as bad for us as if the area had been captured by force. To my mind, this is the case where the theory of

Dulles' speech aroused such immediate and detailed criticism and had such a deleterious effect on confidence abroad that remedial action had to be taken. This took the form of a personal statement, which ultimately appeared as an article under the Secretary of State's name in the April 1954 issue of *Foreign Affairs*. In this article, entitled "Policy for Security and Peace," Dulles explained the new military policy of the United States in language that reduced the more extreme implications of his "massive retaliation" address. For instance, he now said "massive atomic and thermonuclear retaliation is not the kind of power which could most usefully be evoked under all circumstances." (In a piece in *Life* magazine Dulles referred to the new policy as "brinksmanship"; we were willing to go to the brink with nuclear weapons if necessary to stop Soviet expansion.)[13]

The events that led Dulles to correct himself have since been largely overlooked by officials and scholars who maintain that the U.S. under the Eisenhower Administration had a policy of "massive retaliation." In fact, as Louis J. Halle, a former State Department official, points out in his detailed and incisive study of the period, "the United States cannot be said to have ever had a policy of 'massive retaliation,' any more than it ever had a policy of 'liberation' as opposed to the policy of 'containment.'"[14]

Nevertheless, many informed observers both inside and outside the U.S.

'retaliation' falls down." "You put your finger on the weak point in my presentation," Dulles replied, promising to remedy the situation in the final draft of an article for *Life* magazine. The published article did not clarify matters, however. Consequently, Eisenhower had to warn again that "exclusive reliance upon a mere power of retaliation is not a complete answer to the broad Soviet threat." When Dulles allowed the offending phrase "retaliatory striking power" to creep into the Republican platform, the President was furious: "I'll be damned if I run on that," he told amazed aids at the Chicago convention. The offending phrase was quickly removed, but this was not the end of the matter. See John L. Gaddis, *Strategies of Containment: A Critical Appraisal of Postwar American National Security Policy* (New York: Oxford University Press, 1982), p. 128.

13. See Michael A. Guhin, *John Foster Dulles* (New York: Columbia University Pres, 1972). One major difficulty with many critiques of Dulles' "massive retaliation" policy is that they usually involve reconstructions made only from public statements of how he thought and saw reality in general and certain situations in particular.

14. Louis J. Halle, *The Cold War as History* (New York: Harper & Row, 1967), p. 283. Eisenhower reluctantly accepted Dulles' language in the Republican platform in 1952 condemning the "negative, futile and immoral policy of 'containment' which abandons countless human beings to a despotism and godless terrorism." But he felt obliged to remind Dulles during the campaign that "liberation" could only come by "peaceful means" — a point later made by Dulles himself in an article in *Life* magazine.

government believed that the United States was now relying on a deterrent posture known by its popular, if inaccurate, name "massive retaliation." For example, Henry Kissinger, whose book *Nuclear Weapons and Foreign Policy* represents a devastating critique of "massive retaliation," early questioned the predominance of fiscal considerations in the national security policies of the Eisenhower Administration. Kissinger noted that the budgetary process "by giving priority to cost over requirement... subordinated doctrine to technology."[15]

A second major criticism of the policy change had to do with the credibility of the U.S. threat. To skeptics, the "massive retaliation" strategy was not credible (except possibly against a devastating all-out nuclear attack on American cities) and thus would not serve as an adequate deterrent. As one student of nuclear policy wrote "the efficacy of a massive and undifferentiated threat to influence minor issues" was simply not believable to an adversary such as the Soviet Union.[16]

Lastly, critics of the policy maintained that it tended to make a nuclear war more likely, not less. These strategic thinkers noted that SAC bombers were concentrated on a small number of bases — all of which could be struck by a well-timed and coordinated "Pearl Harbor" attack.[17] Administration officials attempted to alleviate this threat by dispersing the bombers to more bases, but even after this was accomplished the B-47s and B-52s flown by SAC were still based at less than fifty locations. Even with a substantial air defense, it was entirely possible that at least one Soviet bomber per base might get through, and with nuclear bombs aboard, that one Soviet bomber could completely destroy the base. Given this situation, U.S. officials — at least as the Soviets saw it — might be tempted to use the Strategic Air Command pre-emptively rather than risk having it destroyed on the ground during a crisis. This awareness could, it was feared by some, cause the Soviets to strike first in desperation.

Strategic Vulnerability

The Dulles strategy relied heavily for deterrence on the planes of the Strategic Air Command of the U.S. Air Force. But as time went by, U.S. policymakers became increasingly concerned with their vulnerability to a surprise Soviet attack. For deterrence to work, they claimed, the Kremlin

---

15 Henry Kissinger, *Nuclear Weapons and Foreign Policy* (Garden City, N.Y.: Doubleday, 1958), p. 230.

16 See Laurence Martin (ed.), *Strategic Thought in the Nuclear Age* (Baltimore: The Johns Hopkins University Press, 1979), pp. 4-15.

17 See Richard K. Betts, *Surprise Attack* (Washington, D.C.: Brookings, 1982).

must never attain the ability to disarm the United States by striking first. This hypothetical capability came to be called, in the strategic lexicon, a "first-strike" capability.

Since there is much confusion today over the meaning of this phrase, it behooves us to discuss it in detail. Many uninitiated observers of the arms race think a "first-strike" capability means the ability to strike first. It does not mean that at all. A "first-strike" capability simply means the ability of one state to launch a disarming strike against an adversary; that is, one state, by striking first and hard, would be able to destroy an adversary's ability to strike back with any effectiveness.

Strategic thinkers put it another way. These analysts urge that the United States must always make sure that it has a "second-strike capability." This is not just the ability to strike back after being attacked; rather it is the ability to retain enough operating forces after being attacked to strike back *effectively* (i.e., to inflict "unacceptable damage" on the attacker).

"Unacceptable damage" has been defined in several ways. In the 1960s, Secretary of Defense Robert McNamara defined it conservatively as from 20 to 25 percent destruction of the population and 50 percent of industrial capacity. At the time McNamara made this definition, the U.S. possessed over 10,000 nuclear warheads. With only four hundred of these, McNamara noted, the U.S. could destroy at least 30 percent of the Soviet population and 76 percent of its industrial capacity.[18]

In summary, then, a successful deterrence strategy rests — in the view of its proponents — on the ability of the U.S. to retain a secure, second-strike force. Thus, what counts is not the total size of the American strategic arsenal but how much of it can survive a surprise nuclear attack and still penetrate the defenses of an adversary. From the point of view of a potential adversary, only that part of one's nuclear force that does survive and does reach its target is a real threat.[19]

Critics of "massive retaliation" maintained that it did not adequately take the above-mentioned principles into account. For instance, U.S. strategic forces were much larger than were necessary to destroy every important target in the Soviet Union (assuming that these forces remained intact and that all of them were used). But they were not deployed in such a way as to enhance their survivability in the event of a full-scale Soviet attack.

---

18 See U.S. Congress, House Committee on Armed Services, *Hearings on Military Posture*, 90th Congress, 2nd Session, April 3-27, 1968, p. 8507.

19 On the importance of "second-strike" forces see Albert Wohlstetter, "The Delicate Balance of Terror," *Foreign Affairs*, Vol. 37 (1957), pp. 211-234.

"Graduated Deterrence"

To some students of nuclear strategy, "massive retaliation" was one way — if not the best way — to handle the kinds of "limited wars" that were expected to occur in light of the Korean experience. Another way was "graduated deterrence," which was debated heatedly in the 1950s as an alternative to the threat of launching an all-out nuclear war.[20]

Basically, this strategy relied on America's superiority in "tactical" nuclear weapons. The idea was that the U.S. and its allies could resist any future Korean-size offensive by using relatively few nuclear weapons against enemy troops on the battlefield without having to expand the area of conflict geographically.[21] The idea was attractive to some specialists in national security policy, including Henry Kissinger for awhile, because in theory at least the U.S. government would avoid the high cost burden of a large standing army. Moreover, under graduated deterrence, the U.S. might also be able to avoid having to initiate a "massive retaliation" strike against the U.S.S.R. or China.[22]

To be sure, the proposed strategy posed a number of problems, which led to a lessening of enthusiasm for it. In his psychological analysis of limited nuclear warfare in the 1950s, Kissinger, for one, was criticized for manifesting what has been described as "a Talmudic mind." The famous psychoanalyst Erik Erikson tells a joke about a Jew who met another Jew in a Polish railroad station. "Where are you going?" asked the first. "To Minsk," said the other, "To Minsk!" exclaimed the first, "you say you are going to Minsk so that I should believe you go to Pinsk! You are going to Minsk anyway — so why do you lie?"

To critics, Kissinger resembled the first Jew on the train when he argued:[23]

A strategy of limited war adds to deterrence for the very reason usually invoked against it. The danger that a limited war may expand after all works both ways. An aggressor may not credit our threat of massive retaliation because it would force us to initiate a course of action which will inevitably involve enormous devastation. He may calculate, however, that once engaged in war on any scale neither he nor we would know how to

---

20 One of the earliest and most influential essays of the postwar period on how to deal with limited war was written by Bernard Brodie, "Unlimited Weapons and Limited War," *The Reporter*, Vol. II (1954), pp. 16-21.

21 See Robert E. Osgood, *Limited War* (Chicago: University of Chicago Press, 1957.

22 See William W. Kaufmann, "The Crisis in Military Affairs," *World Politics* Vol 10, pp. 579-603.

23 Henry Kissinger, *Necessity for Choice*, p. 60.

limit it, whatever the intentions of the two sides. The stronger the limited war forces of the free world, the larger will have to be the Communist effort designed to overcome them. The more the scale of conflict required for victory approaches that of all-out war the greater will be the inhibitions against initiating hostilities. In this sense a capability of limited war is necessary in order to enhance the deterrent power of the retaliatory force.

The contradictory "finesse" of such arguments aside, the limited war theory suffered considerable shortcomings, so much so that Kissinger was later forced to repudiate it. In the first place, the strategy put the United States in the undesirable position of being the *first* to convert a conventional conflict into a nuclear war. This predicament did not bother some national security experts who favored Thomas C. Schelling's idea of viewing limited war as a kind of tacit "bargaining" process in which each side bargained with the other about what the "ground rules" should be by deliberately escalating the conflict a certain amount but no more.[24] But others doubted whether a limited war could, in fact, be limited once nuclear weapons were introduced. These security specialists believed that the "firebreak" (or "threshold") between nuclear and conventional weapons should never be crossed, because no one could guarantee that the process of escalation could be halted.[25]

The debate over "graduated deterrence" was still raging when President John F. Kennedy entered office in 1961. But the young "New Frontiersman" was generally skeptical of any use of nuclear weapons. So he picked new people, like Secretary of Defense Robert S. McNamara, who would put the President's own ideas into policy.[26]

---

24 See Thomas Schelling, *The Strategy of Conflict* (Cambridge: Harvard University Press, 1960).

25 See Bernard Brodie, *Escalation and the Nuclear Option* (Princeton: Princeton University Press, 1966).

26 Ambassador Martin J. Hillenbrand, former Assistant Secretary of State for European Affairs, would comment here: "I think you draw too sharp a distinction between 'graduated deterrence' and 'flexible response.' At least as used in the NATO context, 'graduated deterrence' was also conceived to operate at the conventional level and did not involve automatic use of tactical nuclear weapons. In fact, some NATO types saw the whole thing as essentially a change of nomenclature rather than of doctrine. Americans involved in NATO never liked the tripwire concept advanced by some British generals. In any event, the more sophisticated conceptualization of 'flexible response' could be viewed within the NATO context as a logical evolution of 'graduated deterrence.'" Letter to this writer, May 22, 1984.

"Flexible Response"

President Kennedy was personally distressed with some of the harsh and, in his view, "irresponsible" rhetoric of the Dulles period. Although it was deliberately ambiguous, it seemed to suggest at times that the United States might initiate a nuclear war over a relatively minor intrusion upon a rather illdefined line demarcating what U.S. officials called "the free world." Generally, he tended to view such a policy as dangerous. If it were a bluff, the U.S. might be left embarrassed and helpless.[27] If the policy were not a bluff, it was even more dangerous because it might trigger a nuclear holocaust. Kennedy came into office determined to change Administration policy in the field of nuclear weapons; in particular, he wanted to make sure such weapons of mass destruction were never used. "We must face the fact that the United States is neither omnipotent nor omniscient," the young New Frontiersman said. "[W]e can not impose our will on the other ninety-four per cent of mankind."[28]

During the 1950s, while developing his campaign strategy, JFK became greatly influenced in his thinking on nuclear weapons policy by two well-known defense experts who had held highlevel positions in the Eisenhower Administration. The first was James M. Gavin, who had headed the Army's Research and Development Program. The second was Maxwell D. Taylor, who had served as Army Chief of Staff. Both were very critical of the nuclear policies of the Eisenhower Administration (which pundits derided as "more bang for the buck"). After leaving military service they wrote bestselling books detailing this criticism.

Lt. General Gavin published his book, *War and Peace in the Space Age*, shortly after he resigned in 1958.[29] He argued that for the United States to fight a limited rather than a global war, it must be prepared to expand its resources to permit maximum mobility and flexibility. In effect, this meant increasing the size of a standing army, rather than cutting down on manpower, as the Defense Department under President Eisenhower had insisted.

---

27 For background see Bernard Brodie, *Strategy in the Missile Age* (Princeton: Princeton University Press, 1959).

28 *The New York Times*, November 17, 1961.

29 A knowledgeable Pentagon official claims the above is a distortion of the record. This person confides: "In the spring of 1958 Lt. General Gavin went in to see the Secretary of the Army Bruckner and applied for promotion to Full General, commanding the United States Continental Army Command (CONARC). Bruckner would not commit himself because this was the Chief of Staff's prerogative. Whereupon Gavin said: 'If I do not get it, I'll retire.' Bruckner said: 'You will be retired next week.' Lesson: Do not ever apply to be promoted in the Army."

When Gavin's book was brought to his attention, Kennedy picked it up and read it enthusiastically. In a review, he described the author as "imaginative, probing and sensitive to the imperatives of a space and missile age." Upon becoming President in 1961, JFK appointed the former paratroop leader American Ambassador to France.

John Kennedy was particularly taken with General Maxwell Taylor's book, *The Uncertain Trumpet*, which came to his attention in 1959. In his treatise, the retired four star general who had made his reputation during World War II as commander of the "battered bastards of Bastogne," described as "nonsense" the idea that limited war with conventional weapons was impossible in the NATO area. Taylor maintained that a Soviet attack could be met by an expanded army capable of "flexible response."[30]

Taylor's "flexible response" idea was adopted by President Kennedy, who set out the broad objectives of this new strategy in his first message to Congress on defense matters, in March 1961. These goals were "to deter all wars, general or limited, nuclear or conventional, large or small — to convince all potential aggressors that any attack would be futile — to provide backing for the diplomatic settlement of disputes — to insure the adequacy of our bargaining power for an end to the arms race."

To be sure, Dulles and Eisenhower had sought similar objectives — but at a minimal cost. Consequently, they had been prepared to run the risk either of not acting at all or of responding at levels beyond the original provocation. JFK, who possessed an economic rationale for disregarding costs, placed his emphasis on minimizing risks by giving the U.S. sufficient choice between "inglorious retreat or unlimited retaliation." On the one hand, this new strategy would require a capability to act at all levels — ranging from diplomacy through covert action, guerilla operations, conventional and nuclear war. On the other, it would require careful control — what the Administration came to call "fine tuning" (ensuring that actions taken were appropriate to the situation) and "integration" (applying to the tasks at hand all available instruments in a coordinated and purposeful manner). Most importantly, top priority went to decreasing the reliance on nuclear weapons to deter limited aggression that had been such a prominent feature of the strategy of the Eisenhower Administration.

Upon taking office, the President began to push the idea of "flexible response" on a reluctant Defense Department.[31] There it was developed in

---

30 JFK was so taken by some of Taylor's ideas that he used them in his attacks on the Eisenhower Administration. Then, following the aborted Bay of Pigs invasion in April 1961, he called in General Taylor to serve on his staff as Military Representative for Foreign and Military Policy. Later, the President made Taylor Chairman of the Joint Chiefs of Staff.

31 McGeorge Bundy informed Kennedy shortly after his inauguration that "existing

113

great depth by Robert McNamara's staff, which incorporated the doctrine in the Secretary of Defense's strategic guidance to the Joint Chiefs of Staff. Essentially, it stressed keeping America's military options open in the event of war. No longer would the Administration threaten to launch an immediate, all-out nuclear attack on an adversary guilty of encroaching on America's vital interests. Instead the enemy would be faced with a wide range of military responses on the part of the United States, including the possible use of nuclear weapons.[32] In this way, the Administration hoped to force the aggressor to confront costs and risks disproportionate to his initial objectives and to ensure that local clashes would not automatically escalate to all-out nuclear war.

As the advocates of "flexible response" saw it, America's nuclear forces served primarily a deterrent function. On the strategic level, the American strategic nuclear arsenal would deter the Soviet (and later) Chinese strategic arsenal. Whereas on the tactical level, U.S. capabilities for using nuclear weapons would deter Soviet (and Chinese) capabilities of the same kind. The policy was thought to be workable because of the perception that a stable deterrent balance was emerging between East and West on these two levels. Thus, "flexible response" was seen as serving to promote crisis stability.

At a tactical level, such as a potential conflict in Central Europe, the strategy called for the United States and its NATO allies to increase the size of their conventional forces, which would make credible a policy decision to postpone the early use of nuclear weapons. The idea was that these conventional forces should be large enough to deter the Soviet Union (and its Warsaw Pact allies) from launching a massive conventional attack. However, should deterrence fail, the American President theoretically would not be faced with an agonizing choice between accepting defeat or resorting to the use of nuclear weapons.

High-level officials in the Eisenhower Administration had been opposed to the development of a large conventional force because of the cost. But

> war plans placed a debatable emphasis (1) on strategic as against limited-war forces, (2) on 'strike-first', or 'counter-force' strategic planning, as against a 'deterrent' or 'second strike' posture, and (3) on decisions-in-advance, as against decisions in light of all the circumstances. These three forces in combination have created a situation today in which a subordinate commander faced with a substantial Russian military action could start the thermonuclear holocaust on his own initiative if he could not reach you (by failure of communication at either end of the line)."
> (Bundy to Kennedy, January 30, 1961, Kennedy Papers, NSC file, Box 313, Folder 2, "NSC Meetings, 1961, Nr. 475.")

32 General Bruce Clarke, Commander in Chief of United States Army, Europe, 1960-62, writes "I always doubted if the strategy of 'flexible response' would go so far as to use nuclear weapons." Letter to this writer, December 3, 1978.

the advocates of "flexible response" maintained that the European allies had recovered from most of the ill effects of World War II and were now economically able to bear an increasing share of the burden. Their contributions, plus additional American soldiers, would constitute a sizeable NATO conventional force.[33]

The deterrent strategy of "flexible response" was aided by the discovery soon after Kennedy entered office that the real potency of the Red Army in Europe had been exaggerated all along. The "whiz kids" in the Pentagon drew attention to the fact that the total populations of the NATO states were far larger than those of the Warsaw Pact. As Andrew Cockburn writes: "They realized that the United States alone could potentially field far greater hordes of soldiers than the Soviet Union, since half the Soviet population was engaged in agriculture, presumably producing the food to feed the entire population, whereas no more than 10 percent of the U.S. population was fulfilling the same task."[34] Further re-examining the obvious, McNamara's aides wondered how it was that the U.S.S.R. could field an army of 175 divisions and the U.S. a mere sixteen when the Red Army was only about twice as large in terms of manpower (approximately two million to one million).

Robert Amory, former Deputy Director of the CIA, explains in his oral history at the JFK Library how the U.S. came to exaggerate Soviet troop strength opposing NATO forces. "For years," he says, "the [U.S.] Army had a very liberal estimate of the enemy's order of battle system." This estimate tended to maximize Soviet conventional military strength. According to the way it worked, if the Army "ever had any evidence of a division" (a Soviet division is a somewhat smaller unit than a U.S. division) it continued "to carry it" until positively reassured that it had been deactivated. This meant that the Army carried "175 Soviet divisions year after year, as sort of a sacred number," even when it hadn't heard about one of these

---

33 McNamara initially thought that additional conventional forces would not be necessary. But during the 1961 Berlin crisis he became convinced that additional regular troops were in fact needed — both as a sign of U.S. resolve to the Soviets and as a way of increasing the number of escalatory steps that could be taken prior to the resort to nuclear weapons.

"For McNamara," writes Richard J. Barnet, "Berlin was the place to test the new 'flexible response' doctrine he was trying to have adopted as the new NATO strategy. Only after the Soviets had repulsed a 'probe' by ground forces down the Autobahn would nuclear weapons be introduced. This strategy would provide a 'pause' in the rush of events to permit everyone to come to his senses before all-out war occurred." See *The Alliance* (New York: Simon & Schuster, 1983), p. 227.

34 Andrew Cockburn, *The Soviet Threat: Inside the Soviet Military Machine* (New York: Random House, 1983, p. 104.

divisions since 1952 or 1950. Moreover, the Army "didn't pay enough attention to how many of them were really cadres." (These "were no more important than our National Guard outfits or our Reserve outfits that have a few regular officers attached to them and some people drilling weekends...")[35]

Following the creation of the Defense Intelligence Agency in mid-1961, the Army lost its "stranglehold on this problem." A joint task force "was set up from the DIA and the CIA to review every single Russian division and its evidence, and to appraise both its existence and, if it existed, [to determine] how strong it was." As Amory recalls, the findings of this task force were astounding. They "came out with, as I recall, 121 as the maximum number of which some 50 were in various stages of incompleteness. So you essentially cut the estimate by a solid half."

During this time, officials in the new Administration increasingly questioned the reliability of Warsaw Pact forces. They concluded that there was substantial doubt whether the Kremlin's allies in Eastern Europe would fight in a Europeanwide war. Moreover, the serious prospect existed that some Soviet troops might even have to be diverted to keep their satellites under control while the fighting occurred.

Finally, improvements in technology seemed to enhance the feasibility of the "flexible response" strategy. More and larger units, with their equipment prepositioned in Europe, could be flown from the United States to the battlefield in Europe. This meant that some important military units could be stationed in the U.S. (thus saving money)[36] and still be transported quickly to the scene of the fighting. At the same time, advances were being made in the technology of communications, so that U.S. forces could be centrally commanded and controlled down to smaller units.

NATO Implementation of "Flexible Response"

President Kennedy authorized his Secretary of Defense Robert McNamara to propose at a meeting of the NATO ministers in Athens in May 1962 to substitute the strategy of "flexible response" for the existing

---

35 One senior U.S. Army officer makes the following point: "This is a faulty comparison. Our National Guard units are much better than Soviet cadre units."

36 A former high-level U.S. Army officer attached to USAREUR headquarters and privy to its studies on comparative cost savings argues that the savings of having U.S. military units stationed in the continental U.S. instead of Europe is not as great as many people believe.

doctrine of "massive retaliation."[37] McNamara recalled later: the "proposed change in NATO's strategy met with strong opposition."[38] Some opponents argued that the "United States was asking to 'decouple' itself from the defense of Europe." These critics shared the view of the Kennedy Administration that a "tactical" nuclear war in Europe would quickly escalate to a strategic exchange involving the U.S. and Soviet homelands. But as McNamara says: "they saw this danger as the primary factor which deterred Soviet aggression." Any reduction in this prospect, they argued, "might cause the Soviets to believe that hostilities could be confined to Central Europe, and thus tempt them into adventures."

Other critics maintained "that the proposed buildup of NATO's conventional forces was totally beyond what the Alliance would be willing to support." Still others "argued that we had greatly exaggerated the dangers of limited uses of nuclear weapons."

The argument raged for five years, McNamara recalls. "It was not until 1967 that NATO (formally) adopted the strategy of 'flexible response,' inscribing it in a document known as MC 14/3."[39]

The revised strategy adopted by NATO in 1967 proposed to deter aggression by maintaining forces adequate to counter at whatever level the aggressor chose to fight. Should such a direct confrontation not prove successful, McNamara recalls, "the strategy proposed to escalate as necessary, including the initial use of nuclear weapons, forcing the aggressor to confront costs and risks disproportionate to his initial objectives." At all times, however, "the flexible response strategy specified that efforts should be made to control the scope and the intensity of combat." Thus, for example, initial "nuclear attacks presumably would be made by short-range tactical systems in an attempt to confine the effects of nuclear warfare to the battlefield." Even so, the strategy "retained the ultimate escalatory threat of a strategic exchange between U.S. and Soviet homelands to make clear the final magnitude of the dangers being contemplated."

---

37 The text of McNamara's remarks has now been declassified. See "Remarks by Secretary McNamara, NATO Ministerial Meeting, 5 May 1962, Restricted Session.

38 Robert S. McNamara, "The Military Role of Nuclear Weapons: Perceptions and Misperceptions," *Foreign Affairs*, Vol. 62, No. 1 (Fall, 1983), p. 64. 'McNamara was, of course, the driving force behind the full development of 'flexible response' as official NATO doctrine," writes Ambassador Martin J. Hillenbrand. "The extent to which his thinking and that of NATO as a whole was influenced by Berlin contingency planning has never been adequately discussed." Letter to this writer, May 22, 1984.

39 According to one former U.S. official who was involved, the delay was due in part "because NATO had to wait until General de Gaulle withdrew from the military part of the organization."

A Critique of the Strategy

As critics have noted, and these now include McNamara himself, there are a number of major problems with the "flexible response" strategy. In the first place, the West Europeans, even if they finally did go ahead and formally approve the doctrine in 1967, were never quite convinced of its utility. Generally, they viewed the unwillingness of first the Kennedy, and later the Johnson, Administration to use nuclear weapons first in the defense of the region as evidence of a lack of a commitment to defend Western Europe. This was particularly true of General de Gaulle, who decided in the late 1950s to develop an independent nuclear force. In the second place, President Kennedy had difficulty winning the support of the U.S. military for his new policy. For instance, the NATO Commander, General Lauris Norstad, was asked to resign by Kennedy because he resisted the adoption of "flexible response."

Perhaps the most telling *status quo* military argument against the policy had to do with conventional force requirements. To work, at least in theory, "flexible response" demands larger and better equipped Allied conventional forces in Europe than are presently stationed there. While overwhelming Soviet superiority in the area may be a myth,[40] the perception in Allied circles was (and is) that a conventional defense of Europe — without the use of nuclear weapons — is impossible without considerable improvement in Allied forces. This view assumes that the Soviets intend to launch a massive surprise attack against Western Europe or that a conflict would somehow result from misunderstanding or events elsewhere in the world.

"Flexible response" has remained NATO's official deterrent doctrine for over 15 years. Yet, as McNamara himself now recalls, its "essential element ... has never been achieved." This is the development of "sufficient conventional capabilities to offset those of the Warsaw Pact." Indeed, he continues, "during the late 1960s and early 1970s, the Alliance may have fallen farther behind its opponent..." Moreover, the "substantial raising of the 'nuclear threshold,' as was envisioned when 'flexible response' was first conceived, has not become a reality."[41]

There are some other difficulties with the doctrine of "flexible response," as applied today. As McNamara points out: "The nuclear balance has changed substantially since the Kennedy Administration first proposed [the strategy]." Both sides "have virtually completely refurbished their in-

---

40 See for example Alain C. Enthoven, "U.S. Forces in Europe: How Many Doing What," *Foreign Affairs*, Vol. 53, No. 3 (April, 1975), p. 518.

41 Robert S. McNamara, "The Military Role of Nuclear Weapons: Perceptions and Misperceptions," *Foreign Affairs*, Vol. 62, No. 1 (Fall, 1983), p. 65.

ventories, increasing the number of weapons of all three different types — battlefield, intermediate-range and strategic — and vastly improving the performance characteristics of both the weapons themselves and their delivery systems." Because the U.S.S.R. was "so far behind the United States in the early 1960s, the quantitative changes, at least, appear to have been more favorable for the U.S.S.R."

In short, "a key element of the flexible response strategy has been overtaken by a change in the physical realities of the nuclear balance." With huge survivable arsenals on both sides, "strategic nuclear weapons have lost whatever military utility may once have been attributed to them. Their sole purpose, at present, is to deter the other side's first use of its strategic force."[42]

The "flexible response" policy was never tested in Europe where U.S. officials saw its implementation as most appropriate. But the weaknesses of the policy were dramatically highlighted by U.S. failure in Vietnam. By restricting the American response there to the other side's initiative, U.S. policymakers relinquished the initiative to the other side. This left the enemy with the ability to make the real decision as to the commitment and disposition of one's forces. The "controlled" U.S. escalation of the conflict and the communist response raised the disturbing question: How could one indefinitely sustain such a strategy without greatly undermining not only the domestic economy but also the political consensus any government must have in order to function successfully.

The U.S. failure in Vietnam also suggested that the strategy of deterrence cannot be counted on to dissuade an adversary who is determined to achieve his goals. In this case, the North Vietnamese were apparently prepared to absorb practically any amount of punishment U.S. officials threatened to inflict on them to achieve the unification of the country under the domination of Hanoi.[43] Thus, the United States was in large part defeated

---

42 Colin S. Gray, President of the National Institute for Public Policy, maintains that "NATO's military strategy, force posture and deployments do not, and are not really intended to, make military sense ... Many people in the United States and in Western Europe make the grave error of criticizing NATO strategy on military grounds — as if that strategy were designed on military grounds to serve narrow military ends. The key principles of NATO strategy, which are forward defense and flexible response, are political not military in origin." See his "NATO Defense and Arms-Reduction Proposals," *Military Review*, Vol. 63, No. 10 (October, 1983), p. 63.

43 A French professor teaching in Hanoi in 1966 told one Western visitor that North Vietnamese authorities assumed that U.S. bombers would sooner or later totally destroy their cities and industries. However, these officials were convinced that this alone would not ensure their defeat. It would just bring their nation back to where it had been when it had defeated the French in 1954. Once hostilities were

in Vietnam because American policymakers could not understand that the communists used a cost-benefit calculus which was radically different from that of the United States. (In his book *On Thermonuclear War*, Herman Kahn had written that American security must henceforth depend upon "a willingness to incur casualties in limited wars just to improve our bargaining position moderately.")

Summary

Postwar American foreign policy toward the Soviet Union has been characterized by a persistent theme: deterrence. The possibility of Soviet aggression against the security interests of the United States was seen for a long time as requiring an imbalance of terror in favor of the West. U.S. officials relied on American nuclear superiority, enhanced by the dynamism of its technology, to keep feared Soviet expansionist tendencies in check. When American superiority began to erode seriously, the utility of nuclear weapons for the West as an instrument of general deterrence was threatened. Large nuclear stockpiles, accumulated by the Soviet Union and the United States, would cancel each other out resulting in a new balance of terror. Or so it was believed.

Differences in deterrent doctrine between the Truman and Eisenhower Administrations revolved largely around the question of symmetrical versus asymmetrical response. As John L. Gaddis writes in his insightful study of U.S. foreign policy during this period: "The Truman Administration, of course, had emphasized symmetry: deterrence would work by creating certainty in the mind of the adversary both as to the inevitability and the limits of an American response — the United States would counter, but not exceed the initial provocation." Under the Eisenhower Administration, the U.S., "embracing asymmetry, sought to combine the certainty of a response with uncertainty as to its nature. The idea was to open up a range of possible responses so wide that the adversary would not be able to count on retaining the initiative." Lacking this, "it was thought, he would come to see the risks of aggression as outweighing the benefits."[44]

Thus, under the Eisenhower Administration, overwhelming nuclear superiority and fiscal considerations led U.S. policymakers to adopt in the main a rather primitive strategy:[45] an act of communist aggression could

> over, they believed reconstruction would be rapid as was the case in North Korea after the Korean War. See Bernard Fall, "The Other Side of the 17th Parallel," *The New York Times Magazine*, March 16, 1966.

44 John L. Gaddis, *opus cit.*, p. 151.

45 John J. Gilligan of the University of Notre Dame would insert here: In discussing

elicit from the United States a devastating response by means and in places of its own choosing. In this way, the possible use of nuclear weapons — rather than deployment of major ground and air forces — became the declaratory American deterrent posture against possible Soviet and other aggression.

Recently declassified U.S. government documents from the early Eisenhower Administration reveal that this public position was not a bluff. The Administration apparently was prepared to *consider* the use of nuclear weapons in a wide range of circumstances. Thus, NSC 162/2, the top secret policy statement underlying the "New Look" strategy approved by President Eisenhower, in 1953, stipulated that in the event of hostilities with the Russians or the Chinese, "the United States will consider nuclear weapons to be as available for use as other munitions." The general idea, Eisenhower informed Congressional leaders late in 1954, was "to blow hell out of them in a hurry if they start anything."[46]

Actually, this policy of "massive retaliation" (which was seen by some

---

the development of "the Cold War psychology and strategy in the United States during the periods of the Truman and Eisenhower Administrations, you do not, in my judgment, give sufficient weight to the enormous influence of public opinion which was almost hysterically anti-Communist upon the actions and statements of elected officials and their appointed subordinates. America's fear of Communism did not begin after World War II, but really antedated the Russian Revolution, and a climate of fear and suspicion had been cultivated in this country for decades, which made infinitely more difficult the organization of labor unions, or diplomatic recognition of the Soviet Union, or even the passage of social welfare legislation. In a nation whose highest public officials are acutely sensitive to public opinion, and whose actions are always open to public attack by partisan opponents, the conduct of foreign policy — especially of a foreign policy which might be designed to cultivate a somewhat more sympathetic understanding of our erstwhile adversaries is an extremely hazardous business. Demagogy is not only a frightfully effective weapon in the domestic political arena, it is also the most formidable obstacle to real statesmanship . . ." Letter to this writer, April 2, 1984.

46 At one point Eisenhower even considered the idea of preventive war. He wrote Dulles in September 1953 that "we would have to be constantly ready, on an instantaneous basis, to inflict greater loss upon the enemy than he could reasonably hope to inflict upon us. This would be a deterrent — but if the contest to maintain this relative position should have to continue indefinitely, the cost would either drive us to war — or into some form of dictatorial government. In such circumstances, we would be forced to consider whether or not our duty to future generations did not require us to *initiate* war at the most propitious moment that we could designate." (Eisenhower to Dulles, September 8, 1953, Eisenhower Papers, Whitman File: International Series, Box 33, "Dulles/Korea/Security/Policy.") At a press conference on August 11, 1954, Eisenhower said: "[F]rankly, I wouldn't even listen to anyone seriously that came in and talked about such a thing." Quoted in John L. Gaddis, *opus cit.*, pp. 149-50.

Washington policymakers as "cost-effective") contained a number of structural flaws. A number of these were perceived almost immediately, and in the end they led to the general discrediting of the policy associated with the name of Secretary Dulles. Perhaps the most serious shortcoming of the deterrent posture was the problem of credibility it posed. The "all or nothing" character of the policy was simply not credible against any but the most improbable contingency — a devastating all-out nuclear attack on American cities. And even in this "worst-case" scenario Soviet conventional superiority in Central Europe raised serious questions about the credibility of this aspect of the nuclear threat.[47]

As Henry Kissinger has noted in his book *Nuclear Weapons and Foreign Policy*, the efficacy of a massive and undifferentiated threat to influence minor issues was highly suspect from the beginning. For it allowed the Soviets "to nibble away the status quo bit by bit and impose a series of piecemeal defeats on the West." Kissinger contended that if the Soviet Union could present its challenges in less than all-out form, it might well gain important advantages.

More or less the same point was made by President Eisenhower who found much that was "interesting and worth reading" in Henry Kissinger's "very provocative book." Privately, the Chief Executive expressed his personal reservations of the Dulles' strategy. Thus, in 1955, he said: such a monolithic strategy "offers, of itself, no defense against the losses that we incur through the enemy's political and military nibbling. So long as he abstains from doing anything that he believes would provoke the free world to an open declaration of major war, he need not fear the 'deterrent.'" Moreover, whatever the impact of the threat to use nuclear weapons had on adversaries, such threats had the disconcerting effect of frightening friends. For these and others reasons, the President made a point of reminding his Secretary of State that "when we talk about ... massive retaliation, we mean retaliation against an act that means irrevocable war."[48]

If the policy of "massive retaliation" was suspect from the beginning, the U.S. deterrent posture would grow increasingly questionable over time, particularly as the Soviet Union developed a nuclear arsenal capable of delivering devastating attacks against American urban-industrial targets. As Henry Kissinger stated not too long ago: "Logically, once the Soviet Union acquired the capacity to threaten the United States with direct nu-

47 Dulles admitted as much privately when he wrote: "Our deterrent striking power does not, today, have anywhere near the reassuring power of which it is capable because no one knows whether, when or where it would be used." (Dulles memorandum, June 25, 1952, Dulles Papers, Box 57, "Baldwin" folder.)

48 See for instance Eisenhower-Dulles conversation, July 20, 1954, Eisenhower Papers, Whitman File: Diary Series, Box 2.

clear retaliation, the American pledge to launch an all-out nuclear war on behalf of Europe was bound increasingly to lose its sense — and so would the Alliance's defense strategy..."[49] What U.S. leader would accept the destruction of major American cities with enormous casualties to prevent Soviet encroachment in Western Europe or elsewhere, encroachments that by themselves might not threaten the U.S. directly?

The policy of "massive retaliation" rested on the implausible assumption that the Soviet leadership exercised tight control over the world revolutionary process. It also assumed that the Soviets might be amendable to govern its actions by American texts, however unreasonable this might seem to the U.S.S.R. For all these reasons — and others — this deterrent strategy was clearly unsatisfactory — not only as a declaratory policy but as planning and procurement guidelines. In the words of William W. Kaufmann, a policy so obviously incredible would "result only in deterring the deterrer."[50]

At the time, the long-term implications of depending on weapons of mass destruction for national security worried only a politically insignificant minority in the West. Generally, Western governments found in nuclear weapons so convenient a solution to their budgetary problems that they were adopted with little serious public debate. The Europeans — to take the most important case — saw themselves as getting defense on the cheap. In the process they deluded themselves and effectively abandoned responsibility for their own defense. As one British scholar has noted: The armed forces of the West European states, which "have always had the social role of embodying national self-consciousness and will to independent existence, became almost peripheral, part of a mechanism for nuclear deterrence, the ultimate control of which lay elsewhere."[51]

During the 1950s, U.S. strategic thinkers flirted with the idea of "graduated deterrence" (limited nuclear war) as an alternative to the threat of launching all-out nuclear war, which was involved in the Dulles policy of "massive retaliation." Henry Kissinger, among others, was tempted by this theory, which promised to restore some relationship between policy and military power. But after initially embracing it, he came to realize its impracticality. As he recently wrote, part of the problem with the limited

---

49 Henry A. Kissinger, "Strategy and the Atlantic Alliance," *Survival*, Vol. 24 (1982), p. 195.

50 Kaufmann's critique first appeared in 1954 as a monograph distributed by the Center for International Studies at Princeton University. It was later reprinted as a chapter "The Requirements of Deterrence," in Kaufmann (ed.), *Military Policy and National Security* (Princeton: Princeton University Press, 1956), pp. 17-23.

51 Michael Howard, "Reassurance and Deterrence: Western Defense in the 1980s," *Foreign Affairs* (Winter, 1982-83) pp. 312-13.

nuclear war doctrine — as applied to Europe — was that "from the European perspective, the distinction between limited and general nuclear war was not as clear cut as on the American side." A "relatively few nuclear weapons could produce catastrophe and chaos difficult to distinguish from what only total war could do to America." In summary, limited nuclear options do not look very attractive to those who are likely to be affected most by them.

The dangers inherent in a policy of relying primarily on nuclear weapons to ensure Western security were emphasized by John Kennedy before he took office in 1961. He was deeply troubled, among other things, with a policy which presented U.S. decision-makers with only two major military options in a crisis: do nothing or risk having to use nuclear weapons. In the attempt to avoid this dilemma, President Kennedy chose early in his Administration to expand the range of possible retaliation by implementing unilaterally the policy of "flexible response."[52] Under this deterrent strategy, which emphasized a buildup of conventional forces, it was hoped that lesser communist threats would be deterred by lesser and therefore more credible American responses — spanning the spectrum of possible military action.

The policy of "flexible response" became official NATO policy in 1967, but it was only reluctantly accepted by the West Europeans after pressure by the U.S. Basically, the NATO countries were not happy with a strategy that, among other things, explicitly implied the possibility of limited nuclear war in Europe. Whether the fighting involved large conventional forces only, or included nuclear weapons, the damage would be suffered mainly by Europeans. From the European view, it was all too easy to visualize an outcome where the United States and the U.S.S.R. both emerged from a war relatively unscathed, while Europe lay in shambles. This point highlighted a fundamental flaw in the deterrent strategy (which is still U.S. and NATO policy): A doctrine that one side implements because it is "more credible" is sure to be offensive to someone else on grounds that it makes war "more likely."

The "flexible response" strategy was premised on the development of larger and somewhat more expensive conventional forces. Theoretically, this would allow NATO to contain just about any conceivable enemy action. However, the strategy fell short in Europe because the NATO allies

52 In the publicly expressed Soviet view, the initial manifestation of Washington's attempts to adapt to the changing correlation of forces brought about by the emerging military strength of the Soviet Union was the replacement of the doctrine of massive retaliation with that of flexible response. See Morton Schwarz, *Soviet Perception of the United States* (Los Angeles: University of California Press, 1978), p. 122.

refused for various reasons to take the necessary steps to adequately build up their conventional military forces.

The much-vaunted policy of "flexible response" (which between 1960 and 1968, tripled the number of nuclear warheads in NATO to seven thousand) suffered from other equally serious — but less visible — weaknesses. For instance, it rested on such highly questionable notions as control of escalation through threshold recognition and target distinctions, willingness to compete with an adversary in pain endurance and risk-taking and war termination through intrawar bargaining. In the main these theoretical shortcomings in the deterrent policy only became apparent in the Vietnam War because the deterrent posture was never tested in Europe.

The use of calibrated pressures did not work in Vietnam.[53] In part, this was due to a persistent lack of clarity as to who or what was being deterred. But more importantly the Vietnam experience dramatically showed that even when the adversary is identified and threatened, a deterrent strategy is useless against an opponent who is single-mindedly committed to his goals. The "flexible response" policy did not work well in the jungles of Vietnam mainly because the North Vietnamese, aided by their allies in the South, considered unification of their country worth practically any amount of death and destruction. And the U.S. public and Congress were not prepared to pay the price of a protracted war of attrition.

In Vietnam, the U.S. was presented with the spectacle — to use the words of William Whitworth, a writer for the *New Yorker* — of the theory "eating its own tail." In the beginning, flexible response, as applied to the situation in Asia, seemed full of promise. As Maxwell Taylor, Kennedy's chief adviser on paramilitary activities, stated upon returning from his famous mission to South Vietnam in the early 1960s: "Nothing is more calculated to sober the enemy and to discourage escalation in the face of the limited initiatives proposed here than the knowledge that the United States has prepared itself soundly to deal with aggression in Southeast Asia at any level."[54] However, it was not long before Americans saw the expansion of means to honor a commitment made as a substitute for means. They saw the justification of that commitment in terms of a balance of power made shaky by its very existence. They saw the defense, in the interest of credibility, of policies destructive of credibility. Finally, they witnessed the search for a domestic consensus by means that destroyed that consensus. All of these paradoxes reflected the basic failure of "flexible response" to proceed in the neat theoretical manner of its proponents —

---

53 See William C. Moore, "History, Vietnam, and the Concept of Deterrence," *Air University Review*, Vol. 20, No. 6 (September-October, 1969), pp. 58-63.

54 Quoted in Fred Kaplan, *opus cit.*, p. 329.

through the stages of identifying interests, perceiving threats and selecting appropriate responses. Instead, as John Gaddis has pointed out, "both threats and responses became interests in themselves, with the result that the United States either ignored or forgot what it had set out to do in Vietnam at just the moment it was resolving, with unprecedented determination, to do it."[55]

In short, the major doctrines of nuclear deterrence adhered to by the United States in the 1950s and 1960s suffered debilitating weaknesses. These severely undercut — if they did not thoroughly discredit — the practical effectiveness of U.S. nuclear deterrence policy. For the most part, the structural flaws inherent in the policies of "massive retaliation" and "flexible response" have been noted and analyzed by critics. But some of these shortcomings have also been observed — and this is less well known — by the initiators of these policies. In the case of Secretary of State Dulles, he was compelled to modify the nuclear deterrent posture associated with his name as the perception of overwhelming U.S. superiority waned before his death in the late 1950s.[56] It is significant to note that Dulles in his 1954 *Foreign Affairs* article, already listed alliances ahead even of nuclear deterrence as the "cornerstone of security for the free nations." Later Dulles talked more openly about "selective retaliation," although some would say that Dulles thought that he was always talking about "selective retaliation."[57] In the case of Secretary McNamara, he chose to wait some fifteen years after leaving office to criticize severely the deterrent policy — "flexible response" — with which he was at one time closely identified. All of these are examples of what psychiatrist Robert J. Lifton has called "nuclear backsliding" — a "retreat from, and often a condemnation of, that contemporary religion of power that had so held one in thrall."[58]

Again we can not know with certainty what Soviet intentions were during this period. But a close study of the historical record for these years would seem to show that the Soviet Union (and other Communist powers) were not seriously deterred by the various nuclear deterrent postures of the United States if they were clearly concerned by their implications and

---

55 John L. Gaddis, *opus cit.*, p. 243.

56 On Dulles' change of heart concerning the strategy of "massive retaliation," see the interviews with George Kennan and Maxwell D. Taylor, Dulles Oral History Project, Princeton University.

57 See Colin S. Gray, "The 'Racing Syndrome' and the Strategic Balance," in Lawrence L. Whetten (ed.), *The Future of Soviet Military Power* (New York: Crane, Russak & Co., 1976), p. 31.

58 See Robert J. Lifton and Richard Falk, *Indefensible Weapons: The Political and Psychological Case against Nuclearism* (New York: Basic Books, 1982), p. 98.

American nuclear superiority.[59] To be sure, "Dulles was a worthy adversary," Nikita Khrushchev later recalled. "It always kept us on our toes to match wits with him."[60] But despite America's overwhelming nuclear deterrent, great-power conflicts — which could well have escalated to nuclear war — marked the landscape of this Cold War era. To name but a few areas where U.S. interests were subject to serious challenge, one could cite Vietnam, 1954-65; the Middle East, 1956; Berlin, 1958-62, and Cuba, 1962. As Harvard University's Adam Ulam writes in his highly regarded study of Soviet policy, "America's possesion of nuclear weapons (during this period) was *not* a source of urgent concern to the Russian leaders . . . The Russians seem to have assumed between 1953 and 1962 that, short of a catastrophic miscalculation or a cataclysmic accident, an American nuclear attack was out of the question."[61]

Thus, from the perspective of hindsight, it may be — as Richard Barnet has written — "that for much of the cold war the United States [was] running an arms race with itself." It was "always possible that the Soviet Union would launch a nuclear attack on the United States." But "everything we know about the nature of nuclear weapons, budgetary restraints,

---

59 In April 1969, an article by Anatoly A. Gromyko, the son of the Soviet Foreign Minister and a distinguished "American expert" in the Soviet Ministry of Foreign Affairs, appeared in *Military Thought*, the important confidential journal of the Soviet General Staff. Articles in this journal by non-military contributors are rare. The thrust of Gromyko's argument was that American reaction to the buildup in Soviet strategic power had led to the need for the U.S. to shift from a policy of "massive retaliation" to that of "flexible response." See Anatoly A. Gromyko, "American Theoreticians Between 'Total War' and Peace," *Voyennava mysl'*, No. 4 (April, 1969), pp. 86-92.

60 Nikita Khrushchev, *Khrushchev Remembers*, Vol. II (Boston: Little, Brown & Co., 1970), p. 410. Earlier Khrushchev reminisced: "There was a time when American Secretary of State Dulles brandished thermonuclear bombs and followed a 'positions of strength' policy with regard to the socialist countries . . . That was barefaced atomic blackmail, *but it had to be reckoned with at the time* because we did not possess sufficient means of retaliation, and, if we did, they were not as many and not of the same power as those of our opponents." *Pravda*, August 12, 1961 (italics mine). Lest this statement be misunderstood, Arnold L. Horelick and Myron Rush write: "At some point after deposing Malenkov from the premiership early in 1955, Khrushchev must have drastically reduced his estimate of the threat to Soviet security posed by superior United States strategic power, *for the foreign and military policies that evolved under his leadership were to be grounded in the assumption that the mere existence of such American superiority did not gravely threaten the Soviet Union."* (Italics mine.) See Horelick and Rush, *Strategic Power and Soviet Foreign Policy* (Chicago: University of Chicago Press, 1966).

61 Adam Ulam, *Expansion and Coexistence: Soviet Foreign Policy 1917-1973* (New York: Praeger, 1974), p. 610.

political pressures in the Soviet Union and Communist ideology suggests that it was *highly unlikely.*"[62]

If one were to draw one major lesson from the American experience with nuclear deterrence doctrine as practiced in the 1950s and 1960s, it might be this: We have to realize that there can be no easy military (or other) solution to the problems of our time. To be sure, defense will continue to be a necessity in a world of sovereign states. But we must stop relying primarily on the "quick fix" of nuclear deterrence which, at best, is highly questionable. To deal with the complicated security dilemma of our time we need clear heads, moral courage, human compassion and, above all, a sense of proportion. This unfortunately, may be the most difficult requirement of all.[63]

---

62 Richard Barnet, "The Illusion of Security," *Foreign Policy*, No. 3 (Summer, 1973), p. 71.

63 One critic disagrees with this analysis. "You condemn flexible response but have no alternative but prayer and a 'sense of proportion.' With all the criticism, no one has yet presented an alternative to flexible response, by which I mean having a variety of capabilities and planning options. The argument is not over flexible response but the emphasis to be given various components, diplomacy, economic pressures, conventional forces, theater nuclear weapons, and strategic nuclear weapons.

"Massive retaliation worked for a short while, but only until we began to fear Soviet capabilities to hurt the U.S. Even in 1962, our nuclear power was so overwhelming that the Soviet leaders were scared to death.

"Today nuclear weapons can only be used to deter the other side's using them. The question, in view of this reality, is what we should do about our conventional forces. The West Europeans are at this time prepared to do less than the U.S., since they are not seriously concerned about a war in Europe. I hope they are right."

I. Development of U.S. Intercontinental Ballistic Missile Technology

Missile	Deployed	Warheads	Comments
Intercontinental ballistic missile (ICBM)	1960	Single	First ICBMs outfitted with one warhead each. Soon multiple warheads added. Early ICBMs were liquid-fueled.
ICBM with multiple reentry vehicles (MRVs)	early 1960s	Several	Strength of missile increased by adding more warheads. Multiple warheads still landed on *same* target, doing more damage but not increasing number of targets missile could hit.
ICBM with multiple independently targeted reentry vehicles (MIRVs)	1970	Several to many	A missile's flight consists of three phases (1) boost phase; (2) coast-through-space phase; and (3) reentry-through-earth phase. After missile's motors burn out, they are separated from front section (called "bus") which contains MIRVed warheads. As bus passes through space, it is oriented toward particular target and warhead drops off. As it coasts further, it is reoriented and drops off another warhead. And so on until all warheads are dropped off. Most modern ballistic missiles today are MIRVed. This has effect of multiplying number of warheads deliverable by single booster to separate aiming points.
ICBM with maneuverable reentry vehicles (MARVs)	1983	Several to many	Warheads with propulsion systems giving them ability to maneuver during re-entry. Basically two kinds of MARV's: (a) evader MARV – e.g. Navy's MK-500 designed to overcome ballistic missile defenses; and (b) very accurate MARV with counterforce mission – e.g. Army's Pershing II.

II. Pictorial Representation of Development of Long Range Ballistic Missile Technology

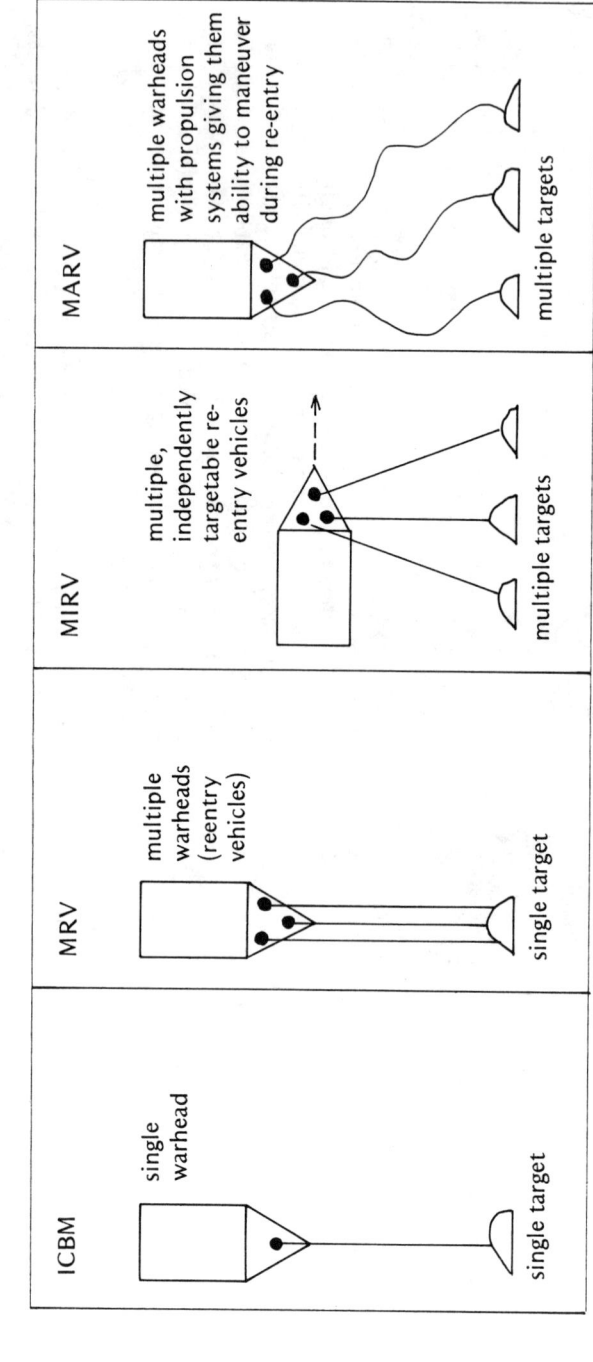

130

> While we tend to talk of deterrence as though it were in continuous operation, it is doubtful if the leaders of the great nuclear powers ask themselves on a daily basis whether they feel deterred. It is only in circumstances of confrontation and crisis that the credibility of the deterrent comes under test. At that point, what may have seemed like a plausible threat under normal conditions may appear grossly inadequate or inappropriate to the situation at hand.
>
> *Secretary of Defense James R. Schlesinger,*
> *Annual Defense Department Report, FY 1976.*

V. FROM MAD TO NUTS

The nuclear deterrent strategies pursued by the United States have not been constant or uniform. In fact, a study of American strategy doctrine over the past twenty-five years or so reveals numerous variations of the theme of nuclear deterrence. Some reflect technological breakthroughs. Others represent shifts in geopolitical assessment. This chapter attempts to portray the assumptions underlying these strategies, the reasons for their adoption and the problems they pose. The basic research focus takes the form of the following question: Have these nuclear policies increased or reduced the likelihood of nuclear war with the Soviet Union?

The Impact of the "Missile Gap"

Kennedy came into office in 1961 on the crest of charges about a "missile gap" between the United States and the Soviet Union.[1] The "missile gap" had been a major issue in the presidential campaign (which had been won by a very slim margin) and had been the subject of much public con-

---

1 The first U.S. National Intelligence Estimate (NIE) ascribing a huge missile arsenal to the U.S.S.R. was released in November 1957. It projected that the Soviets would have 500 ICBMs by the end of 1962 or, if they embarked on a "crash program," the end of 1961. However, there was no solid proof for this erroneous estimate. When the NIE was released on February 9, 1960, the date by which the Soviets could have 500 ICBMs was pushed back to mid-1963 and even later, insiders say.

cern. Generally, the impression outside the U.S. government at the time was that the strategic forces of the United States were distinctly inferior to those of the Soviets. However, the truth was, as Kennedy soon discovered, that there was a "missile gap," but it was distinctly in favor of the United States.[2]

Allegations of a "missile gap" arose in the late 1950s soon after the U.S.S.R. launched Sputnik, the world's first artificial satellite, in October 1957. This Soviet space achievement was followed within a few weeks by two more satellites which were much heavier than anything the U.S. would be able to launch into orbit for several years. Circumventing the globe about every ninety minutes, the Soviet satellites became an instant propaganda success, advertising to nations everywhere Soviet technological prowess.

The impact of this Russian achievement on U.S. strategic planning has been analyzed by a number of scholars. One of the more perceptive statements is by Richard Smoke. He writes: "Throughout the West, Sputnik generated anxiety about overall American technological leadership, of which the 'space race' instantly became the premier symbol."[3] This anxiety was "to go on for years, and to become a source of major shifts in U.S. government policy..."[4] This fear was renewed three years later, when the Soviets launched the first man into orbit, Yuri Gagarin.[5]

2 On September 6, 1961, the CIA issued a special National Intelligence Estimate reporting that the agency now believed "that our present estimate of 50-100 operational ICBM launchers as of mid-1961 is probably too high." The CIA was now of the view that the Soviets "deliberately elected to deploy only a small force of first-generation ICBMs in 1960-1961, even though they had the capability to deploy ICBMs in considerably greater quantity." What led the CIA to make this reassessment? According to Walt Rostow, the decisive evidence was provided by spy satellite photography. Letter to this writer. (The first completely successful SAMOS spy satellite launch was on January 31, 1961, from Point Arguello, California. It orbited the earth, passing over the Soviet Union several times a day. It radioed enough intelligence information back to earth to inventory Soviet ICBM strength.)

3 Richard Smoke, *National Security and the Nuclear Dilemma: An Introduction to the American Experience* (Massachusetts: Addison-Wesley Publishing Co., 1984), p. 97.

4 Two years after Sputnik, President Eisenhower commented that the Soviet space spectacular had given a "surge to defense spending from which we have not recovered." Quoted in John L. Gaddis, *Strategies of Containment: A Critical Appraisal of Postwar American National Security Policy* (New York: Oxford University Press, 1982), p. 186.

5 "Other factors which contributed to Western anxiety in the later 50s were the collapse of 'rollback' in the aftermath of the failed Hungarian Revolution of 1956 and the Suez fiasco of the same year," adds Ambassador Martin J. Hillenbrand. Letter to this writer, May 22, 1984.

Historian John L. Gaddis is more specific. "As a revelation of unexpected threat, the shock of Sputnik rivaled only Pearl Harbor and Korea." All at once "the entire United States [and much of the rest of the world] appeared to be within range of a Soviet nuclear attack." Warning time, "a matter of hours when the means of delivery had been bombers, would now be at most thirty minutes." Worst of all, as Eisenhower publicly acknowledged, "there was no known defense against a ballistic missile strike." Official estimates had been that the U.S.S.R. "would not have an operational ICBM capability until 1960 or 1961, by which time it was thought, the U.S. would have one too." Now "it looked as if the nation would have to suffer through several years of dangerous vulnerability . . ."[6]

Soon after Sputnik was launched, Khrushchev began to trumpet publicly the boast that the Soviet Union had attained strategic superiority over the United States. High Soviet military and civilian officials began a steady and systematic campaign to deceive the West in practically all their public statements regarding the East-West military balance. For the most part, these pronouncements were widely reported in the Western media, generating growing public concern.

Riding high on the euphoria of Soviet space achievements, Khrushchev instigated a severe crisis over West Berlin in November 1958 (which continued into 1959 and later into 1961-63). On its face, the Soviet aim was to drive the Western Powers (Britain, France and the United States) from the occupied city, and Khrushchev now used claims of strategic superiority to support his "cold war" tactics. In this regard, he was seen by some diplomatic historians as following American strategy earlier in the "cold war" period when the U.S. had used its strategic superiority to intimidate the Soviet Union.

During the late 1950s, when allegations of superior Soviet nuclear strength began to appear with increasing frequency, the Republican Administration was in a difficult position to respond. Generally, its knowledge of Soviet nuclear military activity was quite detailed, but this could not be admitted for it came mostly from a secret source — the high-flying U-2 aerial reconnaissance over the Soviet Union, which began in 1956.[7]

---

6 John L. Gaddis, *opus cit.*, p. 183.

7 "Operation Overflight," as it was called, began in 1956 with the deep penetration of Soviet airspace by America's new superspy plane, the high-flying U-2. Between 1956 and 1958 about twenty "deep penetration" missions were reportedly carried out by the CIA. By 1959, the U-2 pilots discovered that the Soviets were regularly tracking their flights and were also making concentrated efforts at shooting them down. Because of the higher risks, the U-2 flights were temporarily curtailed. However, in May 1960, two missions were scheduled from Pakistan across the Soviet Union to Norway. This was the first time that a U-2 pilot would

The secret overflights were considered by the Soviets to be illegal, but they could not do much about them until May 1960, when a U-2, piloted by Francis Gary Powers, was shot down. Subsequently, Premier Nikita Khrushchev, taking advantage of this incident (Eisenhower denied at first that Americans were flying spy missions over the U.S.S.R.), forced the collapse of a summit conference with President Eisenhower, General DeGaulle and Prime Minister Macmillan.

The Development of the Triad

If the dramatic victory of launching a satellite into space seemed to capture the public imagination, U.S. national security analysts were seriously disturbed by the discovery some months earlier that the Soviet Union had tested a prototype long-range intercontinental ballistic missile (ICBM). For all American intelligence officials could tell, it appeared that the Soviet Union — and not the United States — was going to be the first country to deploy an ICBM.[8]

The fact that the Soviets were on the verge of deploying an ICBM force was interpreted by many American officials as evidence of their determination to attain a "first-strike" capability over the United States. The Soviet ICBMs could be launched over the North Pole, striking targets in the U.S. in about thirty minutes. Since the United States had no defense or early warning radar at this time for spotting their approach, many U.S. officials leaped to the conclusion that within the near future the Soviets might well be able to destroy practically all of the U.S. Strategic Air Command before it could be launched.[9]

To meet this frightening possibility, U.S. officials pressed ahead with a new radar system called the Ballistic Missile Early Warning System (BMEWS). This system, which provided about fifteen minutes warning of an incoming missile attack, began to be deployed shortly after the Soviet

fly from south to north across Soviet territory. The CIA suspected that the U.S.S.R. was about to deploy its first intercontinental missile, and it was determined to schedule more U-2 flights and cover as many targets as possible. When Francis Gary Powers, one of the CIA's best pilots, was shot down he was on a mission that was to take him deeper into Soviet territory than any U-2 had ever been. For details see David Wise and Thomas B. Ross, *The U-2 Affair* (New York: Random House, 1962) and Francis Gary Powers, *Operation Overflight* (New York: Holt, Rinehart & Winston, 1970).

8 The U.S. had two ICBM models under development in 1957, but neither was ready yet to be test flown. See Edmund Beard, *Developing the ICBM* (New York: Columbia University Press, 1976).

9 Robert Levine, *The Arms Debate* (Cambridge: Harvard University Press, 1963).

ICBMs became operational. At the same time, U.S. defense officials decided to implement a policy which would keep a certain number of intercontinental bombers with nuclear weapons in the air ready to attack the Soviet Union on short notice.

As things turned out, the "worst-case" scenario of U.S. defense experts did not develop. As American satellite photographs showed, the Soviet leadership decided *not* to push development of ICBMs as quickly as possible. Instead, Kremlin officials decided to concentrate their resources on producing a more reliable and technologically advanced second-generation ICBM. By 1960 the Soviets had actually only deployed a very small number of intercontinental ballistic missiles.[10] If the U.S.S.R. had only four operational ICBMs in 1960, the United States had 18.[11]

Even though Kennedy and his advisers knew that a real missile gap had not materialized, they decided to improve the strategic posture of the United States.[12] First, the Administration asked Congress for an additional allocation of money for defense. Though some of this money would be spent on upgrading America's conventional strength in line with the doctrine

---

10 The exact number is in dispute. Daniel Ellsberg, who has had access to top secret information, says that the actual number of Soviet ICBMs deployed in early 1962 was four. See his "Introduction: Call to Mutiny," in E.P. Thompson *et. al.* (eds.), *Protest and Survive* (New York: Monthly Review Press, 1981). Other scholars maintain that the Soviets had deployed approximately fifty to sixty of their earliest ICBMs by this time. Fred Kaplan, who has interviewed several persons familiar with the "Codeword-classified" Annex of the CIA's National Intelligence Estimate of September 6, 1961, confirms the number four — just four SS-6 missiles. He says another twenty newer SS-7 and SS-8 sites were under construction, but none of them, nor any more SS-6s, "would be deployed for the rest of the year." See Kaplan, *The Wizards of Armageddon* (New York: Simon & Schuster, 1983), p. 289.

11 "Missile Gap: 1957-1960," Center for Defense Information, unpublished paper, 1981, p. 3.

12 For background see William W. Kaufmann, *The McNamara Strategy* (New York: Harper & Row, 1964). This book is interesting because, among other things, the author pretends to be simply an MIT professor attempting to explain McNamara's strategy "in his own words wherever possible" since "McNamara is well able to speak for himself (p. x)." The ordinary reader has no idea that Kaufmann played a major role in devising strategy and wrote several of the speeches that he quotes." In his memors McNamara has this to say: "Since we could not be certain of Soviet intentions, since we could not be sure that they would not undertake a massive build-up, we had to insure against such an eventuality by undertaking a major build-up of our own Minuteman and Polaris forces ... But the blunt fact remains that if we had had more accurate information about planned Soviet strategic forces, we simply would not have needed to build as large a nuclear arsenal as we have today." McNamara, *The Essence of Security* (New York: Harper & Row, 1968), p. 58.

of "flexible response," much of the additional funding went to accelerating programs that would strengthen the U.S. "second-strike" strategic force. Then the Administration put the SAC bomber force on a heightened alert status, which called for about half the planes to be prepared for take-off on approximately fifteen minutes warning. Finally, the Adminstration pressed ahead with plans for the deployment of America's first generation ICBMs — the *Titan* and *Atlas* — some of which had already entered the U.S. strategic force. Importantly, these early ICBMs were deployed above ground because the technology of constructing hardened, underground silos had not been fully developed.

The early American ICBMs were much less sophisticated than the ones deployed today. For one thing, they used liquid rather than solid fuel. Liquid fuel missiles such as the kind the Soviets had (and still do) could not be kept fueled at all times. They had to be filled with liquid fuel after the order came down the chain of command to launch them. Since this was a difficult and time-consuming procedure, the Soviets were for a long time at a major disadvantage with their long-range missiles. Eventually, this problem was solved as storable liquid fuel was developed. Today, American solid-fuel missiles have their fuel prepacked in a relatively stable form, which has the potential of lasting a long time.

As the first-generation ICBMs were being developed by the Kennedy Administration, work was already well underway on the development of a second-generation Intercontinental Ballistic Missile. Called the *Minuteman*, it was solid-fueled and could be fired on approximately one minute's notice. It differed from the *Titan* and *Atlas* in a number of ways, but perhaps most importantly, it was designed to be launched from underground hardened silos, making it less vulnerable to attack. The Kennedy and Johnson Administrations purchased this ICBM in large quantities, making it the backbone of the land-based U.S. intercontinental ballistic force.[13]

Another solid-fuel missile being planned at this time was the *Polaris*, which had the advantage of being fired from submarines. The *Polars* missile seemed to ensure for a very long time in the future a highly secure "second-

13 Basically, the U.S. approach was to ensure high unit quality. In this respect, it differed considerably from the Soviet approach which stressed numbers. Thus, the U.S.S.R. rarely removed old missiles to make way for new ones as was the American tendency. What seems on the surface to be a technical matter had important ramifications as the SALT talks were to show. It is interesting to note that even after these negotiations got underway and aggregate numbers were obviously going to be relevant, this policy continued. As far as the American public is concerned, it is entirely possible that had the United States not withdrawn from service almost 1000 ICBMs and over 300 B-52s between the early 1960s and the mid-1970s, a quite different image of U.S. nuclear strength *vis-a-vis* the Soviet Union would have prevailed.

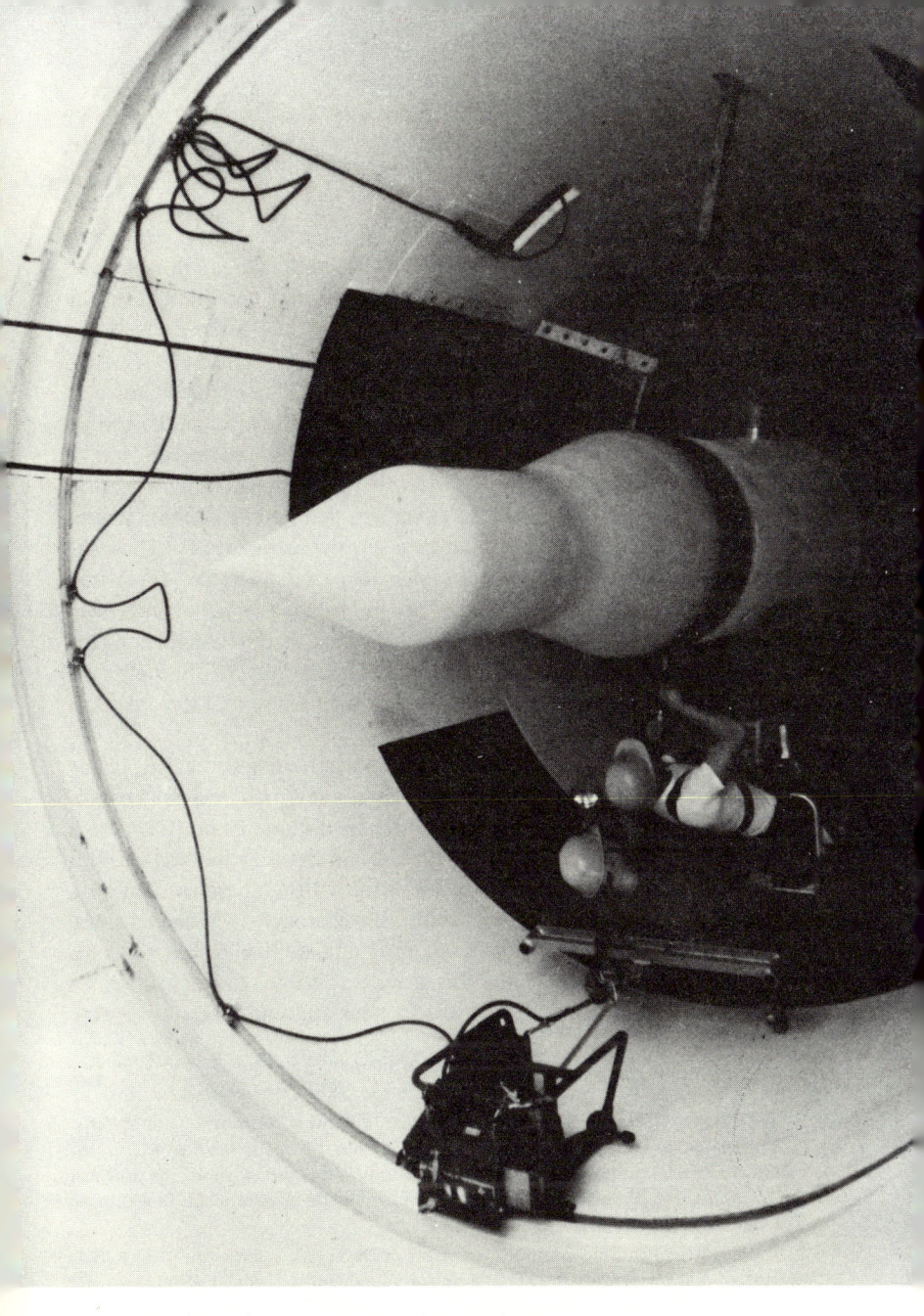

Figure 2: *Whiteman Air Force Base, Missouri — Two missile maintenance crewmen perform an electrical check on a Minuteman III (LGM-30G) intercontinental ballistic missile in its silo.*

strike" capability on the part of the United States. The first *Polaris* submarine launched ballistic missiles (or SLBMs, as they were called) became operational in 1961.[14] Very quickly thereafter the United States rolled them off the assembly line.

In the 1970s the *Polaris*,[15] which had an "intermediate" range of some 1,500 miles, was replaced with a new SLBM called the *Poseidon*, which has a longer "intercontinental" range.[16] With each enlargement in range, more targets could be reached, but more importantly, the submarines would have a much larger body of water to hide in.

With the development and deployment of a land-based ICBM force in the 1960s, along with a highly mobile submarine missile force, the United States adopted what became known as a "triad" strategic force. That is, the U.S. deterrent force became significantly dispersed into three "legs" or components. The idea behind this system was that no two of these groups of nuclear forces could be wiped out by a surprise Soviet attack. Thus, the United States was guaranteed of an invincible "second-strike" force that would bolster the U.S. deterrence posture by making the Soviet leadership realize that a nuclear attack would be suicidal. (In this connection, the term "synergism" was discovered; it referred basically to the deterrent effect of the combined triad which was greater than the sum of its individual parts.)

While the triad concept generally found favor among strategic thinkers in the Kennedy Administration, each element in the triad possessed particular advantages and disadvantages. For instance, the land-based ICBM force was now more secure underground than it had been on the surface. But even a hardened, underground silo could not withstand a direct hit by a Soviet warhead. The SAC bombers could deliver a payload accurately, and they could be recalled after a false-alarm — unlike missiles. But the SAC force was highly vulnerable on the ground. Finally, though American missile-firing submarines were difficult to track and thus target, they were

14 According to James Fallows, the first *Polaris* submarine was launched in 1959. See his *National Defense* (New York: Random House, 1981), p. 164.

15 One U.S. government insider would add this interesting footnote to the *Polaris*. "During the early 1960s, the warhead of the Polaris ballistic missiles would not detonate. This failure was not detected for some time. When it was, the problem proved immune to numerous solutions. Meanwhile, the missiles might as well have carried rocks in their warheads."

16 In 1968, Dr. Enthoven, Assistant Secretary of Defense (Systems Analysis) stated: "One of the big factors in the Poseidon development decision made three years ago (1965) was the conclusion that Poseidon would be the most effective way possible of guaranteeing against the threat of accurate Soviet missiles." Quoted in Ted Greenwood, *Making the MIRV: A Study of Defense Decision Making* (Cambridge: Ballinger Publishing Co., 1975), p. 101.

not as accurate as bombers, and when submerged they had major problems communicating with the mainland.

The Whiz Kids at the Pentagon decided in the end to begin the gradual phasing out of the 1,500 B-47 bombers that, in early 1961, formed the backbone of SAC. They reasoned that B-52s were better than B-47s and missiles better than bombers. As might be expected, General Curtis LeMay, who succeeded Tommy White as Air Force Chief of Staff was unhappy with this decision. According to one account, LeMay was horrified when Harold Brown, McNamara's thirty-four-year-old R&D director, tried to tell him which bomber the Air Force should really want. "Why, that son of a bitch was in junior high school while I was out bombing Japan!" LeMay exclaimed.[17]

Ultimately, Kennedy and Johnson chose to deploy approximately one thousand *Minutemen* and forty-one *Polaris* submarines, each of which could carry up to sixteen missiles (for a total of 656 long-range missiles). With the fifty-four *Titans* that remained in place (they were to be phased out in the early 1980s), this meant that by the mid-1960s the United States possessed a strategic missile force of some 1,710 ICBMs and SLBMs. This force remained in service well into the 1970s, although major improvements were made in such vital areas as accuracy, payload and reliability.

In the early 1980s the United States added a new element — or fourth leg — to its triad of strategic forces. This was the long-range cruise missile. In effect a small, pilotless aircraft, it can be launched from air, sea or land. Its small size and its capability to fly at low altitudes helps it to penetrate the extensive air defense of the Soviet Union. The chief military advantage of the cruise missile is that it is cheap and, hence, can be produced in large enough numbers to saturate the defense. However, from an arms control perspective, the cruise missile is a nightmare because it is so small and almost impossible to detect. Moreover, it is virtually impossible to tell whether the cruise missile has a conventional or nuclear warhead.

For their part, the Soviets lagged way behind in the 1960s.[18] Despite continued strident propaganda claims of superiority and an assertive (if not aggressive) attitude in the area of foreign policy, the Soviet leadership did not deploy many ICBMs in the first half of the 1960s. Some analysts maintain that this was because the Soviets experienced technical difficulties in perfecting their second-generation missiles, but one should be skeptical of this argument, given what is now known of Khrushchev's reining in of the military. By 1965, for example, the Soviets still had only approximately

---

17 Quoted in Fred Kaplan, *The Wizards of Armageddon* (New York: Simon & Schuster, 1983), pp. 255-56.

18 See Institute of Strategic Studies (London), *The Military Balance 1962-63*.

two hundred ICBMs, and they had not yet deployed any SLBM forces nor did they yet have a jet bomber with intercontinental range. However, the depth and configuration of Soviet nuclear forces would change remarkably over the next decade.

The Single Integrated Operations Plan

Probably the most secret document in the Pentagon is the Single Integrated Operations Plan (SIOP, pronounced "sigh op") for the conduct of nuclear war. In fact, the SIOP is so secret that the contingency plan has its own security classification: "Extremely Sensitive Information." The SIOP assigns every nuclear weapon to a specific target under any given set of circumstances. This targeting plan is in the hands of the Joint Chiefs of Staff, who are responsible for following the policy guidelines of each Administration.[19]

During the Eisenhower Administration, the contingency plans for bombing the Soviet Union were in the hands of the Joint Strategic Target Planning Staff (JSTPS), an uneasy grouping of representatives from all the armed services. The primary task of this staff was to eliminate duplication of bombing operations. Until this time, the U.S. Navy and Air Force had been permitted their own independent targeting. It was estimated that between 200 and 300 Soviet targets were on the target lists of both services so that, in the outbreak of war with the U.S.S.R., several Soviet cities and ports would have received two nuclear raids, one from the Navy and another from SAC's bombers. Eisenhower thought it was dangerous, foolish and wasteful for the U.S. government to have so many different targeting plans.

With the creation of the Joint Strategic Target Planning Staff, the SAC commander was made its director and an admiral his deputy. But this compromise did not resolve interservice bickering. The generals and admirals continued to argue endlessly over how many representatives there should be from each service. In the end, the Strategic Air Command won. Of a total of 269 seats, SAC received 219, the Navy 29, the Army 10, the Air Force (separate from SAC) 8 and the Marines 3. Importantly, of 34 positions in which key decisions were made on target selection, SAC and the Air Force obtained 51 percent, a controlling interest.[20]

The origins of the SIOP can be traced back to December 1960 when, for the first time, the Defense Department drew up a plan to coordinate

---

19 See Peter Pringle *et al., S.I.O.P.: The Secret U.S. War Plan for Nuclear War* (New York: W.W. Norton, 1984).

20 For details see Peter Pringle *et al.*, pp. 11-12.

ICBMs, SLBMs and bombers in the event of a single, massive nuclear attack. In 1961 and 1962, the SIOP was modified to make more limited attacks possible — especially separate attacks on military and industrial targets.[21] However, if the entire force were launched, the attack would involve 3,423 nuclear weapons, totaling approximately 7,847 megatons.

The need for more flexibility in targeting was indelibly drilled into the mind of one McNamara aide, William Kaufmann, as a result of a "briefing" he had received at SAC headquarters in Omaha on December 12, 1960, a few months before the new Democratic Administration took office. Officially, Kaufmann was at SAC Headquarters to present his own counterforce briefing to the Air Force generals. Hardly two minutes into his lecture, General Tommy Power interrupted with a long, angry tirade against practically everything that the MIT professor was saying.

"Why do you want us to restrain ourselves?" bellowed General Power. "Restraint! Why are you so concerned with saving *their* lives? The whole idea is to kill the bastards!" Several minutes later the general exclaimed: "Look. At the end of the war, if there are two Americans and one Russian, we win!"

His patience almost exhausted, Kaufmann replied: "Well, you'd better make sure that they're a man and woman." At that point, the angry General stalked out of the room. The briefing was over.[22]

"No-Cities" Doctrine

In 1962, at Ann Arbor, Michigan, Secretary of Defense McNamara proclaimed a "no-cities" doctrine. This policy, which was enhanced by advances in reconnaissance capabilities which made it possible to pinpoint key enemy targets, represented a major shift from the "city-busting" emphasis of the 1940s and 1950s. In case of a major attack by the Soviet Union on Western Europe, he stated, the principal objective of the American nuclear response should be "the destruction of the enemy's military forces, not his civilian population."[23]

---

21 Albert Carnesale *et al., Living With Nuclear Weapons* (New York: Bantam Books, 1983), p. 84. According to one U.S. government insider familiar with SIOP, "from beginning to end, SIOP greatly exaggerated the number and size of bombs and warheads needed to damage all types of targets."

22 Fred Kaplan, *The Wizards of Armageddon* (New York: Simon & Schuster, 1983), p. 246.

23 For details see Desmond Ball, *Politics and Force Levels: The Strategic Missile Program of the Kennedy Administration* (Berkeley: University of California Press, 1980).

Thereafter, U.S. military planners put primary — thought not exclusive — emphasis on military targets, including nuclear and conventional forces. Now the idea was that the U.S. could conceivably respond to a Soviet attack in Europe, for instance, with a nuclear attack on Soviet military targets, without necessarily initiating a mutual exchange of attacks against cities.[24]

For the first time, a certain portion of the U.S. nuclear force would be held in reserve. The idea had an instant appeal to Secretary McNamara, who preferred having "options" available to the President, especially options that would leave possible pauses for diplomatic exchanges during the fighting.[25]

Assured Destruction

Growing American missile superiority in the early 1960s, combined with already existing U.S. superiority in long-range bombers, led officials to redefine the purposes for U.S. strategic nuclear forces. While their basic function was still most fundamentally explained in terms of deterrence theory, American officials began to stress that deterrence rested on the

---

24 It is frequently overlooked that McNamara's "city-avoidance" strategy, heavily predicated on U.S. superiority, was a "damage limitation" strategy that envisaged both massive targeting of Soviet strategic forces and the possibility that the United States might launch first. To be sure, official Defense Department pronouncements tended to avoid calling attention to this point. However, it could scarcely have been missed by any attentive observer of the policy of the Kennedy Administration. As one McNamara aide reportedly observed: "[T]here could be no such thing as primary retaliation against military targets after an enemy attack. If you're going to shoot at missiles, you're talking about a first strike." Quoted in Henry L. Trewhitt, *McNamara: His Ordeal in the Pentagon* (New York: Harper & Row, 1971), p. 115. President Kennedy stated the case even more authoritatively when he said that "Khrushchev must *not* be certain that, where its vital interests are threatened, the United States will never strike first." *Newsweek*, April 9, 1962.

25 McNamara subsequently ordered a revision of the Basic National Security Policy to include counterforce strikes and controlled responses, and a new version of the first SIOP appeared in the summer of 1961. As Peter Pringle and William Arkin point out in their study of SIOP: "It had five options, plus various sub-options. The U.S. attacks were to proceed according to the following plan: (1) Soviet strategic retaliatory forces — missile sites, bomber bases, submarine pens, ets.; (2) Soviet air defenses away from cities, for example, those covering U.S. bomber routes; (3) Soviet air defenses near cities; (4) Soviet command and control centers; and (5) if 'necessary,' allout 'spasm' attack. By the end of 1961 the United States had an official policy of not targeting Soviet cities." See Peter Pringle *et al.*, *SIOP: The Secret U.S. Plan for Nuclear War* (New York: W.W. Norton & Co., 1984), p. 121.

capacity of the U.S. to retain a secure "second-strike" capacity which could devastate the U.S.S.R. In the lexicon of strategic thinkers, this capability was now referred to as the "assured destruction" mission of U.S. forces.

The term "assured destruction" was first used in 1964. It replaced the phrase "assured retaliation," which some in the Pentagon thought was too bland. Technically, an assured destruction capability was defined as the ability to deter a deliberate nuclear attack upon the United States or its allies by maintaining at all times a clear and unmistakable ability to inflict an unacceptable degree of damage upon any aggressor, or combination of aggressors — even after absorbing a surprise first strike [sic].[26]

To put it another way: the "assured destruction" formula was originally developed merely as a sizing criterion for U.S. strategic force structure planning. Only later did it become enshrined as a preferred objective of strategic retaliatory planning.[27]

To the proponents of assured destruction, the basic postulates of this strategy seemed self-evident and irrefutable. But to the critics, the new deterrence doctrine was fatally flawed. As Benjamin S. Lambeth, a strategic analyst formerly with the CIA, put it:[28]

Although commonly called a strategy, assured destruction was by itself an antithesis of strategy. Unlike any strategy that ever preceded it throughout the history of armed conflict, it ceased to be useful precisely where military strategy is supposed to come into effect: at the edge of war. It posited that the principal mission of the U.S. military under conditions of ongoing nuclear operations against [the continental United States] was to shut its eyes, grit its teeth, and reflexively unleash an indiscriminate and simultaneous reprisal against all Soviet aim points on a preestablished target list. Rather than deal in a considered way with the particular attack on hand so as to minimize further damage to the United States and maximize the possibility of an early settlement on reasonably acceptable terms, it had the simple goal of inflicting punishment for the Soviet transgression. Not only did this reflect an implicit repudiation of political responsibility, it also risked provoking just the sort of counterreprisal against the United States that a rational wartime strategy should attempt to prevent.

Other critics focused on what they saw as duplicity in the strategy of "assured destruction." As Richard Falk of Princeton argues: "The pretense

---

26. Alain C. Enthoven *et al.*, *How Much is Enough? Shaping the Defense Program, 1961-1969* (New York: Harper & Row, 1971), p. 174.
27. See Benjamin S. Lambeth, *Selective Nuclear Options in American and Soviet Strategic Policy* (Santa Monica: The RAND Corporation, 1976), p. 14.
28. *Ibid.*

has been that our preoccupation with nuclear weapons is a defensive one, centering on deterring a nuclear Pearl Harbor or, at the very least, some massive instance of Soviet aggression." Actually, the "nuclear weapons policy of the United States has always included various offense minded ideas about how to translate its national nuclear advantage into beneficial political results in the context of rivalry with the Soviet Union."[29]

This hidden emphasis, which so disturbs Falk and others, has been expressed by Lynn E. Davis, a defense specialist close to official sources. She writes:[30]

This 'Assured Destruction' concept was attractive from the point of view of determining the size and characteristics of American strategic forces, since American planners could establish quantitative criteria to measure the effectiveness of these forces. However, the actual plans for the use of American nuclear forces have been kept secret. Most people assumed that the war plans simply incorporated the Assured Destruction criteria, but in fact, having relied on well-hedged planning assumptions when acquiring strategic forces, <u>the United States ended up with more weapons than it needed to carry out the Assured Destruction task. The actual war plans included large-scale attacks against enemy military targets (nuclear and conventional) as well as against military plus urban/industrial targets.</u> (emphasis mine).

Mutual Assured Destruction

During the Kennedy Administration, the public was left with the impression (which was not correct) that the bulk of America's strategic forces was targeted against Soviet cities.[31] The same was said to be true of Soviet targeting, which allegedly served to hold American cities hostage. The situation which resulted from this strategy became known to strategic

---

29 Robert J. Lifton and Richard Falk, *Indefensible Weapons: The Political and Psychological Case Against Nuclearism* (New York: Basic Books, 1982), p. 175.

30 Lynn E. Davis, *Limited Nuclear Options: Deterrence and the New American Doctrine* (London: Institute for Strategic Studies, 1975-76), p. 1.

31 As Secretary of Defense Harold Brown stated in August of 1980: "The U.S. has never had a doctrine based simply and solely on reflexible, massive attacks on Soviet cities. Instead, we have always planned both more selectively (options limiting urban-industrial damage) and more comprehensively (a range of military targets). Previous administrations, going back well into the 1960s, recognized the inadequacy of a strategic doctrine that would give us too narrow a range of options." See his "Remarks Delivered at Convocation Ceremonies for the 97th Naval War College Class," U.S. Naval War College, Newport, Rhode Island, August 20, 1980, p. 7.

planners as the "mutual assured destruction" deterrent strategy. Or "MAD" for short.[32]

The MAD strategy was advanced by Secretary of Defense Robert McNamara. From his viewpoint, the strategy had several attractive features. In the first place, the policy would save money in the long run because it did not depend on America's continued striving for superiority against a foe who was willing and able to match U.S. forces and expenditures. As McNamara put it in 1966, "The country can reach a point when, in buying more military hardware, it is no longer buying more security for itself, and we have reached such a point."[33] Secondly, the strategy had the advantage of ruling out the use of nuclear arms as levers of political influence, because their use could not credibly be threatened. Finally, with the MAD strategy in place, the U.S. would have an incentive to begin seriously seeking arms limitation agreements with the Soviet leadership.

The doctrine of "mutual assured destruction" and of accepting strategic parity rose rapidly to prominence in the literature on U.S. nuclear weapons' strategy in the latter part of the 1960s, *even though there was little evidence to support the view that the Soviet Union subscribed to such a policy*. For a while the debate over strategic doctrine seemed to be a matter of the past. But in the early 1970s more and more strategic thinkers became critical of the MAD policy, which they maintained was militarily unacceptable in addition to being immoral.

The policy was unworkable, critics maintained, because it was based on the false assumption that the Soviet leadership subscribes to the strategy of mutual deterrence. In actuality, however, critics noted, the Soviets are vehemently opposed to such a strategy which would, in effect, make the U.S.S.R. dependent on the goodwill and designs of the United States. Moreover, the MAD concept is generally rejected by the Kremlin because it implies the enshrinement of the *status quo*, something which is alien to known Soviet political, ideological and historical doctrine.

Many critics, such as Fred C. Ikle, formerly head of the U.S. Arms Control and Disarmament Agency (now Under Secretary of Defense), regard the MAD doctrine as immoral because it signifies a policy of leaving "mass slaughter" as the only option should deterrence fail. Basically, the strategy holds millions of innocent Soviet citizens hostage to the provocative acts

---

32 Acronyms are a favorite tactical weapon in debates among deterrence theorists in the United States. The acronym MAD was reportedly coined by the late Donald Brennan at the Hudson Institute. He clearly disliked the idea of preserving peace through mutual vulnerability and tried to discredit the policy by coining the acronym MAD.

33 Quoted in Morton Schwarz, *Soviet Perception of the United States* (Los Angeles: University of California Press, 1978), p. 71.

of their leaders, over whom they have no control.[34] Ultimately, the most energetic critics of MAD argued that the best way to deter the Russians was to convince them that the U.S. was capable of winning a nuclear war at any level of intensity.[35]

With the signing of the Anti-Ballistic Missile Treaty in 1972, the U.S. accepted a state of mutual vulnerability with the Soviet Union in which the populations of one country would be "held hostage" by the other. Nevertheless, while recognizing this condition of mutual assured destruction, U.S. military planners continued to develop other targeting options. These served as the basis for a "counterforce" strategy, as embodied in the highly classified Single Integrated Operations Plan for nuclear retaliation.

"Counterforce" Strategy

Two terms that occupy an important place in the jargon of modern strategic theory are "counter*value*" and "counter*force*." These terms refer both to the nature of the target of a strategic weapon and also to a nuclear deterrent strategy. Technically, "countervalue" means that one's principal targets are objects of national "value," specifically the population and industrial centers of the adversary. To threaten them is to counter what each superpower values most. U.S. military planners usually use the term "counterforce" to mean that the principal objectives of one's nuclear missiles are the enemy's forces — that is, his launchers as well as the related command and communications facilities.

In view of the predominantly defensive (i.e. retaliatory) character of U.S. policy through much of the post-war period, U.S. officials seemed naturally predisposed to a counter*value* targeting strategy. The basic idea behind this nuclear deterrent policy was that should the U.S.S.R. dare to launch a surprise attack against the United States, the U.S. would use its surviving missiles to lay waste Soviet cities and industrial areas. This strategy virtually took for granted that no country would consciously expose itself to the terrible risk of having its urban and industrial centers destroyed. In this respect the policy operated on a set of assumptions which were derived from British military theory of the 1920s and 1930s, and which influenced the Royal Air Force to concentrate on strategic bombing raids on German cities and industrial areas during the Second World War.[36]

34 Fred C. Ikle, "Can Nuclear Deterrence Last Out The Century?," *Foreign Affairs* Vol. 51 (January, 1973), pp. 267-85.

35 See for example, Colin S. Gray *et al.*, "Victory is Possible," *Foreign Policy*, No. 39 (Summer, 1980), pp. 14-27.

36 See Richard Pipes, "Why the Soviet Union Thinks It Could Fight and Win a Nuclear War," *Commentary*, Vol. 64. No. 1 (July, 1977), p. 32.

Many people believe that the idea of "counterforce" targeting is a relatively new concept. Actually, it extends back to the 1960s when the United States was coming to possess much more strategic power than was needed for "mutual assured destruction." It was at this time that U.S. military planners began to focus attention on supplementary deterrent strategies which would put this extra power to "good" use.

After studying the matter, theorists came up with what soon became known as a "damage limitation" strategy. The objectives of this strategy were to retain the superiority of American forces and to keep the United States essentially invulnerable. Without this invulnerability, it was maintained, America's commitments to its allies in Europe would appear less than credible.[37]

The basic idea behind the "damage limitation" strategy was that the damage the United States and its allies might sustain in the event of a nuclear war could be reduced both defensively and offensively. In the former case, air defenses, ballistic missile defenses and civil defense could theoretically curtail the destruction of nuclear war. In the latter case, damage might be limited by possessing nuclear weaponry capable of destroying Soviet missiles and bombs before they could be launched. It was on this second capability that most attention now came to be focused.

At this time, Soviet bomber bases were thought to be vulnerable to an attack by U.S. missiles. At the same time, Soviet ICBM forces, which were deployed for the most part above ground (or in only semihardened silos), were considered vulnerable. The same was true for Soviet tactical air bases and other military sites. In the strategic lexicon, these targets were now termed "counterforce" targets because to attack them was to counter the forces of the enemy; they were not of ultimate value in the same way as population centers.

Soon a substantial portion of the rapidly growing U.S. nuclear force was given a "damage limiting" mission against Soviet counterforce targets. The deterrent strategy that stressed the importance of striking targets before any cities were attacked came to be known as a "counterforce strategy."

Secretary McNamara first announced this new strategy publicly at the University of Michigan in June 1962. At that time, he said: "Nuclear war should be approached in much the same way that more conventional military operations have been regarded in the past." He asserted that weapons should be aimed at a variety of targets to ensure that the United States would be able to deter a number of different kinds of threats. Basically,

---

37 See Roger D. Speed, *Strategic Deterrence in the 1980s*. (Palo Alto, Calif.: Hoover Institution Press, 1979), p. 8.

McNamara argued that an announced strategy of refraining from striking cities early in a nuclear war (but retaining the option to hit these targets if necessary) would give the Soviets a strong incentive not to attack American cities.

The basic strategic rationale behind the "counterforce" strategy was that it would provide a more credible deterrent than a "countercity" doctrine because an authoritarian regime was said to place a higher value on its military forces than on the lives of its citizens. Thus, a threat to destroy its ability or will to wage war would prove more effective than a threat against other types of targets, including urban or industrial centers. Counterforce advocates further insisted that should deterrence fail and a nuclear war break out, striking at the adversary's military targets rather than cities was the least immoral policy. This was because it not only minimized the loss of civilian lives in an actual war but also because it was the only policy short of pacifism that was consistent with the "just war" doctrine that noncombatants must not be held hostage. Such a deterrent strategy also gave the opponent an incentive to avoid cities, thereby potentially reducing loss of life on both sides.

If the new "counterforce" doctrine (which did not replace MAD but served to supplement it) seemed plausible to U.S. strategic thinkers, the critics had a field day with it. In the first place, they questioned the deterrent effect of a policy which is aimed at destroying the enemy's military forces so as to eliminate its ability to wage war. Such a policy, they argued, was counterproductive and destabilizing because, by threatening the enemy's retaliatory (second-strike) forces, it gave the enemy an important incentive to strike first in times of crisis. Second, the critics attacked the policy on moral grounds, since it seemed to imply that the United States, while trying to deter the Soviet Union in this way, might well initiate a nuclear war. Third, the strategic doctrine seemed to rest on highly dubious "armchair" scenarios involving "controlled" escalation, which presumably would spare the general population from devastation. Actually, as critics pointed out, "counterforce" options were illusory; any strategic exchange, however limited, would entail ghastly consequences for both sides. Moreover, whatever its intentions, the United States would quickly find it impossible to limit strategic nuclear war to avoid counter-city exchanges. Finally, the skeptics feared that by fostering the illusion that a general nuclear war could be controlled and limited, the counterforce policy would make political leaders more reckless and hence weaken American inhibitions.

During the second half of the 1960s the Soviets began to react to these very threatening developments by embarking on substantial improvements in their nuclear forces. For one thing, they began to build hardened, underground missile silos. For another, they started to increase substantially their landbased ICBM force. These ICBMs jumped from some 200 in 1964 to 340 in 1966 to 730 the following year. By 1969 the Soviet leadership had improved its ICBM force to such an extent that approximate parity with the U.S. was now reached; the U.S.S.R. now had over one thousand ICBMs.

This major build-up on the part of the Russians caused officials in the Johnson Administration to rethink the prudence of pursuing a "damage limitation" strategy. To be sure, the "counterforce" doctrine was not completely abandoned, but because it offered less and less as Soviet forces were expanded, U.S. authorities reverted to an emphasis on "mutual assured destruction." The thinking now was that the U.S. should take all necessary measures to protect its "second-strike" forces so that it would not make any major difference how large Soviet forces might grow. The Soviets would still be deterred, it was believed, because the U.S. would still be able, under the worst-case scenario, to inflict unacceptable damage on the Soviet Union.

Declaratory Versus Action Policy

Given the public confusion and misunderstanding of U.S. deterrent policy over the years, it is probably best here to distinguish between *declaratory* policy and *action* policy. This distinction, first articulated publicly by Paul Nitze,[38] is crucial to any intelligent understanding of the debate over the pros and cons of specific strategies. During the McNamara era, U.S. declaratory policy did gradually move away from "counterforce" options toward a posture of assured destruction. *But on the level of war plans, the action policy of the U.S. was never revised to reflect this shift in declaratory policy.*[39] Secretary of Defense McNamara never had any counterforce options removed from U.S. strategic war plans (technically known as SIOP). And as new counterforce targets appeared, new American weapons were allocated to these targets. Operationally, McNamara and his successors never incorporated assured destruction as an action policy.[40]

---

38 Paul H. Nitze, "Atoms, Strategy and Policy," *Foreign Affairs*, Vol. 34, No. (January, 1956), pp. 187-98.

39 See David N. Schwartz, *NATO's Nuclear Dilemmas* (Washington, D.C.: The Brookings Institution, 1983), p. 175.

40 See the testimony of Alain Enthoven, head of the Office of Systems Analysis in the Department of Defense under Robert McNamara, before the Senate Armed Services Committee in April 1968. At that time he said: "Our targeting policy, as reflected in the guidance for the preparation of the targeting plan, has not changed. From 1961-62 on, the targeting plan has been based on the principle that we

This situation, which will no doubt surprise many people, raises an intriguing question. Why did Secretary McNamara shift declaratory policy if he was unwilling to codify assured destruction in the actual war plans of defense planners? There is no easy answer to this question, although some speculative answers have been suggested. One emphasizes McNamara's desire to calm domestic and European fears that a counterforce deterrent strategy was provocative. Another has to do with the bureaucratic battles the Defense Secretary was engaged in with the Air Force over the size and composition of the strategic nuclear force. Briefly, the Air Force — which was reluctant to accept the new planning guidelines set forth in 1961 — became more enthusiastic when it realized that these "counterforce" guidelines left the calculation of strategic requirements somewhat open-ended. Any target of military importance could be pressed for inclusion in the war plans on the grounds that its destruction would reduce the capability of the Soviet leadership to wage war against the U.S. Thus, as the Soviet strategic nuclear arsenal grew, the Air Force could press for higher rates of missile deployment.[41] For his part, McNamara was faced with competing claims on a constrained defense budget, so he could not easily authorize such procurement. But by latching on to the policy of assured destruction — which asserted that the U.S. only needed to maintain the capability to destroy 25 percent of the Soviet population and about 70 percent of its industrial capacity — McNamara was able to put a limit on the procurement requests of the Air Force. In this way, by the time the Secretary of Defense left office, each leg of the strategic triad was outfitted to meet the assured destruction criteria but not much more.[42]

From Superiority to Sufficiency

When Richard Nixon became President in 1969, he accepted McNamara's idea of the desirability of "parity" or rough equivalence with the U.S.S.R. in strategic forces. Subsequently, the principle of "sufficiency" became

> should have different options that target the strategic forces and cities." U.S. Congress, Senate, Committee on Armed Services, Preparedness Investigating Subcommittee, *Status of U.S. Strategic Power*, Hearings, 90th Congress, 2nd Session (Washington, D.C.: U.S. Government Printing Office, 1968), p. 138.

41 This point is taken up in Alain C. Enthoven *et al.*, *How Much is Enough? Shaping the Defense Program, 1961-1969* (New York: Harper & Row, 1971), pp. 165-96. McNamara has commented favorably on this book.

42 Desmond J. Ball, *Déja Vu: The Return to Counterforce in the Nixon Administration* (Los Angeles: California Seminar on Arms Control and Foreign Policy, 1975), pp. 201-02.

the watchword of the Administration.[43] In practice, "sufficiency" meant that the security of U.S. strategic forces would be maintained, and U.S. strategic power would not be allowed to become inferior to that of the Soviet Union.

Reportedly, Nixon was greatly influenced on this point by Henry Kissinger, who served first as Special Assistant to the President for National Security Affairs and then as Secretary of State. Kissinger had apparently never held the view, fashionable among defense intellectuals in the 1960s, that maintaining the balance of power required indefinitely expandable means. Such profligacy, he believed, was more likely in the end to destabilize the international order. "No country," he wrote in 1968, "can act wisely simultaneously in every part of the globe at every moment of time."

The problem was, as historian John L. Gaddis explains, that objectives "tended to expand as means did, thereby producing not only eventual exhaustion but also increasing resistance from other nations who would see in a quest for absolute security absolute insecurity for themselves."[44] The beginning of wisdom in human, as well as international, affairs was "knowing when to stop."

Given this understanding by Kissinger, it is hardly surprising that one of his earlier priorities was to shift the emphasis in official thinking on defense policy from "superiority" to "sufficiency."[45] Whereas the terminology itself referred to the strategic weapons balance, the underlying assumptions had wider ramifications. In the past, efforts to surpass the Russians had only provoked comparable efforts on their part. Thus, the official thinking now was that the interests on both sides might best be served by exhibiting mutual restraint.

---

43 It is interesting to note that President Eisenhower leaned toward this basic idea as early as 1955. By way of illustration, Eisenhower said on March 2, 1955: "There comes a time, possibly, when a lead is not significant in the defensive arrangements of a country. If you get enough of a particular type of weapon, I doubt that it is particularly important to have a lot more of it." See Dwight D. Eisenhower, cited in *Public Papers of the Presidents of the United States 1955* (Washington, D.C.: U.S. Government Printing Office, 1959), p. 303. Perhaps surprisingly, one should note that John Foster Dulles seemed to go along with this concept. Care should be taken, he told the Cabinet in the State of the Union address in January 1958 to avoid emphasis on military "superiority" because that concept could only lead to "invidious comparisons." He preferred to "stand on the concept of having sufficient military power to deter aggression." See Notes, Cabinet meeting of January 3, 1958, Eisenhower Papers, Whiteman File: DDE Diary, Box 18, "Staff Notes — Jan. 58".

44 John L. Gaddis, *Strategies of Containment: A Critical Appraisal of Postwar American National Security Policy* (New York: Oxford University Press, 1982), p. 279.

45 See Nixon's press conference, January 27, 1969, in *Public Papers of the Presidents: Richard M. Nixon* (Washington, D.C. Government Printing Office, 1969), p. 19.

Economic necessity had already more or less led the Johnson Administration, in the area of nuclear weapons, to this same conclusion. However, it was not until Nixon and Kissinger arrived on the scene, Gaddis writes, that this wisdom was "elevated to the status of doctrine."[46]

It is important to note that "sufficiency" never meant unilateral restraint. Moscow would just regard this as weakness, Kissinger was convinced, and thus would try to exploit it.[47] However, it did mean that quests for "superiority" were recognized as likely to be costly and self-defeating. Moreover, the hope was that a combination of pressures and inducements aimed at convincing the Soviets that "sufficiency" was in their own best interest would, simultaneously, best serve the interests of the United States.

Sufficiency Versus Finite Deterrence

Since people sometimes confuse a deterrent strategy based on "sufficiency" with a doctrine known as "finite deterrence," we shall spend a few minutes distinguishing the two. Under "finite deterrence," once a given level of nuclear weapons is reached, no more are deemed necessary. That is, all a state must do to deter an adversary under finite deterrence is to maintain enough nuclear forces to inflict "unacceptable damage" on a foe. Theorists differ on what exact level this should be, but Secretary McNamara once estimated it at 20 to 30 percent of the population and 50 percent of the industry of an opponent. (Contrary to widespread impression, the industrial activities of the Soviet Union are more concentrated than those of the United States; therefore, far fewer weapons would be needed for the equivalent destruction.) McGeorge Bundy, Special Assistant to President Kennedy for National Security Affairs, implied it could be set much lower when he declared: "One bomb on a city would be a catastrophe without precedent."[48]

The theory of "finite deterrence" (sometimes called "minimum deterrence") suggests that more than the minimum level of force needed to deter is actually bad, since excessive levels might indicate that one side is not really interested in simply deterring war. For example, a foe might believe that the U.S. was building toward the development of a disarming "first-strike" capability. This situation might cause the Soviets, for instance, to engage in more building of their own and thus fuel the arms race.

The essence of "finite deterrence" is that populations must be exposed

---

46 John L. Gaddis, *opus cit.*, p. 280.

47 Henry Kissinger, *White House Years* (Boston: Little, Brown, 1979). p. 535.

48 McGeorge Bundy, "To Cap the Volcano," *Foreign Affairs*, Vol. 48, No. 1 (October, 1969), p. 10.

to retaliatory attack. In effect, then, major population centers are considered to be held "hostage" under this strategy. (Nuclear weapons are targeted on them as in the MAD policy.) Because cities are generally large and undefended, American missiles need not be very big or accurate according to this theory.

The strategy of "sufficiency" differs from "finite deterrence" in two major ways. In the first place, under the former policy, the U.S. would not be allowed to become inferior to the Soviet Union in strategic forces. This would not be true under the latter policy. For under "finite deterrence" one could be distinctly inferior to the U.S.S.R., and still be able to inflict "unacceptable damage" on it. In the second place, "sufficiency" accepts various kinds of targeting strategies, whereas finite deterrence rejects all but a "countercity" targeting strategy.[49]

Finite deterrence is not without its critics, who raise some important points. For one thing, they argue, finite deterrence reduces the usefulness of military force solely to one purpose; this is the supposed prevention of an all-out attack on the U.S. But, as these people see it, this is the least likely thing to happen. The U.S.S.R. would have nothing to gain from a wanton devastation of American cities. Moreover, Moscow has never indicated any interest in pursuing such a goal. In the view of these critics, the more likely danger is a threat to U.S. vital interests, such as the oil fields in the North Sea, or piecemeal attacks, such as a move into the Persian Gulf region. Under these circumstances finite deterrence would not credibly deter the Soviet leadership. In fact, they maintain, if the U.S. relied on such a strategy, it would be at the mercy of the Soviet Union, which possesses a substantial conventional capacity in addition to its stalemating nuclear stockpile.

There are additional questions with finite deterrence, which stresses that weapons intended to destroy other weapons are "bad," whereas weapons that are designed to destroy people are "good." As previously mentioned, there is serious question whether finite deterrence would even prevent a direct attack on the U.S. Here the following scenario is outlined: The Soviet Union continues to construct more missiles once the U.S. stops at the minimum number. At some point the U.S.S.R. would have nuclear superiority. Thus, if the leaders of the Kremlin chose to strike first, they would target some of their weapons at the U.S., leaving others in reserve. The idea is that after launch the Soviets would not have destroyed all our weapons, but the United States would not have many left. Importantly,

---

[49] For a now dated popular discussion of this whole subject see Ralph E. Lapp, *Kill and Overkill* (New York: Basic Books, 1962). For a more sophisticated and critical treatment see Phillip Greene, *Deadly Logic: The Theory of Nuclear Deterrence* (Columbus: Ohio State University Press, 1966), pp. 282-83.

because their attack was directed at American weapons and not American cities, most major U.S. population centers would be intact. In this situation, the President would face an awful dilemma. Because he would not have enough missiles left to destroy their remaining missiles, he would have to aim American missiles at Soviet cities. "But this would do us no good," says Professor David Ziegler, "and would in fact only guarantee that the Soviets would use their remaining missiles to attack our cities."[50] In this situation the President might well choose not to retaliate at all.

Critics of finite deterrence maintain that relying on this minimum deterrent posture, particularly if the self-imposed ceiling is set very low, makes the "balance of terror" vulnerable to a sudden technological upset. For instance, the U.S. could decide to dismantle part of its strategic triad of bombers and land-based ICBMs and rely exclusively on missile-carrying submarines (SLBMs). But a sudden break-through in anti-submarine warfare could put the U.S. deterrent force in jeopardy overnight.

Critics of President Nixon's embrace of the "sufficiency" construct stress the ambiguity of the concept, particularly as it was understood by various high-level officials in his Administration.[51] They note that Secretary of Defense Melvin Laird, a hard-liner, who had once written a book advocating the development of a first-strike capability, added an important qualification: the use of the term should in no way be taken to suggest that we have given up "the idea of superiority."[52] More blatant disregard for the meaning of the word, they point out, was demonstrated in the candid and undoubtedly revealing remark made by then Deputy Secretary of Defense Vance Packard when pressed by reporters for a definition of sufficiency "It means," said Packard, "that it's a good word to use in a speech. Beyond that, it doesn't mean a God-damned thing."[53]

50 David W. Ziegler, *War, Peace, and International Politics*, 2nd ed. (Boston: Little, Brown & Co., 1981), p. 230.
Ambassador Martin Hillenbrand writes here: "Your quotation from Ziegler's 1981 book was, of course, essentially the argument used earlier by Paul Nitze against ratification of SALT II." Letter, May 22, 1984.

51 See John P. Leacacos, "Kissinger's Apparat," *Foreign Policy*, No. 5 (Winter, 1971-72), pp. 3-27. The Administration's policy was laid out in National Study Memorandum (NSSM) 3, although the targeting policy was not fully crystallized. According to Desmond Ball, there was some official doubt about the "sufficiency" of a deterrent posture based almost exclusively on the threat of indiscriminate nuclear retaliation against Soviet urban-industrial centers. See his *Déja Vu*, p. 5.

52 Quoted in Michael E. Sherman, "Nixon and Arms Control," *International Journal*, Vol. 24 (Spring, 1969), p. 335. Laird's book is entitled *A House Divided: America's Security Gap* (New York: Henry Regnery, 1962). At the time he was appointed Secretary of Defense, he was asked about this book. He said that it had been written during a time of confrontation which was now passed.

53 *The Washington Post*, June 16, 1969.

Soviet officials, their skepticism of the doctrine of "sufficiency" notwithstanding,[54] seemed impressed by the general changes in world view pursued by the Nixon Administration. One Soviet analyst chose to highlight the change in America's self-image by comparing the following statements made by two U.S. Presidents a decade apart:

Let every nation know, whether it wishes us well or ill, that we shall pay any price, bear any burden, meet any hardship, support any friend, oppose any foe, to assure the survival and success of freedom. (John Kennedy, 1961).

America cannot — and will not — conceive all the plans, design all the programs, execute all the decisions, and undertake all the defense of the free nations of the world. (Richard Nixon, 1970).

Such declarations, from the Soviet point of view implied a major change in official American thinking. As Professor Henry Trofimenko of the Soviet USA Institute wrote at the time, it is in terms of the essentially "psychological framework of deterrence" that the concept of sufficiency introduced by the United States assumes significance. Thus, he notes, "President Nixon emphasized that one of the particular criteria of 'sufficiency' was the necessity of a deployment of U.S. strategic forces which the Soviet Union could not view as a provocation. 'Sufficiency,' Nixon stated, 'also signifies that the number, specifications, deployment of our forces will not provide the Soviet Union with grounds for interpreting them as an intention to threaten the USSR with attack in order to disarm it.'"[55] Washington, in Trofimenko's view, had finally come to recognize that the security of both the United States and the U.S.S.R. must be based on the Principle of equality.

---

54 During the course of the SALT I negotiations in the early 1970s, the Soviet delegation indicated concern over U.S. strategic programs for improving the accuracy of missiles to the extent of giving them counterforce capabilities. In line with stated U.S. policy at the time, the American delegation vigorously argued that it was not American policy to seek such accuracies, which would be destabilizing. A publicly released letter from President Nixon to Senator Brooke was cited. This communcation stated that the United States would not develop such capabilities. In 1974, however, President Nixon reversed this policy, and programs were announced and pursued to attain the very capabilities previously denounced as destabilizing.

55 See Morton Schwarz, *opus cit.*, p. 111.

"Flexible Targeting"

The "sufficiency" policy of the Nixon Administration meant in effect, that the U.S. would now stress maintaining sufficient forces to deter a Soviet attack. However, upon becoming President in 1969, Nixon discovered that his Administration had inherited a much larger strategic nuclear force than was needed to destroy Soviet (and even Chinese) cities. The fact of the matter was that the surplus remained targeted as before on Russian military sites (that is, "counterforce" targets).

Around 1970 new *Poseidon* and *Minuteman* III missiles went on station. These long-range missiles were equipped with several warheads, each of which could be targeted separately. This new technology, called MIRV for "multiple independently-targetable re-entry vehicle," is a system that has the effect of multiplying the number of warheads deliverable by a single booster to separate aiming points. The impact of this new technology can readily be seen when it is applied to our submarine force. Before MIRV, 41 nuclear submarines, with 16 nuclear missiles apiece, could carry a total of 656 warheads. After the breakthrough in MIRV technology they could deliver more than 5,300. Since no more than 200 Soviet cities then had a population of over 100,000, the U.S. possessed a significant "overkill" capability with MIRV.

The primary rationale for developing a MIRV capability had been the alleged threat posed by the limited construction of an ABM (anti-ballistic missile) system around Moscow and Leningrad in the 1960s.[56] (Actually, the Soviet ABM sites were needed more against the unpredictable Chinese than anyone else.) Nevertheless, U.S. planners, operating again on a "worst-case" basis, projected a Soviet expansion of this system, and, as a consequence, it was thought many more missiles would be needed to penetrate

---

56 "MIRV has frequently been described as a prime example of an interactive action-reaction process driving the nuclear arms race," writes Ted Greenwood in his study of the MIRV decision. "Because the Soviet Union seemed to be deploying an ABM system, the explanation goes, the United States reacted by developing and deploying MIRVs. The motivation of the early inventors, the timing of the initiation of full-scale development, the changes in the numbers and types of re-entry vehicles that each system would carry and the foregoing analysis of the motivations of senior decision-makers all point to the important influence of intelligence information and intelligence estimates about Soviet activities. The linkage existed, although it was far from the sole determinant of the programs." Importantly, Greenwood says, "the word 'reaction' can only be used with great care. The United States did not wait until the Soviets had taken steps that required countermeasures, nor did it even wait until there was significant evidence that they would take those steps ... *It was the anticipation of potential actions that helped generate support for MIRV.*" See Ted Greenwood, *opus cit.*, pp. 103-5. (Italics mine.)

an expanded and improved ABM system than to destroy undefended Soviet cities.

Since only the U.S. was close to deploying the MIRV technology during the early stages of the Strategic Arms Limitation Talks (which began after Nixon entered office), no attempt was made to seek a trade-off with the Soviets which would eliminate this dangerous technology. In fact, in order to get the uninformed military to defend SALT I, Kissinger is reported to have promised to support the deployment of MIRV.[57] The irony was, however, that SALT I, which was signed in May 1972, removed any prospect for a large, effective Soviet ABM system. Yet the United States was now saddled with a new and destabilizing technology (it also increased the threat to Soviet landbased systems which represent the bulk of the Soviet strategic triad), and the Soviet Union now had an incentive to develop the MIRV technology as well, which it did some five years later.

With the development of MIRV, U.S. strategic planners had to rethink their deterrent strategy. How could the new surplus in warheads be put to "good" use? The answer came to public attention in January 1974, when Secretary of Defense James R. Schlesinger announced at several news conferences the American intention to modify its nuclear deterrent strategy to possible strikes *only* against Soviet military targets. The Secretary's announcements gave the public the impression that U.S. officials intended to develop a wider range of strategic options (increased flexibility) than those which the policy of Mutual Assured Destruction provided.[58]

The basic idea behind the new policy, as it was explained publicly, was that in a moment of national crisis, the President needed options other than doing nothing or launching an all out attack against the Soviet Union. The specific scenario outlined by Schlesinger, who was the first professional civilian strategist to become Secretary of Defense, was that the Soviet leadership might decide at some point to launch a handful of missiles

---

57 According to one U.S. State Department official who specializes in military-political affairs: "MIRVs were originally developed as a counter to the Soviet ABM threat. By the time the ABM treaty was concluded, MIRVs were too far advanced to stop. In 1969, some of us tried to get the testing of MIRVs held up until we could see if we could work out a deal with the Soviets not to MIRV. In State, we could not get Dean Rusk to move. He maintained that this was McNamara's problem. I understand that there was a similar move in the Pentagon, with the same results. I have read somewhere that Rusk has said that this was a mistake, but his wisdom came a bit late. Ambassador Smith's book on SALT I, *Doubletalk*, contains an interesting account of the 'effort' to negotiate a MIRV agreement."

58 The Schlesinger flexible options were eventually codified as National Security Decision Memorandum No. 242, or NSCM-242, and a new contingency plan for nuclear war was drawn up known as SIOP-5. See Peter Pringle *et al.*, *SIOP: The Secret U.S. Plan for Nuclear War* (New York: W.W. Norton, 1984), p. 179.

against American military targets — but not cities. In this case, the U.S. government needed to be able to retaliate in kind.[59]

In his formal presentations, Schlesinger did not explain why the Soviets would take the terrible risk of launching such a limited nuclear attack in the first place. Nor did many people ask for a detailed explanation. Schlesinger's arguments were mostly accepted by a distracted public which was still sorely divided over Vietnam.

As the critics did not hesitate to point out, the hypothetical firing by the Soviets of several missiles was a highly questionable notion for two main reasons. In the first place, if the Kremlin chose to initiate limited nuclear war, the Soviets would have no assurance that the American response would be equally limited. In the second place, a limited Soviet attack on the United States was unrealistic because, even if American retaliation were also limited, it could still be more severe. In that case, hostilities would not be likely to end there. In short, as far as Schlesinger's opponents were concerned, the hypothetical circumstances used to justify publicly the targeting doctrine of selectivity and flexibility could not stand close scrutiny.[60]

Schlesinger's strategy was given the official name "flexible targeting." (Critics called it a "little nuclear war looking for a place to happen.") But there was some ambiguity about it.[61] For instance, the public was not told explicitly whether the new policy (which was sometimes called the strategy of "selective options") meant the capability to strike Soviet military targets in *general* or Soviet land-based missile silos in *particular*. A clarification on this matter was urgent, for if the new policy meant the U.S. would now target Soviet ICBM sites, this represented — in Richard Smoke's words — "a great change in American strategy."[62] In effect, it meant the revival of

---

59 See Agatha S.Y. Wong-Fraser, *Symmetry and Selectivity in U.S. Defense Policy: A Grand Design or a Major Mistake?* (Lanhan, Md.: University Press of America, 1983).

60 See Robert C. Aldridge, *First Strike! The Pentagon's Strategy for Nuclear War* (Boston: South End Press, 1983), pp. 33-34.

61 When a Senate committee asked Schlesinger if this newly announced policy would have a destabilizing effect on the current round of SALT talks, the reply was: "We have no *announced* counterforce strategy, if by counterforce one infers that one is going to attempt to destroy silos. We have a new targeting doctrine that emphasizes selectivity and flexibility." (Italics mine.) See *Fiscal Year 1975 Authorization for Military Procurement, Research and Development, and Active Duty, Selected Reserve and Civilian Personnel Strengths,* Hearings before the Senate Armed Services Committee (Washington, D.C.: U.S. Government Printing Office, 1974), Part I, p. 265.

62 Richard Smoke, *National Security and the Nuclear Dilemma: An Introduction to the American Experience* (Massachusetts: Addison-Wesley Publishing Co., 1984),

something like the old "counterforce" strategy of the 1960s, whereby U.S. military planners had threatened to destroy Soviet missiles on the ground before they were launched.

Secretary Schlesinger maintained publicly that the new "flexible targeting" strategy was adopted to support nuclear deterrence. But privately he was skeptical of the idea that the "balance of terror" could ensure the peace. It was his personal view that the U.S. nuclear deterrence posture represented the "fatal flaw in our Western alliance system."

At the time, Schlesinger appeared greatly concerned about the credibility of America's far-flung alliance commitments, especially as its interventionary policy was coming under increased attack at home. The focus of attention was Vietnam and the potential credibility crisis it presented. The situation was deteriorating there — the United States was about one year away from facing up to a communist victory — and some outspoken critics on the right were charging the Administration with letting Vietnam "go down the drain" without using nuclear weapons. Schlesinger may have been implying by his public statements — though this is speculation — that the United States had learned this lesson and that nuclear weapons would be available for use in the future, possibly in Korea if another war were to erupt there.

In any case, the thrust of Schlesinger's argumentation seemed to rest on the assumption that a nuclear war could be kept limited. However, a number of people both inside and outside government were unconvinced. They cited Henry Kissinger, who wrote in 1965: "No one knows how governments or people will react to a nuclear explosion under conditions where both sides possess vast arsenals."[63]

---

p. 199. Schlesinger hinted in a BBC radio interview on October 24, 1974 that the limited use of *strategic*, rather than tactical, weapons might be the nuclear option of *first* resort in a NATO contingency. The essence of his argument maintained that if the goal is to stop the invasion of Western Europe without destroying America's allies in the process, why not induce the Soviets to halt by inflicting increments of pain on their own homeland?

63 See Kissinger's introduction to his edited book of readings, *Problems of National Strategy* (New York: Praeger, 1965), p. 6. Fred Kaplan tells the following story about Henry Kissinger in the White House. "In the spring of 1974, Kissinger asked the JCS to devise a limited nuclear option that the President might order in the hypothetical case of a Soviet invasion of Iran. A few weeks later, two JCS generals briefed the results to Kissinger . . . The JCS solution was to fire nearly 200 nuclear weapons at military targets — air bases, bivouacs and so forth — in the southern region of the U.S.S.R. near the Iranian border. Kissinger exploded: 'Are you out of your minds?' he screamed. 'This is a *limited* option?'" See Kaplan, *opus cit.*, pp. 370-71.

A Return to "Counterforce" Strategy

The American "counterforce" strategy was temporarily abandoned in the late 1960s when the Soviets put a substantial number of their land-based missiles in underground silos in order to protect them better. Since neither side possessed highly accurate long-range missiles in the 1960s and early 1970s, American and Soviet land-based systems were considered practically invulnerable in the main. However, this situation did not last long. Beginning in the 1970s technology was moving so rapidly that U.S. scientists predicted that it would be just a matter of years before warheads could be perfected that could strike directly at Soviet silos and vice versa. Once these new improved warheads could be put on missiles, it was said, each side might come to believe that it could attack and destroy most of the other's silos. In this context, the old "counterforce" targeting strategy was resurrected, and the U.S. began to move in the direction of developing a "hard target kill" or "silo busting" capacity.

The formal adoption of the "counterforce" deterrent strategy posed a number of dangers, however. In the first place, by insisting on the capability for a "surgical strike," the policy tended to move strategic nuclear weapons closer to the tactical arena. Thus, it blurred further the distinction between "tactical" and "strategic" nuclear strikes. This erosion of the "firebreak" was adamantly deplored by those who believe that even small nuclear weapons for a "surgical strike" would inevitably lead to escalation and nuclear holocaust.

In the second place, the "counterforce" strategy was criticized because it tended to make the dubious notion of a "surgical strike" acceptable. In the view of the critics, no nuclear weapons, no matter how accurate and small, could be used in or near urban complexes — where most of the militarily interesting targets actually lie — without extremely detrimental effects to the civilian populations. Therefore, any strategy which had as its effect the establishment of the "surgical strike" as an option available to the military, appeared to be a reckless and unnecessary escalation of the dangers inherent in the nuclear confrontation between the United States and the Soviet Union.

Finally, the "counterforce" strategy was attacked on the grounds that it gave legitimacy to the very questionable proposition that a nuclear war could be fought and "won." In making nuclear war more "flexible," the policy made it more thinkable, more tolerable and consequently more probable.

Improving Delivery Systems and Warheads

As the years moved along, both the Soviet Union and the United States made substantial improvements in their delivery systems and warheads. For their part, the Russians put about three-fourths of their total warheads (which were heavier than those of the U.S.) on land-based missiles, most of which came to be outfitted with MIRV technology. The Americans, on the other hand, put the bulk of their power on missile-firing submarines because submarines are very difficult to target. Generally, Russian and American missile-firing submarines were considered far less accurate than land-based long-range missiles and were not usually thought to be the kind of weapons one would use to target the silos of the adversary. Consequently, this led to a situation in which the United States had more silos to shoot at with fewer ICBMs, and the Soviets had fewer silos to shoot at with more ICBMs.

The fact that the Soviets could now use their new MIRV technology to over-target American land-based ICBMs caused a great deal of concern to some U.S. strategic thinkers. Many of these people banded together to form, in 1976, the "Committee on the Present Danger." Their major argument, which was later taken up by Ronald Reagan in the 1980 presidential campaign, was that the growing vulnerability of American land-based ICBMs to large numbers of Soviet MIRVed warheads was creating a so-called "window of vulnerability." (It was called a window on the assumption that the U.S. should rush to correct the nuclear imbalance — to close the window — leaving the Soviet leadership with only a few years to exploit its advantage here.) One of the boldest projections of the Committee on Present Danger in this respect was that in the early 1980s the Soviets would be able to destroy ninety percent of the U.S. Minuteman and Titan land-based missiles, while retaining a portion of their ICBMs in reserve.[64]

Problems of Missile Accuracy in Wartime

There are a number of technical factors which complicate translating *theoretical* accuracy and an overtargeting advantage into a practical operational advantage under wartime conditions. These include the accuracy of the attacking missiles, the explosive "yield" of their warheads and the relative "hardness" of the missile silos that would be attacked. Some stra-

---

64 See Warner R. Schilling, "U.S. Strategic Nuclear Concepts in the 1970s", *International Security*, Vol. 6 (Fall, 1981), p. 69. He argues that the "Soviets will shortly have the theoretical ability to destroy about 90% of the U.S. ICBM force."

tegic thinkers attach precise values to these variables, but in reality there is a very large degree of uncertainty.[65]

One of the most important of these factors is "bias," or the tendency of warheads to drift to one side of their targets because of anomalies in the shape of the earth, its gravatational field and other factors. What makes "bias" an extremely important consideration is the fact that nuclear explosions tend to do most of their damage through shock waves (or "overpressure"). An overpressure of some five pounds per square inch is usually enough to flatten a house. Generally, U.S. missile silos are designed to withstand overpressures of some two thousand pounds per square inch or more. But a Soviet nuclear warhead can only create that kind of pressure by scoring a direct hit on the silo after travelling many thousands of miles.

Soviet missiles coming from the U.S.S.R. and attacking U.S. land-based systems have to come over the North Pole. So far no missile has ever flown this route and been exposed to its unique bias. Thus, one can not know with certainty what impact this flight path will have on missile accuracy.

Strategic thinkers mean something quite different from laymen when they talk about the "accuracy" of a missile. The important point is that it does not mean technically what it is often assumed to mean: how close the warhead will come to its target. The formal measure of the accuracy of a missile is its "circular error probable" (CEP). The CEP has been explained in this way: If one were to fire twenty missiles and draw a circle around the center of the impact pattern that contained half the impact points, the radius of that circle would be the CEP. Thus, the CEP — as formally defined — has little to do with the target point. It is a measure of the consistency of the missiles — that is, *whether they fall in roughly the same place.*

Perhaps the most persuasive statement on missile accuracy comes from former Secretary of Defense James Schlesinger, a proponent of the "counterforce" strategy. While he was in office, he offered secret testimony to the Arms Control Subcommittee on the Senate Foreign Relations Committee on March 4, 1974. Since then, his testimony has been declassified. Here is what he said on the issue of missile accuracy:[66]

I believe there is some misunderstanding about the degree of reliability and accuracy of missiles ... It is impossible for either side to acquire the degree of accuracy that would give them a high confidence first strike, because we will not know what the actual accuracy would be like in a real world contest. As you know, we have acquired from the Western Test Range a fairly precise accuracy, but in the real world we would have to fly

65 See, for instance, James Fallows, *National Defense* (New York: Vintage Books, 1981), pp. 148-57.
66 Quoted in Alexander and Andrew Cockburn, "The Myth of Missile Accuracy," *New York Review of Books,* November 20, 1980.

from operational bases to targets in the Soviet Union. The parameters of the flight from the Western Test Range are not really very helpful in determining those accuracies to the Soviet Union. We can never know what degrees of accuracy would be achieved in the real world . . .

The point I would like to make is that if you have any degraduation in operational accuracy, American counter-force capability goes to the dogs very quickly. We know that, and the Soviets should know it, and that is one of the reasons that I can publicly state that neither side can acquire a high confidence first strike capability. I want the President of the United States to know that for all the future years, and I want the Soviet leadership to know that for all the future years.

The importance of Schlesinger's testimony cannot be overstated, for it would seem to pull the rug out from under those proponents of a large strategic buildup. In short, there are just too many uncertainties about the degree of reliability and accuracy of Russian and American missiles to believe that the leadership of the U.S.S.R. or the U.S. would actually be persuaded to take the dangerous gamble of launching a surprise nuclear attack on land-based systems with only theoretically accurate ICBMs.

Expanding the U.S. "Nuclear War-Fighting" Capability — PD-59

In 1977, Jimmy Carter came into office with a quite different approach to national security. "We must replace balance-of-power politics with world order politics," he told an interviewer from the New York *Times* in June 1976. The candidate proposed a five-to-seven-billion dollar cut in the military budget. Seven months later he declared in his inaugural address: "We will move this year toward our ultimate goal — the elimination of all nuclear weapons from this earth."[67]

Less than three years later, Carter committed himself to a five percent annual increase in defense spending and a more risky — in the eyes of his critics — plan to expand the "counterforce" deterrent strategy of previous administrations. This later decision took the form of Presidential Directive (PD) 59, which was issued in July 1980.[68]

67 Roger Speed, *Strategic Deterrence in the 1980s* (Stanford: Hoover Institution Press, 1979).

68 According to Roger Molander, a former member of the National Security Council staff under Zbigniew Brzezinski, PD 59 was drafted at the insistence of Brzezinski. The Department of State, then under Edmund Muskie, was apparently not included in the process. According to Walter Slocombe, then Deputy Under Secretary of Defense, who was Co-Director of the committee that dealt with the issue of revised military targeting that led eventually to the drafting of PD 59, believers in nuclear war-fighting were a distinct minority in the Carter Administration.

Of all the American presidents since Harry Truman, Jimmy Carter took the greatest interest in the contingency plans for nuclear war. "Within weeks of arriving at the White House," one knowledgeable source writes, "Carter, a former member of a submarine crew, ordered a full review of the presidential procedures for the release of nuclear weapons."[69] Carter's preoccupation with these plans was shared by his National Security Adviser Zbigniew Brzezinski, and within a year a review of the whole nuclear response procedures was well under way. The result was a series of presidential directives, the most noted of which was PD-59.

Presidential Directive No. 59 represented the first executive order requiring the armed forces of the U.S. to be able to fight a prolonged nuclear war. Highlights of this classified document were subsequently made public by Secretary of Defense Harold Brown in a speech at the Naval War College on August 20, 1980. At that time, Brown called for strengthening U.S. nuclear "war-fighting" capability in order to provide an added measure of deterrence by demonstrating America's ability to respond in credible fashion without having to escalate immediately to an all-out nuclear war. The goal of U.S. nuclear defense strategy, he said, was to convince the Soviets "that no . . . use of nuclear weapons — on any scale of attack and at any stage of conflict — could lead to victory, however they may define victory."[70] The key innovation was thinking in terms of limited strikes against political and economic targets rather than exclusively against military targets.

The objectives of the new deterrent posture, which had the effect of formally enshrining in official doctrine the concept of "limited nuclear war," were summarized in the Defense Department's *Annual Report*, which was published in January 1980. According to this unclassified document, successful deterrence required the U.S. to maintain the MAD policy as "the bedrock of nuclear deterrence." However, since the new policy assumed that a nuclear war might last days, weeks and even longer, the U.S. would henceforth "fine-tune" its nuclear responses, particularly against military targets, with the intention of escalating gradually and of holding a large portion of warheads in reserve in any nuclear conflict. Thus, the Carter Administration was moving toward a "shoot-look-shoot" capability

69 Peter Pringle *et al., opus cit.*, p. 39.
70 *The New York Times*, August 21, 1980. According to the *Chicago Sun Times* of February 12, 1979, PD 59 was preceded by an 18-month study ordered by the White House. This study reportedly sought to (a) determine the nuclear strategy that would eliminate the USSR as a functional national entity; (b) investigate promoting separatism by destroying areas in the USSR which support the present Soviet government; and (c) identify the targets which would "paralyze, disrupt and dismember" the Soviet government by annihilating the ruling group.

for its strategic forces in the jargon of those proponents of a nuclear warfighting strategy.

In commenting on PD-59, some critics were quick to point out that the new policy was proclaimed in the aftermath of the revolutions in Iran and Nicaragua and the Soviet invasion of Afghanistan. They noted that the "Carter Doctrine" represented a more general diplomatic statement of national resolve to safeguard control over the oil-producing region of the Persian Gulf by a readiness to use *whatever* military means might prove necessary. Despite the prominence given to the decision to develop a *Rapid Deployment Force* as an instrument of effective intervention in the Persian Gulf states, it was evident to the critics that such a defense could not succeed in the face of serious challenge. Thus, PD-59 and the Carter Doctrine appeared more like expressions of diplomatic desperation than a shift in nuclear weapons policy.

One of the most important statements of the new deterrent strategy, which was officially termed a "countervailing" strategy, was made by Walter Slocombe, a young lawyer, an alumnus of the International Institute for Strategic Studies in London, who had started his political life campaigning for George McGovern, later had become a Kissinger aide, and who now served as Deputy Undersecretary of Defense for Policy Planning in the Carter Administration. He writes:[71]

Under the countervailing strategy, as before, the fundamental U.S. objective is and remains deterrence — but not just of massive attacks on U.S. cities. The United States needs to consider also how to make U.S. nuclear power contribute to deterrence of less than all-out attacks, and particularly how to disabuse the Soviets of any belief that a large-scale but still limited aggression, e.g., an attack on U.S. ICBMs, or an attack on Europe, could work to their advantage.

Importantly, the new policy now assigned priority to targeting the hardened underground shelters that would be used by Soviet leaders in the event of a nuclear war. In this way, the United States began to emphasize what John Steinbruner, a defense specialist, has termed "nuclear decapitation." (Decapitation is an early surprise attack on an enemy's civilian and military headquarters and communications facilities. It aims to destroy the political and military leadership of an adversary as well as to prevent communication between the leadership and forces in the field.)[72]

---

[71] Walter Slocombe, "The Countervailing Strategy" *International Security*, Vol. 5 (Spring, 1981), p. 21. See also Louis René Beres, *Mimicking Sisyphus: America's Countervailing Nuclear Strategy* (Lexington, Mass.: Lexington Books, 1983).

[72] John D. Steinbruner, "Nuclear Decapitation," *Foreign Policy* No. 45 (Winter, 1981-82), p. 16. According to Steinbruner, "command vulnerability is the most significant problem of modern thought."

Little information is available in the unclassified literature on the sensitive subject of the Soviet system of "command, control, communication and intelligence" — what is referred to in the vernacular of strategic theorists as "C^3I." Pronounced C-cubed-I, this cryptic formula designates the capability which would enable the Soviet national command authority (NCA) to detect a nuclear attack, assess its extent and direct a retaliatory response. In general, the Soviet command-and-control network seems to be similar to that of its American counterpart. However, while the Soviets have emphasized building multiple hardened bunkers, U.S. officials have stressed airborne command posts which are less vulnerable.

From what we know from open sources, the first-echelon C^3I centers for Soviet government and military officials are dispersed within an eighty-mile radius of Moscow. These include some seventy-five underground command posts within the ring-road system alone. Main and alternate centers of command are linked to Soviet strategic forces through extensive networks or landlines, microwave and other radio systems and satellites. These latter systems now carry the bulk of Soviet military communications.

The hardened underground bunkers are backed up by a fleet of airborne command posts. These are operated by the Soviet Air Force and have been observed during exercises and in crisis situations.[73] Generally, the Soviet airborne command posts are technically less sophisticated than their American counterparts. But protection of the Soviet military and political leadership is more extensive. Moreover, the redundant communications links would seem to make it difficult for any American strike to isolate the Soviet command authorities entirely from their strategic forces.

Critics of the new strategy of targeting Soviet command-and-control systems maintain that it is a most dangerous development.[74] For four reasons.[75] First, the counterforce capability to destroy hard targets during a limited nuclear exchange is indistinguishable from that needed to launch a knockout nuclear blow against the Soviet Union. Second, the Kremlin could be expected to follow the American lead — as they have so often done in the past. Third, if the leadership of each side felt that it was in imminent danger of being annihilated in the middle of a crisis, there might be a compelling logic to launch a pre-emptive strike. Finally, the threat to

---

73 See "Strategic Command and Control," *IISS Strategic Survey* (London: Neil Moore, 1980), p. 13.

74 See Desmond Ball, *Can Nuclear War be Controlled?* (London: IISS, 1981).

75 Ambassador Martin J. Hillenbrand writes here: "An additional argument beyond those you list against targeting Soviet command-and-control systems is that war termination, if we can think in such terms, becomes more difficult if not impossible when there is no command-and-control system with which we could communicate." Letter, May 22, 1984.

C^3I and to the national command centers of both superpowers would contribute to East-West tensions and make it more likely that nuclear war might occur by accident or miscalculation.[76]

The decision by the Carter Administration to develop a nuclear "decapitation" strategy was but one of the areas of the new policy to draw the fire of critics. Some skeptics were particularly incensed by the idea that there should be enough of a residual force to carry out a war "for a substantial period after a strategic exchange." In the view of these people, if the official function of the American nuclear force was to target the weapons of an adversary and to keep hitting him months after a "strategic exchange," no set number of nuclear bombs and missiles conceivably would be sufficient.

The implications of the Administration's logic were also disturbing to critics. Every nuclear weapon the Soviets built must be matched by the United States. Every technological improvement developed in their defense (e.g. the achievement of greater accuracy or reduced vulnerability) must be offset. Finally, the decision to continue to regard the American strategic nuclear force as a "war-fighting" instrument meant that the arms race became a never-ending, very costly contest — and all for a purpose that increased the chances of a holocaust, or so the critics argued.

Professor Richard Pipes of Harvard, a former advisor to Ronald Reagan on the Soviet Union, takes issue with this analysis: There "is something innately destabilizing in the very fact that we consider nuclear war unfeasible and suicidal for both (the United States and the Soviet Union), and our chief adversary views it as feasible and winnable for himself."[77] But critics respond: "Would stability be enhanced if *both* superpowers operate on the assumption that a nuclear war is feasible and winnable?"

The Carter Administration's emphasis on targeting weapons rather than

---

76 Some proponents of deterrence were opposed to the new strategy on the grounds that it contradicted the basic concepts of "intrawar deterrence" and "escalation dominance," on which the countervailing doctrine is based. "Intrawar deterrence" presupposes the ability to negotiate after a limited nuclear exchange in order to control further escalation and preserve nonmilitary targets. "Escalation dominance" refers to the strategy of maintaining a margin of superiority at each rung of the escalation ladder so that the Soviets would be deterred from escalating a nuclear conflict because it could achieve no rational objective by doing so. Under a "decapitation" policy the destruction of the enemy's national command structure would preclude all such bargaining and with it, according to these theorists, the hope of terminating hostilities at a level below that of mutual assured destruction. See Richard K. Bets, "Nuclear Surprise Attack," *Jerusalem Journal of International Relations*, Vol. 5, No. 3 (1981), p. 193.

77 See Richard Pipes, "Why the Soviet Union Thinks it Could Fight and Win a Nuclear War," *Commentary*, Vol. 64 (July, 1977), pp. 21-34.

Table A
Distribution of U.S./Soviet Nuclear Warheads 1981[78]

Leg of Triad	U.S.	U.S.S.R.
Land-based (ICBMs)	24%	75%
Submarine-based (SLBMs)	50%	20%
Air-based (Long-range bombers)	26%	5%
	100%	100%

cities was explained publicly as being morally motivated. The idea was that it is more moral to hit missiles rather than people. But, as critics were quick to point out, in fact, an expanded "counterforce" strategy meant preparing to hit missiles *and* people — a lot of them.

A report made by NBC several years ago analyzed some of the destruction that would occur from a limited Soviet strike involving some three hundred missiles against 150 Minuteman missiles at the Whiteman Air Force Base in Sedalia, Missouri. According to NBC, which based its report on information provided by Pentagon officials, the "zone of total destruction" would exceed the size of the state of Delaware. However, if westerly winds prevailed (as they usually do), fallout would reach St. Louis, where half of the population would die. Louisville and Cincinnati would also lie in the track of the hypothetical "counterforce" attack. NBC concluded that "millions would be poisoned by radiation," but it did not take into account the devastation that would accrue to the interdependent web of systems that sustain the life of the planet.

The decision by President Carter to broaden the scope of the "counterforce" strategy was a consequence of what former CIA Director William Colby calls the "paper and pencil war." U.S. military strategists, using sophisticated computer technology constantly, strive to increase their "options." In theory, the side with the better options wins. Paul Nitze, a staunch advocate of the "counterforce" strategy, put it this way: "it is possible to think of highly plausible scenarios, assuming a position of Soviet superiority, and a deterioration of crisis stability, in which, should the balloon go up, the outcome would be highly one-sided."[79] But this is only in theory. Reality, critics maintain, might be much different.

---

78 *Annual Report* of the Department of Defense (1981).
79 Quoted in Alan Tonelson, "Nitze's World," *Foreign Policy* (Fall, 1979), pp. 78-79.

Prevailing in a Nuclear War?

When Ronald Reagan became President in 1981, he took office with plans for a major strategic build-up, including a further modification of the "counterforce" doctrine. As the President told a group of visiting editors at the White House on October 16 of that year, a nuclear exchange could occur "without it bringing either one of the major powers to pushing the button." When asked five days later at a press conference whether he still subscribed to this belief, he became somewhat uncomfortable. After making what some described as a long, rambling response, the President concluded with the statement that a limited nuclear exchange was a "possibility".

He added: "You could have a pessimistic outlook on it or an optimistic [outlook]. I always tend to be optimistic."[80]

In 1982, Secretary of Defense Caspar Weinberger informed the armed services to prepare for the possibility of fighting a protracted nuclear war involving a series of carefully "managed" nuclear exchanges over a period of several months. Presidential Directive 59 was now replaced with National Security Decision Directive 13, which some informed "insiders" said privately projected a "winnable" nuclear war-fighting strategy.[81]

This modification of the U.S. deterrent posture had a major impact on American strategic command, control, communications and intelligence systems (C^3I). Essentially, it required the development of a strategic C^3I system not only capable of enduring a succession of "limited nuclear attacks," but of controlling a wide spectrum of escalatory actions. These ranged from the execution of "limited nuclear options" through a full-scale nuclear strike. Furthermore, the new Administration came to view effective C^3I capabilities as a kind of "force multiplier" in a controlled nuclear war. Theoretically, it would enable the National Command Authority to get more utility out of the weapons held in reserve than if they were employed in an uncoordinated fashion.

The concern of Reagan Administration officials over American C^3I vulnerability led to a review procedure which culminated in National Security Directive No. 12. This stated that C^3I would now and in the future enjoy a resource-allocation priority at least equal to that of major new strategic weapons systems.[82] On October 2, 1981, the President announced

---

80 Quoted in the *Boston Globe*, November 11, 1981, p. 1.
81 For details see Robert Scheer, *With Enough Shovels: Reagan, Bush and Nuclear War* (New York: Random House, 1982).
82 "Why C^3I Is the Pentagon's Top Priority," *Government Executive* (January, 1982), p. 12.

his "strategic connectivity package," which called for making the nation's ground-based and space-based C^3I systems sufficiently hardened and redundant to function "during all levels of conflict," including protracted nuclear war. The Administration subsequently requested $ 18 billion in fiscal 1982 dollars over the following six years of C^3I modernization. Eventually, according to "insiders," the request may reach $ 25 billion.

That the Reagan Administration was moving in the direction of perfecting a nuclear war fighting capability was made clear by Lieutenant General James W. Stansberry. Stansberry is Commander of the Electronics Systems Division of the U.S. Air Force and is responsible for running much of the American C^3I program. As he stated in October 1981:[83]

In previous years the concept for C^3I was that it only had to be able to get off a launch of U.S. strategic weapons in response to a first strike before damage was unacceptable. The idea that there was no way to win a nuclear war exchange sort of invalidated the need for anything survivable. There is a shift now in nuclear weapons planning, and a proper element in nuclear deterrence is that we be able to keep on fighting.

When asked about the plans of the Reagan Administration to improve massively American strategic C^3I capabilities in order to perfect a nuclear war-fighting capability, former Secretary of State Cyrus Vance responded: "I think it is sound and proper to have a command and control which could hopefully survive a nuclear attack."[84]

However, to take the next leap, that it is important to have a command and control that is survivable so that you can fight a nuclear war, is a wholly different situation . . . I happen to be one of those who believe it is madness to talk about trying to fight a continuing nuclear war as though it were like fighting a conventional war, and that one could control the outcome with the kind of precision that is sometimes possible in a conventional war situation. It is a totally different world, a world that is hard for any of us to conceive, because none of us knows what a nuclear war is like. But by extrapolation, we can have some idea of the incredible devastation that would come from it and the almost unimaginable consequences that would flow from it.

One of the favorite arguments used by officials in the new Administration for pursuing what seems to many to be a very dangerous policy is that the Soviets are allegedly moving in the direction of developing a more sophisticated nuclear war-fighting strategy of their own. And indeed the Soviet leadership seems committed to improving what may be regarded as "counterforce" capabilities — by building more accurate warheads and

---

83 Quoted in *Aviation Week and Space Technology,* October 26, 1981.
84 Quoted in Robert Scheer, *opus cit.,* p. 33.

adding to its growing stockpile of more powerful missiles that can knock out missiles. Actually, however, the situation is more complicated than this, as critics are quick to point out.

It is by no means certain that the Soviets have adopted a counterforce deterrent strategy. In fact, their public statements today indicate that they view such a policy as highly dangerous and running counter to détente. As the Director of the Soviet Institute of the United States and Canada G.A. Arbatov wrote soon after Secretary Schlesinger proclaimed the doctrine of "limited nuclear options" in 1974, Schlesinger fell victim to "strategic scholasticism." His military doctrines were not only "completely divorced from reality" but, more dangerously, they increased rather than reduced the threat of general nuclear war.[85] (More about this later in Volume Two, *Soviet Nuclear Strategy*.)

Ever since the details of the nuclear war-fighting plans of the Reagan Administration were leaked to the press, they have been the center of a great deal of controversy.[86] Nobel physicist Hans Bethe, who headed the Theoretical Physics Division of the Los Alamos Scientific Laboratory during the Manhattan Project in World War II, said that they come "close to a declaration of war on the Soviet and [contradict] and may destroy President Reagan's initiatives toward nuclear arms control."[87]

On June 19, 1982, the Washington *Post* reported that General David C. Jones, who had retired as Chairman of the Joint Chiefs of Staff, "left office yesterday with the warning that it would be throwing money in a 'bottomless pit' to try to prepare the United States for a long nuclear war with the Soviet Union." The *Post* stated that Jones doubted that any nuclear exchange between the U.S. and the U.S.S.R. could be contained, but would

---

85 Quoted in Morton Schwarz, *Soviet Perceptions of the United States* (Los Angeles: University of California Press, 1978), p. 71. In evaluating the significance of Arbatov's remarks, it is important to note that the general assessment over the years of the Defense Department by members of the USA Institute has been largely negative. The Department of Defense is seen generally to be a powerful force in American political life, with a vital stake in the continuation of the arms build-up.

86 Alexander Haig has this to say about leaks in the Reagan Administration: "Leaks were not merely a problem, they were a way of life ... Leaks constituted policy," because the "president's closest aides were essentially public relations men ... consummate professionals — 'wizards' is not too strong a word." Reagan's men, Haig says, "exercised their intangible power. They opened the doors to the workshop and escorted reporters inside in a way hitherto unknown in Washington. They literally told them everything. For the first time in living memory, you could actually believe almost everything you read [in the media]." See *Caveat: Realism, Reagan, and Foreign Policy* (New York: Macmillan Publishing Co., 1984), p. 19.

87 Quoted in Robert Scheer, *opus cit.*, p. p.

escalate into an all-out war. According to the newspaper, Jones said: "I don't see much of a chance of nuclear war being limited or protracted... I see great difficulty in keeping any kind of nuclear exchange between the United States and the Soviet Union from escalating."

In general, the proposed strategy of the Administration was vehemently opposed on the following grounds:

First, in a crisis, it places on Moscow the burden of making a rational moral choice about whether to escalate, and this may not be the way to ensure American security, some critics note.

Second, none of the nuclear war-fighting weapons are likely to perform with the degrees of accuracy and reliability that the scenarios require.

Third, "limiting" a nuclear conflict depends on assured communications — not only with the adversary but with one's own forces as well. And this is likely to be impossible in the radioactive frenzy of the nuclear battlefield.

Fourth, efforts to negotiate meaningful arms control agreements under such a strategy will be surely overtaken by the rush to develop new war-fighting systems on both sides.

And this brings us to the final fatal weakness of the Reagan Administration's enhanced "counterforce" strategy: It is destabilizing because it encourages technological developments which endeavor to cancel out the effects of the other superpower. There is no point where either side can call halt and say, "O.K. we're strong enough; let's stop here."

Most of the critics of Reagan's deterrent policy challenge the "window-of-vulnerability" scenario from which it derives a great deal of impetus.[88] One variation unfolds somewhat like this: The Soviets initiate a pre-emptive nuclear strike against U.S. silo-based missiles but hold back a sizeable portion of their land-based ICBM force to deter American retaliation. According to U.S. military planners, the President, knowing that most of the American land-based force was destroyed, would be in a terrible predicament. If he ordered retaliation against Soviet cities by less accurate U.S. submarine forces or by bombers which might be able to penetrate the sophisticated Soviet air defense system, he would surely trigger a Soviet response which could well lead to all-out destruction. The alternative would be: to do nothing.

The critics attack this scenario on two major grounds. They first note that the theoretical window of vulnerability was slammed shut by President Reagan's Scowcroft Commission. This commission, chaired by retired Air

---

88 "The wholesale vulnerability of fixed ICBMs has thus become the driving assumption of Western strategic planning," says William H. Kincade, "Over the Technological Horizon," *Daedalus*, No. 110 (Winter, 1981), p. 110.

Force General Brent Scowcroft, was formed in early 1983 to salvage the MX missile, which was then facing Congressional defeat. The problem of the Commission was primarily a political and public relations one of how best to sell the MX to a skeptical Congress and public so as to gain enough support to begin producing the missile. Their solution was to link the missile to arms control, promote it as the symbol of American national will, and recommend a follow-on missile in the 1990s. Consequently, the Commission recommended putting at least 100 of the MX missiles in the same Minuteman silos which members of the Committee on the Present Danger (a number of whom became high-level officials in the Reagan Administration) had been saying for years were vulnerable to a Soviet pre-emptive strike. In this way, critics conclude, the "window of vulnerability" has gone the way of the "bomber gap" and the "missile gap."

Table B
Soviet Union Buildup, Nuclear and Conventional Forces, 1964-81[89]

	1964	1981
Strategic Forces		
Intercontinental ballistic missiles	190	1,398
Submarine-launched ballistic missiles	29	989
Bombers	170	150
Total weapons (warheads)	400	7,000
Land Forces		
Tanks	30,000	55,000
Divisions	145	187
Artillery tubes/rocket launchers	11,000	20,000
Tactical Air Forces		
Fighter/attack aircraft	3,500	5,000
Naval Forces		
Major surface combatants and amphibious ships	260	378
Other naval vessels	1,440	1,200
Total military manpower	3,400,000	4,200,000
Total defense spending[90]	105	185

89 Sources: U.S. Department of Defense; U.S. Central Intelligence Agency; International Institute for Strategic Studies.
90 Figures are in billions of 1980 dollars.

Lastly, the critics maintain, feverish military preparations to counter nuclear war by being prepared to fight and win it actually make nuclear war by miscalculation more likely. These people are extremely disturbed in this connection by reports that consideration is now being given secretly to a "launch-under-attack" strategy. The Pentagon's 1980 *Posture Statement* already indicated how U.S. military planners tend to view the problem. In part, it reads as follows: "Very low survivability of ICBMs in the early 1980s will leave us with very little effective quick-response hard-target kill capability unless we were to adopt a launch-under-attack policy..."

To be sure, even the most unabashed proponents of "counterforce" deterrence see the dangers (even if their analysis is different than that of critics). As Paul Nitze told the House Armed Services Committee not too long ago:

An important issue surrounding the launch-under-attack option is launch what against what Soviet targets — upon what degree of evidence that an attack of what size is under way against U.S. targets? Extremely difficult considerations are involved in answering that complex question. Should the President be asked to resolve them in the few minutes which may be available to him, or should the answers be preprogrammed into a computer? Neither alternative is without immense dangers.

Other high-level officials in the Reagan Administration, such as Fred C. Ikle, have publicly acknowledged the problem. As the former head of the U.S. Arms Control and Disarmament Agency told one interviewer, a "launch-under-attack" system puts "incredible responsibilities on some tech sergeant in the innards of the system. The more quick and automatic it is, the more you're turning over decisions — the most fateful decision in the nation's history — to people far removed from the President and the Joint Chiefs."[91]

"Horizontal Escalation"

At the same time the Reagan Administration was expanding the nuclear war-fighting capability of the United States, it implemented (without much public fanfare) a two-fold global policy of actively deterring Soviet military pressure and maneuvering. The first component of this new strategy was dubbed "horizontal escalation" by Pentagon enthusiasts. Basically, it consisted of a plan to deter Russian attacks against vulnerable American military interests by threatening to retaliate against equally important — and militarily vulnerable — Soviet interests elsewhere. The second component

---

91 Quoted in Richard J. Barnett, *Real Security: Restoring American Power in a Dangerous Decade* (New York: Touchstone Books, 1981), p. 30.

Figure 3: *Groton, Connecticut — A starboard bow view of the progress of construction of the nuclear powered fleet ballistic missile submarine Michigan, SSBN-727.*

was called "simultaneity" by Defense Department officials and was based on the Pentagon's assessment that the U.S. had to be prepared for combat simultaneously on all fronts. According to one U.S. military analyst, "The two concepts constituted the Reagan Administration's clearest break with Carter's non-nuclear defense policies and buttressed the administration's plans for naval expansion."[92]

Basically, the two policies grew out of Reagan's frustration with President Carter's handling, in 1979, of the disclosure that Soviet troops were in Cuba (they had been there since the Cuban missile crisis in 1962). Carter's policy, Reagan charged then, was to react to Soviet aggression. "The Soviets move in one place and we react in that place. Why don't we give them some problems to worry about?" In Reagan's view, it was time for the United States to flex its muscles and fashion policies to circumscribe the freedom of movement enjoyed by the Soviets.

Secretary of Defense Caspar Weinberger outlined the so-called "horizontal escalation" concept in the 1983 *Annual Report*. "We might choose not to restrict ourselves to meeting aggression on its own immediate front," the Pentagon head stated. "A wartime strategy that confronts the enemy, were he to attack, with the risk of our counter-offensive against his vulnerable points strengthens deterrence."

Weinberger later suggested that a particularly vulnerable Soviet point was its potentially fractious empire of satellite countries. But other than this hint, he revealed no details as to how U.S. officials might stir up anti-Soviet elements to divert Soviet leaders from other plans. In view of American military preponderance in the Caribbean basin, however, some champions of "horizontal escalation" hinted darkly of threats against Cuba as one likely application of such a policy. It was not until the invasion of Grenada by U.S. forces in October 1983, however, that this policy saw its first application.

Perhaps the most influential advocate in the Pentagon of this new policy is Navy Secretary John F. Lehman. The senior defense official generally views the Navy's aircraft carriers, ship-launched cruise missiles and Marine landing units as being ideally flexible weapons for putting Soviet interests at risk on all fronts. To Lehman, the doctrine of "horizontal escalation" is a key element in the commitment of the Administration to maritime supremacy.[93]

At the present time, Lehman wants to procure three more "big deck"

---

92 Quoted in Michael Glennon *et al.* (eds.), *The Soviet Union* (Washington, D.C.: Congressional Quarterly, Inc., 1982), p. 101.

93 Michael Wormser (ed.), *U.S. Defense Policy*, 3rd ed. (Washington, D.C.: Congressional Quarterly, Inc., 1983), p. 148.

aircraft carriers — at a cost of $ 2.4 billion each. This will give the United States a total of fifteen of these nuclear-powered vessels. The new super-carriers will form core units of new, exceptionally potent naval squadrons. Each carrier holds approximately ninety planes and represents a formidable weapons system. These are designed to "go for the jugular" and to strike directly at the heart of Soviet defenses, specifically the Kremlin's second-strike and withholding sanctuary in the Barents Sea and adjacent Arctic waters.[94]

The Congressional Budget Office explains:[95]

The specifics of these plans are based upon a maritime offensive strategy that emphasizes strikes against enemy waters and their supporting base structure, including strikes in enemy waters against its home territory.

The critics are extremely uncomfortable with Lehman's plans. Many experts both inside and outside the Navy are convinced that even F-14 jet fighters designed especially for the task cannot adequately defend the carriers against a determined attack by Soviet Backfire bombers. The result is a Navy built around a mission it cannot perform — and needlessly expensive for lesser missions.

More importantly, however, critics view Lehman's strategy as likely to provoke Soviet use of nuclear weapons against the battlegroups. They consider the strategy to be dangerously provocative in a nuclear-armed world and very hazardous to the American carriers even if a nuclear exchange is avoided.

As far as the critics are concerned, the Navy does not need to destroy the Soviet fleet in port to maintain control of the high seas. Two-thirds of the Soviet Navy is stationed in the Barents Sea, and it must pass through the gap between Iceland and the United Kingdom in order to threaten U.S. control of shipping lanes. This is a gap that the American Navy can close with a combination of mines, submarines and land-based aircraft.

Capacity for a "Simultaneity" of Wars

Like "horizontal escalation," the policy of "simultaneity" reflected a basic difference in strategy from that of the Carter Administration. According to one Reagan "insider," Carter had been willing to accept a smaller U.S. force on grounds that U.S. forces could be shifted from one theater of hostilities to another, dealing with threats one at a time.

94 See C.G. Jacobsen, "Soviet American Policy: New Strategic Uncertainties," *Current History*, October, 1982.
95 Congressional Budget Office, *Building a 600 Ship Navy: Cost, Timing and Alternative Approaches* (Washington, D.C.: U.S. Government Printing Office, 1982).

For most of the 1950s and 1960s, U.S. strategy rested on the assumption that the United States might have to fight "two and a half wars" simultaneously — against the U.S.S.R. in Europe, China in Asia and guerrillas somewhere else. To be sure, manpower and equipment were never adequate to such a task, but U.S. generals tended to rely on the overwhelming superiority of the U.S. to plug the gaps. By 1969, it was apparent that the People's Republic of China was far more likely to go to war with the Soviet Union than with the United States. So the strategy shrank to accommodate one and a half wars — a major conflict with the Soviets in Europe and a minor one somewhere in the Third World.

According to Secretary of Defense Weinberger, that strategy is clearly outmoded. By steadily increasing its defense spending over the past two decades — while the U.S. spent billions on a futile war in Vietnam — the U.S.S.R. pulled ahead of the U.S. in many categories essential to conventional warfare. "The Soviets are now militarily capable of having two and a half wars going at once," argues Weinberger.[96] Consequently, the worst-case scenario now envisions the U.S. fighting major wars against the U.S.S.R. in both Europe and the Persian Gulf and a brushfire battle against Soviet proxies in El Salvador.

Just like "horizontal escalation," "simultaneity" implies that any conventional U.S.-Soviet conflict would be dealt with on many fronts at once. Basic to its development is the notion that the U.S. could force a multi-front war on the Soviet Union. In that event, Reagan officials would not have time to shift forces from one region to another.

In June 1984, media reports indicated that the Pentagon would like to move its rapid-deployment headquarters from Florida to the Middle East. Now called the U.S. Central Command (USCENTCOM), the Rapid Deployment Force established in November 1983 a 20-man, floating forward command post on a ship of the Navy's Middle East Force in the Gulf. According to Admiral James Watkins, Chief of Naval Operations, there is an inestimable value in being close to the scene. So far, however, the Arab states — who would like the U.S. to keep a low profile in the region — have not extended an invitation.[97]

---

96 Quoted in *Newsweek*, June 8, 1981.
97 See *Newsweek*, June 18, 1984.

Summary

Many Americans have come to regard nuclear deterrence as stable. It is an awesome threat, to be sure, but one so very unlikely to be executed that under its shadow, people carry on, in reasonable security. Or so many people think.

However, the findings of this investigation remind one that the stability allegedly provided by nuclear deterrence is more apparent than real. A nuclear war could come to pass in a number of different ways. It might start through a nuclear accident which, despite all precautions, will always have some possibility of occurring — but more so now with the ever increasing numbers of deployed nuclear weapons ostensibly justified in the name of maintaining deterrence. It might come about in a crisis through an act of desperation by a supposedly "rational" leader. It might begin by the deliberate firing by an overzealous subordinate or a deranged statesman. A catalytic nuclear war might also be started by a "have-not" smaller power without a great deal to lose (at least in the mind of its leader) or by some middle-level power driven by some perverted value of gaining more than a superpower could imagine. It might come about inadvertently through the outcome of competition in risk-taking. Most plausible, of course, is the interaction of several of these elements at an inopportune moment.

For some time these terrible possibilities seemed remote. However, the debate over nuclear deterrence policies has focused attention on the dilemma posed by the existence of large nuclear arsenals. In the main, this is because the various deterrent strategies employed by the United States have not reduced the probability of the use of these weapons to an acceptably low level.

Basically, the United States has had two deterrent policies since the early 1960s: a *declaratory* and an *action* policy. Frequently, this distinction is not realized by public commentators and others who debate the pros and cons of various deterrent strategies. But an understanding of this dichotomous situation is crucial to any evaluation of American nuclear deterrence strategy from the 1960s through the present day.

From 1962 to 1984 the *declaratory* policy of the United States on the use of nuclear weapons changed significantly. During the mid-1960s Secretary of Defense Robert McNamara increasingly stressed what he called an "assured destruction" strategy. Under this strategy, the United States counted at one point on being able to destroy in a massive nuclear retaliatory strike one quarter to one-third of the Soviet population and fifty to seventy-five percent of Soviet industry. If the U.S. retained that capability, it was asserted, nuclear deterrence would work.

The exact definition of "assured destruction" has over the years varied from Administration to Administration. In the event of an all-out war, present policy calls for the destruction of some high percentage of the economic, political and military targets in the Soviet Union as well as the destruction of most of its large population centers.

On the surface, the "assured destruction" strategy seems to be the opposite of the "no-cities" strategy McNamara had articulated in 1962. But, in fact, the shift in declaratory policy was not matched by a shift in targeting policy. The Secretary of Defense never had any counterforce options removed from U.S. strategic war plans.

Apparently, McNamara proposed his new assured destruction strategy not to destroy Soviet cities in wartime but to hold down the American military budget in peacetime. It would have been enormously expensive for the U.S. to counter Soviet military forces weapon for weapon; an assured destruction strategy had the major advantage of setting a ceiling on military requirements which could be met at the level then achieved by U.S. strategic forces.

Despite this *declaratory* policy, throughout the 1960s U.S. nuclear forces remained targeted primarily against Soviet military forces. Indeed, during the early 1960s, American superiority was so great that Soviet nuclear forces could have been substantially destroyed in a first strike. In fact, certain U.S. military officials even proposed such an idea, which was rejected by President Kennedy and Secretary McNamara.[98] However, by the end of the decade, the growth of Soviet strategic forces had decisively reduced their vulnerability. Both superpowers now had strategic forces which could not be substantially destroyed by a first strike. The era of mutual assured destruction (MAD) had arrived.

Mutual assured destruction — the ability of each side to first absorb an attack on its nuclear forces and still retaliate massively against the other side — is no longer official U.S. policy. But as Richard Falk has pointed out, "MAD has never been more than the option of last resort, the least likely nuclear scenario, as official policy has evolved over the years."[99] The Soviet leadership has understood this situation. Thus, the Soviets have sought to convey the impression that they are resolved to treat any limited

---

[98] During the 1950s, when the United States still enjoyed nuclear superiority, there was some talk and even planning by some U.S. government officials regarding a first-strike option. Daniel Ellsberg, who worked on strategic planning in the Kennedy Administration, claims that a first strike was actively considered during JFK's first year in office. Indeed, as late as 1962, the U.S. Air Force was urging President Kennedy to allocate resources for such a capability. But, as then Secretary of Defense McNamara recalled recently, he and the President rejected such a proposal. See Robert Scheer, *opus cit.*, p. 10.

[99] Robert J. Lifton and Richard Falk, *opus cit.*, p. 182.

nuclear strike as producing an irresistable upward pressure to escalate to all-out war.

The doctrine of mutual assured destruction was developed in an era when the United States still enjoyed numerical superiority in nuclear weapons over the Soviet Union. However, by the late 1960s this superiority was rapidly declining and no longer operative — if it ever had been. As Henry Kissinger stated in 1965: "This situation reflects the basic paradox of contemporary technology. Power has never been greater; it also has never been less useful."[100]

As more and more nuclear warheads were added to the American arsenal in the 1960s and 1970s, U.S. officials began to target more and more military (counterforce) targets.[101] Since all large cities in the U.S.S.R. were already earmarked, targeting was extended to military installations of all kinds. Although the Kennedy Administration was the first to develop the concept of counterforce, this doctrine was extended and elaborated upon by successive administrations.

American counterforce policy was first publicly explained in the context of Defense Secretary McNamara's "damage limitation" strategy. Damage limitation is a tranquilizing term introduced by U.S. military planners to mean counterforce. On its face, damage limitation sounds like a reasonably restrained approach to nuclear strategy; its military aim is to limit damage to cities in the United States. The problem is that to achieve this end, the strategy requires in the main the destruction of the assault forces of the opponent *before* they can be used. Thus, one man's damage limitation, at a certain point, becomes another man's feared first strike.[102]

---

100 Henry A. Kissinger (ed.), *Problems of National Security* (New York: Praeger, 1965), p. 5.

101 It is important to note here that the race to acquire new warheads was accompanied by a shift toward smaller yields. Freeman Dyson explains: "First, as the numbers of weapons on both sides increased, the military planners rapidly ran out of targets for huge bombs. There is not much satisfaction, even for the most bloodthirsty general, in using ten megatons to wipe out an airfield or a city when a tenth of a megaton would do the job just as well. Second, the accuracy of missiles improved dramatically. So long as missiles were inaccurate, with aiming errors measured in miles, it made sense to use high-yield weapons on small targets. As soon as the errors were reduced to a small fraction of a mile, small targets could be attacked more effectively by accurate low-yield weapons than by inaccurate monsters. Third, and most important, new means of delivery were developed which tilted the balance of costs decisively toward low-yield weapons..." See Dyson, *Weapons and Hope* (New York: Harper & Row, 1984), p. 38.

102 Former Secretary of Defense Donald Rumsfield made more or less the same point when he stated shortly before his resignation in early 1977: "The most ambitious [damage limiting] strategy dictates a first strike capability against an enemy's strategic offensive forces which seeks to destroy as much of his megatonnage as

As the Harvard Nuclear Study Group writes: "An American ability to attack all Soviet military forces might greatly increase Soviet incentives for a preemptive attack. Soviet missiles are also generally deployed close to population areas, and the Soviets could well interpret an American damage-limiting attack as a major damage-creating attack."[103]

According to some accounts, Secretary McNamara became convinced during his tenure in office that his "city-avoidance" strategy, which was designed to minimize civilian casualties in a nuclear war, was unworkable both on physical and military grounds. Civilian casualties were still apt to number in many millions, and one could not be sure the opponent would also follow a city-avoiding strategy. Instead, an adversary might choose to target centers of population.[104]

During the early 1970s, Secretary of Defense James Schlesinger stressed the importance of the U.S. having the capability to respond to Soviet aggression with a variety of "limited nuclear options." Ostensibly, this policy was designed to make the U.S. deterrent posture more credible. However, it reflected the political reality that the United States no longer had the ability it possessed earlier in the 1960s to launch a disarming first strike against Soviet nuclear forces.

At the time Secretary Schlesinger announced his "flexible targeting" policy, which was embraced with anything but uniform enthusiasm throughout the U.S. military establishment,[105] he implied that the United States then had only massive retaliation against Soviet cities as a response option. But this was stretching the truth a bit. Since its inception, the SIOP — the blueprint for actual U.S. targeting policy — contained counterforce options.

On the surface, the Nixon-Schlesinger targeting doctrine seems more humane than obliterating population centers. Aiming at military targets sounds at first like the way a war should be run. And if it is limited, so much the better. But the chance of such a war remaining limited is very small, if not virtually zero.

>
> possible before it can be brought into play ..." *Annual Defense Department Report Fiscal Year 1978* by Secretary of Defense Donald H. Rumsfeld (January 17, 1977), pp. 76-77. "Most damage limiting strategies represent an effort," Rumsfeld said, "by one belligerent to maximize the damage to his enemies and minimize it to himself."

103 Albert Carnesale *et al.*, *Living with Nuclear Weapons* (New York: Bantam Books, 1983), p. 146.

104 See Wolfgang K.H. Panofsky, "The Mutual-Hostage Relationship Between America and Russia," *Foreign Affairs*, Vol. 52, No. 1 (October 1973), p. 111.

105 See Benjamin S. Lambeth, *Selective Nuclear Options in American and Soviet Strategic Policy* (Santa Monica: The RAND Corporation, 1976), p. 7.

A number of careful studies over the years, even when posed in essentially military and political terms, have expressed grave doubts about limited nuclear war. This point was effectively made by the four prominent authors of the article on "Nuclear Weapons and the Atlantic Alliance" in the Spring issue of *Foreign Affairs*:[106]

It is time to recognize that no one has ever succeeded in advancing any persuasive reason to believe that any use of nuclear weapons, even on the smallest scale, could reliably be expected to remain limited. Every serious analysis and every military exercise, for over 25 years, has demonstrated that even the most restrained battlefield use would be enormously destructive to civilian life and property. There is no way for anyone to have any confidence that such a nuclear action will not lead to further and more devastating exchanges. Any use of nuclear weapons in Europe, by the Alliance or against it, carries with it a high and inescapable risk of escalation into the general nuclear war which would bring ruin to all and victory to none.

The assumption underlying Schlesinger's "flexible targeting" strategy was that if deterrence fails, damage limitation could best be achieved by what is called "intrawar deterrence" — that is, by mutual restraint in the choice of targets and weapons. However, intrawar restraint requires the cooperation of both parties. And as a RAND study concludes, Soviet strategic thinking is hardly inclined toward a cooperative damage limitation strategy.[107]

Historically, the various nuclear war-fighting policies of the United States have been justified on grounds that they serve to deter the Soviet Union. In actuality, however, they increase rather than decrease the possibility of all-out nuclear war. For instance, they create the dangerous

---

106 According to a study reported by the International Institute for Strategic Studies in London in November 1981, it would be "most unrealistic" to expect "a relatively smooth and controlled progression from limited and selective strikes to major counterforce exchanges or a breaking off of the war prior to large-scale attacks on urban-industrial areas." Controlled nuclear war is described as a "chimera" or an illusion. See Desmond Ball, *Can Nuclear War be Controlled?* (London: The International Institute for Strategic Studies, 1981). The present U.S. Commander of NATO states the case more bluntly. The use of "theater nuclear weapons," he says, "would in fact escalate to the strategic level and very quickly." See *Defense Daily*, November 12, 1981.

107 Jack L. Snyder, *The Soviet Strategic Culture: Implications for Limited Nuclear Options* (Santa Monica: The RAND Corporation, 1977), p. v. "It would be dangerous to assume that Soviet crisis decision-makers will tailor their behavior to American notions of strategic rationality," this report concludes. "Soviet criticism of the limited strategic options doctrine is consistent with deeply rooted patterns of Soviet strategic thought."

illusion that low casualty, surgically fought nuclear wars are possible. One only has to recall Defense Secretary James Schlesinger's remarks in his 1974 *Annual Report* that nuclear attacks against U.S. military installations might result in "relatively few civilian casualties."[108]

To the extent that this illusion is believed, it lowers inhibitions against the use of nuclear weapons. Moreover, such war-fighting strategies give the Soviets the impression that the United States, in a crisis situation, is prepared to initiate nuclear war — at least on a limited basis. Given this situation, the Soviet leadership might in a severe crisis be encouraged to strike first. Finally, former Secretary Schlesinger himself has admitted that "Soviet military doctrine does not subscribe to a strategy of graduated nuclear response,"[109] so once war begins, escalation may be inevitable, regardless of any American restraint.

Despite the obvious shortcomings of the counterforce concept, it has persisted. Indeed, President Jimmy Carter, after first rejecting the concept, appeared to embrace it toward the end of his Administration. In 1980, Secretary of Defense Harold Brown elaborated on Schlesinger's idea of limited nuclear options. Brown now stressed greater flexibility in targeting, the ability to change targets during the course of a prolonged nuclear war and the central importance of securing facilities for command, control, communications and intelligence (C^3I). The new American deterrent posture, officially termed a "countervailing strategy," was designed to persuade the Soviets that there was no level of aggression at which they could succeed. Under this policy, the U.S. would have adequate forces — and the plans for employing them — to deny the Soviets victory at any level of engagement, given any plausible definition of victory.

Presidential Directive No. 59 — or PD-59 — was only a few pages long, but it did two main things to the contingency planning for nuclear war: "It shifted some of the emphasis from economic targets onto military targets, particularly Soviet political and leadership targets *and* military command and control targets, it required instead that the U.S. forces be able to "endure" a protracted nuclear war, one that might last perhaps months instead of the few days imagined under the older doctrines that incorporated massive, or "spasm,' responses to a Soviet attack..."[110] In short,

---

108 Since Schlesinger's conclusion generated considerable skepticism among members of Congress, the Office of Technology Assessment of the U.S. Congress was subsequently asked to evaluate the Department of Defense calculations.

109 Contrast this statement with that made by Schlesinger on January 10, 1974 at an Overseas Writers Association luncheon in Washington, D.C. that "in the pursuit of symmetry we cannot allow the Soviets unilaterally to obtain a counterforce option which we ourselves lack."

110 Peter Pringle and William Arkin, *SIOP: The Secret U.S. Plan for Nuclear War*

however important the new document was, the changes merely incorporated "evolutionary" variations on the counterforce theme of U.S. strategic policy.

Whatever the intent of the Carter Administration, PD-59 represented an important expansion of the counterforce doctrine. Nevertheless, the Reagan Administration went even further. According to testimony by "insiders," NSDD 13, which superceded PD-59, specifically proclaimed that the goal of U.S. policy is to *prevail* in a protracted nuclear war.[111] The document adopted by the Carter Administration expressly stopped short of a declaration that nuclear war could actually be won.

Following the findings of the Scowcroft Commission, much of the talk about the so-called "window of vulnerability," which Reagan had used so effectively during the presidential campaign, died down. But the Administration continued to press its case for the development of what is called a "second strike counterforce capability." This means having missiles, such as the larger MX-Peacekeeper and the more accurate Trident II, that can survive a pre-emptive attack from the U.S.S.R. Such survivable missiles would be launched during the "trans-attack" and "post-attack" periods, which theoretically range from a few days to a few months. As the rest of the U.S. nuclear force and the country disintegrates, this "secure reserve force" will ensure "victory."

However, there are some substantial objections to the development of such a capability. In the first place, the idea of destroying Soviet missile silos during a second (retaliatory) strike was justified as a necessary precaution against a hypothetical Soviet pre-emptive strike. But in fact such a capability may create the conditions under which such an attack would be launched. In a very real sense, then, the second-strike counterforce scenario is a self-fulfilling prophecy.

More importantly, though, despite all the loose talk about the need by the U.S. of a second-strike counterforce capability, there is no practical difference between such a capability and a first-strike counterforce capability. As Robert C. Aldridge, a former design engineer for the Polaris and Trident missile systems, writes: "If the U.S. can destroy a sizeable portion of the Soviet ICBM force after absorbing a Soviet (preemptive) strike under

> (New York: W.W. Norton & Company, 1984), p. 185. The authors report that "By the time PD-59 leaked to the press in the summer of 1980, SIOP-5 had been through four regular revisions . . . The 1980 war plan, SIOP-5D, included a staggering 40,000 potential targets." Besides the expected Soviet targets, these included "thousands of targets in the Warsaw Pact nations, in China, in Cuba, and in Vietnam, and even some targets in unspecified 'allied and neutral territory.'" (p. 188)

111 See Robert Scheer, *opus cit.*, p. 12.

the stress of a going war and when atmospheric conditions created by nuclear explosions are far from favorable, then it would have a far greater chance of destroying all Soviet silo-based missiles with a pre-emptive first strike when the element of surprise and choice of time are in its favor and Soviet missiles are not in a high state of readiness. This is a first strike [sic] capability even if the intention is not there to use it."[112]

To combat actively a perceived military imbalance in the Soviet-American relationship, President Reagan is presiding over the largest peacetime expansion of U.S. military forces since World War II. The President says U.S. strategic forces should be able to ensure "the margin of safety necessary for our security" — codewords for obtaining military superiority over the Soviet Union. But it is unclear whether this will have any practical meaning in view of the Soviet intention to match the United States in this crucial area. All previous Administrations and many strategic thinkers agree that U.S. foreign policy requires that American strategic forces have overall capabilities that are perceived as roughly equal to Soviet capabilities.[113] But military superiority is a different matter altogether.

The huge military build-up of the Reagan Administration, which was originally projected to cost approximately $ 1.5 trillion over five years, embraces a number of major new weapons systems. Among the most important, at least as far as U.S. strategic forces are concerned, are the two new ICBM systems — the MX (Missile Experimental) and the Midgetman. But there is also the new generation of Trident submarines being developed which can deliver their lethal warheads on "hard" targets — that is, those that are deeply entrenched and coated with thick concrete — in less than ten minutes if deployed near the Soviet coastline; an extensive cruise missile system, which can be deployed by air, sea or land, and two enormously expensive strategic bombers — the B-1B and the so-called "Stealth" bomber. Altogether, according to one independent analysis of the budget

---

112 Robert C. Aldridge, *First Strike! The Pentagon's Strategy for Nuclear War* (Boston: South End Press, 1983), p. 39. A similar conclusion is reached by a confidential Congressional Budget Office background paper made available to this writer: "... There may be an inescapable dilemma in the procurement of second strike counterforce capability: a U.S. arsenal large enough to attack Soviet ICBMs after having absorbed a Soviet first strike (sic) would be large enough to threaten the Soviet ICBM force in a U.S. first strike. Moreover, the Soviet Union, looking at capabilities rather than intentions, might see a U.S. second-strike capability in this light. Faced with a threat to their ICBM force, Soviet leaders facing an international crisis might have an incentive to use their missiles in a preemptive strike before they could be destroyed by the United States."

113 Albert Carnesale *et al.*, of the Harvard Nuclear Study Group, *Living with Nuclear Weapons* (New York: Bantam Books, 1983), p. 152.

request of the Reagan Administration, the Pentagon plans to build 17,000 more nuclear warheads and bombs during the decade of the 1980s.[114]

Many of the proposed weapons systems in the present military buildup are redundant. Does the Pentagon really need the land-based MX, for instance, when it also plans to have the submarine-based Trident D-5 aimed at Soviet targets? What about the B-1B bomber, which will soon be out of date as the new "Stealth" bomber is built?[115] According to a recent Brookings Institution analysis, the U.S. government could carve $46 billion out of the defense budget by 1989 without damaging American national security at all.[116]

Along with these plans for a massive strategic build-up, the Administration has developed plans for further expansion of the counterforce "deterrent" doctrine. However, the emphasis is now on "prevailing" in a nuclear war, which could theoretically last many months. Reagan's top secret NSSD is the first declaratory policy statement of a U.S. Administration to proclaim that U.S. strategic forces must be able to win a protracted nuclear war. Thus, the Reagan Administration goes considerably beyond the nuclear war-fighting strategies of past Administrations.

There is an unfortunate element in present U.S. policy which appears to assume that the fiercer the visage the United States presents, the better the deterrent. The problem with this very negative kind of thinking is that it is strikingly unrealistic. As Louis René Beres points out: "It generates a spiraling pattern of fear and mistrust which progressively inhibits opportunities for general cooperation, freezes hostilities into fixed and intransigent camps, and ultimately explodes into general warfare. At the same time, this fear and mistrust feeds back to world leaders and reinforces the commitment to a 'get what you can' philosophy of international conduct."[117]

---

114 "Science and the Citizen," *Scientific American* (May, 1981), p. 92.
115 According to some Pentagon planners, the Stealth bomber is only the beginning. These sources foresee a whole arsenal of "nearly invisible" equipment, from tanks to satellites. See *U.S. News and World Report*, June 11, 1984.
116 See Alice Rivlin et al., *Economic Choices 1984* (Washington, D.C.: Brookings Institution, 1984). Rivlin is a former director of the Congressional Budget Office.
117 Louis René Beres, "Nuclear Strategy and World Order: The United States Imperative," *Alternatives — A Journal of World Policy*, Vol. 8, No. 2 (Fall, 1982).

> Policy-making officials in the United States, the United Kingdom and other Western countries can often be heard saying that the best guarantee against a new war is the "balance of fear." Means of destruction and annihilation have become so powerful, argue the proponents of this view, that no state will run the risk of starting a nuclear war since it will inevitably sustain a retaliatory nuclear blow ...
>
> But to base the policy of states on a feeling of universal fear would be tantamount to keeping the world in a permanent state of feverish tension and eve-of-war hysteria. In such an atmosphere, each state would fear that the other side would lose its nerve and fire the first shot. Would not this create the temptation to prevent the opponent from gaining a lead?
>
> *Soviet Foreign Minister Andrei Gromyko,*
> *Speech to the U.N. General Assembly,*
> *September 21, 1962.*

VI. SOVIET VIEWS OF DETERRENCE*

Many proponents of deterrence seem to assume that the Soviet leadership has accepted nuclear deterrence in the same way as the United States. But do the political and military leaders in the Soviet Union accept mutual deterrence? The continuing Soviet military buildup and the continued expressions in published Soviet military writings of a war-fighting doctrine have convinced some — and troubled others — as to Soviet views on this important — and controversial — question.

This chapter attempts to illuminate Soviet thinking on the subject of deterrence. In particular, it will consider the interrelationship of Soviet ideological beliefs, political imperatives and calculation, military views and doctrine and their reconciliation in Soviet policy.

---

* This chapter draws heavily on the contributions to the literature by John Erickson, Roman Kolkowicz and Benjamin Lambeth. Their research on the subject is highly regarded by students of Soviet nuclear strategy.

An American View of the Soviet Mind

American officials often describe deterrence as the ability to influence the Soviet mentality. Thus, in formulating its definition of deterrence, the Joint Chiefs of Staff *Dictionary of Military and Associated Terms* (JCS Pub. 1) refers to "a state of mind." In view of this situation, one would think that if the United States were seriously attempting to implement a policy of deterrence *vis-a-vis* the Soviet Union, high Administration officials would pay close attention to the evidence on how Soviet leaders and military officials think on this crucial matter. While some obviously do, the following statement by Defense Secretary Caspar Weinberger is not very encouraging: "it's very hard to get inside the Soviet mind. I have not attempted to do that."[1]

Of course, there is no such thing as the "Soviet mind," just as the notion of the "American mind" is a myth.[2] However, Soviet military and political leaders do hold certain strategic views, although differences of opinion obviously exist in the U.S.S.R. as they do anywhere else. In the past, public references by U.S. officials to "the Soviet mind" were frequently made for contriving the most simplistic and self-serving assumptions about Soviet intentions. Only recently are more and more observers coming belatedly to realize that Western leaders may have made a major mistake in assuming that Soviet officials think like them on the crucial issue of deterrence.

John Erickson, Director of Defense Studies at the University of Edinburgh, puts it this way. For a long time, the Americans took a "markedly condescending" attitude towards the Russians, whom they generally assumed thought like they did. This "disdain shown towards the quality (or lack of quality) in Soviet strategic thinking was a marked feature of the 1960s." It was "rooted in the supposed intellectual superiority of American sophistication in matters of 'deterrent theory.'" And it encouraged "the notion that during the SALT I process the US would perforce initiate the Soviet Union into the mysteries of deterrent theory and the complexities of nuclear war."[3]

To general "discomfiture, it soon became apparent that the U.S.S.R.

---

1 Quoted in *The Defense Monitor*, Vol. 12, No. 3 (1983), p. 5. General Andrew J. Goodpaster, President of the Institute for Defense Analyses, adds here: "the Soviet leaders, both military and civilian, are intelligent people, and . . . we are not without a lot of evidence of how they view a great many of their problems, and how they act on them . . ." Letter to this writer, June 22, 1984.

2 Professor Robert C. Tucker might disagree. See his book *The Soviet Political Mind: Studies in Stalinism and Post Stalin Change* (New York: W.W. Norton & Co., 1971).

3 John Erickson, "The Soviet View of Deterrence: A General Survey," *Survival*, Vol. 24, No. 6 (November-December, 1982), p. 242.

needed no tutoring in matters pertaining to war in general and nuclear war in particular." There was "a singular cogency to Soviet strategic thinking and ... [the] Russians did not necessarily think like Americans."[4] Apparently, the impression was not lasting. For Western specialists in strategic theory continued in Professor Erickson's words "to refine their concepts of deterrence into ever more complex (and arcane) theorems, a kind of nuclear metaphysics." And the Russians continued to work "much more closely within classically configured military concepts, inducing at once a much greater degree of military and political realism into what, in American parlance, is termed their 'mind-set.'"

To this day, Western preferences in deterrent thinking are frequently superimposed on the Soviet scene.[5] Many Americans not only continue to believe in their ethnocentric fashion that the Soviets think like they do in matters involving deterrence. But they even go so far as to interpret Soviet weapons programs in terms of a *Western* rationale for such programs.

The process of American misunderstanding of Soviet strategic thought is long established, although it is now subject to some limited change. But, as Professor John Erickson points out, it "has had damaging, not to say dangerous results..."[6] At the very least it has had a deleterious effect on effective arms limitation and arms control. But more importantly, it has led many U.S. officials to exaggerate American "vulnerabilities" and distort Soviet intentions — all within the framework of what Professor Erickson terms a sort of "strategic demonology."

Differing Conceptual Perceptions

To many Western strategic thinkers, Soviet concepts and doctrines of strategic and limited warfare appear strangely simplistic, anecdotal and "soft" in contrast to the "logically impeccable" and "tightly-reasoned" Western theories of deterrence and war-fighting strategies. Generally, they find Soviet military writings to be excessively politicized and historical as well as subordinated to the prevailing values and whims of political elites. In short, their "primitive" and "unsophisticated" approaches tend to exasperate many Western analysts.

4 *Ibid.*
5 Raymond L. Garthoff, a distinguished American scholar and former U.S. Ambassador to Bulgaria, maintains that the Soviets "seek to stabilize and maintain mutual deterrence." See his article "Mutual Deterrence, Parity and Strategic Arms Limitation in Soviet Policy," in Derek Leebaert (ed.), *Soviet Military Thinking* (London: Allen & Unwin, 1981), pp. 92-124. For a critique of Garthoff's view, see Donald G. Brennan, "Commentary," *International Security* (Winter, 1978), pp. 193-98.
6 John Erickson, *opus cit.*, p. 242.

Some of this exasperation is reflected in the commentary of the American editors of the classic Soviet work on *Military Strategy* which was put together by Marshal V.D. Sokolovsky. This volume represented the first major work on strategy by Soviet writers since the 1920s,[7] and it was taken by many in the West as defining the new consensus that had emerged through the post-Stalin debate on nuclear strategy and the more recent arguments with Nikita Khrushchev.[8] The editors of this work write: "Nowhere in this book, as in most Soviet literature as well, are there to be found signs of serious professional interests in concepts like controlled response and restrained nuclear targeting, which have been widely discussed in the West." The editors appear frustrated by the persistent "theme of automacity [sic] of global nuclear war," which they interpret not only as serving to reinforce the credibility of Soviet nuclear retaliation "but also to discourage the United States and its allies from entertaining ideas that ground rules of some sort might be adopted for limiting the destructiveness of a war, should one occur."[9]

This Western exasperation with Soviet strategic thinking is reciprocated. Many Soviet military and political writers dismiss much of Western strategic and limited-war theory as pretentious, pseudo-scientific and even metaphysical.[10] The following statement by G.A. Arbatov, Director of the Institute of U.S.A. and Canadian Studies, is not atypical: "The idea of introducing rules and games and artificial restrictions by agreement seems illusory and untenable. It is difficult to visualize that a nuclear war, if unleashed, could be kept within the framework of rules and would not develop into an all-out war. In fact, such proposals are a demagogic trick designed to reassure public opinion."[11] The authoritative publication, *Marxism-Leninism on War and Army*, puts it this way: It is a "cynical and deliberate falsehood" that "the prudence of the opponents will make it possible to coordinate their nuclear targets against which these weapons should be aimed."[12] A prominent (now deceased) Soviet military theorist, Major General Nikolai Talensky, summarizes a major Soviet school of thought: "When the security

---

7 A. Svechin's *Strategy* was published in 1926.

8 See Lawrence Freedman, *The Evolution of Nuclear Strategy* (New York: St. Martin's Press, 1983), p. 264.

9 The first edition of this book was translated with an introduction by Herbert Dinerstein, Leon Goure and Thomas Wolfe of the RAND Corporation. See *Soviet Military Strategy*, Rand edition (Santa Monica, Calif.: Rand Corporation, 1963), pp. 44-45.

10 Jonathan S. Lockwood, *The Soviet View of U.S. Strategic Doctrine* (New Brunswick, N.J.: Transaction Books, 1983).

11 G.A. Arbatov, *Problemy mira i sotsializma*, No. 2 (February, 1974), p. 46.

12 Marxism-Leninism on War and Army (Moscow: Progress Publishers, 1972), p. 100.

of a state is based on mutual deterrence with the aid of powerful nuclear weapons . . ., it is directly dependent on the goodwill and designs of the other side, which is a highly subjective and indefinite factor."[13]

The Abstract Nature of Western Military Doctrines

Soviet analysts generally find Western strategic sophistries unacceptable on the grounds that politics is in effect subordinated to more narrow technological and bureaucratic imperatives and to the abstract notions of game theory and formal logic. As Marshal Grechko, the former Soviet Minister of Defense, wrote shortly before his death, the "bourgeois military theorists . . . propagate a different viewpoint from that of communist military analysts." Western military theorists "regard war as a mere armed clash between the two sides . . ." In other words, "they emasculate the political content of the concept of war."[14]

One student of Soviet military policy, writing on the differing Soviet and American views of deterrence, notes that American strategic thinkers tend to emphasize the belief that "deterrence stability (hence U.S. security) is best served by a strategic environment of mutual vulnerability. The Soviets reject 'mutual vulnerability' out of hand as an abdication of political responsibility." Benjamin S. Lambeth goes on to point out that Soviet analysts generally dismiss such common Western strategic notions as "demonstration attacks," "Limited nuclear operations" and slow-motion "counterforce duels." Soviet military writers, he says, tend to treat such American conceptualizations of strategic issues "with alternating bemusement, perplexity and sarcasm."[15]

13 N. Talensky, "Anti-Missile Systems and Disarmament," in John Erickson (ed.), *The Military-Technical Revolution: Its Impact on Strategy and Foreign Policy* (New York: Institute for the Study of the USSR, 1966), pp. 225-27. The late Major General Nikolai Talensky was a former editor of the influential military theoretical journal, *Military Thought*, and an outspoken "revisionist." In 1965, he argued: "In our day there is no more dangerous illusion than the idea that thermonuclear war can still serve as an instrument of politics, that it is possible to achieve political aims by using nuclear weapons and still survive." Several Soviet military writers subsequently attacked General Talensky's position. They maintained that while his position was not theoretically wrong, it was practically dangerous because it undercut the rationale for maintaining large military forces. Today, a number of Soviet military writers have made a rather sharp turn toward accepting views like Talensky's which they previously criticized.

14 A.A. Grechko, *The Armed Forces of the Soviet Union* Moscow: Progress Publishers, 1977).

15 Benjamin S. Lambeth, "The Political Potential of Soviet Equivalence," *International Security*, (Fall, 1979), p. 27.

The Status Quo Nature of Deterrence Theory

A major problem the Soviets have with Western deterrence strategies is that they tend to reinforce the territorial *status quo*. As Alexander George and Richard Smoke have written: "deterrence is a policy which, if it succeeds, can only frustrate an opponent who aspires to changing the international status-quo."[16] As the leadership of the Soviet Union, a quasi-revolutionary power, sees things, the *status quo* reflects the interests of the imperialistic West. Thus, it should come as little surprise that the Russians should find pernicious the Western attempt to impose its own rules of the political and strategic game upon socialist countries and on countries in the Third World that are trying to emancipate themselves from colonial or imperialistic shackles.

A recent Rand study has observed that the Soviets pay "no homage whatsoever to the abstract concept of stability" assumed in Western strategic thought under the concept of a *mutual* assured destruction relationship.[17] Other studies have revealed likewise that, generally speaking, the concepts of "equivalence" and "balance" were seen as "unnatural" by the Soviets because they imply "the enshrinement of the status quo, something alien to every known tenet of Soviet political, ideological and historical doctrine."[18] Nowhere in the public record of official Soviet utterances is there any indication that the Soviet leadership has endorsed "essential equivalence" — at least as it is understood by U.S. officials — as the desired endpoint of the SALT process or of Soviet weapons acquisition.

The preferred Soviet formulation is "equal security." This is a far more ambiguous and subjective concept that admits considerably broader and more ambitious definitions of Soviet force requirements than faithful adherence to the more restrictive "essential equivalence" construct allows.[19]

16 Alexander George *et al.*, *Deterrence in American Foreign Policy* (New York: Columbia University Press, 1974).

17 Jack Snyder, *The Soviet Strategic Culture: Implications for Limited Nuclear Operations* (Santa Monica, Calif.: Rand Corporation, 1977), p. 18.

18 Benjamin S. Lambeth, *opus cit.*, p. 28.

19 One of the more thoughtful Soviet writers on military affairs, retired Army Colonel V.M. Kulish, has stated that the ultimate measure of strategic adequacy "is the result of a complicated opposition of forces which is impossible to express in terms of simple qualitative indices, even though it may prove impossible to analyze the balance of forces in the absence of such indices." See his *Military Force and International Relations* (Moscow: Izdatel'stvo Mezhdunarodnye Otnosheniia, 1972), p. 29. One critic would point out here: "Remember that political analyses published in the Soviet Union are never 'value free' research efforts aimed at discovering the 'truth.' Rather, they are always positions intimately related to matters of policy. They are designed more to win debates and bolster policy preferences than to set forth individual perceptions."

The Soviets explicitly disavow any intention to seek "superiority" over the United States.[20] But they have made it clear in the context of SALT and elsewhere that they believe that their unique "geopolitical problems" (namely China and Western Europe) entitle them to compensating forces over and above those required for maintaining just "equal security" with the United States.[21] For obvious reasons, such intimations have failed to elicit much sympathy in official Western circles. But they nevertheless do indicate that to Soviet policy makers, acceptable security genuinely entails not merely "equivalence" with the United States, but a significant *de facto* margin of strategic advantage.[22]

20 The Reagan Administration appears to believe that the Soviet leadership is inexorably committed to the permanent achievement of strategic superiority over the United States. In fact, Ronald Reagan was the first U.S. President to state publicly that "On balance, the Soviet Union does have a definite margin of superiority." However, there is good reason to believe that while the Soviets find themselves comfortably superior to the United States in some categories of power they find themselves distressingly inferior in others. Given the considerable economic resources, technological capabilities and political determination possessed by the U.S. to neutralize any Soviet attempt to acquire a posture of manifest strategic advantage, there is ample cause to doubt whether the Soviet leadership believes it is able to achieve a goal of permanent strategic authority. For an analysis of Soviet respect for American capabilities here see Morton Schwartz, *Soviet Perceptions of the United States* (Berkeley: University of California Press, 1978), p. 165.

21 One U.S. official observes here: "The Soviet claim for equal security against all perceived adversaries combined means they are superior to each one individually." Dimitri K. Simes points out: "Soviet perceptions of their legitimate defense needs may well differ from American views." Many Soviet officials believe that a superpower has and should have the right to act in areas of its perceived national interest. Generally, these officials express a willingness to recognize that the U.S. has this right, but they feel that the United States is unwilling to reciprocate. The prominent "Americanologist" Georgi Arbatov has elaborated on this point: the arguments about what defense needs are legitimate in another country are dubious. No country has the moral or political right to determine what another country's defense needs really are. Each country must do this for itself. The Soviet Union is forced to think seriously about its security and defense in order to meet the challenge by the military potential of the United States and Western Europe and . . . China. . . . It would be interesting to see how those who criticize the Soviet Union would talk about legitimate defense needs if they were in this country's position. Quoted in Burns H. Weston (ed.), *Toward Nuclear Disarmament and Global Security: A Search for Alternatives* (Boulder, Colo.: Westview Press, 1984), p. 8.

22 Benjamin S. Lambeth, "The Political Potential of Soviet Equivalence," *International Security*, (Fall, 1979), p. 26. General Goodpaster: "I believe there is evident in Soviet action a desire for stable security in the sense of avoiding nuclear war as well as nuclear disadvantage in the 'arms race." At the same time, there is no evidence of which I am aware to suggest that they would not be happy to enjoy strategic superiority. Next, although there are numerous Soviet statements express-

Soviet acceptance of the Anti-Ballistic Missile Agreement in 1972 is frequently cited as testimony to some acceptance of the principle of stability governing strategic behavior. However, it is much more probable that the agreement was attractive to the Soviet leadership because superior American ABM technology, plus superior U.S. ABM penetrating technology, would have given the United States a major advantage during the mid to late 1970s. Thus, from the Soviet viewpoint, the 1972 ABM accord was most likely seen as "stabilizing" a process of strategic catchup against a serious risk of reversal. But it did not necessarily imply acceptance of the American principle of stability.[23]

For a long time U.S. strategic thinkers have been relatively sensitive to the potential of technology jeopardizing specific deterrent formulae for achieving stability. The Soviets, too, have generally been sensitive to destabilizing technologies. However, they tend to accept the destabilizing dynamism of technology as an intrinsic aspect of the strategic dialectic. For them, the underlying engine of this dialectic is a political competition not susceptible to stabilization.

The Self-Constrained Nature of Western Doctrines of War

Soviet military analysts are especially critical of Western claims concerning the ability to control, limit and "fine tune" the applications of force inherent in the "counterforce" deterrent strategy. In fact, they seriously question the whole idea of limited nuclear war. As Jack Snyder points out: "If there is little convergence in Soviet and American writing on deterrence, there is even less complementarity in their standards on limited nuclear war."[24]

Generally, Soviet analysts disbelieve claims to omniscience, omnipotence and ubiquity of cool reason and rationality that are implicit in many Western studies on limited war.[25] As one military publication concludes: "To lull the vigilance of the peoples, the U.S. militarists are discussing the pos-

   ing views on the inexorability of escalation from any initial nuclear exchange, however limited, to all-out nuclear war, the evidence is by no means conclusive as to just what they think in this regard or just what they would do. There is a strong strain of Soviet concern over the damage to the Soviet people and territory that would occur as a result of such escalation." Letter, June 22, 1984.
23 See Derek Leebaert (ed.), *Soviet Military Thinking* (London: Allen & Unwin, 1981), pp. 58-59.
24 Jack Snyder, *opus cit.*, p. 19.
25 Roman Kolkowicz, "U.S. and Soviet Approaches to Military Strategy: Theory vs. Experience," *Orbis*, (Summer, 1981), p. 314.

sibility of limiting nuclear war."[26] Soviet writers are skeptical of the notion that prudent opponents will coordinate their nuclear strikes, thus keeping material losses and human suffering at a minimum. For they would have to "rely on the chance that the aggressors will be prudent and will impose certain limits on the use of nuclear weapons."[27]

In the writings of Western strategic theorists, the "counterforce" strategy presupposes certain types of cooperation, coordination and self-denial by the opposing sides. Generally, the Soviets find curious and unrealistic the notion that a nuclear war could remain contained, that it would resist pressures to escalate and that it would come to a conclusion through Schelling's idea of "intra-war bargaining" or compellance, which underpins much of the American writing on limited nuclear war. A survey of official Soviet pronouncements and writings on the "controllability" of escalation and the possibility of limitation in nuclear conflict continues to indicate "no Soviet acceptance of restraint once that threshold has been crossed."[28]

Most importantly from the Soviet perspective, American deterrence doctrine with its increased emphasis on nuclear war-fighting is designed to give legitimacy to nuclear war. By making limited nuclear war more feasible, U.S. policy has the effect of making it "more acceptable." Assessing the gist of U.S. deterrent doctrine, General Secretary Leonid Brezhnev stated in 1980 that it "actually boils down to making the very idea of nuclear war more acceptable, as it were, to public opinion."[29]

Professor Henry Trofimenko, Head of a Department at the Institute of U.S.A. and Canadian Studies, Academy of Sciences of the U.S.S.R., questions the practice of American leaders of ascribing counterforce intentions to the Soviet Union. He says this "now definitely appears to have been a gimmick used by the U.S. strategists to prepare an American public for the announcement of Washington's own counterforce strategy." In this respect, "the American campaign to call attention to the alleged counterforce threat" is nothing more than a "public relations smokescreen." Each time the U.S. Defense Department "intends to strengthen a new component of its forces, or to introduce a new strategy," he says, "it invariably sets about to 'prove' that 'the Soviets have already acquired such a capability,' and hence, that the United States must follow suit . . ."[30]

---

26 Marxism-Leninism on War and Army (Moscow: Progress Publishers, 1972), p. 99.

27 *Ibid.*, p. 100.

28 Benjamin S. Lambeth, *Selective Nuclear Operations and Soviet Strategy* (Santa Monica, Calif.: Rand Corporation, 1975).

29 *Pravda*, August 30, 1980.

30 Henry A. Trofimenko, "Counterforce: Illusion of a Panacea," *International Security*, Vol. 5, (Spring, 1981), pp. 28-49. If counterforce is not the official *policy* of the Soviet Union, as many U.S. officials maintain, it is nevertheless true that the

The Soviet Union, Professor Trofimenko argues, "has emphasized repeatedly that it does not advocate [a] counterforce strategy, as it does not support the first-strike concept."[31] It is "indisputable that [a] counterforce strategy — a strategy of strikes against bomber and submarine bases and against military command and control centers — is an offensive, aggressive strategy," he insists. "All of the so-called Soviet counterforce strategies that are discussed in the U.S. press are strategies imputed to the Soviet Union by American theoreticians who fraudulently like to play out their own counterforce war scenarios on the premise of a 'Soviet attack against the U.S.A.'" This scheme "makes them look more innocent, while, at the same time, they manage to frighten the public at large into loosening their purse-strings for the sake of a new offensive arms build-up."

Trofimenko argues that certain U.S. strategists "ascribe to the Soviet Union the intention to deal the first strike and picture the U.S. *counterforce* strike as merely 'retaliatory.'"[32] However, he points out that "if the bulk of the Soviet strategic forces will be used already in the first strike what is the United States planning to retaliate against?"

"Obviously," Soviet strategic forces "also have components capable of precision strikes against hardened point targets," Trofimenko admits. But "the introduction of such systems into the arsenals of nuclear powers," he claims, "is an inevitable result of qualitative improvements in strategic armaments..."[33]

If Soviet writers like Trofimenko would have Americans take at face

> number of strategic warheads on each side far exceeds the number of significant non-military targets, so that the majority of weapons can be assumed to be aimed at military (i.e., counterforce) targets.

31 Here Trofimenko cites the Declaration adopted by the Summit Anniversary Conference of the Political Consultative Committee of the Warsaw Treaty Member States, which was held in Warsaw in May, 1980. The member states solemnly reaffirmed that they "have never sought and will never seek military supremacy; they have invariably declared for military equivalence being ensured at increasingly lower levels, for lessening and ending military confrontation in Europe. We do not have, never had and will not have a different strategic doctrine, but a defensive one; we did not and will not have any intention to create a first nuclear strike potential." (*Pravda*, May 16, 1980).

32 John Spanier, a former U.S. Foreign Service Officer, writes in his book: "The Soviet Union has thus been building a first-strike or counterforce capability, rather than a second-strike, or retaliatory, counter-city (or economy) force. Its leaders had adopted a 'war fighting' strategy while the United States was thinking only of deterrence. The result is that, instead of war being 'unthinkable,' as Americans proclaimed, it has become 'thinkable' and will be a genuine option for Soviet policy makers by the middle 1980s." See his *Games Nations Play*, 4th ed. (New York: Holt, Rinehart & Winston, 1983), p. 191.

33 Henry Trofimenko, *opus cit.*, p. 30.

value their protestations of innocence for their share of responsibility for the arms race and the deterioration of détente, it is nevertheless true that the Soviet leadership rejects the notion of "limited" nuclear war that is implied in the counterforce deterrent strategy. To a large extent, the Soviet position on this controversial matter is based on the political idea that political objectives — not military goals or the performance of certain weapons systems — determine the scope of war.[34] In addition, the Soviets are skeptical of the kind of American strategic thinking that lies behind the so-called "limited" nuclear war. The Soviets point out that whatever the technical aspects of the weapons involved, American objectives are not unlimited. In fact, the Soviets see the U.S. as employing strategies such as "escalation dominance" in order to maximize "some or other — real or only apparent" — American edge over the U.S.S.R. So no nuclear war operation could be limited in this sense.

The Correlation of Forces Versus the Balance of Power

In the United States and most of the West international relations are seen in the context of the central notion of a "balance of power." To be sure, this core concept of interstate behavior is often disparaged by many academics.[35] But as Henry Kissinger's memoirs reveal, for all its obvious problems it is still generally adhered to by U.S. statesmen. As John Spanier writes, a balance of power is seen as desirable because it is "most likely to deter an attack." By contrast, "possession of disproportionate power might tempt a state to undertake aggression by making it far less costly to gain a predominant position and impose its will upon other states."[36]

If the notion of a power balance underlies much of deterrence thinking in the West, this is not the case in the Soviet Union. There a more subtle concept, known as the *correlation of forces*, acts as the driving force behind much of contemporary Soviet analysis of international affairs. From the perspective of the Kremlin, this idea serves as a tool for measuring the relative capabilities of competing forces or groups of forces. Essentially, it

---

34 Roman Kolkowicz, *opus cit.*, p. 314.

35 As Kenneth N. Waltz writes, the "balance of power is the hoariest concept in the field of international relations. Elaborated in a variety of analyses and loaded with different meanings, it has often been praised or condemned, but has seldom been wholly rejected." See his "International Structure, National Force, and the Balance of World Power," *Journal of World Affairs*, Vol. 21, No. 2 (1967), pp. 215-231.

36 John Spanier, *American Foreign Policy Since World War II*, 9th ed. (New York: Holt, Rinehart and Winston, 1983), p. 2.

is a multifaceted concept. Soviet sources specifically cite numerous socioeconomic, political, ideological, and military factors when the "international correlation of forces" is debated. But other quantitative and qualitative factors are also involved.[37]

Generally, the Soviet leadership undertakes its assessment of the correlation of forces on at least three different levels. These include (1) the global relationship between the capitalist and socialist countries; (2) regional relationships between movements, alliances or other groups of states; and (3) specific relationships between individual countries. Usually when Soviet officials declare that the correlation of forces is shifting in favor of the socialist states, they are stating their view of the long-term trend of the aggregate of global quantitative and qualitative factors. As the Soviets see things, national or regional correlations may *temporarily* move against the Marxist-Leninist tide. However, the overall correlation of forces cannot. This is taken as an article of faith in the U.S.S.R.

Many Soviet commentators maintain that a significant shift in the correlation of forces took place during the Brezhnev era (1964-1982). In the main this shift is linked to the growth of Soviet military capabilities, especially the attainment of strategic nuclear parity with the U.S. According to this view, the attainment by the Soviet Union of strategic parity forced the United States leadership to accept the U.S.S.R. as its military equal. Consequently, these Soviet spokesmen contend that intersystemic competition shifted from the military to socioeconomic, political and ideological planes.

As Brezhnev's close associate — and now General Secretary — Konstantin Chernenko recently put it: "the times of imperialism's omnipotence in international relations, when it could unceremoniously and with impunity throw its weight around in the world . . . have receded irretrievably."[38] As "imperialism" has been tamed, the sense of threat and alienation experienced for decades by the Soviet leadership has lessened somewhat.

From the Soviet perspective, public acknowledgement by the United States of the existence of strategic parity and American recognition of the constraining influence exercised by parity on U.S. foreign policy are as important as parity itself. As G.A. Arbatov, the head of the Institute of the United States and Canada in the Soviet Union, wrote as early as 1972: only in conditions of nuclear parity will American policymakers be com-

---

37 For a detailed discussion of the correlation of forces see Michael J. Deane. "The Soviet Assessment of the 'Correlation of World Forces': Implications for American Foreign Policy," *Orbis* (Fall, 1976), pp. 625-36.

38 Konstantin Chernenko, "Constantly Strengthening the Ties with the Masses," *Sovetskaja Moldaviia*, February 27, 1979, pp. 1-3, in Foreign Broadcast Information Service, *Daily Report: Soviet Union*, Supplement, March 20, 1979, p. 71.

pelled to "adapt to reality" and curb their instinctive resort to military force.[39]

If the Soviets realize that they are no longer number two in the world, this does not mean that they subscribe to the "parity principle" either as a touchstone of their weapons acquisition program or as a preferred basis for nuclear deterrence. As Benjamin S. Lambeth wrote recently: For the Soviets, "parity is less an ultimate goal than a transitory and permissive springboard for testing Western resolve and pursuing whatever additional accreditions of strategic power the structures of SALT and American tolerance will allow."[40]

In the view of some Western analysts, the shift in what the Soviets term the correlation of forces has ideological consequences. Most importantly, it is said to have "lessened" the relevance of Leninism and the "Bolshevik" image of the world.[41] Traditionally, many students of Soviet behavior have operated on the assumption that "the views of the Soviet leaders are so rooted in an unchanging ideology and 'national character' that they are entirely resistant to change.[42] But as important studies by William Zimmerman[43] and Jan Triska and David Finley[44] have documented in detail, the *Weltanschauungen* of Soviet officials — particularly those who have carried major occupational responsibilites for the conduct of foreign policy — have been modified. As Zimmerman concludes from his ten-year study of Soviet scholars work in the major foreign policy institutes, these experts "no longer let Lenin do their thinking," *though they continue to use Lenin to legitimize their arguments.*[45]

---

39 G.A. Arbatov, "Sobytie Vazhnogo mezhdunarodnogo znacheniya" ("An Event of Important International Significance"), *SShA*, No. 8, August, 1972, pp. 3-12.

40 Benjamin S. Lambeth, "The Political Potential of Soviet Equivalence," *International Security* (Fall, 1979), p. 25.

41 See Robert H. Donaldson, "Soviet Conceptions of 'Security,'" in Burns H. Weston (ed.), *Toward Nuclear Disarmament and Global Security: A Search for Alternatives* (Boulder, Colo.: Westview Press, 1984), p. 293.

42 See for instance Nathan Leites, *A Study of Bolshevism*, pp. 25-25, 29. and Richard Pipes, "Détente: Moscow's View" in Pipes (ed.), *Soviet Strategy in Europe*.

43 William Zimmerman, *Soviet Perspectives on International Relations, 1956-1967.*

44 Jan Triska and David Finley, *Soviet Foreign Policy*, especially Chapters 3-4.

45 William Zimmerman, *opus cit.*, p. 287. "It is a very tricky thing," states Ambassador Martin Hillenbrand, "to calculate the role of Marxist-Leninist ideology in Soviet strategic thinking, or to factor in the Soviet proclivity for disinformation in writings directed to the West. Nor does there seem to be much coherence in what one can describe as Soviet views on deterrence and their actual deployment of weapons. The Soviets are surely not so unsophisticated as to suppose that the kinds of weapons they have deployed are not liable to be taken by the U.S. as related to intentions, no matter how much they protest to the contrary. Both

Soviet Emphasis on Deterrence by Denial

Theorists have explained the general American deterrence doctrine in an oversimplified way as *deterrence by punishment*. In Soviet eyes, it reflects an offensive posture and commitment that is both military and political. Moreover, it is directly related to "escalation dominance," which relies on U.S. military superiority. Thus, as the Soviets see it, the U.S.S.R. is to be "deterred" into accepting a situation that basically implies political and global dominance by the United States.

If the American deterrence posture may be explained as deterrence by punishment, by way of contrast the Soviet position is sometimes explained as *deterrence by denial*. Obviously, this is a somewhat oversimplified description. But it does help to distinguish the two policies.[46]

Deterrence by denial is essentially the policy of traditional defense. It is based on the ability of the defender to convince a potential aggressor that his attack will be met by a military response sufficient to prevent him from gaining his objectives. By way of contrast, deterrence by punishment, which hopes to influence an adversary's estimate of possible costs, does not postulate a direct link between the original defense and the response, and might have little effect on his chances for territorial gain.[47]

It should be noted that the terminology used in the Soviet Union to discuss "deterrence" tends to reflect this dichotomy. Thus, in the 1960s and at present, the Western deterrent concept has been defined as *ustrashenie*, which has a clear hint of threatening intimidation. On the other hand, the Soviet stance has been indicated by the word *sderzhivanie*, which conveys a sense of constraining a foe. Frequently, the word "defense" *(oborona)* is used in the context of official Soviet "deterrent" doctrine. On the face of it, this may seem like mere semantic hair-splitting, but this is not the case at all.[48]

> sides protest that they have no war-initiating intentions with respect to the other, but neither side apparently believes this in the case of the putative opponent."

46 General Goodpaster states here: "Denial of gain has for a long time been an important part of my own view regarding deterrence, and I believe I have seen it reflected (as your chapter indicates) on the Soviet side . . . I would add a reminder, as I put it, that the Soviets seek the fruits of war without the costs of war." Letter, June 22, 1984.

47 For more on this distinction see Glenn Snyder, *Deterrence and Defense* (Princeton: Princeton University Press, 1961).

48 Here Professor John Erickson observes: Deterrence as a *concept* has never held much appeal for the Soviet military: the terms *ustrashenie* and *zderzhivanie* are rarely used, while *oborona* (defense) increasingly denotes the "deterrent concept . . . From the outset the Soviet military never accepted the nuclear weapon as an absolute". . . See his "The Chimera of Mutual Deterrence," *Strategic Review* (Spring, 1978), p. 14.

Some authorities have explained the origins of the Soviet view of deterrence on the basis of its experience during the Great Patriotic War (World War II). As a result of the near catastrophe of June 1941, when German armies steamrolled their way across the Soviet Union to the outskirts of Moscow in *Blitzkrieg* fashion, the Soviet leadership has been little inclined to countenance a deterrent strategy which tolerates the absorption of any initial strike. Never again will the Soviet leadership endorse a policy which commits the Soviet Union to remaining inert and then lashing out in punitive response. For such a policy contradicts this historical lesson which remains indelibly marked on the minds of the aged Politburo leadership.

In light of the experience gained in the Second World War, it should not be surprising to learn that the Soviet leadership puts a premium on defense in the first instance. Thus Soviet defense and "deterrence" go hand in hand.[49]

As the Soviet leadership generally sees it, the massive Soviet defense buildup — both active and passive — needs little or no advertising. But it, of course, has been the cause of much misgiving and misunderstanding. Paradoxically, the Soviet interest in taking steps to protect itself (including more than just a passing interest in civil defense planning) has fueled American apprehension that the Soviets were determined to develop a first-strike capability. For their part, many Soviet officials saw in the lack of a defense program in the United States more than just a hint that U.S. policy was basically one that emphasized pre-emptive and even first-strike attack, which would deliver a paralyzing blow that would perforce eliminate any retaliation.

The Soviets are, of course, prepared to wage nuclear war. Indeed, the Soviet leadership regards the capability to wage nuclear war as a crucial element of a visible "deterrent." However, "this does *not* indicate any preference for, or inclination towards, regarding nuclear war as a rational instrument of policy." Even more, Soviet deterrent policies "are designed

---

49 Some Western military strategists have drawn the wrong conclusion from the tremendous Soviet losses in World War II — approximately 7.5 million military personnel and some 12.5 million civilian dead. As Albert Wohlstetter has written: "Russian casualties in World War II were more than 20 million. Yet Russia recovered extremely well from this catastrophe. There are several quite plausible circumstances in the future when the Russians might be quite confident of being able to limit damage to considerably less than this number . . ." See his "The Delicate Balance of Terror," *Foreign Affairs*, Vol. 37, No. 2 (January, 1959). General Thomas S. Power, former Commander of the U.S. Strategic Air Command, puts it more bluntly: "With such grisly tradition and shocking record in the massacre of their own people, the Soviets cannot be expected to let the risk of even millions of Russian lives deter them from starting a nuclear war . . ." See his *Design for Survival* (New York: Coward-McCann, 1964), p. 111.

to minimize the incentives for attacking the USSR and, above all, are aimed at preventing the outbreak of hostilities, 'denial' in an absolute sense."[50]

Thus Soviet "deterrence" rests on Soviet capabilities rather than on enemy rationality or goodwill. It relies on retaining the initiative and is skeptical of scenarios that are "managed," especially when the crisis is, or could be, apocalyptic. In this way, the Soviets display a commitment to "war-denial" in their deterrence policy.

The Soviet concept of deterrence by denial serves several theoretical purposes. First, it would prevent the U.S. from actually initiating hostilities. Second, it would reduce the prospect of the United States making military gains at the expense of the Soviet Union and its allies. (This latter objective may be partly responsible for the Soviet Union's determination to play a global role.) Third, it would ensure the survival of the Soviet system. Finally, through the development of a war-fighting capability it would minimize the incentives for attacking the Soviet Union by guaranteeing a substantial counterstrike.

In summary then, Soviet "deterrence" doctrine may be seen in a positive, active cast. The essence of the policy is not the avoidance of war so much as *preventing it from happening in the first place.* Here the impressive military capability of the U.S.S.R. plays a prominent role. Soviet "deterrence" then is supposed to restrain the imperialists.[51]

The Notion of Mutuality

The notion of "mutuality" or "reciprocity" is very much a part of the American nuclear deterrent doctrine. However, from the Soviet point of view there are some fundamental problems with this concept. To be sure, in one sense there is mutuality of deterrence. That is, Soviet officials — like their American counterparts — recognize that both sides have an overwhelming capability to inflict "unacceptable damage" on each other if nuclear war were initiated. But this realization of political reality should

---

50 John Erickson, *opus cit.,* p. 245. Ambassador Hillenbrand states here: "I think you sometimes engage in hair-splitting, for example where you try to distinguish between the essence of Soviet deterrence and the assumption of enemy rationality. Whether or not the Soviet view of deterrence be called 'deterrence by denial' as distinguished from 'deterrence by punishment,' the underlying assumption must still be of rationality or the whole concept of deterrence collapses." Letter,. June 4, 1984.

51 As G.A. Arbatov, a leading Soviet commentator stated in 1974, "the concept of deterrence itself cannot be defended — it is a concept of 'peace built on terror,' which will always be an unstable and a bad peace." See his "The impasses of the Policy of Force," *Problemy Mira i Sotsializma,* No. 2 (February, 1974).

not be construed as the Soviets "accepting the posture of hostage and thus denying any initiative to the Soviet Union..."[52]

In general, a natural and logical skepticism pervades the Soviet view of MAD. This is partly because the strategy runs counter to the Soviet idea of avoiding having to rely on a potential adversary for Soviet security. But more importantly, Soviet skepticism is due to the fact that they see the notion of mutuality, as it is embodied in "assured destruction" (MAD), as something which is nothing more than a front for what is viewed essentially as an American "counterforce" — and pre-emptive strike — policy.

The reasoning behind Soviet suspicions of the alleged pre-emptive nature of the present U.S. counterforce strategy has been stated authoritatively by Major General R. Simonyan, Director of Military Science. He observed just a few years ago:[53]

Indeed, a power which sets itself the aim of destroying the 'potential enemy's' [strategic] military facilities must [sic] be the first to deliver a strike, because otherwise its nuclear charges will land on empty missile launch silos and airfields. (emphasis added)

Here the Soviets point to the obvious discrepancy between the *declaratory* policy of the United States, which for a long time was "mutual assured destruction" (MAD), and its *action* policy, which was much different. From the Soviet vantage point, the latter policy was designed to increase its counterforce capabilities. Hence the MX missile program, the Trident submarine program and improvements in Western forward based systems (FBS). Generally, the Soviets see all of these developments as calculated to "outflank" the SALT agreements.

The following statement, penned almost ten years ago by two Soviet military writers, provides some insight into how certain military analysts in the U.S.S.R. view nuclear deterrence.[54]

Of course, the concept of 'nuclear deterrence,' which presupposed the existence of enormous nuclear forces capable of 'assured destruction' is not an ideal solution to the problem of peace and the prevention of nuclear conflict.

The authors of the above statement reject such ideas as "acceptable" limited nuclear options, "selective targeting" concepts and the like, which are combined in the U.S. counterforce policy. They maintain that "Prevent-

---

52 John Erickson, *opus cit.*, p. 247.
53 R. Simonyan, "In Search of a New Strategy," *Krasnaya zvezda*, March 19, 1979.
54 Lt. General M.A. Mil'shtein and Colonel L.S. Semeyko, "The Problem of the Inadmissibility of a Nuclear Conflict (on New Approaches in the United States)," *SShA*, No. 11 (November, 1974), p. 4.

ing nuclear war in any of its forms, large or small, and the limitation of the arms race, are the central problems of Soviet-American relations."[55]

Soviet View of Pershing II and Cruise Missile Deployment

A number of discussions in the official Soviet media since these authors wrote have reflected disappointment and concern with the U.S. deterrent position and its increased emphasis on nucelar war fighting. As Secretary General Leonid Brezhnev put it in a speech in May 1977:[56]

I am convinced that not a single statesman, or public figure, or thinking person can avoid his share of responsibility in the struggle against the threat of war, for this means responsibility for the very future of mankind itself. I shall not conceal the fact that our concern over the continuing arms race, including the strategic arms race, has grown in connection with the positions adopted in these matters by the new American Administration.

Brezhnev's remarks and other more recent statements by Soviet military and other leaders indicate a growing Soviet concern over increased U.S. counterforce capabilities but also as to *why* this continued increase in capabilities is being sought. As Raymond L. Garthoff, a senior fellow at the Brookings Institution and a noted expert on Soviet military policy writes, "To be sure, some of these expressions of concern doubtless serve other purposes, such as the argument to support requested Soviet military programs. But many have the ring of sincerity about them and many cite incontrovertible evidence to support their arguments on capabilities . . ."[57]

In the Soviet perception, the United States has continued, SALT and detente notwithstanding, to seek military superiority. Thus, the NATO two-track deployment decision of December 1979 is viewed by Soviet military analysts as another step in this direction. Of course, these officials also see this move as an attempt to tie NATO even more closely into Amer-

---

55 *Ibid.*, p. 9. See also Colonel D. Proektor, "Two Approaches to Military Policy," Novoye vremya, No. 48 (November, 1978). General Goodpaster adds: "I too feel there is evidence to support the Soviet desire to prevent nuclear war. I would add there is also evidence that they want a free hand to pursue adventures in other areas, and to pursue their hostility to Western political-socio-economic systems while the use of nuclear weapons is avoided, or successfully deterred. Somewhere during the past years, the concepts of deterrence advanced by U.S. writers (although not, however, the programs of actual practioners) seem to have become unduly narrow and arcane." Letter, June 22, 1984.

56 L.I. Brezhnev, *Radio Moscow*, May 29, 1977.

57 Raymond L. Garthoff, "Mutual Deterrence, Parity and Strategic Arms Limitation in Soviet Policy," in Derek Leebaert (ed.), *Soviet Military Thinking* (London: Allen & Unwin, 1981), p. 111.

ican strategic nuclear planning while deflecting or diverting Soviet counteraction towards Europe — rather than against the United States itself.

The Soviet objection to this new capability of the NATO allies to strike targets deep inside the Soviet Union is not merely propaganda. It reflects "a real perception and concern," according to Raymond L. Garthoff.[58] We shall cite but one remark from General of the Army Sergei F. Akhromeyev, First Deputy Chief of the General Staff:[59]

The Soviet Union is not setting for itself the task of striving for military superiority over the United States, but it cannot remain indifferent to the increase in US military potential and cannot permit the existing parity of forces to be upset.

Akhromeyev notes that the Pershing II and theater cruise missiles are being deployed so as to make it possible "to destroy targets over a considerable part of Soviet territory — up to the Volga... (Thus the) Soviet Union must regard them as weapons of strategic significance." Finally, he says, such "actions automatically call for reflection as to whether they accord with the aims of the negotiations and agreements on limiting strategic offensive arms."[60]

In this context, the newly deployed intermediate-range-nuclear Pershing II is regarded as a pre-emptive, counterforce weapon. The Soviets note that it substantially surpasses the capabilities of the Pershing I and is capable of destroying not only ICBM sites but also centers of command and control. However, what disturbs Soviet officials most is the short flight time of the missile which nullifies any Soviet resort to launch under warning or even launch under attack.

Thus the Pershing II together with the ground-launched cruise missiles heighten the Soviet sense of vulnerability. As the Soviets see things, the ongoing deployment of these weapons amount to an American push for superiority *tout court*. But they also represent the attempt, from the Soviet viewpoint, to implement a "Eurostrategic" strategy of limited nuclear war. Thus, in the European context, a so-called "Eurostrategic" nuclear war might be pursued which would leave the Soviet Union open to attack but which would give sanctuary to the United States.

58 Raymond L. Garthoff, "Mutual Deterrence, Parity and Strategic Arms Limitation in Soviet Policy," in Derek Leebaert (ed.), *Soviet Military Thinking* (London: Allen & Unwin, 1981), p. 118.

59 Sergei F. Akhromeyev, "Dangerous US Aspirations to Nuclear Supremacy," *Horizont* (East Germany), No. 3, January, 1980, p. 3. This article is based on a *Novosti* interview which was originally issued on December 24, 1979 in Moscow.

60 *Ibid.* See also G. Dadyants, "Operation Pershing II," *Sotsialisticheskaya industriya*, October 19, 1979; Lt. General N.F. Chervov and V. Zagladin on *Radio Moscow*, Domestic Service, October 20, 1979; and Colonel L. Semeyko, "Where 'Eurostrategy' is Aiming," *Krasnaya zvezda*, October 28, 1979.

Figure 4: *Cape Canaveral, Florida — The US Army launches a Pershing II missile on a long-range flight down the Eastern Test Range at 2:55 p.m. EST. This is the eighth test flight in the Pershing II engineering and development program and the fifth flight from the Cape Canaveral Air Force Station.*

Given this view of the situation in Europe, the Soviets responded to the Pershing II and cruise missile deployment in a predictable way. They sent the message to Washington that recourse to limited war would produce general war. And they let the West Europeans know that recourse to a limited war would mean the end of Europe.

Summary

As we have seen, one does not need to accept at face value official Soviet protestations of innocence regarding their share of responsibility for the arms race and the deterioration of detente, nor their accusations of American culpability, in order to realize that the Soviet perception of nuclear developments differs significantly from our own. To be sure, both Soviet and American approaches in the nuclear era *appear* to be similar. For instance, the military technologies employed by the two sides are similar. Each side generally understands the quantitative and qualitative aspects of the weapons systems of the other side. And both superpowers have been engaged in protracted diplomatic and technical negotiations on strategic arms limitations, with certain mutually acceptable results. Yet the differences between American and Soviet doctrinal views on the role of strategic forces, once largely ignored or dismissed by most Western analysts, are very real. Essentially, they boil down to a fundamental divergence in outlook between U.S. and Soviet elites on the nature of the modern nuclear predicament and the requirements for successfully dealing with it in terms of national security and foreign policy. Within this context, there is a sharp divergence in view over the controversial notion of nuclear deterrence which, from the Soviet vantage point, attempts to compel the U.S.S.R. to follow a foreign policy behavior to the likings of Washington.

In the main, the disparity in doctrine is due to the asymmetrical nature of the two belief systems and different cultural, historical and political influences.[61] American and Soviet views are neither strategically nor politically comparable quantities — except in particular and carefully defined senses. There is no indication that they have identical strategic aims or similar nuclear weapons policies.

Historically, nuclear deterrence was politically attractive to a conservative power like the United States which possessed a vested interest in preserving the post-war *status quo*. The doctrine seemed advantageous to a state with

61 Roman Kolkowicz, Director of the Center for International and Strategic Affairs at the University of California, puts it this way: "We are dealing with two orthodoxies, mutually exclusive by their nature, each claiming a monopoly on scientific truth." Kolkowicz, *opus cit.*, p. 119.

far-flung economic interests and designs and enjoying strategic superiority. Indeed, the policy appeared ideal for dealing with a troublesome and dangerous, but weaker, adversary by making harsh threats of punishment in order to appeal to a bully's sense of survival.[62]

At its heart, Soviet strategy is a strategy of both confrontation and negotiation. Its conceptual underpinning is provided by the concept of the changing correlation of forces, a more subtle variation of the "balance of power" notion. Basically, Soviet strategy rejects the stark choice provided by the American emphasis on deterrence — either stable peace or nuclear incineration.

Soviet officials have adopted a strategy that appears suitable for a quasi-revolutionary power whose particular interests lie in changing the international *status quo*. It seems a proper strategy for a state that emerged on the international scene after the Second World War as a strategic inferior and whose historical tradition favors the brute force of massed armies, guided primarily by continental strategies of defense and possessing a defensive coastal navy. Furthermore, it appears appropriate for a country having little experience in massive projection of its forces beyond the Eurasian land mass. Soviet strategy appears advantageous, also, to a country with universal ideological and global political interests and aspirations. Moreover, it seems attractive to a state that is not in a hurry, believing that history and time are on its side.

It is clear from this discussion that there is a serious lag in Western, particularly American, appreciation for the Soviet view of nuclear deterrence. Too many U.S. military analysts still evaluate Soviet doctrine using sources which, if not actually outmoded, have become passé. Of particular note here is the stylized recourse to Marshal Sokolovky's *Military Strategy*, which was first published over twenty-two years ago. This book shows Soviet military recognition of the emergence of mutual deterrence (as well as an equivocal and changing view on its public embrace.) Indeed, in the first edition, which appeared in 1962, there is even a passage which not only attributes the concept to Western strategists and leaders, but also endorse it. However, Soviet military doctrine and its view of deterrence have evolved since the early 1960s.

The authority that Western analysts attribute to Soviet military writings, naturally enough, shapes their ensuing conclusions about Soviet intentions. This is particularly true in the debate in Western circles over the role of war-fighting in Soviet nuclear planning. Already in 1959, Lt. General James Gavin described the classic work of Clausewitz as the Rosetta Stone to un-

62 "I would note," says General Goodpaster, "that some in the U.S. had hoped that 'deterrence' could deter much more than Soviet nuclear attack, war in Europe, or Soviet tactics of threat and bullying." Letter, June 22, 1984.

derstanding Soviet military thinking. This is a metaphor that unfortunately has been used many times since. Gavin, among others, argues that the Soviet conception of both nuclear and conventional force is intertwined with the famous proposition by Clausewitz that war is the continuation of politics by other means. However, the situation is much more complicated than this simplistic portrayal would have us believe.

This preoccupation with outdated source material has contributed in large part to lack of official U.S. recognition that Soviet realism and adherence to military orthodoxy has led to the development of a persistent skepticism towards the "metaphysics" of deterrence. This is particularly true as it finds expression in the present nuclear war-fighting policy of the Reagan Administration, which was largely justified on grounds that the Soviets had moved toward the development of an extended counterforce strategy. Actually, the Soviets do not generally favor a deterrent posture that views nuclear war as a "rational" instrument of policy — or a process that is "winnable." Why should they? Soviet acknowledgement of limited war scenarios would mean in effect conceding the results of American nuclear advantage, thereby subjecting themselves to nuclear blackmail.

In general, the role of military power is seen from the Soviet point of view as a major instrument in impressing on the "imperialist camp" that military means cannot solve the historical struggle between the two opposing social systems. Moreover, the Soviets want to be able to reduce — if not actually eliminate — the prospect of military gain that could be obtained at the expense of the "socialist camp." While U.S. analysts fret over Soviet military advantages, the undertone in Soviet writings is different. The Soviet Union may no longer be number two. But it is still the United States that shapes the terms of the competition between the superpowers. To put this in the context of deterrence theory, it may be said somewhat simplistically that the Soviet position is one of "deterrence by denial." This contrasts sharply with "deterrence by punishment," which is practiced by the U.S.

To be sure, the Soviet leadership regards the capability to wage nuclear war *(in terms of military preparation)* as a crucial element of its visible "deterrent." But this does not reflect any preference, or inclination, to regard nuclear war as a rational instrument of policy. In short, Soviet "deterrent" policies are designed to minimize the incentives for attacking the U.S.S.R. but, above all, to prevent the outbreak of hostilities. Thus denial becomes a very real function of Soviet "deterrent" strategy. The following statement by the late Major General Nikolai A. Talensky of the U.S.S.R. remains as true today as when he wrote it in the 1960s:[63]

63 N.A. Talensky, "Anti-Missile Systems and Disarmament," in John Erickson (ed.), *The Military-Technical Revolution* (New York: Praeger, 1966), p. 227.

History has taught the Soviet Union to depend mainly on itself in ensuring its security and that of its friends . . . After all, when the security of a state is based only on mutual deterrence with the aid of powerful nuclear rockets it is directly dependent on the goodwill and designs of the other side, which is a highly subjective and indefinite factor.

SECTION II
THE NUCLEAR DETERRENCE STRATEGIES OF NATO

> And therefore I would say — what I might not say in office — that our European allies should not keep asking us to multiply strategic assurances that we cannot possibly mean or if we do mean, we should not want to execute because if we execute, we risk the destruction of civilization.
>
> Henry Kissinger, 1979

VII. THE EVOLUTION OF NATO'S NUCLEAR DEFENSE

The U.S. deterrent policy has been an integral part of NATO's military strategy virtually from the inception of the Alliance in 1949. This chapter attempts to put NATO nuclear strategy in historical perspective. Specifically, it seeks to answer the following questions: (1) How did nuclear weapons become a permanent feature of NATO's strategy? and (2) What role has nuclear deterrence played in the Alliance? An analysis of these issues will help set the scene for the discussions which follow on "no first use" of nuclear weapons and the 1979 "dual track" NATO decision to station Pershing IIs and cruise missiles in Europe.

The Early Postwar Period

One of NATO's earliest tasks was to arrive at estimates of the size of Soviet conventional forces and the nature of the threat from the East. This analysis, which is continually updated, served as the basis for developing NATO's military strategy and force structure.[1]

At the end of World War II, Western military planners concluded (erroneously we now know) that the Soviet Union could muster as many as 175 divisions against Western Europe.[2] In order to mount a credible defense,

---

1 For details see Lawrence Freedman, *The Evolution of Nuclear Strategy* (New York: St. Martin's Press, 1983), p. 283.
2 For a valuable brief history of NATO's conception of the role of nuclear weapons see J. Michael Legge, *Theater Nuclear Weapons and the NATO Strategy of Flexible Response* (Santa Monica: RAND Corporation, 1983).

NATO strategists decided that the Alliance would require 96 of its own divisions. This estimate was formally accepted by the NATO ministers in February 1952 at their annual meeting in Lisbon.

As things turned out, the members of NATO were unwilling to meet these so-called "Lisbon force goals." Michael Howard of Oxford University explains: "In the judgment of the political leaders of Western Europe, the danger of the Soviet military attack did not appear great enough to warrant the costs involved in building up the kind of defensive forces that, on a purely military calculus, would be needed to deter it."[3]

Instead, the Alliance deliberately turned to nuclear weapons as a substitute for the sacrifices in financial and manpower support that would have been necessary for the deployment of an adequate conventional defense. The long-term implications of depending upon weapons of mass destruction for national security apparently concerned only a politically insignificant minority.[4]

Some of the early criticisms of the NATO decision to rely primarily on nuclear weapons to forestall Soviet conquest of Europe are largely forgotten today. But they bear upon the current state of nuclear defense. For instance, in one of the earliest articles concerning nuclear defense in Europe, which appeared in 1949, General Omar N. Bradley, then Chairman of the Joint Chiefs of Staff, was very critical of a nuclear defense of Western Europe:[5] *This train of thought represents so much compound folly that it is hard to answer it patiently . . . It foolishly assumes that the atom bomb is omnipotent. It fails to explain how, if some millions of invader troops moved into Western Europe and were living off the country, we could use the bomb against them without killing ten friends for every enemy foe.*

General Bradley's recognition that nuclear defense could entail the destruction of Western Europe was an early surfacing of an intractable dilemma that lasts through today. Perhaps surprisingly, the West Europeans themselves did not fully appreciate the implications of nuclear defense. Opinion polls taken in West Germany in the early 1950s indicated that the public there believed Soviet aggression was *not* deterred by America's nuclear arsenal but by the fear of the industrial mobilization capability of the United States.[6] But this belief was to change considerably as the new

3   Michael Howard, "Reassurance and Deterrence: Western Defense in the 1980s," *Foreign Affairs* (Winter, 1982-83), p. 312.
4   For the importance of budgetary considerations in the decision by NATO to rely on nuclear weapons see the statement by then Secretary of State John Foster Dulles in Department of State *Bulletin,* January 25, 1954, p. 108.
5   *The Saturday Evening Post,* October 15, 1949.
6   Hans Speier, *German Rearmament and Atomic War* (Evanston, Ill.: Row, Peterson & Co., 1957), pp. 112-113, 132-140.

Western Europe, NATO, and the Warsaw Pact

Of all overseas regions, Europe remains the most important to the security of the United States. The United States is firmly committed to NATO (Map I-3) and maintains strong forward-deployed forces in Europe and the adjacent seas as evidence of its determination to do whatever is necessary to deter attacks on the Alliance or restore allied territorial integrity in the event of aggression. The security of NATO depends on the ability of the United States and its allies to maintain a full range of conventional and nuclear forces. To maintain a credible conventional defense capability, the Alliance must be able to reinforce forward-deployed forces rapidly and apply its significant advantages in resources, technology, and cohesion productively. Chapter IV contains a detailed discussion of the military balance in Europe.

Middle East and Southwest Asia

US strategic interests in the Middle East and Southwest Asia center on oil resources. The United States is committed to regional stability and the reduction of tensions that carry risks of wider involvement by the major oil producing countries.

WESTERN EUROPE, NATO AND THE WARSAW PACT

NATO   WARSAW PACT

* DOES NOT PARTICIPATE IN INTEGRATED MILITARY STRUCTURE

AS OF 1 JANUARY 1984

MAP I-3

Source: Joint Chiefs of Staff, United States Military Posture FY 1985.

Eisenhower Administration came to emphasize the strategy of "massive retaliation."

Implementation of "Massive Retaliation"

In support of the NATO decision, President Eisenhower issued a directive known within the U.S. government as NSC-162/2. Basically, this "Top Secret" National Security Council document ordered the Joint Chiefs of Staff to plan on using nuclear weapons whenever it would be to the American advantage to do so. Subsequently, radical changes were made in the organization and plans of the U.S. Army so that it would be better able to fight on a nuclear battlefield. By late 1953, the first tactical nuclear weapons were deployed in Europe. These included substantial numbers of artillery shells, bombs, short-range missiles and nuclear mines. Just as the French government decided in the 1930s to release films of the Maginot Line for deterrent effect, so was there a great deal of television, newspaper and magazine publicity surrounding the deployment of these tactical nuclear weapons by the U.S. Army.

The first nuclear weapon deployed on the European continent by the U.S. Army was the 280-millimeter "Long Tom" atomic cannon, which reached Bremerhaven, West Germany in October 1953. It was a cumbersome weapon whose symbolic value far exceeded its military capability, as Premier Khrushchev later found out after the Soviets had produced some of their own. This buildup of NATO tactical nuclear weapons continued steadily, peaking in the mid-1960s at around 7,000 weapons. (In the early 1980s, this number was unilaterally cut by one thousand as some old systems were phased out.)[7] Although large numbers of conventional forces were retained on the continent until the early 1960s, their main purpose then was twofold: to contain an attack long enough for nuclear strikes to defeat a potential aggressor and to convince the Europeans that the United States was committed to defend them.

If there were any doubts about NATO's policy of relying primarily on nuclear weapons in the 1950s, they should have been dispelled in late 1954 when General Bernard Montgomery, the Deputy Supreme Allied Commander in Europe, said:[8]

---

7 "In 1983," says one U.S. government insider, "NATO also agreed to withdraw another 1,400 warheads over the next several years on a unilateral basis. Both the 1,000 and 1,400 are in addition to the one-to-one warhead exchange for the Pershing IIs and ground-launched cruise missiles."

8 Quoted in Robert E. Osgood, *NATO: The Entangling Alliance* (Chicago: University of Chicago Press, 1962), p. 110.

I want to make it absolutely clear that we at SHAPE are basing all our operational planning on using atomic and thermonuclear weapons in our own defense. With us it is no longer: They may possibly be used. It is very definitely: They will be used, if we are attacked.

By December 1954, the NATO ministers apparently felt comfortable enough with the nuclear strategy to reduce their force level objective from 96 to 30 active divisions. Two years later, the Alliance formally adopted the policy of "massive retaliation" in a secret document known as MC 14/2. In this way NATO forces came not to be built *around* nuclear arms; instead, nuclear arms were built *into* traditional military organization. This is the main way in which theater nuclear weapons differ from strategic nuclear forces.

If the *general* defensive policy of NATO during the 1950s was based on the primacy of nuclear weapons, the *tactical* situation on the ground in the late 1950s was more complicated than the policy would suggest. The Supreme Allied Commander in Europe (SACEUR), General Lauris Norstad, introduced the idea of a "pause," which modified the overall policy. Under this concept, a Soviet invasion of Western Europe would be met initially by non-nuclear resistance. But this would only be a short duration — just long enough to test Soviet intentions and afford the Soviet leadership an opportunity to draw back from the brink before NATO ignited the nuclear fires.[9]

A Change to "Flexible Response"

It is, of course, debatable whether or not the balance of forces between the Warsaw Pact and NATO, as it was developing during the mid-1950s, provided adequate justification for NATO's adoption of this nuclear strategy. In any case, after John F. Kennedy took office in January 1961, he ordered a detailed study of the strengths and weaknesses of the policy of "massive retaliation." This investigation revealed two major deficiencies in the reasoning behind the adoption of MC 14/2. In the first place, the relative balance between NATO and Warsaw Pact conventional forces was far less unfavorable from a Western perspective than had been thought; the power of Soviet forces, in particular, had been overestimated.[10] In the second

---

9 See William W. Kaufmann, *The McNamara Strategy* (New York: Harper & Row, 1964), pp. 102-34.

10 A book by two assistants to Secretary McNamara states: [B]y 1965, we knew that a Soviet division force cost only about a third that of a US division force, had only about a third as many men, and (we had strong reason to believe) was only about one-third as effective. . . . In short, eliminating paper divisions, using cost

place, there was great uncertainty whether nuclear weapons could be utilized to the best advantage of NATO, and if so, in what manner.

Determined to avoid relying on a policy that stressed the early use of nuclear weapons, President Kenndy authorized then Secretary of Defense Robert McNamara to propose a substitute. This McNamara did at a classified meeting of the NATO ministers in Athens in May 1962.[11] His suggestion, which had the endorsement of the President, was to replace the existing doctrine of "massive retaliation" with the strategy of "flexible response."

As McNamara recalls: "The new strategy required a buildup of NATO's conventional forces, but on a scale that we believed to be practical on both financial and political grounds." Instead of the early massive use of nuclear weapons, "it permitted a substantial raising of the nuclear threshold by planning for the critical initial response to Soviet aggression to be made by conventional forces alone." (This assumed, of course, that the initial Warsaw Pact attack was non-nuclear.) The strategy was "based on the expectation that NATO's conventional capabilities could be improved sufficiently so that the use of nuclear weapons would be unnecessary." But, under the new doctrine "even this expectation turned out to be false. Any use of nuclear weapons would be 'late and limited.'"[12]

McNamara remembers that his "proposal of the new strategy was the result of the recognition by U.S. civilian and military officials that NATO's [then] vastly superior nuclear capabilities, measured in terms of numbers of weapons, did not translate into usable military power." Moreover, "we understood that the initial use of even a small number of strategic or tactical nuclear weapons implied risks which could threaten the very survival of the nation." Consequently, "we, in effect, proposed confining nuclear weapons to only two roles in the NATO context:

— *deterring the Soviets' initiation of nuclear war;*

> and firepower indexes, counts of combat personnel in available divisions, and numbers of artillery pieces, trucks, tanks and the like, we ended up with the same conclusion: NATO and the Warsaw Pact had approximate equality on the ground. Where four years earlier it had appeared that a conventional option was impossible, it now began to appear that perhaps NATO could have had one all along. See Alain C. Enthoven and K. Wayne Smith, *How Much is Enough? Shaping the Defense Program 1961-1969* (New York: Harper & Row, 1971), Chapter 4.

11 McNamara's address, entitled "Remarks by Secretary McNamara, NATO Ministerial Meeting, 5 May 1962, Restricted Session," was declassified on August 17, 1979. For a discussion see David N. Schwartz, *NATO's Nuclear Dilemmas* (Washington, D.C.: The Brookings Institution, 1983), pp. 156-165.

12 Robert S. McNamara, "The Military Role of Nuclear Weapons: Perceptions and Misperceptions," *Foreign Affairs*, Vol. 62, No. 1 (Fall, 1983), pp. 63-64.

— as a weapon of last resort, if conventional defense failed, to persuade the aggressor to terminate the conflict on acceptable terms.[13]

The policy of "flexible response" has remained the official deterrent doctrine of NATO for more than fifteen years. It was officially accepted by NATO in 1967 as outlined in the Military Committee (MC) 14/3 document.[14] Its essential element, however, as McNamara notes, "has never been achieved." This is the development of sufficient conventional capabilities to offset those of the Warsaw Pact. Indeed, during the late 1960s and early 1970s, the Alliance may even have fallen further behind its opponent as a result of a Soviet military buildup and the weakening of U.S. forces in Europe during the Vietnam War.[15]

In more recent years NATO has made considerable strides in improving its conventional posture, but many military experts in the West believe the conventional balance in Europe continues to favor the Warsaw Pact. Some Western analysts thus conclude that a Warsaw Pact attack with conventional forces would require the use of nuclear weapons, most likely within a very short time. The former operational war plans of NATO reflected this belief, as Harland Cleveland, formerly U.S. Ambassador to NATO, reveals. As he points out, the substantial raising of the nuclear threshold, as was envisioned by "flexible response," has not become a reality.[16]

A Joint NATO Nuclear Force?

Proposals for a jointly controlled NATO nuclear force were put forth in Europe in the late 1950s. But they elicited only a perfunctory response from the United States. However, the Skybolt controversy of December 1962 triggered a series of events that made it seem likely that U.S. officials might respond positively to such a proposal if it were brought up again.[17]

---

13 Robert S. McNamara, *opus cit.*, p. 64.

14 See Colin S. Gray, "NATO Defense and Arms-Reduction Proposals," *Military Review*, Vol. 63, No. 10 (October, 1983), p. 63. According to Gray, MC-14/3 is "one of the great ambiguous documents of all times." He says it was "designed to satisfy every major interest in the alliance that needed to be satisfied for peacetime acquiesence." To translate "very freely indeed, MC-14/3 says that NATO will seek to hold a Warsaw Pact invasion with conventional forces. Should that fail, nuclear weapons will be employed within the theater, and, should that fail to dissuade, then strategic nuclear forces will intervene."

15 See General Bernard W. Rogers, "Enhancing Deterrence — Raising the Nuclear Threshold," a presentation to the ministerial session of the Defense Planning Committee at NATO Headquarters on December 1, 1982.

16 Personal conversation with Harland Cleveland, Fall, 1983.

17 The "Skybolt controversy" concerned a two-stage ballistic missile being developed

Subsequently, the proposal for the creation of a multilateral force of nuclear-armed ships with integrated crews drawn from the NATO membership was put forth by the U.S. and debated for a number of years. The West German government under Chancellor Ludwig Erhard, in particular, expressed considerable interest in participating in a multilateral nuclear force (MLF). Washington, which hoped that the MLF would vitalize NATO and harness nuclear proliferation by preserving the "nuclear centralization" of the Western Alliance, also gave it initially a great deal of support.[18]

However, as military planners eventually discovered, the MLF idea did not make much military sense. (President Kennedy himself viewed it as a fake.)[19] Moreover, its anticipated political value turned out to be even more doubtful. This was because in reality European control-sharing in a nuclear force would not have been increased substantially had the MLF idea been implemented. U.S. officials would still control the buttons. Moreover, though Bonn had shown an early interest in the collective nuclear force concept and later became its only real enthusiastic European supporter, the MLF program was designed in part not to satisfy but to forestall the alleged desire of West Germany to become a nuclear power.

Eventually, the proposal for a multilateral force was replaced by the assignment of U.S. Polaris submarines to NATO. This step was followed by the creation in Brussels of an interallied Nuclear Planning Group.[20] How-

jointly by the United States and the United Kingdom. After extensive cost-effectiveness evaluations, Washington decided to scrap the project, which meant, in effect, the British would either have to abandon plans for an independent nuclear capability or develop the Skybolt on its own at very high cost. "The British already had an independent nuclear capability on a small scale," interjects Ambassador Martin J. Hillenbrand. "Skybolt was needed, the British thought, to modernize their delivery capability." Letter to this writer, June 4, 1984.

18 A comprehensive account of the debate leading up to this proposal may be found in T.C. Wiegele, "The Origins of the MLF Concept, 1957-1960," *Orbis* (Summer, 1968). "The MLF was initially an American proposal in response to what the U.S. felt was a European psychological need to have a finger on the trigger," affirms Ambassador Martin Hillenbrand. "We tried to sell it to the Europeans."

19 Wolfram F. Hanrieder et al., *The Foreign Policies of West Germany, France, and Britain* (Englewood Cliffs, N.J.: Prentice-Hall, Inc., 1980), p. 13. "I don't believe 'fake' is the right word," states Ambassador Hillenbrand. "After all, Kennedy knew his own government was pushing it. The President doubted that the MLF would serve a suitable military purpose, but accepted that it was psychologically desirable." Letter to this writer, June 4, 1984.

20 NATO established the Nuclear Planning Group in December 1966. It was designed in the main to provide a forum in which non-nuclear alliance members could share information and participate in nuclear planning and decisionmaking. It consisted of four standing members (the United States, the United Kingdom, Italy and West Germany), three to four rotating members drawn from the other NATO members

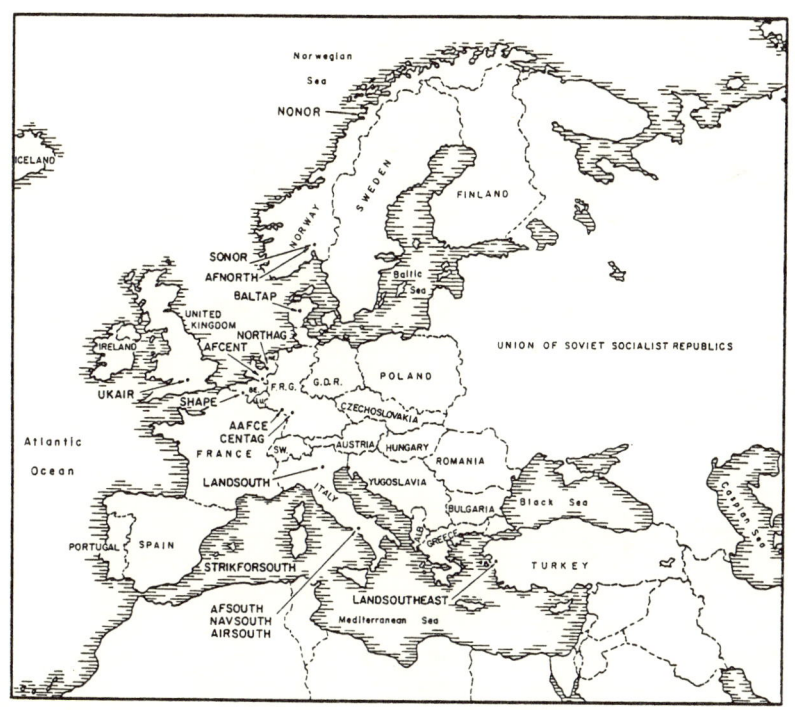

ALLIED COMMAND EUROPE

SUPREME HEADQUARTERS ALLIED POWERS EUROPE   SHAPE

ALLIED FORCES NORTHERN EUROPE	AFNORTH	**ALLIED FORCES SOUTHERN EUROPE**	AFSOUTH
Allied Forces Baltic Approaches	BALTAP	Allied Land Forces Southern Europe	LANDSOUTH
Allied Forces North Norway	NONOR	Allied Land Forces Southeast Europe	LANDSOUTHEAST
Allied Forces South Norway	SONOR	Allied Naval Forces Southern Europe	NAVSOUTH
ALLIED FORCES CENTRAL EUROPE	AFCENT	Allied Air Forces Southern Europe	AIRSOUTH
Northern Army Group	NORTHAG	Naval Striking and Support Forces Southern Europe	STRIKFORSOUTH
Central Army Group	CENTAG		
Allied Air Forces Central Europe	AAFCE	**UNITED KINGDOM AIR FORCES**	UKAIR

ever, not much else was accomplished in the nuclear field in Western Europe until the 1970s.

In both the 1950s and 1960s, NATO kept itself together more by mutual political confidence than by plausible nuclear war-fighting plans. The situation became somewhat acute in the 1970s, as succeeding American administrations gave impetus to new doctrine and new deployments, one result of which was to increase fear of nuclear war in Europe, and even of American officials as its possible initiators.

Before turning to the arguments that have been raised for and against the present "first use" policy, we would do well to take a close look at the conventional balance. For any decision one way or the other seems to be closely related to how this balance is perceived.

The Question of Conventional Superiority

There is a great deal of controversy about the actual numbers and what they mean in the debate over the conventional balance of forces in Europe. Most official U.S. and NATO sources give the impression of a tremendous disparity in forces between the Warsaw Pact and NATO.[21] While such an imbalance may exist, it is by no means as great as Western publics are often led to believe. A lot depends on what one chooses to emphasize.

In the spring of 1982, NATO headquarters in Brussels published a booklet entitled *NATO and the Warsaw Pact: Force Comparisons*. This booklet was introduced by Joseph Luns, the NATO Secretary General, who pointed out that "the numerical balance of forces has moved slowly but steadily in favor of the Warsaw Pact over the past two decades. During this period the members of the North Atlantic Alliance have lost much of the technological advantage which permitted NATO to rely on the view that quality could compensate for quantity."

Despite Luns's statement in his introduction that this publication was "factual, objective, and unbiased" in presentation, any such assessment can hardly be "objective," as critics have noted, since it is made up of facts

which would serve terms of nine to eighteen months. The Secretary General of NATO would act as Chairman.

"Today," one U.S. official says, "all NATO states but Iceland are permanent members."

21 Former NATO Commander Alexander M. Haig, Jr. writes in his memoirs, for instance, that "It is common knowledge that the U.S.S.R. and the Warsaw Pact have always enjoyed a very large numerical superiority over NATO in conventional military forces." See his *Caveat: Realism, Reagan, and Foreign Policy* (New York: Macmillan, 1984), p. 224.

bolstered by prejudices which are assembled toward a particular end. This end has traditionally been to minimize the impact of one's own forces while maximizing the impact of those of the enemy.

Most Pentagon reports on the conventional balance in Europe, which are released for public consumption, portray Warsaw Pact divisions as equivalent or near equivalent to Soviet divisions. They also generally fail to take into account that fact that Soviet divisions are substantially smaller than U.S. divisions. (U.S. divisions average about 18,300 soldiers, whereas Soviet divisions average about 14,000.) Finally, despite the CIA discovery back in the 1960s that many of the 175 divisions the Pentagon then ascribed to the Warsaw Pact forces only existed on paper, a 173-division figure still keeps cropping up in U.S. public documentation of the threat from the East.

In June 1984, NATO published a new study that indicates that in the past the Alliance has exaggerated the numerical superiority of Warsaw Pact forces in Europe. On announcing this study, Luns said the rules for counting had been changed to give "a more complete picture of those land forces which could actually be brought to bear" in an East-West war. The number of Warsaw Pact divisions in Europe reinforced by rapidly deployable forces was revised to 115, compared with 173 given in the 1982 study. The number of NATO divisions was increased from 84 to 88. The new balance was reportedly calculated by excluding Soviet forces that would not be available immediately because of a low state of readiness or distance from the area of dispute.[22]

The Warsaw Pact nations insist that the total number of their forces is 815,000 ground troops, However, NATO says the total is 960,000 or almost 18 percent higher. Most of the difference is accounted for by Soviet manpower. According to NATO, there is 530,000; by the Warsaw Pact's count, the figure is 446,000.[23]

NATO has some 790,000 ground troops in the comparable area of West Germany, Luxembourg, the Netherlands and Belgium. Of the total, about 195,000 are Americans.

In counting NATO forces, it is important to note that the two French divisions and supporting troops stationed in West Germany (nearly 50,000 strong) are not included in official NATO figures.[24] (The same is true for

22 See *The International Herald Tribune*, June 22, 1984.
23 According to the highly respected *Defense Monitor*, "NATO leads the Warsaw Pact in total manpower in uniform, total ground forces, and total ground forces in Europe." Altogether, the "Warsaw Pact has 253 active divisions and NATO has the equivalent of 143 divisions when independent brigades are included." See *The Defense Monitor*, Vol. 11, No. 6 (1982).
24 One NATO official notes here: "Many people forget that in the 1970s Secretary

those forces belonging to Spain, which joined NATO in 1982.) Although technically a NATO member, France since 1966 has refused to allow its forces to be integrated into the NATO command structure.[25] If the entire French army were included, the number of NATO forces would be higher than that of the Warsaw Pact forces.[26] (Under President François Mitterand, French military doctrine has shifted from a narrow Gaullist definition based on a defense of national territory to a wider one that includes protection of the eastern borders of West Germany in the event of a Warsaw Pact invasion.)

The case of Spain is interesting. Spain joined NATO in May 1982 with a center-right government in power. The opposition Socialists vehemently attacked this decision and were elected that October on a program which included an essentially anti-NATO stance. Pending a promised referendum on membership, they froze integration into NATO's military structure.

Shortly before taking office, Prime Minister Felipe Gonzalez stated in an interview: "We have never been opposed to NATO. What we are against is Spain's joining NATO."[27] Since 1982, his public comments have followed a graceful arc. He has noted that Spain has a defense agreement with the United States and has contributed to Western defense for two decades by providing the U.S. with military installations. In December 1983, he said that "as things are here and now, Spain cannot be a neutral country." More recently, he affirmed: "Spain belongs to NATO but isn't militarily integrated into it."[28]

---

of Defense James Schlesinger in his annual report to Congress counted the five French divisions as part of NATO forces."

25 Under President François Mitterand, the French have taken a number of practical steps to reassure the West Germans and support NATO. One was the replacement of short-range Pluton nuclear weapons, which were not capable of reaching targets beyond the battlefield in West Germany, with the longer-range Hades, capable of striking enemy forces in East Germany. Another step was the creation of a Rapid Intervention Force of 47,000 men that can be mobilized in a matter of hours — and this includes its equipment and 150 anti-tank helicopters.

26 During a recent trip back to the United States, General Bernard Rogers, the NATO Commander, talked about NATO's relations with France. "We work very closely" with the Chief of Staff of the French armed forces, Rogers declared, "and over the years we have made great progress. Some things we talk about. Some things we don't talk about... We have plans for use of the First French Army as a reserve for Central Army Group... Those plans... have been exercised in command-post exercises. The allied air force of Central Europe works very closely with the tactical air force of France. [There is] a very close relationship between the navies in the Mediterranean..." See *The Christian Science Monitor,* April 26, 1984.

27 Quoted in *The International Herald Tribune,* June 14, 1984.

28 *Ibid.*

Quantity Versus Quality?

But even if the NATO forces are outnumbered in terms of military manpower in Europe,[29] this does not tell the whole story. Generally, an aggressor — if he is expected to be successful in a conventional attack against conventional forces — must have a two-to-one or three-to-one advantage in manpower, even though the attacker usually has the advantage of surprise. Moreover, the conventional force figures for Europe do not complete the picture. Together, the U.S. and NATO have about 5.9 million personnel under arms at home and abroad. By way of contrast, the Soviets — even including some one million Warsaw Pact troops of doubtful reliability — have only about 4.9 million. So the problem is not only what to count, but where to count it.[30]

The U.S. Defense Intelligence Agency describes the Soviet Army as "the most powerful land army in the world." But no one knows whether it is also the best. Moreover, in assessing the Soviet threat to NATO what many people forget is that the Soviets face a hostile Chinese Army — the largest in the world — on their eastern flank. If the Soviets were to contemplate an attack on Western Europe, they would have to take into account their vulnerability to a threat posed by the Chinese.[31]

One of the greatest worries to NATO planners is the large number of tanks possessed by Warsaw Pact forces. At the present time, the Warsaw Pact is said to enjoy at least a three-to-one advantage in tanks.[32] However,

---

29 In January 1980, Secretary of Defense Harold Brown stated: "In the Central Region of Europe, a rough numerical balance exists between the immediately available non-nuclear forces of NATO [including France] and those of the Warsaw Pact." Quoted in *The Defense Monitor*, Vol. 11, No. 6 (1982).

30 In 1983, according to the Center for Defense Information, NATO spent some $ 288 billion to maintain 5.9 million troops and their equipment. During that same year the Warsaw Pact spent an estimated $ 200 billion for 4.9 million troops and equipment.

31 "You make no mention of the U.S. problem of having to cross 3,500 miles of ocean," says one American official. "What about the quality of Turkish, Greek or even Dutch troops?"

32 Various estimates have been given publicly of the tank balance in Central Europe. At one time, President Reagan asserted the Soviets enjoyed a five-to-one advantage in this area. However, one should bear in mind that while the Soviets enjoy a substantial advantage in this crucial area, tank counting is not an exact science. Satellites cannot peer into tank sheds. Consequently, the "bean counters" must calculate the number of tanks a shed could hold and then multiply that number by the number of sheds that are portrayed in photographs. At the time satellite photographs are taken there is, of course, no guarantee that the sheds are full.
One former Pentagon official notes: "Despite their huge inventory of about 50,000 tanks, the Soviets are stuck — at any given moment — with more brokendown tanks than all of ours put together."

what many outside observers fail to consider is that NATO outnumbers the Warsaw Pact in anti-tank weapons. NATO deploys over fifty types of anti-tank weapons and a total of almost half a million.[33] "Since the purpose of NATO is defensive," Richard Barnet, a former consultant to the Defense Department, concludes: "it makes sense to invest in technology to stop tanks [rather] than to engage in a tank-collecting contest."[34]

Ambassador Jonathan Dean, who was in charge of the U.S. Delegation to the Mutual and Balanced Force Reduction talks (MBFR) from 1978 to 1981, puts it this way. "Despite the concerns of recent years over trends in Soviet and Warsaw Pact forces, NATO forces in Central Europe today have important advantages in specific areas [that are frequently overlooked]."[35] For example, NATO air forces maintain an impressive edge over Warsaw Pact units in many categories including payload. The pilots flying for NATO have also logged more hours and are better trained than their counterparts in the East. Moreover, NATO has about twice as many modern fighter-bombers as Pact forces and maintains a lead in anti-tank guided missiles and helicopters.[36] These fighter bombers in Europe can strike all Warsaw Pact nations with nuclear weapons.[37] "We are in the strongest position

---

33 *The Defense Monitor*, Vol. 11, No. 6 (1982). "Anti-tank weapons do not equal tanks," maintains an experienced U.S. tank commander. Retired German General D. Christian Krause disagrees. Today attacks by large numbers of Soviet tanks supported by small infantry units "would be easy prey to improved anti-tank weapons."

34 Richard J. Barnet, *Real Security: Restoring American Power in a Dangerous Decade* (New York: Touchstone Books, 1981), p. 38. One U.S. official with first-hand knowledge of the problem observes: "Many of these anti-tank weapons cannot be effective against the new Soviet T-80 tank which has special armor."

35 Jonathan Dean, "Beyond First Use," *Foreign Policy*, No. 48 (1982), pp. 37-53. It is often alleged that the Soviets are closing the gap in military technology. However, this is by no means clear. Edward Jayne, former Assistant Director for National Security and International Affairs in the Office of Management and Budget, has stated: "I'm absolutely persuaded that not only do we have the technological edge, but that the edge is getting greater. In the important area of new precision-guided weapons, which William Perry, President Carter's Undersecretary of Defense for Research and Engineering, has called "the most significant application of technology to modern warfare since the development of radar," Dr. Perry said in 1981 that the U.S. has a "substantial lead." See *The Defense Monitor*, Vol. 11, No. 1 (1982).

36 According to the June 1948 NATO booklet *Force Comparisons*, NATO has 1,960 fighter-bombers versus 2,250 for the Warsaw Pact.

37 "NATO's counter to the numerical superiority of the Warsaw Pact ground and air forces has always rested to a large extent on the high quality of its air power," notes one former NATO official. "NATO air forces have the ability to bring heavy concentrations of fire to bear with extreme rapidity and accuracy at virtually any point in the battle. Air power offers the ability to strike hard and repeatedly at

that we've ever been in when it comes to tactical aircraft," states Brigadier General Del Jacobs of the U.S. Air Force.[38]

As things now stand, NATO air power would most likely cause great damage to Warsaw Pact aircraft. Not unaware of this possibility, the Pact has fielded enormous flak forces. In East Germany, western Czechoslovakia and Poland the Soviets have reportedly 16,000 surface-to-air missile launchers and 2300 interceptors. More than two-thirds of this force is deployed in East Germany.[39]

On the ground NATO forces possess important advantages accruing to a force defending its own soil. It has prepared defensive positions. It controls a relatively favorable terrain; it has greater knowledge of its own area, and is supported by friendly forces. And it has higher morale. NATO also benefits from the aforementioned general requirement that the potential attacker must have considerable overall superiority to insure success.[40]

In assessing the conventional balance in Central Europe, one is advised to be skeptical of the emphasis on numbers.[41] Here it is perhaps worthwhile to recall the Nazi-Soviet experience of World War II. On the eve of the outbreak of the German invasion of the Soviet Union in June 1941, the Russians reportedly outnumbered their enemies by 6 to 1 in tanks, 5 to 1 in aircraft and 2 to 1 in submarines. Yet, by the end of 1941, much of this enormous arsenal was destroyed. Superior German tactics, training and equipment more than made up for the disparity in numbers.

---

the choke points along the frontier of the two Germanies through which a massive Soviet land offensive would have to squeeze." This official adds: "Tactical air power could also be projected strategically, that is, large numbers of U.S. tactical aircraft would be able to fly into Europe from the United States in times of crisis." According to the Center for Defense Information, "NATO and the Warsaw Pact have approximately the same number of total combat aircraft." *The Defense Monitor*, Vol. 11, No. 6 (1982).

38 Quoted in *The Washington Post*, June 6, 1982. One U.S. official with NATO responsibilities would observe here: "NATO has fewer airfields than the Warsaw Pact; thus its forces are more vulnerable and less survivable. Also, the Soviets have a preponderance of fighter-bombers in central and eastern parts of the Soviet Union which can be easily moved west. As to helicopters, the Soviets are building them at a rate twice ours. Have you talked to some U.S. military men in Europe? The morale of our troops is spotty."

39 According to one U.S. intelligence officer, "at night or in bad weather only 2000 of the enemy missiles and few of the aircraft are usable."

40 One former U.S. Army officer attached to NATO headquarters says: "The CENTAG area generally favors the defenders, but this is not true of the North German plain."

41 "Military officials are often too close to their work to make objective appraisals," says one former NATO diplomat.

In short, although the Warsaw Pact forces may enjoy a manpower advantage in Central Europe, Ambassador Dean concludes, "it does not appear to create a decisive advantage for the Pact in conflict." Indeed, the 1982 NATO report concludes: "NATO forces are well trained and, given the full range of capabilities at their disposal, are capable of presenting a credible defense of Alliance territory."[42]

Soviet Military Weaknesses

To be sure, the Soviet Union has vast military strength and objectives harmful to the West. But it also suffers from grave weaknesses. These include the more well-known shortcomings, such as a stagnant economy, a chronic food shortage and technological backwardness. But very debilitating also are some other important but lesser-known problem areas.[43]

One of these is the lack of experienced manpower. The Soviet armed forces relies more heavily on conscripts than do most Western armies. The Red Army is about 77 percent conscript. When fully mobilized, the Russian Army is approximately 85 percent conscript. In about a third of its divisions, the conscript rate is about 95 percent. The majority of noncommissioned officers are appointed conscripts. Soviet Army officials, all volunteer and professional, perform much of the supervision which is carried out by NCOs in Western armies.

Since the Soviet birthrate is declining, the Red Army can no longer pick and choose the men and women it wants. According to U.S. intelligence estimates, by 1990 the number of eighteen-year-olds in the Soviet Union

---

42 Quoted in *The Defense Monitor*, Vol. 11, No. 6 (1982). Americans often are unaware of the extent of the European contribution to NATO. This includes 90 percent of the ground forces, 80 percent of the combat aircraft and 75 percent of the ships dedicated to the alliance. General Bruce C. Clarke, who served as U.S. Army Commander, Europe as well as Commander-in-Chief of Central Army Group NATO, in the early 1960s, states: "I was in Germany two years ago (1982) and received a top secret briefing. I would say that our forces in Germany are 50% stronger than when Carter left office ..." Letter to this writer, March 15, 1984. Lower-ranking Army officers tend to agree with Clarke, but they point out some of the problems with the new equipment the Army in Europe is receiving. "The new M-1 tank," one U.S. Army officer confides, "is ready-made for Europe, but it cannot be rapidly airlifted to other critical areas such as the Persian Gulf. It is so big and heavy that only one tank at a time can be transported by the Air Force's biggest plane, the C-5A." In 1981, the Pentagon wanted 7,000 M-1 tanks even though the United States had only 77 C-5A planes at the time.

43 See the remarks made by Sir Oliver Wright, the British Ambassador to the United States, in St. Paul, Minnesota as reported in *The Minneapolis Star and Tribune*, April 26, 1984.

will fall by approximately 20 percent — to about 2.1 million. And this is not enough to cover projected military needs.

At the same time that the overall birthrate in the U.S.S.R. is declining, the birthrate of the non-Russian population of the Soviet Union is growing rapidly.[44] This is a potential problem because these persons are generally regarded as unsatisfactory soldiers. Few Soviet Asians speak Russian well, and this is the language of the Red Army. Moreover, because their schooling tends to be poor, they are difficult to train in technical fields.

Some Western military experts assert that the training of most Soviet troops is a holdover from the 19th century. Therefore, it does not meet the needs of a modern army steeped in the latest technology. Basic training is still designed to "break" recruits, and the rigid hierarchy of the Red Army subjects them to harsh punishment. These practices, in addition to racial discrimination and service in relatively isolated areas, undermine the motivation of an effective fighting force.

Another weakness of the Red Army is its logistics. Western military experts estimate that five percent of the Soviet army is now tied down by the bloody, unsuccessful Afghanistan war. However, the U.S.S.R. is using about one-fourth of its air transport capability to supply the needs of this invasion force.

In the view of U.S. military experts, the lower echelons of the command structure of the Soviet armed forces are too inflexible. This weakness is seen as the result of years of conditioning. By way of contrast, Western unit commanders are expected generally to follow mission-type orders, which encourage NATO forces which enjoy considerable freedom of action to take initiatives. Soviet military leaders emphasize, in the main, central control over even small maneuvers although less so than in Stalin's time.

The U.S.S.R. has a large number of divisions, but its ground combat forces, as a whole, are in a poor state of readiness. Aside from those Soviet divisions stationed in the restive East European countries, barely ten percent of the other Soviet ground divisions are combat-ready. And two-thirds are at greatly reduced strength, as Secretary of Defense Caspar Weinberger reported in the October 1981 version of the Pentagon's booklet, *Soviet Military Power*. The Defense Intelligence Agency has also stated: "The So-

---

44 The ethnic Russian population increased only 6.5 percent between 1970 and 1979, while the Muslim population increased by 24 percent in the same period. If the high birthrate of the Muslims continues, they will make up close to one quarter of the Soviet population by the year 2000. At the same time the overall Soviet birthrate is declining, death rates for almost every age group are increasing in the Soviet Union, while male life expectancy has declined by five years in the past two decades. According to a recently published study, this trend, which is unique in the developed world, is due to adverse living conditions and widespread, chronic alcoholism. See *The Wall Street Journal*, October 18, 1982.

At a Glance: Military Resources of NATO*, Warsaw Pact, and People's Republic of China

	NATO	Warsaw Pact	China
Population	626 million	380 million	1 Billion
GNP	$ 5,975 Billion	$ 2,020 Billion	$ 552 Billion
Military Spending	$ 256 Billion	$ 202 Billion	$ 57 Billion
Military Manpower	5.8 million	4.8 million[+]	4.9 million
Strategic Nuclear Weapons	10,000	7,800	Several Hundred
Total Nuclear Weapons	31,000	20,000	Several Hundred
Tanks	29,000	63,000	11,600
Anti-tank Weapons	400,000	data not available	
Other Armored Vehicles	54,000	83,000	4,000
Heavy Artillery	17,000	24,000	18,000
Combat Aircraft	12,000	12,000	6,100
Helicopters	12,400	4,500	350
Major Surface Warships	428	281	32
Attack Submarines	232	298	104

* NATO totals include France and Spain
Sources: NATO, IISS, DOD, CIA, CDI.
Chart by Center for Defense Information

[+] Excludes some 560,000 Soviet border guard, internal security, railroad, and construction troops.

Source: Center for Defense Information, 1982.

viets rely on mobilization of reserves to supply much of their war-fighting capability."[45]

These and other problems were revealed during the Polish crisis in the early 1980s. CIA officials monitoring developments there observed that the Red Army was unable to bring its forces to readiness as expected.

---

45 See Rear Admiral Gene R. LaRocque, "Preparing to Fight a Nuclear War ... The Reagan Arms Budget," in Congressman Ronald V. Dellums, *Defense Sense: The Search for a Rational Military Policy* (Cambridge: Ballinger, 1983), pp. 109-124. Admiral LaRocque, who is Director of the Center for Defense Information, concludes: "My conclusion is that the picture of the Soviet war machine as poised to march tomorrow to victory on battlefields around the world is absurd."

According to one "insider," the attempt in 1980 to set up a force ready to invade Poland resulted in chaos. For instance, reservists called up for this crisis deserted in such large numbers that it became impractical to punish them all. In the view of this high-level official, these problems — more than anything else — contributed to the Soviet decision not to invade Poland.

Western military experts generally agree that in the event of a Warsaw Pact attack on NATO by those Eastern countries aligned with the Soviet Union, they would be even less effective than Soviet forces.[46] Dozens of Red Army divisions are needed even now just to keep some Pact members from weakening or renouncing their ties to the U.S.S.R.[47] "This is serious in warfare," declares General Bruce C. Clarke, a vigorous tank man of long standing who served as Commander-in-Chief of Central Army Group NATO (CENTAG) in the early 1960s.[43]

These considerations are hardly ever mentioned in the public debate over the nature and extent of the Soviet threat to NATO. Yet they bear directly on the military balance of power and the question of "no first use" of nuclear weapons.[49]

46 John Erickson, one of the leading authorities on the Red Army in the West, maintains that it is very unlikely "that any non-Soviet national force would be allotted an independent operational role on any scale." The Soviets might therefore have serious problems because they would be forced to disperse their own divisions, thus limiting the number available for the principal attack. See Erickson, "Soviet Military Capabilities in Europe," *Journal of the Royal United States Institute*, No. 120 (March, 1975), p. 66.

47 Professor Bialer would note here: "what we are witnessing now is the beginning of the decline of the Soviet 'external empire.' Economically, the Soviet bloc is already a burden on the Soviet Union. Militarily, the size of the Soviet forces that, in case of war, would have to keep Eastern Europe subjugated is probably already larger than the size of the elite units of the Warsaw Pact countries, which would be trusted to participate effectively and offensively in a Soviet strike against Western Europe. Incidentally, one of the most important and overlooked consequences of the Polish events was the creation, for the foreseeable future, of a power vacuum in the central link of the Warsaw Pact forces confronting NATO. Politically, the situation in Eastern Europe is more and more an embarrassment to the Soviet Union, costing them much of whatever influence they have left over Communist parties abroad and potentially endangering détente with Western Europe."

48 Letter to this writer, March 15, 1984.

49 Alfred A. Hormel, in a letter to the New York *Times*, April 13, 1984, raised the following question in this context: Why would the Russians attack NATO in the first place? "A glance at any map shows that Germany has been divided in half, and the Soviet Union (sic) has constructed a most elaborate barrier between the two halves precisely so that 'their' Germans won't rush in vast hordes to West Germany. "Glance further down the map and see one East European country after another (Poland being but the latest) which has battled to get out from under Soviet domination — countries that, far from being allies of Russia, are kept in line

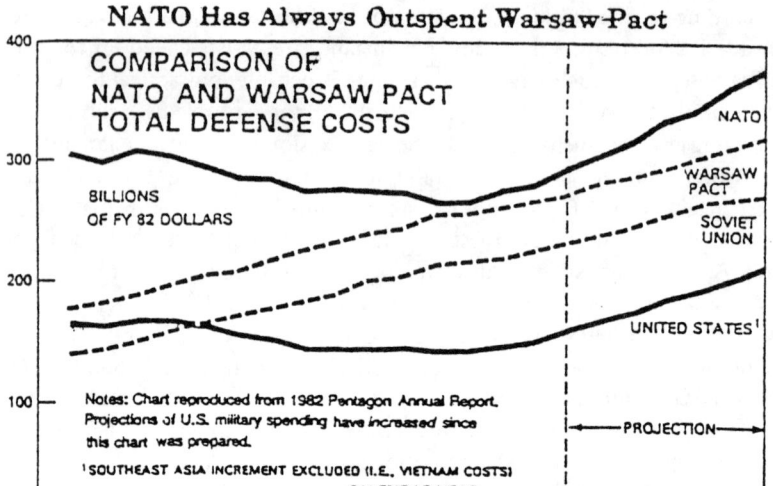

Source: Center for Defense Information, 1982.

The Nuclear Picture in Europe Today

The nuclear balance has changed substantially since the early 1960s when the Kennedy Administration introduced, and NATO accepted in 1967, the strategy of "flexible response."[50] Both the United States and the Soviet Union have almost completely refurbished their inventories of nuclear weapons.[51] They have increased the number of weapons of all three

> only by the threat of the Russian Army and serve at best as buffers should the West ever decide to march into the Soviet Union. You might even ponder the case of Yugoslavia, clearly a thorn in the side of Russia. Yet Russia has not even dared to move into that small country. "Then glance at Russia's other borders — an endless battle going on with Afghanistan and a virtually limitless border with antagonistic China, incredible numbers of troops poised on both sides and skirmishes erupting with some regularity. "Now, assuming that Russia is not run by total imbeciles, can somebody explain why they would wish to take over Western Europe? ...."

50 A good review of various conceptualizations of theater nuclear forces can be found in Harold A. Feiverson, "The Dilemma of Theater Nuclear Weapons," *World Politics*, 23 (January 1981), pp. 282-98.

51 One NATO official states: "The majority of U.S. nuclear weapons are over ten

types — battlefield, intermediate-range and strategic. In the process they have vastly improved the performance characteristics of both the weapons themselves and the delivery systems. Because the U.S.S.R. was so far behind the U.S. in the early 1960s the quantitative changes seem to many to be more consequential for the Soviet Union.

As the Soviet Union has now achieved rough parity in strategic and intermediate-range forces, a central element of the "flexible response" strategy has become less and less credible. With huge survivable arsenals on both sides, strategic nuclear weapons have lost whatever military utility that may once have been attributed to them. As McNamara has observed, "Their sole purpose, at present, is to deter the other side's first use of its strategic forces."[52]

The roughly 6,000 nuclear warheads now deployed by NATO in Europe are American-owned and controlled. They are provided for Allied delivery vehicles under a series of *bilateral* treaties and agreements between the United States and the various host nations and are known as Programs of Cooperation. It is important to note that the weapons deployed on Allied delivery vehicles are governed *not* by a multilateral NATO instrument, but instead by individual arrangements made between various states and the U.S.[53] The exact nature of these agreements is kept highly secret, as indeed are the deployments of American-owned nuclear warheads on foreign soil.

The procedure by which the United States maintains physical control of the warheads in the host states is the so-called "dual-key" control mechanism.[54] Not really a key at all (though it once was), it is simply the procedure of maintaining the warheads under U.S. custodial control. One "key" is the warhead; the other is the foreign-owned delivery vehicle. In order to be launched, or fired, the nuclear warhead must be matched to the delivery vehicle, so it is as if both keys were turned together. Reportedly, about half of the six thousand nuclear weapons in NATO are under dual-key control.[55]

American warheads deployed for use by U.S. troops on European soil do not have this control feature. They are maintained at storage depots

years old; the majority of Soviet weapons are less than five years old. This is true for strategic as well as theater nuclear weapons."

52 Robert S. McNamara, *opus cit.*, p. 68.
53 See Irving Heymont, "The NATO Nuclear Bilateral Forces," *Orbis*, Vol. 9 (Winter, 1966), pp. 1025-41.
54 "The use of the term 'dual key' may be confusing to your readers," states one U.S. official familiar with nuclear-release procedures. "The nuclear-release system is dual-control. This means that two people are necessary to release key codes for nuclear weapons use. When you use the term 'dual key' control, you mean dual national control."
55 *The New York Times*, November 1, 1979.

and would have to be dispersed to the delivery units before they could be used.[56]

The most important point to be made here is that the great diversity of theater nuclear weapons *is controlled by the U.S.* through seven national command organizations, representing six different languages. To be sure, joint planning can ease some problems of coordination. But the political reality inevitably will influence the extent to which coordination can occur. Each national military organization is under separate national control. Thus, for example, Turkish forces serve under Turkish command in peacetime — not under any direct NATO command. Combat forces are not released from national control until a state of emergency. Therefore nuclear weapons and launchers must be maintained and guarded by national troops. The U.S. holds the nuclear warheads and the host states the launchers.[57]

In the case of West Germany, the situation is more complicated. In 1955, the Federal Republic was made a full and equal partner in NATO after agreeing to establish a national contingent of twelve divisions wholly under NATO command. In return, the members of NATO pledged to use all diplomatic means to support reunification and to regard the West German government as the only legitimate spokesman for all of Germany.[58]

There is one major exception to this organizational picture. The NATO "quick reaction alert force" (QRA) of aircraft is under control of the NATO Commander, traditionally always an American. The quick-reaction alert force is kept constantly on a very high alert status, even in peacetime. Reportedly, the planes are armed with their nuclear weapons on board.[59] The purpose of the force is to deter a Soviet surprise attack by maintaining a fully ready nuclear strike force for instant retaliation.

American-owned warheads in Europe consist in the main of warheads for air-defense missiles,[60] nuclear warheads for shorter-range missiles, nu-

---

56 U.S. nuclear warheads are stored at more than 100 sites in Europe guarded by American troops. About a third of the sites are for warheads to be used by United States forces; the remaining two-thirds are for warheads to be used by Allied forces in the event of war.

57 The foregoing information was obtained by means of off-the-record interviews with U.S. diplomatic and military officials.

58 See Wolfram F. Hanrieder *et al.*, *The Foreign Policies of West Germany, France and Britain* (Englewood Cliffs, N.J.: Prentice-Hall, 1980), p. 7.

59 Paul Bracken, *The Command and Control of Nuclear Forces* (New Haven: Yale University Press, 1983), p. 152. According to one insider, those aircraft on quick reaction alert are loaded with nuclear weapons supplied by the United States, supervised by American guards who are under strict orders not to permit the aircraft to move without a properly authenticated release order.

60 "These nuclear warheads are being phased out with conventional replacements," says one knowledgeable U.S. official.

clear bombs, nuclear artillery projectiles and those nuclear warheads for Pershing IIs and cruise missiles. These weapons come in all shapes and sizes. They have been named after great figures in American folklore (Davy Crocket), famous generals (Pershing) and weapons of an earlier age (Lance).

In 1981, the North Atlantic Assembly published a rough estimate of the distribution of these weapons. This list, which is published below, does not take into account the 464 ground-launched cruise missiles, with one warhead each, and the 108 Pershing II missile launchers and warheads that are being deployed over a five-year period which began in the fall of 1983.[61]

U.S. Nuclear Warheads[62]
Located in Europe in 1981

Bombs to be delivered by aircraft	1069
Artillery Shells (203 mm and 155 mm)	2000
Missiles: Pershing 1A	270
Lance and Honest John	910
Air Defense and Atomic Demolition Charges	1750
Total	5999

Nuclear artillery shells constitute the largest portion of the tactical nuclear weapons stockpile. Comprising about one-third of the total, they are also the weapons that are the greatest concern to NATO political leaders. For years rumors of the existence of Soviet nuclear artillery were circulated, but it was not until 1977 that U.S. Army intelligence confirmed their

---

61 See Special Committee on Nuclear Weapons, North Atlantic Assembly, *Second Interim Report on Nuclear Weapons in Europe*, Report to the Committee on Foreign Relations, U.S. Senate, 98th Congress, 1st session (Washington, D.C.: Government Printing Office, 1983), p. 59. One NATO official would add here: "You should note that the 1979 NATO decision to deploy Pershing IIs and cruise missiles will not raise the level of warheads in Europe. With the 1980 and 1983 reductions of 1,000 and 1,400 nuclear warheads respectively, each Pershing II and ground launched cruise missile replaces five warheads taken out."

62 According to one U.S. government "insider," a recent confidential report to Congress by the Pentagon shows that before the recent deployment of the Pershing IIs and cruise missiles to Europe there were 5,845 warheads in the tactical nuclear weapons arsenal in Europe. The report, classified secret, reveals that the European stockpile holds 150 warheads less than previously was publicly known. The United States and its Western European allies have agreed to withdraw almost 2,000 warheads from this stockpile over the next five years. With the increase in warheads made available by the recent deployment of the Pershing IIs and cruise missiles the net loss to the nuclear stockpile in Europe will be 1,400 warheads.

actual presence.[63] However, very little information is available about Soviet nuclear advancement in this area.

Basically, nuclear artillery shells in the NATO inventory are of two types. There are those designed for use by 155 mm and 203 mm howitzers. What many people do not realize, however, is that the howitzers are "dual capable." This means they can be used to fire shells containing conventional explosives as well as nuclear munitions. Thus, these weapons contribute to a distinct lowering of the nuclear threshold (i.e. that point at which nuclear weapons would be used).[64]

During the extended public debate over the "neutron bomb" in the late 1970s, one of the main arguments used by critics against the introduction of enhanced radiation warheads was that they are nuclear warheads which can be fired by conventional means. They were, therefore, dangerous because they blurred that all important distinction between conventional weapons and nuclear weapons.[65]

The exact ranges of the 155 m and 203 mm howitzers are a classified military secret. Most published accounts give them an approximate range of ten miles. Because of the relatively short range of these weapons, the artillery pieces and their nuclear shells tend to be deployed near the potential front lines of a conflict in Central Europe. There are, in effect, about 2,000 of these short-range nuclear warheads with an approximate yield of two kilotons. They are concentrated at a few sites close to the East German border.[66]

The nuclear mines, which are known officially as atomic demolition munitions or ADMs, are the source of special concern to U.S. and NATO officials. For the most part, these nuclear weapons are stored in West Germany, Turkey, Greece and Italy. They are approximately twenty-five years old and probably are no longer reliable. There are conflicting reports about Soviet possession of nuclear mines.

Historically, they were intended to destroy bridges and tunnels and to

---

63 U.S. Department of the Army, Office of the Assistant Chief of Staff for Intelligence, *Understanding Soviet Military Developments*, Pub. AST-11005-100-77 (1977), p. 71. This document also implies the development of nuclear mortar rounds for use by the Soviet infantry. See also Robert Kennedy, "Soviet Theater Nuclear Forces," *Air Force*, March 1981, p. 78.

64 Stanley H. Hoffmann of Harvard University, for one, maintains that the barrier between conventional and nuclear force use should be kept as wide as possible. He sees the recent INF deployment as reducing that barrier.

65 The Reagan Administration has eliminated production money in the fiscal 1985 budget for the controversial new 155 mm nuclear artillery shell. This action apparently ends the 15-year-old program.

66 *The Defense Monitor*, Vol. 12, No. 4 (1983), p. 5.

block mountain passes and other "choke points" along potential Soviet invasion routes. However, if used, their detrimental effects would be felt on NATO countries. Moreover, to be most effective they would have to be emplaced *before* a war actually was initiated.[67] But such a move could very well aggravate a crisis and could possibly contribute to the starting of actual hostilities. From the point of view of NATO planners, directed to implement a policy of "flexible response," their use would in fact seriously undermine the basic point behind such a strategy, which is to postpone the use of nuclear weapons until the ability of NATO conventional forces could be tested in the containment of a Warsaw Pact invasion.

Somewhat similar problems bedevil old and probably unreliable nuclear-armed air defense systems. Intended for use at the onset of a conflict they are to disrupt the large-scale attack that could be expected to accompany a Warsaw Pact invasion. Thus, they too negate the main purpose behind the strategy of "flexible response."[68]

In a crisis, it is desirable to have a configuration of forces that contributes to "crisis stability." However, in an acute international situation in which the risk of war appears to be rising, the forementioned characteristics of nuclear artillery, mines and air defense systems are such that they would tend to put pressure on the political leaders of NATO, particularly the American President, to delegate the authority to release these weapons to the military commanders on the scene. Each host NATO country for the U.S. weaponry retains a veto over the use of these nuclear weapons. However, only the U.S. President can authorize their release.

The question of presidential release aside, it is the characteristics of these weapons that have led many observers in the West to predict that the Alliance would most assuredly use tactical nuclear weapons within hours of the beginning of a war in Central Europe.[69]

---

67 In July 1973, testimony published by the Joint Congressional Atomic Energy Committee indicated that West Germany had refused the United States permission to dig holes for hundreds of atomic demolition mines. According to the U.S. Army the successful use of these mines requires that the holes be dug in advance, so that atomic demolition crews could in an emergency rush in, drop the mines in "prechambered holes" and then fall back and detonate the mines at "choke points" along the likely invasion routes that would be used by the Warsaw Pact. For details see *The New York Times*, July 15, 1973.

68 "These nuclear-armed air defense systems are being phased out and replaced by conventional systems," says one U.S. official.

69 "There will unquestionably be doubts and hesitations in the Alliance over the initiation of nuclear release," observes one former NATO official. "For instance, widespread unwillingness to allow the use of battlefield weapons on West German territory can be counted on in the Federal Republic, for the effect of battlefield weapons there would only differ in degree from that of strategic attack on the home territory of the Soviet Union and the United States."

In effect, NATO leaders would be faced with "a use them or loose them" situation. That is, they would be faced with the likely choice of either having to use these battlefield nuclear weapons or see them overrun or destroyed by the rapidly advancing aggressor.

According to Harland Cleveland and Robert McNamara, NATO has not been able to devise plans that would make practical use of the alleged military utility of such weapons as nuclear artillery. No official scenario has been developed that would both assure a clear advantage to the Alliance and at the same time avoid the very high risk of escalating to all-out nuclear war.[70]

Current Guidelines on NATO Nuclear Use

Current guidelines on the initial use of nuclear weapons by NATO date from the early 1970s. The Alliance's nuclear policies are defined in a secret document entitled "Concepts for the Role of Theater Nuclear Strike Forces in ACE (Allied Command Europe)." This document was originally adopted by the North Atlantic Council in 1970 and later revised. On the basis of this document, NATO headquarters has drawn up what is called a general strike plan and lists of targets.

The general strike plan provides for different categories of nuclear warfare. *All* levels of nuclear warfare require consultations among the allies as well as approval by the President of the United States. Importantly, within what is known as the selective category the Supreme Allied Commander Europe (General Rogers, an American) has the capability for deliberate escalation with which he can expand the scope or intensity of combat in order to strengthen his defensive effort or to insure the survival of his forces within the scope of the authority the President has authorized him to use.[71]

---

70 "Their existence alone," states one NATO observer, "complicates Soviet conventional planning, e.g., massing for a breakthrough in NATO defenses."

71 In an interview in 1978, General Andrew Goodpaster, NATO commander from 1969-1974, spoke of "differences of concept and preference" among the NATO allies on the use of nuclear weapons. The general said that there are "realistic" plans for "selective use . . . accepted up to a [certain] degree." The one thing that the NATO allies agreed upon, Goodpaster stated categorically, was the deterrent value of the weapons.

Dwight Eisenhower, first as NATO commander and then as President, "had a clearer recognition of deterrence rather than use" as the prime benefit of tactical nuclear weapons, General Goodpaster stressed. "It was Eisenhower's concept that by building up this force, it was unlikely we'd have to employ it." See *The International Herald Tribune*, December 16-17, 1978.

For a long time, there were no accepted "fire plans" — specific weapon-firing orders — for using most of the roughly 7,000 nuclear artillery shells, ground- and air-defense missile warheads, tactical bombs and other atomic devices in the NATO stockpile. There were, however, agreed-upon rules for what weapons should not be used (at least not on Western European territory). Technically called "NATO constraints," these highly classified orders dating from the early 1960s reportedly set a limit of ten kilotons as the highest yield that can be exploded on NATO territory, declining to zero in built-up urban areas. In this way, nuclear weapons were (and are) barred from use in large sections of Europe.[72]

In 1978, a special committee, called the High Level Group, was established by the Alliance to examine once again the nuclear posture of NATO and the practical feasibility of all weapons in the U.S. stockpile in Europe. However, according to a former member, that body was unable to agree (despite discussions lasting for years) on guidelines for the subsequent use of nuclear weapons if a first attempt to communicate NATO's intentions through a controlled demonstration use did not succeed in persuading the adversary to halt hostilities."[73]

Two major problems confront NATO planners. The first issue is related to the assumption that NATO would in a conflict be responding to a Warsaw Pact invasion of Western Europe. In this case, since Western artillery has such short range, nuclear explosions would most likely occur on NATO's own territory with devastating effects. For instance, a 100-kiloton tactical nuclear weapon would be needed to destroy a regiment of tanks (some 50 to 100 in dispersed formation).[74] But such a weapon would create general destruction of structures and people in a circle with a diameter of 4.5 miles (an area of about 15 square miles). In a typical West German region, a blast circle of this size would be likely to include several villages or towns of several thousand people. Furthermore, depending on the nature of the weapon and the height of the air burst, a much larger area could be affected by the fallout.[75] (It should be remembered that West Germany is about

---

72 These constraints reportedly prohibit use in NATO territory of ground-burst bombs and warheads because their fireballs would create a radioactive fallout cloud that could not be controlled.

73 Special Committee on Nuclear Weapons, North Atlantic Assembly, *Second Interim Report on Nuclear Weapons in Europe*, Report to the Committee on Foreign Relations, U.S. Senate, 98th Congress, 1st Session (Washington, D.C.: Government Printing Office, 1983), p. 7.

74 "Show me artillery that can deliver 100 kilotons," one former U.S. NATO official challenges.

75 See Seymour J. Deitchman, *New Technology and Military Power* (Boulder: Westview Press, 1979), p. 12.

the size of Oregon, with a population density more than twice as great as the northeastern United States.)

Several hundred such tactical nuclear weapons would probably be required to counter an armored development in Central Europe. However, if a substantial number of the 2,000 nuclear artillery shells were fired, not only would Warsaw Pact forces suffer heavy casualties, but large numbers of friendly civilian and military personnel would also probably be killed and injured. And this does not take into account the considerable collateral damage that would be done to property, farmland and urbanized areas.

The second major problem relates to the expected response of the Warsaw Pact to a limited nuclear exchange initiated by NATO. As McNamara has stated, "there is no reason to believe that the Warsaw Pact, now possessing tactical and intermediate-range nuclear forces at least comparable to those of NATO, would not respond to NATO's initiation of nuclear war with major nuclear attacks of its own." These attacks "would probably seek most importantly to reduce NATO's ability to fight a nuclear war by destroying command and control facilities, nuclear weapon storage sites, and the aircraft, missiles, and artillery which would deliver NATO's nuclear weapons." Direct support facilities such as ports and airfields "would likely also be attacked in the initial Warsaw Pact nuclear offensive." Thus, "the war would escalate from the battlefield to the rest of Western Europe and probably to Eastern Europe as well, as NATO retaliated."[76]

It is this situation which led Helmut Schmidt to comment once that the use of tactical nuclear weapons "will not defend Europe, but destroy it."[77]

The reaction of many Europeans to what they generally see as the suicidal nature of nuclear weapons use on their soil has had a direct effect on the approach to security taken by NATO. Norway and Denmark, for instance, have refused permission for any nuclear weapons to be installed in their territory in peacetime.[78] For its part, West Germany has insisted on a strategy of "forward defense"; this means in theory that any military hostilities would be conducted immediately on the East German border. Officials in Bonn have repeatedly stressed that they oppose a defense in depth which, with tactical nuclear weapons, would devastate East and West Germany.[79]

76 Robert McNamara, *opus cit.*, p. 70.
77 Helmut Schmidt, *Defense or Retaliation?* (New York: Praeger, 1962), p. 101.
78 Nils Orvik and Niels J. Haagerup, *The Scandinavian Members of NATO*, Adelphi Paper No. 23 (London: The International Institute for Strategic Studies, 1965).
79 Federal Republic of Germany, Federal Minister of Defense, *The Security of the Federal Republic of Germany and the Development of the Armed Forces* (Bonn, 1976).

Precision Guided Munitions

In view of the many problems connected with defending Western Europe by threatening to use (or using) tactical nuclear weapons, NATO military experts are now taking a hard look at a vigorous and fast growing area of military technology called precision guided munitions (PGM). These new weapons are small accurate missiles with non-nuclear warheads. They are designed in the main to knock out tanks and airplanes. PGM are of many shapes and sizes. Some are small enough to be fired by infantry; others can be carried in armored personnel carriers, helicopters, airplanes and ships.[80]

Precision guided munitions were first seen in action on a large scale during the 1973 war in the Middle East. At that time, PGM supplied by the Soviets to Egypt and Syria inflicted heavy losses on Israeli tank forces. Since 1973, the technology of precision guided munitions has developed much further, not only in the United States and the Soviet Union but in other states as well.

Existing PGM technology fits well into the tradition of David and Goliath. Precision guided munitions are light and very mobile, and importantly they are comparatively cheap. In fact, they may well prevail in the end, the experts say, just because they are more cost-effective. Tanks, on the other hand, which PGM "kill", are heavy, clumsy and expensive.

These new weapons combine advanced guidance and target-detection systems with new explosive technologies. They are capable of engaging the enemy with great precision and saturating large areas. As Senator Sam Nunn noted in a report to Congress in 1982: "Long-range conventional weapons are now being developed that begin to approach the destructive potential of small yield (two to three kiloton) battlefield nuclear weapons."

Experts disagree about the extent to which precision guidance weapons have revolutionized land warfare. Some U.S. military men believe that these new weapons will destroy tanks in the future as decisively as airplanes defeated battleships during the last world war. Other authorities dispute this. They maintain that tanks will survive if they are supported by friendly infantry and precision guided munitions. In any case, there is little doubt that the new weapons have brought to a close an era in which tank armies won easy victories.

---

80 For one of the better accounts of the possibilities of PGM, see Norbert Hannig, *Abschreckung durch konventionelle Waffen: Das David-Goliath Prinzip* (West Berlin: Berlin Verlag Arno Spitz, 1984).

Summary

The policy of nuclear deterrence has been an integral part of NATO's overall military strategy virtually from the formation of the Alliance. The problem, then as now, was the accurate assessment of the threat and the determination of the appropriate measures for the defense of Western Europe. Early in the "cold war" period, the NATO allies concluded that the Soviet Union enjoyed such overwhelming conventional superiority that it could only be deterred by relying on the threat to launch an immediate and overwhelming nuclear blow against Soviet territory. An important consequence of this policy was that the total NATO forces on the continent were kept below the level required for conventional defense. NATO did not wish to tempt Soviet conventional aggression by doing anything to suggest that a Western response would be limited to non-nuclear means.

It is, of course, debatable whether or not the balance of forces in Central Europe was such as to provide adequate justification for NATO's adoption of a first-use nuclear strategy. But even operating on the worst-case basis, there was a great uncertainty in NATO circles how nuclear weapons could be utilized to the best advantage of NATO. Determined to avoid relying on a policy that emphasized the early use of tactical nuclear weapons (which by the early 1960s had reached several thousand in number), Presidents Kennedy and Johnson pressed a policy of "flexible response" on reluctant NATO allies.

"Flexible response" was based on the notion that Soviet aggression could best be deterred in Europe if the adversary was confronted with a ladder of escalation which began with conventional weapons and ended with a nuclear exchange. The hope was (and this was the real rationale for the policy) that NATO's conventional forces could be improved sufficiently so that resort to nuclear weapons would be unnecessary. But this expectation never materialized. Paradoxically, the doctrine, which was designed in the main to make the use of nuclear weapons unnecessary, came to rest on the requirement that made a nuclear response at an early stage essential in the eyes of NATO military planners.[81]

The present accumulation of almost 6,000 nuclear warheads in Western Europe today (excluding those on ships and submarines) has created an extremely difficult if not dangerous situation, as Henry Kissinger and others readily admit. Among other things, the forward deployment of tactical

---

81 One former American official with first-hand knowledge of NATO war plans would observe here: "The nuclear posture in Europe has long been irrational, with too many weapons in the wrong location. The whole thing is based on a bluff, the assumption that there will be no war. This is probably correct, but if it proves wrong, the consequences would be terrible."

nuclear weapons in Europe could lead the NATO allies to become inadvertently embroiled in a nuclear conflict. Presidential permission to use nuclear weapons would be difficult to deny when forward-deployed nuclear forces were in the process of being overrun.[82]

To date there have been no instances of tactical nuclear weapons in Europe being fired because of ambiguity of command or accident. But there have been cases of what could at least be called uneasiness about an indistinctness in command relationships. In 1974, for instance, when Turkey invaded Cyprus, there was considerable concern in the United States about American nuclear weapons stored in Turkey and Greece. Both governments were severely divided at this time about national policies. The situation became so serious at one point that U.S. Marines with the Sixth Fleet in the Mediterranean were put on alert and prepared for a helicopter assault on the storage sites for nuclear weapons in Turkey in order to maintain U.S. possession.[83] At the same time nuclear weapons kept on alert aboard the quick-reaction aircraft of the Greek and Turkish air forces were removed from the planes because of American anxiety that stability of command could not be maintained.[84] To be sure, the vital security of Greece and Turkey was not in jeopardy over the Cyprus dispute, but the crisis served to underline the potential danger of these tactical nuclear weapons.

Certainly nuclear warheads on the spot in Europe provide an obvious, sobering reminder of the unpredictable consequence of any large attack on NATO. But the obvious reality is that there are more than enough of them already in place to do this job. Moreover, their deterrent potential is questionable. In any case, they are much less important for the overall credibility of the ultimate American commitment to NATO than the some 320,000 Americans stationed in Western Europe.

A number of NATO experts who doubt the utility of defending Western Europe with tactical nuclear weapons have been quick to embrace the development of a new generation of powerful conventional munitions — PGM. Some observers have even gone so far as to suggest that development of these "near-nuclear" conventional weapons will strengthen deterrence and "raise the nuclear threshold" by enhancing the capacity of NATO to

---

82 "Any war we have with the Soviet Union," Admiral Gene R. LaRocque, Director of the Center for Defense Information, states, "will inevitably be a nuclear war because we have nuclearized our Army divisions, our air wings, and our Navy warships, over 70 percent of which carry nuclear weapons. Nuclear weapons have become the conventional weapons of our armed forces today."

83 "Cyprus Stirred U.S. to Protect Atom Arms," *New York Times*, September 9, 1974, p. 10; "Cooling Off the Nukes," *Newsweek*, August 12, 1974, p. 17.

84 "U.S. Weighs Status of Nuclear Warheads in Greece," *New York Times*, September 11, 1974, p. 12.

repel a conventional attack by the Warsaw Pact with conventional weapons. However, what these well-intentioned persons tend to overlook is the fact that deployment of such conventional weapons by the West will almost be certainly matched by a similar action in the East. The net result may lead NATO to increase rather than decrease its reliance on an already dubious nuclear deterrent. At the same time, it is doubtful whether these weapons will indeed contribute to the raising of the nuclear threshold. As Colonel Trevor N. Dupuy, a U.S. military theorist, wrote in a recent issue of *Armed Forces Journal:* "I suspect . . . that the more effective and destructive conventional weapons have become, the inhibitions on using nuclear weapons are lowered correspondingly."[85]

Nevertheless, if there are good reasons to be skeptical of the promises of this new technology, it is still too early to render a definitive answer. As Freeman Dyson writes: "If equipment alone could guarantee a successful defense, France would not have been overrun by a numerically inferior force of German tanks in 1940. Warfare is always a gamble, for the defenders as well as for the attackers." The question we should be asking ourselves, "is whether the risks of a PGM defense would be smaller than the risks of our present reliance on nuclear weapons." Although this question cannot yet be answered with certainty, Dyson says," there are strong reasons to believe the answer will be affirmative."[86]

---

85 For an interesting discussion see John J. Mearsheimer, *Conventional Deterrence* (Ithaca: Cornell University Press, 1983). This book examines an extremely important question: How do conventional forces deter? Unfortunately, it is marred by poor supporting evidence and factual errors of magnitude.

86 Freeman Dyson, *Weapons and Hope* (New York: Harper & Row, 1984), p. 50.

> Should NATO stake the future on a deterrent strategy that is 'either a bluff or a suicide pact (?)'
>
> *Field Marshal Lord Michael Carver,
> former Chief of the British Defense Staff*

VIII. THE NO FIRST USE DEBATE

One of the most hotly argued issues in the deterrence debate is the question of "no first use" of nuclear weapons. The position of the present Administration is clear. As Secretary of Defense Caspar Weinberger stated in early 1983: "The nuclear option [i.e. early first use of nuclear weapons] remains an important element in deterring Soviet attack."[1]

The "Foreign Affairs" Debate

Proposals that NATO should consider renouncing the "first-use" of nuclear weapons attracted a great deal of attention at about the time the "nuclear freeze movement" was gaining momentum in the United States. But the first major contribution to the debate by former high-level U.S. government officials came in a controversial article in the Spring 1982 issue of *Foreign Affairs*. The authors were McGeorge Bundy, Special Assistant to the President for National Security Affairs from 1961 to 1966, George F. Kennan, U.S. Ambassador to the Soviet Union in 1952, Robert S. McNamara, Secretary of Defense from 1961 to 1968 and Gerard Smith, Chief of the U.S. Delegation to the Strategic Arms Limitation Talks (SALT) from 1969 to 1972. They asserted that the "first use" policy of the United States needs *re-examination*. (Contrary to the public impression, they did not call for the implementation of a "no-first-use" policy). Stubborn adherence to "first use," they argued, might divide the Alliance while its deterrent credibility steadily erodes.[2]

1 Secretary of Defense, *Annual Report to the Congress, FY 1984* (Washington, D.C.: Government Printing Office, 1983).
2 McGeorge Bundy et al., "Nuclear Weapons and the Atlantic Alliance," *Foreign Affairs*, (Spring, 1982), pp. 753-68.

The first-use policy, they argued, was first established at a time when the American nuclear advantage had been overwhelming. But that "advantage has long since gone and cannot be recaptured."

Regarding the contemplated use of nuclear weapons in the European area they argued: "it is time to recognize that no one has ever succeeded in advancing any persuasive reason to believe that any use of nuclear weapons, even on the smallest scale, could reliably be expected to remain limited." Every serious analysis and "every military exercise, for over 25 years, has demonstrated that even the most restrained battlefield use would be enormously destructive to civilian life and property."

The crucial point for Bundy, Kennan, McNamara and Smith was preservation of the "threshold" or "firebreak" between conventional and nuclear weapons: To keep "that firebreak wide and strong is in the deepest interest of all mankind."

The advantages that would accrue from a no-first-use policy would outweigh the political risks, the authors asserted. In the main, such a policy would decrease the danger of conventional war escalating into a nuclear war in Western Europe. In addition, such a policy would promote political coherence in the Alliance, which is sorely divided over the question of using nuclear weapons. At the same time, it would help in U.S. relations with the Soviet Union which has repeatedly offered to join the West in declaring a no-first-use policy. Finally, such a posture "could help to open the path towards serious reduction of nuclear armaments on both sides" and "bring hope to everyone in every country whose life is shadowed by the hideous possibility of a third great twentieth-century conflict in Europe."

Haig and Jones Argue Against the No First Use Concept

The majority response, official and otherwise, to the no-first-use proposal has been "unambiguously negative" to use the words of Jonathan Dean, Ambassador in charge of the U.S. Delegation to the Mutual and Balanced Force Reduction talks in Europe, 1978-1981.[3] The idea was especially criticized by officials in the Reagan Administration who are concerned with the development of a nuclear war-fighting capability that would allow the U.S. to prevail in such a war. In May 1982, the NATO Foreign Ministers also officially expressed their implied disapproval by re-endorsing the first-use strategy.

3 Jonathan Dean, "Beyond First Use," *Foreign Policy*, No. 48 (1982), p. 37-53. In this piece, Dean argues that "NATO's nuclear deterrent strategy is no longer credible to a large number of West Europeans whom it seeks to defend and is not acceptable as a means of defense to many of those who do not find it credible."

Foremost among the critics of the suggested policy change was Secretary of State Alexander M. Haig. He sternly addressed the issue in a major speech on April 6, 1982 at the Center for Strategic and International Studies at Georgetown University. At that time, the former NATO Supreme Commander made it clear that the major problem with the idea was that, in his judgment, its conventional substitute would require huge amounts of money and manpower to implement. This made it unrealistic. "Those in the West who advocate the adoption of a 'no-first-use' policy," he declared, "seldom go on to propose that the United States reintroduce the draft, triple the size of its armed forces, and put its economy on a wartime footing." Yet, "in the absence of such steps, a pledge of no-first-use effectively leaves the West nothing with which to counterbalance the Soviet conventional advantages and geopolitical position in Europe."[4]

From Haig's perspective, the Soviets would have a greater advantage in a conventional war. A no-first-use policy, he noted, had been suggested by the Soviets on numerous occasions. But such a pledge would be "tantamount to making Europe safe for conventional aggression."

On April 28, 1982, General David C. Jones, Chairman of the Joint Chiefs of Staff, made a speech addressing the no-first-use proposal. Like Haig, he focused most of his attention on the possibility of conventional war under such a pledge. The "no-first-use proposal fails to account for the conventional force imbalance," Jones claimed. Although there "is an understandable debate as to how great a margin of superiority the Warsaw Pact has in conventional forces — and I for one believe that the margin is often overstated — I know of no serious analyst in the West who does not conclude that one exists." If in a political crisis the Soviets believed "that they could launch a successful conventional attack against NATO without fear of a possible nuclear response," Jones maintained, "their incentive to do so — and thus the probability of armed conflict — would be greatly increased." Paradoxically then, "a declaratory policy of no-first-use may well lead to the very outcome its proponents seek to avoid — an increased likelihood of conflict and escalation to nuclear warfare."[5]

No First Use Pledge by the Soviet Union

In June 1982, the Soviets entered the debate on "no-first-use" by declaring that they would not be the first to use nuclear weapons. Speaking at the Special Session on Disarmament at the United Nations on June 15,

---

4 See *The New York Times*, April 7, 1982.
5 *The New York Times*, April 29, 1982.

President Leonid Brezhnev affirmed that "The Union of Soviet Socialist Republics assumes an obligation not to be the first to use nuclear weapons. He expected other countries with nuclear weapons to "assume an equally precise and clear obligation." That, he declared would be "tantamount to a ban on the use of nuclear weapons."[6]

In his speech, Brezhnev added an important qualifier that many people have subsequently overlooked. He said that the Soviet Union "will naturally continue to take into account how the other nuclear powers act." This statement was interpreted by most Western analysts as an escape clause that would enable the Soviets to renounce their promise if the United States, Britain and France did not follow suit. (China already pledged that it would not use nuclear weapons first after exploding its initial device in 1964).

Official American response to the Soviet proposal was predictably cool. When asked for reaction to the Soviet presentation at the UN, the State Department referred reporters to the statement on this subject the previous April by Secretary of State Haig.

By way of contrast, Robert McNamara said that he was delighted by the Russian proposal: "They recognize that this policy is in their interest, and we believe it is in our interest."

"Foreign Affairs" Dispute Continues

In the Summer 1982 issue of *Foreign Affairs*, General Bernard W. Rogers, Supreme Allied Commander, Europe, maintained that a central element in deterring Soviet aggression was Moscow's uncertainty about NATO's readiness to cross the nuclear threshold. Removing that uncertainty by a no-first-use pledge would leave Europe exposed to conventional attack.[7] NATO should "also not lose sight of the tactical advantage to the defender resulting from his threatened use of nuclear weapons." This serves "as a restraint on the tactical massing of Warsaw Pact forces preparatory to an attack."

"Another inherent danger of declaring no-first-use is that many in Europe and the United States would see such a policy as a limitation on the American commitment to European security," Rogers wrote. "This might well create a situation in which the final guarantor of deterrence — the U.S. strategic nuclear arsenal — would be viewed as divorced from the fate

---

6 See *The New York Times*, June 16, 1982.
7 General Bernard W. Rogers, "The Atlantic Alliance: Prescriptions for a Difficult Decade," *Foreign Affairs*, Vol. 60, No. 5 (Summer, 1982), pp. 1145-56.

of Europe." The possibility of using nuclear weapons should be retained as a deterrent, at least until NATO and the Warsaw Pact countries negotiate an equitable and verifiable balance of conventional forces at the ongoing Mutual and Balanced Force Reduction (MBFR) talks in Vienna.

*

Four West German experts on military policy also responded to the no-first-use proposal in an article in the Summer 1982 edition of *Foreign Affairs*. The authors of the article were Karl Kaiser, Director of the Research Institute of the German Society for Foreign Affairs; Georg Leber, a member of the Social Democratic Party and Vice President of the West German Bundestag; Alois Mertes, a member of the Christian Democratic Party and its legislative spokesman on foreign policy; and General Franz-Josef Schultze (ret.), Commander-in-Chief of Allied Forces Central Europe from 1977 to 1979.[8]

They argued that the NATO strategy of "flexible response" worked to deter the Soviets by confronting them with an incalculable risk. But a policy of renouncing the first use of nuclear weapons would allow the Soviet leadership to more easily calculate the response of the West. Thus, such a policy would make a conflict in Europe more likely rather than less likely. They added that any conventional conflict probably would escalate into a nuclear confrontation in any case.

*

In the same issue of *Foreign Affairs* in which the article by Rogers appeared, McGeorge Bundy and his colleagues responded to their critics. They commented on "what is probably the most frequently and deeply held objection to a no-first-use policy." This is the argument that NATO should try to "keep the Russians guessing" by maintaining a policy of uncertainty about the possibility of first use. Their response was "that this threat is steadily declining in credibility, while its political costs within the Alliance are growing." A continued *"reliance on threats that it would be disastrous to execute strikes us as morally insupportable and empty of logic."* (Italics mine.) In their view, it made more sense to build up NATO's conventional strength in order to deter the other side. It is "more credible, more unifying, more civilized — and attainable."

The very vulnerable position of West Berlin was singled out by one of

---

8   Karl Kaiser *et al.*, "Nuclear Weapons and the Preservation of Peace," *Foreign Affairs*, Vol. 60, No. 5 (Summer, 1982), pp. 1157-1170.

their critics as evidence of the need to retain a first-use policy. But the authors maintained that the freedom of West Berliners "is defined today not by any expectation that a coup-de-main there would unleash nuclear war." Rather it is protected "by full Soviet awareness of the greatly destabilizing consequences that would follow a breach of the Quadripartite Agreement of 1971, which is correctly regarded by both sides as a major landmark in East-West relations." Whatever "may have been the role there of nuclear deterrence in earlier years — and the question is far from simple — we think it is clear that the freedom of West Berlin has rested, for more than a decade, on a much wider and primarily political base."[9]

*

In the fall 1983 edition of *Foreign Affairs*, Robert S. McNamara raised the debate over the use of nuclear weapons to a higher — and more provocative — level by declaring that "Nuclear weapons serve no military purpose whatsoever. *They are totally useless — except to deter one's opponent from using them."*

"The question of what deters Soviet aggression," he said, "is an extremely difficult one. To answer it, we must put ourselves in the minds of several individuals who would make the decision to initiate war." We must ask "what their objectives are for themselves and their nation, what they value and what they fear." We must "assess their proclivity to take risk, to bluff, or to be bluffed." We must "guess at how they see us — our will and our capabilities — and determine what we can do to strengthen their belief in the sincerity of our threats and our promises."

But most difficult of all, "we must evaluate all these factors in the context of an acute international crisis." Our problem "is not to persuade the Soviets not to initiate war today. It is to cause them to reach the same decision at some future time when, for whatever reason — for example, an uprising in Eastern Europe that is getting out of control, or a U.S.-Soviet clash in Iran, or conflict in the Middle East — they may be tempted to gamble and try to end what they see as a great threat to their own security."

There are some additional factors to be considered here, argues

---

9 General Bruce C. Clarke, Commander-in-Chief of U.S. Army forces in Europe during the 1961 Berlin crisis, has this to say about the defense of West Berlin: "Four or five years ago Vice President Mondale was in Berlin. In a TV talk to the Berliners he stated to the effect that if the Russians attacked Berlin the U.S. would come to its aid with all it had. I wrote to him in the White House and said that, as an ex-C-in-C of the Army in Europe, I would like to know how the U.S. would do that with 20 Russian divisions between West Germany and Berlin? He did not answer me. I still would like to know how to do it? Letter to the author, March 5, 1984.

McNamara. "Whether it contributes to deterrence or not, NATO's threat of 'first use' is not without its costs." Not only is it a "most contentious policy, leading to divisive debates both within individual nations and between the members of the Alliance." But it "reduces NATO's preparedness for conventional war . . . and it increases the risk of nuclear war."

Preparing for tactical nuclear war, McNamara maintained, "limits NATO's ability to defend itself conventionally in several ways." Nuclear weapons are "indeed 'special' munitions." They "require special command, control and communications arrangements." They "require special security precautions." They "limit flexibility with which units can be deployed and military plans altered." Operations on a nuclear battlefield "would be very different from those in a conventional conflict." Thus, NATO planners, "must take those differences into account."

Moreover, "since most of the systems that would deliver NATO's nuclear munitions are dual-purpose, some number of aircraft and artillery must be reserved to be available for nuclear attack early in a battle, if that became necessary." Under these circumstances, they would not be available for delivering conventional munitions.

Most importantly in the view of McNamara, though, is that "the reliance on NATO's nuclear threats for deterrence makes it more difficult to muster the political and financial support necessary to sustain an adequate conventional military force." Both publics and governments "point to the nuclear force as the 'real deterrent', thus explaining their reluctance to allocate even modest sums for greater conventional capabilities."

To the extent that the nuclear threat has deterrent value, McNamara argued, "it is because it increases the risk of nuclear war." However, "Soviet predictions of such a risk, in fact, could lead them to initiate nuclear war themselves." For one thing, "preparing themselves for the possibility of NATO nuclear attacks means that they must avoid massing their offensive units." This "would make it more difficult to mount a successful conventional attack, raising the incentive to initiate the war with a nuclear offensive." Moreover, "if the Soviets believe that NATO would indeed carry out its nuclear threat once they decided to go to war — whether as a matter of deliberate choice or because the realities of the battlefield would give the Alliance no choice — the Soviets would have virtually no incentive not to initiate nuclear war themselves."

McNamara emphasized that "this would only be the case if they had decided that war was imminent and believed there would be high risk that NATO's threats would be fulfilled." But if those two conditions were valid, "the military advantages to the Warsaw Pact of preemptive nuclear strikes on NATO's nuclear storage sites, delivery systems, and support facilities could be compelling." He concluded by urging NATO to modify its basic strategy, starting with a summit announcement that it intends to meet Soviet conventional aggression with non-nuclear forces only."

Reactions to McNamara's Nuclear Assessment

McNamara's assessment of the "first-use" policy stirred up quite a controversy in Europe, particularly in West Germany. Some critics construed his remarks as an invitation to the Soviets to step up actions against the West, thus increasing the risks of war rather than lessening them. Others, like Kurt Biedenkopf, formerly General Secretary of the ruling Christian Democratic Party,[10] agreed that existing strategic doctrine should be reexamined, particularly in light of Europe's reliance on the U.S. extended nuclear deterrent at a time when America has lost its global superiority. The result of his proposal would be a shift away from primary reliance on nuclear deterrence to reliance on conventional options.[11]

General Bernard Rogers conceded that the West should not have to rely so heavily on quick use of nuclear weapons for its defense if deterrence fails and that there are no "obvious indications" that the Soviets intend to attack Western Europe. However, he said he believes the Soviets are intent on using their superior military position to intimidate Western Europe and that a better balance of conventional forces would lessen this threat.[12]

Report by the Union of Concerned Scientists

Following the publication in the spring of 1982 of the aforesaid article in *Foreign Affairs* the Union of Concerned Scientists sponsored a detailed study of the first-use option. This study was directed by John M. Lee, a retired Vice Admiral of the U.S. Navy. He was assisted by Kurt Gottfried, Professor of Physics at Cornell University, and Henry W. Kendall, Professor of Physics at the Massachusetts Institute of Technology. In addition, a number of retired senior military officers and former civilian defense officials on both sides of the Atlantic took an active part in the project and endorsed the final report. Their findings were published in *Scientific Amercan* in March 1984.[13]

---

10 In his book *Die Atomschwelle* (Raise the Nuclear Threshold), he underpins his view that preserving the peace with arms depends on public approval.

11 See *Die Welt*, February 4, 1984.

12 *The Washington Post*, December 15, 1983.

13 Kurt Gottfried *et al.*, "'No First Use' of Nuclear Weapons," *Scientific American*, Vol. 250, No. 3 (March, 1984), pp. 33-41.

It is generally agreed, they reported, that NATO "would resort to nuclear weapons only if an offensive by the Warsaw Pact appeared to be on the verge of success." Accordingly, "military casualties already number in the thousands, and the rapidly shifting front would run somewhere through densely populated West Germany." Under these circumstances, "the use of tactical, or short-range, nuclear weapons could lend effective support to troops on the battlefield only if the commanders were able to make rapid decisions on the basis of accurate intelligence and if the weapons could be promptly released for use."

However, as the scientists noted, formidable obstacles would stand in the way of such NATO operations. For one thing, the intricate system NATO relies on for command control communications and intelligence (C^3I) "is highly vulnerable to attack and would presumably be a prime target for the Warsaw Pact forces from the very beginning of hostilities." At present, they stressed, the "nuclear threshold" cannot be crossed by NATO field commanders acting alone. "The highest political leaders of the NATO countries are supposed to agree on the timing, magnitude and location of any nuclear attack." For this reason "NATO has set up an elaborate procedure for reaching such decisions."

However, "NATO's military and political requirements are in direct conflict with each other." From the military standpoint, it "is essential to take prompt action while the C^3I system is still able to provide reliable data and before the NATO armies, which have been trained to depend on nuclear weapons, begin to disintegrate." From the political standpoint, the decision to use nuclear weapons "would require a consensus capable of withstanding the unprecedented strains inherent in initiating and sustaining a nuclear attack." But such a consensus "could be brought only with time, whereas the military situation could deteriorate to the point of collapse if the political leadership delayed — or refused to allow — the use of nuclear weapons."

These and other considerations led the scientists to conclude that "there is no plausible scenario for the use of nuclear weapons in a conflict between the two superpowers that does not carry with it the danger of catastrophic escalation." They noted that, to some, this conclusion "merely emphasizes the value of the first-use doctrine as a deterrent." Others, however, have come to believe NATO cannot stake the future on a strategy that is "either a bluff or a suicide pact" to quote Field Marshal Lord Carver, former Chief of Staff of the British Defense Staff. In view of the foregoing, the scientists devoted the bulk of their attention to an investigation of the assertion that a no-first-use policy would provide a more sound foundation for defense.

The scientists began their inquiry by attacking the "widespread misperception" that the U.S.S.R. has an overwhelming superiority in conventional forces, a premise which has led some critics to dismiss outright the no-first-use option as utopian. They point out that the way in which the conventional balance of forces is usually portrayed, "it ignores the fact that NATO's task is to defend, not to attack." They concede the controversial point that the Warsaw Pact is stronger in conventional arms than NATO. But they say "it must be remembered that in a conflict between armies of comparable competence an attacker must hold a substantial advantage to be confident of success." The disparity between the Warsaw Pact and NATO armies "is not of such proportions."

At present, the scientists argue, the prevailing first-use policy tends to make many people in Western Europe "more frightened by their own defense than they are by the potential attack." This fear "threatens the entire Alliance with political paralysis and *has created concern in military circles that NATO may already have a de facto no-first-use policy without any of the requisite preparation."* (Italics mine.) In the view of the scientists, a "no-first-use policy that has been deliberately prepared and agreed on in peacetime would lead to more confident and coherent decisions in a crisis . . ."

In assessing the overall balance of forces, the scientists discuss several uncertain military and political factors. One of these is whether or not the NATO countries "would be able to act quickly and in unison in the event of an attack." Another uncertainty concerns the role of France. Although France "is formally a member of the Alliance, it does not participate directly in the NATO military-command structure." At the present time, France maintains two active divisions and support troops in West Germany, and it is unlikely that France would remain neutral in the event of an attack by the Warsaw Pact.

The scientists point out here the questionable reliability of non-Russian Warsaw Pact forces. This is a serious problem for the Soviet Union. Would Polish and Czech troops, for instance, participate fully in combat not directly linked to their own defense? Could East German troops be used in an invasion of West Germany? Indeed, they suggest, "it is possible that the U.S.S.R. would have to commit its troops to guarantee the loyalty of its allies in a war against NATO." Furthermore, the Soviet leadership would have to plan "for the possibility that China would take advantage of the hostilities in Europe." This would limit the ability of the U.S.S.R. to call on its strategic reserve for the European theater.

The scientists emphasize that certain weaknesses and inadequacies in NATO's conventional defenses must be corrected "if NATO is to face the Warsaw Pact confidently without the option of first use of nuclear weapons." The steps that should be taken fall into four categories. First, NATO "must be able to make quicker political decisions and to deploy supporting forces and reinforcements promptly from Europe and overseas." Second, a number of operational improvements should be made. These include the construction of tank obstacles and field fortifications and better organization of reserve forces to cover the threat of a long war." Third, NATO "should improve its present advantage in advanced technology." Finally, NATO's ability to sustain military operations "should be strengthened."

The estimated cost for improving the ability of NATO's conventional forces to withstand any invasion of Western Europe without resorting to nuclear weapons would add up to less than $ 100 billion over six years, the scientists estimate. The $ 100 billion figure they project would entail an annual increase of approximately two percent in real terms of NATO's total annual defense expenditures of $ 300 billion. Importantly, "this increase would be below the current level of three percent that NATO members agreed to in 1978 and considerably below the four percent recently advocated for the 1983-88 period by General Bernard Rogers.[14]

The scientists suggest that funds for implementing these improvements could come from a restructuring of NATO's military priorities. In particular, "funds allocated to nuclear-weapons procurement could be shifted to meet the cost of many of the higher-priority conventional programs." To illustrate, they say that the cancellation of the MX missile program could save more than $ 20 billion.

In summary, the scientists conclude that the adoption of a no-first-use policy would be to NATO's military and political advantage. It could be taken independently of actions by the Soviet Union and its allies. Therefore it is not contingent on negotiations. A no-first-use policy would strengthen the cohesion of the Alliance and make relations with the Soviet Union less perilous in times of crisis. Most importantly, it would markedly lower the risk of nuclear war.[15]

14 In June 1984 Defense Secretary Caspar Weinberger sent a classified report to Congress stating that West European military spending is falling below NATO's goal of a 3-percent real annual increase. According to one U.S. insider, West European spending rose on average by just over one percent after inflation last year. According to Senator Sam Nunn (D-Geogia), U.S. financial support for NATO has been increasing by between 4.9 percent and 9 percent during the last four years. The present American share of the conventional defense of Europe is about $ 115 billion for 1984, or 42 percent of the $ 274 originally requested for defense by the Reagan Administration.

In order to signal the Europeans that "We cannot permit ... this situation [to continue] endlessly into the future," Nunn proposed to cut U.S. troop commitments to NATO in stages by 90,000, or nearly one-third, by 1990 unless changes were made in the funding of conventional forces. As the Senate worked on a $ 299-billion defense authorization bill for fiscal 1985, that body voted 55-41 to reject Nunn's proposal. See *The International Herald Tribune*, June 21, 1984.

15 For a very recent study along similar lines see F.W. von Mellenthin *et al.*, *NATO*

Henry Kissinger Joins the Debate

In the March 1984 issue of *Time* magazine former Secretary of State Henry Kissinger entered the debate with a number of highly controversial proposals. "An alliance cannot live by arms alone," he wrote. "To endure it requires some basic agreement on political aims that justify and give direction to the common defense." If "military arrangements provide its only bond, it will sooner or later stagnate."

According to Kissinger, four main problems are gnawing at the Alliance. The first is the "lack of a credible strategy." The "flexible response" strategy, he notes, "remains NATO's official doctrine." But in today's circumstances it has a "fatal weakness." Neither existing nor projected NATO conventional ground forces are adequate to repel a major Soviet conventional attack." Therefore, the "doctrine would require a nuclear response at an early stage." Yet strategic nuclear parity "deprives the threat of strategic nuclear war of much of its credibility; mutual suicide cannot be made to appear as a rational option," he says.

The second major problem faced by NATO has to do with the arrival of the new Pershing IIs and cruise missiles in late 1983. Their arrival should "properly be hailed as a major success," Kissinger argues, for "if public demonstrations and Soviet pressure had succeeded in blocking that deployment, the Soviet Union would in effect have achieved a veto over NATO's military dispositions." But "unless the alliance clarifies the purpose of these missiles, the accomplishment is likely to be transitory, since the basic European attitude toward the missiles is that of a host toward a now unwanted guest whose invitation to dinner it would be too awkward to withdraw."

European ambivalence, Kissinger says, "makes it excruciatingly difficult to define 'progress' toward arms control." Moreover, the "nearly desperate eagerness with which progress is pursued makes its attainment less likely." Significant segments of European opinion persist in blaming the U.S. for the deadlock in arms control talks, he says. In time, this attitude must "erode the public support needed not only for missile deployment but also for coherent arms control."

The third major problem confronting NATO pertains to East-West relations. "Too many Europeans," Kissinger maintains, "accept the caricature of a U.S. run by trigger-happy cowboys whose belligerence has provoked Soviet intransigence." On the other hand, many Americans "consider such European notions naive." They "believe that together with the pacifist and

Under Attack: Why the Western Alliance Can Fight Outnumbered and Win in Central Europe Without Nuclear Weapons (Durham: Duke University Press, 1984).

neutralist demonstrations, they reflect a trend toward appeasement that encourages Soviet intransigence."

The last major problem Kissinger indentifies focuses on relations with the Third World, and U.S. and West European competition there.

These differences, Kissinger argues, have led to mutual recrimination and have created opportunities for Soviet political warfare. "The Politburo is obviously convinced that the West has become so paralyzed concerning nuclear weapons that there is no urgency about nuclear arms control; the Soviets can simply wait for a while to harvest the fruits of Western anxieties."

Kissinger goes on to say that the "present NATO structure is simply not working, either in defining the threat or in finding methods to meet it." Thus, an "explicit act of statesmanship" is needed to give new meaning to Western unity and a new vitality to NATO. He supposes that the current difficulties in NATO are at least indirectly affected by a state of affairs where one country (the United States) "dominates the alliance on all major issues..." So he proposes to provide (1) a more significant role for Europe within NATO; (2) a reform of the NATO organization; and (3) a reassessment of current NATO deployment.

A New Role for Europe

During the entire post-World War II period, Kissinger writes, "it has been an axiom of American policy that for all the temporary irritation it might cause us, a strong, united Europe was an essential component of the Atlantic partnership." The United States applied that principle, insofar as it depended on American actions, in "all areas except security." With respect to the defense of Western Europe, "the U.S. has been indifferent at best" — at least since the failure of the European Defense Community in the early 1950s. Many U.S. officials "seemed to fear that a militarily unified Europe might give less emphasis to transatlantic relations or might botch its defense effort and thus weaken the common security." The "opposite is almost certainly the case."

Today "the vitality of the Atlantic Alliance requires Europe to develop greater identity and coherence in the field of defense." The present allocation of responsibilities fails to bring the allies to "reflect naturally about either security or political objectives." Since drift "will surely lead to unravelling — if more imperceptibly — statesmanship impels a new approach."

Structural reform of the alliance, Kissinger points out, "cannot substitute for a sense of purpose and clear doctrine." But if "pursued with care and sensitivity, it can help catalyze the development of shared political purposes." The former Secretary of State proposes in this context four major changes.

I. *Europe Should Assume Major Defense Burden.* "By 1990 Europe should assume the major responsibility for conventional ground defense," Kissinger suggests. This, he says, is "well within the capability of a group of countries with nearly one and one-half times the population and twice the size the G.N.P. of the Soviet Union."

II. *NATO Commander Should Be European.* With an increased participation of Western Europe in its own defense, the planning for Europe's defense becomes "more explicitly" a European task. A European officer should take over the post of Supreme Allied Commander, traditionally an American honor, Kissinger says. A U.S. military man could probably serve as a Deputy Commander.

III. *NATO Secretary-General Should Be American.* In the new reformed NATO structure, with greater emphasis on political coordination, the post of NATO Secretary-General should go to an American. (Traditionally, the individual responsible for NATO's political machinery has been European.)

IV. *Europe Should Take Over Certain Arms Control Negotiations.* Kissinger notes that the INF talks with the Soviets on intermediate range missiles and the MBFR talks on conventional forces have heretofore been conducted by American delegations. Both of these negotiations "should be 'Europeanized' as quickly as possible, with a European chairman, an American deputy and a mixed, though predominantly European, delegation."

The structure that Kissinger proposes "would enable Europeans to confront — on their own initiative and in their own context — issues that have been evaded for at least two decades." These include the "precise definition of an adequate conventional defense; the nature of the so-called nuclear threshold; and the relationship between strategy and arms control." Since nuclear weapons would presumably be used only if conventional defense failed, "Europe would be responsible for setting the nuclear threshold by its own efforts..." It "could relieve its nuclear anxieties by the simple expedient of augmenting its conventional defenses."

The issue of redeploying American forces touches raw European nerves "like no other," writes Kissinger. But if the allies refuse to play a greater role in their own defense, then the United States should "draw certain conclusions." If Europe "by its own decision condemns itself to permanent conventional inferiority," then the United States should withdraw up to one-half of its 320,000 military personnel in Europe. The proposed "redeployment" would leave intact air and naval forces, as well as intermediate-range missiles "so long as Europe wants them."

For a "son of Europe reared on the existing NATO orthodoxy, the very idea of even a partial redeployment is painful — all the more so after Leba-

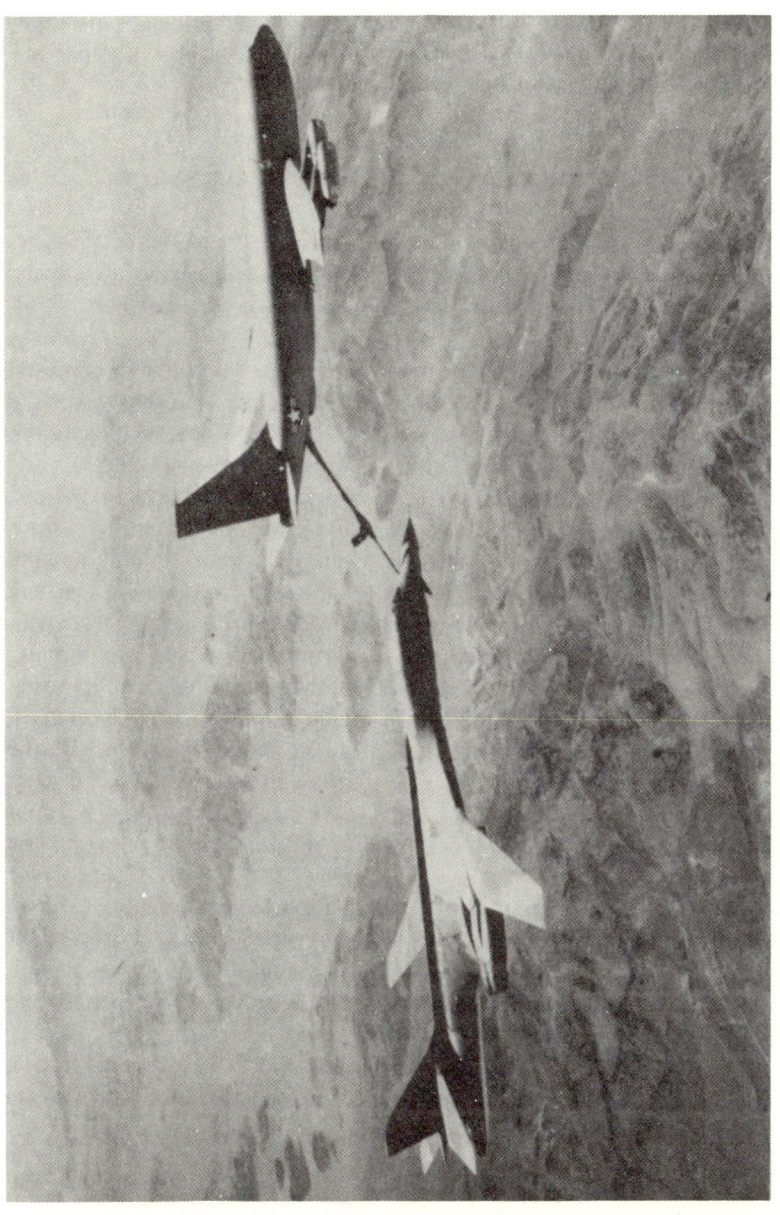

Figure 5: *A US Air Force B-1 prototype being refueled by a KC-135 tanker aircraft. The successful B-1 flight test program had provided valuable technology that will form the basis for the Air Force's new B-1B Long Range Combat Aircraft.*

non," Kissinger states. "But we will not be fulfilling our obligations to the West if we fail to put forward an initiative to forestall the crisis that will otherwise confront us in much worse circumstances."

Allied Reaction to Kissinger's Proposals

Kissinger's ideas provoked immediate controversy in Western Europe. In part this was because he is perceived as a possible successor to Secretary of State George Shultz[16] and also a man who wields great influence within the Reagan Administration.[17]

Many West German newspapers spread Kissinger's proposals across their front pages. The conservative daily *Die Welt* called it "a shot across the bow." The pro-government *Frankfurter Allgemeine* headlined the story "Bonn Concerned About Anti-European Mood in America."

Alois Mertes, Minister of State *(Staatssekretär)* in the West German Foreign Office, criticized Kissinger for what he described as his "irrational pessimism." This was more damaging to the alliance than useful, he said. Mertes rejected Kissinger's suggestion for the restructuring of NATO and dismissed the threat to substantially reduce American conventional strength in Western Europe if the West Europeans did not assume more responsibility for the defense of the continent. Mertes said that Europe could not possibly assume a responsibility that exceeded the limits of its power. He also criticized Kissinger's remarks that the Europeans should negotiate with the Soviets over nuclear missiles recently deployed by U.S. forces in Britain, Italy and West Germany. "How can we, in negotiating with the Soviet Union, conduct negotiations dealing with weapons we do not own," he asked.

Mertes agreed with Kissinger on the need to beef up conventional forces in Europe. But he felt the remarks by the former Secretary of State might give the overall impression that NATO was in the midst of a deep crisis. In reality, said Mertes, the Alliance has recently proven its inner unity and strength.[18]

In a talk with reporters, Chancellor Helmut Kohl ruled out the idea of a German military commander in charge of NATO forces. This would create too many political difficulties with the European Allies, he said.[19]

16 "This is a European perception that many in Washington would not share," says Ambassador Martin J. Hillenbrand. Letter to this writer, June 4, 1984.
17 Just a short time before, the President had appointed Kissinger head of the Foreign Intelligence Board, which oversees the American intelligence community.
18 *The Week In Germany*, March 2, 1984.
19 *The Washington Post*, February 29, 1984.

Interestingly, high-level members of the opposition Social Democratic Party in Bonn welcomed the Kissinger proposals for a greater European role in determining the nature of Allied defense in Europe. The Social Democrats had previously refused to support the deployment of the Pershing IIs and cruise missiles in Europe. And this fact had been cited by some critics as evidence of a drift toward neutralism.

Writing in *Die Zeit*, a major West German newsweekly, former Chancellor Helmut Schmidt (SPD) personally welcomed Kissinger's piece, although he took issue with some of his ideas. "Kissinger's critics," he stated, "overlook his correct and urgent appeal for the development of a common comprehensive strategy regarding East-West problems." Schmidt went on record as being opposed to a no-first-use policy, but he did strongly support "an improved conventional balance of power."[20]

The net effect of the Kissinger article was to heighten Allied, particularly German, sensitivities toward mounting American exasperation with the NATO alliance. Even though Kissinger stressed that his ideas were designed to counter the neutralist and pacifist trends he saw in some European countries, West Germany and other NATO members warned that such notions might have the reverse effect, by encouraging such ideas.

Emphasis on European Responsibility

Uncertainty about U.S. foreign policy and controversial comments coming out of Washington on military matters have prompted the European Allies to accelerate plans to bring a greater measure of European identity and decision-making to their military policies. Seven of the NATO Allies, led by France, Britain and West Germany, are now planning a meeting of their foreign and defense ministers in the fall of 1984 to discuss what some of the group term "Europeanization." This idea is roughly defined as Western Europe taking greater control of its own defense while maintaining its military relationship with the United States.[21]

The Fall 1984 meeting represents the first wide-ranging discussion by West European foreign and defense ministers in years to take place outside of the NATO alliance and without the United States. Predictably, the American response has not been enthusiastic although *publicly* the U.S. government welcomed the initiative, provided it did not try to take over NATO's function.

The major short term goal of the group seems to be cooperation in

---

20 *Die Zeit*, March 16, 1984.
21 See *The New York Times*, February 26, 1984.

building new weapons in the face of what West European officials acknowledge is a widening technological gap between Europe and the United States. In the long run, the West Europeans want to develop a closer strategic relationship with one another.

The Western European Union (WEU) is to be the principal organizational framework for the new European defense initiative.[22] The WEU was set up in 1954 in succession to the Brussels Pact, which was concluded in 1948 by Britain, France and the Benelux countries. The original purpose of this group was to monitor the rearmament of West Germany and to ensure that there would never be a recurrence of German policies of aggression. Subsequently, the Federal Republic and Italy, another World War II adversary, were included in the WEU.

Under the terms of the accession agreement, both states were subjected to strict restrictions on their production of arms and exports. For its part, West Germany undertook a commitment not to manufacture atomic, biological and chemical weapons.[23] Over the years, some of these restrictions have been lifted. For instance, in 1980, the tonnage limit permissable for submarines and warships built in German yards was waived. Three years later, the WEU's parliamentary body proposed a motion for the waiving of WEU treaty provisions mainly regarding the manufacture of long-range bombers and missiles.

This recommendation was approved by the Western European Union's Council of Ministers in late June 1984.[24]

For many years the WEU was greatly overshadowed by NATO. However, the Western European Union assumed greater importance when France withdrew from the military organization of NATO in 1966. The WEU then became both a vehicle that continued to link France with the North Atlantic Treaty Organization and a forum in which the Europeans could discuss defense and arms issues among themselves.

The recent ugprading of the WEU has reportedly given rise to some

22 Unlike NATO, the WEU binds every member to automatic intervention against aggression from any quarter whatsoever. See Josef Joffe, "Europe's American Pacifier," *Foreign Policy*, No. 54 (Spring, 1984), p. 71.

23 According to one source, Secretary of State Dulles told Franz Josef Strauss, Chancellor Konrad Adenauer's Minister of Defense, when the Federal Republic of Germany renounced nuclear weapons in 1954 that the *rebus sic stantibus* principle of international law could be invoked if the other European powers went nuclear. See Richard J. Barnet, *The Alliance* (New York: Simon and Schuster, 1983), p. 222.

24 In March 1984, France proposed that remaining restrictions on the West German manufacture of conventional weapons be lifted. Jacques Chirac, a neo-Gaullist leader, has implied that he favors giving the Federal Republic of Germany some participatory voice in the use of nuclear weapons. See *The Wall Street Journal*, March 15, 1984.

mistrust in Washington. But the Europeans are moving cautiously. They acknowledge privately that European political cooperation is now low. Moreover, they realize that European economic stagnation and military budgets that often contain a decline in real spending are not encouraging signs for new joint military efforts.

Summary

As this chapter makes clear, the debate over the question of the first-use of nuclear weapons in Europe has important implications for the larger issue of deterrence.[25] For the early first-use of nuclear weapons still remains a central element in America's strategy of deterring Soviet aggression in the European region.

As we have seen, the opponents of "no first use" have marshalled impressive arguments in their behalf. However, those military experts, who would contemptuously dismiss the idea of a no-first-use declaration on the ground that "declarations like that get put aside in the first moments of conflict," fail to understand what a no-first-use declaration is intended to do. *Its purpose is not to restrict the use of weapons in wartime so much as to restrict the deployment of weapons in peacetime.*

Freeman Dyson explains the significance of this crucial point. "When Country A signs a no-first-use declaration, the effect is to compel the military authorities in Country A to take into account the possibility that the political authorities in Country A may actually mean what they say." This means "that Country A is forced to go to the trouble of hardening and concealing its weapons or withdrawing them from exposed positions where they would be vulnerable to preemptive attack." The effect "is to make Country A's deployments more survivable and at the same time less threatening to neighboring countries. The risk of war is reduced by these

---

25 One U.S. official with some thirty years experience in military-political matters would comment: "In my view, the first-use debate is of limited value. It is not so important what one says. The important thing is what weapons do you have where, and what plans you have for using them. The U.S. must reconcile itself to the reality that the Europeans are not prepared to build up a credible conventional defense. The question it must ask itself is whether it is prepared to take the risks involved in the present strategy and force posture. While at times I am inclined to leave the Europeans to their own devices and let them defend themselves, in my more sober moments I am unwilling to do this — simply because I have little confidence that the Europeans can run their own affairs. I wish this were wrong, but I am unwilling to take the chance. When my father's generation turned its back on Europe, I found myself twenty years later fighting here to liberate the continent from Hitler."

changes in peacetime deployments, not by any possible direct effect of a no-first-use declaration in wartime."[26]

The major advantage for NATO in making such a declaration is that it will direct Western deployments strongly in the direction of stability but will not detract substantially from the defensive value of NATO weapons as seen by the Soviet Union. At the present time, tactical nuclear weapons in Western Europe and elsewhere are not subject to no-first-use constraints, with the net result that they are far more exposed and vulnerable. Since tactical nuclear weapons are more likely than strategic weapons to cause a great deal of trouble, a no-first-use declaration covering these weapons would greatly reduce the danger.

Adoption of a "no-first-use" policy by NATO has specific implications for its "forward defense" strategy. This tactical concept was imposed on the Alliance when West Germany agreed to re-arm during the Korean War. At that time Chancellor Konrad Adenauer insisted that no amount of FRG territory should be ceded in a war, even as part of an opening gambit designed to allow sufficient time for mobilization and counter-attack.[27] Subsequently, "forward defense" has been interpreted by different NATO members according to how far back they are from the front, but it is still taken literally by West Germany. The U.S. military, in particular, was never happy with this concept. It generally favored tactical concepts suitable for mobile units, based far from the front and yet ready to move rapidly forward to confront an aggressor at the time and place of most favorable circumstances for the defender. This more fluid tactical defensive strategy did not involve a commitment to hold a particular line.

Even with a conventional buildup, it is difficult to see how a "forward defense" could be guaranteed. A fortified border would certainly help, but such an idea in the past was deemed politically unacceptable because a barrier would acknowledge the permanence of a divided Germany. It was also dismissed on military grounds because of a similarity with the French Maginot of the inter-war period, the failure of which in 1940 was taken as evidence of the inadequacy of the notion. Given domestic concerns about the political wisdom of relying primarily on nuclear weapons for defense/ deterrence, perhaps the time is now ripe for German leaders to consider seriously a mobile defense.

Those on both sides of the first-use debate recognize that the actual use of tactical nuclear weapons would very probably result in the devastation

---

26 Freeman Dyson, *Weapons and Hope* (New York: Harper & Row, 1984), pp. 278-79.

27 This position, held by Chancellor Adenauer during 1951 and early 1952 in all negotiations leading to FRG rearmament, was not agreed to by the U.S. government.

of a substantial part of NATO's own territory. At the same time, they realize that any use of nuclear weapons by NATO carries with it a high and inescapable risk of escalation into general war which would bring ruin to all and victory to none. The brutal fact is that NATO planners have not, in all these years, been able to devise contingency plans that would make practical use of weapons with such pervasive after-effects that are clearly advantageous to the Alliance.

The major concern of proponents of a "first-use" strategy is that a change in policy might make NATO forces more vulnerable to an attack from the East. However, an objective assessment of the current balance of forces in Central Europe would lead us to conclude that neither side could be guaranteed a favorable outcome should war break out in Europe. Assuming that the Warsaw Pact began to mobilize for war before NATO did, its greatest military advantage would exist in the first few days of a crisis. Thereafter, as a number of defense experts have pointed out,[28] if an uninterrupted buildup of forces were to continue on both sides, the ratio of opposing forces available in Europe would continue to shift in the favor of NATO unless the Soviet leadership were willing to move large numbers of troops from its Central, Southern and Far Eastern military districts — a doubtful development given the Soviet concern over the threat posed by China. In the very long term, the ratio might even shift in NATO's favor because of the far larger population and economic base it enjoys and consequently its greater potential for raising and supporting military forces.

Because of these disadvantages, the most attractive strategy for the Warsaw Pact, if it decided to go to war under a NATO no-first-use policy, would appear to be an attempt to achieve victory in the shortest possible time — by surprise.[29] However, it is unrealistic to assume that the ground forces of the Warsaw Pact could launch a major conventional attack without any warning.[30] U.S. intelligence officials report that Eastern Europe army units are generally manned in peacetime at less than 75 percent full strength. At the same time, the normal peacetime activities of Soviet ground

---

28 See Barry Blechman et al., *The Soviet Military Buildup and U.S. Defense Spending* (Washington, D.C.: Brookings Institution, 1977), p. 28. The authors are still of this opinion.

29 See Joseph D. Douglas, Jr., *Soviet Military Strategy in Europe* (New York: Pergamon Press, 1980).

30 It is important to note that, given the intelligence-gathering capabilities of NATO, the Warsaw Pact would not be able to mobilize its forces in any significant way without being detected, so complete surprise would be impossible. See the speech delivered by Bobby Inman, former Deputy Director of CIA, before the ninety-sixth annual convention of the American newspaper Publishers Association, San Francisco, April 27, 1982.

forces in Eastern Europe (which are believed to be almost fully manned) include training and maintenance activities that at most times would inhibit their immediate availability. Finally, supplies that would be consumed fairly quickly in combat, particularly ammunition and fuel, would have to be distributed to combat units in advance of an attack. In short, Soviet preparations for an attack would most likely take several days at the least and East European preparations somewhat longer.[31] Mobilization would be noticed almost immediately in the West.

Moreover, the frequently cited danger that NATO members would receive this strategic warning but be unable to react because of political indecision seems exaggerated.[32] To be sure, a political decision calling for NATO to mobilize would take time — perhaps days. But military commanders have the authority to cancel training and begin preparing for war long before that. In fact, such steps as loading vehicles, conducting last-minute maintenance and updating and reviewing operational plans should allow NATO ground forces to begin to move almost immediately after a political decision is reached.[33]

In summary, then, the Soviet Union and its Warsaw Pact allies could threaten NATO militarily in a number of ways under a no-first-use policy. If all of these possibilities are unlikely, they cannot be ignored. Currently, NATO forces would have a good chance of conducting a conventional defense if the attack occurred after some period of tension and mobilization on both sides or if the U.S.S.R. received less than full co-operation from its Warsaw Pact allies. There is room for worry about NATO's capa-

31 Until the mid-1970s, U.S. and NATO policy planners reportedly projected an official warning time of 23 days — time enough for Alliance mobilization and reinforcement from the continental United States, Canada and the United Kingdom. However, when confronted with increasing evidence of a Warsaw Pact capability to launch an attack against Western Europe without prior reinforcement, Allied planners generally concurred that NATO's warning time of an impending attack had been drastically reduced. See Jacquelyn K. Davis *et al.*, *Soviet Theater Strategy: Implications for NATO* (Washington, D.C.: United States Strategic Institute, 1978), p. 9.

32 General Bernard Rogers and the outgoing NATO Secretary-General of NATO, Joseph Luns, disagree. Following a secret exercise in March 1984, there were reports that as mock intelligence reports of Soviet activity poured into NATO headquarters, officials representing several West European governments were reluctant to respond with mobilization, arguing that such a move could precipitate a war. Later Luns said: "One of the worries ... that I take with me is that warning time will not be used by governments of the alliance under the false pretext that if we mobilize it might increase the crisis. In fact it might be the last possibility to defuse the crisis." *The International Herald Tribune*, June 29, 1984.

33 "These are trivial measures in face of a Soviet mobilization," states one former NATO official.

bility, however, if all Warsaw Pact forces were committed on short warning — or if NATO were slow to mobilize. In these cases, the Warsaw Pact would have a fair — though by no means certain — chance of forcing NATO to make some hard choices including the loss of large amounts of territory. For these reasons, NATO's first priority must be to increase its conventional capabilities as it begins the consultative process within NATO leading to the adoption of a no-first-use policy.[34] In the meantime, NATO should make a clear statement of intent to rely on conventional forces in event of war.

*

Today the debate over first-use turns on the issue of deterrence. Those who argue in favor of retaining the present policy generally see real deterrent value in it, even though the development of strategic nuclear parity deprives the policy of much of its credibility. Basically, they see the policy as lessening the risk of war because of the increased risk to the Warsaw Pact forces. Those who would change the policy point out that some 19,000 nuclear weapons are estimated to be allocated directly on *both* sides for nuclear war in Europe.[35] Given this situation, these people tend to see the present policy as either a bluff or a strategy to commit mutual suicide (to use Lord Carver's words).[36] And in their eyes neither should be made to appear as a rational option to policy makers.[37]

34 According to General Bernard Rogers, there is an existing congressional ceiling of 315,600 American military personnel in Europe. In the Federal Republic of Germany, one West German official says, "defense spending has increased to 28 percent of the budget, which is arguably the limit to what Germany is able and willing to contribute." Lord Carrington's appointment in June 1984 as NATO's Secretary-General is seen by many observers as giving new emphasis to the matter of increasing NATO's conventional capabilities. The former British foreign and defense secretary replaced Joseph Luns who, even to many NATO officials, seemed after 13 years in the stewardship to lose touch in later years with changing public opinion and the importance of the need for more conventional defense efforts. "I think Carrington will try to make the generals more responsive to political reality," a senior NATO official said at the time. *The International Herald Tribune,* June 25, 1984.

35 See Steven Canby and Ingemar Dorfer, "More Troops, Fewer Missiles," *Foreign Policy,* No. 53 (Winter, 1983-84), p. 9.

36 Michael Carver, "No First Use: A View From Europe," in Suzanne P. Ogden (ed.), *World Politics 84/85* (Guilford, Ct.: Dushkin Publishing Group, 1984), pp. 198-202.

37 See John D. Steinbruner *et al.*, (eds), *Alliance Security: NATO and the No-First-Use Question* (Washington, D.C.: Brookings, 1983).

Whatever one's view of this debate, the following points should be borne in mind: To pose an unacceptable risk to a nuclear-armed adversary *automatically* poses the same risk to one's own side. Any policy that would turn to some form of limited nuclear war to reduce this risk and thereby make the threat more credible tends to make the unacceptable risk appear more acceptable — and thus less of a deterrent.

The more acceptable nuclear war, however limited, seems to the leaders of the superpowers, the more likely it is that nuclear war will actually come about. Even if nuclear war results in only a few exchanges, the effects will be catastrophic to those individuals who reside in the territory in which the nuclear weapons are exploded. To term these results "defense" or "security" is to make a mockery of these terms.[38]

This military reality has been perceived by a number of Western defense planners, who now realize that existing strategic doctrine should be reexamined.[39] Since the existing strategy of NATO was adopted in 1967, the world has undergone great change. Besides specific changes in theater capabilities of both the Warsaw Pact and NATO forces outlined in this chapter, there has been a basic change in the strategic nuclear balance. This change has been from dominant Western superiority, upon which present NATO strategy is based, to what many people now view as "rough" or essential equivalence, *at best.* If current trends continue, and indicators are that they probably will, some basic changes seem unavoidable.

The most important change may well come in the area of NATO conventional forces. There seems to be general agreement now that NATO's conventional forces should be quantitatively and qualitatively improved — even if this may not be easy to achieve. The likely result of such a develop-

---

38 It is often forgotten in the debate over "no-first-use" that both the United States and the United Kingdom pledged themselves in 1978 not to use nuclear weapons against any non-nuclear-weapon states that are parties to the Non-Proliferation Treaty. The only exception to this obligation would be in the case of an armed attack on Britain and the U.S., their forces or their allies by such a state in association or alliance with a nuclear-weapon state. To be sure, this formula (termed "negative security assurance") does not rule out initial use of nuclear weapons in the event of a conflict between NATO and Warsaw Pact forces. Indeed, it was deliberately worded not to preclude this option. However, the guarantee does provide an undertaking not to use nuclear weapons against third parties in almost all other likely situations. Furthermore, NATO members as a group have underlined their commitment to the "no-first-use of force" undertaking in the U.N. Charter by repeating that NATO "has never and will never initiate the use of force." See Nuclear Planning Group Ministerial Communiqué, Colorado Springs, March 23, 1982.

39 The official quest for a new alliance strategy was started by General Bernard Rogers more than two years ago.

ment would be a shift away from primary reliance on nuclear deterrence to reliance on a defense by conventional means.[40] In the end, such a reduced dependence on a strategy based primarily on the use of nuclear weapons should lessen the risk of a nuclear confrontation.

The debate over "no-first-use" has had a positive effect on the European members of the NATO Alliance, official American concerns notwithstanding.[41] Most importantly, it has forced them to pay more attention to their own role in the defense of Western Europe. The United States, instead of being suspicious, should applaud and support West European efforts toward greater defense cooperation and self-reliance. For far too long, American officials proclaimed their hope for real European unity and independence — and then resented it when the Europeans took them at their word. As the late French philosopher Raymond Aron wrote just three years ago: "By its very nature, Western Europe's dependence on the U.S. for its own defense is unhealthy." To too many West Europeans, the American nuclear umbrella and its alleged deterrent effect have made the European military largely irrelevant. It has also encouraged many Europeans to adopt a more passive (some would say "neutralist") stance than might otherwise have been the case.

To be sure, the West European-American destiny will continue to be a common one, despite particularist concerns on both sides of the Atlantic.[42] In the words of Arthur Schlesinger, Jr.: "Americans may indeed be standing tall these days, as our president assures us, but it isn't going to help much if we stand tall all by ourselves. We continue to need allies, not only to temper our own messianic delusions, but also for the eminently practical

---

40 Samuel P. Huntington of Harvard University and a former adviser to the Reagan Administration recently proposed a strategy for fighting a conventional weapons war with the Soviet Union and its Warsaw Pact allies. Huntington argued that should the Warsaw Pact embark on an offensive into Western Europe, the North Atlantic Treaty Organization should retaliate with an offensive into East Germany and Czechoslovakia. His proposal is one of the most recent in a series, aired on both sides of the Atlantic, which seeks a Western strategy that does not involve nuclear exchanges. Huntington's view is questioned by some military experts who maintain that, once a Soviet offensive into West Germany began, it would not be deterred by any NATO strike into East Germany and Czechoslovakia unless the strike severed Soviet lines of communication.

41 One U.S. State Department official observes here: "Europeans want to escape dependence on an America they can't understand and that doesn't seem to want to understand them."

42 Josef Joffe, a West German military expert, wrote recently with brutal insight in *Foreign Policy* about the U.S. role in keeping the Europeans together. He describes the United States as "Europe's pacifier," the outside force that has brought extraordinary cohesion in the area of security among powers that had fought for a thousand years.

reason that there are few foreign policy objectives in the real world that we can attain by going it alone."[43]

Nevertheless, salesmen of the *status quo*, with their heavy reliance on the American nuclear deterrent, play into Soviet hands. From the Soviet point of view, the current arrangement, with the United States and Western Europe bound together in a severely frayed consensus that may be on the verge of breaking down, offers numerous opportunities to exploit. Thus, a friendly political, economic and military relationship, based on mutual respect and appreciation for divergent views, resulting in a reinvigorated, partially (but hopefully increasingly) united, more powerful Western Europe is better for the West.[44]

---

43 *The Wall Street Journal*, March 5, 1984.

44 Just recently, former Chancellor Helmut Schmidt proposed that France and West Germany undertake a "major security initiative" that would in effect merge their armed forces and curtail Europe's military dependence on the United States. Schmidt argued that the two countries could, by mobilizing reserves, field 30 divisions that would be "sufficient to defend the Western part of Europe and deter any attack." He said it would take up to five years to equip French and West German divisions with enough weapons and munitions to form a credible defensive force. Schmidt delivered his appeal during a West German parliamentary debate in late June 1984. See *The International Herald Tribune*, June 29, 1984.

> ... the grave risks of perpetuating the notion that more nuclear weapons in NATO Europe are synonymous with greater security makes it, I believe, advisable now to dissipate the myth of a nuclear nostrum. If kidding ourselves only means kidding our potential adversary as well, the fact that our nuclear doctrine may be unrealistic poses no serious threat to NATO's security. But if adherence to nuclear illusions threatens to promote divisiveness with NATO, to afford the Soviets' protracted opportunity for mischief, and to stimulate Soviet consideration of destabilizing strategies such as launch on-warning, then it is time to get serious and explicit about the role that nuclear weapons can play in the defense of Western Europe.
>
> *Paul C. Warnke*

IX. THE EUROSTRATEGIC CONTROVERSY

The role of American nuclear weapons in the defense of Western Europe has been the subject of intense debate almost since the creation of the NATO Alliance itself in 1949. After all, as Andrew J. Pierre, Director of the Project on European-American Relations for the U.S. Council on Foreign Relations, writes: "what is at issue is the fundamental link between Western Europe's security and that of the United States, and therefore the credibility of the American nuclear guarantee."[1]

Between 1979 and 1984 the debate reached a new height of controversy over the NATO decision to deploy 572 U.S. intermediate-range nuclear missiles to Western Europe while at the same time undertaking arms control negotiations with the U.S.S.R. The deployments began in the midst of massive demonstrations in Europe in November 1983, but they are not scheduled to be completed until 1988. After making clear its strong opposition to the deployments, the Soviet Union walked out of the talks on intermediate-range nuclear forces (INF) in Geneva. This Soviet exit was soon followed by the departure of the Russians from both the strategic arms negotiations (START) and the deliberations on mutual and balanced

---

1   Andrew J. Pierre (ed.), *Nuclear Weapons in Europe* (New York: Council on Foreign Relations, 1984), p. 1.

force reductions (MBFR) in Vienna which deal with the conventional arms balance.

The fact that NATO continued to rely primarily on the American nuclear deterrent at a time when the United States had lost its superiority in ICBMs was a principal reason for the controversial NATO decision of December 12, 1979. The vulnerability of American ICBMs had made it appear less likely to the European allies that the U.S. would agree to a policy of nuclear retaliation to defend Europe if the Soviets could destroy a large portion of U.S. land-based missiles in North America. Many West Europeans questioned whether the United States would risk its own survival to defend its allies.

This chapter attempts to explore the historical background to these major events. In particular, it seeks to answer the following important questions: (1) Was the NATO deployment decision in 1979 a wise decision? (2) What was the nature of the threat NATO was responding to? (3) What impact has the decision had on the NATO allies? (4) What role has the issue of deterrence played in the controversy over deployment?

Eurostrategic Forces

Before one can begin to understand the significance of the 1979 NATO deployment decision, it is first necessary to come to grips with the various categories of nuclear delivery systems within the context of the overall East-West balance. Traditionally, nuclear weapons have been divided into two basic categories, based largely on their range, the size of their payload, and planned target. These are so-called "tactical" and "strategic" nuclear weapons. Generally, those missiles possessing shorter ranges and smaller warheads for use on or near the battlefield to destroy military forces have been termed "tactical" nuclear weapons. By way of contrast, those longer-range, more destructive nuclear missiles targeted against important centers in the homeland to destroy the war-making ability of the opponent have usually been labeled "strategic" weapons. However, it should be noted at the outset that this distinction is somewhat artificial and theoretical. In fact, as one strategic expert would point out, "The boundary between these two classes of nuclear weapons has never been precisely defined..."[2]

We can see this most clearly in the case of NATO nuclear-capable aircraft. Frequently, they are referred to as "strategic" weapons. But this is an oversimplification. For although many do indeed possess the capability

2 Richard Burt, "The SS-20 and the Eurostrategic Balance," *The World Today* (March, 1977).

Intermediate-range Nuclear Missiles
(March 1983)

	USSR			U.S.	
	SS-4	SS-5	SS-20	Pershing II	GLCM[1]
Warheads	1	1	3 MIRV	1	1
Range (KM)	2,000	4,000	5,000	1,800	2,500
Operational Flight Time	Minutes	Minutes	Minutes	Minutes	Hours
Operational Mode	Fixed	Fixed	Mobile	Mobile	Mobile
Global Numbers Deployed	232	16	351[2]	0[3]	0[4]
Year Operational	1959	1961	1977	1983	1983

1. Ground-launched cruise missiles.
2. About 108 targeted on Asia, the rest on Europe.
3. 108 Pershing IIs scheduled for deployment beginning December 1983.
4. 464 GLCMs scheduled for deployment beginning 1983.

Source: Joint Chiefs of Staff, *United States Military Posture*, fiscal 1984 (Washington, D.C.: U.S. Government Printing Office, 1983). SS-20 figures updated.

to carry out strategic missions in Europe or the Soviet Union, most are assigned tactical roles. (Before November, 1983, nuclear attacks on the Soviet Union could have been carried out from Western Europe only by 162 British and French nuclear missiles and some NATO aircraft.)[3]

If the traditional distinction between "strategic" and "tactical" weapons is becoming less meaningful, we should take note of another distinction which is taking on added significance. This is the division between superpower and regional strategic weapons. The superpower strategic weapons possess intercontinental ranges and are based, for the most part, within their territory. These nuclear delivery systems include land-based ICBM forces, long-range bombers and submarine-based ballistic missiles. On the other hand, regional strategic weapons do not generally have the capability for intercontinental strikes. Thus, these systems tend to be stationed in, or targeted against, Western Europe. This type of "Euro-strategic" nuclear force is made up of a far more diverse group of delivery systems. For the most part, these are NATO and Warsaw Pact nuclear-capable aircraft, Soviet medium-range bombers, Soviet and French Intermediate Range Ballistic Missiles (IRBMs) and the British and French submarine-based missile systems. ("Eurostrategic" nuclear weapons do not technically include the some 6,000 shorter-range nuclear weapons designed primarily for use in the European theater in tactical roles, such as nuclear artillery or surface-to-surface tactical missiles like the U.S. *Lance*.)[4] Despite the fact that one would be hard put to distinguish between an IRBM attack on London and Bonn from an ICBM attack on Washington, these Eurostrategic weapons have only recently received some of the attention they deserve. However, the tendency on the part of many people is still to lump them together with "tactical" nuclear weapons.

Characteristics of the Pershings and Cruise Missiles

The decision to upgrade NATO's Eurostrategic capability resulted in the phased deployment to Europe beginning in December 1983 of some 108 Pershing II ballistic missiles and 464 ground-launched cruise missiles (GLCMs). Varying amounts of these missiles were installed in the United Kingdom, Italy and West Germany, which is to receive all the Pershing IIs and approximately one-fourth of the cruise missiles. Belgium and the

---

3 In the Warsaw Pact the Soviet Union maintains control over all its nuclear weapons. The Pact has no nuclear weapons of its own.

4 In 1983, at a nuclear planning group meeting in Ottawa, NATO decided to scrap about 1,400 of its approximately 6,000 tactical nuclear weapons in Europe. The Europeans, one insider revealed, initially wanted to scrap about 2,500.

Netherlands, which were originally to be candidates for the new missiles, have meanwhile expressed serious reservations and have postponed deployment.[5]

The exact operational range of these nuclear weapons is a government secret. However, knowledgeable observers estimate the range of the Pershing IIs to be about 1,100 miles and that of the ground-launched cruise missiles about 1,800. Unlike the new Soviet MIRVed SS-20, the Pershing II carries a single "selectable" warhead, which allows the yield to be adjusted to the magnitude of the target. The ground-launched cruise missiles are descendants of the old Matador and Mace cruise missiles; they have, however, a terrain contour-mapping navigation system that makes them among the most accurate nuclear delivery vehicles.

The ground-launched cruise missile is a single-warhead missile with pinpoint accuracy. What is rarely mentioned in the unclassified literature, however, is the fact that this missile can also be outfitted with multiple warheads and is fired from a reloadable launcher. Although it would take the ground-launched cruise missiles several hours to reach certain high priority targets in the U.S.S.R., its miniscule size and "microscopic" radar signature make it a threat to all Soviet sites.

Contrary to public impressions, cruise missiles are not new. The earliest cruise missile was the German V-1 "buzz bomb," which was used against the United Kingdom in the final years of World War II. It was slow and inaccurate and was utilized primarily as a terror weapon.

By the mid-1950s both the U.S. and the U.S.S.R. had deployed somewhat more capable cruise missiles. Some of these were even armed with nuclear weapons. One of these was the "Snark," a subsonic, high-altitude intercontinental cruise missile whose accuracy was measured in miles. But

---

5 In mid-June, 1984, the Dutch Parliament, after two days of intense debate, voted to approve the Cabinet's plan to deploy 48 intermediate range cruise missiles unless the Soviet Union immediately halts its nuclear buildup in Eastern Europe. Under terms of the government's compromise plan, the final decision on deployment would be delayed until November 1985 and installation of the missiles would move from late 1986, as originally planned, to 1988. Although this plan is the first substantive commitment by the Dutch to deploy the missiles, it also represents the first serious break from the timetable set by the North Atlantic Treaty Organization. See *The International Herald Tribune,* June 15, 1984.

When asked to clarify the Dutch position on the deployment of the cruise missiles, Ruud Lubbers, Prime Minister of the Netherlands, told an interviewer: "In the first place there is no question of delay, because the Netherlands never committed itself to deploy the missiles. This is a misunderstanding that should be corrected. Since 1979, Holland has left open the possibility of deployment, and everyone within the alliance was fully aware of that stand. Now we have made a decision in favor of deployment based on certain conditions . . ." *Newsweek,* June 18, 1984.

it was rendered obsolete soon after it was deployed by the advent of the faster ICBMs which were harder to counter. Indeed, ballistic missiles replaced cruise missiles in all U.S. forces by the late 1960s.

The cruise missiles staged a comeback, however, soon after SALT I was signed. In large part, this was due to the development of miniature electronics and advanced engine technology. These breakthroughs made it possible to produce a small, accurate missile that was difficult to detect. Moreover, this missile could carry a nuclear warhead 1,500 miles or more — that is, from bases in Great Britain, ground-launched cruise missiles have the range to cover most of the high priority targets in the U.S.S.R., *including Moscow.*[6]

If the cruise missile is now a formidable weapon, the Pershing II has special attributes that make it a lethal battlefield weapon. Perhaps its most important characteristic is its deadly "pin-point" accuracy. The precision of the Pershing IIs, though not tested over ranges in which they might be used in a nuclear war, is attributed in part to the evolution of inertial guidance systems. These are like advanced gyroscopes that can tell a missile where it is while it is in flight. The Pershing II represents the first deployment by the U.S. of a high-accuracy MARV weapon.[7]

As agreed upon by the Allies, the United States alone is to control the Pershing IIs and cruise missiles as well as pay for them. Washington initially offered "dual key" (joint control) of the weapons to any NATO partner willing to share the cost, originally estimated at $ 5 billion. But the Allies showed little interest in the proposal.[8]

Technically, the Pershings and the cruise missiles were termed Long-Range Theater Nuclear Forces or LRTNF for short.[9] These are weapons

---

6 George M. Seignious II and Jonathan P. Yates, "Europe's Nuclear Superpowers," *Foreign Policy*, No. 55 (Summer, 1984), pp. 40-53.

7 The maneuverable reentry vehicle, or MARV, is defined by a recent Library of Congress report as a "ballistic missile warhead or decoy whose accuracy is improved by terminal guidance mechanisms." However, there are basically two types of MARVs. One is an evader MARV (e.g., the Navy's MK-500) designed to overcome ballistic missile defenses. The other is a very accurate MARV with a counterforce mission such as the Pershing II. For a good discussion see Robert J. Bresler *et al.*, "The Bargaining Chip and SALT," *Political Science Quarterly*, Vol. 92, No. 1 (Spring, 1977), pp. 84-85.

8 Michael D. Wormser (ed.), *U.S. Defense Policy*, 3rd ed. (Washington, D.C.: Congressional Quarterly, Inc., 1983), p. 75. The West Germans stated categorically that they would not accept the two-key system whereby a decision to send a nuclear weapon toward the Soviet Union would be shared by the United States and Germany. Thus, a decision to launch these weapons would be an American decision *even though these weapons are now based in Europe.*

9 During the second half of 1981 the Reagan Administration adopted new terminology for these weapons. This new wording, which was subsequently approved by

with ranges from 1,000 to 5,000 kilometers. (Weapons with ranges from 200 to 1,000 kilometers are called Medium-Range Theater Nuclear Forces or MRTNF, and those of less than 200 kilometers are named Short-Range TNF or "battlefield nuclear weapons.") The dispatch of Long-Range Theater Nuclear weapons to Western Europe had been planned for four years to deter or, if necessary, to counter any attack on the NATO Allies, by Soviet intermediate-range ballistic missiles or conventional forces. Generally, there was concern that NATO's longer-range nuclear systems — all of them aircraft — were aging and becoming increasingly vulnerable to a Soviet pre-emptive attack. Moreover, the build-up of Soviet SS-20 medium-range missiles in the western part of the Soviet Union caused some worry that the U.S.S.R. was obtaining what strategic theorists like to call "escalation dominance."[10] This is technical nuclear war-fighting jargon for the ability of one side to control the level of exchange by effectively deterring the other side from escalating. Hence, the U.S. and its NATO Allies decided that this development would have to be offset by new, more survivable and equally medium-range missiles, capable of reaching targets in the Soviet Union. (The Pershing II has a range not comparable to the SS-20).[11]

The SS-20 Threat

Because NATO based its controversial decision to deploy American Pershing II and cruise missiles to Europe primarily on the Soviet decision in the 1970s to deploy the SS-20 in the western part of the Soviet Union, we would do well to take a close look at possible Kremlin motives. The Soviets generally say that the SS-20s, which can reach every part of Western Europe, are the centerpiece of a justifiable and long overdue program to replace their obsolete IRBM force in Europe and to counter U.S. forward-based sys-

> NATO, did away with the name *theater nuclear forces*. Instead, these forces are now described according to their range capability: longer-range intermediate-range nuclear forces (LRINF), shorter-range intermediate-range nuclear forces (SRINF) and short-range nuclear forces (SNF). The LRINF category is a rough equivalent to the old LRTNF category. This cumbersome change was made at the behest of the West Europeans, who were offended by the view that looked upon the European continent as merely a "theater." My decision to retain the older terminology is not based on any wish to offend Europeans. Rather, I prefer the older terminology because it seems more descriptive of the location and mission of these forces.

10 The concept of escalation dominance was first developed by Herman Kahn in *On Escalation: Metaphor and Scenarios* (New York: Praeger, 1965).

11 For details see Christoph Bertram, "The Implications of Theater Nuclear Weapons in Europe," Foreign Affairs (1983), pp. 305-26.

tems.[12] The two IRBMs that previously made up the force — the SS-4 and SS-5 — were both over 15 years old and reflected Soviet missile technology of an earlier period. Western analysts agree that both systems, totalling 315 in number, were obsolete by Western standards. They possessed unwieldy, liquid-fuel propulsion systems and inaccurate guidance devices, and they required extensive logistical support. Thus, their replacement could probably have been justified on grounds of cost-effectiveness alone. But the Soviets also argued that their growing vulnerability posed an inviting target for a pre-emptive attack by Western forces.

The vulnerability issue is widely recognized by Western experts. While the Soviet ICBM force is now housed in hardened, underground silos, most of the previously existing Soviet IRBM force was deployed above ground in "soft" sites. In Soviet military eyes, it was their stationing above ground that made them extremely vulnerable. The SS-20 represented a vast improvement in this area because it is a solid-fuel missile, which can be easily transported and launched; thus its vulnerability is reduced because it is much harder to hit.

Most Western analysts seem willing to concede that, from the Soviet point of view, modernization of their IRBM force was a logical step. Deployed aboard a mobile launcher, the SS-20 greatly enhances the ability of Soviet Eurostrategic forces to survive attack from the West.[13] However, the United States and its NATO Allies contend that Moscow has used its modernization program as a cover for rapidly developing a superior nuclear IRBM force. Together with the increase in the advanced Russian medium-range bomber, the Tu-26 (code-named "Backfire" by NATO intelligence) which, with in-flight refueling, has an intercontinental range and a new generation of Soviet long-range fighter aircraft, the new SS-20s are generally seen by U.S. officials as intended not simply to deter attack but to intimidate nations on the Soviet periphery. This, in turn, undermines the allies' faith in the American security guarantee and ultimately could force their accomodation to Soviet interests.

Here Administration spokesmen note the qualitative jump in destructive capability that the SS-20 represents. Fitted with multiple, independently targeted re-entry vehicles (MIRV) and possessing improved accuracy, the SS-20 makes existing targets in Western Europe more vulnerable to attack.

12 See Michael Tatu, "U.S.-Soviet Relations: A Turning Point?," *Foreign Affairs (America and the World 1982)*, p. 594. "The SS-20 has a range of some 5,000 kilometers (3,000 miles)," notes one U.S. government insider. "It is capable of striking any city in Western Europe, the Middle East or North Africa from bases on either side of the Ural Mountains."

13 For a discussion of Soviet motives here see George Ginsburgs *et al.* (eds.), *Soviet Foreign Policy Toward Western Europe* (New York: Praeger, 1981).

At the same time, this larger number of smaller, more accurate warheads enables the Soviets to place a larger range of Western European assets at risk and with greater discrimination.[14]

In order to understand fully the controversy that rages over the Soviet Euromissiles, we must recount a little history. Basically, the dispute has its roots in the 1950s, when the Soviet Union and the United States each began developing a significant nuclear strike force. Then, as now, differences in geography, technological capabilities and strategic philosophy meant the two opposing sides were far from "mirror" images of each other. In the late 1950s and early 1960s, the United States concentrated on building long-range intercontinental ballistic missiles. But the Soviet Union, instead of following the American pattern (which has so often been the case), focused its attention on building intermediate-range missile forces aimed at countries near the borders of the Soviet sphere of interest.

Why the Soviet leadership chose to concentrate on Eurostrategic, rather than superpower strategic, forces during this period is unclear. In part, the answer may be that IRBMs were less technically demanding than longer-range missiles. Perhaps the Soviet Union simply lacked the skills to compete with the United States in long-range missile procurement in the early 1960s (a situation that changed radically in the latter half of that decade). But other considerations may have also been at work. As some writers have suggested, the early Soviet emphasis on regional nuclear forces could very well have reflected their concern over the decision by the United States to concentrate initially much of its nuclear force in "forward based systems" — that is, bombers and medium range missiles in Europe, Turkey and the Far East.[15]

According to Western figures, the Soviet Union had by the early 1960s about 700 medium-range SS-4 and SS-5 missiles aimed at targets along its periphery. 600 of these were targeted on Western Europe. Large, sluggish and vulnerable, these liquid-fueled missiles stood on exposed launch pads and required roughly a full day to prepare for launching. These were all important factors that made them unlikely candidates for carrying out a surprise nuclear attack on Western Europe.

In contrast, the United States never had more than 60 medium-range Thor missiles in Britain and another 45 Jupiters in Italy and Turkey. All were withdrawn in 1963. This was at a time when the American intercontinental ballistic missile force was greatly superior to that of the Soviet

---

14 See Edwina Moreton *et al.*, (eds.), *Soviet Strategy Toward Western Europe* (Winchester, Mass.: Allen & Unwin, 1984).

15 See William Hyland, "Soviet Theatre Forces and Arms Control Policy," *Survival* (September -October, 1981), pp. 194-99.

Union, and NATO governments in Europe had relatively few doubts that this force conferred equal protection on them.

During the next decade European missiles became a "backwater" issue for the Kremlin. Leonid Brezhnev was consolidating control at home, and the Soviet leadership was proceeding to close the gap in ICBMs that had so humiliated the Soviets in the Cuban Missile Crisis of October 1962.

Two main developments caused the Soviets to re-focus their attention on regional nuclear forces. One was the growing obsolescence of its SS-4s and SS-5s. The second, ironically, was the first strategic arms limitation agreement in May 1972 and the continuing talks on strategic arms reductions. Under the SALT I Treaty, which allowed the U.S.S.R. to achieve strategic parity with the United States, U.S. officials refused to count American European-based aircraft and British and French missiles in limits on strategic forces. Since these medium-range forces were thus unrestrained, the Soviet leadership began strengthening its own.[16]

During the late 1960s, the Soviet military developed the less than successful mobile, solid-fuel ICBM that NATO dubbed the SS-16. As things worked out, this "white elephant" of an intercontinental ballistic missile was transformed into a fearsome new weapon. The first two stages of the SS-16 became the SS-20, which was outfitted now with three independently targeted warheads. With its 3,000-mile range, it was counted as a Eurostrategic weapon, and thus it was not included in the SALT II talks.[17]

From the Soviet perspective, the mobility of the SS-20 and its solid-fuel system bypassed the vulnerabilities of the old SS-4 and SS-5.[18] But from the view of the West, its three highly accurate warheads made the new missile look disturbingly like a potential pre-emptive strike weapon designed to intimidate Western Europe. Consequently, offsetting that danger became the rationale for deployment of the Pershing IIs and ground launched cruise missiles which would enable NATO's nuclear forces in Europe to strike deep into Soviet territory.[19]

16 Marsha M. Olive et al., *Nuclear Weapons in Europe: Modernization and Limitation* (Lexington, Mass.: Lexington Books, 1983).

17 The SS-20 has apparently also been tested with a single lightweight warhead at ranges exceeding the 5,500 km limit established in the 1972 SALT I Interim Agreement as the upper limit of a so-called "tactical" nuclear weapon. See *Aviation Week and Space Technology*. Vol. 31 (May 1976), p. 12.

18 The SS-4 was first deployed in 1959; it carries a single, one megaton warhead to a maximum range of 1,900 kilometers. In 1983, some 340 SS-4s were believed to be still operational. The SS-5 was initially deployed in 1961; it carries a single, one megaton warhead to a maximum range of 4,100 kilometers. In 1983, some 40 SS-5s were still in service. See Burns H. Weston (ed.), *Toward Nuclear Disarmament and Global Security: A Search for Alternatives* (Boulder, Colo.: Westview Press, 1984), p. 11.

Yet Western analysts are not united in the belief that the Soviet leadership actually intended a political mission for the SS-20.[20] Some analysts, and they seem to be in the minority, maintain that the Soviets were doing no more than following their old paranoid and simplistic instincts, which indicated that more weapons meant more security. "Certainly the Soviet Union would prefer a 'margin of safety' or advantage in the [European] theater balance, and would welcome any inhibitions this might place on NATO self-confidence," writes Raymond Garthoff, a senior fellow at the Brookings Institution in Washington and a long-time student of Soviet military policy. "But there is no evidence to support the idea that the Soviet leaders saw a political 'option' flowing from their SS-20 military deployment decision, or that such a political purpose even entered into their consideration in making such a decision. And there is considerable indirect evidence that it did not."[21]

The first SS-20s were installed and made operational by late 1977. Today, according to U.S. officials, 361 are in place. 243 of them are located in the western part of the Soviet Union and are aimed at Western Europe. The rest are deployed in the eastern part of the U.S.S.R. and are aimed at China, Japan, etc. Combined with the more than 340 older SS-4 missiles still in operation, the SS-20s more than double the number of Soviet warheads on intermediate-range ballistic missiles targeted on the NATO nations of Europe.

---

19 Richard Burt has argued that the SS-20 possesses an additional danger. In his view the fact that the SS-20 is comprised of the two upper stages of an ICBM raises the possibility that, in time of crisis, the missile could be converted to ICBM status by adding an additional rocket stage. See his "The SS-20 and the Eurostrategic Balance," *The World Today* (March, 1977).

20 William G. Hyland, a long-time U.S. expert on the Soviet Union, believes that the SS-20 was developed as an instrument of intimidation against the West Europeans and the Americans. But he suggests other possible (i.e. additional) interpretations of SS-20 deployment. For instance, it could be argued "that the explanation for this behavior lies in the bureaucratic politics in the Kremlin. A major program once begun is almost impossible to reverse. It could be that Brezhnev, in political maneuvering involving his successors, chose not to challenge or test his political position in a debate over a military program." See Hyland, "The Struggle for Europe: An American View," in Andrew J. Pierre (ed.), *Nuclear Weapons in Europe* (New York: Council on Foreign Relations, 1984), p. 31.

21 *The New York Times*, December 4, 1983. Former Secretary of Defense Robert McNamara argues here: "Each side got into these deployments for political rather than military reasons. That doesn't mean there hasn't been a rise in military risk."

The Politics of the Dual-Track Decision

References to the existence of the Soviet SS-20 program first emerged in official Western statements during 1975. But the missile did not receive widespread attention from the Western press until September 1976. At that time Fred Ikle, then Director of the U.S. Arms Control and Disarmament Agency, argued in a speech that its deployment was "unwarranted" and that it could jeopardize East-West arms control efforts.[22]

However, as far as NATO was concerned, the immediate spark to intra-Allied debate was a German initiative.[23] This was a speech made by West German Chancellor Helmut Schmidt to the London International Institute of Strategic Studies in October 1977.[24] At that time, Schmidt warned of the growing significance of the European nuclear balance, given a U.S.-Soviet strategic parity regulated by SALT and increasing Soviet deployment of SS-20 mobile missiles.[25]

Why did Chancellor Schmidt make the remarks he did in the way he did? One can only speculate, but it appears the West German leader was particularly disturbed by disclosures of an early Carter Administration analysis of NATO strategy. Known as Presidential Review Memorandum 10, this document recommended trading off much of the Federal Republic of Germany for a securer defense perimeter close to the Rhine. (In the aftermath of serious protest from Bonn, Presidential Directive 18 restored the "forward defense" of West Germany.) Schmidt was also concerned about rumors before the signing of SALT II that President Carter was prepared to bargain away the cruise missile. Such a move would abandon the very weapons system that the Chancellor and others believed could revolutionize the defense of NATO. In any case, Schmidt's London speech, which he came to regret, turned out to be one of the most important of his career.

Lengthy discussion in NATO soon followed Schmidt's public speech. It

22 Richard Burt, "The SS-20 and the Eurostrategic Balance," *The World Today* (March, 1977), pp. 43-51.
23 "It is important to emphasize," writes William Hyland, "that Schmidt's call for a reexamination of the European balance was not the original impetus that eventually led to the famous dual-track NATO decision of December 1979, though it certainly contributed. The dual-track decision flowed initially from an American critique in the mid-1970s of the consequences for Europe of the declining credibility of the U.S. nuclear guarantee . . ." See Hyland, "The Struggle for Europe: An American View," in Andrew J. Pierre (ed.), *Nuclear Weapons in Europe*, p. 19.
24 See Helmut Schmidt, "The 1977 Alastair Buchan Lecture," *Survival*, Vol. 20, No. 1 (January-February, 1978), pp. 2-10.
25 It is important to note here that, contrary to popular belief, Chancellor Schmidt did not refer specifically to the Soviet SS-20 missile at this time or suggest that NATO needed to expand its own Long Range Tactical Nuclear Force capability.

resulted in the creation of a group of Allied representatives called the High Level Group (HLG). This body involved all interested governments and met frequently throughout 1978 and 1979. At the insistence of European representatives, a second parallel group was set up nearly a year later. Called the Special Consultative Group, its duty was to prepare simultaneous proposals for East-West limitations on Long Range Tactical Nuclear Force deployments. The work undertaken by both these groups resulted in the Pershing and cruise missile package presented and broadly approved by the NATO Council in December 1979.[26]

It is important to note here that as NATO leaders debated possible hardware responses to the SS-20 through 1978 and 1979, Soviet and East European officials grew visibly alarmed. In the obvious attempt to pre-empt a NATO deployment decision, in October 1979 Soviet President Leonid Brezhnev offered — on the condition that no new medium-range NATO systems were deployed — to reduce the deployment of Soviet medium-range missiles and begin negotiations immediately on this category of weapons. At that time, fewer than 100 SS-20s were targeted on Western Europe. The United States could have cashed in the Pershings and the cruise missiles right then, but NATO's collective leadership lumbered on to its double decision.[27]

In part, the NATO deployment decision reflected the enthusiasm of American and West European elites, who tended to view cruise missiles in these early days almost like wonder weapons. The cruise missile represented the brightest of the emerging military technologies, which could be used in the West's continued search for means to offset the East's increased military power. Diffusion to the NATO Allies would be gradual and in proportion to national military and economic resources, with the United States — as always — in the lead.[28]

If cruise missiles, and especially the GLCMs were viewed in these early discussions as the most promising new military technology, they also were generally seen by NATO as offering a qualitative edge in the East-West theater balance. The Allies did consider a range of other systems (including the new medium-range ballistic missiles) and other basing modes (sea-launch-

---

26 For background on the U.S. role see Cyrus Vance, *Hard Choices: Critical Years in American Foreign Policy* (New York: Simon & Schuster, 1983). The deployment decision was taken at a meeting of NATO's Nuclear Planning Group (NPG). This Group, which formulates NATO's nuclear policy, included the U.S., Canada, West Germany, Britain, Italy, Belgium, The Netherlands, Denmark, Norway, Greece and Turkey.

27 *The Christian Science Monitor*, January 13, 1984.

28 Some of this enthusiasm is recaptured by Richard Burt in his article "New Conventional Weapons and East-West Security: Part II," *Adelphi Papers*, No. 145 (London: International Institute for Strategic Studies, 1978).

ed or tactical air-launched cruise missiles). But in the view of many participants, the result was largely pre-ordained by broad political concerns. Especially important here were visibility (thus, ground not sea-based systems) and timeliness (the earliest possible initial operating capabilities).[29]

The most difficult issues to resolve were political. Of special importance was the satisfaction of West Germany's long-standing policy of "non-singularity."[30] Chancellor Helmut Schmidt asserted from the outset that any new deployments must not increase German political vulnerability or unduly threaten its *Ostpolitik* (its rapprochement with the Soviet Union and Eastern Europe). Thus, any NATO plan had to ensure the participation of at least one non-nuclear European state beyond the Federal Republic of Germany and include the explicit support of *all* Alliance states including those (like France) which did not permit the stationing of U.S. nuclear weapons on its territory in peacetime.

The original Western plan called for deployment of 108 Pershing II ballistic missiles and 464 ground-launched cruise missiles over a five-year period, beginning December 1983. This long lead time was worked out because deployment was to be used mainly as a "bargaining chip" to induce the Russians to reduce the large number of their SS-20 missiles trained on Western Europe.

In one major respect, the December 1979 NATO decision was unique:[31] The decision to procure new nuclear arms was linked with the understanding to negotiate their limitation through bilateral American-Soviet arms control. Unfortunately, only two weeks after the NATO ministers issued their joint communiqué, Soviet forces moved into Afghanistan effectively putting bilateral détente "on ice."

Many West European leaders now claim, in fact, that they never expected to see the American missiles deployed in large numbers. Thus, they tend to blame the Carter,[32] and now the Reagan, Administration, for not

29 Catherine M. Kelleher, "The Present as Prologue: Europe and Theatre Nuclear Modernization," *International Security*, Vol. 5 (Spring, 1981), p. 153.

30 See Catherine M. Kelleher, *Germany and the Politics of Nuclear Weapons* (New York: Columbia University Press, 1975).

31 See Communiqué of the Special Meeting of Foreign and Defense Ministers in Brussels on 12 December 1979.

32 One former American diplomat with long experience in NATO matters would point out here: "You do not indicate that the Carter Administration was unenthusiastic about the deployment of missiles to Europe and argued against it. Hence the David Aaron visit to NATO." Personal relations between President Carter and Chancellor Schmidt were not good as Carter and Brzezinski detail in their memoirs. Schmidt, who has yet to write his, found it unsettling to have the American leader suggest to him that "you and I have to get the Russians out of Berlin." Here is a man, the Chancellor told Theo Sommer, the editor of *Die Zeit*,

being willing to negotiate seriously with the Soviets on the matter. In that Reagan was committed privately to a policy that emphasized a military build-up *before* undertaking serious talks with the Soviets on arms reductions, they had reason to be upset with the official American position, for it did not seem to reflect an adequate appreciation for their domestic pressures.

In retrospect, many American officials admit privately that the so-called "dual-track" approach, which called for prior negotiations to ban the weapons altogether and make their deployment dependent on a failure of the negotiations, was a tactical blunder. Henry Kissinger writes: "Experience with arms-control negotiations — or Soviet diplomacy — should have warned that an unambiguous outcome of such talks was nearly impossible." Instead, "the decision guaranteed a domestic crisis in most of the countries slated to receive missiles." Indeed, "it almost surely supplied an incentive for the Soviets to procrastinate and thus test the resolve of Western governments." Even more important, "the NATO decision caused the debate about the reasons for deploying the missiles to become bogged down either in domestic politics or in all the evasions and contradictions of the general NATO controversy." Opponents, "appealing both to fears and nationalism, invented the argument that the intermediate-range missiles reflected our desire to confine a possible war to European territory. This was absurd. We already had thousands of short-range tactical weapons in Europe."[33]

The INF Negotiations

In view of the importance the West European leaders attached to negotiations as a means of limiting Soviet and NATO Eurostrategic forces, we should spend some time briefly recounting the history of the INF talks, as they were called. The acronym INF stands for Intermediate-Range Nuclear Forces.

The arms control discussions mandated by the second track of the 1979 NATO decision opened in October 1980 during the final days of the Carter Administration after the Soviets dropped the precondition that NATO agree not to deploy while the talks went on. Little, however, was accomplished in this round.[34]

"who knows everything and understands nothing." Quoted in Richard J. Barnet, *The Alliance* (New York: Simon and Schuster, 1983), p. 375.
33 Henry Kissinger, "Arms Control and Europe's Nuclear Shield," *The Wall Street Journal,* January 31, 1984.
34 In early December 1979 the Soviets began to implement plans to withdraw some 20,000 troops and 1,000 tanks from East Germany as "a gesture of good will."

During the first weeks of 1981, when the Reagan Administration took office, the American negotiating position was considerably weakened by indecision and bureaucratic "infighting." At a meeting in February, Richard Perle, the congressional staffer who would soon become Assistant Secretary of Defense for International Security Policy, reportedly termed the NATO initiative that had been approved by President Carter "a lousy decision if ever there was one." Perle, who had the reputation in Washington as a "hawk's hawk," also expressed "misgivings about the cost-benefit wisdom" of the LRTNF deployment. Scoffing at the idea of paying billions of dollars for 572 weapons, he is said to have commented: "That's a hell of a price tag for a marginal military fix." For his part, Fred Ikle, who had recently joined the government as Under Secretary of Defense for Policy, feared that lining up the Europeans to accept the missiles would cause more political trouble within the Atlantic Alliance than the missiles were worth.[35]

The feelings of both these powerful U.S. officials were shared by others in the Reagan Administration. As one American insider recalls: "There was a movement early in the Reagan Administration to scrap the INF deployment, but it did not succeed."

Apparently, the influence wielded by Secretary of State Alexander Haig, who regarded the White House "as mysterious as a ghost ship," was decisive.[36] The former NATO commander felt it would be disastrous "to pull the plug on a promise that NATO made to itself." The new Administration was already in trouble in Western Europe for its strident rhetoric toward the Soviet Union. Cancellation of the December 1979, dual-track NATO decision might, it was felt, be taken as proof of President Reagan's opposition to arms control and of his insensitivity to America's Allies.

There was significant opposition in the government to beginning serious negotiations on theater nuclear weapons. Secretary of Defense Caspar Weinberger, for one, argued that the U.S. should make no such move until

---

Before this withdrawal Western intelligence officials estimated that the Soviet Union maintained some 400,000 troops and 7,000 tanks in the GDR. See *The New York Times*, December 6, 1979.

35 This account is based for the most part on Strobe Talbott's forthcoming book on the INF negotiations.

36 See Alexander M. Haig, Jr., *Caveat: Realism, Reagan, and Foreign Policy* (New York: Macmillan, 1984), p. 85. The full quote reads: "But to me, the White House was as mysterious as a ghost ship; you heard the creak of the rigging and the groan of the timbers and sometimes even glimpsed the crew on deck. But which of the crew had the helm? Was it [Edwin M.] Meese [Counselor to the President], was it [James A.] Baker [White House Chief of Staff], was it someone else? It was impossible to know for sure."

the huge rearmament program that Reagan was in the process of launching was well under way. "What the alliance wants, or at least what it needs," Weinberger reportedly told Haig at the Pentagon in early April, is "leadership, not compromise."

Later, Haig wrote in detail of Weinberger's tendency to "talk off the top of his head on issues of war and peace." Haig "prayed he might overcome" his penchant "to blurt out locker-room opinions in the guise of policy". But if "God heard, He did not answer in any way understandable to me. The arduous duty of constructing the meaning of Cap Weinberger's public sayings was a steady drain on time and patience."[37]

Generally, Weinberger and other "hard-liners" in the Administration saw Haig as showing signs of "clientitis." That is, they believed the former NATO commander was too concerned with mollifying the West Europeans. In the end, however, Haig got his way by appealing directly to the President, who was still recovering from the March 1981 assassination attempt. Consequently, Reagan agreed to let Haig announce in Rome that the INF negotiations would begin by the end of 1981.

If the Secretary of State more or less had his way over the issue of opening these talks with the Russians, he did not get his way on the vital question of who would represent the U.S. in the negotiations. Haig and other high-level State Department officials wanted a career diplomat who would be under their control. But instead, Paul Nitze, a veteran defense specialist who had helped found the Committee on The Present Danger,[38] was chosen. Although there was some concern in the State Department that Nitze's "notorious hawkishness" would scare off the Allies, he received the crucial backing of National Security Adviser Richard Allen, who claimed: "We need a heavy hitter, not a utility infielder."

Once the issue of who would head the U.S. negotiating team in Geneva was resolved, the debate over what proposal to make in the INF talks intensified. Ultimately, however, the hard-liners in the Administration, who believed that it would be almost impossible to secure an agreement with the Russians before the LRTNF weapons were in place, prevailed. As Richard Burt, then Director of the Bureau of Political-Military Affairs in the State Department, argued: the U.S. needed a proposal that would look equitable to the West Europeans but would also shore up their resolve to move ahead with deployment of the new weapons in the face of a stalemate in Geneva. "The purpose of the whole exercise," Burt told his staff, "is

---

37 Alexander M. Haig, Jr., *opus cit.*, p. 87-88.
38 The Present Danger Committee is a private group of conservative Democrats and Republicans who had opposed the SALT Treaty of 1979 and urged an American arms build-up.

maximum political advantage. It's not arms control we're engaged in, it's alliance management."[39]

On November 18, 1981, the President unveiled the "compromise" proposal worked out by the bureaucracy. His proposal was to offer to forego deployment of the two types of missiles if the Soviet leadership agreed to dismantle all of its European targeted SS-20s, SS-4s and SS-5s. This proposal, which came to be known as the "zero option" plan, was cautiously endorsed by America's NATO Allies, who tended to view it merely as an opening gambit.[40] Subsequently, talks on Intermediate-Range Nuclear Forces — the official name of the negotiations on theater nuclear forces — began on November 30, 1981 in Geneva, Switzerland.[41]

---

39 Just a short time before leaving the New York *Times* for the State Department Burt wrote an article which forcefully denounced the arms control process and held out little hope for its future success. "Arms control," Burt wrote, "has developed the same kind of mindless momentum associated with other large scale government pursuits ... There are strong reasons for believing that arms control is unlikely to possess much utility in the coming decade." See his article "The Relevance of Arms Control in the 1980s," *Daedalus* (Winter, 1981).

40 While recognizing that the zero option was "clever public relations and did indeed put the U.S.S.R. on the defensive," William G. Hyland believes that the zero option proposal "could have created a serious problem" for NATO. If accepted, it would have left "the U.S.S.R. free to deploy an unlimited number of shorter range weapons against most European targets" while "barring the United States from any new weapons capable of attacking Soviet territory." This "new tactical imbalance in Europe" would have made "any nuclear exchange virtually suicidal for West Germany. Even if the United States had compensated by shifting its cruise missile deployment to sea-based systems, NATO would have lost the tangible coupling with American strategic forces." See Hyland, "The Struggle for Europe: An American View," in Andrew J. Pierre (ed.), *Nuclear Weapons in Europe*, p. 36.

41 Alexander Haig writes in his memoirs that the "zero option" plan was a German idea. "The Schmidt government huckstered an ingenious basis for negotiation: the United States would not deploy new missiles in Europe if the Soviets would dismantle the SS-20s and perhaps the SS-4s and SS-5s they already had in place. This came to be known as the Zero Option. It was enthusiastically championed by the Department of Defense. I opposed it ... The fatal flaw in the Zero Option as a basis for negotiations was that it was not negotiable. It was absurd to expect the Soviets to dismantle an existing force of 1,100 warheads, which they had already put into the field at the cost of billions of rubles, in exchange for a promise from the United States not to deploy a missile force that we had not yet begun to build and that had aroused such violent controversy in Western Europe." See Haig, *Caveat: Realism, Reagan, and Foreign Policy* (New York: Macmillan, 1984), p. 229. One U.S. official familiar with the Zero Option proposal would add here: The Zero Option was "developed by the SPD Left around Karsten Voigt and adopted by the Social Democratic Party at its 1979 Party Congress."

The Walk-in-the-Woods Agreement

During the first two rounds of negotiations on the Reagan plan little progress was made. The Soviets, who made it clear that they intended to use the negotiations as a way of inducing the West Europeans to postpone acceptance of the new missiles, rejected out of hand the so-called zero-option proposal. "Both sides," President Leonid I. Brezhnev declared during a visit to Bonn in November 1981, "should, for as long as the negotiations last, refrain from stationing new medium-range systems in Europe and from modernizing already existing ones."[42]

During subsequent sessions Paul Nitze and Yuri Kvitsinsky, the chief negotiator for the Soviet side, sparred and probed. Meeting privately, they eventually worked out the "ground rules" for a climactic breakthrough in their talks, which took place on July 16, 1982. The two men traveled to a spot high in the Swiss Jura Mountains, near the French border. As they strolled along a wooded path, they conducted a lengthy, sometimes tense bargaining session. While both men reserved the right to disavow the deal later, only Nitze was operating completely on his own. He had learned the hard way that it would be impossible to obtain formal approval in advance from Washington for all the necessary trade-offs, so he had decided to risk "going it alone."

The outcome of this informal bargaining session became known as the "walk-in-the-woods" agreement. Its essential features were as follows: The Soviets would give up their insistence on cancellation of the U.S. LRTNF deployment and on compensation for British and French forces. The number of Soviet SS-20s would be reduced from 243 to 75 in Europe and frozen at 90 in Asia. The U.S. would only be allowed to install 75 land-based cruise missile-launchers, with four warheads each, for a total of 300 warheads. In addition, the U.S. would cancel its plans to deploy Pershing IIs in West Germany.

From the Soviet perspective, the Pershings were the most worrisome of the two prospective nuclear weapons systems because they could reach targets in the Soviet Union much more quickly than cruise missiles, which fly at subsonic speeds (about 450 miles an hour). Also, the Soviets have a long standing fear of German fingers anywhere near the nuclear trigger. From the American perspective, the agreement was advantageous because it finally sanctioned the introduction of new U.S. LRTNF weapons in Western Europe. By agreeing to this proposal, the Soviets would have tacitly

---

42 On March 16 and May 17, 1982, the Soviets sought to influence world opinion and the INF negotiations by declaring a unilateral moratorium on intermediate-range missiles. See *Pravda*, March 17, 1982 and May 18, 1982.

conceded that they had created an imbalance and that the West was entitled to redress it. At the same time, the Soviets would have abandoned their claim to compensation for the British and French nuclear forces. Moreover, a freeze on Asian-based SS-20s would have enabled U.S. officials to assure China, Japan and South Korea that European arms control was not being conducted at their expense.[43] Under this tentative agreement, the United States would have ended up with more warheads on its cruise missiles than the Soviets would have had on their remaining SS-20s in Europe, and the U.S.S.R. would have agreed not to deploy any long-range ground-launched cruise missiles of its own. This entire package would all have been in exchange for one basic U.S. concession: the sacrifice of the Pershing II.

Subsequently, Nitze returned to Washington and furiously set about trying to persuade the Administration to accept the bargain he had worked so hard to achieve. In his immediate superior, Secretary of State Haig, Nitze had a formidable opponent. As Haig wrote later: "If the objective of the talks is a balanced reduction in missiles, if the aim of Western policy is deterrence, if the American goal in Western Europe is to allay the anxieties of our allies and restore their confidence in our leadership, then the 'walk in the woods' proposal works against our purposes on all three counts."[44]

Shortly a group of national security specialists was set up to study the deal carefully and make recommendations. Its chairman was Robert McFarlane, then Deputy to William Clark, the President's National Security Adviser who had taken over after the resignation of Richard Allen. McFarlane, a former Marine officer, was particularly taken aback by the idea that Nitze had "wandered off the reservation." Consequently, he drafted a memorandum reprimanding Nitze for exceeding his instructions. At the same time, McFarlane prompted the President to ask the Joint Chiefs of Staff whether they could live without the Pershing II.

---

43 The significance of this concession seems not to have been comprehended by many in the West. But William G. Hyland, a former aide to Henry Kissinger, highlights the "new" importance of the Far East to the U.S.S.R. He writes: "The Soviets began redeploying some short-and medium-range nuclear forces to the Far East in the 1970s. The Far East subsequently became a distinct theater for operations with a new independent command. The number of SS-20s deployed in the Far Eastern command has been 108 launchers, or 324 warheads... The Soviets argue that the separation between European Russia and the Far East is legitimate and reflects a genuine security concern... To include the Far East deployments in U.S.-Soviet negotiations would thus involve Soviet concessions to the United States for the benefit of China... The Far Eastern factor thus sets a sharp limit on Soviet freedom to negotiate..." See Hyland, "The Struggle for Europe: An American View," in Andrew J. Pierre (ed.), *Nuclear Weapons in Europe*, p. 33.

44 Alexander M. Haig, Jr., *Caveat: Realism, Reagan, and Foreign Policy* (New York: Mcmillan, 1984), p. 232.

The Joint Chiefs of Staff knew that the strictly military rationale of the weapon's deployment was highly questionable. For one thing, despite the Soviet build-up in Eurostrategic weapons, America's lead in deliverable nuclear warheads remained impressive. For another, the new theater-based systems would at best only make a marginal difference. (Every target in the U.S.S.R. could be covered by existing American nuclear weapons.) Finally, the Joint Chiefs were aware that the Soviet build-up in Europe only added to military options that their force of medium and intermediate-range missiles had enjoyed from the late 1960s, rather than creating new ones as some Administration officials liked to maintain.

On September 13, 1982, a National Security Council meeting was convened to rule on Nitze's package deal. At this time, Ambassador Nitze defended for his compromise agreement, and Defense Secretary Weinberger argued vociferously against it. The President, who was still attached to the simplicity of the original zero option proposal, seemed confused. Why, he asked, could the Soviets not live without SS-20s if the U.S. could live without its new missiles in Europe?

Nitze took special pains to answer the President on this crucial point. There was a big difference, he said, between not deploying a weapons system still under development and dismantling one that was already perfected and in place. In his view, it was inconceivable that the Soviets would ever accept a proposal that required them to remove every last one of their most modern intermediate-range missiles. That was asking for too much.

Following the debate, the President gave his decision. "Well, Paul," Reagan said, "you just tell the Soviets that you're working for one tough son of a bitch."

A New Soviet Proposal

Once the Soviets learned of the President's decision, they moved *publicly* to repudiate the deal struck by their negotiator Kvitsinsky. Confidentially, the Soviets complained that they had been tricked into tipping their hand on their own ultimate fallback position. However, most importantly, they emphasized that Nitze had first raised the possibility of a breakthrough in the context of a Reagan-Brezhnev summit which the Soviet President, who was then in failing health, appeared to want, perhaps as a last hurrah of statesmanship. Whatever the case, the summit never materialized, for within weeks, Brezhnev was dead. (Brezhnev died on November 10, 1982).

Soon after Brezhnev died, Yuri Andropov, formerly head of the KGB, emerged as the new Soviet Communist Party leader. A great goal of Andropov's foreign policy before he in turn died fifteen months later was to induce the Western Europeans to reject deployment of the new American missiles.[45] He told the West Germans that the two Germanies would be divided by a "palisade of missiles" if Bonn accepted the U.S. weapons. Then, in December, 1982, Andropov made a live television address, in which he offered to trim the European SS-20s from 243 to the number of intermediate-range missiles (162) deployed by Britain and France.[46] Andropov also offered at this time to re-deploy the remaining Soviet missiles at sites about 700 miles further east, on the far side of the Ural Mountains.

It should be noted here that the vast bulk of British and French nuclear weapons are targeted on the Soviet Union. The British have sixty-four missiles, carrying three warheads each, on four submarines. In addition to these submarine-launched ballistic missiles, they have long-range bombers carrying nuclear weapons. The French have eighteen land-based missiles plus eighty submarine-launched ballistic missiles on five submarines as well as long-range "nuclear-capable" aircraft.

For all practical purposes, the Soviets regard the British and French nuclear arsenals as part of the NATO organization.[47] But the situation is actually more complicated than that. France is a member of the Atlantic Alliance, but since the latter part of the 1960s has not participated in its military organization. Therefore, Paris does not coordinate its nuclear weapons policies with NATO. By way of contrast, the United Kingdom plays a central role in NATO's nuclear planning, and all its forces are formally assigned to the Alliance. But British governments have always reserved the right to use these forces independently in a moment of supreme peril.[48]

Andropov's proposal was quickly rejected by the United States as well

---

45 At the height of the confrontation in fall 1983 over deploying the U.S. missiles in West Germany, Soviet representatives hinted that the Kremlin might consider a de facto incorporation of West Berlin and even move toward acceptance of German reunification if the Federal Republic rejected the deployment. See Jonathan Dean, "How to Lose Germany," *Foreign Policy*, No. 55 (summer, 1984), pp. 54-72.

46 For the Soviet viewpoint on including the British and French nuclear weapons systems in the INF talks see Valentin Falin, "Counting Europe's Nuclear Powers," *World Press Review*, July, 1983.

47 France, under General de Gaulle, withdrew from the control structure of NATO in 1966, but the Soviets have always included the French weapons in their NATO statistics.

48 See Richard H. Ullman, "Out of the Euromissile Mire," *Foreign Policy* (Spring, 1983), p. 40. "The British," says one U.S. official, "have assigned their submarine-based weapons to NATO command permanently, but their bomberdelivered weapons remain under their own command until released to NATO at time of war. France keeps its forces completely under its own command and is not obligated to release them to NATO command in time of war."

as by the United Kingdom and France. For their part, the British and French governments were indignant about the idea that their nuclear weapons should be on the table in Geneva at all. In their view, the two superpowers had no license to bargain over the independent national nuclear weapons systems of other countries. But to many West Europeans, Andropov's proposal sounded like a major concession, for it amounted to a tacit admission that the Soviets already had a large excess of SS-20s.[49]

Allied Criticism

While America's NATO Allies continued officially to support Reagan's zero option plan, they let it be known confidentially that they preferred a more flexible negotiating position at the INF talks. The West Germans, in particular, began expressing anxiety over whether other more balanced proposals would follow. (Former Chancellor Helmut Schmidt was personally in favor of the "walk-in-the-woods" formula). Most West European leaders, however, contended that the Soviet leadership would never accept the Reagan plan unless it were modified.

Corresponding to the continuing "hardline" taken by the Reagan Administration in the INF negotiations, more and more European leaders were coming to view the LRTNF deployment as an attempt by the United States to impose unwarranted nuclear weaponry on its NATO allies.[50] In the first place, there was never any agreement on the military function of theater nuclear forces in NATO's strategy. Secondly, they noted, there was never any agreement on the kinds and amounts of theater nuclear forces required. Thirdly, the proposed deployment of new medium-range missiles inferior in numbers to the Soviets seemed to lack any operational rationale. In fact, many suspected that the deployment was aimed at saving the United States from having to resort to its central strategic forces in case of Soviet use of the SS-20s. Finally, the Allies were perturbed that the important arms control aspects of the deployment decision had been neglected.[51]

For these reasons and others, a number of West Europeans were skeptical

---

49 For an excellent discussion of Soviet INF data by one of the best West German analysts of Soviet military and political behavior, see Gerhard Wettig, "The Soviet INF Data Critically Reviewed," *Aussenpolitik*, English edition Vol. 34, No. 1 (1983), pp. 30-42.

50 See Eliot A. Cohen, "The Long-Term Crisis," *Foreign Affairs* (Winter, 1982-83), p. 339.

51 Stephen S. Rosenfield, "Testing the Hard Line," *Foreign Affairs (America and the World 1982)*, p. 505.

of the Reagan Administration's policy from the beginning. But they were especially incensed in late 1981 when President Reagan suggested that he could envisage a nuclear war limited to Europe. This rather naive observation was immediately picked up by some West Europeans and touted as a cynical confession that America would perch safely on the sidelines while Europe was incinerated.[52]

Fairly or unfairly, Reagan came to be generally viewed in nuclear matters as casual and insensitive. When sensible, he was considered untutored, more concerned about establishing credibility with the Kremlin than winning the confidence of his European Allies. Nor were his very real and perceived gaps in this crucial area viewed as well covered by his chief aides. For instance, Secretary of Defense Caspar Weinberger was known in certain circles in Europe as the adviser who had sold a befuddled Reagan on the MX by showing him a cartoon.[53]

Some European leaders were further disturbed by other related actions of the President. Many denounced (more privately than publicly) his decision to forego further talks on a comprehensive nuclear test ban treaty. This was a negotiation that had been carried forth by every President since Eisenhower and was considered integral to American obligations under the nuclear proliferation treaty. Instead, the President undertook a warhead testing program suspected of being designed to cross over the 150-kiloton limit of the threshold nuclear test ban treaty (which had been signed but not ratified.) In short, the impression spread in Europe that the President was rather simplistic in his thinking, particularly in his vitriolic anti-communist stand, and that his Administration was creating a very dangerous international situation.

---

52 One former U.S. official with knowledge of NATO war plans observes here: "If this is a naive statement, so are U.S. military plans, for they conceive of this possibility. That is, there is no automaticity about escalation from the use of theater nuclear weapons to strategic."

53 According to the October, 1981 edition of *Armed Forces Journal International*, Defense Secretary Weinberger had taken to briefing President Reagan on complex defense matters with the help of cartoons prepared by the graphics department of the Pentagon. For example, information about the differing sizes of various strategic nuclear forces was conveyed to the Commander-in-Chief by means of a chart showing different-sized mushroom clouds.

Figure 6: *Ground Launched Cruise Missile (GLCM). The US Air Force's GLCM (a BGM-109), which is being deployed in Europe, is a variant of the US Navy's Tomahawk cruise missile.*

A Crucial Election in Germany

The dissatisfaction of many West Europeans resulted in a concession from the Reagan Administration. The zero option proposal, U.S. officials now said, was not intended as a "take-it-or-leave-it" offer. Arriving in Geneva on January 26, 1983, for a new round of INF negotiations, Paul Nitze declared that Washington was "certainly not locked into zero option." And shortly before he left on a 12-day trip to seven European nations January 30, Vice President George Bush proclaimed that the United States remained "open-minded."

Germany's support of NATO's Pershing II and cruise missile deployment was generally viewed by U.S. officials as crucial. (Many of the GLCMs and all of the Pershing IIs were to be deployed in West Germany.) Consequently, the Reagan Administration waited with bated breath as the issue was put to the test on March 6, 1983, the date of the West German parliamentary election.

Almost from the beginning, an especially vocal segment of public opinion had expressed itself negatively about the installation of the Pershing IIs and cruise missiles in West Germany, a country that has renounced ownership of nuclear weapons. Impressive demonstrations took place to protest as strongly as possible the stationing of these new weapons on home soil. In some respects, the public outcry over these weapons reminded U.S. officials of the heated public debate in 1978 over the proposed deployment in Europe of so-called enhanced radiation warheads, popularly known as "neutron bombs." Although public pressure eventually caused the Carter Administration to defer production of the weapon, that controversial attempt to strengthen European forces led many U.S. officials to distrust West European resolve and Europeans to suspect an American overreadiness to fight a war — probably a nuclear war — in their homeland. To this day, the NATO Allies refuse to accept the stationing of neutron weapons on their soil, even though Reagan proceeded to reverse Carter's production decision.[54]

---

54 Proponents of the neutron bomb saw the weapon as one way of countering the threat of a potential Soviet invasion of Western Europe, particularly a *Blitzkrieg* of tanks and armored personnel carriers rolling into West Germany with little or no warning. Advocates note that armored vehicles are resistant to the blast and heat of a "regular" nuclear explosion. Moreover, Soviet vehicles, unlike their NATO counterparts, are equipped to shield their crews from radioactive fallout. The advantage of neutron weapons, from this point of view, is that they could circumvent Soviet defenses. The bombs reduce the physical destruction of most nuclear devices, thereby limiting the radius of explosive blast, fire and fallout. However, they increase the momentary wave of neutron radiation that kills people without harming the structures. To the critics, one of the major problems with the

Opposition in West German political circles to the new missiles ran especially deep. Many members of the Social Democratic Party (SPD) joined the demonstrations against deployment. For the most part, these persons represented the left wing of the SPD, but they also included some more moderate figures such as Willy Brandt, the former Chancellor of Germany and Mayor of West Berlin during the height of the "cold war" period. Most acutely affected by this split within the SPD, however, was Helmut Schmidt, who had been replaced by CDU Chairman Helmut Kohl as Chancellor in October, 1982. Schmidt, together with his Foreign Minister Hans-Dietrich Genscher (FDP), had steadily supported NATO policy on the Pershing II and cruise missile deployment. During the *Bundestag* debate on a referendum on the issue in November, 1983, Schmidt tossed a paper airplane labeled "Pershing II" as if to show contempt for current Social Democratic policies. But in the end he refused to vote with the Kohl-government because he disputed the Christian Democratic claim that the U.S. had made sufficient efforts to bring about an agreement with the Soviets.[55]

Significantly, early in 1983, West German polls indicated that 61 percent of the respondents favored the postponement of American Pershing II and cruise missile deployment, even if Soviet-American negotiations on this issue failed.[56] Given this groundswell of negative opinion against the Pershings and cruise missiles, it came as a surprise to many outside observers that the "pro-deployment" coalition of Christian Democrats (CDU/CSU) and the Free Democrats (FDP) retained its majority in the election on March 6, 1983. At that time, incumbent Christian Democratic Chancellor Helmut Kohl won a resounding victory in the national parliamentary elec-

---

neutron weapons is that their use on the battlefield tends to further erode the all important threshold between conventional and nuclear weapons. (The neutron bomb is a nuclear weapon, but it is fired by conventional means.) In their view, such weapons which have the effect of lowering this threshold are extremely dangerous because of the risks of escalation once any nuclear weapon is used. If deployed, it was feared, these weapons might be viewed by the military as another type of conventional weapon and used accordingly in a crisis with far-reaching consequences. After lengthy debate and an intense Soviet propaganda campaign against the weapons, President Carter announced his decision on April 7, 1978 to defer production of the neutron bomb.

55 *Time*, December 5, 1983.
56 *Times-Picayune* (New Orleans), January 14, 1983. According to a survey carried out in November/December 1982, three percent of the West German population was actively involved in the peace movement and 29 percent sympathized with the movement. Of the younger generation (16-29 year-olds), six percent was involved in the peace movement with 44 percent expressing their support for this movement. See *Allensbacher Archiv*, IFD-Survey 1018, November/December 1982.

tions over Social Democrat Hans-Jochen Vogel, who had called for reconsideration of the missile deployment decision. However, the "Greens," a maverick party made up of a diverse group of ecologists and anti-nuclear left-wingers adamantly opposed to deployment, polled 5.6 percent of the votes and thus were able to be represented in the *Bundestag* for the first time.[57] Although economic and other domestic considerations were probably more important in affecting Kohl's election success, the outcome was nevertheless widely interpreted as one of the most significant in decades in terms of NATO policies and East-West relations. Both Soviet and American officials had lobbied hard to influence the outcome. (The Soviets, through party links in West Germany, were particularly active in attempting to mobilize support of anti-nuclear leftwing groups. So much so that many German analysts believe the perception of Soviet meddling and pressure tactics helped elect Helmut Kohl.)[58]

The Modified Zero Option Proposal

Following Kohl's election victory, European pressure mounted for the development of a more flexible U.S. bargaining position in the INF talks. Both British Prime Minister Thatcher and Chancellor Helmut Kohl desired a new, more reasonable looking U.S. proposal to help outflank their political opponents and quiet their domestic constituencies. In West Germany, the opposition Social Democrats urged resurrection of the walk-in-the-woods scheme, and Kohl hinted privately that he, too, thought the plan was worth a second look. But U.S. National Security Adviser Clark favored hanging tough on the zero option, and Caspar Weinberger agreed, saying "We don't want it to look as though we're letting the West German left push us around."

Nevertheless, Reagan decided to respond cautiously to West European pressures, and on March 30, 1983, he modified his zero option proposal. Essentially, the new scaled-down plan, which was drafted after intense consultations with the NATO Allies, called for the United States and the Soviet Union to have an equal number of warheads deployed on IRBMs "on a global basis." This latter phrase was chosen to include SS-20s stationed in the eastern part of the Soviet Union aimed at China and Japan.

As many hard-liners in the Administration expected, the Soviet reaction was negative. Radio Moscow termed the new U.S. proposal the "notorious

57 *Relay from Bonn,* March 11, 1982.
58 See *Newsweek,* March 26, 1984. One U.S. diplomat familiar with the German scene emphasizes that "the March 1983 elections were not a referendum on the missiles. Other factors were much more important."

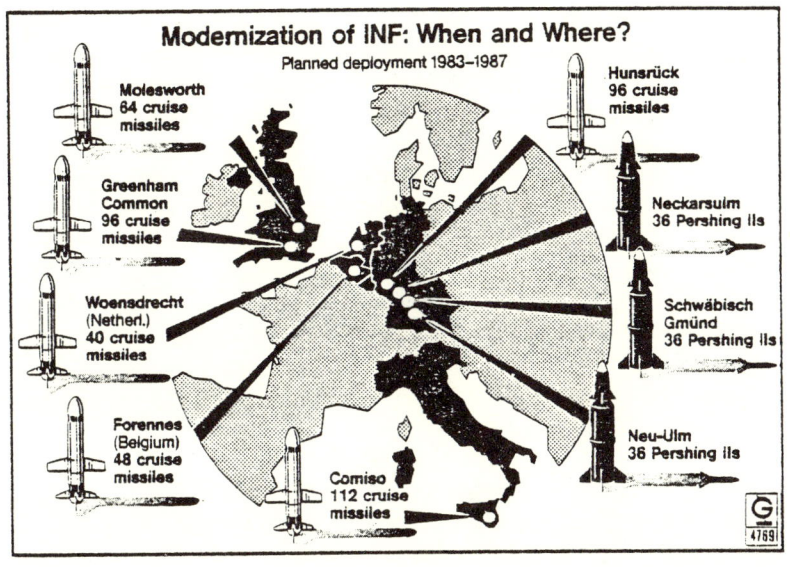

'zero option' in a new wrapping," which did not take into account the "other type of intermediate nuclear arms or the American nuclear-capable bombers deployed in Western Europe." Soviet Foreign Minister Andrei A. Gromyko dismissed Reagan's proposal on April 2 as "unacceptable." He said the inclusion of Soviet Asian-targeted IRBMs was a "tall order."

Reagan's proposal was aimed not so much at the Soviets but at two other audiences. One was Congress and the American public, where the nuclear "freeze" idea was receiving more and more support. The other audience was Western Europe, especially West Germany, where many people were strongly opposed to the deployment of the Pershing IIs on their territory. The President's proposal was designed in part, to defuse further demonstrations in Europe against the initial deployment of the missiles. About five months later, the Soviets tabled their new proposal in response to the Reagan initiative. On August 26, President Andropov said that the U.S.S.R. would not only agree to reduce its European SS-20s from 243 to 162, but it would be willing to "liquidate" the remaining 81 rather than redeploy them in Asia. The Soviet leader, however, still held out for zero U.S. missiles in Europe. Moreover, should the British and French governments reserve the right to pursue plans to modernize their own nuclear arsenals by adding multiple warheads to their submarine missiles, the Soviet Union would reserve the right to increase its SS-20 force.[59]

Generally, the Soviet proposal was viewed by Administration hardliners as a "trick," because of the qualification regarding the British and French nuclear forces. But as neutral observers hastened to point out, the Soviets had cause for concern about these forces which were in the process of transition. The British, for instance, planned to replace their 64 old Polaris missiles with modern, longer-range American Trident II (D5) missiles, each of which would carry 8-10 relatively accurate MIRVs. For their part, the French were also determined to put multiple warheads on their 80 submarine-launched missiles and perhaps on their 18 land-based missiles as well. They are already building a sixth 16-missile submarine.[60]

A Test of NATO Unity?

As Administration officials debated how to respond to the Soviet initiative, disagreement over the U.S. negotiating stand in the INF talks led to the dismissal of Eugene Rostow, the Director of the U.S. Arms Control and Disarmament Agency. Rostow, a Yale Law School Professor, had served as Under Secretary of State for Political Affairs in the Johnson Administration and was a founding member of the Committee on the Present Danger. But, although a "hard-liner," he was considered not tough enough.[61]

These developments, as well as the bourgeoning peace movement in Western Europe, portended a serious danger for NATO cohesion. Consequently, even those former U.S. government officials like Robert McNamara who were critical of the initial deployment decision reluctantly came to agree with Reagan Administration officials that the United States had to go through with its decision if only to demonstrate to the Soviets that they could not exercise a veto over NATO modernization plans. Thus, the

59 As of April 1984, there were 378 SS-20 missiles aimed at Europe and Asia, according to one U.S. government insider.
60 Richard H. Ullman, "Out of the Euromissile Mire," *Foreign Policy* (Spring, 1983), p. 51.
61 For background see Duncan L. Clarke, "Arms Control and Foreign Policy under Reagan," *The Bulletin of the Atomic Scientists* (November, 1981), pp. 12-19. At his confirmation hearings Senator Claiborne Pell of Rhode Island asked Rostow this critical question: "In the event of nuclear exchange between the Soviet Union and the United States, do you envision either country surviving?" Rostow replied: "The human race is very resilient, Senator Pell." Rostow went on to explain that there might be "10 million dead on one side and 100 million on the other, but that is not the whole population." See Confirmation Hearings, Committee on Foreign Relations, U.S. Senate, June 22, 23, 1981.

deployment decision soon came to be seen as a test of NATO unity in the face of a propaganda campaign orchestrated by Moscow.[62]

Shooting Down of the Korean Airliner

Relations between the United States and the Soviet Union were already deteriorating when Yuri Andropov took office the previous year (November 1982). Following the deadlock over the Euromissiles in Geneva, the atmosphere grew even colder. In general, it provided a constant pretext for one side to label the other "dangerous," "obstinate" or both. Neither President Reagan nor General Secretary Andropov missed many opportunities.

There was a brief summer thaw in the relationship. The Soviet leader took the first step. He released two families of Siberian Pentacostals, who had lived since 1978 in the basement of the U.S. Embassy, demanding the right to emigrate. The two superpowers signed a grain agreement. But these tentative signs of a lessening of tension ended abruptly when, on September 1, 1983, Soviet fighters shot down a Korean airliner, which had passed over Soviet territory. All 269 passengers were killed.

The destruction of the airliner was the nadir of Andropov's first year. According to some sources, it demonstrated lack of firm command and poor judgment. The Soviet leader was not consulted before the Soviet military, acting on standing orders, used brute force to stop a violation of Soviet airspace.[63] But he bore responsibility for the stance the Soviet Union adopted after the plane crashed into the sea.

For six days, Soviet officials refused to acknowledge even that they had shot down the commercial airliner. Soviet silence on the matter, which drew world-wide outcry, continued even though the Reagan Administration had already made public tape recordings of Soviet pilots describing the kill. The official Soviet stonewall compounded the calamity, and Soviet-American relations went downhill thereafter.

---

62 For an up-to-date discussion of the major issues in the debate on "tactical" nuclear weapons in East-West relations see the Atlantic Council, *The Credibility of the NATO Deterrent* (Washington, D.C., 1981). One U.S. government insider would remark here: "François Mitterand was deeply affected by the groundswell of pacifist sentiment in the Federal Republic. He repeatedly hectored Helmut Kohl to stand firm on the NATO deployment decision."

63 This statement is based on Soviet sources. See *Newsweek*, February 20, 1984.

The Soviet Walkout from the INF Talks

Two months later, in November 1983, the first Pershing IIs and cruise missiles arrived in Europe. This action triggered a long-threatened move by the Soviet delegation to walk out of the tenuous two-year dialogue on the troublesome INF issues. For its part, the Reagan Administration tended publicly to make light of the Soviet walkout, which also extended to the START talks and eventually to the negotiations on Mutual Balanced Force Reductions (MBFR.)[64] At a follow-up press conference, Paul Nitze stressed that the Soviet walkout should not be viewed as a death knell for the talks. He added that the United States is prepared to continue the negotiations at any time.[65]

Not too long after the Soviet walkout, U.S. intelligence officials received hard evidence indicating that the Soviet leadership was preparing in late 1983 to deploy new "tactical" medium-range missiles (dubbed by NATO the SS-22) for the first time in East Germany and Czechoslovakia.[66] A U.S. report to NATO in November 1983 had said that the Soviets had already dispatched to East Germany more than thirty SS-21 mobile missiles with a range of about 75 miles. This force was reportedly growing by about four launchers a month.

The SS-22 has a range of about 560 miles and is capable of carrying nuclear or conventional warheads. The missile was under development for many years as a replacement for the older SS-12 missile. When it was first introduced, it was stationed — like the older SS-12 model — along the boundaries of the Soviet Union. Now, however, there were concrete signs

---

64 The Soviets agreed to resume European troop — but not nuclear arms — reduction talks in mid-January, 1984. See *The Christian Science Monitor*, March 16, 1984.

65 *Time*, December 5, 1983. NATO and the Warsaw Pact entered into the MBFR talks in 1973 with the aim of reducing the numbers of troops on both sides. Over the next decade, these negotiations — termed "Mutual Balanced Force Reductions" in the West — dragged on without major breakthrough. For their part, the Soviets would not agree to the Western notion of "balance" and omitted this word from their name for the deliberations. As NATO officials saw it, the Soviets wanted equal *cuts*, which would leave their margin of superiority relatively more important. The Western side insisted on differential cuts down to equal final *levels*. Later, a major dispute arose over what forces actually exist. The Soviets argued that NATO overstated Warsaw Pact totals and maintained that the French forces should be counted on the Western side. Just this last year (1984) the Reagan Administration agreed not to insist any longer that the Soviets accept Western estimates of Warsaw Pact totals.

66 *The Washington Post*, January 26, 1984. One U.S. intelligence official insists here that the CIA "has been reporting since about 1981 Soviet preparations to deploy the new short-range missiles, the SS-21, 22 and 23."

that support equipment for the new missiles was being moved into Eastern Europe — a radical departure from previous Soviet practice.

The introduction of SS-21s and SS-22s in East Germany and Czechoslovakia was but one of a series of countermeasures planned by the Soviets in response to the deployment of the Pershing IIs and cruise missiles.[67] Other planned responses included the end of a self-imposed "moratorium" on the deployment of additional Soviet SS-20s in Europe and the deployment near U.S. shores of Soviet submarines carrying new long-range (1,500-mile) depressed-trajectory ballistic missiles.[68]

The SS-20 Missile Threat Reconsidered

With the breakdown in the talks, U.S. critics began to intensify their broadsides at the Reagan Administration. Some retired American military leaders argued that U.S. officials, by emphasizing the threat posed by the SS-20s as justification for the Pershing II and cruise missile deployment, had deliberately manufactured an artificial crisis. "The fact of the matter is," they said, "the Soviet Union for more than 20 years has been able to devastate all of Western Europe with nuclear weapons just as we have been able to devastate the Soviet Union." In their view, the "SS-20 missile has made no substantial change in the nuclear threat to Europe." For "even if the Soviets got rid of all their SS-20s they could attain the same target coverage of Europe using their ICBMs." Moreover, the United States, Britain and France "have enormous nuclear capability in Europe to which the Pershing II and the ground-launched cruise missile will add no increased capacity." By creating an "artificial nuclear crisis in Europe," these sources maintain, "we have given ourselves a black eye and the Soviets a propaganda bonanza."[69]

The already sensitive feelings of the West Germans were not allayed

---

67 One former NATO official makes the point here: "Soviet plans to deploy the SS-21 and 22 preceded the 1979 decision; the failure of the INF talks just provided a convenient excuse."

68 One U.S. official would point out here: "The Soviet Union began routinely in the early 1970s to base strategic nuclear ballistic submarines (SSBMs) off the American coast." Nevertheless, as General John Vessey, Jr., Chairman of the Joint Chiefs of Staff, stated in February 1984, there has been a substantial surge in the number of Soviet missile-firing submarines cruising off the East Coast of the United States. Vessey said that the Soviet activity was part of the long-promised Soviet reaction to the U.S. deployment of Pershing IIs and cruise missiles. The new subs were identified as Delta-class submarines, which usually operate in the northern Atlantic or the Berents Sea. See *The Minneapolis Star and Tribune*, February 15, 1984.

69 *The Defense Monitor*, Vol. XII, No. 4 (1983).

much when it was learned, in 1983, that the U.S. Army planned secretly to place 216 Pershing II missiles in the Federal Republic instead of the 108 originally agreed upon by NATO. The U.S. military plan was to consign a reload missile to each Pershing II launcher in West Germany. However, when Chancellor Kohl found out about this secret plan, he reportedly became furious and refused to accept any more missiles than the number agreed upon.[70]

The Pershing IIs Versus Crisis Stability

Other critics of the installation of the Pershing IIs and the cruise missiles argue that these systems will not defend Germany, for example, against a Soviet ground attack. From a purely military point of view, these new missiles are counterproductive because they could actually contribute to the destruction of Europe.

From a political point of view, the Pershings undermine what strategic

70 *The Defense Monitor*, Vol. 12, No. 7 (1983), p. 12.

theorists call "crisis stability." This is an extremely important concept, which simply means reducing incentives for pre-emptive nuclear attack. Most U.S. officials recognize that crisis stability, which inherently includes deterrence, is one of the foremost goals to be sought by the United States.[71] Essentially, the concept means that in a crisis that might escalate to nuclear warfare, government leaders should find that the configurations of forces on both sides encourage moderation and restraint, particularly unhurried and careful decision-making. Most importantly, force configurations should not encourage rapid or major escalations or snap decisions.

Let us reflect on this some more. As Richard Smoke writes, "It is well understood ... that both the content of the decisions that leaders make in a crisis, and the rationality of the process by which they formulate and make their decisions, are heavily influenced by the characteristics of the forces on both sides." For example, "one or both sides may have important forces that are vulnerable to attack by accurate missiles, by strike aircraft, or perhaps by ground assault in the case of systems based near their borders. Once fighting has begun, leaders may feel strong pressure to employ those forces quickly, to 'use them or lose them.'" But often using them "would mean escalating the crisis and perhaps triggering a much bigger war." The goal of crisis stability, therefore, is to create "ahead of time, forces that will not generate this or similar kinds of escalation pressures."[72]

This logic of strategic thought applies to the Pershings and SS-20s or indeed to any nuclear forces. From the perspective of crisis stability, the goal of the superpowers requires, among other things, that each side's forces be as secure as possible for as long as possible. In this way, the two leaders will not feel they must "use them or lose them," and therefore they will be able to make difficult unhurried decisions during unusually tense moments.

The Pershings significantly undercut crisis stability, in the main because they are so obviously suited for a preemptive strike. As Paul Bracken, a political scientist at Yale University and author of a book on the command and control of nuclear forces, says: "They must look to Soviet military men exactly like the kind of weapon needed to attack their high command before it has time to react." Bracken states that he has no doubt that the

---

71 One U.S. official would note here "that crisis stability is extremely important, but it is not the only goal of American strategy. For instance, a U.S. ability to attack Soviet forces may reduce crisis stability by increasing Soviet fears of pre-emptive attack, but such a U.S. counterforce capability may also enhance the credibility of the U.S. retaliatory threat."

72 Richard Smoke, *National Security and the Nuclear Dilemma: An Introduction to the American Experience* (Reading, Mass.: Addison-Wesley Publishing Co., 1984), p. 230.

Russians are trying to exploit the Pershing deployment "as a propaganda measure." But "that doesn't mean it is not a real military issue as well."

The Pershing IIs are relatively vulnerable even to conventional weapons. Once removed from their storage depots, the missiles would have no hardening to protect them. Although mobile, they would not move swiftly nor be easily concealed on the crowded highways of West Germany. In other words, the danger that in a mounting crisis the Pershings would attract a pre-emptive Soviet threat is another major reason why some critics are distressed by their deployment.[73]

Launch on Warning Threat

The Pershing II is viewed by former Secretary Robert McNamara as an especially dangerous nuclear weapons system for another reason. With a range of about 1,100 miles, this mobile missile will be able to deliver a 10-20 kiloton warhead to within 65-130 feet of its target. While it may not be able to reach Moscow, the Pershing II will still be able to strike many key targets such as hardened command bunkers and nuclear storage sites in the Western U.S.S.R.

Because the Pershing warheads could hit targets in the Soviet Union less than ten minutes after launch, the Soviets have threatened to adopt a "launch on warning" policy.[74] Launch on warning simply means that a state plans to launch its counterstrike as soon as its radars and computers indicate that an enemy attack is on its way. Thus, such a policy represents, in a sense, the ultimate answer to anxiety that one's own missiles or command and control centers may be vulnerable.[75]

Under a policy of launch on warning one does not wait for the enemy

---

73 Michael D. Wormser (ed.), *U.S. Defense Policy* (Washington, D.C.: Congressional Quarterly, Inc., 1983), pp. 74-75.

74 Soviet officials say that any attack upon the U.S.S.R. by the Pershings would give them no more than six minutes' warning. U.S. officials maintain there would be about twelve minutes. The Soviets contend that the Pershings in West Germany could reach Moscow, roughly 1,200 miles away. The Reagan Administration has said publicly that they could not.

75 "There is some reason to believe that in practice this [i.e. launch on warning] would control the policies of both the U.S. and the U.S.S.R., once the warning is believed to be clear and unmistakable," says Ambassador Martin Hillenbrand. "In the case of the United States, the authority to command the firing of nuclear weapons still remains with the President, and one can assume that some analogous arrangement for central control also exists in the Soviet Union. A really dangerous new development would be any move towards automatic response simply on the basis of a warning recorded by computers." Letters to this writer, June 1, 1984 and July 31, 1984.

to strike and wreak its damage. Rather, one fires while one's forces and command centers are still intact. In contrast, a policy of "launch under attack" calls for waiting until the last moment and then launching just before the enemy strike arrives.

Henry Kissinger, for one, believes that the Soviet argument about the shortened warning time caused by the Pershing IIs is for the "gullible."[76] As he writes in *The Wall Street Journal:* "A Pershing takes 8 to 10 minutes to reach the Soviet Union from Western Europe. An ICBM takes 25 to 30 minutes from the U.S.; a submarine-launched missile, depending on its location, requires 15 to 20 minutes. Were the Pershings to be removed, what would the Soviets do with the extra few minutes of warning time?"[77]

In his article, Kissinger explains the real reason for the deployment of the Long-Range Theater Nuclear Forces.[78] He says these weapons which could reach beyond Europe were dispatched to West Germany because they helped prevent the nuclear blackmail of Europe. This they would do by linking their strategic defense with that of the U.S. "With intermediate-range American weapons in Europe," he argues, "the Soviets could not threaten Europe selectively." Any "nuclear attack and any successful conventional attack would trigger an American counterblow from European installations." Thus, "the Soviets would have to calculate, even in the case of conventional attack, that we would use our missiles before they were overrun." Hence, "the Soviets would have to attack the missiles if they used even conventional weapons in Europe." That in turn "would trigger our strategic forces."

---

[76] William G. Hyland, a former aide to Kissinger, also tends to discount shrill Soviet claims of a special threat of a surprise attack because of the short flight time of the Pershing IIs. "A separate attack of 100 Pershings is too foolish to contemplate," he says. "Moreover, the Pershing's range is too limited to attack all Soviet command and control centers. It could not even attack all of the SS-20 sites." See Hyland, "The Struggle for Europe: An American View," in Andrew J. Pierre (ed.), *Nuclear Weapons in Europe,* pp. 33-34.

[77] Henry Kissinger, "Arms Control and Europe's Nuclear Shield," *The Wall Street Journal,* January 31, 1984. Herbert Scoville, Jr., a former official with the U.S. Arms Control and Disarmament Agency, attempts to answer that question: "It forces you to go one step further, of trying to guess when there would be an attack and then trying a pre-emptive strike."

[78] Kissinger's view here is somewhat different from the opinion he expressed in an interview with *The Economist,* February 3, 1979.
Question: We have no real answer, do we, at the moment in the European theatre to the SS-20?
Answer: No.
Question: Which is, if you are a European, a little worrying.
Answer: If you assume that every weapon aimed at Europe must be answered by a weapon stationed in Europe. *That is not self evident.* (Italics mine.)

The Soviets, Kissinger maintains, "grasped the significance of the new deployment immediately." They "threatened that any use of these weapons would be answered with an attack on the U.S."[79]

Does LRTNF Deter?

Robert McNamara disagrees with Henry Kissinger on the European deployment of the Pershing IIs and cruise missiles: "There is no military requirement for NATO to deploy the Pershing II and cruise missiles in order to maintain a stable deterrent... The 300,000 U.S. troops in Europe already guarantee [that the United States would come to the defense of Europe if the Soviets attack] and deployment of Pershings and cruise missiles will not add to the guarantee."[80]

McNamara challenges Henry Kissinger on the essential point of "coupling" our strategic forces with the forces deployed in Europe. He maintains that the "coupling" strategy is more apparent than real. For "the same reason that led Henry Kissinger to recognize that a U.S. President is unlikely to initiate the use of U.S.-based strategic nuclear weapons against the U.S.S.R., so a President would be unlikely to launch missiles from European soil against Soviet territory."[81]

Even though McNamara is opposed to the deployment of Long-Range Theater Nuclear Forces, he notes that there is a problem of perception. He states that some European leaders feel there is a political requirement to deploy these weapons. Although he doesn't give any names, he argues that these persons "are convinced the weapons will strengthen the belief that the United States would come to the defense of Europe if the Soviets attack." McNamara maintains that the "Europeans are operating on a misperception, but as long as it is held, it must be treated as a reality."

The practical upshot of all this, from McNamara's perspective, is that now that the weapons are in Europe we should keep them there — but "only for as long as it takes to convince the Europeans that these weapons are serving no military purpose. Then they should be withdrawn unilaterally." However, when we withdraw them, "we should make it clear that we are not removing them in response to Soviet pressure, which could be taken as a sign of weakness..."

79 *Ibid.*
80 Robert S. McNamara, "We Do Not Need The Pershing II," *Newsweek*, December 5, 1983. McGeorge Bundy, former National Security Adviser to Presidents Kennedy and Johnson, also sees INF deployment as unnecessary, even dangerous.
81 Robert S. McNamara, "We Do Not Need The Pershing II," *Newsweek*, December 5, 1983.

In the view of other critics, a serious problem with the deployment of the ground-launched cruise missiles in Europe is that the missiles do not have the psychological barrier of ballistic missiles. Land-based ICBMs and SLBMs have become the symbols of nuclear war and global extermination; their use is therefore somewhat constrained by their image, in the minds of political and military leaders, as the vehicles of ultimate folly and catastrophe. Cruise missiles, on the other hand, are often thought of in a more casual and benign manner. A decision to use them might appear much less forbidding. Thus, the missiles stationed in Europe, which could carry either a conventional or nuclear warhead, have the potential to make war more casual and less politically responsible. At the same time, they greatly increase the possibility of war as well as its quick transmutation from a conventional tactical encounter to a nuclear confrontation.

By far the most serious disadvantage of the cruise missiles (which represent a technology that the Soviet Union will not have in such advanced form until later in the 1980s)[82] is their impact on arms limitation efforts. The obvious pre-requisite of any international agreement limiting one or more weapons systems is that the agreement can be verified by national technical means (e.g. satellites). Being quite small, cruise missiles are easily concealed away from their launchers. Moreover, ground-launched cruise missiles can be released from small, less visible platforms. They can be stockpiled clandestinely in large numbers much more easily than the larger, heavier Pershing IIs and thus evade an arms control agreement. Admittedly, in the relatively open societies of the West, concealment might be difficult. But would the U.S. Congress accept Soviet assurances, the critics ask, that they had no hidden stockpiles? Until the initial deployment of the cruise missiles no long-range ground-launched cruise missiles had been deployed anywhere. Therefore, for arms control reasons, it made sense not to deploy any and to attempt to negotiate an agreement with the U.S.S.R. forbidding them. Or so the critics argued.

Anti-Nuclear Missile Movements in Warsaw Pact Countries

If the Soviet walkout of the INF talks in November 1983 was a major cause for concern among West Europeans, the same was true for an increasing number of East Europeans who, for the first time, are protesting the military threat posed by *both* superpowers. Generally, the East Europeans are worried about the prospect of becoming targets in a nuclear war.

---

82 In August 1984 *Prawda* announced the first successful testing of a long-range cruise missile.

Furthermore, they are concerned about the Soviet decision to counterplant nuclear weapons in their countries. Finally, they are apprehensive that the Soviet response would further strain their beleaguered economies and jeopardize business and social relations with the West.

Not surprisingly, the sharpest rise in anti-nuclear sentiment comes in the two countries where the Soviets planned to station their new SS-21s. Both East Germany and Czechoslovakia are being compelled to accept and pay[83] for the Soviet missiles, even though they are reluctant to do this. In Czechoslovakia, various groups of workers, students and clergymen have produced petitions against nuclear arms "anywhere in the world." In East Germany, a synod of the Lutheran Church in Thuringia has issued a "letter to the parishes" criticizing the nuclear build-up by both superpowers, and more than 100 residents of Rostock have signed an open letter, in which they objected to the prospect of nuclear missiles in their backyard.

Official reaction to the anti-nuclear movement has differed sharply from one country to the next. In Romania, President Nicolai Ceausescu has actually made the repudiation of both superpower missile build-ups official policy of the government. However, in other Warsaw Pact countries, less independent leaders have generally stuck publicly to the Soviet party line that Washington alone is to blame for the Euromissile crisis. In private remarks, however, these leaders have made it plain that they don't relish the prospects of nuclear missiles on East European soil. In Czechoslovakia, high government and party authorities have been grumbling to Western diplomats. And in East Germany, a country closely allied to the U.S.S.R., Communist Party Chief Erich Honecker has conceded in interviews that "no one will cheer" when the Soviet missiles arrive.

Recently, Honecker gave his views to Canadian Prime Minister Pierre Trudeau. The East German leader informed Trudeau that he had seen "The Day After." He complained that the end of the TV film pulled punches by leaving some characters alive. "In any superpower nuclear exchange," he said, "East Germany would be obliterated because neither Washington nor Moscow would be able to control escalation." Honecker reported that the Soviets had not kept him informed of developments in the nuclear arms race in Central Europe. And he argued that Yuri Andropov's warning that new U.S. deployments would put a "palisade of missiles" between the two Germanys — an image calculated to pit German national aspirations against the interests of Western security — was an exaggeration.[84]

Most East Europeans are skeptical of any real breakthrough in negotiations when both sides return to the negotiating table. Generally, they

---

83 See *Newsweek*, March 5, 1984.
84 *Newsweek*, March 5, 1984.

acknowledge that election-year politics may encourage President Reagan to moderate his anti-Soviet rhetoric. But they believe that the U.S. will not make any hard concessions until Moscow sharply modifies its bargaining strategy. The death of President Andropov in February, 1984, and his replacement by Konstantin Chernenko did not seem to alter this view.

Summary

With the first phase of INF deployment well under way in early 1984, NATO officials were able to breathe "a collective sigh of relief." The great danger of a successful Soviet exploitation of Alliance division appeared to have been averted. However, this was the short-term view; the long-term assessment may well be different.

The controversy surrounding the dual-track NATO decision of 1979 has revealed the basic quandary of NATO strategy: How to insure that U.S. strategic nuclear forces are credibly coupled to the defense of Western Europe.

Broadly speaking, American military planners tend to approach the problems of defense "as essentially technical tasks, to be mastered by the application of energy, physical resources, planning, and organization." On the other hand, European military officials tend to regard the problems of defense "as essentially political, to be solved by calculations of interest and political purpose, and to be decided in large part by structuring political relationships and interests."[85] Lagging behind the United States in innovations in strategic thought, the Europeans tend to be skeptical of some of the "sophisticated" concepts of the Americans like "intra-war deterrence," which the formidable Franz Josef Strauss, West Germany's Defense Minister from 1956 to 1962, once described as "conceptual aids for the precalculation of the inconceivable and incalculable nature of the specific."[86]

This difference in approach was well demonstrated in the NATO decision to install intermediate-range missiles in Europe. Thus, deterrence is the major reason for the installation of the intermediate-range missiles by NATO. To be more precise, deterrence is to be enhanced at all levels by raising the cost of attack for the Soviet Union. Or so many West Europeans see things, and it is reasonably clear from the record that the main impetus

---

85 Frederick S. Wyle, "U.S., Europe, SALT, and Strategy," in Morton A. Kaplan (ed.), *SALT: Problems and Prospects* (Morristown, N.J.: General Learning Press, 1973), pp. 142-43.

86 Quoted in Catherine McArdle Kelleher, *Germany and the Politics of Nuclear Weapons* (New York: Columbia University Press, 1975), p. 282.

for the deployment came from Europe rather than the United States, even though some European statesmen in the wake of subsequent events came to have serious second thoughts about the political wisdom of the original NATO decision.[87] In general, the Europeans did not regard the problems of deterrence as difficult as the United States. Most Europeans did not feel the U.S.S.R. was gearing up for major aggression. Generally, it was felt that so long as the Russians knew that any aggression would entail a modicum of serious risk they would remain content with peaceful coexistence.

In retrospect, it seems clear that the NATO deployment decision left a lot to be desired.[88] As national security specialists Steven Canby and Ingemar Dorfer write, "None of the Atlantic Alliance's decisions designed to deter Soviet aggression has caused more problems . . ."[89]

Not only did the decision escalate tensions with the Soviets, who are especially sensitive to the decapitating threat posed by these weapons to their command-and-control apparatus.[90] But the way in which the decision was carried out served almost to guarantee a large public outcry in those West European countries that were scheduled to receive the new weapons. Indeed, the net cost may be the loss of West German postwar consensus on security, as a recent staff report to the Senate Foreign Relations Committee concludes.[91]

The way in which the 1979 NATO decision was carried out by the Reagan Administration saw a sharp clash between two fundamentally different *political* approaches in dealing with the Soviet Union.[92] The Americans were generally very skeptical of the policy being pursued by West Germany — that of the "outstretched hand," to use Foreign Minister Hans-

87 To use the words of Michael Howard of Oxford University, the new missile deployment was to "assuage the fears of Western Europeans that, confronted by a threat that did not extend to their own continent, the Americans would be effectively deterred from intervening." Quoted in Leon Wieseltier, *Nuclear War, Nuclear Peace* (New York: Holt, Rinehart & Winston, 1983), pp. 62-63.

88 This is shown e.g. by the stance of Belgium and the Netherlands held throughout 1984. See also footnote 80.

89 Steven Canby and Ingemar Dorfer, "More Troops, Fewer Missiles," *Foreign Policy*, No. 53 (Winter, 1983-84), pp. 3-17.

90 William V. Garner, *Soviet Threat Perceptions of NATO's Eurostrategic Missiles* (Totowa, N.J.: Rowman & Allanheld, 1983). This is the conclusion reached by this detailed and scholarly study based on actual readings of Soviet literature and press accounts.

91 See *The Christian Science Monitor,* March 7, 1984.

92 See Uwe Nerlich, "Western Europe's Relations with the United States," *Daedalus*, (Winter, 1979), pp. 87-111 and Theo Sommer, "Europe and the American Connection," *Foreign Affairs*, Vol. 58, No. 3 (Winter, 1980), pp. 622-636.

Dietrich Genscher's phrase. It was designed in the main to keep the dialogue with Moscow alive even as NATO proceeded to redress the Euromissile imbalance. The idea was to preserve as much of détente as possible. Bonn wanted to keep open the possibility of cooperation as well as confrontation.

The U.S. Administration was not as suspicious of fledgling conservative Chancellor Helmut Kohl as it had been of Chancellor Helmut Schmidt and his Social Democrats. After all, the West German Christian Democrats came into office in October 1982 swearing loyalty to the United States, and it was not long before they were putting up the additional NATO "infrastructure" funds that the Schmidt government had balked at. Nonetheless, Kohl's government soon began to formulate policies that were not so unlike those of Helmut Schmidt, much to the discomfiture of Washington. New Defense Minister Manfred Wörner's supporting arguments about not inflaming the domestic peace movement sounded to some in the Reagan Administration like "kowtowing to nationalist neutralist sentiment," as one U.S. official put it.

As a number of high-level officials in the Reagan Administration saw things, the West Germans were soft on the Soviet threat. They were afraid of the new SS-20s and were ready to pay any price rather than to stand up to them. They were being tempted to dilute their loyalty to the Atlantic Alliance by the chimera of reunification. In effect, they were being blackmailed into incipient "Finlandization" by the lure of improved relations in Central Europe.[93] Finally, as those in Washington saw it, the ungrateful West Germans and the other Allies were getting a free ride on defense while selfishly trying to preserve their own unusual "island of détente" in the midst of superpower confrontation.

The different American and West German approaches reflected two radically different sets of assumptions. To be sure, both the U.S. and the FRG agreed that the U.S.S.R. was a military threat (if the precise definition of the threat deviated). And both agreed that the Soviet Union was a military giant while at the same time "an economic and social runt." However, that was where major similarity in the two views ended.

For its part, the Reagan Administration, for some time under the strong

---

93 Despite the deterioration in Soviet-American relations, relations between East and West Germany have improved. In the last year a stream of leaders from the Federal Republic visited East Berlin. These high-level officials included the archconservative Bavarian party leader of the CSU, Franz Josef Strauss. In 1983, the West Germans loaned East Germany a billion DM, and talks for a new loan are now under way. In a speech to the *Bundestag* in March 1984, Chancellor Kohl spoke earnestly of the improved relationship between the GDR and the FRG. *Presently (August 1984) East German Communist Party leader Erich Honecker in scheduled to visit the FRG in the fall of 1984.*

influence of Harvard historian Richard Pipes, regarded the Soviet Union as an implacable foe which must be dealt with harshly from a position of military superiority. Only when the entire internal Soviet system and dynamics were radically transformed could there be any hope that the U.S.S.R. would join the community of "civilized" nations and accept peace in the world.

The American position was, of course, the antithesis of the West European, particularly West German, view of conflict management. In Europe, memories of the horrors of the First and Second World Wars are deeply etched in the consciousness of national leaders. As Karsten D. Voigt, currently Social Democratic Party leader in the Foreign Affairs Committee of the West German *Bundestag*, notes: "Anyone living, as do the Germans, along the borders separating the NATO countries from the Warsaw Pact nations is aware that even a war waged solely with conventional weapons leaves few chances of survival. This is all the more true of a war fought with nuclear weapons — even if 'only' with so-called tactical nuclear weapons..."[94]

Given this different historical and cultural context, the more realistic European aim was to work directly through negotiations and economic deals to lessen tension between East and West. The hope was to divert Moscow from military adventures abroad by using both "carrots and sticks" in the mode of Henry Kissinger during the early 1970s. The long-term objective was focused on turning potential military opponents into partners seeking a common security.

If the Administration/Pipes strategy was to enhance the crises within the "tottering" Soviet economy and the world's only surviving 19th Century empire, the Europeans took a different view. Their more modest goal was to control world crises so they would not explode. For the most part, the West Europeans — conscious of their limited means and limited interdependent sovereignty and aware that Europe would likely be the first battlefield in any nuclear war — shared little of the American "can-do" enthusiasm for transforming the character of the Soviet Union or hastening its demise. Moreover, they were extremely skeptical that the nearly autarchic Soviet economy, with its huge resources and pliant population, could be "brought to its knees." Their view was that any such attempt would be counterproductive. It would simply let the Soviet leadership rally its people in a xenophobic wave of patriotism. Indeed, many were aghast by the idea of "horizontal escalation" and the arbitrary overturning of the hard-won post-war stability in Europe. For many Europeans, the major concern was to preserve a *modus vivendi* in which neither side went to war with the other.

94 Karsten D. Voigt, "Nuclear Weapons in Europe: A German Social Democrat's Perspective," in Andrew Pierre (ed.), *Nuclear Weapons in Europe*, p. 98.

Differences between the Europeans and the Americans aside, one can certainly question the necessity of the new missiles in Europe. As Paul C. Warnke, formerly Director of the U.S. Arms Control and Disarmament Agency, emphasizes: "The 464 ground-launched cruise missiles and 108 Pershing II missiles can add nothing militarily significant to the ability to blow up Soviet and East European targets. All important military, industrial and urban facilities in the Warsaw Pact's geographic area are redundantly covered by the 10,000 warheads now carried on American intercontinental and submarine-launched ballistic missiles and strategic bombers."[95]

To be sure, the Pershings and the cruises are remarkable weapons. But neither provides substantially new capabilities or options. Indeed, the ground-launched cruise missiles function more or less as air-launched and sea-launched land-attack cruise missiles do. They differ mainly in details of storage and basing.

Likewise, the Pershing IIs can not carry out any major tactical mission that cannot be performed by weapons now in the American nuclear arsenal. The only important theoretical advantage to be gained by having these missiles in Europe is a strategic one: The Pershing IIs can arrive so quickly and so accurately on targets in the Soviet Union that they could serve as an adjunct to central strategic forces in certain kinds of strategic nuclear exchanges. However, U.S. war-planners do not seem to have designed this missile or scaled the overall program with this aim in mind. Moreover, about the same military advantage could probably be obtained in other less provocative ways.[96]

Important European opinion on this matter has been nicely summed up by the British social historian E.P. Thompson. "U.S. scenarios for limited

---

95 Paul C. Warnke, "The Illusion of NATO's Nuclear Defense," in Andrew J. Pierre (ed.), *Nuclear Weapons in Europe*, pp. 76-77.

96 Andrew Cockburn argues that at the same time the Soviets were in the process of deploying their new SS-20 as a replacement for the antiquated SS-4s and SS-5s, the Americans were developing new medium-range missiles of their own. The SS-20 "provided a welcome justification for the production of these new systems [the Pershing II and the cruise missiles]. As with the neutron bomb, Schmidt was encouraged to play his part by requesting their deployment in Europe. Before long, this deployment had become a 'test' of the cohesion and strength of will of the Atlantic alliance." Consequently, some observers "came to believe that the SS-20 represented the 'real issue' as far as the Soviet military threat was concerned..." In this respect, they were guilty "of ignoring the fact that Western nuclear policy regarding Europe is and has always been predicated on the assumptions that NATO is incapable of defending itself against Soviet conventional forces without resorting to nuclear weapons, and that in the event of a Soviet conventional attack the NATO response must be nuclear, whether the Pershing II and cruises are deployed or not." See his *The Threat: Inside the Soviet Military Machine* (New York: Random House, 1983), pp. 201-02.

war in the European theater do not amuse us," Thompson complains. "This is where we happen to live."[97]

The need for the Pershings and cruises has been explained publicly in terms largely of the threat posed by the SS-20.[98] Yet, according to one authority, the SS-20 did not initially excite U.S. specialists nor the Europeans at whom it was aimed. In fact, the top officials of the Carter Administration were initially cool to the idea of a buildup in Western Europe to balance the Soviets. As Brzezinski confided to a colleague, there never has been such a thing as a "Eurostrategic balance." Europe had survived years of overwhelming Soviet superiority in middle-range missiles during the peak of the cold war. Why worry unduly about it now in the context of détente, however shaky it might be?

Scholars Steven Canby and Ingeborg Dorfer point up a degree of duplicity that marked the NATO deployment.[99] The real reason for the NATO decision, they say, was concern by the Europeans, particularly the West Germans, "that their increasingly unreliable U.S. ally might abandon them in the face of Soviet blackmail." To prevent such an American retreat, "the effort to modernize U.S. nuclear weapons based in Western Europe needed to satisfy three criteria." First, NATO needed *land-based* nuclear missiles capable of reaching Soviet territory "to insure that the Soviet Union would not be a nuclear sanctuary in a European war." Second, "these missiles had to be unambiguously owned and operated by the United States to make sure that the United States could not escape the consequences of their use." Finally, the missiles "were to be deployed in a vulnerable enough way that Washington would have to use them early in a conflict or lose them." The basic idea was that the American missiles "would act as a trigger for U.S. strategic weapons should the United States hesitate to keep its promise to defend Western Europe." (For this reason the sea-based mode, originally favored by officials in the Carter Adminis-

---

97 Quoted in Leon Wieseltier, *Nuclear War, Nuclear Peace* (New York: Holt, Rinehart & Winston, 1983), p. 57.

98 U.S. Ambassador Raymond L. Garthoff argues that the development of the strategic cruise missiles is a prime example of "bargaining chipology." "There was no strategic need" to begin research and development on strategic cruise missiles back in 1972, he says, "but the research looked technically promising, relatively inexpensive, and was part of the pursuit of everything not explicitly limited." Moreover, "it could 'always' be used as a bargaining chip." In 1976, Dr. Kissinger, "one of the authors of this approach, wondered: 'How was I to know the military would come to love it [the strategic cruise missile]?' He admitted that he himself had pushed the Pentagon to develop cruise missiles as a bargaining chip several years earlier." See Raymond Garthoff, "SALT I: An Evaluation," *World Politics* (1978), p. 22.

99 Steve Canby *et al., opus cit.*, pp. 6-7.

tration, was unattractive to many West Europeans. Submarines and ships have the capacity for turning around and going home, should American officials decide that their previous commitment was unwise.)

Yet, Bonn "felt that this thinking had to be hidden from Western, particularly U.S., public scrutiny." Thus, the "coupling forces were described as a response to an allegedly new threat, the SS-20, which was in fact a replacement for much older and unwieldy SS-4s and SS-5s." The introduction of the U.S. missiles "was further legitimated by the simultaneous offer of arms control talks." Because they "concealed their true coupling rationale, however, West German officials were forced publicly to advocate the need for a number of theater nuclear weapons too large to best achieve coupling." A few dozen weapons, after all, "would have satisfied West German coupling requirements."

While a small number of missiles increases coupling, Steve Canby and Ingemar Dorfer note, a large number, such as 572, "decreases coupling by the prospect of a Eurostrategic balance and the limited nuclear war this balance would theoretically make possible." This, of course, "is the last thing that West Europeans, and the West Germans in particular, want. And the "specter of limited nuclear war united the West European peace movement and swayed public opinion against the INF deployment."

In the end, there was only a minimal relationship between the final numbers for deployment and conventional military criteria. Indeed, as William Hyland relates, "the final number for deployment — 108 Pershing II missiles and 464 cruise missiles — was arbitrarily selected by Zbigniew Brzezinski and his staff. The higher end of the range of possibilities was chosen in order to provide fat for negotiating purposes..."[100]

Negotiations over Eurostrategic forces began in October 1980. But little could be accomplished until after the presidential election in the United States. However, since President Reagan and his close advisers entered office believing that the United States and the West were inferior to the Soviet Union, it is not surprising that they did not regard opening serious negotiations as an urgent priority.

The so-called "walk-in-the-woods" agreement, which Paul Nitze subsequently arrived at informally with his Soviet negotiating partner, represented the kind of a solution the West German government had in mind. It would have created the assurance of continued coupling. At the same time, it would have limited Soviet SS-20 deployments. But President Reagan, who was now focused on the magnitude of the SS-20 threat, refused to endorse this informal agreement. This decision was a tragic mistake, for the accord held out the promise of substantial Soviet concessions — in exchange for

---

100 See William G. Hyland, "The Struggle for Europe: An American View," in Andrew J. Pierre (ed.), *Nuclear Weapons in Europe*, p. 20.

the foregoing of the deployment of an unnecessary American missile, the Pershing II.[101]

Despite allegations to the contrary — and the obvious propaganda advantages the Soviets have derived from the continued deployment of the Pershing IIs and cruise missiles, —[102] the Kremlin leadership seems genuinely concerned about the implementation of the 1979 NATO decision. In this connection, one need only recall the Soviet warning made in 1982. At that time, General Secretary Brezhnev emphatically warned that a decision by the United States to violate the twenty-year-old "understanding" that neither side deploy shorter-range missiles to firing locales from which they could strike the other's homeland would compel the Kremlin to proceed with "analogous" deployment.[103]

From the viewpoint of the U.S.S.R., it really makes little difference if an attack on its territory comes from American land-based ICBMs or from European-based Pershing IIs or ground-launched cruise missiles.[104] However, there is no doubt that a counterforce Pershing strike against Soviet command and control centers could arrive faster than U.S. ICBMs. While such a contemplated pre-emptive strike might not have seemed plausible at some other time, 1983 was just the time when Reagan Administration officials were talking loudly about the general policy of nuclear war-fighting and the U.S. intention to prevail in a "controlled" nuclear war.[105]

101 In the view of William G. Hyland, it may well be "that the entire [walk-in-the-woods] episode will be seen as an important lost opportunity." Other former U.S. officials such as Paul C. Warnke, are more emphatic. See Hyland, "The Struggle for Europe: An American View," in Andrew J. Pierre (ed.), *Nuclear Weapons in Europe*, p. 38.

102 While most attention has focused on the Pershing II, the cruise missile is acknowledged by the experts also to be a most lethal weapon. According to former Defense Secretary Harold Brown, the cruise missile "would probably be the best weapon against hardened targets because it would take eight hours to get there, but at [censored] feet accuracy *it has the highest kill probability against hard targets of any of our forces.*" See "Air-Launched Cruise Missile Shows Promise but Problems could Result in Operational Limitations," unclassified digest furnished in lieu of a secret GAO report, C-MASAD-82, February 26, 1982, p. iii.

103 According to one U.S. government "insider," this understanding derived from the Cuban missile crisis of October 1962. At that time the Soviets dismantled their installations in Cuba, and in 1963 the Americans withdrew their missiles from Turkey.

104 Reports that the Pershing II will carry an "Earth Penetrator" warhead suggest to the Soviet leadership that the missile is designed to attack command and control centers. See John Erickson, "The Soviet View of Deterrence: A General Survey," *Survival*, Vol. 24, No. 6 (November-December, 1982), p. 250.

105 One of the best analyses in the open literature of why the planning for controlled, limited nuclear warfare is not feasible is that by Desmond Ball, *Can Nuclear War Be Controlled?* (London: International Institute of Strategic Studies, 1981).

U.S. nuclear policy towards Western Europe appears founded on a myth. This is that the Pershing II and cruise missile deployments will create a potential "escalatory ladder that provides a variety of response options below the strategic level and helps to insure the linkage between lower response options and the strategic nuclear forces."[106] However, such deployments are likely to produce in a nuclear exchange not an "escalatory ladder" but *escalation*.

The belief of some U.S. military planners that the escalation of a nuclear war, once under way, could be restrained and that, in the thick of fighting, they would be free and able to terminate the hostilities and de-escalate in a controlled manner is just an article of faith — nothing else. So long as the threat of selective nuclear strikes could even remotely lead to a major nuclear war and thus to mutual destruction, the threat itself — by rational standards — is not credible.

In late 1983 the crusading American columnist, Jack Anderson, disclosed the contents of a top secret State Department cable warning that existing U.S. submarine-launched ballistic missiles assigned to NATO could not do the INF job because "they are generally regarded as strategic systems whose use prior to General Nuclear Response might convey an overly escalatory signal to the Soviet Union."[107] The notion that the Soviet leadership would take a pre-emptive strike with Pershing IIs or ground-launched cruise missiles less seriously would be laughable if it were not so dangerous.[108]

President John Kennedy certainly understood this when he observed that "inevitably the use of small nuclear armaments will lead to larger and larger nuclear armaments on both sides, until the worldwide holocaust has begun."[109]

In summary, then, the NATO deployment decision, which was made in the main to enhance deterrence, is based on some very questionable — if not dubious — assumptions.

106 Quoted in Burns H. Weston (ed.), *Toward Nuclear Disarmament and Global Security: A Search for Alternatives* (Boulder, Colo.: Westview Press, 1984), p. 227.
107 *The Washington Post*, September 8, 1983.
108 See Paul C. Warnke, "The Illusion of NATO's Nuclear Defense," in Andrew J. Pierre (ed.), *Nuclear Weapons in Europe*, p. 87.
109 One former high-level NATO official has this to say: "Personally, I was unenthusiastic about the 1979 decision, perhaps because of my experiences with our allies in the 1960s. Something, however, had to be done to counter the SS-20s. Once the decision was made, we had no real choice but to go ahead. We can't have the European left and the Soviets dictating NATO's weapons programs. My main thought, however, is that all the energy spent on the Euromissiles could better have been directed to a buildup of NATO's conventional forces — and the problem of the Persian Gulf. These are NATO's real problems."

SECTION III
THE UBIQUITY OF NUCLEAR DETERRENCE

I don't want some young Colonel to decide when to drop an atomic bomb.

Harry Truman

X. CHAIN OF COMMAND AND COMMUNICATIONS PROBLEMS

American reliance on nuclear deterrence is based on the assumption that the U.S. must be prepared to use its nuclear weapons if the President decides. This readiness is deemed essential if the "balance of terror" is to be credible. Consequently, an elaborate nuclear chain of command structure has been set up which would facilitate operations in a crisis situation.

How reliable is this system? How would it function in case of a surprise nuclear attack? These are serious questions, and they provide the focus for this chapter.

The Worldwide Military Command and Control System

Under the American system of government, the President bears the awesome responsibility to his fellow Americans, to his Allies, and indeed to all mankind, of deciding when — if ever — to use some or all of the vast arsenal of U.S. nuclear weaponry. According to law, only the President (the Commander-in-Chief of the armed forces) can give the launch order.

In facing his responsibility for nuclear weapons use since 1945, the American President has had two major concerns. One is keeping the ultimate decision in his own hands; the other is avoiding the possibility of an accidental nuclear war. Both problems thrust the Chief Executive into a complex of mechanisms and procedures regulating the release of nuclear weapons — a process which is far too little understood by many Americans.[1]

---

1 Some of the best unclassified source material on WWMCCS are the congressional hearings and reports, beginning in the early 1970s. See especially *Review of Defense*

This complex begins with the system of strategic command, control communications and intelligence known in the strategic lexicon as "C^3I." This system is designed to enable the National Command Authority (NCA) of the United States to assess the extent of any nuclear attack and direct a retaliatory response. The NCA is comprised of the President, the Secretary of Defense and the Chairman of the Joint Chiefs of Staff (or their designated successors).[2]

The American C^3I system is known collectively as the Worldwide Military Command and Control System (WWMCCS, pronounced "wimex"). Basically, this system is composed of a network of command posts, communications centers, satellites and data-processing links employed by the National Command Authority to direct the U.S. armed forces. Within the continental United States, the National Military Command comprises the installations that direct U.S. strategic forces. These include the National Military Command Center, a series of office suites on the third floor of the Pentagon; the Alternate National Military Command Center, a backup command post situated deep inside Raven Rock Mountain in southern Pennsylvania about 70 miles from Washington, the North American Aerospace Defense Command (NORAD) headquarters dug into the center of the Cheyenne Mountains near Colorado Springs, Colorado, and the Strategic Air Command headquarters situated in an underground bunker at Offutt Air Force Base outside Omaha, Nebraska. Command posts are also situated overseas that control tactical and intermediate-range nuclear weapons stationed in Europe and the Pacific regions.[3]

Generally, intelligence of ballistic-missile attack is provided by a combination of early-warning satellites and radar installations. But it may also be possible to obtain strategic warning of an imminent attack by detecting changes in the deployment and alert status of Soviet nuclear forces. In the

---

Worldwide Communications, Phase I produced on May 10, 1971 by the House Armed Services Investigating Subcommittee. *Phase II*, which was published on October 12, 1972 and *Phase III*, published on February 7, 1975. Also useful is the General Accounting Office's *Report to Congress: The Worldwide Military Command and Control System — Major Changes Needed in Its Automated Date Processing Management and Direction*, LCD-80-22, December 14, 1979, and GAO *Report to Congress: The WWMCCS — Problems in Information Resource Management*, MASAD-80-2, October 19, 1981.

2 U.S. Congress, *Authority to Order the Use of Nuclear Weapons*, Report Prepared for the Subcommittee on International Security, House Committee on International Security, House Committee on International Relations (Washington, D.C.: U.S. Government Printing Office, 1975).

3 For this information the author is indebted to Jonathan B. Tucker, "Strategic Command-and-Control Vulnerabilities: Dangers and Remedies," *Orbis*, Vol. 26, No. 4 (Winter, 1983), pp. 943-45.

main, tactical warning of a pre-emptive attack would be given by the network of satellites in the Defense Support Program (DSP). These satellites are able, for instance, to detect the thermal plumes of rising Soviet missiles about thirty seconds after launch. Then they would immediately transmit a prompt warning to NORAD, SAC headquarters and the other national command posts. Subsequently, confirmation and the tracking of incoming warheads would be undertaken by several ground-based radar installations. These include the Ballistic Missile Early Warning System (BMEWS) in Thule, Greenland, England, Alaska, the Cobra Dane phased-array radar in the Aleutian Islands, and the Pave Paws phased-array radars now operating in Massachusetts, in California (and soon in Florida). The Pave Paws radars are designed to track those missiles fired from submarines.

This detection system is supplemented by the Integrated Operational Nuclear Detection System (IONDS). This system will eventually be carried by all eighteen of the new Global Positioning System (NAVSTAR) satellites being developed by the U.S. The location and magnitude of a nuclear explosion in the atmosphere or in space will be detected by combinations of signals from ultraviolet and x-ray sensors.

To avoid an accidental nuclear war, policymakers, generals, psychologists, sociologists and physicists charged with the responsibility of tightening the safety factor must deal with several types of human error. Therefore, a critical aspect of the nuclear early-warning system is the concept of "dual phenomenology." This is the idea that intelligence of a surprise attack must be confirmed by a multiple and "redundant" means so as to remove any doubts about the reality of the threat. A number of times in the past, the network of Defense Support Program satellites has been fooled by spurious signals created by such phenomena as sun glare, fires in the Siberian oil fields, and even the Northern Lights. In the aftermath of several well-publicized false alarms, this system has incorporated more elaborate testing and redundancy procedures.

Through the Worldwide Military Command and Control System, the President has several different ways of dispatching an Emergency Action Message (EAM). This is the authorization that would release nuclear weapons for an actual launch. In an emergency, the President could employ such diverse systems as priority telephone, teletype, landlines, microwave relay, radio transmitters and communications satellites.

Despite the redundancy of strategic C^3I capabilities, nearly all of the above channels are highly vulnerable to the effects of nuclear weapons. One expert on the system has observed: "As offensive nuclear arsenals continue to improve in accuracy, number of warheads and dispersal of delivery systems, it seems plausible that surprise attack directed at the adversary's C^3I network could delay receipt of the EAM by the strategic

The U.S. Chain of Command*

```
                    ┌─────────────────────┐
                    │     PRESIDENT       │
                    │ SECRETARY OF DEFENSE│
                    └──────────┬──────────┘
  ┌──────────────┐             │
  │ JOINT CHIEFS │─────────────┤
  │   OF STAFF   │             │
  └──────────────┘             │
       ┌─────────────┬─────────┼─────────┬──────────────┐
       │             │         │         │              │
  COMMANDER     COMMANDER  COMMANDER  COMMANDER    COMMANDER
  STRATEGIC     PACIFIC    NORTH      ATLANTIC     EUROPEAN
  AIR COMMAND   COMMAND    AMERICAN   COMMAND      COMMAND
                           AEROSPACE
                           COMMAND
```

Subordinate units:
- Commander Strategic Air Command: Fifteenth Air Force, Eighth Air Force
- Commander Pacific Command: Fifth Air Force, Eighth Army, Seventh Fleet
- Commander Atlantic Command: Third Fleet, Second Fleet
- Commander European Command: Seventh Army, Sixth Fleet, Third Air Force

* For reasons of space not all units are included.

forces for hours or even longer, thereby impairing or even preventing the execution of a prompt retaliatory strike."[4]

In the effort to make military communications more secure, the U.S. now routes about seventy percent of its messages through satellites. But given the superpower race to develop anti-satellite weapons, it won't be long before these vital communications links will be vulnerable as well.

The Chain of Command

Suppose the President of the United States goes "crazy," or suppose he singlehandedly decides to reverse national policy and launch a pre-emptive strike against the Soviet Union. What then?

During the Watergate crisis in the early 1970s, President Nixon once mentioned to a group of Congressmen that he could walk into his office and push a button and thirty minutes later, we could find ourselves in a nuclear war. According to newspaper reports, the mental instability of the President during this crisis was a real concern to certain high level civilian leaders in the Pentagon, and they took steps in great secrecy to thwart any such desperate act.

The point here is that (contrary to the impression many people have) the President is subject to checks in this crucial area. Even he cannot simply pick up his telephone or push a button and order "go." From what is known about the authorizing process from the unclassified literature, a "fail-safe" mechanism ensures that nuclear weapons are not armed until a coded authorization has been received.

Wherever the President goes, he is accompanied by a warrant officer who carries a black briefcase popularly known as the "football." This briefcase is so named because an early U.S. nuclear strike plan against the Soviet Union was code-named "Dropshot."[5] Recently, U.S. intelligence sources thought they identified the military aide to the late Soviet President Yuri Andropov who was charged with a similar responsibility.

The "football" contains a summary of U.S. nuclear war plans, which, in a crisis situation, could enable the President to select among various options for nuclear strikes against the Soviet Union and/or China, as well as communist retaliation. There are also "Gold Codes," which are highly

---

4   Jonathan B. Tucker, *opus cit.*, p. 945.
5   The plan, related documents and commentaries are published in Anthony C. Brown, *Dropshot: The American Plan for World War III with Russia in 1957* (New York, 1978). Contingency plans for a war beginning in 1955-56, code-named Charioteer, are contained in U.S. Joint Chiefs of Staff Records, "USSR" Series (3-2-46), Section 6.

secure and would only be made available to American SAC bombers, ICBMs and missile-firing submarines after the President had authorized the release of nuclear weapons.

The National Security Agency changes the Gold Codes, a jumble of baffling numbers and letters, each day. At the same time, at nuclear command posts all around the world, duty officers receive their own sealed copies of the same codes. This procedure has been followed since 1962, when President Kennedy signed a highly classified National Security Action Memorandum changing the process for presidential release of nuclear weapons.

Since the Reorganization Act of 1958, the President does not have complete control over the release of nuclear weapons. In practice, he would order the Secretary of Defense to employ these weapons. He, in turn, would direct the Chairman of the Joint Chiefs of Staff to execute the strike plan that has been selected. Thus, the President cannot by himself authorize the use of nuclear weapons without the cooperation of two other high-level officials.[6]

There are elaborate plans for removing the President from Washington in the event of a surprise nuclear attack. According to the contingency plan, the President would, in a crisis, be immediately flown the ten miles to Andrews Air Force Base by helicopter. There he would be put aboard the National Emergency Airborne Command Post (NEACP, pronounced "Kneecap"). This "doomsday" aircraft is an E-4B, a modified Boeing 747 with blacked-out windows and an interior crammed with computers and high-powered transmitters. Code named "Nightwatch", it is on ground alert around the clock. If necessary, this plane can stay aloft for more than ten hours without refueling, but it can also be refueled by airborne tankers. The Nightwatch aircraft is fully equipped to oversee at least the initial stages of a nuclear exchange.

Theoretically, the President would be airborne before the White House and the airfield itself were destroyed in a nuclear attack. But this is only theory. Who knows how long it would take the President to get from whereever he was — out riding horses, playing golf or even in bed or in the bath — to the "doomsday" plane?[7]

Security adviser Zbigniew Brzezinski has recounted in his memoirs an

[6] Vice Admiral G.E. Miller, "Existing Systems of Command and Control," in Franklin Griffiths *et al.* (eds.), *The Danger of Nuclear War* (Toronto: University of Toronto Press, 1979), p. 56.

[7] The President's personal helicopter squadron is parked at Quantico Marine Corps Base, approximately thirty miles south of the White House. Theoretically, one of these helicopters can arrive within a few minutes and whisk the President to Andrews Air Force Base some twenty miles away and the waiting "doomsday" plane.

attempt to put the evacuation plan into action soon after Jimmy Carter took office.[8]

"I called in the person responsible for evacuating the President in the event of a crisis. I obtained a detailed account of how long it actually would take to evacuate the President by helicopter . . . I ordered him to run a simulated evacuation right now, turning on my stopwatch.

"The poor fellow's eyes . . . practically popped," Brzezinski records. "He looked so surprised. He said, 'Right now?' and I said, 'Yes, right now.' He reached for the phone and could hardly speak coherently when he demanded that the helicopter immediately come for a drill." Brzezinski continues: "I took one of the secretaries . . . along to simulate Mrs. Carter, and we proceeded to the south lawn to wait for the helicopter to arrive. It took roughly two and a half times as long to arrive as it was supposed to. We then flew to a special site from where another evacuation procedure would be followed." To make a long story short, "the whole thing took roughly twice as long as it should have." Moreover, "on our return we found that the drill somehow did not take into account the protective service and we were almost shot down."

In reviewing the above account, it is worth noting that a missile launched in a depressed trajectory from a Soviet submarine off the East coast could reach Washington in five to ten minutes. So any plan to evacuate the President would seem, in some circumstances at least, to be doomed to failure.[9]

Should the President be killed in a nuclear attack, the authority to release nuclear weapons automatically passes down the line of succession, beginning with the Vice President, the Speaker of the House, the President *pro tempore* of the Senate and the members of the Cabinet. But again this is only theory. In his best-selling book *The Death of a President*, William Manchester contends that the assassination of President Kennedy in 1963 caught Vice President Lyndon Johnson so poorly briefed on his responsibilities as Commander-in-Chief that if a Soviet nuclear attack had been launched that afternoon, it could have crippled the American capability to retaliate. However, security officials who were on duty at the time immediately challenged this account.[10]

More recently, the attempted assassination of President Reagan in April

---

8 Zbigniew Brzezinski, *Power and Principle: Memoirs of National Security Adviser 1977-1981* (New York: Farrar, Straus, Giroux, 1983), p. 15.
9 According to one Carter Administration insider, Presidential Directive 41, which was adopted after a study of presidential evacuation plans, concluded: "[I]t may not be possible to evacuate those members of the National Command Authority in town at the time to either hardened ground bases or airborne command posts."
10 See Louis W. Koenig, *The Chief Executive* (New York: Harcourt, Brace and World, 1968), p. 259.

STRATEGIC OFFENSIVE FORCES

ICBMs

US		USSR	
40	TITAN	SS-11	550
450	MINUTEMAN II	SS-13	60
550	MINUTEMAN III	SS-17	150
1040		SS-18	308
		SS-19	330
			1398

SLBMs

US		USSR	
304	POSEIDON	SS-N-5	45
288	TRIDENT I*	SS-N-6	368
592		SS-N-8	292
		SS-N-17	12
		SS-N-18	224
		SS-N-20*	40
			981

BOMBERS

US		USSR	
168	B-52G	BEAR	100
96	B-52H	BISON	45
61	FB-111	BACKFIRE**	230
325			375

APPROXIMATE TOTALS

	US	USSR
DELIVERY VEHICLES		
• MISSILES	1632	2379
• BOMBERS	325	375

* INCLUDES SLBMs POTENTIALLY CARRIED ON TRIDENT AND TYPHOON SSBNs ON SEA TRIAL

** INCLUDES SOVIET STRATEGIC AIR FORCE AND NAVAL AVIATION BACKFIRE AIRCRAFT

AS OF 1 JANUARY 1984

Source: Joint Chiefs of Staff, United States Military Posture FY 1985.

1981 provoked renewed discussions in the government over who should have the authority to order the use of nuclear weapons or direct other military actions when the President is disabled or otherwise isolated from military communications. According to one report, Vice President Bush "automatically" inherited the authority to act for the President in a "narrow range" of contingencies, presumably including nuclear war, while Ronald Reagan was put under anesthesia as he underwent extensive surgery to remove the bullet lodged in his chest.[11] But a number of still unresolved problems surround this issue. For example, what if the Secretary of Defense or the Chairman of the Joint Chiefs of Staff could not be reached in a nuclear emergency? What then would be the situation?

The Presidential Succession Act of 1947, not the U.S. Constitution, specifies that after the Vice President, the presidency passes to the Speaker of the House, then to the President *pro tempore* of the Senate, then to the Secretary of State, and then down through the Cabinet.

One of the most sensitive of White Hause plans provides for the contingency of a disarming first-strike attack which would obliterate the U.S. chain of command. In this case, the commanders of U.S. *Poseidon* and *Trident* submarines would at some point be able to retaliate *on their own* after such a "decapitating" attack. This contingency plan is known officially as "permissive action," and it is highly classified.

Communications with U.S. Ballistic Missile Submarines

1. Poseidon and Trident Submarines

Currently, the United States possesses some 34 ballistic missile submarines: 31 *Poseidon* and 3 *Trident*. The first *Polaris* missiles had "only" an intermediate range of 1,500 miles or so. They were later replaced with longer-range missiles. In the 1970s, these missiles were replaced again with a new SLBM termed the *Poseidon*, which had an intercontinental range. Each improvement in range meant that more targets could be reached. But more importantly, it meant that the submarines would have a larger area of the ocean in which to hide. Also, since a rotating part of the U.S. submarine fleet is in port at any one time, longer range meant that in an emergency the submarines in port could be dispatched to their duty station and could reach their cruising areas quickly.[12]

---

11 See *The New York Times*, April 4, 1981.
12 The United States maintains about 60 percent of its 34 ballistic missile submarines at sea at all times. By way of contrast, only about eleven percent of the Russian

The U.S. has just completed the retrofitting of *Trident* I missiles on 12 of 31 *Poseidon* submarines. The weapons on these new missiles have 60 percent longer range, are two and one-half times more powerful and are more accurate than the weapons on the *Poseidon* missiles they replaced. The *Trident* I missiles, which will also be deployed on new *Trident* subs, will provide 3,000 new nuclear weapons for the American strategic arsenal in the 1980s.

Currently, the United States is moving forward with the *Trident* II (D-5) missile. This long-range missile will give U.S. submarine-launched missiles the ability to destroy hardened Soviet missile silos for the first time.[13]

President Reagan's five-year plan calls for the building of 15 *Trident* submarines. Each *Trident* submarine is bigger than the Washington Monument and alone will carry enough weapons to target every Soviet city of over 100,000 people.[14]

Several years ago Norman Cousins pointed out in an editorial in the Saturday Review that, next to the leaders of the Soviet Union and the United States, a *Trident* submarine commander is "the third most powerful man in the world."[15] He controls more destructive power than the military establishments of Britain, Italy, Spain, Brazil, Argentina, West Germany, Japan, the Philippines, India and Pakistan — all put together. To put it another way: Each *Trident* submarine commander has in his missiles an explosive force equal to some two thousand "Hiroshimas."

Some of the troubling aspects of the *Trident* were stated candidly by President Carter in his 1979 arms control impact report. This document indicated that " . . . the potential impact of the *Trident*-2 missile on strategic stability . . . may be negative, due to the significant hard target kill capability it may have . . ." This "hard target capability could stimulate negative effects on Soviet reactions, which, in turn, could lead to instabilities

> submarine fleet is reportedly at sea on any normal day. Even during periods of international crisis, the Soviets usually maintain more or less the same deployment rate, unlike the United States, which increases the number of submarines at sea to almost 100 percent. The low rate of Soviet submarine deployment is due to a number of factors, including the shortage of trained crews and inadequate maintenance facilities. Unlike the Soviet Union, the United States maintains two crews for each submarine. See Honoré (Marc) Catudal, *Soviet Nuclear Strategy* (Berlin: Berlin Verlag, 1985).

13 See J.S. Wit, "American SLBM: Counterforce Options and Strategic Implications," *Survival*, Vol. 24, Nos. 4-5 (July-October, 1982), pp. 163-74. These deadly accurate weapons pose a grave danger to Soviet land-based missiles, which constitute almost 75 percent of the total Soviet strategic nuclear arsenal.

14 *The Defense Monitor*, Vol. 11, No. 6 (1982), p. 4.

15 Norman Cousins, "The Third Most Powerful Man in the World," *Saturday Review*, April 17, 1976, p. 4.

Figure 7: *Identification View (aerial) of USS John Marshall (SSBN-611), Port Bow.*

in the strategic balance and complicate strategic arms limitation efforts." The *Trident*-2 SLBM "also could be perceived as a first strike weapon with a significant hard target kill potential against time-urgent targets . . ."[16]

2. One-way Communications with Submarines

During peacetime, communications are maintained with U.S. submarines via a system of redundant transmitting stations at fixed sites around the world.[17] In order to avoid detection, these submarines never have to report to base while they are on patrol. This arrangement provides the commander with a unique degree of autonomy. Although he is supposed to maximize the time he spends within range of the Soviet Union and his submarine's targets, he alone decides whether his "time on station" is causing an unnecessary risk of detection.

Under current conditions, all communication with U.S. submarines is one-way. The submarine commander receives messages frequently from the Joint Chiefs of Staff and the National Command Authority, but there is no requirement that he acknowledge receipt of the message or identify himself, as this might give away his position. These messages usually contain information on the location of Soviet naval and anti-submarine warfare units, changes in the targeting plans, weather and water conditions, changes in the patrol route, new regulations, promotions and news from home. Each member of the crew is allotted only a "handful" of short messages from home during the entire period in which his submarine is at sea.

Submarine communications are the most sensitive of all links with the strategic forces of the United States. The radio operators have special "Circuit Mayflower" clearances, and they are ordered to adhere rigidly to procedures to avoid transmissions that might reveal the position of the submarine. In response to a simple warning, the missile-firing submarine on alert slows down and proceeds to move close to the surface where it can deploy a special antenna enabling it to pick up the "go code."

In over 2,000 U.S. submarine patrols since 1960, the U.S.S.R. has never succeeded in completely tracking one, say U.S. insiders. However, when a submarine commander fires one of his missiles, he immediately betrays his position to the enemy and this presents a serious problem to the submarine. In an all-out attack, of course, the missiles would be fired consecutively — at intervals of about twenty seconds. But some attack options in the SIOP

---

16 *Fiscal Year 1979 Arms Control Impact Statement* (June, 1978), pp. 40-41.

17 Given the fact that shore-based systems are vulnerable to attack and jamming, there is an airborne system known as TACAMO ("Take Charge And Move Out"), which functions as an emergency communications link between the National Command Authority and submerged submarines.

require only some of the missiles to be fired. None the less, as one submarine commander puts it, "If you fire one, you want to fire them all. The tendency is wanting to save your ass."[18]

3. Launching Specifications for Nuclear Submarines

American submarine commanders reportedly have thick briefing books which contain pages of highly classified "attack options" represented by three-letter codes. All that is needed for the National Command Authority to authorize a specific strike plan is to transmit the proper code word four times.

U.S. missile-firing submarines have a verification code which is reportedly changed every hour. It is transmitted to the submarine along with the launch order and must be verified by the submarine skipper, the executive officer and the weapons officer.

It is unclassified knowledge that the crews of U.S. landbased missiles and SAC bombers can only release their nuclear weapons after receiving the National Command Authority authorization that would release nuclear weapons for use and its authenticators.[19] However, a different situation exists regarding nuclear submarines, which are considered to be the most survivable leg of the strategic triad. For instance, it has been learned that the electrical firing circuit on board the submarines can be activated by means of a complex, collaborative action within close time tolerances on the part of several men on board who are considered "reliable."[20] (U.S. missile-firing submarines also differ from the other legs of the triad in that their missiles can be retargeted autonomously.)

According to one well-informed source, at least four of the twelve officers usually on board a missile-firing submarine would have to turn switches — or "vote," as crew members put it, and all at the same time — in order to effect nuclear release. "Four switches must be turned on for the firing circuits to be properly armed before the missile can be launched." Both the captain and the weapons control officer "have keys for their switches, but the navigations officer must throw a switch and the launch control officer must pull a large lever, called the trigger." In order to protect

---

18 Quoted in Peter Pringle *et al., S.I.O.P.: The Secret U.S. War Plan for Nuclear War* (New York: W.W. Norton, 1984), p. 160.
19 Safety features, called "permissive action links," are reportedly attached to all U.S. nuclear weapons in silos. These devices can only be remotely opened by a code transmitted with the launch order so that a missile crew cannot arbitrarily fire the weapon. See Robert C. Aldridge, *First Strike! The Pentagon's Strategy for Nuclear War* Boston: South End Press, 1983), p. 246.
20 L. René Beres, *Apocalypse* (Chicago: University of Chicago Press, 1980), p. 39.

against wrongful use of the missiles, "the launch control officer, the weapons control officer, or the navigator may officially refuse to obey the captain's order to fire, and the alternate launch officer, the executive officer who must verify the captain's commands and the communications officer who must decode the orders, may intervene if they believe that for some reason the proper orders were not received."[21] These fail-safe procedures make missile-firing submarines the only instance in the U.S. Navy where mutiny is officially sanctioned.

Strategic Air Command

The United States possesses about 325 operational strategic bombers. All are high-speed jet aircraft. The U.S. also has over 40 long-range bombers in active reserve and over 200 in storage. In addition to strategic bombers, the U.S. has over 400 strike aircraft which are equipped with nuclear weapons aboard its aircraft carriers.

The United States is in the process of adding about 4,350 nuclear-tipped air-launched cruise missiles (ALCMs) to enhance the capability of its strategic bomber force. Sixty B-52Gs are now outfitted with ALCMs, improving considerably their penetration capability against increasingly dense and sophisticated Soviet air defenses.[22]

The U.S. is also building a fleet of at least one hundred B-1B bombers. At the same time, it is moving ahead with plans to develop an advanced technology ("Stealth") bomber to replace the B-1. The super-secret "Stealth" technology would make U.S. heavy bombers "invisible" to Soviet radar, or at least much harder to detect.

The origins of the Strategic Air Command can he traced back to World War II and the strategic bombing of Germany and Japan. At that time, the American Air Force was part of the Army. After the war, when tensions between the United States and the Soviet Union began to mount, the new Air Force, which now existed as a separate branch of the armed forces, created a special bomber force aimed at the U.S.S.R. Popularly known as SAC, it was put under the charge of General Curtis LeMay of the Japanese bombing campaign.

With his mandate from the U.S. government, General LeMay quickly gathered together scattered and decrepit B-29 squadrons that had little or

21 See Peter Pringle *et al., S.I.O.P.: The Secret U.S. War Plan for Nuclear War* (New York: W.W. Norton, 1984), p. 161.
22 Joint Chiefs of Staff, *United States Military Posture for FY 1985* (Washington, D.C.: Pentagon, 1984), p. 25.

no operational capability and quickly whipped aircraft and airmen into shape. Headquarters was established in Omaha, Nebraska, and many SAC bases were set up in the Midwest. The idea was that their location in America's heartland would put them at the greatest distance from the perceived Soviet threat.

During the 1950s the Strategic Air Command was the mainstay of America's national security. In recognition of this military reality, Congress routinely gave about fifty percent of the defense budget to the Air Force.

It was also at this time that SAC obtained the generally recognized status of an elite corps. Discipline was tight, and LeMay demanded superior performance. Frequently, SAC pilots and crew members had to stay so long on ready-alert that they did not see their families for weeks at a time.

During much of the 1960s, U.S. strategic bombers were kept on air alert. This means that they were permanently on patrol with their nuclear weapons, waiting for the "go code." One of the most controversial practices of these bombers was to make periodic runs — with hydrogen bombs at the ready — to so-called "fail-safe" points near the Soviet border. Critics severely attacked this practice because they believed it increased the risk of nuclear war.

In 1968, a series of accidents occurred which drew worldwide attention to the problems connected with maintaining strategic bombers on constant airborne alert. The first one involved a B-52 flying over Greenland. It crashed, spewing plutonium and uranium over a large area. The second tragedy occurred later that year. This time a B-52 collided in mid-air with its refueling tanker. The two planes exploded and crashed into the sea off Palomares, along the coast of Spain. The U.S. Navy recovered three nuclear bombs, but a fourth fell into water over five hundred feet deep and disappeared. These accidents, which were highly publicized at the time, led to an investigation and the recommendation that the airborne patrols be ended. Now the aging B-52s never fly with nuclear weapons on board unless they are scrambled by a genuine alert.[23]

If U.S. strategic bombers are no longer on constant alert, they can be scrambled relatively quickly. According to U.S. military sources, about sixty-eight aircraft could be in the air with five minutes notice. A second wave of approximately ninety-five bombers could be airborne within fifteen minutes. Assuming that the Soviets were to attack all nineteen U.S. bomber bases, the Pentagon expects that half of the bomber force would survive.[24]

23 See David A. Anderton, *Strategic Air Command* (New York: Charles Scribner's, 1977).

24 The Strategic Air Command maintains flying command posts, with continuous eight-hour airborne alert shifts. These planes, originally termed "Looking Glass"

The B-52s flying time to the Soviet Union is anywhere between six and nine hours. This fact of life gives the National Command Authority the unusual luxury of being able to recall them if necessary. Their recall potential, in fact, makes them the most controlable of all U.S. nuclear delivery vehicles.[25] In view of this easy-recall situation, the SAC Commander, a four-star general, is authorized to launch his bombers and put them in a holding pattern (known technically as "positive control") after receiving an alert from NORAD and before any orders are transmitted from the President.

Most B-52s on genuine alert today are armed with four nuclear bombs and four short-range attack missiles (SRAMs). Should the order come down to attack the Soviet Union, the SRAMs would be used to help destroy Soviet air defenses. The remaining larger bombs would be dropped on any targets that had not already been destroyed by land-based ICBMs and submarines such as missile silos, airfields, dockyards, Soviet command and control posts and other military targets or, if the President authorized execution of this option, urban and industrial complexes.

Those nuclear weapons delivered by aircraft today are generally considered more accurate than those launched from land- or sea-based systems. With the assistance of sophisticated electronic aiming devices, they can be dropped precisely on target. Or at least that is the theory. The reality is somewhat different as B-52 pilots know."It's still like throwing a marble into a paper cup from a moving bicycle," one attests.

There is a great deal of controversy about the reliability of this leg of U.S. strategic nuclear forces. "Most are older than the pilots who fly them," asserts one Defense Department official. To be sure, in the past the bombers had to be able to penetrate thick Soviet air defenses in order to reach their targets in Eastern Europe or the U.S.S.R. And despite a vast array of countermeasures against radar, attacking missiles and fighters, they were given only a fifty-fifty chance by some knowledgeable insiders of arriving over their targets. Now, however, as more and more B-52s are being outfitted

because they were able to do aloft what the underground command posts could do below, have direct communications with the Joint Chiefs of Staff through the Pentagon command post and SAC bomber and missile bases. Each "Looking Glass" plane is reportedly commanded by a SAC general and each is said to have the ability to launch the entire land-based ICBM force in case a nuclear attack were to result in the total loss of civilian control. See Roger Speed, *Strategic Deterrence in the 1980s* (Stanford: Hoover Institution Press, 1979).

25 One former U.S. official with experience in these matters disagrees. "The most controlable are the submarines, some of which would take days to get on station. The bombers must either be used in a matter of hours or one risks losing them if there were no place for them to land."

with air-launched cruise missiles, which can be fired from outside the borders of the Soviet Union, and the new Stealth technology is being applied, the situation has changed, and the air arm of U.S. strategic forces is assuming greater importance.

Princeton Professor Richard Falk, who visited the SAC headquarters in the fall of 1970, describes his encounter with the Commander of the Strategic Air Command[26] in a hollowed-out granite mountain in the Rockies, which in the days of less accurate missiles, was considered "bombproof."[27] Perhaps aboveground was situated SAC's flying command post, a silver Boeing 707 code named "Cover All."

On a desk in front of the SAC Commander's chair is a bewildering array of telephones — all different colors. A gold phone links the four-star general with the Pentagon. In case of enemy attack, the Joint Chiefs would use this line to relay commands from the President to SAC. Theoretically, the President might use it to seek the advice of his nuclear commanders before taking any precipitous measures.

As was the case with many of the higher-ranking officers the Princeton University professor met that day, the SAC Commander "exhibited an extreme preoccupation with the malicious designs and great capabilities of the Russian bear." Nothing unusual so far. The SAC commander told Falk and his fellow visitors how glad he was that prominent Americans could be reassured firsthand about U.S. readiness to defend "the free world" against nuclear attack. The general was eloquent in his description of SAC morale and of the need for public support. Then, Falk reports, the general "said something I have never forgotten. He said he wished that during the Cuban Missile Crisis of 1962 the Soviet Union had attacked Florida because then we could have 'wipe[d] them off the face of the earth' and that this would have 'finally pull[ed] this country together!'" (Falk's visit coincided with a peak time of Vietnam-related domestic unrest.)

To be sure, what the SAC Commander Falk was talking about is not typical of those who figure in the current command and control structure. And the present command structure presiding over the growing array of Amer-

---

26 Robert Jay Lifton and Richard Falk, *Indefensible Weapons: The Political and Psychological Case Against Nuclearism* (New York: Basic Books, 1982), pp. 130-31.

27 See Office of the Historian, *Strategic Air Command, Development of Strategic Air Command, 1946-1976* (Offutt Air Force Base, Nebr.: Strategic Air Command, 1976), pp. 58-59. SAC built its underground command post in 1957 and maintains that this gave the U.S. a hardened, survivable command system in the 1950s. Some experts, however, dispute this. Paul Bracken, for instance, says "Even a small, inaccurate Soviet nuclear weapon could have destroyed it." See his *The Command and Control of Nuclear Forces* (New Haven: Yale University Press, 1983), p. 186.

ican nuclear weaponry is less prone to such grandiose impulses. But the prevailing attitudes of war gamers and military planners do seem disturbingly oriented toward the expectation of nuclear war — when, not if, deterrence fails.

Land-Based ICBMs

The United States currently maintains 1,040 ICBMs (down from 1,054 in the early 1970s). The bulk of these intercontinental ballistic missiles consists of solid-fuel Minuteman II (450) and Minuteman III (550) missiles. The Air Force is in the process of phasing out its remaining 40 aged *Titan* liquid-fuel missiles.[28]

The distinction here between liquid and solid fuel missiles is extremely important. Solid fuel missiles have their fuel prepacked in a stable form that lasts a long time. They are always ready for launch and can be fired on very short notice. Liquid-fuel missiles, on the other hand, are problematical. These missiles, which make up about 95 percent of the strategic nuclear forces of the Soviet Union, are very unstable. For instance, the fuel has a tendency to corrode its containers and even to explode at unpredictable moments. The first-generation of Soviet liquid-fuel missiles could not be kept fueled at all times. They had to be filled with liquid fuel after the command came down to be ready for launch. As the technical experts note, this was a time-consuming and somewhat difficult procedure. The experience of the U.S. Air Force with its huge *Titans*, which carry the largest single warhead in the entire American arsenal, provides a clear example of the kind of dangers liquid-fuel rockets pose.

In September 1980, an airman working on a *Titan* at a base in Damascus, Arkansas dropped a 9-pound wrench, which fell some 66 feet down the silo and punctured the "skin" of the missile. From that time on the fuel began to leak. Nine hours later the missile exploded. The force of the explosion blew the 750-ton concrete lid a distance of approximately 1,000 feet. Sergeant Kennedy, who had just emerged from the silo, was thrown some 150 feet. The nine-megaton warhead broke into several pieces but did not explode.[29]

Since all liquid rocket fuels — American and Soviet — are highly toxic when exposed to the atmosphere and thus dangerous to handle, it is not

28 Joint Chiefs of Staff, *United States Military Posture for FY 1985* (Washington, D.C.: Pentagon, 1984).

29 For details see Andrew Cockburn, *The Threat: Inside the Soviet Military Machine* (New York: Random House, 1983).

surprising that the U.S. Air Force would want to eliminate the old-fashioned liquid-fuel *Titans* and the Soviets should be in a hurry to develop solid-fuel missiles for the bulk of their strategic forces. (U.S. intelligence officials have learned of numerous accidents involving Soviet liquid-fuel missiles, but the most spectacular occurred on October 24, 1960, when an experimental 8-K-63 rocket blew up. According to one report by a Soviet Army officer who defected to the West, "the commander-in-Chief of the Strategic Rocket Forces, Chief Marshal Nedelin, and his entire staff were burned alive ....")[30]

As a general rule, U.S. *Minuteman* missiles are deployed several miles from each other in reinforced concrete silos ninety feet deep. These concrete shields are reportedly able to withstand the blast and pressure of nuclear explosions exceeding twelve times normal atmospheric pressure. The United States has just completed hardening these silos and has installed an improved guidance system which doubles accuracy.

Some 550 *Minuteman* ICBMs have been MIRVed. That is, they have been outfitted with multiple independently targeted re-entry vehicles. Soon the U.S. will complete retrofitting 300 of these missiles (900 nuclear weapons) with the MK12A warhead. This will double each weapon's explosive power and increase lethality.

The Reagan Administration has plans for deploying at least 10 highly accurate MX ("Peacekeeper") missiles. These hydraheaded heavy missiles are very accurate and can carry at least ten MIRVed warheads. Recently, however, the U.S. Congress dealt a setback to these plans, allowing only a very limited number to be built only if the Soviets refused to return to the negotiating table in the START talks.[31]

ICBMs are the most accurate nuclear weapons in the U.S. strategic arsenal. Like missile-firing submarines, but unlike heavy bombers, they are almost certain to reach their targets. However, unlike SLBMs, land-based missiles and bombers have redundant and reliable communications links with the National Command Authority.

According to one well-informed source, this is how the command and control system for U.S. ICBMs works.[32] Two *Minuteman* launch control

---

30 See Viktor Suvorov, *Inside the Soviet Army* (London: Hamish Hamilton, 1982), p. 58. This book contains a wealth of information about the Soviet military, but it has to be used with caution, for it contains many factual errors, oversimplifications and obvious distortions.

31 For an excellent discussion of the MX controversy see Herbert Scoville, *MX: Prescription for Disaster* (Cambridge: MIT Press, 1981).

32 The following account relies heavily on the detailed report by Peter Pringle and William Arkin, *SIOP: The Secret U.S. Plan for Nuclear War* (New York: W.W. Norton, 1984), pp. 164-68.

officers, situated in a missile control capsule fifty feet below ground, "oversee ten missiles, with five launch control centers in each Strategic Missile Wing." During an alert "they strap themselves into red padded chairs, sitting at right angles from each other and separated by the regulation spacing of twelve feet. They each face identical computer consoles that monitor the status of the missiles and would be used to launch them." Generally, the missiles maintain a 98 percent alert rate, and "any change in their status is immediately reported to wing headquarters and SAC at Offutt [Air Force base] and appears on the SAC command post diplay screens."[33]

The two launch control officers are in regular contact with crew members inside the five launch centers. These centers are located just outside the missile control capsule, but are sealed off from the outside by four-ton blast doors.

Inside each of the five launch centers is the so-called "red box." This container is perched on a shelf between the two *Minuteman* crewmen and is a replica of the red boxes inside missile submarine command and control centers and B-52 cockpits. It is secured with two combination locks. Inside the red box are the "validation codes," which would authenticate a "nuclear control order," and two keys for missile release.

During an actual attack, an alarm bell inside the missile control capsule sounds in response to the initial alert command originating from the SAC controller at Offutt. The two *Minuteman* missile crewmen then "button up." They close the blast doors and switch to emergency air and power. Next, the senior crew member picks up the red phone, which is the primary alerting system for SAC, and talks with a member of the Strategic Missile Wing command post. He is told that an authorized launch instruction (officially called an "emergency action message") has been received and will soon be transmitted over the SAC automated command and control system to the center. Almost immediately an oral number and letter code follows. The crew commander proceeds to copy the message down, verifying it with the launch codes for that particular day. At the same time, a "hard copy" confirmation of the oral message is received over a small teletype machine. Each crew member begins to open one of two locks on the red box, removing the special sealed instructions for firing the missiles (the "emergency war order"). The crew members also remove their firing keys.

Then the two launch officers jointly "validate" their launch instructions sent over the red telephone. If the letters or numbers in the emergency action message are not matching, the crew will reject it as an invalid message. After validation is complete, the launch officers wait for the "nuclear

---

33 U.S. intelligence sources believe that the alert rate for Soviet ICBMs is much lower.

control order." This communication may tell them to launch some of their missiles, all of their missiles or just prepare them for launching.[34]

In the unusual case that the missile crew is instructed to change the targets of its missiles, this action is undertaken without the two ever having to leave the launch control center by simply dialing a new set of numbers into the memory of the missile. The crew members never know what the change means in terms of the actual names of the targets.

Not all the checks have been exhausted at this point. Before the launch officers are authorized to "turn their keys," thereby launching their missiles, a second crew in one of the other four launch control centers attached to the squadron must duplicate the same procedures. This process, known as "voting," positively indicates that the command to launch is valid. Ultimately, any one of the crews in the other four capsules of the squadron can prevent a launch if it believes the launch is being made under an invalid order. In practice, this mechanism performs mostly a delay function, for it is automatically cancelled after only a few minutes, although it can be reintroduced any number of times.

Finally, to fire a missile (or missiles), the two crewmen must turn their keys simultaneously, maintaining them in position for at least five seconds. During this elaborate control procedure, the lit panels on the crewmen's consoles have passed through several launch sequences. These began with "strategic alert" and passed through "warhead armed" to "launch in progress," ending with "missiles away." Once "missiles away" has been reached, the chance for recall does not exist.

The Delegation of Presidential Authority

Many people believe that only the President can authorize the use of nuclear weapons and that this authority must not be delegated. However, a 1975 study conducted by staff members of the Library of Congress states "we have been unable to find any constitutional or statutory basis supporting [this belief]." In fact, the authors of this investigation conclude that the authority to release nuclear weapons "may be delegated to subordinate officers in the chain of command virtually without limitation."[35]

---

34 Originally, *Minuteman* missiles were designed to fire only in groups of fifty missiles at a time, but in 1961 they were outfitted with a selective launch capability in accordance with the new strategic doctrine that not all missiles should be launched at the outset of a nuclear conflict. See Desmond Ball, *Politics and Force Levels* (Berkely, Calif.: University of California Press, 1980), p. 194.

35 Congressional Research Service of the Library of Congress, *Authority to Order the Use of Nuclear Weapons*, a report prepared for the House International Relations Committee, December 1, 1975, p. 1.

A close examination of the public record reveals substantial evidence that others than the President have access to the "nuclear button." During the presidential campaign of 1964, for instance, it was learned that in September 1957 General Earl E. Partridge, formerly Commander of NORAD, had stated in an interview that his command was authorized to launch nuclear weapons under certain circumstances *without specific approval* by the President.[36] Nineteen years later Vice Admiral Gerald E. Miller, retired former Deputy Commander of the Joint Strategic Target Planning Staff, substantiated Partridge's testimony when he advised a congressional committee that the NORAD commander "has been delegated such authority only under severe restrictions and specific conditions of attack."[37]

Interestingly, Admiral Miller alluded to reports that Presidents Eisenhower and Kennedy had delegated nuclear release authority to regional commanders, but he acknowledged that he was not able to confirm them. For his part, Daniel Ellsberg, a former Defense Department consultant and the person who leaked the Pentagon Papers, maintains that he personally saw secret letters signed by President Eisenhower authorizing commanders overseas to use nuclear weapons under certain circumstances Ellsberg claims that this delegation of authority remained in effect during the Kennedy period and probably through the Administrations of Presidents Johnson and Nixon.[38]

One of those regional commanders who allegedly had been given nuclear release authority is Admiral Harry D. Felt, then Commander of the Pacific Theater. But if Ellsberg can be believed, that authority also trickled down the chain of command. Ellsberg recalls that a major in the U.S. Air Force in Korea told him that he would put his dozen nuclear-armed planes in the air if he thought he was under enemy attack. According to what the major reportedly told Ellsberg, it was possible for one of the major's pilots to misunderstand instructions and touch off World War III.[39]

---

36 This interview is reprinted in *U.S. News & World Report*, October 5, 1964.

37 *First Use of Nuclear Weapons: Preserving Responsible Control*, Hearings before the Subcommittee on International Security and Scientific Affairs of the House Committee on International Relations (Washington, D.C.: U.S. Government Printing Office, 1976), p. 49.

38 Opening address by Daniel Ellsberg at a "Whistleblowers Conference" in the Rayburn House Office Building, May 19, 1978.

39 *Ibid.* In the early 1980s, U.S. Army representatives reportedly made a secret presentation to Congress, in which they requested clearance in advance to use tactical nuclear weapons in Europe. According to the Washington *Post* reporter who leaked the story, this presentation was entitled "AirLand Battle 2000." See *The Washington Post*, July 21, 1982.

Launch on Warning

One of the most controversial issues affecting the command and control systems of the United States and the Soviet Union is the concept of "launch on warning." The notion received a great deal of publicity in the context of the 1979 NATO decision to deploy Pershing IIs and cruise missiles to Europe. These missiles pose a severe threat to Soviet command and control systems due to their accuracy and, in the case of the Pershing II, their extremely short flight time.

Launch on warning has an aura of mystery around it. However, the concept, as it may be recalled, simply means that a state plans to launch its counter-strike as soon as its radars and computers indicate that an enemy attack is on the way. Thus, such a policy represents in a sense the ultimate answer to fears that one's own missiles or command headquarters may be vulnerable to surprise attack.[40]

The United States has never had a launch-on-warning policy. So far as it is known, the Soviets have never adopted this policy either, although some U.S. military planners suspect now that the Russians may have moved close to it. The main reason such a policy is so widely opposed is that it is extremely dangerous. One false alarm in the radar and/or computer system of a defending state with such a policy could automatically result in a launch of its forces. The net effect might be accidental nuclear war, since the other side, faced with a real nuclear attack, would probably feel compelled to respond.[41]

The notion that a nuclear war could begin by accident has been with us for a long time. The problem was dramatized in the popular novel and movie, *Fail Safe*. In this story, a U.S. nuclear attack on the U.S.S.R. was

---

40 It has been suggested that a possible "launch-on-warning" policy was alluded to by former Secretary of State Henry Kissinger in a footnote to a speech delivered before the Commonwealth Club in San Francisco on February 3, 1976. In 1977, then Defense Secretary Harold Brown was asked during Congressional testimony if the United States would not launch its missiles until after it had been attacked and Soviet warheads had actually exploded on U.S. soil. "I am not answering that question one way or the other, Mr. Chairman," Brown said. "I think it is not our doctrine to do so — neither is it our doctrine that under no circumstances would we ever do so." See *Department of Defense Appropriations for 1978*, Hearings before the Defense Subcommittee of the House Appropriations Committee (Washington, D.C.: U.S. Government Printing Office, 1977), Part 7, p. 155.

41 One U.S. official says here: "Actually, a launch-on-warning policy does not require any computers or radars, even though as a practical matter these are necessary to implement it smoothly. Also, launch on warning can include cases where military authorities are given emergency authority to use nuclear weapons in advance of hostilities and are instructed to use this authority if there are indications of attack."

triggered by a "statistically impossible" double mechanical failure that sent American bombers to Moscow. The city was destroyed, and only by the reciprocal sacrifice of New York general war was avoided. This best selling novel of the early 1960s was so influential that the philosopher Sidney Hook felt compelled to issue a refutation. He argued that the technical dangers were exaggerated and that such irresponsible writing encouraged a greater fear of the American nuclear deterrent than the Soviet desire for world domination.[42]

To be sure, this tragic tale played fast and loose with the actual facts of U.S. command and control arrangements. But it did point up some of the inherent risks involved in mechanical and electronic systems.

In the United States, the record of publicly reported false alarms goes back at least two decades. In the 1950s, a flock of Canadian geese led U.S. officials to believe for a time that the United States was about to be attacked by Soviet bombers. In 1960, a meteor shower was interpreted as an assault by enemy missiles. In 1977, a Pentagon test of its multi-billion dollar Worldwide Military Command and Control System — the computer nerve center of the entire United States military apparatus — failed 62 percent of the time.[43] In 1980, a 46-cent computer chip malfunctioned, leading to a warning of a possible Soviet submarine attack on the United States.[44]

---

42 Sidney Hook, *The Fail-Safe Fallacy* (New York: Stein & Day, 1963).

43 Louis René Beres, Nuclear Strategy and World Order: The United States Imperative," in Burns H. Weston (ed.), *Toward Nuclear Disarmament and Global Security: A Search for Alternatives* (Boulder: Westview Press, 1984), p. 241.

44 This incident led to a Senate investigation, which was directed by Gary Hart and Barry Goldwater. Their findings, which were published in October 1980, concluded: "In no way can it be said that the United States was close to unleashing nuclear war . . ." However, the Senate inquiry revealed that the computer chip malfunction was by no means an isolated accident. In March, 1980 a Soviet submarine on a training exercise in the vicinity of the Kurile Islands, north of Japan, fired four missiles, one of which "generated an unusual threat fan," the Senate report stated matter of factly. Some lesser alarms — totaling 3,703 in the 18-month period to the end of June 1980 — were all routinely and successfully weeded out by U.S. early-warning systems. See Recent False *Alerts from the Nation's Missile Attack Warning System*, Report of Senator Gary Hart and Senator Barry Goldwater to the Committee on Armed Services (Washington, D.C.: U.S. Government Printing Office, 1980). An investigation by the House of Representatives produced *Failures of the North American Aerospace Defense Command's (NORAD) Attack Warning System*, Subcommittee of the Committee on Government Operations (Washington, D.C.: U.S. Government Printing Office, 1981). A third report from the House is entitled *NORAD Computer Systems Are Dangerously Obsolete*, 23rd Report by the Committee on Government Operations (Washington, D.C.: U.S. Government Printing Office, 1982).

These famous incidents are by no means isolated events as those familiar with the shortcomings of U.S. command and control systems are only too painfully aware. The Center for Defense Information in Washington, D.C. reports that there is evidence of many other nuclear weapon accidents that have gone unreported or unconfirmed. In the words of a recent Center publication, *The Defense Monitor*, "Serious students of the problem estimate that an average of one U.S. nuclear accident has occurred every year since 1945, with some estimating as many as thirty major nuclear accidents and 250 'minor' nuclear accidents during that time."[45]

Today, such accidents are generally discounted by American military officials who speak "on the record." These authorities maintain that the U.S. government has adopted a number of precautions to avert the accidental use of nuclear weapons. These measures are highly secret, but they are known to include strict custodial control of these weapons and a considerable array of redundant safety features. Most of these features are incorporated into the chain of command and into the weapons themselves.

The principal safety feature in the chain of command is the so-called "two-man" concept. Under this rule, no one individual is able to perform the task of arming and firing nuclear weapons. At least two people are required to work with nuclear weapons of any kind whether on a submarine or a bomber, in a silo or a storeroom. In addition, every person with a responsibility for nuclear weapons must be formally cleared by the "Human Reliability Program."[46]

The exact release procedures for nuclear weapons are also classified information. But it is known that safeguards against accidental nuclear firings do vary from one weapons system to another. For instance, all tactical nuclear weapons that are situated overseas include mechanical or electrical devices that would prevent their firing in the absence of a specially coded signal passed down through the chain of command.[47]

---

45 *The Defense Monitor*, Vol. 4, No. 2 (February, 1975).

46 Richard Falk, who has read some classified studies of "human reliability," observes that personnel chosen to operate the sensitive equipment associated with nuclear weapons are "supposed to be selected, in part, on the basis of their *absence* of moral scruple. The express idea [is] that individuals with an active conscience might hesitate in a crisis to follow orders leading to nuclear war, that such soldiers would, in this decisive military sense, be unreliable." See Robert Jay Lifton and Richard Falk, *Indefensible Weapons: The Political and Psychological Case Against Nuclearism* (New York: Basic Books, 1982), p. 130.

47 See U.S. Department of Defense, Directive No. 5030.15, *Safety Studies and Reviews of Nuclear Weapons Systems* August 8, 1974, pp. 3-4.

The Soviet Launching Set-up

At present, the power to launch a nuclear war on the part of the Soviet government rests with the Politburo through the National Defense Council.[48] However, should the Soviet leadership decide to formally adopt a launch-on-warning policy, this could well mean that the power to authorize a retaliatory nuclear strike could be turned over to computers or regional commanders. Such lower-ranking personnel, it is feared, would have very little, or no, time to confer with their superiors over what could be a false alarm.

Officials in the Soviet Union are known to have been discussing the merits of adopting a policy of launching a retaliatory nuclear strike on receiving a warning by radar, satellites and computers that the missiles of an adversary are on the way. But so far the Soviets have not indicated publicly that they have decided on such a launch-on-warning policy.

With the first phase of the deployment to Europe of the Pershing IIs and cruise missiles now complete, military experts inside and outside the Administration have doubted whether such deployment could force the Soviet Union to reconsider its retaliatory policy. Proponents of deployment maintain that it has not brought any new problem. In their view, the Soviets have had to face the proximity of potentially hostile nuclear weapons ever since U.S. missile-firing submarines have patrolled abroad. However, those opposed to the Pershings disagree. They contend that the deployment of these advanced weapons on land minutes away from the Soviet Union could be a new deciding factor.

Soviet officials insist that any attack upon the U.S.S.R. by the Pershings would give them no more than six minutes warning time. U.S. authorities maintain there would be about twelve minutes. However, this is still much less than the half hour or so required for an intercontinental ballistic missile to reach the Soviet Union from the U.S. It is, however, close to the same time that it would take Soviet missiles to reach Western Europe.

The Kremlin complains that the Pershings in West Germany could reach Moscow, which is about 1,200 miles away. Washington, which tends to portray Soviet concern as a ploy to sow dissention among the NATO allies and interfere with future deployment plans of the new missiles on the Con-

---

48 The National Defense Council is an obscure and highly secret body that has ultimate responsibility for all areas of defense. It is unclear if the Chairman of the Defense Council, Soviet Party leader Konstantin Chernenko, can actually launch missiles on his own, although his long-time mentor Leonid Brezhnev may have used the threat of a surprise attack to arrogate such power to himself, when he was Chairman of the Council. See Honoré (Marc) Catudal, *Soviet Nuclear Strategy* (Berlin: Berlin Verlag, 1985).

tinent, has said publicly they could not. However, the position of the Reagan Administration is weakened somewhat because U.S. officials do not see fit to release the actual range of the new missiles.

As Paul Bracken of Yale University sees things, the main reason why the deployment of the Pershings in Europe is so dangerous (or for that matter the Soviet response, which has been to increase the number of missile-firing submarines off U.S. coasts)[49] is "not the physical damage they can do but rather that they inject ambiguity into the command of nuclear weapons." They "threaten decapitation, and the reaction is likely to be the adoption of a range of extremely dangerous operating policies..."[50] U.S. military experts say these policies would involve Soviet retaliation before any enemy missiles could arrive over the U.S.S.R. These sources say that the initial detection of hostile missiles might be made by one of nine Soviet early-warning satellites. These satellites, like those of the United States, probably utilize infrared sensors to detect hot exhaust from missiles. Enemy launching might be confirmed, these "insiders" say, by large ground-based radar on Soviet borders, and a final warning could possibly come from radar installations around Moscow.

Soviet systems are presumed to rely on computers that are less modern than those of the United States. American officials point to numerous instances of slow and mistaken Soviet identifications of aircraft. Perhaps the most noted is the case of the South Korean airliner that was shot down on September 1, 1983 after flying unmolested through Soviet airspace for approximately two hours.

It is important to note here that Soviet nuclear forces are, for the most part, technically far less ready to fire than their American equivalents. The Australian defense scholar Desmond Ball suggests that this is because "the Soviet Union lacks the very complex and expensive command systems re-

---

49 In late May 1984, Dimitri Ustinov, the Soviet Defense Minister, announced that the Soviet Union had increased the number of submarines carrying nuclear missiles off the coasts of the United States and that the weapons could strike U.S. targets in 8 to 10 minutes. Presumably to allay public fears, Reagan Administration officials scoffed at Soviet claims of improved nuclear submarine capability off U.S. coasts. They said the increase in such deployment increased the Soviet submarine fleet off U.S. coasts from five to seven and was not significant. Speaking off the record, U.S. insiders said the Soviets have long deployed three Yankee-class submarines off the East Coast and two others off the West Coast. Each of these subs can fire 16 missiles, which have a range of about 1,000 miles. According to these sources, the Soviets have added off each coast one Delta-class submarine, which also has 16 missiles but with a range of some 4,000 miles. See *The Minneapolis Star and Tribune,* May 22, 1984.

50 See Paul Bracken, *The Command and Control of Nuclear Forces* (New Haven: Yale University Press, 1983).

quired to combine a high state of launch readiness with adequate safeguards against unauthorized firing."[51] However, an important factor that influences Soviet reaction time is the fact that the vast bulk of their nuclear forces are liquid, rather than solid, fueled. It takes longer to prepare a liquid-fueled missile for launch. Most Soviet submarines are liquid-fueled, although the Soviets have been working for some time on solid-fueled replacements.

If Soviet early-warning systems leave a lot to be desired, this is not true for actual physical control of nuclear warheads. Nuclear stockpiles in the Soviet Union are under the control not of the regular armed forces but of the KGB. According to U.S. intelligence officials, Soviet missile silos contain four men: two servicemen, who launch the rocket, and two KGB soldiers, who carry out the separate function of arming the weapon's nuclear warhead. In earlier years, Soviet safety precautions extended to keeping the warheads physically separated and under KGB protection away from the actual missiles that would carry them.[52]

Until recently, the Soviets were loathe to maintain any nuclear weapons outside their own territory.(The Soviet decision in 1962 to station medium-range and intermediate-range ballistic missiles in Cuba was a major exception, and this is one of the reasons why the U.S. intelligence community was caught by surprise at the time.) Thus, the short-range missiles, artillery pieces and bombers based in Eastern Europe that would launch or carry nuclear warheads and bombs were without their ammunition. For the most part, the warheads were stored in the Soviet Union and only matched with the delivery systems in times of urgent crisis or during nuclear exercises. With the introduction of short-range SS-21s and 22s in East Germany and Czechoslovakia in late 1983 and early 1984, the Soviets radically departed from previous practice, and NATO intelligence was keen to learn if support equipment for the tactical missiles was also being moved into those two countries. According to a secret U.S. report to NATO, there were concrete indications that this indeed was the case.

Vulnerability of C^3I Systems

The possibility of nuclear accidents aside, another major problem in the area of command and control systems is the prospect that sensors and communication lines would be vulnerable to attack in time of crisis. At the present time, the Administration is giving top priority to the strengthening

---

51 See Desmond Ball, *Can Nuclear War be Controlled?* (London: International Institute for Strategic Studies, 1981).

52 See John Barron, *KGB* (New York: Reader's Digest, 1974), p. 13.

and rebuilding of U.S. communications and control systems, but still substantial problems will remain for some time.

John Steinbruner, a senior analyst with the Brookings Institution, has spent considerable time studying this problem area. He calls "command vulnerability" the "most significant problem of modern strategic thought." Although there is no prospect of a technical solution, certain protective measures can be taken — but only at great expense.

Steinbruner states that the quick launching of a nuclear weapon from a submarine and its detonation some 300 miles above the earth could create an intense burst of eletromagnetic energy. Known technically as "eletromagnetic pulse," it would flash across a continent and burn out communication links.

The probable "failure of land lines would interrupt the transmission of warning information and high-data-rate military communications," writes Steinbruner in the January 1984 issue of *Scientific American*. "With only partially disseminated warning signals and disrupted communications, normal command procedures would almost certainly delay protective firing."

Jonathan B. Tucker, a former member of the Board of Editors of *Scientific American* and a specialist in science, technology and international affairs, takes an equally negative position in regard to C^3I vulnerability. He concludes: "Because of ... inherent uncertainties, the reliability of strategic C^3I cannot be assumed to the extent necessary to make a doctrine of controlled escalation and protracted nuclear war credible as a deterrent."[53]

Summary

"Without communications," stated SAC Commander General Thomas Power in the 1950s, "all I command is my desk." It should be clear from the foregoing analysis that the American C^3I system has become an enourmously elaborate and complex set-up since those words were uttered.

The sophisticated command and control system has also become very expensive to maintain. One insider estimates that it now costs some $ 30 billion a year just to operate and to maintain the Worldwide Military Command and Control System. But this is not the whole story. "It will cost tens of billions of dollars over the next ten years, above and beyond what we are spending today," says Charles Zraket, Vice-President of the Mitre Corporation, the U.S. Air Force's C^3I "think tank." (The Reagan Administration asked for $ 31 billion for improving C^3I systems in 1983.)

---

53 Jonathan B. Tucker, "Strategic Command-and-Control Vulnerabilities: Dangers and Remedies," *Orbis*, Vol. 26, No. 4 (Winter, 1983), p. 958.

In theory, the C^3I system can be counted on to detect a surprise nuclear attack and to provide the President with enough information for him to make the "right" decision. Its early warning system, which includes a number of redundant features, is designed to filter out false alarms from the real thing. However, this is mainly theory, although impressive measures have been taken in recent years to develop a "fail-safe" system.

The limitations of the C^3I system have been painfully discovered and re-discovered many times since 1957, when the Russians successfully tested their first full-range intercontinental ballistic missile. The brutal fact of the matter is that the Pentagon, until the late 1970s, never gave the C^3I problem the attention it deserved.[54] It was much more satisfying for generals to order up a new generation of missiles, bombers and the like rather than devote their time and efforts to new generations of computers. Indeed, only a handful of generals bothered to learn the ins and outs of communications. No doubt, this was because such knowledge would not have enhanced their career prospects.

All this changed with the Carter Administration. As one senior official remarked: "Protection of key government functions during a crisis is as much of a deterrent to nuclear war as building new strategic nuclear systems."

Of all American Presidents, Jimmy Carter showed the greatest interest in the chain of command structure for nuclear war and the contingency plans for responding to a surprise nuclear attack. Carter's immersion in these procedures included a ride in the Nightwatch plane, the first such ride in the presidential command post by a President. The result was considerable skepticism. For instance, the President was concerned that his "doomsday" plane would not be able to withstand the blast, heat and electromagnetic affects of a nuclear attack and that few American airports could receive the large plane. (Even with the aid of refueling tankers the plane can reportedly remain airborne only for a maximum of 72 hours.)

Carter was especially interested in the civilian chain of command in case the President should become incapacitated. Thus, he was astonished to discover that the Vice President, the next commander in line, had never been involved in any Administration, in any of the highly secret briefings about America's attack options in the event of a nuclear war. Subsequently, Carter ordered a full review of presidential procedures for the release of nuclear weapons.[55]

---

54 President Carter's chief military aide, General William Odom, used the words "benign neglect" to describe the state of the U.S. command and control system during the earlier years.

55 See Executive Office of the President, *President's Reorganization Project*, October

A former Director of the White House Military Office confirms that matters of nuclear war had low priority in all Administrations from Lyndon Johnson to Jimmy Carter. This can be be seen in their attitudes toward the "football":[56]

No new President in my time ever had more than one briefing on the contents of the Football, and that was before each one took office, when it was one briefing among dozens. Not one President, to my knowledge, and I know because it was in my care, ever got an update on the contents of the Football, although material in it is changed constantly. Not one President could open the Football — only the warrant officers, the military aides and the Director of the Military Office have the combination. If the guy with the Football had a heart attack or got shot on the way to the President, they'd have to blow the goddamn thing open.

As a result of Carter's thorough review of nuclear matters, a series of presidential directives were issued which, among other things, provided for a greatly improved C^3I system. According to the President, the nation needed a command and control system that could "endure" a prolonged nuclear war. To many in the Pentagon, this was interpreted as meaning that computers, satellites, radars and communication links suddenly had equal importance to missiles, airplanes and submarines.

With the election of President Reagan, even greater emphasis was placed on enhancing the capabilities of C^3I. The new Administration now saw such technical improvements in the context of fighting nuclear wars and actually winning them. When asked how the U.S. might be able to "win" a nuclear war with the Soviets, Vice President Bush was quoted as replying: "You have a survivability of command and control, survivability of industry, protection of a percentage of your citizens, and you have a capability that inflicts more damage on the opposition than it can inflict upon you. That's the way you have a winner."[57]

Thus committed to an enhanced nuclear war-fighting strategy, the new Administration required greatly strengthened strategic C^3I capabilities, which would not only be able to endure a succession of limited nuclear attacks, but also to control a spectrum of escalatory actions ranging from the execution of "limited" nuclear options through full-scale nuclear war. In addition, the Reagan Administration considered effective C^3I systems as a "force multiplier" in a controlled nuclear war, which would enable the National Command Authority to make better use of those nuclear weapons held in reserve than if they were utilized in an uncoordinated fashion.

25, 1978, and E.L. Dreeman, *Leader National Security Team Federal Data Processing Reorganization Project* (Office of Management and Budget, 1978).
56 See Bill Gulley, *Breaking Cover* (New York: Warner Books, 1980), p. 225.
57 Quoted in Peter Pringle *et al.*, *opus cit.*, p. 40.

In short, substantially improved C^3I capabilities were now regarded as the *conditio sine qua non* for a credible nuclear war-fighting "deterrent" strategy.

To make deterrence "more credible," the Reagan Administration has launched the largest-ever C^3I program. This is being done despite the considerable skepticism among experts as to whether any amount of investment would produce a communications system able to endure a nuclear attack. As things now stand, C^3I has become a separate and seemingly limitless part of the arms race.

It is not putting it too strongly to say that preoccupation today with C^3I has become a fad with many military planners. And this situation has some distressing consequences. Perhaps the most important is the diffusion of nuclear command and control authority in certain situations. Regrettably, the current emphasis on nuclear war-fighting scenarios, in which C^3I vulnerability plays an integral part, no longer allows for the luxury of comprehensive presidential control.

Many U.S. citizens are not aware of this, but for some time now it has been physically possible for high-level military officers to circumvent the system and launch nuclear weapons without a presidential order. While there is no reason to suspect that loyal military officials would want to do this, present procedures are such — no matter how many built-in safeguards there are — that an unauthorized launching of missiles, possibly triggering a nuclear war, could occur.

To be sure, some military planners give the general public the confidence that C^3I can somehow ensure the continuity of civilian control over nuclear weapons from peacetime to wartime. And in peacetime, it is difficult to argue against further improvements in command and control, such as keeping pace with weapons safety or computer technology. However, there is no "perfect" communications system, invulnerable to the tremendously disruptive aftereffects of nuclear weapons explosions. And all attempts to create one, which will "control" the course of a nuclear war, are based on a faulty premise.

No matter what the Administration does, the presidential-decision time after receiving warning of a surprise nuclear attack on Washington, D.C. is very short. In case such an attack emanates from a Soviet submarine off the East Coast, the President will have less than ten minutes to react. Given this harsh reality, it would seem to make more sense to invest money in preventing nuclear war, such as improving techniques for recognizing and dealing quickly with erroneous information that an attack is underway when in fact none is taking place, rather than pour considerable resources into the illusion of developing a communications system that could survive and control a prolonged nuclear war.

The fact of the matter is that, should Washington be the subject of a Soviet pre-emptive nuclear attack, it would probably be impossible to determine which officials in line of succession had been killed. Former Secretary of State Alexander Haig's account of the events surrounding the attempted assassination of President Reagan (an account that is disputed by Secretary of Defense Weinberger) points up the kind of government confusion that is likely to occur in such a situation, magnified many times over. Most probably, policymakers would not be able to determine who should take over the role of the President in this crucial area.

To be sure, the Reagan Administration has proposed a central locator system that would be of some help. Devised by the Federal Emergency Management Agency (FEMA) and run by the White House, this system has the task of keeping tabs on every official in the constitutional line of succession, so that executive power could theoretically be maintained in the worst case-scenario that the President and his immediate successors were killed.

But even if the right individual could be found in the midst of a nuclear holocaust, it is by no means certain whether the survivor would accept such authority or whether he would be able to act responsibly under such chaotic conditions. Very likely, there would be a serious breakdown of government authority and order.

One solution to this problem has been the development of a contingency policy known as "permissive action." This policy allows the commanders of missile-firing submarines to retaliate on their own, according to certain procedures after a decapitating nuclear attack. Procedures have also been established which would allow officers of airborne command posts to authorize the launching of missiles and SAC bombers should they be at the highest level of command surviving a pre-emptive nuclear strike.

The "permissive action" policy is inextricably linked with the present U.S. deterrent strategy. The basic idea is that the Soviets would never dare to launch a surprise nuclear attack against Washington if they knew that even if the nation's top political leadership were destroyed, from the President on down, elements of the U.S. military could still, acting autonomously, retaliate with a devastating nuclear blow.

The main problem with this "permissive action" policy is that it tends to compromise the strict and even vital centralization of nuclear authority. This state of affairs is known to the Soviets, who might in a crisis situation be provoked rather than deterred by the policy. In any case, they now have some grounds to fear that the American National Command Authority might lose control of its strategic forces under circumstances less than a severe crisis.

Pre-delegation of authority for use of nuclear weapons also raises some important constitutional questions. The Constitution provides that Congress is responsible for declaring war. More than just a superficial examination of the problem would seem to indicate that a major — or even a minor — use of U.S. nuclear weapons, even in retaliation, would constitute an act of war. Of course, the "founding fathers" never had to entertain the prospect of an all-out war waged in less than an hour.

The American historian and editor of the *Eisenhower Diaries*, Robert E. Ferrell, points out that President Eisenhower, for one, was troubled by the possibility in the nuclear era of having to override constitutional considerations in an emergency. During Ike's tenure, the basic problem was that the SAC bombers might have to be launched on short notice without time for Congress to convene and vote on a declaration of war, even though the U.S. would technically land the first blow in a pre-emptive strike.[58]

In summary, then, the problems of nuclear command and control are very serious. "Permissive action," in particular, is a dangerous policy and one that seems incompatible with the democratic form of government in the United States. While concerns about strategic decapitation are genuine, "permissive action" hardly represents an adequate solution to the immensely complex technical difficulties of C^3I vulnerability.

A tightening of centralized control seems highly disirable. In this regard, the idea proposed by Jonathan B. Tucker should be taken as a starting point for discussion of significant reform of the current system. While no arrangement will guarantee 100 percent security against unauthorized or accidental launch of nuclear weapons, the problem of command and control deserves a fresh approach and certainly more attention than the Carter and Reagan Administrations have given it.

A Proposal to Ensure Central Command Authority

The United States could proceed unilaterally to reduce the vulnerability of executive authority in any contingency. This could be done, Tucker suggests, "by having one Cabinet-level official always on 'vacation' in an undisclosed location (to be changed frequently), where he would have access at all times to military communications." In the event of a confirmed nuclear attack in which the civilian head of government was cut off (including the entire constitutional succession above the Cabinet level), this official would inherit presidential authority in the area of nuclear release.

The Soviet Union "would be informed through the news media of this

---

58 See Robert E. Ferrell (ed.), *The Eisenhower Diaries* (New York: Norton, 1981), pp. 311-12.

overall strategy, but not the specific details of the plan." In this way, "Soviet leaders would be convinced of the futility of seeking to forestall prompt retaliation through a decapitating attack on the American [National Command Authority], thereby removing a possible incentive for preemption in a crisis."[59]

To some, this idea may seem farfetched, and there are some problems connected with it. But it does point up the fact that there are imaginative ways of dealing with what seems, on its face, to be an intractable dilemma.

---

59 Jonathan B. Tucker, *opus cit.*, p. 961.

> The distinguishing feature of modern American defense has been the pursuit of the magic weapon.
>
> *James Fallows*

XI. DETERRENCE MOVES INTO SPACE
THE ABM CONTROVERSY

"The central problem of nuclear deterrence," writes Colin Gray, once a strong advocate, "is that no offensive deterrent, no matter how fearsome, is likely to work forever, and the consequences of its failure would be intolerable for civilization."[1]

On March 23, 1984, President Reagan delivered a major television address to the nation in which he seemed to agree with this statement. Suggesting that the policy of nuclear deterrence through the threat of strategic nuclear retaliation is inadequate, he called upon the vast U.S. technological community to consider the potential for effective defense against ballistic missiles:[2]

Would it not be better to save lives than to avenge them? Are we not capable of demonstrating our peaceful intentions by applying all our abilities and our ingenuity to achieving a truly lasting stability? I think we are — indeed we must.

After careful consultation with my advisers, including the Joint Chiefs of Staff, I believe there is a way. . . . It is that we embark on a program to counter the awesome Soviet missile threat with measures that are defensive. Let us turn to the very strengths in technology that spawned our great industrial base. . . . I know this is a formidable technical task, one that may not be accomplished before the end of the century. Yet, current technology has attained a level of sophistication where it is reasonable for us to begin this effort.

1   Keith B. Payne and Colin S. Gray, "Nuclear Policy and the Defensive Transition," *Foreign Affairs,* Vol. 62, No. 4 (Spring, 1984), p. 822.
2   The complete text of President Reagan's speech is in *The York Times,* March 24, 1983.

The President's speech may go down in history as one of the most important of the entire post-war period. For it was immediately interpreted as a direct challenge to the offensive concept of deterrence that has dominated American strategic policy for decades. President Reagan's announcement suggested that vulnerability to Soviet attack, the lynchpin of the deterrent policy of Mutual Assured Destruction, is not an acceptable condition in the long term and that the U.S. would seriously examine ways to counter the threat of nuclear missiles, such as the development of an orbiting anti-missile system that could deflect a Soviet nuclear attack with lasers and other high-tech devices. Such a shift in strategy, the President said, holds out the "promise of changing the course of human history."

This chapter attempts to analyze the pros and cons of the President's plan, putting it into historical perspective. Specifically, it proposes to answer the following crucial questions: (1) Is the plan feasible? (2) What impact will it have on U.S. nuclear deterrence policy? and (3) How might it affect U.S. relations with the Soviet Union?

The ABM Issue in Historical Perspective

The idea of developing a comprehensive anti-ballistic missile defense is not new. In May 1946, a board of scientists had already recommended to the U.S. Army that one be built. However, the idea of maintaining such a system in space gives it a new and more serious twist.[3]

For over twenty years, intragovernmental battles have been fought to prevent an ABM system from being developed and deployed. Back in the mid-1960s much of the uniformed military, led by the Joint Chiefs of Staff, pressed hard to get President Johnson to develop an ABM system to "defend the country" against the Soviet missile threat. Opposed to the ABM were Secretary of Defense Robert McNamara and Secretary of State Dean Rusk, as well as the head of the Arms Control and Disarmament Agency. They believed that the decision to deploy an ABM would seriously aggravate a spiraling and costly arms race and would destroy chances for a stabilization of the American-Soviet deterrent balance.[4]

---

3 "Don't forget to mention the Pentagon's 'Project Defender,' a study done twenty years ago," advises one U.S. official in the Department of Defense. "It argued also for a space based system."

4 See Morton Halperin, "The Decision to Deploy the ABM: Bureaucratic and Domestic Politics in the Johnson Administration," *World Politics* (October, 1972), pp. 62 ff.

For his part, McNamara believed that an American decision to deploy the ABM would virtually preclude any possibility of initiating arms limitations talks with the Soviets. The Defense Secretary was also skeptical of the technical feasibility of the proposed system: in order to be effective, it would have to be 100 percent foolproof. Finally, McNamara was concerned with the cost. In his view, it would always be cheaper for the Soviets to build more missiles and better decoy devices than it would be for the United States to further improve an ABM system to counter them. Therefore, if the U.S. developed an ABM system, a competition could begin in which the Soviets added more and more to their missile forces and the U.S. more and more to its ABM system. At each successive stage in the race the new increment of threat would be cheaper for the U.S.S.R. than the extra ABM defense for the United States. The end would be bankruptcy.

The Nobel physicist Hans Bethe, who headed the Theoretical Physics Division of the Los Alamos Scientific Laboratory during the Manhattan Project in World War II, put it this way:[5]

Against missiles there is no defense. This is a subject on which I have worked quite carefully and industriously for many years before '68, looking at many ways how to tell decoys from missiles, and so on. Whatever you did, the offense could always fool the defense and could do it better. So antiballistic missiles for city defense are technically nonsense . . .

In arguing their cases, proponents and adversaries emphasized different factors. Supporters pointed out that the Soviets had already begun to develop an ABM system. They argued that it threatened the American deterrent capacity and that such a system would save lives. Furthermore, they insisted that a favorable ABM decision would provide the U.S. with an extra "bargaining chip" in any negotiations on mutual defensive-weapons limitation. For their part, opponents were less concerned with the Soviet deployment (which was seen by some as a possible Soviet hedge against the developing Chinese nuclear threat) than about the potential for an arms race. Finally, there was the price tag: Estimates of the cost of an ABM system ranged from $ 40 billion.[6]

The debate put President Johnson in a difficult spot. For one thing, he wanted to maintain unity within his Administration. But he and his

---

5   Interview with Hans Bethe in the Los Angeles *Times*, April 11, 1982.
6   The case against the ABM is developed by Abram Chayes and Jerome B. Weisner (eds.), *ABM: An Evaluation of the Decision to Deploy an Anti-Ballistic Missile System* (New York: Harper & Row, 1969), pp. 17-24, 57-60. The case for ABMs is developed by D.G. Brennan and Johan J. Holst, *Ballistic Missile Defense: Two Views* (London: Institute for Strategic Studies, 1967).

Secretary of Defense, who tended to view the ABM decision as a direct confrontation between himself and the Joint Chiefs of Staff, were headed on a collision course over this issue. (The two men already differed over Vietnam policy, which would culminate in the resignation of the Secretary of Defense.) For another, the President was under a great deal of pressure from Congress. A negative decision on the ABM would have alienated key senators who were also long-time friends and colleagues whose views and convictions Johnson respected.[7] At the same time, the President was concerned with his re-election, and the Republicans were already talking of an "ABM gap." They seemed to be threatening to do to him what Kennedy and Johnson had done to Nixon in 1960 — to utilize the powerful charge of neglecting the defense of the nation.

In view of these conflicting pressures and the penchant of the President for compromise, the critical question soon became: "What would be the nature of this compromise?" Part of the answer subsequently became clear at a meeting between Johnson and Soviet Premier Kosygin at Glassboro, New Jersey, in June 1967.[8] At this time, Johnson pressed the Soviet leader for a firm date for the opening of the arms limitation talks. Such a statement would allow the President to postpone the decision on the ABM. But Johnson did not receive a specific answer.

"When I have trouble sleeping nights," Kosygin told McNamara, who had been lecturing him on how ABMs would only prompt an offense-defense arms race, "it's because of your offensive missiles, not your defensive missiles."[9] The Soviet leader characterized the Soviet ABM as a defensive weapon and therefore unobjectionable. It would not destabilize

---

[7] With the benefit of hindsight, it now appears that President Johnson may have been in error in his belief that sentiment on the Hill in favor of ABM deployment was wide and growing. Apparently, LBJ was particularly influenced by Senator Richard Russell and several other Southern Democrats who were among those in favor of the ABM as well as large military programs in general.

[8] In 1966, President Johnson had already authorized the late U.S. Ambassador to Moscow Llewellyn Thompson to propose bilateral talks on strategic arms limitations, specifically to limit ABM systems. This proposal led to further exchanges in early 1967 after Johnson indicated in his State of the Union message that the United States had decided to defer deployment of an antimissile defense in the hope that the Soviet leadership would follow. The 1967 exchanges proposed broadening the talks to include offensive missiles, but there were no immediate signs of rapid progress toward serious negotiation. See Raymond L. Garthoff, "SALT I: An Evaluation," *World Politics* (October, 1978), p. 1, and John C. Campbell, "Soviet-American Relations: Conflict and Cooperation," *Current History*, Vol. 53 (October, 1967), p. 201.

[9] Fred Kaplan, *The Wizards of Armageddon* (New York: Simon & Schuster, 1983), p. 346.

the arms balance and was therefore not a proper subject for a SALT Treaty. Robert McNamara's major objection to the ABM had been refuted by Kosygin. So the President no longer saw the ABM as a possible stumbling block to beginning talks on strategic arms limitations.

In July 1967, LBJ announced his minimal decision: The United States would move to adopt a small ABM system. His Secretary of Defense, in a speech which was viewed by some critics as somewhat contradictory, subsequently explained the decision to deploy the Nike-Sentinel system in fifteen sites. On the one hand, McNamara said that the most effective way to overcome a Soviet ABM system was to saturate the defense with offensive missiles. On the other hand, should the Chinese be as irrational as their militant revolutionary rhetoric suggested (China was still in the throes of the Cultural Revolution, which was little understood in the West) then a small ABM system might help to deter a limited Chinese nuclear strike.[10]

From one point of view, it looked like the Defense Secretary had won a major victory over the Joint Chiefs of Staff and those energetic supporters of the ABM in Congress who favored the development of a nationwide anti-Soviet (and much more costly) Anti-Ballistic Missile system. At least McNamara could plausibly argue that the President's decision left open the possibility that the system would never be deployed if the Russians agreed to a limitation on mutual defensive systems. His position was bolstered in this respect because Johnson had *not* supported deployment but only increased funding for the procurement of certain ABM components that would require a long lead time.

For their part, the supporters of ABM in Congress and the military tended to view the public change in the Administration's position as a victory for their cause. Generally, they saw Johnson's decision as a hopeful sign that their goal would eventually be realized. Thus, there were as yet no real "winners" and no real "losers." Johnson's compromise had seen to that.

The fight over the ABM continued into the next Administration. President Nixon proposed to deploy around American cities a nuclear ABM system called Sentinel. However, opposition to this deployment was widespread and stormy. In the end, the combination of environmental, personal and technical opposition was strong enough to convince Nixon

10 According to sources close to Robert McNamara, the Secretary of Defense had offered the Chinese threat as a possible rationale for the ABM as early as 1961, before he turned against the system. Since then, these people say, he had never taken it very seriously. He only offered the Chinese threat later to make sure that if ABM production were forced on him, the official rationale would support only limited deployment.

that was a fight he very likely could not win. Consequently, he withdrew his proposal to deploy Sentinel before it came to a vote in Congress and came up with an alternative plan. In the effort to pacify suburban housewives, he suggested moving Sentinel away from cities and converting the system into one concentrated around offensive missiles based in Montana and North Dakota. The President also had a new name for the ABM system: Safeguard.

Consideration of the system came at a time when the Soviets were rapidly expanding their offensive missile forces. Consequently, many military planners were now predicting that the Russians soon would be able to attack American land-based missiles with a large number of warheads. Many officials in the Nixon Administration believed that the Safeguard system would be able to shoot down a high percentage of incoming Soviet missiles, thus protecting many of the ICBMs.

Generally, White House staffers expected little public objection to locating the ABMs in unpopulated areas. The new Safeguard system would only be deployed near the missiles it would protect, which were already located in the least populated parts of the country. But the President and his advisers misjudged the mood of the country. Those opponents of high-spending Pentagon defense plans, having been successful in defeating Johnson's ABM proposal, were not about to accept Safeguard lying down. Consequently, they maintained a drumfire of criticism. They questioned the expense of the system, its alleged effectiveness and the possibility that the Soviet threat to U.S. land-based missiles was being exaggerated. The upshot was that these opponents, aided by the anti-war and anti-military mood in American politics, were successful in delaying Congressional approval of the system for some time. In the end, the Safeguard system was approved in a halfhearted fashion by Congress, and a small fraction of the system was actually deployed. As Freeman Dyson writes, "it was understood by all concerned that the Safeguard system as it finally emerged was only a token deployment, not a real ABM defense. Nixon had lost the battle for a real ABM deployment, and the public knew it."[11]

During the early 1970s the two superpowers discussed ways to limit deployment of Anti-Ballistic Missile systems. While an absolute prohibition against each side constructing ABM systems was impossible because both had already begun to construct small ones, the two sides were interested in preventing these systems from expanding across the country. For their part, the Soviets knew that they could overwhelm a limited Safeguard system, and the Americans knew that they could penetrate the systems around Moscow and Leningrad and destroy these cities. Both

---

11 Freeman Dyson, *Weapons and Hope* (New York: Harper & Row, 1984), p. 75.

sides had a vested interest in a prohibition on further ABM work, since otherwise the two countries would reserve the option of building larger offensive forces certain of penetrating possible expanded ABMs of the future.

In May of 1972, during President Nixon's visit to Moscow, U.S. and Soviet officials signed their treaty on ABMs as well as an interim agreement on offensive missiles. The Senate subsequently approved the two accords.

The 1972 ABM Treaty established the first qualitative arms control limitations in a series of agreed prohibitions on various types of ABM systems. For instance, the testing and deployment of land-mobile, sea-based, air-based and space-based ABM systems were banned. Moreover, MIRVed and other multiple ABM warheads were forbidden, and rapid reload systems were banned. Finally, the deployment of *future* systems substituting for ABM radars, missiles or launchers (e.g., laser interception systems) was effectively prohibited unless agreed upon by both parties. Importantly, the ABM Treaty, which is of indefinite duration, limits each side to anti-missile deployments at strategically insignificant levels. Both the United States and the Soviet Union are restricted to two anti-missile complexes with a maximum of 100 interceptors for each site — not enough to provide meaningful defense for a country's population. One site could be located around the nation's capital and a second in the vicinity of offensive missiles. A subsequent amendment of the treaty limited the number of permissible sites in each country to one with 100 interceptors.[12]

The one U.S. ABM site was shut down in 1976 by order of Congress. The demise of the Grand Forks, North Dakota complex was justified primarily on economic grounds. It was maintained that continued operation of the system was not worth the cost. For their part, the Soviets chose not to expand their relatively crude ABM system of 64 interceptor missiles (codenamed Galosh by the U.S.) around Moscow.[13] (There have been recent reports that the U.S.S.R. is now modernizing this site.)

12 This protocol was ratified in 1976. See Raymond L. Garthoff, "Negotiating with the Russians: Some Lessons from SALT," *International Security*, Vol. 1, No. 4 (Spring, 1977), pp. 3-24. It is important to note that the Soviets have to date not even built up to the low level of 100 permissable missiles.

13 See Nils H. Wessel, "Soviet-America Arms Control Negotiations," *Current History* (May, 1983), p. 213. Andrew Cockburn explains some of the problems with the Soviet ABM system: "The designers are not optimistic enough to imagine that they can actually hit the incoming warheads or even get close enough to destroy them with a conventional explosion. ABMs are therefore designed to carry nuclear warheads, so that their blast will be sufficient to destroy everything within a radius of several miles." Unfortunately, "a nuclear

The Implications of Reagan's Proposal

Since the limited ABM treaty went into effect, there has been debate over what is legally permissible in the area of research and development of advanced ABM systems such as the space-based one supported by President Reagan. For one, Morton A. Kaplan, an arms control expert at the University of Chicago, believes that there "is nothing in the ABM treaty that prevents research and development of advanced ABM systems including laser types."[14] But Gerard C. Smith, a middle-of-the-road Republican who was the chief U.S. negotiator during the SALT I talks, has observed that the only objective interpretation of the 1972 ABM treaty is that "any exotic system is banned." The Soviets seem to agree.

More to the point, a number of august members of the U.S. strategic community echoed Bernard Brodie and some twenty years of civilian wargamers. They declared that attempts to defend the United States with "Buck Rogers" weaponry against nuclear attack were folly. Stalemate, they maintained, was the best the U.S. could expect in the age of nuclear weapons. Defense was offense, they argued. ABMs would only increase the likelihood of war. Either the "have" side would be tempted to launch a pre-emptive nuclear strike without fear of retaliation. Or the "have-not" side would launch first to pre-empt ABM development.[15]

Upon learning of Reagan's proposal for a space-based ABM system, then Soviet President Yuri Andropov labeled it as "irresponsible."[16] It would "open the floodgates to a runaway race for all types of strategic arms, both defensive and offensive." Andropov added that in embarking

> explosion generates more than just a blast; it also creates a huge cloud of electronically charged particles, which, among other things, renders the sky totally opaque to radar." Thus, "the first Galosh might just possibly be able to destroy one enemy warhead; but thereafter, the entire system around a particular target, such as Moscow, would be entirely 'blind' and therefore useless." See his *The Threat: Inside the Soviet Military Machine* (New York: Random House, 1983), p. 223.

14 Morton A. Kaplan, *SALT: Problems and Prospects* (Morristown N.J.: General Learning Press, 1973), p. 17.

15 Walter A. McDougall, "How Not to Think about Space Lasers," *National Review* May 13, 1983.

16 See the interview in *Pravda*, March 27, 1983. The following statement by Andropov is especially important: "All attempts at gaining military superiority over the U.S.S.R. are futile. The Soviet Union will never allow them to succeed. It will never be caught defenseless by any threat. ... Let there be no mistake about this in Washington. It is time they stopped devising one option after another in search of the best ways of unleashing nuclear war in the hope of winning it. Engaging in this is not just irresponsible, it is insane."

on arms control negotiations the two superpowers had "agreed that there is an inseverable interrelationship between strategic offensive and defensive weapons." He stated it was "not by chance" that the Anti-Ballistic Missile (ABM) Treaty of 1972 was signed simultaneously with the SALT I accord limiting strategic arms. The Soviet leader concluded with the warning that the U.S.S.R. would never allow "the development of ABM systems that could render our ICBMs impotent."

From the perspective of Moscow, one of the greatest dangers inherent in the Reagan proposal had to do with the offensive capability it would give the United States. In the view of Soviet military leaders, the possession by the United States of a system thought to be a foolproof missile defense system might lead U.S. officials to feel they could launch a surprise nuclear attack against the Soviet Union, confident that a retaliatory blow could be stopped or deterred with their own defensive missiles. From the perspective of some American arms control experts outside the Administration, such a situation might sorely tempt the Soviet leadership to launch a pre-emptive nuclear strike before the U.S. was able to put in place an effective ABM system.

Reagan acknowledged these problems and others associated with a decision to go ahead and develop a missile defense in space. "I clearly recognize that defensive systems have limitations and raise certain problems and ambiguities," the President said in his speech on March 23, 1983. "If paired with offensive systems, they can be viewed as fostering an aggressive policy, and no one wants that."

As might be expected, the President's bold, futuristic scheme has encountered a mixed response from American politicians and Allied officials who question whether "Buck Rogers" weaponry, however attractive in a visionary sense, offers practical exit from Western strategic doldrums. Some have noted with perhaps a touch of cynicism that Reagan has spent most of his public life opposing arms-control agreements and has pressed for bigger and better weapons systems.

Most domestic critics seriously question what they call "Reagan's challenge to America's scientists to achieve a technological miracle that would make the successful race to the moon child's play by comparison." For their part, many members of Congress are deeply concerned about the potentially destabilizing effect of the President's proposal on the arms race. Senator Edward Kennedy (D-Mass.) has termed the plan a "reckless Star-Wars scheme." Senator Mark Hatfield (R-Oregon) has declared that Reagan "has, in effect, called for the militarization of the last great hope for international cooperation and peace - outer space."[17] A number of

17 *U.S. News and World Report,* April 4, 1983.

European commentators have expressed fears that emphasizing a U.S. missile defense system aimed primarily at Soviet ICBMs would "decouple" Western Europe from the American security umbrella.

The West German Government of Chancellor Helmut Kohl in particular is keenly concerned about the international implications of the Reagan Administration proposal. Among the most serious doubts are those raised by his Defense Minister Manfred Wörner. He discussed his skepticism about the Reagan ABM program at a gathering of NATO defense ministers in the spring of 1984. At that time Wörner is said to have told Secretary of Defense Caspar Weinberger and other officials that the development of anti-missile defense could lead to a "Fortress America" mentality in the United States and leave the Western European allies, who confront a wider spectrum of threat than does the United States, with inferior defenses. In several interviews after his return from the NATO gathering, Wörner indicated with a sense of urgency his feeling that the United States and the Soviet Union should open negotiations "before space becomes the next area of the arms race."[18]

The Social Democratic opposition in West Germany's parliament has been even more outspoken. Karsten Voigt, spokesman on security affairs for the SPD, has warned that if the United States develops statellite and missile killers in space, the storm of American-European argument that will break out will make the recent NATO debate over Euromissiles seem like a spring breeze.[19]

Background to Reagan's Decision

President Reagan's decision to move toward the development of a space-based ABM system reflects a view that was advocated in a monograph, *High Frontier: A New National Strategy*. This study was published in February, 1982 by the Heritage Foundation, a conservative think tank. The director of the study was Lt. General Daniel O. Graham, a former head of the Pentagon's Defense Intelligence Agency.[20]

Graham's study declares: "If both East and West can free themselves from the threat of disarming nuclear first strikes both sides will have little compulsion to amass ever larger arsenals of nuclear weapons. And it will

---

18   The *New York Times*, April 14, 1984.
19   See *The Christian Science Monitor*, April 12, 1984.
20   The "High Frontier" project was subsequently undated and published by Devin-Adair in 1984 under the title *A Defense That Defends: Blocking Nuclear Attack*.

allow us to avoid leaving to future generations the horrendous legacy of a perpetual balance of terror." These ideas were repeated by the President in his speech.

The "High Frontier" study says its main objectives are to "nullify the present and growing threat to the U.S. and its allies which is posed by Soviet military power; replace the dangerous doctrine of mutual assured destruction (MAD) with a strategy of assured survival; and provide security and incentive for realizing the enormous industrial and commercial potential of space." The study argues that "Cruise missiles become a more attractive option in a new strategic setting that include defenses against ballistic [missiles]."

The authors of the "High Frontier" study maintain that the strategy they advocate — which has now been adopted in the main by the President — will "confront the U.S.S.R. with precisely the sort of armaments competition that the Soviet leadership most fears." Secondly, it will "severely tax, perhaps to the point of disruption, the already strained Soviet technological and industrial resources." And thirdly, it will "seriously threaten the very foundations of the strategic structure the U.S.S.R. has built at great cost over the past twenty years."

If the President was especially influenced by the vision of a new world described in the "High Frontier" study,[21] it is also true that his decision to adopt a space-based ABM system repeated a call, sounded for a number of years, by a small but energetic group of conservative military experts, scientists and others. One of its leading spokesmen in Congress was Senator Malcolm Wallop (R-Wyo.), who claimed that new breakthroughs in anti-missile technology made Reagan's proposal feasible. Writing in *The Washington Post* on February 6, 1983, Wallop said: "I believe a variety of good defenses against ballistic missiles is possible ... The technology of space-based lasers gives substantial hope that attacking Soviet missiles could be defeated, or at the very least severely thinned, just after they rose out of the atmosphere."

Advocates of the so-called "defense dominance" school estimated that by 1990 the United States could field satellites able to destroy Soviet missiles shortly after they were launched. An article appearing in *The Washington Post* on March 27, 1983, discussed a classified study undertaken by the General Accounting Office for the Pentagon in 1981 that criticized the low level of funding for high-energy laser weapons in outer

---

21 Former National Security Adviser William Clark told aides during his tenure in the White House that the notion of a space-based, antiballistic missile system intrigued the President long before New Right leaders started touting the concept of "High Frontier." *Newsweek,* April 4, 1983.

space.²² According to the *Post*, the GAO study predicted that a laser weapon could be tested by 1993 and that the full system would cost $ 30 billion.

In the view of many experts outside the government, the $ 30 billion projected by the GAO was much too low. They estimated the cost of such a system anywhere from $ 50 to $ 100 billion and even higher.²³

Reagan's idea that science could provide the U.S. with an "Impenetrable umbrella" which would obviate the strategic vulnerability of America's cities and towns is based on the development of such new technologies as laser and particle beam weapons. Such weapons, however, present some enormous technical problems which have yet to be resolved.

Lasers are a little like flashlights, except that the beam of light is very intense, highly focused and entirely of one wavelength. As a result, laser devices can produce powerful beams that travel great distances without spreading. But laser systems suffer, among other things, from the fact that they can only operate in good weather, since clouds interfere with the beam. (What happens when one tries to blast an intense laser beam through a heavy rainstorm? Steam.) Moreover, current laser generators are much too heavy; the laser beam is not intense enough; and it is extremely difficult to point the laser accurately at a target.²⁴ Finally,

---

22 One retired career Department of Defense official, frustrated over what he saw as "foot-dragging" on lasers during the Carter Administration, attributed it confidentially to the fact that "Carter's top defense aides had backgrounds in nuclear physics."

23 Thomas Karas, author of a forthcoming book on space warfare, *The New High Ground*, estimates that "a full-scale antiballistic-missile system, designed to offer the kind of protection against all Soviet missiles that space-laser enthusiasts endorse, would cost about 500 billion dollars." The late futurologist Herman Kahn estimated the cost of a comprehensive ABM system with today's "primitive" technology at $ 200 billion, plus a $ 50 billion annual maintenance fee.

24 Of all the "exotic" weapons now being studied by the Reagan Administration, nuclear-pumped X-ray lasers appear to offer the most promise, according to outside experts. To be sure, much information on the X-ray laser remains classified. However, the Lawrence Livermore National Laboratory reportedly created an X-ray pulse with the system in a recent underground test. Nevertheless, George Keyworth, II, the President's chief science adviser, has conceded privately that "it is still an embryonic technology. . . . I don't see any clearcut systems application at this time. It's premature. It's at the science stage." There appear to be no unclassified technical articles by U.S. insiders in this field. So readers may wish to consult the results published by the Soviets on this issue. See F.V. Bunkin *et al.*, "Specification for Pumping X-Ray Laser with Ionizing Radiation," *Soviet Journal of Quantum Electronics* (July, 1981), pp. 971-72.

warheads coated with highly reflective paint can diminish the usefulness of laser beams.[25]

Similar problems inhibit the development of a particle-beam weapon.[26] This would, in the imagination of military planners, be a device that could focus and project atomic particles at the speed of light to intercept and neutralize re-entry vehicles.[27] Scientists have been producing high-energy particle beams in cyclotrons and other devices for decades. But the laboratory devices require a vacuum, and even large accelerators produce only a weak beam of particles which cannot penetrate the atmosphere. To be used in space, such a weapon would have to have access to large supplies of power for the extraordinarily large amount of energy it would consume. Particle-beam weapons are still in the conceptual stage.[28]

Spurgeon M. Keeny, Jr., former Assistant Director of the U.S. Arms Control and Disarmament Agency, and Wolfgang K.H. Panofsky, a former member of the President's Science Advisory Commission, analyze in more detail some of the immense problems associated with the development of these kinds of weapons in a space-based ABM system. To begin with, they argue, such a system to work effectively must virtually be "leakproof," since the penetration of even a single warhead would cause tremendous destruction. Here, they argue, it "is worth repeating the often stated, but little comprehended fact that a *single* modern strategic weapon could have a million times the yield of the high explosive strategic bombs of World war II, or one hundred to a thousand times the yield of

---

25   Michio Kaku, "Wasting Space: Countdown to a First Strike," *The Progressive*, June 22, 1983. Kaku is professor of nuclear physics at the Graduate Center of the City University of New York. See also Kosta Tsipis, "Laser Weapons," *Scientific American*, Vol. 245, No. 6 (December 1981), pp. 51-57.

26   For details see John Parmentola *et al.*, "Particle-Beam Weapons," *Scientific American*, Vol. 240, No. 4 (April, 1979), pp. 54-65.

27   See Clarence A. Robinson, Jr., "Soviets Push for a Beam Weapon," *Aviation Week and Space Technology*, May 2, 1977, pp. 16-61.

28   One recognized authority, Kosta Tsipis, writes:
   There is a difference... between lasers and particle beams. While the basic laws of nature simply forbid the use of charged-particle beams in outer space, and make the production and aiming of a neutral-beam ABM system in outer space technically unfeasible, the same is *not* true for lasers. There seem to be fewer technical difficulties with lasers used as weapons. The entire field of laser physics is largely new and unexplored, unlike the field of particle beams, which is rather well understood and exploited. So the physics of lasers may hold surprises for us. One day in the future a discovery *may* be made that will make practical laser weapons possible.
   See Tsipis, *Arsenal: Understanding Weapons in the Nuclear Age* (New York: Simon and Schuster, 1983), p. 211.

the atomic bombs that destroyed Hiroshima and Nagasaki, killing 250,000 people."[29]

Moreover, a space-based ABM system involves "putting a very complex system with a large power requirement into orbit." Analysis "indicates that a comprehensive defensive system of this type would require literally thousands of space shuttle sorties to assemble." It has been "estimated that such a system would cost several hundred billion dollars." Finally, even "if the control mechanisms were available to operate such a system, there are serious questions as to the vulnerability of the satellites to physical attack and to various measures that would interfere with the system's operation." In short, they conclude, "no responsible analysis has indicated that for at least the next two decades such 'death ray weapons' have any bearing on the ABM problem . . ."[30]

Despite this criticism, Defense Secretary Caspar W. Weinberger said at a news conference a week after Reagan's speech that he was "confident" U.S. scientists could develop a space-based antiballistic missile defense. And he said that the Administration might redirect some funding to lasers and other space weapons.

Scientific Recommendations

Following President Reagan's ABM speech, National Security Directive 6-83 mandated a study of the technology that could be used to eliminate the threat posed by nuclear ballistic missiles to the security of the United States. Consequently, two investigations were undertaken between June and October 1983, in which the technical and policy ramifications of a national commitment to ABM defense were examined. James C. Fletcher, former administrator of the National Aeronautics and Space Administration, was put in charge of a Defensive Technologies Study Team. And Fred S. Hoffman, Director of Pan Heuristics, an organization for policy

---

29   Spurgeon M. Keeny, Jr., et al., "MAD Versus NUTS," *Foreign Affairs* (Winter, 1981-82), p. 291. One arms control expert in the Reagan Administration would point out here that "the largest weapon in the U.S. inventory is nine megatons. It will be gone by 1985. All remaining U.S. weapons will be in the kiloton range (i.e., possessing the equivalent explosive power of thousands of tons of TNT). Not so for the Soviets who will retain multimegaton warheads."

30   This view is supported by a recent important book, which *Foreign Affairs* hailed as "the most informative and judicious analysis to date of one of the most critical strategic nuclear questions of the next two decades." See Ashton B. Carter et al. (eds.), *Ballistic Missile Defense* (Washington, D.C.: Brookings, 1984).

analysis based in California, headed an extragovernmental Future Security Strategy Study. A senior interagency group integrated the two investigations. Their findings and recommendations were subsequently outlined in a highly classified report, which was forwarded in the fall of 1983 to Ronald Reagan on behalf of Defense Secretary Weinberger and William P. Clark, the President's outgoing National Security Adviser.[31]

The interagency group reportedly stressed the importance of demonstrating that the United States is determined to explore and has the competence to develop the required technology for ballistic missile defense. Specifically, the group is said to have urged the President to back an accelerated five-year research and development program that would cost from $ 18 billion to $ 27 billion and would develop space-based and other advanced defensive weapons for intercepting nuclear missiles fired at American or other Western targets. Subsequently, some of the details of the report were published in *Aviation Week and Space Technology*, a periodical with long-standing and close ties to official U.S. Air Force thinking.[32] According to this source, the interagency report argued that these new defensive weapons would enhance strategic stability and the deterrent quality of the U.S. nuclear arsenal.

George A. Keyworth, Scientific Adviser to the President, later stated in a speech that the Pentagon's scientific-study panel had recommended a "multi-tiered array" of defensive weapons.[33] These weapons, which would cost approximately $ 95 billion by the year 2,000, could attack Soviet warheads all along their flight path, from the moment they were boosted off their rocket launchers to their point of detonation over American or allied targets.

The technologies, which are to be studied further, cover a broad spectrum. They include space- and ground-based laser weapons, especially the notorious "X-ray" laser powered by a nuclear blast in outer space. Other weapons considered in the system include powerful infrared sensors and laser pointing and tracking equipment effective at a range of several thousand miles. One senior American weapons scientist who participated in the study said that many of the technologies recommended for "fast track" development would be based on earth or used in the atmosphere. These include so-called "hypervelocity projectiles" and "shotgun" projectiles to knock down Soviet warheads once they enter the atmosphere.

31 Keith B. Payne *et al., opus cit.*, p. 821.
32 *Aviation Week & Space Technology*, October 17, 1983.
33 "According to one White House insider, George Keyworth was a skeptic, who lamented spending most of his time in 1981 resisting congressional pressure, led by Senator Malcolm Wallop, to proceed with laser stations."

While the President was still pondering the implications of the report, his political opponents and others were urging him to reconsider his decision, which they saw as committing the nation to a new arms race in space. In this respect, one former high-level government official advised Reagan to ponder the following sad and cautionary historical episode before approving the report.

A Lesson from History

Back in 1963, Soviet Premier Nikita Khrushchev wrote President Kennedy a letter (which is still highly classified at the JFK Library in Massachusetts), in which he noted that talks on a comprehensive ban on all nuclear testing had bogged down on the issue of "on-site" inspection within the Soviet Union. However, so important did the Soviet leader consider such a ban, that he decided to accept three on-site inspections a year. This was a significant concession for Khrushchev to make as the Russian military was paranoid about the intelligence ramifications of regularly allowing a U.S. team of experts into the U.S.S.R. to check Soviet compliance with a treaty banning all nuclear testing. (Khrushchev had once highlighted this problem in his folksy way: "You can't let a cat into the kitchen and expect it just to drink the milk.")

The President was generally sympathetic with Khrushchev's proposal. But the U.S. position was reportedly determined in the end by the Joint Chiefs of Staff. They argued that seven inspections a year would be necessary to ensure the Russians would not cheat on such an important treaty.

As remembered by Franklin Long, who was then Assistant Director of the Arms Control and Disarmament Agency, President Kennedy believed the United States could afford to accept the Soviet offer or seek a compromise at four or five annual inspections. But Kennedy could not convince the JCS, who were determined to continue nuclear testing anyway. Nor did the President think he could win Senate approval of a comprehensive test-ban treaty if the Joint Chiefs opposed it. As a result, he settled for the limited test-ban treaty of 1963.[34] While this treaty was

---

34 The Partial Test Ban Treaty of August 1963 was signed by representatives of the United States, the Soviet Union and the United Kingdom. It bans nuclear weapons tests in the atmosphere, in outer space and under water. It permits underground nuclear tests so long as such explosions do not pollute the environment with radioactive debris outside the territorial limits of the state conducting the tests. In early 1984, it became known that the Reagan Administration had for about a year been concealing an unknown number of nuclear ex-

significant, it was far less than the important achievement it could have been. (As it was, it required no on-site inspections and allowed underground nuclear testing to continue unabated.)

In Long's view, "a great chance" was missed merely because of the difference between three and seven on-site inspections a year. At the time, American nuclear technology was far superior to that of the Soviet Union. Thus, the Soviets would have gained from a comprehensive test ban that would have prevented — in Long's view — most of the menacing developments in that technology. In retrospect, Carl Kaysen, Deputy Special Assistant to the President for National Security Affairs, has called this one of the four great "missed opportunities" of the nuclear era.

Antisatellite Weapons

In the eyes of the critics, the Reagan Administration is proceeding on a course which may well condemn it to repeat a past it appears not to remember. For all one can tell, U.S. officials are ready to take another great long-range risk in order to avoid what they consider an immediate risk. For example, the Administration insists that the United States has to develop an effective anti-satellite weapon (ASAT) before the Russians do, thus seizing the initiative in what the White House believes is an inevitable expansion of the arms race into outer space.[35] (The U.S. antisatellite weapon is closely tied to the Reagan Administration's keen interest in developing an Anti-Ballistic Missile defense system). But the fact of the matter is, as experts have testified to Congress, the Soviets have only a primitive, low-orbit ASAT that has failed at least half its operational tests.[36]

In 1978 and 1979 the United States and the Soviet Union had begun to negotiate an agreement to limit or prohibit each other's ability to de-

plosions at an underground test site in Nevada. These undisclosed tests signified a break with previous U.S. policy of announcing all tests that had taken place since 1975. Critics immediately protested the secret tests which eroded public confidence in the government's programs.

35 For background see Geld Steinberg, "The Ultimate Battleground Weapons in Space," *Technology Review* (October, 1981).

36 See *The Christian Science Monitor*, January 11, 1984. In 1976, Major General George Keegan, chief of U.S. Air Force intelligence, sounded the alarm about Soviet research in this area. By 1981, the Soviets had repeatedly tested their conventional anti-satellite system and appeared to have launched a prototype battle station armed with clusters of infrared homing rockets capable of knocking out U.S. military satellites.

stroy satellites in outer space. Each side was making increased use of military satellites for reconnaissance, communication, navigation and other purposes. Without a treaty limiting the development of ways to destroy these satellites, it was feared that great uncertainties would be produced about each other's intentions and capabilities. These uncertainties could greatly increase international tensions and lead to an arms race in space. However, the ASAT talks became stalled as a result of the Soviet invasion of Afghanistan, and the last negotiating session was held in Vienna from April to June, 1979.[37]

The Soviets would like to avoid extending the arms race into space because, among other things, of the enormous cost and their technological disadvantage in this area. Thus, in 1983, they presented at the United Nations a draft treaty which would prohibit the testing and deployment of space-based weapons and announced a "unilateral moratorium" on launching antisatellite weapons. Shortly before he died, the Soviet leader Yuri Andropov informed a group of visiting U.S. Senators that he personally favored the conclusion of a treaty to limit the arms race.

In the view of many outside experts, such es Admiral Noel Gaylor, the proposed Soviet draft treaty suffers from a number of flaws (e.g., the totally unnecessary and unacceptable provision "not to test, nor use, for military, including counter-satellite ends, any manned spaceships"). But otherwise the Soviet draft provides a suitable basis for beginning serious negotiations and early agreement.

While there is good reason to be wary of Soviets bearing disarmament initiatives, there is no reason, these experts say, for refusing to probe them further. Yet the Reagan Administration dismissed Soviet ASAT feelers out of hand. Publicly, the U.S. government denigrated Soviet overtures as a public relations ploy. However, it was clear to most critics that the U.S. rejection was due in part to a shortsighted and amnesiac confidence in the superiority of "American high tech" and in part to the Administration's deep-seated distaste for arms control of any kind.

Assertions by critics that no program of strategic defense should be launched without the establishment first of a comprehensive arms-control program that places sharp limits on offensive weapons notwithstanding, the Reagan Administration is moving further and further ahead to control the "high ground" of space. For one thing, the Joint Chiefs of Staff are reported to have recommended that the services form a unified command for developing and "controlling" military activities in space. (Already in September 1982, twenty-five years after the launch of Sputnik I, the U.S.

---

37 See Thomas A. Halsted, "Arms Control and Disarmament in the Nuclear Age," in Bruce W. Jentleson *et al.*, *Perspectives 1981* (Washington, D.C., 1982), p. 203.

Air Force had established a Space Command, the first organizational unit at that level devoted exclusively to the operational use of space.)[38] Congress, responding to Administration pressures, has appropriated $19.4 million for testing the nation's first space weapon.[39] This is an air-launched anti-satellite missile much more advanced than its Soviet counterpart.[40]

Like many American weapons, the U.S. ASAT warhead — a onefoot cylinder — is much smaller than the Russian model. It simply homes in on the infrared signature of the target. Using a sophisticated guidance mechanism and small course-correction rockets, it rams the target at a blistering 30,000 miles an hour.

It is interesting to note the semantic difference used by Pentagon officials when they refer to U.S. or Soviet antisatellite weapons. Soviet interceptor satellites are always called "killer satellites," whereas their U.S. counterparts are named SAINT, an acronym for satellite interceptor.

To critics, antisatellite weapons are especially provocative. Development of them threatens the very satellites the U.S. relies on for warning of attack, for monitoring arms-control agreements and for military command, control and communications. As Peter A. Clausen, Senior Arms Analyst of the Union of Concerned Scientists, writes: "The vulnerability of such satellites to attack would be a highly provocative factor in future U.S.-Soviet confrontations, and would reduce the chances of bringing hostilities under control if nuclear conflict actually began."[41]

38 Albert Carnesale, *et al.*, *Living with Nuclear Weapons* (New York: Bantam Books, 1983), p. 181. The U.S.S.R. has had a counterpart organization (a branch of national air defense) since the mid-1960s.

39 Actually, the United States tested its first ASAT twenty-five years ago. Subsequently, it deployed some nucleartipped anti-satellite missiles of limited military value. These were dismantled in 1975.

40 The Soviets have been testing a low-altitude ASAT system since 1967. It is now credited with the capability to damage enemy satellites as high as 1,500 miles up. However, high-orbit navigation, communications and early-warning U.S. satellites remain invulnerable 22,000 miles above the earth. From time to time, U.S. officials have stated publicly that the U.S.S.R. is ahead in ASAT technology. But this point is dubious. As U.S. Air Force Chief of Staff Lew Allen stated in 1979, the Soviet antisatellite weapons system has "a very questionable operational capability." Quoted in *The Bulletin of Atomic Scientists*, Vol. 40, No. 5 (May, 1984), p. 35.

41 *The Minneapolis Star and Tribune*, April 13, 1984. For background see James Cana, *War in Space* (New York: Harper & Row, 1982). The U.S. antisatellite weapon is launched from a small missile carried by an F-15 fighter plane. Once operational, this weapon would be very difficult to monitor. This is because there are no obvious differences between F-15s equipped with the device and those that are not. By way of contrast, the Soviet antisatellite weapon is placed in orbit by a huge booster rocket operating from known launch sites. Such a weapon presumably could not be clandestinely deployed.

Critics also attack the development of an extensive ASAT capability on grounds that such a capability will increase the likelihood of accidental and uncontrollable nuclear war. As Daniel Deudney, a senior researcher at the Worldwatch Institute, observes: "Because the eyes and central nervous system of the high-strung nuclear strike forces are already in space, every satellite malfunction will have to be treated as the harbinger of surprise attack. Whatever the usefulness of limited shows of force, it makes little sense to start a preliminary shoot-out among the systems that must remain intact to control escalation and maintain crisis communications. The Archduke Francis Ferdinand of World War III may well be a critical U.S. or Soviet reconnaissance satellite hit by a piece of space junk during a crisis."[42]

Experts on both sides of the issue generally agree that the United States is much more reliant than the Soviet Union on satellites for military purposes such as photographic and electronic intelligence. Moreover, it is generally acknowledged that U.S. satellites are more capable. For this reason, critics say, the United States should press for a ban on antisatellite weapons.

But the Reagan Administration does not want to reach agreement with the Soviet Union on a ban of these ASAT weapons.[43] This would

> Neither American nor Soviet antisatellite weapons can now attack the key communications and early-warning satellites stationed in high orbits. But this situation could change if ASAT weapons development continues.

42 Daniel Deudney, "Unlocking Space," *Foreign Policy*, No. 53 (Winter, 1983-84), pp. 100-01.

43 U.S. officials have admitted as much privately, but the Administration cannot state this publicly because of Congressional pressure. In the spring of 1984, the President sent Congress a legally required report which gave the impression that he is serious about negotiating with the Soviets a treaty limiting antisatellite weapons systems. This report stated that the Administration has not found any new proposals for limiting space weapons that it considers "in the overall interest of the U.S. and its allies." The report goes on to argue that it would be extremely difficult to verify any agreement with the U.S.S.R. outlawing antisatellite weapons. In addition, the report says the U.S. would have a hard time stopping the Soviets from testing existing weapons systems to determine whether they could be converted into satellite-killing weapons during war. "Until we have determined whether there are, in fact, practical solutions to these problems," the report declares, "we don't believe it would be productive to engage in formal international negotiations toward banning anti-satellite weapons." By filing this report, the White House took the first step toward freeing $19.4 million in funds for developing a U.S. anti-satellite weapons system. Congress had approved the money, but said it could not be spent until 45 days after such a report was submitted by the executive branch. See *The Wall Street Journal*, April 3, 1984.

just interfere with American efforts to develop a space-based ABM system which would intercept and destroy attacking nuclear missile warheads.[44]

In late January 1984, the U.S. Air Force announced that it had conducted the first test in flight of a missile designed to destroy satellites. The missile (which is designed to be operational by 1987) was fired from a high-flying F-15 fighter plane near Vandenberg Air Force base in California. Almost immediately after the test, a group of scientists denounced it as a very dangerous "escalation of the arms race." They also noted that the year before, when Congress approved the Pentagon's appropriations, it banned tests "against objects in space" until U.S. officials tried to negotiate a ban of such weapons with the Soviet Union. However, Defense officials interpreted the language to allow the first round of anti-satellite tests.[45]

Reagan's Decision

On January 6, 1984, President Reagan did what many political observers had expected him to do. He signed a new National Security Decision Directive (No. 119). This document formally set in motion a stepped-up multibillion-dollar research program designed to determine if a new space-based or other advanced ABM system could be developed to thwart an enemy missile attack. Politically astute, the President's advisers made this decision known publicly late in January. They portrayed it in the context of alleged concerns that the Soviets were accelerating their work on missile defense.[46]

White House officials minimized the enormous political ramifications connected with the President's decision to sign the new missile-defense directive. They claimed, for instance, that it did not set in motion any "crash program." But the critics were skeptical, given what they knew of the President's personal enthusiasm for the program.

Administration authorities also took pains to argue that the President's decision was not incompatible with the 1972 Anti-Ballistic Missile Treaty with the Soviet Union. They said the new directive involved research rather than the development of components for anti-missile systems. Therefore, they maintained, it did not violate the 1972 treaty, which they said only limited the development, testing or deployment of certain kinds of new systems.

44 *The Christian Science Monitor,* April 4, 1984.
45 *The New York Times,* January 22, 1984.
46 *The Washington Post,* January 26. 1984.

In an "off-the-record" briefing, journalists were given some additional details of the new directive. Briefly, they were told that the specific language of National Security Decision Directive No. 119 called for the "initiation of a focused program to demonstrate the technical feasibility of enhancing deterrence and thereby reducing the risk of nuclear war through greater reliance on defensive strategic capability." Specifically, the purpose of the new directive was "to move technology to a point where a decision could be made" to move ahead with development and production.

Such a missile defense would have three layers. The first, based in space, would attempt to aim laser beams at Soviet missiles moments after they take off. A second system would attempt to hit any missiles that escaped the initial defense response. These missiles would be knocked out into space before they could dispense the load of individually targeted nuclear warheads carried in their noses. Finally, a third terminal defense around targets in the United States would attempt to knock out any warheads that survived.

Administration officials deliberately worded the directive in a way to ease fears that the U.S. was moving toward ultimately abrogating the ABM treaty. For instance, White House aides described the directive as a "strategic defense initiative" rather than as work on a new ABM system, which would link it to the 1972 treaty. Similarly, other sources said the directive used the word "demonstrate" rather than "test" and referred only to "research" rather than to "research and development."

Opponents quickly responded by arguing that the Administration was involved in a "game of words" to cover up its responsibility for moving away from the ABM treaty. Specifically, they pointed to such words as "research" as constituting an euphemism, for it was understood by officials that some development work would take place. This, according to the critics, would represent an obvious violation of the ABM treaty.

A number of critics were disturbed by the way in which the President's decision was portrayed publicly. The Administration seemed to insinuate that the American plan was deemed necessary because the Soviets are "ahead" in ABM technology. Actually, this issue is the subject of heated debate, they pointed out.

According to U.S. government insiders, allegations of Soviet superiority in this area rest heavily on a single piece of disputed evidence. These sources reveal that in 1972 Major General George Keegan, then Director of U.S. Air Force intelligence, alleged that satellite photos of a Soviet base some sixty kilometers south of Semipalatinsk provided conclusive evidence that the Russians were further ahead of the U.S. in the development of particle beam weaponry. As one U.S. intelligence official recalls,

"Keegan cited four large holes in the ground and two spherical structures that he insisted were energy storage tanks for particle beams."

CIA officials were skeptical, and they undertook an investigation of their own into the matter. This study reportedly concluded that the evidence provided by Keegan was marginal and inconclusive. The Central Intelligence Agency referred to the Soviet facility as URDF-3, which stood for "unidentified research and development facility number three." This decision left the Air Force general virtually without substantial backing for his claim that the Soviets possessed a twenty-year edge on the United States. However, with the election of President Reagan, the charges made by Keegan received a new, sympathetic hearing.

Some of the old arguments brought up by critics focused on the questionable effectiveness of the President's initiative and its exorbitant price tag. For one thing, they said that missile defense could not be made effective enough to stop some 7,500 warheads lofted toward the United States by Soviet missiles. By the same token, opponents said, Reagan risked removing the stability that theoretically came from an Anti-Ballistic Missile treaty; this essentially left both homelands hostage to missile attack under the MAD policy. Also, they maintained that since the Russians feared U.S. technological superiority, they would now be stampeded into an all-out offensive and defensive missile race. In addition, they zeroed in on the "staggering" cost of the President's program, which in the end could well be over $100 billion.[47] Finally, they argued that defending against missile attack at a time when the United States had little defense against bombers or cruise missiles would set off a new multibillion-dollar effort to beef up defenses against these weapons as well.

Deterrence, ABM Defense and Nuclear War Fighting

Over the years, the American philosophy and approach to ballistic missile defense have undergone significant change. During the late 1960s and early 1970s the argument centered on the impossibility of preventing a nuclear attack from penetrating ABM defense. And it was probably responsible in large part for agreement by the superpowers in 1972 to sign the Anti-Ballistic Missile Treaty.

As Herbert York, former Director of Defense Research and Engineering

---

47 Originally, Pentagon officials had planned to spend between $15 billion and $18 billion on space-based weapons in the first five years. In May 1984, the Pentagon produced a new estimate which would spend $26 billion over the same period. See *The New York Times*, May 10, 1984.

in the Pentagon, recalls: in 1967, when ABM fever was at a high pitch, President Johnson summoned his top military and science advisers. Discussion proceeded, and the President eventually was led to ask two simple questions: "Will it work and should it be deployed?" All present agreed that the answers were no.[48] For the President was keen on knowing whether it was possible to devise a system that could destroy *all* incoming warheads. As Johnson saw things, it was not sufficient to destroy, say, one in every two, since if only one warhead penetrated the system it would be enough to destroy Washington, D.C.

U.S. officials now publicly argue, however, that the real purpose of any ABM defense is not to make an attack impossible but to make it more difficult and costly. Theoretically, a significant proportion of incoming enemy warheads could be destroyed through ballistic missile defense. Thus, one side cannot be certain of destroying the entire retaliatory force of the other. This uncertainty, it is said, will enhance deterrence.[49]

If this is the "good reason" offered for public consumption, there are some other important, more controversial considerations. They are to be found largely buried in the arcane theories and peculiar ratiocinations of the nuclear warfighting strategists who wield great influence in the Reagan Administration. As Michio Kaku of New York University points out, "The laser ABM, with all its limitations, may have effective applications in conjunction with the launching of a preemptive [nuclear strike]."[50]

"The arithmetic is simple," Professor Tatu says. "The Soviet Union has about 8,000 strategic warheads aimed at targets in the United States. In the near future, the land-based MX missile and the submarine-launched Trident II will be accurate enough to drop two hydrogen bombs on each of the Soviet SS-18 and SS-19 missile silos."

Still there are some uncertainties. But there is a likelihood that "about 1,000 of the 8,000 Russian warheads would still be available to retaliate against the United States." With all its faults, "the laser ABM system can reasonably be expected to handle most of those remaining 1,000 Soviet warheads." The few missiles "that might elude both the (preemptive nuclear) strike and the laser ABM provide the rationale for the Administrations new emphasis on civil defense and relocation plans." The purpose of such programs "is to preserve U.S. industrial capacity for the 'post-attack era.'"

48 Herbert F. York, *Race to Oblivion* (New York: Simon & Schuster, 1970).
49 See *The Christian Science Monitor*, March 20, 1984.
50 See Michio Kaku, "Wasting Space: Countdown to a First Strike," *The Progressive*, June 22, 1983.

State Department consultant Colin S. Gray, an influential nuclear war-fighting strategist, neatly sums up this doctrine: "The United States should plan to defeat the Soviet Union and to do so at a cost that would not prohibit U.S. recovery. Washington should identify war aims that in the last resort would contemplate the destruction of Soviet political authority and the emergence of postwar world order compatible with Western values ... A combination of counterforce offensive targeting, civil defense, and ballistic missile and air defense should hold U.S. casualties to approximately 20 million, which should render U.S. strategic threats more credible."[51]

In other words, the objectives of the proposed ABM system must be seen in a larger context. A space-based ABM system, combined with a comprehensive mix of counterforce targeting and civil defense measures purport to guarantee, in the Administration's view, that the United States will be able to "prevail" in a nuclear exchange with the Soviet Union.

Summary

The immensely important debate over how to avoid nuclear war entered a new phase in March 1983. The focus was now on the following issue: Should the United States develop and deploy a space-based system for defending itself against Soviet missiles so as to deter the Kremlin from ever contemplating such an attack?

Just about 18 months ago, the President surprised the nation, and many experts in his own government as well, by calling for an all-out program — along the lines of the Manhattan Project, which developed the atom bomb — to build a defense system in space. Reagan's address may, as some observers have already noted, rank in history with Winston Churchill's "iron curtain" speech and John F. Kennedy's proclamation in 1961 to land a man on the moon within the decade. However, neither of these two famous speeches had the ominous implications for humanity that the 1983 presidential proposal for a space-based ABM system has.

To be sure, this was not the express intention of the President, who was counting on his proposal selling well with U.S. voters. At the time, he called upon the scientific community — "those who gave us nuclear weapons" in the first place — to undertake a "long-term [missile defense]

---

51 Colin Gray, in his most recent discussion of this subject, has toned down his rhetoric considerably. See Keith B. Payne and Colin S. Gray, "Nuclear Policy and the Defensive Transition," *Foreign Affairs*, Vol. 62, No. 4 (Spring, 1984), pp. 820-842.

research and development program to begin to achieve our ultimate goal of eliminating the threat posed by strategic nuclear missiles." But he did not give out any details about the plan. Only later did Administration officials acknowledge that the project would take decades to reach fruition, with no guarantee of success."[52]

The idea for the system, which drew on ideas from the "High Frontier" project, was reportedly planted in the mind of the President by his friend and frequent adviser Edward Teller, the Hungarian-born scientist, often described as the "father of the H-bomb." As *Time* magazine later reported: "Teller's brainstorm became Reagan's dream, and the dream became national policy."[53]

Few would probably deny the appeal of the President's stated long-term goal of "rendering nuclear weapons impotent and obsolete. This goal, which is attractive to large segments of the population of the United States and many of its allies who are becoming increasingly alarmed at the prospect of nuclear war, is made even more attractive politically by recent progress with sophisticated techniques that can shoot down missiles without using nuclear explosives.[54] Moreover, there can be little doubt that the idea of developing an Anti-Ballistic Missile system continues to have a constituency in the arms industry, which sees billions of dollars in contracts over the next two decades. There is nothing surprising about this.

However, there are many pitfalls to the President's plan — now called a Strategic Defense Initiative. Indeed, so many substantial technical obstacles bar the way to the realization of the President's dream that critics quickly dubbed the Strategic Defensive Initiative "Star Wars." This sobriquet suggests a fantasy — not just a dream, but a pipedream. And a potentially dangerous and expensive exercise in self-deception at that.

The case against the President's proposal, which rests on a cluster of mutually reinforcing arguments, seems overwhelming. On technical grounds alone, experts all across the ideological spectrum doubt that a space-based ABM system would work well enough to vindicate Reagan's vision. First, the necessary technology for an effective, space-based ABM

---

52 According to *Newsweek*, "The space-based ABM idea was tacked on to the President's speech just hours before air time." See *Newsweek*, April 4, 1983.

53 *Time*, May 7, 1984.

54 In June 1984, the United States successfully tested its non-nuclear interceptor for the first time. (The three previous tests failed for various mechanical reasons.) A special interceptor rocket fired from Meck Island in the Pacific struck the dummy warhead of a *Minuteman* I intercontinental ballistic missile that had been launched from Vandenburg Air Force Base in California some 30 minutes earlier. See *Time*, June 25, 1984.

system does not presently exist. Nor is its attainment likely in the next decade or even some years thereafter — if ever. There are simply too many scientific "unknown quantities" and technological obstacles to developing an effective, reliable system.

The history of military technology suggests that advances in defensive weapons are frequently superceded by developments in offensive capabilities. In this respect, the ABM system proposed by the Reagan Administration is no exception. An adversary could make use of a whole bag of tricks to neutralize such a space-based system. These include different technological developments such as "killer satellites," space mines and laser cannons.

In June 1984, the Defense Department announced the successful test of a new space warfare device. "We really tried to hit a bullet with a bullet and it worked," one U.S. Army official exalted. To be sure, the test is an achievement; the Air Force's homing vehicle is much more sophisticated than the erratic anti-satellite missile so far tested by the Russians. And intercepting one missile with another when both are travelling at thousands of feet per second is indeed somewhat like "hitting a bullet with a bullet." But that feat was first achieved twenty years ago before the construction of the Safeguard ABM system. Safeguard was abandoned, after expenditures of more than five billion dollars, as it became clear that an attacker could simply overwhelm a defender's "bullets" by a "shotgun" blast. The question ever since has been how to hit a shotgun blast with a shotgun blast.

Another aspect of the problem is even more serious. It has to do with the destructive capabilities of thermonuclear weapons and the size of existing Soviet stockpiles. These are such that even at the most optimistic attrition rate of 99 percent (which is presently regarded by most of the ablest scientific experts as a practical impossibility) can result in tremendous destruction and devastation.[55]

What does it mean for a missile defense of the U.S. population to "work" when one percent of the warheads of the adversary gets through?

---

55 Former Defense Intelligence Agency Director Daniel Graham claims in his new book that "within five years, at a cost of $ 12 billion, the United States could deploy a two-layered fleet of satellites (firing interceptor rockets) that would filter out 98 percent of a Soviet missile launch." But this is a distinctly minority view not shared even by those who support the President's plans in this area. On March 27, 1983, Secretary of Defense Caspar Weinberger said on the "Meet the Press" television program, "The defensive systems that the President is talking about are not designed to be partial. What we want to try to get is a system which will develop a defense that is thoroughly reliable and total, yes. And I don't see any reason why that can't be done."

It means basically that the defender can write off about eighty cities. (The best air defenses the United States has ever built were never more than twenty percent effective.)[56] Then the defensive systems themselves need protection — or they will be sitting ducks. In short, the task assigned to the defense is a technically difficult — if not impossible — undertaking. Indeed, the prospect of such a system ever working as expected is so "remote that it should not serve as the basis of public expectation or national policy," to use the words of a recent report by the Congressional Office of Technology Assessment.[57]

After more than a year of study and refinement in the Executive Branch, the Strategic Defense Initiative now implicitly recognizes the impracticability of a "leakproof umbrella." Instead, it has adopted the somewhat more modest "interim" goal of "enhancing," rather than replacing, deterrence based on offensive weapons. The idea, as it is now explained, is that Soviet plans for attack would be further complicated by even an imperfect U.S. defense.

The role that strategic defense might play in American national security policy is now a contentious issue even among U.S. policymakers. The question still has not been resolved whether an ABM defense should be expected to provide an "astrodome" covering American military forces and cities comprehensively or whether a more limited objective is acceptable, such as only defending U.S. retaliatory weapons.

In a speech before the National Press Club in early May 1984, Caspar Weinberger indicated that a compromise might be in the making. At that time, the Secretary of Defense stated that although the "ultimate goal" of the space-weapons program was to provide "thoroughly reliable defenses" for the U.S. population, this would "not preclude any intermediate deployment that could provide defense of the offensive deterrent forces."[58]

A major drawback to the development of a comprehensive ABM system, whether land- or space-based, is the staggering financial cost. It will always be cheaper for a determined adversary to manufacture offensive capabilities to overwhelm any "Maginot Line" in the sky than to develop a corresponding system for mutual protection against nuclear weapons. Relying on an ABM capability, then, would require the U.S. constantly to keep ahead of each Soviet escalation of offensive weapons with an escalation of defensive ABMs. The cost disadvantage is thus clear. To use

---

56 Jan Lodal, former Director for Program Analysis, National Security Council, *U.S. News & World Report,* April 11, 1983.
57 Quoted in *The International Herald Tribune,* June 14, 1984.
58 *The New York Times,* May 10, 1984.

the words of the late Senator Frank Church, the new ABM system could become "potentially the most expensive sieve in history."

In addition, the proposed space-based ABM system, which for the most part is intended to protect the U.S. mainland from attack by intercontinental ballistic missiles, cannot offer any protection against low-flying bombers and cruise missiles. While the Soviets are behind the United States in this area of technology, it is expected that they will, in a matter of a few years, deploy sophisticated and long-range cruise missiles as the U.S. is now doing. In a world where intercontinental missile attacks can theoretically be warded off, the cruise missile becomes more attractive.

Finally, the decision to move toward the development of an ABM system has grave implications as far as Soviet-American political relations are concerned. Most importantly in this respect, it gives the Soviet leadership the distinct impression that the United States is bent on developing a first-strike capability against the U.S.S.R. Theoretically, a comprehensive ABM system creates the possibility that a state possessing such a capability could strike its adversary first and avoid retaliation by using ABMs to destroy or deflect any retaliatory attack. Thus, the Reagan Administration's decision will at the very least heighten Soviet suspicions and might provide them with an incentive to strike first rather than wait for the "inevitable" strike from a United States protected by an ABM system.

To be sure, the Administration has publicly denied that a final decision has been made with regard to the development of a space-based ABM system. But it is clear that the President has set in motion plans that are gaining added momentum with each passing day. Just recently, for instance, U.S. officials announced plans to spend $ 26 billion by the end of this decade on anti-missile research and technology, and in March 1984 Lieutenant General James A. Abrahamson, an Associate Director of NASA, was named to co-ordinate research on particle-beam weapons and the generation of electric power in space.

For their part, the Russians have indicated that they cannot afford to sit back and do nothing while their main foe gains a significant technological advantage in this crucial area. "If we go ahead on this [ABM development]," warns former U.S. arms negotiator Gerard C. Smith, "the Soviets are bound to match it. Instead of one arms race, we'll have two."[59] This point, in particular, is what bothers a number of America's allies. They are growing increasingly concerned about the international implications of the Reagan Administration's proposals. In particular, they fear that the direction in which the United States is going could

---

59   Quoted in *Newsweek*, April 4, 1983.

start a new arms race and strategically divide the United States from its European allies. Basically, the NATO allies worry that if the U.S. felt its territory was impregnable, the American incentive to defend Europe would be greatly diminished, leaving Western Europe still exposed to Soviet military might.

President Reagan has indicated that the United States would consult with its allies and insure their defense as part of any program it undertakes. But so far the Administration has been unable to alleviate skepticism among the NATO members. For some very good reasons. The fact of the matter is that there is no known way to defend Western Europe against Soviet nuclear artillery or low-flying aircraft used against European targets. No ABM system would prevent this from occurring.

But if the West Europeans are mainly concerned about their own security, they are also worried about the implications for arms control of the American plan. As one West German official said recently, "We got the impression that the Administration has made up its mind on producing these weapons and is not thinking about arms control first."[60]

No matter what the President finally decides on this issue, many knowledgeable students of arms control maintain that the Administration must carefully avoid taking any measures that could lead to renunciation of the 1972 ABM Treaty. This agreement stipulates: "Each party undertakes not to *develop*, test or deploy ABM systems or components which are sea based, air based, space based or mobile land based." (Italics are mine.) This language is about as clear as it can be on a matter of vital importance.[61]

To be sure, the strategic and political rationale for the 1972 ABM Treaty was developed in an era of technology that both superpowers have now surpassed. However, technological innovation does not invalidate that rationale. Nor does it lessen the continuing importance of the treaty.

President Reagan's own Commission on Strategic Forces recognized this point when it issued its report in the spring of 1984. This report specifically warned against tampering with the 1972 Antiballistic Missile

---

60 *The Washington Post*, April 11, 1984. The Reagan Administration has introduced what Richard Perle, Assistant Secretary of Defense for International Security Policy, calls "a fundamental change in the focus on arms control as a way of moderating our requirements." As Perle explains it, the entire arms-control process of the past decade has so harmed American security that the U.S. will no longer make sacrifices to keep the process going. See *Newsweek*, June 8, 1981.

61 Certain U.S. officials have conceded privately that it will be necessary to renegotiate the ABM Treaty if and when the actual development of a space-based missile defense weapons system is deemed feasible.

Treaty by pushing antimissile defense systems. Furthermore, it disputed the cynical view of some White House aides that Moscow is duping Washington through arms control negotiations. The Commission recommended a cautious step-by-step approach to arms control.[62]

Louis René Beres touches on another important point — the ramifications of the President's ABM plans for non-proliferation. "In this connection, there is a real danger that the United States may seek to protect its MX forces by the deployment of a Ballistic Missile Defense System. Should such deployment take place, the resultant ABM Treaty termination would be widely interpreted as U.S. violation of Article VI of the NPT [the Non Proliferation Treaty]. It follows that such deployment would be injurious to a sound U.S. nonproliferational policy."[63]

During the spring of 1984, the Administration came under increasing pressure to negotiate limits with the Soviets on anti-satellite weapons. In late May 1984, the U.S. House of Representatives voted to prohibit the Air Force from conducting further ASAT tests so long as the Soviets refrained from such initiatives. The following month, the Republican-dominated Senate voted to halt testing of anti-satellite weapons until the President tries to negotiate "the strictest possible limitations" on their use. In the wake of these developments, the President began to show some flexibility towards possible negotiations with the Soviets on this issue.

The Soviet-American impasse now turns on one critical question: Should weapons be banned from space altogether or should they merely be limited? On the one hand, the Soviets want a ban on all space arms, starting with anti-satellite weapons. Before negotiations can begin, however, the U.S.S.R. wants a moratorium on ASAT testing. The Kremlin offers to destroy its own primitive ASATs and to accept verification against their replacement. On the other hand, the Reagan Administration proposes not to prohibit but to limit ASAT deployment. It is producing a sophisticated ASAT for deployment by 1987.

The Administration contends that it must proceed with an anti-satellite weapon because a ban could not be reliably verified and would leave the Soviets with possession of the world's only "operational" ASAT. However, the Soviet low-altitude ASAT is primitive and no threat to the most important American satellites which are in high orbit. Moreover, should the Soviet weapon be secretly resuscitated during a ban, it could be readily offset by defensive measures.

62   See *The Christian Science Monitor*, April 4, 1984.
63   Louis René Beres, "Nuclear Strategy and World Order: The United States Imperative," *Alternatives — A Journal of World Politics*, Vol. 8, No. 2 (Fall, 1982).

For its part, the evolving low-altitude American ASAT — once tested and deployed — could not easily be banned. It is launched from F-15 jet fighters. And the flights of this aircraft containing an anti-satellite capability would be hard to distinguish from other F-15 flights the world over.

Its public rhetoric notwithstanding, the American ASAT program is really driven not by fear of a Soviet advantage or even doubt about verification. No. The Administration is convinced that a superior ASAT capability would give the United States an important military advantage. However, this is a serious miscalculation. In lieu of a complete ban on anti-satellite weapons, the Soviets will have little difficulty eventually catching up or even leapfrogging the American effort, ultimately threatening the U.S. most important early warning and communications satellites. And then it will be too late for a verifiable ban. The genie will be out of the bottle.

One only has to recall the experience with MIRV back in the late 1960s. At that time the United States enjoyed an advantage in the development of independently targeted multiple warheads, and the bureaucracy shortsightedly pushed aside attempts to negotiate limits on their deployment. In the end, within a relatively short time, the U.S. advantage was followed by Soviet MIRV deployments that are now seen as a grave disadvantage.

Congress was prudent to require in 1983 that the President seek a Soviet-American ban before testing ASAT against a target in space. The House recently voted to bar such tests for another year, if the Soviet Union also refrains. However, the Reagan Administration is pressing a Senate amendment which would permit tests if the President merely certified that he is seeking strict limits on ASATs. Only if the House of Representatives holds its ground, insisting on retarding flight tests, can the chances for achieving a total ban be preserved and American security interests be better served.

> Nuclear weapons have turned out to be 'ultimate' in an unanticipated sense of the word. No nation's military planners have been able, in 38 years, to think up a way to use such huge explosions with such pervasive aftereffects in ways that are clearly advantageous to their side. This may now be the most important thing about nuclear weapons in the 1980s: that they are militarily unusable.
>
> *Harland Cleveland*

XII. THE BOOMERANG EFFECT

In 1960, the famous American nuclear strategist Herman Kahn published his book *On Thermonuclear War*, in which he described the hypothetical existence of a "Doomsday Machine." This machine was intended to be a *reductio ad absurdum* of the idea of nuclear deterrence. The Doomsday Machine was a device which would deter nuclear war with absolute certainty by making the cost of aggression infinite.

It worked like this: A vast computer would be wired up to a huge stockpile of H-bombs. When the computer sensed that the U.S.S.R. had committed an act defined as intolerable, the machine would automatically set off the Doomsday bombs, which would destroy the earth.

Freeman Dyson in his classic treatise *Weapons and Hope* calls Kahn's Doomsday Machine a myth.[1] Yet recent research, particularly by Carl Sagan, Professor of Astronomy and Space Sciences at Cornell University, and Paul Ehrlich, Professor of Biological Studies at Stanford University, suggests Kahn's basic idea may not be so farfetched after all.

This chapter attempts to come to grips with the findings of scientists in the area of the catastrophic effects of nuclear weapons' use and determine their implications for nuclear deterrence.

---

1 Freeman Dyson, *Weapons and Hope* (New York: Harper & Row, 1984), p. 34.

Putting Things into Perspective

Many knowledgeable people generally agree that a full-scale nuclear war would mean the end of civilization. Yet claims that other kinds of more "limited" nuclear war might cause a regression of civilization to prehistoric levels or even the extinction of the human species have been dimissed as alarmist or, worse, irrelevant. Popular works that stress this "doomsday" theme, such as William Manchester's *Nuclear War: What's In It For You* and Jonathan Schell's *The Fate of the Earth*, have been labeled "disreputable" by some U.S. officials;[2] their apocalyptic charges are rejected out of hand as unsubstantiated and unlikely. It is judged unwise to frighten the public with doomsday talk when nuclear weapons are needed, one is told, to deter the Soviet Union.

Admittedly, it is hard to describe what a postnuclear world would be like. When such major disasters as earthquakes or floods occur in the world today, most of the death and destruction take place at the time of the tragedy or immediately afterward, before help can reach the victims. Given a tragedy such as a major earthquake in southern California, the undamaged towns and cities in the state — and indeed the entire nation — usually respond quickly by providing support and assistance to reduce the suffering and help the survivors recuperate. In a nuclear attack, however, there would hardly be any undamaged areas to provide relief. Moreover, the initial nuclear explosions and huge firestorms could be followed by other dire effects, which U.S. scientists now project would cumulatively produce a "nuclear winter."

To make this nightmare more intelligible we might explain briefly how warfare has changed over the last two centuries. Two hundred years ago, European states relied largely on professional armies to fight their battles. Although many civilians suffered and many were killed as a result of such warfare, most victims were combatants. War was indeed a painful experience for society, but something that could be survived.

The late nineteenth century and particularly the twentieth century saw the development of what came to be called "total war." Modern armed forces were dependent on the strength of their country's economy and society, and that economy and society became legitimate targets in war. Therefore, the ravages of war inflicted on the participants grew geometrically. But still, all in all, society did survive it.

---

2 William Manchester, *Nuclear War: What's In It For You* (New York: Pocket Books, 1982) and Jonathan Schell, *The Fate of the Earth* (New York: Knopf, 1982).

Overcoming Resistance

Resistance to serious consideration of the consequences and effects of nuclear war has to do with two major factors. These are (1) their necessarily theoretical basis and (2) the tendency of people to practice what psychologists call "denial." In the first case, understanding the long-term consequences of nuclear war is not conducive to experimental verification — at least not more than once. In the second case, many people, while they recognize nuclear war as a grave and terrifying prospect on one level of their human experience, frequently put the agonizing problem out of their heads on a day-to-day basis, since they believe they can do nothing about it.

One source of the problem of denial, states the recent Harvard Study Group's publication, *Living With Nuclear Weapons*,[3] is the penchant of civilian strategists, military men and policymakers for euphemisms, the use of innocent language to mask the ugly reality of nuclear war. Thus, the term "counter-value" targeting replaces the disturbing reality of aiming nuclear weapons at the population of the enemy.

Long-Term Effects of Nuclear War

The long-term climatic and biological effects of nuclear war have recently been thoroughly examined by Carl Sagan,[4] Paul Ehrlich,[5] and other lesser known scientists. Their studies, conducted over a two-year period, involved the use of computer models of a variety of nuclear war scenarios, including cases ranging in explosive power from 100 to 10,000 megatons. Their findings, which have been endorsed by a large number of scientists, were presented in detail at a special conference in Cambridge, Mass. on April 22-26, 1983. Their conclusions were subsequently announced at a conference in Washington, D.C. and a detailed summary in layman's language was published in *Foreign Affairs* in the winter of 1983.

One of the most important findings of the Sagan and Ehrlich studies

---

3 Harvard Study Group, *Living With Nuclear Weapons* (New York: Bantam Books, 1983), p. 12.

4 See R.P. Turco, O.B. Toon, T.P. Ackerman, J.B. Pollack and Carl Sagan, "Nuclear Winter: Global Consequences of Multiple Nuclear Explosions," *Science*, Vol. 222, No. 4630 (December 23, 1983), pp. 1283-1292.

5 Paul R. Ehrlich *et al.*, "Long-Term Biological Consequences of Nuclear War," *Science*, Vol. 222 (December 23, 1983), pp. 1293-1300.

is that the long-term consequences of a nuclear war could constitute a global climatic catastrophe. While this has long been suspected by people both inside and outside government, the two scientists also found that even a comparatively small nuclear war could have devastating consequences. In fact, a climatic catastrophe could be triggered by only one side — even if the attacked state did not lift a finger to retaliate.

According to Sagan, there exists a threshold at which severe meteorological consequences are triggered.[6] In the case of nuclear warheads exploding in *surface* bursts against counterforce targets (e.g., missile silos), this threshold is about 2,000 warheads. Given the large number of warheads in the arsenals of the two superpowers (about 50,000 with an aggregate yield near 15,000 megatons),[7] the number of nuclear warheads that could destroy the world is small indeed. As in all calculations of this complexity, Sagan and Ehrlich acknowledge uncertainties. Some factors tend, for instance, to work towards more severe or more prolonged effects; others tend to ameliorate the effects. As Sagan writes, "it is the soot produced by urban fires that is the most sensitive trigger of the climatic catastrophe."

As Sagan and Ehrlich report, the cumulative effects of a nuclear strike of between 500 and 2,000 warheads could trigger a "nuclear winter" and shatter the interconnecting web of systems that sustain life on the planet. Smoke and soot would obscure sunlight, causing temperatures to plunge below freezing levels even in the summer. Food crops and other ecological systems would be wiped out. And radiation would be several times more intense than previously estimated. Finally, when this pall lifted, ultraviolet rays from the sun would reach intolerable levels.[8] In the words of Paul Ehrlich: "The population size of *Homo sapiens* conceivably could be reduced to prehistoric levels or below, and extinction of the human species itself cannot be excluded."

Russian scientists, who were asked to comment on the studies done by Sagan and Ehrlich, discussed new research findings in the Soviet Union similar to those in America. These included the possible creation of a global "toxic smog," unchecked biological epidemics and substantial

---

6 It should be noted that the concept of a "nuclear *threshold*" is disputed even by some of those scientific supporters of Sagan's "nuclear winter" idea.

7 In 1982, the U.S. and its allies possessed approximately 31,000 nuclear weapons and the Soviets about 20,000. Some 26,000 U.S. nuclear weapons were in active inventory, and 4,000 more in active storage. See *The Defense Monitor*, Vol. 11, No. 6 (1982), p. 1. These amounts definitely must be considerably increased for the present (fall 1984).

8 See also C.H. Kruger *et al.*, *Causes and Effects of Stratospheric Ozone Reduction: An Update* (Washington, D.C.: National Academy of Sciences, 1982).

depletion of the earth's oxygen supply. Sergei P. Kapitza of the Physico-Technical Institute in Moscow said he agreed with his U.S. counterparts that recent findings mean that the use of nuclear weapons is "suicidal."[9]

Some Policy Implications

The foregoing probable consequences of a nuclear war, one involving between 500 and 2,000 nuclear warheads, have important implications for doctrine and policy. Some of the most significant are discussed below.

First Strike

Although neither the Soviet Union nor the United States presently possess a first-strike capability (i.e. the ability to launch a disarming nuclear strike), there is constant talk and concern about the possibility of one side or the other obtaining such a capability in the near future. Now, as Sagan and Ehrlich make clear, a first-strike option is rationally out of the question for all time, because the strategic forces of the United States and the Soviet. Union — even if they were all situated at fixed sites — could not be destroyed in a *reliably subthreshold* war. There are simply too many essential targets.[10] The number of U.S. land-based strategic missiles is about 1,050; for the Soviet Union, it is about 1,400. In addition, each side has at least several dozen alternative strategic bomber bases and airstrips as well as command and control facilities, submarine ports and other prime strategic targets on land.

Sub-Threshold War

To be sure, devastating nuclear wars that are significantly below the threshold for severe climatic consequences are possible. But it is important to note here that a sub-threshold pre-emptive strike would leave much of the retaliatory force of the attacked state intact and would serve as a powerful provocation.

---

9 The Russian scientists were led by Evgeny P. Velikhov, Vice President of the Soviet Academy of Sciences, and they were questioned via satellite during the conference in Washington, D.C. on October 31 and November 1, 1983. For details see *The New York Times*, December 9, 1983.

10 One scientist would comment here: "The nature, not the number, of the targets is most crucial."

Transition to Low-Yield High-Accuracy Arsenals

A conceivable response to the prospect of climatic catastrophe might be to continue present trends toward lower-yield and higher-accuracy missiles. These trends might be accompanied by development of technology enabling warheads to burrow into the ground before detonating. Payloads have already been developed for the Pershing II that use radar area-correlators for target recognition and terminal guidance.

The unclassified "targeting probable error" is about forty meters.[11] It is apparent that technologies are emerging that might permit delivery accuracies of thirty-five meters or better over intercontinental range. The present projection is that high-accuracy penetrating warheads in the one-to-ten kiloton range would be able, with high reliability, to demolish even very hardened silos and underground command posts.

From the military viewpoint, a major advantage of this new low-yield sub-surface technology is that it cannot threaten the ozonosphere. The stratospheric ozone layer absorbs biologically dangerous ultra violet radiation from the sun. Thus, the Sagan and Ehrlich study could conceivably be used, by U.S. officials to increase calls for further improvements in high-accuracy earth-burrowing warheads.

However, as critics note, there are some major problems with this prospect. While a world in which the nuclear arsenals of the superpowers were completely converted to a relatively small number of burrowing low-yield warheads would be safer in terms of climatic catastrophe, such warheads are destabilizing. In this view, the weapons would only serve to provoke the Soviet Union. Seeing the United States take a serious interest in such an pre-emptive strike weapon, the Soviet leadership might well conclude that the Administration was moving toward the development of a first-strike capability.

ABM Defense

In the view of some strategic theorists, the prospect of a climatic catastrophe strengthens the argument for the development of an Anti-Ballistic Missile system. But critics deny this. Besides the high technical, cost and policy difficulties inherent in such a proposal, one likely response to an adversary's anticipated deployment of an ABM system would be a proportionate increase in the stockpiles of offensive warheads. Most pertinent to this chapter is the recognition that even the most readily deploy-

---

11 *Aviation Week and Space Technology,* May 15, 1978.

able ABM system will never be 100 percent effective. Moreover, such a system suffers from the disadvantage of generating tremendous explosions and fires as incoming missiles are attacked, triggering in a number of cases "sympathetic detonation."

Other Possibilities

There are a number of other conceivable responses to the prospect of climatic catastrophe. For instance, the leadership of a nuclear power might decide to re-locate its silos and mobile launchers (the latter inviting a barrage attack) to cities and forests to guarantee that a counterforce pre-emptive strike by its adversary would trigger a global climatic catastrophe. Another even more desperate scenario envisions countries with small nuclear arsenals of marginal strategic capability amassing a threshold of some 500 to 2,000 deliverable warheads in order to be taken seriously as a "great power."

The "Nuclear-Winter" Debate

Since publication of Sagan and Ehrlich's findings, U.S. authorities and others have raised questions about the validity of their prediction of a "nuclear winter." State Civil Defense officials, for instance, argue that their projection is based on extreme assumptions which *may* be valid. According to Randy Lanaria, a state radiation specialist in Minnesota, "Their data was insufficient; they said that right in their study. Why did they come all across the newspaper and TV [saying] that this was the final word?"[12]

In response, Paul Ehrlich said the studies were scientifically valid and well-balanced. "Basically, [they're] talking through their hats," he said of State Civil Defense officials.

Other critics zeroed in on the historical data about the climatic effects of large deposits of dust in the upper atmosphere. According to one report, in 1815 a volcanic eruption released over 200 times the energy of the thermonuclear megatonnage that constitued Sagan's "threshold" for triggering a 13-degree centigrade drop in average global temperature; yet this eruption, which blew an estimated 25 cubic miles of debris into the air, led only to a global temperature drop of almost one degree centigrade.

Edward Teller, referred to popularly as the "father of the H-Bomb"

---

12 *The Minneapolis Star and Tribune,* January 21, 1984.

and a noted "hardliner" on nuclear weapons, claimed that Sagan and Ehrlich "may be stating a case two to three times as bad as what would actually happen."[13] But this criticism immediately drew the rebuttal: Should Americans be relieved that only one-third to one-half of the earth would be destroyed instead of all of it?

Probably the most telling criticism came from S. Fred Singer, a geophysicist at the University of Virginia. While he agrees that Sagan and Ehrlich may well be correct, he notes the extreme difficulty of making accurate predictions of the global environmental effects of a nuclear exchange. Singer argues that based on another, yet quite reasonable, set of assumptions, we might actually "have a nuclear summer — dark and hot." And "whatever the temperature effects, they are likely to be quite short-lived."

Unquestionably, some of the findings of Sagan and Ehrlich are new. And, in this sense, they would seem to raise the stakes of nuclear warfare. However, Paul Ehrlich would caution against overstating the case. For many people both inside and outside government have long recognized that nuclear war might very well mean the extinction of the human race. As Ehrlich testified recently, his findings were so extensive and so obvious they constituted a sort of "biological overkill." Further, he said, to ask a biologist what would be the results of a nuclear war was like asking "a physician if everybody in this room put a double-barreled shotgun in his mouth and shot it, what would be the medical consequences?" The result is apparent to all.

As early as June 1947, the Joint Chiefs of Staff gave, in a secret report, their "Evaluation of the Atomic Bomb as a Military Weapon." Here they stated: "If used in numbers, atomic bombs not only can nullify any nation's military effort, but can demolish its social and economic structures and prevent their reestablishment for long periods of time." This study was not radically different from earlier U.S. assessments of the bomb, insiders say, but it possessed a chillingly contemporary ring with its graphic portrayal of the world-ending possibilities inherent in the weapon.

The awesome destructive power of the bomb was in fact recognized immediately after the destruction of Hiroshima and Nagasaki, although attempts were made later by certain groups of people whose interests were directly affected to downplay these effects. For instance, air-power advocate Alexander de Seversky, fearing that the atomic bomb would undermine the rationale for a large Air Force, charged in the February 1946 *Reader's Digest* that an atomic bomb would do no more damage to

---

13 *Time,* December 5, 1983.

a modern city than a high-explosive, ten-ton "blockbuster." A similarly fallacious claim was made at this time by Admiral William Blandy, which prompted a public disclaimer from David Lilienthal, Chairman of the Atomic Energy Commission, who feared that many Americans might henceforth come to dismiss the bomb as just another weapon.[14]

The Soviet View

The official Soviet position toward the bomb and its effects has undergone significant change, as a number of scholars have noted. In the immediate post-war period, Soviet military doctrine, which was determined in the main by Stalin, emphasized the "constantly operating factors" such as manpower, morale and the stability of the home front. In this context, the atomic bomb, while it was condemned as a weapon of mass destruction, was not the ultimate weapon. In keeping with this doctrine *Pravda*, as late as January 1950, was asserting that only 8,400 people were affected at Hiroshima. No public mention was made of the first American explosion of a thermonuclear device at Eniwetok in November 1952. And it was not until 1954 that the first picture of the atomic mushroom cloud was published in the Soviet Union.[15]

Beginning shortly after Stalin died in 1953, a number of efforts (largely by the military) were made to cut the restrictive bonds of "Stalinist military science" and, somewhat belatedly, to adapt to the world of nuclear weapons. Between 1953 and 1957 a debate took place in the pages of Soviet publications which, for all its textual obscurity, indicated to some Kremlinologists that a new school of Soviet strategic thinking had arisen to challenge the conventional wisdom.[16] One of the most articulate spokesmen

14 See "Atomic Bomb Hysteria," *Reader's Digest* (February, 1946), pp. 82-97. For an account of popular attitudes towards atomic energy, see also "Getting Used to the Bomb," *St. Louis Star-Times*, September 8, 1945. Lilienthal wrote to scientist Henry Winnee of this editorial: "I very much fear this is just what a large percentage of our people are doing . . ." Lilienthal to Winnee, September 18, 1945, Correspondence File, Lilienthal MSS. See also Lilienthal to Clar Clifford, December 14, 1948, *ibid*.

15 According to Raymond Garthoff, a long-time student of Soviet military affairs and former U.S. Ambassador to Bulgaria, "not a single article on atomic energy or atomic weapons is known to have appeared in the period from 1947 through 1953 in the Soviet military daily and periodical press, open or restricted in circulation." See his *Soviet Strategy in the Nuclear Age* (New York: Praeger, 1958), p. 67.

16 Herbert Dinerstein has sought to explain the doctrinal discussions of the 1950s as a reflection of internal infighting over the adequacy of Soviet strategic expenditures

of this "new school" was the late Major General Nikolai Talensky, editor of the influential military journal *Military Thought*. He argued that the advent of nuclear weapons, particularly the hydrogen bomb which had just appeared on the Soviet scene, had fundamentally altered the nature of warfare. The sheer destructiveness of these weapons was such that one could no longer talk of a socialist strategy automatically overcoming the strategy of the capitalist countries. In the oblique way in which Soviet debates on issues of great import are invariably conducted, General Talensky was saying in effect that perhaps, after all, war had ceased to represent a viable instrument of state policy.[17]

But more important than Talensky's controversial utterances were the speeches delivered by leading Soviet politicians in the winter of 1953-54. These seemed to support the theses advanced by President Eisenhower in his address before the United Nations of December 1953 — namely, that nuclear war could spell the demise of civilization. In his address delivered on March 12, 1954, Stalin's immediate successor, Georgi Malenkov, echoed the sentiments earlier expressed by Eisenhower. Malenkov said that a new world war would unleash a holocaust which, "with the present means of warfare, means the destruction of world civilization."[18]

This attack on the traditional thinking of the Soviet military establishment triggered a furious reaction. The military leaders of the Red Army were not about to let the Soviet armed forces be relegated to the status of a militia whose principal task was averting war rather than winning it. In the view of several historians of the period, Malenkov's unorthodox views

---

and the influence of this issue on the struggle for power within the Politburo. See his *War and the Soviet Union: Nuclear Weapons and the Revolution in Soviet Military and Political Thinking* (New York: Praeger, 1959), p. 91.

17 Talensky's "heresy" brought an immediate and vehement response from serving Soviet officers, who rushed into the military press to criticize him by name — a move that rarely happens to Soviet general officers. They did not, however, take issue with Talensky's views so much as they did to his having stated them in public. Such loose talk, his opponents made clear, was tactless in the extreme because it dangerously undermined the case for a strong and prosperous military establishment in the U.S.S.R. For instance, General K. Bochkarev, Deputy Commandant of the Soviet General Staff Academy, argued that if ideas like those expressed by Talensky took hold, "the armed forces of the socialist states ... will not be able to set for themselves the goal of defeating imperialism and the global nuclear war which it unleashes and the mission of attaining victory in it, and our military science should not even work out a strategy for the conduct of war since the latter has lost its meaning and its significance ... *In this case, the very call to raise the combat readiness of our armed forces and improve their capability to defeat any aggressor is senseless.*" (Italics mine). See Andrew Cockburn, *opus cit.*, p. 214.

18 *Pravda*, March 13, 1954.

on war may well have contributed to his downfall.[19] In any case, his dismissal in February 1955 as party leader was accompanied by a barrage of press denunciations of the idea that war had suddenly become unfeasible.

There are some indications that the chief rival of Malenkov — Khrushchev — capitalized on the discontent within the military establishment to form with it an alliance with whose help he eventually rose to power. The successful military counterattack appears to have been led by the World War II hero Marshall Georgi Zhukov, whom Khrushchev made his Minister of Defense and brought into the Presidium (as the Politburo was then called).

The guidelines of Soviet nuclear policy during this period of Khrushchev's tenure were formulated during 1955-57 under the leadership of Zhukov himself. They resulted in the rejection of the notion that there existed an "absolute weapon."

During the late 1950s, the Soviet position on nuclear policy changed once again. This was in large part due to Khrushchev's solemn conviction that nuclear war had become politically useless, since there would be no victors and the damage would be so vast and devastating that organized society would cease to exist.[20]

In the aftermath of the Cuban Missile crisis of October 1962, Khrushchev painted this grim picture:[21]

According to the calculations of scientists the very first blow [in a thermonuclear war] would destroy between 700 and 800 million people. All large cities, not only in the United States and the Soviet Union, the two leading nuclear powers, but also in France, Britain, Germany, Italy, China, Japan, and many other countries would be razed to the ground and destroyed. The consequences of atomic-hydrogen bomb war would persist during the lives of many generations and would result in disease, death, and would cripple the human race.

"The atomic bomb," stated the Soviet Party Central Committee in an open letter of July 14, 1963 to the Communist Party of China "does not adhere to the class principle; it destroys everybody within range of its devastating force."[22]

In this context, a study undertaken in the mid-1960s by Thomas W.

---

19 See for instance, Leon Goure et al., *The Role of Nuclear Forces in Current Soviet Strategy* (Coral Gables: University of Miami, 1974), p. xv.

20 See Roman Kolkowicz, "Strategic Parity and Beyond: Soviet Perspectives," *World Politics*, (April, 1971), p. 437. In 1959. Khrushchev remarked that he did "not trust appraisals of generals on questions of strategic importance." Quoted in Lawrence Freedman, *The Evolution of Nuclear Strategy* (New York: St. Martin's Press, 1983), p. 262.

21 *Pravda,* January 17, 1963.

22 *Pravda,* July 14, 1963.

Wolfe, a senior staff member of the Rand Corporation and a faculty member of George Washington University, is worth citing. In analyzing the Sino-Soviet dispute of that era, he wrote: "The Soviet Union ... has charged that the Chinese fail to appreciate the destructive consequences of a nuclear war and have in effect courted it by being willing to provoke the United States. Peking in turn has retorted that the Soviet leaders ... are so afraid of nuclear war that they have allowed this fact to paralyze their policy."[23]

Following Khrushchev's removal as First Secretary in 1964, the "collective leadership" of Party Leader Leonid Brezhnev, Prime Minister Aleksei Kosygin and President Nikolai Podgorny made a number of important changes in Soviet nuclear strategy. However, they did retain the central assumption of Khrushchev's policy that a nuclear war would be a catastrophe for both the East and West.[24]

If the political leadership in the Soviet Union seems to have been the first to recognize the devastating effects of nuclear warfare, there were signs in the 1960s that a number of military men were now willing to acknowledge this reality. For instance, in 1968, Major General L. Bochkarev stated in a confidential Soviet military journal that "it is inadmissible" to ignore the conclusions of scientists on the catastrophic effects of the use of "even a part" of the vast existing nuclear stockpiles.[25]

Just as U.S. officials were observing the evolution of Soviet policy on this important issue, Soviet authorities were following trends in the United States. Writing in 1971, G.A. Arbatov, Director of the USA Institute in the Soviet Union, noted: "Americans today do not doubt the fact that [thermonuclear war] would be suicidal for the American people. The conclusion that a world thermonuclear war has become a 'useless' instrument

---

23 See Wolfe's *The Soviet Union and the Sino-Soviet Dispute* (Calif.: The Rand Corporation, 1965), pp. 16-22. In a famous interview with Edgar Snow in 1965, Mao Tse-tung described how he went to the trouble of reading reports of an investigation of the effects of hydrogen bomb tests conducted over the Bikini Islands in the South Pacific in the early 1950s. Mao became almost lyrical in describing how research workers in 1959 found "mice scampering about and fish swimming in the streams ... foliage ... flourishing, and birds ... twittering in the trees" and vegetation so thick they had to "cut paths through the undergrowth." Although things might have been problematical for a year or two, Mao claimed, "nature had gone on." However, Mao was incorrect. Nature had not quite gone on as he said. Subsequent studies revealed significant radiation effects among some of the people of the islands and lingering dangers from radiation still affecting the habitat. See Robert J. Lifton and Richard Falk, *Indefensible Weapons: The Political and Psychological Case against Nuclearism* (New York: Basic Books, 1982), p. 75.

24 *Ibid.*

25 See L. Bochkarev, "The Question of the Sociological Aspect of the Struggle Against the Forces of Aggression and War," *Voyennaya mysl'*, No. 9 (September, 1968), pp. 8-9.

of policy is now shared by *most* representatives of the ruling circles as well."²⁶

Since the early 1980s, Soviet officials and political leaders have been unanimous in addressing the issue of the devastating effects of nuclear war. The official Soviet policy in this regard did not change during the fifteen-month tenure of Yuri Andropov. And when Andropov died in early 1984, Konstantin Cherenko moved quickly to affirm this policy.

Studying the Effects of Nuclear Weapons

The atomic bombs dropped on Hiroshima and Nagasaki in August 1945 brought home some of the awesome consequences of nuclear warfare. The Hiroshima bomb that killed between 100,000 and 200,000 people was a fission device of some 12 kilotons yield.²⁷ A modern thermonuclear warhead uses a device about as large as the Hiroshima bomb as the trigger — or "match" — for the fusion reaction.

The immediate consequences of a single thermonuclear weapon explosion have been documented since the early 1950s. They are thermal radiation, prompt neutrons and gamma rays, blast and fires.²⁸ Here one should note the experience gained from the Castle/Bravo test that was conducted on February 28, 1954. This device was the largest nuclear weapon ever detonated by the United States. Before it was set off at Bikini Island in the South Pacific, it was expected to explode with an energy equivalent to about eight million tons of TNT. However, as the U.S. government reported, it produced almost twice that explosive power — equivalent to 15 million tons of TNT.

If the power of the bomb was unexpected, so were many of its aftereffects.²⁹ For one thing, there was the unexpected contamination of 7,000 miles of the Pacific Ocean. This surprising development illustrated how even the most limited use of nuclear weapons by one side could produce casualties on a colossal scale — far beyond the "local" effects of

---

26 See G.A. Arbatov, "A Step in the Interests of Peace," *SShA*, No. 11 (November, 1971).

27 It should be noted that the casualty figures for the bombing of Hiroshima and Nagasaki are in dispute.

28 See Samuel Glasstone and Philip J. Dolan, *The Effects of Nuclear War*, 3rd ed. (Washington, D.C.: Department of Defense, 1977).

29 According to one U.S. scientist who talked with a member of the scientific community at Los Alamos, the only nuclear nuclear weapons effect not recognized in 1945 was EMP. The Theory Divisions's predicted yield turned out to be fairly accurate.

blast and fire alone. As Bernard and Fawn Brodie wrote in their classic study *From Crossbow to H-Bomb:* "Until the facts about fallout were released, it was widely believed that while populations in large cities were likely to be destroyed during war, those in smaller towns and in rural areas would remain relatively safe. It is now common knowledge that fallout — the radioactive debris of the materials of the bomb — affects an extraordinary large area, and that the fallout of many bombs can overlap and increase the intensity of the radiation."[30]

A number of other surprises were encountered in September 1962, when a nuclear device was detonated 250 miles above Johnson Island. This test produced what was probably man's most extensive modification of the global environment to date.[31] The 1.4 megaton burst produced an artificial belt of charged particles trapped in the earth's magnetic field. Approximately, 98 percent of these particles were removed by natural processes after the first year. However, traces could still be detected six to seven years later. At the time, a number of satellites in low orbit suffered severe electronic damage resulting in malfunctions and early failure. Also, severe electrical malfunctions occured in Hawaii, some 800 miles away. As Peter Pringle and William Arkin report, "Strings of street lights in Oahu went out and hundreds of burglar alarms in Honolulu were set off when the (electromagnetic) pulse overloaded their circuits."[32]

As a result of this test, it became clear that man had the power to make long-term changes in his near-space environment with the detonation of but a few of the many weapons in his rapidly expanding nuclear arsenal.

The EMP Effect

If scientific interest in the effect of electromagnetic pulse (EMP) was stimulated by American nuclear tests conducted in the early 1960s,[33] this

---

30 Bernard and Fawn Brodie, *From Crossbow to H-Bomb* (Bloomington: Indiana University Press, 1973), p. 267.

31 In 1961, Soviet bomb tests consisted of a series of huge explosions, with many in the ten-megaton class and one with a yield of fifty-seven megatons. The fifty-seven-megaton bomb was carefully designed to produce a relatively small quantity of fallout. Since that time, the trend in both the U.S. and the U.S.S.R. has been toward lower yields, although the Soviet weapons program has moved less rapidly than that of the United States.

32 See Peter Pringle *et al.*, *SIOP: The Secret U.S. Plan for Nuclear War* (New York: W.W. Norton, 1983), p. 230.

33 In 1958, a physicist named Nicholas Christofilos, who was employed at the Lawrence Radiation Laboratory at Livermore, California, calculated that if a nuclear

phenomenon and its ramifications for nuclear deterrence were not fully appreciated by strategic thinkers until sometime later. Only recently has EMP begun to receive some of the public attention it deserves. Unfortunately, the publicity given to the prospect of a nuclear winter arising out of a threshold nuclear exchange has tended to obscure this extremely significant aftereffect.

Briefly, EMP represents a short but intense electrical discharge that can do serious damage to all kinds of electronic circuitry, thus posing a threat to unprotected weaponry and computers. Electromagnetic pulse could, for instance, wipe clean all computer memories that are in range of the electromagnetic effects. EMP has an extremely rapid "rise-time" — ten to twenty nanoseconds and lasts only about a microsecond (one millionth of a second). Technically, this effect is not generated at a single spot like a lightning bolt but is induced simultaneously throughout an entire electrical grid.[34]

All nuclear explosions generate some EMP. However, only bursts high above the atmosphere give rise to pulses whose effects extend beyond the radius of local devastation. As Janet Raloff points out, a blast fifty miles up would affect an area with a radius of six hundred miles. A burst one hundred miles up would affect an area with a radius of nine hundred miles. *A single nuclear detonation centered over the continental U.S. at an altitude of some two hundred miles would cover the entire nation as well as portions of Canada and Mexico with EMP.*[35]

Given the vulnerability of electrical transmission lines and electronic hardware to the destructive effects of rapid voltage surges, a series of EMP pulses would have devastating effects on both civilian and military communications systems. In the view of one expert, John Steinbruner, "several EMP weapons exploded high over the United States could shut down the national power grid for hours or even days and incapacitate large segments of the military command-and-control network."[36]

The chaos-producing effects of electromagnetic pulse have been known for some time by scientists and military communications specialists. But only in the last few years has the American military begun to take major steps to shield or "harden" C^3I systems and other vital electronic equip-

> weapon were fired a few hundred miles above the earth, but within its magnetic field, high energy particles from the detonation would become trapped in that magnetism and a series of electromagnetic pulses would be produced.

34 See Eric J. Lerner, "Electromagnetic Pulse: Potential Crippler," *IEEE Spectrum* (May, 1981), p. 42.

35 Janet Raloff, "EMP: A Sleeping Electronic Dragon," *Science News*, May 9, 1981.

36 John Steinbruner, "Strategic Command and Control Vulnerabilities: Dangers and Remedies," *Orbis*, Vol. 26, No. 4 (Winter, 1983), p. 953.

ment that are considered most critical. The Reagan Administration, in particular, with its emphasis on developing a nuclear war fighting capability that would allow the U.S. to "prevail" in a nuclear war, has been concerned that a dedicated strike by the Soviet Union against the American C^3I network would enhance the effectiveness of a counterforce attack.

Critics are sceptical of recent efforts to pour billions of dollars into schemes that would allegedly protect the American command-and-control system from electromagnetic disruption in a nuclear exchange. They believe the steps now being taken will hardly make the C^3I network invulnerable to EMP weapons, and thus are a great waste of money and resources.

The basic problem, of course, is that since the U.S. stopped testing nuclear weapons in the atmosphere, we have not been able substantially to increase our knowledge of EMP. About the most that the Pentagon can do is simulate the effect, and this is not very satisfactory from a military planning perspective. Therefore, many questions remain unanswered about EMP, but so far there has been little public discussion of this important issue.

This unhappy situation may now begin to change with the release in August 1984 of a major report commissioned by the Defense Nuclear Agency in the Pentagon. This scientific study questioned the U.S. military's method of shielding electrical equipment against the vast pulse of electromagnetic energy that could follow a high-altitude nuclear blast.

The report was prepared by a panel from the National Research Council. It stated that a large pulse could knock out the "nerve system" of the U.S. military command system. Moreover, such a pulse could fire missiles involuntarily and could throw military and civilian computer systems into chaos.

The report maintained that the best method to shield equipment from the devastating effects of EMP was to design complete systems, called shells, to protect entire devices. The report noted that the U.S. military now relies on a system of *selective* shielding, which uses insulators and filters to protect individual components. This system's reliability was called into question by the report.[37]

---

37 See *The International Herald Tribune,* August 10, 1984.

Ozone Depletion

In 1974, the American public was made aware that nuclear war could possibly destroy the ozone layer in the stratosphere. This layer protects all living things from ultra-violet solar radiation that destroys protein molecules. The impact of this "finding" meant that in addition to death, destruction and radiation, extensive ozone depletion could destroy the food chain of plants and animals upon which humankind depends for survival.

In considering the global effects of nuclear war, we should never forget that, although scientists can make certain projections about these effects, it is likely that interactions could take place among these effects so that one type of damage would couple with another to produce new and unexpected hazards. According to a study conducted almost ten years ago by the U.S. Arms Control and Disarmament Agency, the "uncertainties that remain are of such magnitude that of themselves they must serve as a further deterrent to the use of nuclear weapons."[38]

The net effect of all this is that not only the inhabitants of the combatant countries, but virtually the whole population of the world would be the victims of a nuclear war. Therein lies the radical change which nuclear weapons have introduced into the whole concept of warfare.

The Uselessness of Nuclear Weapons

The general uselessness of nuclear weapons is coming to be realized more by individuals both inside and outside government.

As former Ambassador Harland Cleveland, Director of the University of Minnesota's Hubert H. Humphrey Institute of Public Affairs, recently wrote: "Nuclear weapons have turned out to be 'ultimate' in an unanticipated sense of the word. No nation's military planners have been able, in 38 years, to think up a way to use such huge explosions with such pervasive aftereffects in ways that are clearly advantageous to their side. This may be the most important thing about nuclear weapons in the 1980s: that they are militarily unusable."[39]

---

38 U.S. Arms Control and Disarmament Agency, *Worldwide Effects of Nuclear War ... Some Perspectives* (Washington, D.C.: 1975). For an earlier useful study see Atomic Energy Commission, *The Effects of Nuclear Weapons* (Washington, D.C.: U.S. Government Printing Office, 1962).

39 Harland Cleveland, "A Boulder in the Road," *The Christian Science Monitor*, January 18, 1984. This view is also shared by Melvin Laird, Secretary of Defense in the Nixon Administration. According to the Washington *Post* of April 12, 1982,

People who study deeply the effects of using nuclear weapons seem to conclude it is next to impossible to develop a nuclear scenario in which the "solution" is not worse than the problem. As Ambassador Cleveland observes, "I had this experience myself when I worked for four years (1965-69) as the U.S. representative on the North Atlantic Council (NATO's political board of directors)." As a practicing "war gamer, I failed to figure out how either the Soviets or our European allies could believe that the U.S. president would breach the nuclear threshold in response to a conventional attack in Western Europe."

This observation might surprise a lot of people unfamiliar with the way statesmen really think about the utility or, better, disutility of nuclear weapons. But as President Kennedy's former Special Assistant for National Security Affairs McGeorge Bundy wrote as early as 1969:[40]

"There is an enormous gulf between what political leaders really think about nuclear weapons and what is assumed in complex calculations of relative "advantage" in simulated strategic war. Think tank analysts can set levels of "acceptable" damage well up in the hundreds of millions of lives... They are in an unreal world. In the real world of real political leaders — whether here or in the Soviet Union — a decision that would bring even one hydrogen bomb on one city of one's own country would be recognized in advance as a catastrophic blunder; ten bombs in ten cities would be a disaster beyond history; and a hundred bombs on one hundred cities are unthinkable."

Ambassador Cleveland notes that a number of former high level U.S. government officials have recently been saying essentially the same thing. Henry Kissinger said something like this in a speech in London not long after he left office as Secretary of State. Admiral Noel Gaylor has often spoken about the unusability of nuclear weapons since he stepped down as Commander-in-Chief of the U.S. Pacific Fleet. Most recently, Robert McNamara told an Aspen Institute arms control seminar that he would under no conceivable circumstances have given the order to fire a nuclear missile.

In his recent headline-grabbing article in *Foreign Affairs*,[41] which caused quite an uproar in Europe, McNamara was more cautious, but still he said more or less the same thing. The most relevant part of his statement is quoted below:

> Laird said: "A worldwide zero nuclear option with adequate verification should now be our goal ... These weapons ... are useless for military purposes."

40 McGeorge Bundy, "To Cap the Volcano," *Foreign Affairs*, (October, 1969), pp. 9-10.
41 Robert McNamara, "The Military Role of Nuclear Weapons: Perceptions and Misperceptions," *Foreign Affairs*, Vol. 62, No. 1 (Fall, 1983), pp. 59-80.

Having spent seven years as Secretary of Defense dealing with the problems unleashed by the initial nuclear chain reaction 40 years ago, I do not believe we can avoid serious and unacceptable risk of nuclear war until we recognize — and until we base all our military plans, defense budgets, weapon deployments, and arms negotiations on the recognition — that nuclear weapons serve no military purpose whatsoever. They are totally useless — except only to deter one's opponent from using them.
This is my view today. It was my view in the early 1960s. At that time, in long private conversations with successive Presidents — Kennedy and Johnson — I recommended, without qualification, that they never initiate, under any circumstances, the use of nuclear weapons. I believe they accepted my recommendation.

The implications of this revelation seem enormous. Here the man who was identified with the development of U.S. nuclear weapons systems in the 1960s was secretly urging his presidents never to initiate any kind of nuclear exchange. When many old associates read this statement, they raised their brows. Many allied officials were simply astonished.

As some West German commentators have pointed out, the McNamara statement in *Foreign Affairs* is paradoxical. How can one side hope to deter the other side with weapons that are patently useless? As Ambassador Cleveland states: "Deterrence, we have been saying for three decades, consists in the leaders of each superpower being credibly uncertain about what the leaders of the other superpower would do *if*." However, if, as McNamara apparently believes, the use of nuclear weapons would be tantamount to committing suicide, the deterrent posture of the United States has in reality been a bluff — and a dangerous one at that. Or so the critics would argue.

Ambassador Cleveland takes a more positive view of the situation. "In the old Western novels people were sometimes hogtied in a fashion that strangled them if they struggled too hard to escape. Are the nuclear superpowers with their big strategic weapons now in a similar fix? And if so, is this maybe good news for humankind? Could we then get our eye back on the ball — the whole globe, not only the strategic nuclear threat to it?"

Summary

Proponents of deterrence generally focus on one major possible explanation for the fact that no nuclear weapons have been used in warfare since 1945, even though many wars — some involving the United States — have been waged around the world. However, the foregoing analysis suggests that there might be another reason, among others, why nuclear weapons have not been used since at least the mid-1960s (when enough megatonnage existed for Sagan's threshold) which has nothing to do with our deterrent posture. This is the knowledge by the Soviet leadership that a Soviet nuclear strike would be suicide — *even if there was no retaliatory strike by the United States.* As Carl Sagan and Ehrlich have convincingly shown, an attack by the U.S.S.R., using only a small fraction of its existing nuclear warheads, could literally mean the death of the planet and the extinction of the human race. The present French *force de frappe*, said to target Soviet cities exclusively, may itself be adequate to trigger a global nuclear winter.[42]

To put it another way, which approximates the jargon of strategic theorists, a major pre-emptive strike might *in itself* wreak unacceptable damage on the attacker whether the other side retaliated or not. If further study of this "boomerang effect" (Harland Cleveland's words) shows this clearly enough, it might be that the deterring "second strike" is actually contained in the pre-emptive strike. Thus, such a self-inflicted second strike is not "mutual suicide." It is suicide.[43]

---

42 See Carl Sagan's letter in "Comment and Correspondence," *Foreign Affairs*, Vol. 62, No. 4 (Spring, 1984), p. 1001.

43 "Your logic is good," observes Ambassador Hillenbrand, "but I do not think you have established that deterrence is not operative as a causal factor in the superpower relationship. The possible boomerang effect may at *times* also be an operative factor. I come back to my basic definition of deterrence as a *sufficient degree of uncertainty* about what might happen if one resorts to force to make a rational person desist from using force.

> Dig a hole, cover it with a couple of doors and then throw three feet of dirt on top ... It's the dirt that does it ... if there are enough shovels to go around, everybody's going to make it.
>
> T.K. Jones, Deputy Under Secretary of Defense for Strategic and Theater Nuclear Forces

XIII. CIVIL DEFENSE

Since the findings of Carl Sagan and Paul Ehrlich were widely publicized in the fall of 1983, there has been heated debate about their implications for civil defense (CD). Some critics of civil defense find in the studies the conclusion that no one can survive a nuclear war. Thus, any civil defense program is utterly useless, they say. Those in favor of a sustained civil defense effort dispute this. They generally argue that it is "socially irresponsible" not to provide for civil defense, which might also help deter nuclear war. In this chapter, an attempt will be made to explore the arguments for and against CD, analyze Soviet plans in this regard and examine critically the implications of civil defense for deterrence.

The Case for Civil Defense

One of the most forceful cases for civil defense has been stated by Edward Teller, a foreign-born physicist who played a central role in the development of the hydrogen bomb. Teller, who believes that the major problems in building an effective shelter system are human, not technical, is now advising the Reagan Administration.

Recently, the senior research fellow at Stanford University's Hoover Institution summarized the major arguments in favor of elaborate civil defense measures. But he also stated flatly that some "40 million Americans are likely to survive a worst-case, large-scale nuclear attack, even without any protective measures."[1]

---

1 Edward Teller, "The 'Socially Responsible' Course is Civil Defense," *The Minneapolis Star and Tribune*, January 5, 1984. Fred Kaplan tells the story of Teller's

ROUNDOUT TASK 4

RECOGNIZE AND PROTECT SELF AGAINST A NUCLEAR HAZARD
(TASK 031-503-1005)

INSTRUCTIONS TO THE SOLDIER: YOU WILL BE REQUIRED TO RECOGNIZE AND PROTECT YOURSELF AGAINST A NUCLEAR HAZARD. YOU HAVE BEEN TOLD TO EXPECT A NUCLEAR ATTACK IN YOUR AREA. THERE IS NO COVER NEAR YOUR LOCATION SO YOU START WALKING TOWARD A FIGHTING POSITION APPROXIMATELY 50 METERS AWAY. A NUCLEAR BOMB JUST EXPLODED IN THAT DIRECTION.

ROUNDOUT TASK 4   PASS ____ FAIL ____

PERFORMANCE MEASURES: (Sequence is scored.)
(Refer to figure 4-1.)

1. Immediately fall face down in the direction opposite the blast.
2. Place hands and weapon under body.

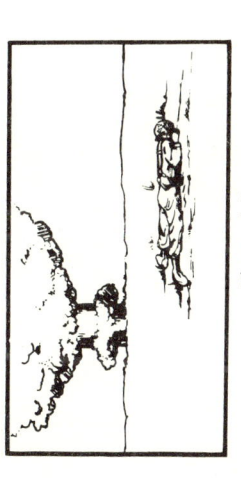

Figure 4-1.

STANDARD: To receive a GO on this test you must pass all performance measures.

GO ☐   NO GO ☐

WAYS TO PROTECT YOURSELF AGAINST A NUCLEAR EXPLOSION

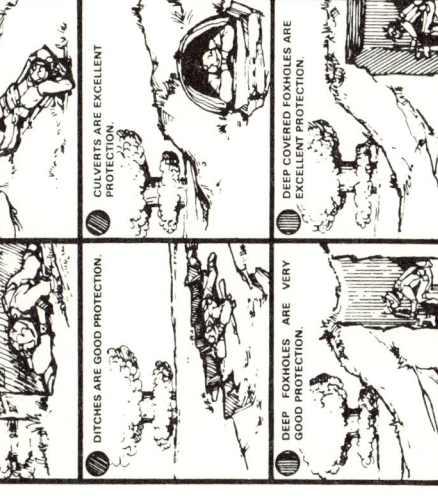

Figure 4-2.

NOTE: An armored vehicle is excellent protection.

Source: Soldier's Manual Army Testing TRADOC Pamphlet No. 600-4, October 1981.

Teller maintains that the "total absence of civil-defense preparations, the public's all-but-complete ignorance of the realities of nuclear war and the consequent potential for an exacerbation of a nuclear tragedy are among the most dangerous characteristics of our present defense effort." While civil defense "cannot dispel the horror of a nuclear war," he contends, "it could save millions of lives and prevent unnecessary suffering." The "father of the H-bomb" further insists that "civil defense planning could reduce the number of American dead from 150 million to 50 million."[2]

Teller downplays the problems associated with the mass evacuation of cities. He says: "We experience considerable 'evacuation' of our cities in a few disorderly hours every holiday weekend — without benefit of planning or one-way exit traffic on major highways." In his view, that experience "indicates that our cities' populations could be evacuated voluntarily in less than 24 hours." Areas supplied with suitable survival plans as well as food, water, shelter, medical goods and tools "could be prepared at reasonable cost." Moreover, survivable education and communication facilities, "sufficient to save millions of lives, could be provided for less than $ 5 per person." All this could "be available in little more than a year, if Congress were willing," he argues.

Since "another war would be the greatest disaster of this war-ridden century," Teller states, "we need to take every opportunity to deter it." The "deterrent effect of a civil-defense program that could be implemented in a year would help to prevent war," he maintains. Its "absence only adds to the probability of war."

attempt in the 1960s to influence the Kennedy Administration on this matter. On November 29, 1961, Teller paid a visit to the White House to try and persuade Jerry Wiesner, Kennedy's science adviser, of the virtues of civil defense. "In his steely Hungarian accent, his thick eyebrows impressively jumping about," Teller narrated his scenario for a massive civil-defense program. "First we will start with fallout shelters," he explained, "but that won't cover everybody, so we will then have to go to blast shelters. But that won't cover everybody, either, so finally we will have to build fire shelters. And if the Russians build bigger bombs, then we will have to dig deeper."

In a "perverse sense," Kaplan recounts, "Wiesner was delighted by this display. In the past few years, Wiesner had undergone a dramatic transformation from a hardline hawk to a passionate advocate of arms control and disarmament . . . he thought the shelter idea was dangerous and self-deluding nonsense." Wiesner, according to Kaplan, "thought that Teller's little lecture was mad, and he knew that any proponent who heard it would reexamine his own position and that anyone still unsure about civil defense would tip decisively to Wiesner's position against it." So with this in mind, Wiesner reportedly encouraged Teller to speak out in support of civil defense. See Kaplan, *The Wizards of Armageddon* (New York: Simon & Schuster, 1983), p. 313.

2 For other estimates, see *Physics and Society*, Vol. 13, No. 2 (April, 1984), pp. 3-4.

Teller points out that other countries have embarked on "considerable civil-defense programs." Here he lists Sweden, Switzerland, China, the Soviet Union and Israel. "Do we not value American lives?," Teller queries. "Must all our deterrence be based on threatening others?"[3]

The Case Against Civil Defense

Perhaps the most forceful case against civil defense is developed in the publication *Freeze: How You Can Help Prevent Nuclear War*. This book was published in 1982 with the backing of Senator Edward M. Kennedy, one of the leading figures in Congress who is opposed to the spiraling arms race and sees, as a viable alternative, the implementation of a freeze on nuclear weapons. The thesis of this book in the area of civil defense is stated neatly by Averell Harriman, a former U.S. Ambassador to the Soviet Union and adviser to five presidents. He declares in the foreword: The truth of the matter is "in a nuclear war you can run, but you cannot hide. Effective civil defense in a nuclear war is utterly impractical."[4]

Why is effective civil defense impractical in the eyes of Senator Kennedy and others? There are several major reasons. First there is the matter of developing adequate shelters. The most ambitious of those kinds of shelters envisioned for civilian populations include food and water for a week or two, modest heating capabilities, rudimentary sanitation and air filtration facilities. However, there would be no provisions for the psychological burdens of a prolonged stay below ground with unknown climatic and ecological consequences developing overhead. Moreover, the kinds of shelters necessary for extended stays at the expected lethal radiation level, subfreezing temperatures and pyrotoxins would have to be very much

---

[3] One former U.S. official would interject here: "Europeans should concentrate on civil defense for conventional war, which is far from satisfactory. This would also provide protection against nuclear weapons. I doubt, however, that it is useful to try to protect against nuclear war, other than to have evacuation plans. In event of a serious crisis, at some point people will evacuate the cities, no matter what the policy is. So governments should be ready for this. I have recently suggested to a friend who is a senior official in WHO that, instead of wringing their hands about the effects of a nuclear war, they should be planning for a nuclear accident or unauthorized firing. Eventually, this will happen, and it can be planned for. A single nuclear explosion is certainly something that the health authorities of the world could cope with. While a lot of people would die, the suffering of those who were not killed immediately could be alleviated and the number of deaths reduced. Today, the whole thing would have to be improvised."

[4] Quoted in Edward M. Kennedy *et al.*, *Freeze: How You Can Help Prevent Nuclear War* (New York: Bantam Books, 1982), pp. xii-xiii.

more elaborate than commonly thought. But for most families, even in the relatively affluent U.S., such shelters, able to service individual families or groups of people, are too expensive. Then there is the consideration that the construction of major government facilities for civilian populations would be tremendously expensive as well as potentially destabilizing. Lastly, the perceived inequity would be great between government leaders and (in some cases) their families, who would be provided elaborate shelters, and the bulk of the civilian population which would be unable even to afford minimally adequate shelters.

The specific shelter program aside, the skeptics argue the tasks of any civil defense organization would be awesome and, if possible at all, extremely difficult to implement. These measures would include giving first aid, providing *uncontaminated* food and water, furnishing transportation, ensuring the continuity of government and burying the millions of dead. Something like three-quarters of the American population lives in or near cities. In the cities themselves there is generally only about one week's supply of food. To be sure, it is conceivable that enough of present grain storage might survive to sustain, on some level, the survivors for more than a year. However, with the breakdown of civil order and transportation systems that could be expected to accompany the cold, darkness and fallout in a nuclear attack, these stores would become largely inaccessible. Thus, vast numbers of those "lucky" enough to survive the initial death and destruction of a nuclear attack would soon starve to death.

Furthermore, the sub-freezing temperatures that might well prevail in the aftermath of nuclear war would probably mean, in many cases, the unavailability of uncontaminated water. Since the ground would tend to be frozen to a depth of approximately a yard in these projected conditions, the millions of dead bodies would likely not be buried for a long while even if the civil organization to do so existed. In addition, fuel supplies to melt the snow and ice would be relatively scarce, and icy surfaces and freshly fallen snow would most likely be contaminated by radioactivity and pyrotoxins.

Finally, the medical reality of a nuclear war would be catastrophic. In the view of Howard Hiatt, Dean of the Harvard School of Public Health, the effects of radiation aside, "Any nuclear war would inevitably cause death, disease, and suffering of epidemic proportions." And "effective medical intervention on any realistic scale would be impossible."[5]

In short, critics of civil defense such as the "Physicians for Social Responsibility" condemn the policy of the U.S. government which has

---

5 Hearings before the Subcommittee on Health and Scientific Research of the Committee on Labor and Human Resources, United States Senate, June 19, 1980.

dissolved, in their view, the line between fantasy and sober assessment. They deplore the decision that has led the Administration, rather than build upon the reality that a nuclear exchange with the Soviet Union would rend the fabric of American society, to spread the news that even nuclear war could be tolerated. There "is no effective civil defense" these physicians maintain. To believe otherwise is to entertain a dangerous illusion.[6]

Experience with Civil Defense in the 1960s

During the 1950s the debate over civil defense was sparked by the writings of Herman Kahn, founder of the Hudson Institute and famous as the author of *Thinking the Unthinkable* and *On Thermonuclear War.* He considered "crazy" the notion that nuclear war was suicidal. In his view, people failed to distinguish between an "incredibly unpleasant experience" and a situation which one could survive. "If 20 million Americans were killed," he opined, "there'd be 200 million survivors."

Kahn did not believe that nuclear war would be the end of the world. He maintained that with an adequate shelter program and certain other civil defense measures more than half of all Americans could survive the blast and radiation in a nuclear war.

To be sure, to Kahn and some others like him, the purpose of a gigantic civil-defense effort was not so much to protect civilians against a Soviet pre-emptive strike. "The whole purpose of the system," he wrote, "is to enable the U.S. to take much firmer positions" in hot and cold wars, to permit the President to engage in pre-emptive strikes ("Type II Deterrence") and tit-for-tat threats ("Type III Deterrence").

"Any power that can evacuate a high percentage of its urban population to protection," Kahn noted, "is in a much better position to bargain than one which cannot do this." Indeed, the 1960s would be so racked with tension that, to Kahn's way of thinking, it was "perfectly conceivable ... that the U.S. might have to evacuate two or three times every decade."

It was this kind of hyperbole that apparently provoked mathematician James R. Newman to write in a review of *On Thermonuclear War* for *Scientific American:* "This is a moral tract on mass murder: how to plan it, how to commit it, how to get away with it, how to justify it."[7]

---

6   See Louis René Beres, "Subways to Armageddon," in Suzanne P. Ogden (ed.), *World Politics 84/85* (Guilford, Ct.: Dushkin Publishing Group, 1984).

7   Kahn reportedly was appalled by this review, believing it grossly misinterpreted his viewpoint. So he wrote to the editor of *Scientific American,* asking for approval to print a rebuttal. However, Kahn was turned down. "I do not think that

For some time many of Kahn's ideas had great impact on U.S. government planners. In 1957, the Presidentially-appointed Gaither Panel recommended a massive shelter program to Eisenhower. However, after extensive review by the National Security Council and the President, the proposal was rejected. Most importantly, it was judged that the program would not save enough lives to justify its costs. Also, there was the consideration that any survivors of a nuclear exchange would emerge into a totally devastated society lacking most of the support systems required to keep them alive even if they escaped immediate injury. President Eisenhower summed up his feelings on the matter in a few cryptic remarks: "You can't have that war," he said. "The living would envy the dead. There would not be enough bulldozers available to scrape the bodies off the street."[8]

When John F. Kennedy became President in 1961, he revived government interest in the moribund American civil defense program. One of his major initiatives in this area was to support the creation of a new, greatly expanded office for civil defense in the Department of Defense. However, when the astronomical costs of developing a "meaningful" shelter program were fully realized, most of his early enthusiasm vanished.

Kennedy was also eventually impressed with the argument that the development of a massive shelter program at this time might be misinterpreted by the Soviet leadership. Instead of seeing such a program as defensive in nature, the Russians might read into it an offensive capability. Specifically, Moscow might view extensive American civil defense efforts to provide a limited measure of protection for its citizens in the event of a nuclear war as evidence of a decision by the Administration to consider seriously the possibility of launching a pre-emptive nuclear strike against the U.S.S.R. In that case, the Soviet leaders might be tempted to strike first before the civil defense program was operational.

Finally, as events were to show, the way the Kennedy Administration sold the shelter program to the public created the conditions for national panic. In a sign of the moral estrangement caused by the issue, some clergymen even justified the right of heads of families to shoot down neighbors who sought to invade their shelters for the purpose of sharing them. In the end, the shelter "craze" disappeared almost as quickly as it began, but it left ugly memories.

> there is much point in thinking about the unthinkable," the editor wrote. "(S)urely it is much more profitable to think about the thinkable ... I should prefer to devote my thoughts to how nuclear war can be prevented. It is for this reason that we must decline your offer to give us your article." Quoted in Fred Kaplan, *opus cit.*, p. 228.

8 Quoted in Jennifer Leaning *et al.* (eds), *The Counterfeit Ark: Crisis Relocation for Nuclear War* (Cambridge, Mass.: Ballinger Publishing Co., 1984), p. xiii.

Civil Defense in the Reagan Administration

Recently, civil defense programs have been given new life. In January 1982, Deputy Under Secretary of Defense T. K. Jones said in a Los Angeles *Times* interview: "Everybody's going to make it [through a Soviet-American nuclear war] if there are enough shovels to go around."[9] Long an advocate of broadening the U.S. civil defense effort, Jones was arguing that deterrence would be improved if the U.S. urban population were trained to protect itself against nuclear fallout by evacuating cities and digging improvised fallout shelters in the countryside. Jones went on to suggest that the United States would recover in two to four years from a nuclear war if it had a Soviet-style civil defense.

In the eyes of some informed observers, Jones's statements were "bizarre" and "outrageous." Ambassador Harriman for one later commented: "I refuse to believe that our common sense has so diminished that we would hand over our fortune to those who say that with civil defense the economies of the United States and the Soviet Union would recover in two to four years."[10] Subsequently, Jones was threatened by the Foreign Relations Committee with a subpoena to come and repeat what he said before it. However, he insisted that his remarks were taken out of context.

A short time later, the Reagan Administration put forth a seven-year, $ 4.2 billion civil defense proposal. Generally, it was taken by critics as evidence not simply of a loose grip but of an actual intent, or at least an intolerable readiness, to countenance nuclear war.[11] "As Robert Scheer, an investigative reporter with the Los Angeles *Times*, has written in his controversial book *With Enough Shovels: Reagan, Bush and Nuclear War:* "Civil defense is the talisman of those who believe that nuclear war is survivable and, what's more, that its consequences can be dealt with strategically, morally and politically in the same manner as conventional war."[12]

With the release of National Security Council Decision Directive 26 (NSDD 26) in March 1982, the Reagan Administration codified its extensive commitment to civil defense. As Louis Rene Beres of Purdue University

---

9 Interview with Robert Scheer, Los Angeles *Times*, January 16, 1982. Jones' phrase was later adopted by Scheer as the partial title of his book on the strange attitude of some officials in the Reagan Administration to nuclear war.

10 Quoted in Edward M. Kennedy *et al., opus cit.*, pp. xii-xiii.

11 Stephen S. Rosenfeld, "Testing the Hard Line," *Foreign Affairs: America and the World* (New York: Pergamon Press, 1983), p. 506.

12 Robert Scheer, *With Enough Shovels: Reagan, Bush and Nuclear War* (New York: Random House, 1982).

writes: "NSDD 26 represents a clear commitment to a national policy of making nuclear war more "thinkable" and calls for "the survival of a substantial portion of the American people in the event of a nuclear attack." The Reagan directive envisions "survival" in a "protracted" nuclear war.[13]

Based largely on the approach taken by T. K. Jones, the Reagan Administration proceeded to develop extensive plans to resist the effects of a nuclear attack.[14] There are now "230 million identified shelter spaces," enough for every man, woman and child, with space to spare. "Crisis relocation centers" have been designated to which the inhabitants of large cities can flee. And special routes have been selected that the evacuees will use to get there. Detailed plans have been laid for the postwar functioning of the banking and postal systems (checks can be drawn on incinerated banks but express mail will be suspended). Moreover, at the first indication of an attack, the Declaration of Independence will be lowered in its case into a specially prepared nuclear blastproof vault beneath the National Archives.[15]

The backbone of the civil defense program in the Reagan Administration is crisis relocation planning (CRP). In 1983, responding to growing popular debate about the feasibility of crisis relocation and the concept of survival after a nuclear war, the Federal Emergency Management Agency (FEMA) subsumed this program under the more general category of "integrated emergency management.[16] This move was accompanied by a declaration to the effect that civil defense for nuclear war embodies disaster management strategies that are applicable to a broad range of natural and technological disasters.

Crisis relocation, of course, is not a new idea. In fact, as Jeremy J. Stone, Director of the Federation of American Scientists, points out, it was raised more than twenty years ago. Stone developed one of the first

---

13 Louis René Beres, "Subways to Armageddon," in Suzanne P. Ogden (ed.), *World Politics 84/85* (Guilford Ct.: Dushkin Publishing Group, 1984), p. 210.

14 The Kyoto Central Hotel in Japan recently promised patrons three extra weeks of life in the event of nuclear war even if the entire world should be destroyed. In recounting the rationale for this new "service" that takes the form of a huge lower basement shelter equipped to take up to 3,000 guests, hotel manager Ryuzo Kutama, stated: This is the first hotel in the world to construct a modern nuclear shelter of this proportion. The shelter was built in line with our policy of providing our guests with the best service and facilities. The shelter was built because our president, Ryuzo Ikeuchi, is pessimistic about the future. He is convinced a nuclear war will break out. See *Japan Times*, April 5, 1982.

15 Ed Zuckerman, "How Would the U.S. Survive a Nuclear War?," *Esquire*, March, 1982, p. 37.

16 Jennifer Leaning *et al.*, *The Counterfeit Ark: Crisis Relocation for Nuclear War* (Cambridge Mass.: Ballinger Publishing Co., 1984), p. xviii.

major relocation plans at the Hudson Institute. He says that he did not agree with the idea then, and the idea makes "even less sense now." This is "because in the interim the Soviet Union has moved from a few bombers and no ICBMs to 6,000 one-megaton warheads." This is more warheads than the U.S. has cities, villages and hamlets. "There are only 5,000 places in [the United States]," he states, "that have even 5,000 citizens in them." And those one-megaton warheads are more than fifty times the size of the Hiroshima bomb."[17]

The basic assumption of American civil defense planners is that any preparedness plan, to be effective, must be preceded by some period of warning. Thus, these officials, operating with the best of intentions, have hypothesized a five- to seven-day period of "heightened international tension" reminiscent of "The Day After." During this period, the President — after evaluating intelligence reports — could decide to order crisis relocation into effect. Thus, the actual time for major population evacuation (taking into account time consumed by national security deliberations) may be reduced to a bare three to five days.

About two thirds of the U.S. population is thought to reside in areas considered to be at high risk of direct thermal and blast effects. Under the Reagan Administration's plans, during the initial phase of crisis relocation, some 150 million Americans are to travel between 50 and 300 miles to designated low-risk rural areas. U.S. government officials estimate that some 80 percent of the population "at risk" will ultimately decide to take this trek. They will join the approximately 75 million people in areas of "relatively low risk" for direct effects. Together they will comprise a potential shelter population of about 190 million people.

A prominent critic of the Administration's emphasis on crisis relocation is H. Jack Geiger, Professor of Community Medicine at the School of Biomedical Education, City College, City University of New York. Geiger maintains that the plan calling for the massive evacuation of people from cities is "more than absurd; it is dangerous." He concedes that "an effective crisis relocation may 'only' require five days warning time." But he says, "people are aware that it takes only twenty-five minutes for a missile to travel in either direction between the Soviet Union and the United States, and only five to ten minutes for submarine-launched missiles."[17a]

Geiger's most devastating criticism of the relocation plan is based on its assumptions. First, the plan "assumes that there will be some definable

---

17 Jeremy J. Stone, "Reagan's Policy Can't Work," in Patrick O'Heffernan (ed.), *Defense Sense: The Search for a Rational Military Policy* Massachusetts: Ballinger Publishing Co., 1983), p. 130.

17a H. Jack Geiger, "The Medical Consequences of Nuclear War," in Patrick O'Heffernan, *opus cit.*, p. 262.

moment in the middle of a crisis when a government can rationally decide that things are serious enough to order a mass evacuation." Second, it "assumes that people will respond as they have in other disasters — hurricanes, floods and the like — that are more familiar, and will behave in an orderly and rational fashion."[18] Third, it "assumes [in Washington, D.C., for example] that people with odd-numbered license plates will leave on a given day and everybody with even-numbered license plates will calmly wait until the following day." Fourth, it "assumes that people will not rush out to fill their automobiles with gasoline and create a huge, enormous traffic jam by that effort alone." Fifth, it "assumes that civil defense planners will know in advance where the bombs will fall." Sixth, it "assumes that one can specify that there are 'safe' areas."

Seventh, it "assumes that there will be adequate shelters for protection against radioactivity, and that shelters will have food, water, and sanitation for people by the millions in the so-called host areas to which citizens are to be transported."[19] Lastly, the plan "assumes also that people in the host areas will be happy to have all of these visitors coming..."

In the view of Professor Geiger, however, the greatest danger lies in the possibility that implementing a civil defense plan for nuclear war "will increase the risk of the very event the plan is designed to protect against." As he says, if "we are involved in a major crisis with the Soviet Union, and in the middle of it we start to evacuate our people, or they start to evacuate theirs, that would be instantly detectible by each other's satellites." And the "most likely response would be for each side to decide that this is being done because 'They are going to fire their missiles and so we had better fire ours now,' or vice versa."

To Professor Geiger, civil defense plans overlook the crucial fact that it takes contemporary technology "only twenty-five or thirty minutes to *retarget* a missile." Thus, if one "really wanted to kill the maximum number of people, one would wait for the middle of the crisis relocation." Then "everybody is out on the highway and the smallest number [is] in shelters, and then [one could] retarget and attack."

There is yet another final possibility, he says. "Suppose crisis fades and is resolved and everybody goes back home. The civil defense agency's own literature acknowledges that [it] would never be able to get people in any significant number to evacuate a second time." This is "because people

---

18 Gallup polls in 1983 indicated that 69 per cent of adult Americans would follow government relocation plans in a crisis. See *The Minneapolis Tribune*, February 26, 1984.

19 One U.S. scientist who basically supports the civil defense efforts of the Reagan Administration would argue here that the point of the crisis relocation plan is to reduce the density of heavily populated areas. This will reduce casualties.

would say: 'I went through that false alarm before, I'm not going through all that again. Nothing happened. I'll take my chances."

Realizing this, enemy planners "could conceivably provoke a crisis, get the United States into crisis relocation, and then back off and have it resolved." Everybody would go back home. "Then, three weeks later an adversary could launch the real attack." Professor Geiger states that he has asked civil defense authorities how they would plan for this contingency, but they "had nothing at all to say to me because they could not think of an answer."

Theoretically, the Reagan Administration's blueprint for civil defense is designed to protect about 80 percent of the U.S. population against a Soviet attack. However, Reagan officials do not tend to stress this point. They contend the program would contribute to deterrence by making the resort to war a "credible" U.S. option.[20] They also say that their "crisis relocation program" is to be used "as a tool in the contest for strategic advantage with the Soviet Union." In this sense, the Administration insists, "it is only an attempt to match what the Russians are doing."[21]

In the view of the Reagan Administration, the Soviet civil-defense program is another indication that the Soviets are following an aggressive strategy, which might well involve the planned use of nuclear weapons.[22] Moscow's plans for evacuation and protection of industry are such — some U.S. officials argue — that the Soviets could suffer "only 5 to 25 million casualties [they suffered 20 million dead in World War II] and recover." General Daniel O. Graham puts it another way:[23]

---

20 One FEMA publication, released in December 1980, states: "With reasonable protective measures, the United States could survive nuclear attack and go on to recovery within a relatively few years." See Handout to Emergency Managers, FEMA, December 1980.

Desmond Ball concludes in his study, published by the International Institute for Strategic Studies in London, that even if the U.S. followed its current counterforce nuclear targeting plan, the destruction of civilians nonetheless would be unavoidably high. Simply by virtue of associated industrial and military targets, all of the 200 largest Soviet cities and 80% of the 886 Soviet cities with populations above 25,000 are included in U.S. war plans. Many of these cities would receive more than 10 warheads. Approximately 60 warheads would be detonated within the Moscow city limits; peak overpressures throughout the central Moscow area would be so severe . . . that not a building or tree would remain standing. See Ball, *Can Nuclear War be Controlled?* (London: The International Institute for Strategic Studies, 1981).

21 See Michael D. Wormser (ed.), *U.S. Defense Policy*, 3rd ed. (Washington, D.C.: Congressional Quarterly, Inc., 1983), p. 67.

22 See O.C. Boileau, "Soviet Civil Defense Prelude to Nuclear War," *National Defense* (May-June, 1977), p. 479.

23 Quoted in Richard J. Barnet, *Real Security: Restoring American Power in a Dangerous Decade* (New York: Touchstone Books, 1981), p. 36-37.

The Soviets evacuate their cities and hunker down. Then they move against NATO or Yugoslavia or China or the Middle East with superior conventional forces.

The United States is faced with the demand to stay out or risk nuclear exchange in which 100 million Americans would die, as opposed to 10 million Russians.

In the view of some critics, the assertion by General Graham that the Soviets think that they could limit their casualties to ten million in a nuclear war that would kill 100 million Americans is the kind of erroneous thinking that could lead the United States into a war. They note that Graham's figures are based on an analysis done by T.K. Jones in the 1970s. Since then, a number of Jones's assumptions have been seriously challenged by knowledgeable officials both inside and outside the U.S. government. In 1979, for instance, the U.S. Arms Control and Disarmament Agency examined the premises that led Jones, now a high official in the Reagan Administration, to conclude that only ten million Russians would die in a nuclear conflict with the United States. In the process, they corrected some of his most dubious assumptions, such as the idea that 61 million Russians were dispersed throughout the "uninhabitable" Arctic wastelands. The ACDA study refuted Jones' major assertion, concluding that he had seriously underestimated the likely range of Russian casualties in a nuclear war.[24]

CIA's Analysis of Soviet Civil Defense Efforts

The Reagan Administration's civil defense effort is based primarily on the fear that the Soviets have an evacuation program that would somehow embolden them. But the Central Intelligence Agency disputes this assertion. In general, CIA officials say privately that they do not believe that the Soviets have put their civil defense program in motion with the idea that they could credibly threaten to survive a nuclear war and use this as part of a nuclear war strategy. But even if this were the case, these sources note, "we could neutralize such an effort."

One high-level CIA official notes in passing that, although the Soviet civil defense program has many ardent admirers in the United States, in truth it is a lowly branch of the service. Telling indication of the overall status of Soviet civil defense is the recent appointment of the recently

---

24 See Office of Operations Analysis, U.S. Arms Control and Disarmament Agency, *Critique of T.K. Jones's Computation of Soviet Fatalities* (Washington, D.C., 1979), p. 5.

disgraced Ivan D. Yershov to be chief of staff of the civil defense troops. His perquisites are quite modest: they include one apartment in Moscow and one dacha of reportedly modest proportions on which he pays rent.

CIA officials point out in private conversations that the Soviet civil defense program has been in existence for a long time (its specific adaptation to the requirements of the nuclear era dates from 1961). But in all this time the Soviets have never conducted an evacuation drill in a major city or entirely emptied even a small town.[25] Moreover, these intelligence officials, who closely monitor the situation in the Soviet Union, say that they have found little evidence of serious efforts at mass indoctrination of the population on civil defense. (In fact, many local citizens seem to take an ironic pleasure from the observation that the acronym for "civil defense" in Russian — "grob" — drawn from the program's full title, *Grazhdanskaya Oborona*, forms the word "coffin.")[26] There is also little evidence that would suggest a comprehensive program for hardening economic installations. Thus, overall, the measures the Soviets have taken to protect their economy would not prevent massive and unacceptable damage from an attack designed to destroy Soviet facilities.[27]

Some officials in the CIA would take issue with the assertion that the much larger Soviet investment in civil defense of some $ billion a year over the past decade indicates the Soviets are preparing not only to survive, but to prevail in a nuclear war. First, these intelligence sources say that $ 2 billion is not really what the Soviets spend; it is only an estimate of what they would spend if they paid their workers at the same wage scale as American workers are paid. Second, they point to a CIA study done in 1978 which discounted the notion that the Soviets believe that their civil defense system gives them a strategic edge. In part this study reads as follows: The Soviets "cannot have confidence ... in the degree of protection their civil defenses would afford them, given the many uncertainties attendant to a nuclear exchange. We do not believe that the Soviets' present civil defenses would embolden them deliberately to expose the U.S.S.R. to a higher risk of nuclear attack."

A study by the U.S. Office of Technology Assessment several years ago concluded that just three Minuteman II intercontinental ballistic missiles and seven Poseidon missiles with multiple warheads could wipe out 73 per

---

25 The U.S. Defense Intelligence Agency disputes this. It claims that on one occasion the Soviets did practice the evacuation of the work force of one industry from one city.

26 See John Burns, "Russians, Too, Joke Sadly on Atom-War Survival," *The New York Times*, June 11, 1982.

27 "Their civil defense program is a turkey, as they are beginning to realize," says Admiral Noel Gayler (ret.), former Director of the U.S. National Security Agency.

cent of the Soviet industrial refining capacity.[28] In this connection, one "insider" would note that about 75 percent of the basic industrial capacity of the U.S.S.R. (primary metals, chemicals, petroleum construction, synthetic rubber, agricultural and railroad equipment and power generators) is concentrated in approximately 400 plants.

According to CIA analysts familiar with the Soviet civil defense program, the problems the Russians face in safeguarding the bulk of their civilian population in a nuclear war are immense if not insurmountable. For instance, Soviet cities are far more concentrated than many cities of the American South and West that developed after the introduction of the automobile and the freeway. The evacuation of these large urban population centers and the even distribution of city dwellers in less populated areas would pose immense logistical problems under the most favorable of circumstances with the world's best transportation. And crisis conditions, such as those which would surely prevail in a deteriorating international situation leading to the contemplation of the use of nuclear weapons, would certainly be less than favorable. And the USSR's creaky public-transportation system is hardly the world's best.

As CIA officials explain, Soviet plans envisage the urban population moving out of the danger areas in trains, in motor vehicles or on foot. Yet there are only about two million cars, two million trucks and approximately 200,000 buses for the entire Soviet Union. Furthermore, there are few roads in that vast and underdeveloped (when compared with the U.S.) country. No more than a third of these have hard surfaces. For the most part, railroads are the preferred method of long-distance travel in the U.S.S.R. However, most of the lines are single-track and most of the trains are loaded with freight at any given time. It is unlikely that the trains would be in the right place at the right time in sufficient quantities to pick up the millions of people in danger and transport them to distant, presumably less dangerous, areas.

Take the case of the Soviet national capital. Present plans for evacuating Moscow call for most residents simply to walk out of the city, since there is inadequate transportation to move approximately eight million people in an expeditious way by train, bus or automobile. According to the CIA, this evacuation would take three to seven days, and the Agency could discover almost immediately that it was happening. (Since this state of affairs would imply that Soviet authorities believed that nuclear war was imminent, it is probable that the Administration would respond by ordering the rapid evacuation of American cities.) Soviet city dwellers would be directed to designated areas in the countryside for regrouping; yet some method of

---

28 U.S. Office of Technology Assessment, *The Effects of Nuclear War* (Washington, D.C.: Government Printing Office, 1979), p. 76.

feeding and sheltering all these people would have to be found. This task would be difficult under any conditions, but particularly so, should evacuation occur in winter. Not surprisingly, therefore, many CIA officials have serious doubts that this system would be implemented effectively amid the breakdown of social order, disruption of services and so forth that would be expected to accompany a nuclear war.[29]

The Soviet program providing for the protection of workers in hardened shelters is also generally viewed with skepticism by the CIA. The shelters are normally located at the sites of major factories, most of which are targeted by U.S. warheads; Russians in such shelters would most probably have a difficult time surviving the multiple effects of nuclear weapons use on or about their shelters. These might well include blast, burial of their shelters under tons of rubble, fire storms and conflagrations that would literally suck the air out of their shelters, denying them oxygen and causing temperatures to rise to unbearable levels.[30]

All of these considerations led Stansfield Turner, when he was CIA Director, to testify before Congress that he was not aware of any civil defense plan in the U.S.S.R. that could conceivably protect the Russian population effectively against nuclear attack. More importantly, he said, he knew of no such plan which would give the leaders of the Soviet Union the delusion that effective protection of their population and industry was possible against nuclear attack.

Frequently, proponents of civil defense in the United States cite official Soviet "publications" as evidence that the Soviet leadership attaches great importance to civil defense measures as a means of ensuring the ability of the U.S.S.R. to survive a nuclear attack and for the attainment of victory. These include handbooks, leaflets and propaganda posters, which have led critics to comment wryly that the "most visible product of the Soviet civil defense bureaucracy is paper."[31] Actually, there is more to it than that,

29 For background see Director of Central Intelligence, *Soviet Civil Defense*, N178-10003, July 1978.

30 For a detailed analysis of Soviet civil defense capabilities see Leon Goure, *War Survival in Soviet Strategy: Soviet Civil Defense* (Coral Gables, Fla.: Center for Advanced International Studies, University of Miami, 1976).

31 See for instance, Andrew Cockburn, *The Threat: Inside the Soviet Military Machine* (New York: Random House, 1983), p. 230. He writes: "The millions of Soviet school-children who attend Pioneer camps (roughly equivalent to boy-scout camps) each summer are given a handbook containing useful hints, such as the standard time for putting on a cotton and gauze mask (2 1/2 minutes), unpacking a 10-foot by 12-foot "trench shelter" (3 minutes for a team of three), and decontaminating irradiated clothing with a soap and oil solvent (7 minutes). It also advises youthful readers that a nuclear blast wave takes 2 seconds to travel the first six-tenths of a mile, while those farther away will have "a few seconds" or more to seek shelter.

say the critics. Just as those publications distributed by civil defense planners in the U.S. give cause for optimism that one could possibly fight and survive a nuclear attack, so do many Soviet C.D. publications paint a generally positive picture. However, as one student of Soviet civil defense has noted, even Soviet publications admit that "civil defense by itself cannot solve the problem of effectively protecting large segments of the population and the essential sectors of the economy from destruction..."[32]

According to Professor Geiger, Russian physicians recently spent two and a half hours on prime time on the Soviet national television network presenting to the Soviet people some of the major consequences of nuclear war. He says that Dr. Ye I. Chazov and his colleagues pointed out "the futility of any defensive measures." This information, he says, "has also appeared recently in Soviet newspapers and magazines."[33]

Summary

The upshot of this analysis is that not everyone is going to make it in a nuclear war even if there are enough shovels to go around. With Soviet nuclear weapons between five and thirty minutes away from impact on virtually every metropolitan area of the United States, no one is safe — no matter how near or how distant the shelter. To believe otherwise is to indulge in a dangerous delusion. Given the devastating multiple effects of nuclear weapons explosions, the dying may well envy the dead in the aftermath of a nuclear attack.[34]

32 Leon Goure et al., *The Role of Nuclear Forces in Current Soviet Strategy* (Coral Gables, Fla.: Center for Advanced International Studies, University of Miami, 1974), p. 119.

33 See Patrick O'Herrernan, *opus cit.*, p. 265. Marshall Shulman, a former adviser to Secretary of State Cyrus Vance and now Director of the Russian Institute at Columbia University, has this to say: "I see nothing in the Soviet literature that leads me to the conclusion that the Soviet leadership believes that a nuclear exchange would be anything less than total catastrophe. The civil defense program isn't of that substantiality. It is by no means of an order that would give the Soviet leadership confidence that they could substantially reduce their casualties, both their immediate casualties and their longterm casualties. They'd have to be out of their minds to think it would do that." Quoted in Robert Scheer, *opus cit.*

34 One "insider" familiar with American nuclear war plans has this to say: "All this argument over whether a nuclear war would destroy all or only half of civilization sickens me. Fortunately, the people who maintain that a nuclear war is survivable do not control the decisions, although under Reagan they are in positions that make me uncomfortable. I know T.K. Jones from SALT. Any remarks I would make on him would be libelous. One thing you should keep in mind is that, for any sane person, the briefing on our nuclear war plans is a very sobering experience.

The same is true for Soviet citizens. Contrary to what some U.S. officials say, the Soviet leadership also seems to recognize the impracticality of implementing civil defense plans on a large scale, even though a large number of persons are apparently involved bureaucratically. The Soviets seem to have plans to protect their top leadership, but they cannot protect the vast majority of their people in the event of nuclear war. In the words of William Hyland, a long-time student of Soviet affairs and a former aide to Henry Kissinger: It is "a mistake to confuse a program to protect leaders and key industrial personnel with effective civil defense for the population."[35]

Former Secretary of Defense Harold Brown put it simply:[36]

The American nuclear arsenal is more than adequate to overcome any civil defense measures that the Soviet Union might pursue. No more than the United States will the U.S.S.R. be able to rely on defense against a nuclear attack to evade the ravages of war.

It is an indisputable fact that the population and economic resources of the Soviet Union are concentrated in a remarkably small number of major urban centers that are extremely vulnerable to nuclear attack. In the view of the CIA, the Soviets have no way of converting their continuing low-level civil defense efforts into a successful nuclear "war-winning" strategy, as some high-level officials in the Reagan Administration fear.

So far, the Administration's seven-year, $ 4.2 billion civil defense program has encountered strong opposition. For instance, Beverlee A. Myers, Director of the Department of Health Services in California, told a public hearing that it would be "unethical" to participate in a plan that "creates the ... illusion that the public health community can offer any assurance of health protection to the cities of California in the event of a malevolent detonation of nuclear warheads." She added that "to plan for a hoax is a disservice to the people of California."[37] The City Council of New York City voted subsequently to reject the crisis relocation plan of the Administration. And the Mayor of New York City, Ed Koch, affirmed that it would be "impossible to evacuate [New York City] in any timely, acceptable way."[38] In the last few years hundreds of local governments throughout the United States have also refused to cooperate with the new federally

---

I cannot imagine anyone knowing what they are and being in any hurry to implement them. If, as I have, one has participated in the annual nuclear war exercise conducted by the JCS, he will be even less enthusiastic. It is a horrifying experience."

35 See *The New York Times*, June 10, 1982.
36 Quoted in *The Defense Monitor*, Vol. 11, No. 1 (1982).
37 *The Los Angeles Times*, March 18, 1982.
38 *The New York Times*, June 10, 1982.

sponsored civil defense program — many of them before it was even funded.[39]

The contention of the Administration that its civil defense program will contribute to deterrence by making the resort to war a more "credible" American option is ill-founded and very dangerous. Not only does the Reagan civil defense plan create the illusion that effective protection of the U.S. population is possible against nuclear attack, but if believed at the top level of government, as seems to be the case, it may well make U.S. policymakers less cautious, thus possibly leading the United States into a war inadvertently. Furthermore, instead of deterring the Soviet Union, it may cause the Soviet leadership to believe that U.S. leaders think the U.S. could survive a nuclear war, and thus the Kremlin might then conclude the Americans are entertaining serious thoughts of striking them pre-emptively. And if the Russians think American leaders are serious about striking first, then Moscow might be tempted to beat them to the punch. The result could be a disastrous nuclear war which no one wanted or intended.

In short, it is wrong to encourage public faith in an inherently non-viable civil defense. Moreover, it is also contrary to our survival needs. The only protection against a nuclear war is not to have one.[40] This not unsubtle reality must not be clouded by futile attempts to make the unworkable work.[41]

---

39 Wolfgang K.H. Panofsky, a former member of President Carter's Science Advisory Commission, wisely advises: "... neither leaders nor serious observers in either country (the U.S. and the U.S.S.R.) should pay much attention to the spuriously precise analyses cranked out by military computers to 'determine' levels of damage from nuclear attack. Such calculations usually take into account only 'prompt' casualties, that is those resulting from blast or prompt radiation. Few analyses consider fallout, and none of those generally used take into account such post-attack effects as fire, damage to food supplies, medical care and productivity, or epidemics. As (former head of the U.S. Arms Control and Disarmament Agency Fred) Ikle notes, the omission of such after-attack effects leads to substantial underestimates. It is another instance of the way in which, in his words: 'The jargon of American strategic analysis works like a narcotic. It dulls our sense of moral outrage about the tragic confrontation of nuclear arsenals, primed and constantly perfected to unleash widespread genocide.'" See Panofsky, "The Mutual-Hostage Relationship between America and Russia," *Foreign Affairs* Vol. 52, No. 1 (October, 1973), p. 114.

40 Freeman Dyson, who is a faculty member at the Institute for Advanced Study in Princeton and the author of one of the best recent books on nuclear weapons, would disagree here. He writes: "The response 'We're all dead anyway, so why bother?' is inadequate. We cannot know in advance that we are all dead. Nuclear war is incalculable..." See Dyson, *Weapons and Hope* (New York: Harper & Row, 1984).

41 This is not to say that the U.S. should make no plans to deal with a small-scale nuclear attack, *one which results from an accidental or unauthorized firing.*

SECTION IV
CASE STUDIES OF NUCLEAR DETERRENCE

> History is not merely what happened; it is what happened in the context of what might have happened.
>
> Hugh Trevor-Roper

XIV. THE FIRST ATOMIC BOMBING

The first atomic bomb was dropped on the Japanese city Hiroshima on August 6, 1945. At least 66,000 people died from the explosion and fire storm that ensued. Many thousands more died in the aftermath — among them twelve U.S. Navy fliers imprisoned in the city jail.[1] Three days later a second bomb was dropped on the city of Nagasaki. Some 40,000 Japanese died immediately, with untold thousands dying later.

The day following the Nagasaki explosion, the Japanese sued for peace, and on August 14 they reluctantly accepted the American terms of surrender in Tokyo.

The rapid collapse of Japan in the wake of the two atomic bombings left the impression on most Americans that the strategic concepts that guided the use of the bombs were valid. However, the accumulation of evidence today suggests this impression to be faulty. Contrary to popular opinion, we now know that in terminating the war the bomb was less important than it appeared at the time.[2]

The American Army-Air Force's own *Strategic Bombing Survey*, published in 1946, reached the conclusion that not even the atomic bomb had proved decisive in the Second World War. "Certainly prior to 31 December 1945, and in all probability prior to 1 November 1945 (the planned date

---

1 The details surrounding the deaths of these fliers were reported in the Boston *Globe*, November 3, 1975, and the Kansas City *Times*, November 20, 1975. To this day, the U.S. government has never officially acknowledged that Americans were killed at Hiroshima.

2 See for instance the study by Ambassador Edwin O. Reischauer, one of America's most knowledgeable experts on Japan, *The United States and Japan* (Cambridge: Harvard University Press, 1957), p. 240. See also Robert J.C. Butow, *Japan's Decision to Surrender* (Stanford: Stanford University Press, 1968). This later work is by the leading student of Japan's decision to surrender.

of the U.S. invasion of Japan), the Japanese would have surrendered, even if the atomic bomb had not been used, and even if no invasion had been planned or contemplated." These words were plainly viewed as a direct challenge by some of the strongest proponents of the bomb. For one, General Leslie R. Groves, who in 1942 was put in charge of the Manhattan Project, rejected the *Survey's* conclusion outright. And Secretary of War Robert Patterson personally "interceded with army historians in 1946 to ensure that the bomb, and not Russia's entry into the war, would be represented in official postwar accounts as decisive in Japan's surrender."[3]

To be sure, President Harry Truman defended his decision in his *Memoirs*. He argued (as others after him have done) that the atomic bombing of Japan not only saved American and allied lives (U.S. estimates at the time expected up to one million Allied lives to be lost in the campaign to seize Japan's home islands) but also Japanese lives (the defenders who would have died). Nevertheless, as Japanese records of the period have been made public and numerous interviews have been conducted with key participants in the decisionmaking process, we now know that the dropping of the atomic bomb was unnecessary because the Japanese were contemplating surrender at the time.

Surrender is a political decision. It is usually controversial, and so it may require a shift in the national power structure before it can be effected. As Lawrence Freedman writes in his widely-hailed study of nuclear strategy, "It was the movement of this shift, dependent on the delicate handling of the hard-line militarists and a hope of tolerable surrender terms, that determined the date of the Japanese surrender. If the bomb did have a role it was in accelerating and intensifying the process of political change."[4]

But even here extreme caution is in order. The atomic bombing was not the only shock that the Japanese absorbed in the four days beginning with August 6, 1945. The devastation of Hiroshima and Nagasaki was accompanied by the entry of the U.S.S.R. into the war against Japan. The surprise Soviet attack, which Stalin had promised Truman at the Potsdam Conference in July-August 1945, dashed any last hopes of Soviet support in mediating more favorable conditions of surrender for Japan.

In other words, the atomic bombing of Japan was like "administering poison on the death bed" to use Freeman's words. By the middle of 1945 Japan was a spent force. Unable to project her power to any important extent beyond her boundaries, she had lost control of both the air and sea.

3   See Gregg Herke, *The Winning Weapon: The Atomic Bomb in the Cold War 1945-1950* (New York: Knopf, 1981).

4   Lawrence Freedman, *The Evolution of Nuclear Strategy* (New York: St. Martin's Press, 1983), p. 19.

Moreover, she was being starved of vital resources by the Allied blockade and was the target of regular and destructive conventional bombing by waves of B-29 bombers.[5] Once the Japanese leaders realized that the path to victory was lost, the problem for them became how to surrender under the most favorable conditions.

The A-Bomb as a Psychological Weapon

The destruction of both Hiroshima and Nagasaki was the result of a single, fateful decision. This was made in late July, 1945 by President Truman, who only a few months earlier had become President upon the death of Franklin D. Roosevelt.

A single B-29 flew over the Japanese city of Hiroshima and dropped an atomic bomb having the explosive force of fourteen thousand tons of TNT. In a matter of moments, this hitherto little-known Japanese city achieved a notoriety so terrible that it stunned men and women the world over and made them reluctant to acknowledge the inevitable horrors of nuclear warfare.

As Vice President, Truman was never informed of Roosevelt's intentions in the matter of atomic policy. As Gregg Herke writes in his critical study of the "winning weapon," Truman "inherited neither the flexibility nor the diplomatic subtlety of his predecessor's planning. He did, however, fall heir to the assumption that the bomb would be used."[6] New to the job, Truman was little inclined to challenge that cardinal assumption of wartime policy.

Truman's first real information about the bomb came from his Secretary of War in a briefing on the afternoon of April 25, 1945. Henry L. Stimson was accompanied on this sensitive mission by Brigadier General Leslie R. Groves, who was in charge of the Manhattan Project. America's war effort in this regard was so secret that the two men entered the office of the Pre-

---

5 Following limited fire-bombing raids in January and February 1945, the U.S. Air Force began a relentless campaign in March with a devastating attack on Tokyo which left over 80,000 dead. General Curtis LeMay, who was in charge of this campaign, wrote in April 1945 that "I am influenced by the conviction that the present stage of development in the air war against Japan presents the (Army Air Force) for the first time with the opportunity of proving the power of the strategic air arm. I consider that for the first time strategic air bombardment faces a situation in which its strength is proportionate to the magnitude of its task. I feel that the destruction of Japan's ability to wage war is within the capability of this command." Quoted in L. Giovannitti *et al.*, *The Decision to Drop the Bomb* (London: Methuen & Co., 1967), p. 35.

6 Gregg Herke, *opus cit.*

sident through a side door, unobserved even by Truman's appointments secretary.[7]

At the Potsdam Conference in July-August 1945, Truman shared some of his knowledge of the bomb and general strategy with Prime Minister Winston Churchill and the Soviet leader Joseph Stalin. When Churchill hinted that the Japanese might be allowed to lay down their arms in a way that would not impair their notions of honor, the U.S. President replied heatedly that Pearl Harbor had shown that Japan had no honor.[8] Upon hearing of the successful test of the atomic bomb at New Mexico, Churchill exclaimed to Henry Stimson: "Stimson, what was gunpowder? Trivial. What was electricity? Meaningless. This Atomic Bomb is the Second Coming in Wrath!"[9]

Truman gave the authorization for the order to drop atomic bombs on Japan on July 24, 1945, the same day that he decided not to tell Stalin in detail about the dawn of the atomic age. This order was general in nature: it simply directed that the bombs be released as soon as they were ready on a predetermined list of target cities until the Japanese government surrendered. The details of implementing this fateful decision were left up to the military.

To throw the enemy off balance, the Japanese would not be given any warning. As Secretary of War Henry L. Stimson later recalled: "I felt that to extract a genuine surrender from the Emperor and his military advisers they must be administered a tremendous shock which would carry convincing proof of our power to destroy the Empire." Thus, the atomic bomb "was more than a weapon of terrible destruction; it was a psychological weapon." Stimson noted that General George Marshall was "emphatic in his insistence on the shock value of the new weapon."[10]

Stimson accepted the suggestion that the most desirable target would be a vital war plant employing a large number of workers and closely surrounded by workers homes. This decision stood in contrast to an earlier

7 *Ibid.*

8 Adam Ulam, *The Rivals: America and Russia Since World War II* (New York: Penguin Books, 1980), p. 81.

9 Quoted in Herbet Feis, *The Atomic Bomb and the End of World War II* (Princeton: Princeton University Press, 1966).

10 Henry L. Stimson and McGeorge Bundy, *On Active Service in Peace and War* (London: Hutchinson, 1948), p. 36, pp. 369-70, p. 373. It is interesting to note that although Stimson apparently never waivered in his determination that the bomb be used (indeed, he even arranged committee deliberations in such a way that this was a foregone conclusion), he was a man with a sensitive conscience. Privately, he referred to the bomb as "the dreadful," "the awful" and "the diabolical." He even went so far as to arrange to have available to him a subordinate whose task was largely to listen to his peined concerns about the weapon.

consensus that the atomic bombing would not concentrate on a civilian area. But as Martin J. Sherwin writes in his highly respected *A World Destroyed*, "No member of the Committee spoke to [this contradiction]."[11] Consequently, Stimson informed President Truman of the advisers' decision.

The use of the bomb was constrained by the lack of key military targets which were available. In the first meeting to discuss bomb use, in May 1943, the Japanese fleet at Truk was thought a suitable target. However, by mid-1945, the Japanese fleet was virtually non-existent.[12] To be sure, the atomic bomb was considered in connection with an invasion of Japan, but such a costly invasion was still the very last thing American policy-makers wanted.[13]

By July 23, the schedule for the atomic attack was fixed. The Secretary of War was informed that a uranium bomb would be available soon after August 1. The first plutonium bomb, the kind tested at Alamagordo on July 16, would be ready for delivery by plane around August 6. A third (plutonium) bomb was anticipated by August 24. Additional atomic bombs would be produced at an accelerated rate "from possibly three in September to perhaps seven or more in December."[14]

Specially trained B-29 crews of the 509th Composite Group were given the responsibility for delivering the first bomb. They were scheduled to do so as soon as weather allowed visual bombing after August 3. The targets: Hiroshima, Kokura, Niigate and Nagasaki.

Two days after the first bombing, as the radioactive dust settled over Hiroshima, the Japanese Ambassador to the Soviet Union entered Foreign Minister V.M. Molotov's study in the Kremlin. Ambassador Naotake Sato hoped to enlist the Soviets as mediators between the Anglo-American and Japanese governments. Consequently, he was caught off guard by the message he actually received: a state of war would exist between the U.S.S.R. and Japan on the next day.

Some two hours later (1:00 a.m. August 9, Tokyo time), Soviet troops crossed the Manchurian border. They immediately engaged the depleted forces of Japan's once powerful army. In this abrupt fashion, the moment of decision had arrived for Japan's military and civilian leaders. But before

---

11 Martin J. Sherwin, *A World Destroyed: The Atomic Bomb and the Atlantic Alliance* (New York: Vintage Books, 1979), p. 209.

12 Lawrence Freedman, *opus cit.*, p. 17.

13 Adam Ulam notes that even "with both a Soviet intervention and use of the bomb, the Joint Chiefs of Staff thought, the invasion would be necessary, although they hoped the struggle would not be so protracted and American casualties so cataclysmic as without them." See his *The Rivals: America and Russia Since World War II* (New York: Penguin Books, 1980), p. 81.

14 Martin J. Sherwin, *opus cit.*, p. 231.

it could be recognized and acted on, a second Japanese city fell victim to the horrors of atomic bombing.[15]

The Hiroshima bombing apparently accelerated Soviet plans to enter the war against Japan. At Potsdam, Stalin had promised Truman he would enter the war by August 15. Soviet troops invaded Manchuria six days early and achieved their objectives there before the war came to an end.

The city of Nagasaki had been an alternate target on August 9th. It was destroyed because of a fluke in the weather. A cloud cover had prevented the American bombardier from making the required visual target sighting on the city of first priority.

The third target in Japan was meant to be either Kokura or Niigata. But these cities were spared by the Japanese peace overtures on August 10. (A third atomic bomb, not yet assembled, would reportedly not have been ready until about the end of the month.) The President, at a Cabinet meeting on the 10th, ordered that further atomic bombing of Japan be suspended. Evidently, the "thought of wiping out another 100,000 people was too horrible," and it outweighed political considerations. However, it was, Truman informed his Cabinet, "to our interest that the Russians not push too far into Manchuria."[16]

The Selection of Japan Rather than Germany

Why was Japan selected as the target for the atomic bombings rather than Germany? There are several reasons, which have been made clear by recently declassified U.S. government documents.

According to the minutes of the Military Policy Committee of May 5, 1943, "The point of use of the first bomb was discussed and the general view appeared to be that its best point of use would be on a Japanese fleet concentration in the Harbor of Truk. General Styer suggested Tokio [sic], but it was pointed out that the bomb should be used where, if it failed to go off, it would land in water of sufficient depth to prevent easy salvage. The Japanese were selected as they would not be so apt to secure knowledge from it as would be the Germans."[17]

---

15 The likelihood that there were American prisoners of war who were among the tens of thousands of Japanese in this "graveyard with not a tombstone standing" is good. As Martin Sherwin writes: "This is suggested by a message from Headquarters, U.S. Army Strategic Air Forces, Guam, to the War Department on July 31: "Reports prisoner of war sources, not verified by photos, give location of Allied prisoner of war camp one mile north of the center of Nagasaki . . ." *A World Destroyed*, p. 234.

16 Quoted in Gregg Herke, *opus cit.*, p. 21.

17 MED-TS, folder 23A.

At a meeting on August 24, 1945, General L. Groves addressed the specific question whether or not the U.S. government would have dropped the bomb on occidentals. He told a committee considering "foreseeable new developments" in warfare that he and the scientists of the Manhattan Project had always known the bomb "would probably be completed too late for use against Germany."

To be sure, there were other reasons that may have contributed to the decision to bomb Japan. First, it was safer to assemble the atomic bomb on a Pacific island than in the United Kingdom. Second, there was the initial absence of B-29 bombers in Europe to carry the weapon. Third, a drop on Japan emphasized "American" primacy in this Anglo-American endeavor. Whatever the case, racism apparently was not one of the reasons for bombing the Japanese instead of the Germans. As General Groves later reported: "President Roosevelt asked if we were prepared to drop bombs on Germany if it was necessary to do so and we replied that we would be prepared to do so if necessary."[18]

Summary

The nuclear era began in August 1945 with the surprise destruction of Hiroshima and Nagasaki. Very soon thereafter Japan capitulated, and World War II was over.

Small by today's standards, the weapons that destroyed Hiroshima and Nagasaki produced explosions equivalent to 14,000 and 20,000 tons of TNT respectively. However, they inflicted so enduring a level of devastation that survivors have experienced what Robert Jay Lifton calls a "permanent encounter with death."[19]

Originally, the bomb was seen as a kind of insurance policy against a successful German atomic project.[20] However, once the American program was well under way, U.S. officials decided that it would be employed against the enemies of the United States regardless of what these adversaries had available in their own arsenals. Of course, it was not until after the first

---

18 On April 23, 1945, Groves told Stimson that "the target is and was always expected to be Japan." MED-TS, folder 25, tab M.
19 See Robert Jay Lifton et al., *Living and Dying* (New York: Praeger, 1974). Also see Committee for the Compilation of Materials on Damage Caused by the Atomic Bombs in Hiroshima and Nagasaki, *The Physical, Medical, and Social Effects of the Atomic Bombings* (New York: Basic Books, 1981).
20 See Leslie R. Groves, *Now It Can be Told: The Story of the Manhattan Project* (New York: Harper, 1962).

test of the atomic bomb in New Mexico in mid-July 1945 that the full importance of atomic power could properly be understood.

To this day, many people believe that the atomic bombings actually compelled the Japanese surrender. However, local government records and interviews with key participants suggest that the unexpected Russian invasion was decisive. Hence, the devastation of Hiroshima and Nagasaki, was neither necessary nor did it exclude the Soviets from Manchuria.

The debate over the atomic-bomb decision still rages today. However, what is often overlooked are the implications of the demand for Japan's unconditional surrender. Unconditional surrender was, of course, devastating to the Japanese, remaining unacceptable to them to the end. Their greatest fear was the Emperor would be held responsible for war crimes and the institution itself would be abolished — as indeed some U.S. policymakers at first insisted it should be.[21] The unconditional surrender decision was a politically unwise act, representing one of the most basic and unnecessary errors of U.S. policy during the war.[22]

In addition, the President should have kept closer control over the scheduling of the bombings. The destruction of Nagasaki, an alternate target anyway, might have been avoided if Truman had not simply instructed that "atomic bombs" be dropped on Japan as soon as possible. The specific initiative had been left with the bomber command on the island of Tinian.[23]

Perhaps surprisingly, these bombings occasioned little criticism from Americans at the time. As the social philosopher Lewis Mumford observed

21 On July 6, 1945, U.S. Assistant Secretary of State MacLeish wrote to Secretary of State James Byrnes: "What has made Japan dangerous in the past and will make her dangerous in the future ... is in large part, the Japanese cult of emperor worship which gives the ruling groups in Japan ... their control over the Japanese society ... to leave that institution intact is to run the grave risk that it will be used in the future as it has been used in the past." See U.S. Department of State, *The Conference of Berlin* (Washington, D.C.: U.S. Government Printing Office, 1956), Vol. I, p. 896.

22 Rather than insisting on unconditional surrender at Potsdam, the Americans and the British could have indicated to the Japanese leadership that it could at least keep the Emperor once the war was over, which the Allies in the end consented to anyway.

23 Martin J. Sherwin, *opus cit.*, p. 233. One former U.S. government official interjects here: "You simply do not understand the psychology of war. Do you think we were engaged in a game of blind man's bluff? No one at that time was concerned about killing Germans and Japanese, particularly if it would save American lives. After eleven months of war in Europe, my division was scheduled for the invasion of Japan. We were all delighted that the bomb was used, and I still think it was a prudent decision."

in late 1945: "Not the least extraordinary fact about the postwar period is that mass extermination has awakened so little moral protest."[24]

Public-opinion polls bear out Mumford's perceptive insight.[25] A Gallup poll taken just two weeks after the destruction of Hiroshima revealed that 85 percent of the American people approved the bombing. Two months after the Japanese surrender, a *Fortune* survey showed that many Americans felt remorse over the bombings, but 53.5 percent still approved.[26] Perhaps most shocking of all is the "wartime emotionalism" that the surveys revealed. Nearly a quarter of those questioned in the *Fortune* poll believed that the United States should have dropped many more A-bombs "before Japan had a chance to surrender."[27] Indeed, 13 percent of those interviewed in a December 1944 Gallup poll favored the wholesale extermination of the Japanese.

As things turned out, the passage of time helped put the atomic bombings in perspective. And major publications, such as John Hersey's *Hiroshima* in 1946, naturally had their effect in modifying public attitudes toward the bomb. A poll taken in 1947 by the Social Science Research Council revealed that a majority of Americans thought the bomb made war less likely, because the new means of warfare possessed by the United States served to deter a would-be aggressor. Still, a majority was still willing to drop the bomb on an enemy, whether or not he used it against the U.S. first.[28]

Acutely sensitive to postwar criticism of his decision to use the bomb, President Truman noted in his memoirs that he "never had any doubt that [the bomb] should be used." Truman was equally blunt and self-assured in a later, personal letter to an actor who had played the part of the President in a Hollywood film on the bomb: "I have no qualms about [the decision] whatever for the simple reason that it was believed the dropping of not more than two of these bombs would bring the war to a close. The Japanese

---

24 Lewis Mumford, "Gentlemen, You are Mad!," *Saturday Review of Literature*, March 2, 1946.

25 See *Public Opinion Quarterly* (Fall, 1945), pp. 385-530. The reaction of American religious leaders is interesting. Generally, Catholics tended to view the atomic bombing as a variant of saturation bombing and condemned it as inhumane. However, it should be noted that conservative churchmen did not necessarily approve it, nor did liberals automatically condemn the bombing. See S.J. Smothers, "An Opinion on Hiroshima," *America*, July 3, 1947; James M. Gillis, "The Atomic Bomb," *Catholic World*, September, 1945; and "America's Atomic Atrocit," *Christian Century*, August 29, 1945.

26 *Public Opinion Quarterly* (Fall, 1945), pp. 385-530.

27 See *Fortune*, December, 1945.

28 Social Science Research Council, *Public Reaction to the Atomic Bomb and World Affairs* (1947), pp. 83-85.

in their conduct of the war had been vicious and cruel savages and I came to the conclusion that if two hundred and fifty thousand young Americans could be saved from slaughter the bomb should be dropped, and it was."[29]

This professed detachment about the controversial decision, however, is contradicted by other, seemingly more important, evidence that has recently emerged. Most relevant is the private journal kept by the President at Potsdam and Truman's comment in the Cabinet meeting of August, 10, 1945. On July 25, 1945, the President noted in his diary: "Even if the Japs are savages, ruthless, merciless and fanatic, we as the leader of the world for the common welfare cannot drop this terrible bomb on the old Capitol [Kyoto] or the new [Tokyo] . . ." Later Truman wrote: "It is certainly a good thing for the world that Hitler's crowd or Stalin's did not discover this atomic bomb. It seems to be the most terrible thing ever discovered, but it can be made the most useful."[30]

Perhaps the most psychologically telling indication of the President's secret doubts about the bomb was his underlining of Horatio's speech in the last scene of *Hamlet*, cited in a book on the decision in Truman's own personal library. The President twice underscored the last line of the following passage:

Of accidental judgements, casual slaughters,
Of deaths put on by cunning and forced cause,
And, in this upshot, purposes mistook
Fall'n on the inventors' heads . . .
But let this same be presently perform'd,
Even while men's minds are wild; lest more mischance,
On plots and errors, happen.

---

29 Quoted in Gregg Herke, *The Winning Weapon: The Atomic Bomb in the Cold War 945-1950* (New York: Knopf, 1981), p. 20.

30 These important papers have now been made public and can be read at the Truman Presidential Library.

> [T]he Chinese intervention in the Korean war provides a good illustration of divergent perceptions in foreign policy decisions ...
>
> John Stoessinger

XV. THE KOREAN WAR

Prelude: Game Theory

"Chicken"

Many sophisticated game-theoretical arguments have been developed to demonstrate the applicability of nuclear deterrence. One of the most interesting is the prototype strategic game known as "chicken." It has been described by Thomas Schelling, one of the leading strategic thinkers in the field of nuclear deterrence theory.[1]

The game consists of two players driving automobiles at 70 miles per hour directly at each other down the center of an isolated road. An audience of peers is closely following the situation. The player who swerves off the center line to avoid a head-on collision is termed "a chicken" and can expect to suffer contempt from his peers.

Using purely rational assumptions, Schelling has provided the following solution to the game: the player will win who first establishes an irreversible commitment to the center of the road. This could be achieved, for instance, by a player who throws his steering wheel out of the window and climbs in the back seat. The other player then faces but two choices: He can suffer a finite loss of honor or death. According to Schelling's scheme of things, there should be little doubt how a rational actor would solve that conflict of values."

Pascal's Wager: Purposeful Uncertainty

The kind of logic employed in the game of "chicken" is said to prevail in the area of nuclear deterrence. The basic idea is that the Soviet leadership, if it is to be discouraged from committing aggression against the

---

[1] See Thomas Schelling, *The Strategy of Conflict* (Cambridge: Harvard University Press, 1960).

United States, an ally or an area in which the U.S. has a vital interest, must believe that America will use nuclear weapons against the U.S.S.R. While some deterrence theorists would argue that the Kremlin must believe with certainty that the U.S. would use nuclear weapons against the Soviet homeland in retaliation, others would simply say that nuclear deterrence rests on a degree of "purposeful uncertainty."

"One should not talk in terms of certainty when talking about the question of nuclear deterrence," Ambassador Martin J. Hillenbrand writes, "If one looks for certitude then, of course, one will never find it. The essence of my view is a sufficient degree of uncertainty about the possible involvement of nuclear weapons so that overriding caution is the dominant psychological feature of decision-makers."[2]

In this context, the logic of Pascal's Wager "continues to be highly relevant," says Ambassador Hillenbrand.[3] "When the possible result of one's action is infinite in its negative implications, in this case not infinite but certainly beyond human conception in the direction of incalculability, then even one chance in many thousands, even millions, that an almost infinite result for practical purposes will be achieved, should, for the rational person, act as a deterrent."

"I do not want to suggest that the Soviet leadership thinks in terms of the calculus of probability, but some rudimentary application of this highly

---

2 Letter to this writer, April 27, 1984.

3 Blaise Pascal (1623-62) was a famous Jansenist mathematician, scientist and spiritual writer. He is perhaps best known in philosophy for his wager which, as originally formulated, represented a unique apologetical argument in support of the belief in God. More recently, the argument has been applied to the question of nuclear deterrence.

Basically, the argument runs like this: there is no clear evidence for the existence of a Supreme Being. "What meets our eye denotes neither total absence nor manifest presence of the divine, but the presence of a hidden God" (*Pensées*, No 233). God is or is not. Which is it?

A game is now on. If one gambles that God does not exist, than that person has nothing to gain and everything to lose should God exist. If, on the other hand, the person wagers that God does exist, that person has everything to gain and nothing to lose. The implication is that if God does exist, the person has lost nothing, since there would be no infinite reward in any case. So as one scholar observes: "to 'bet on' God is to enter a game weighted in the gambler's favor, for the gambler wagers finite stakes with the possibility of infinite returns." (Richard P. McBrien, *Catholicism* (Minneapolis: Winston Press, 1980), Vol. I, p. 310.

To be sure, Pascal's Wager is on its face a compelling theological argument. But it is not one without serious practical flaws. In the main, these shortcomings have to do with the nature of belief and the way one perceives the act of faith. Before Pascal's Wager makes sense, the notion of God has to be a live hypothesis, to quote William James. Martin Luther, who lived before Pascal, put it this way: "I believe in order to know."

sophisticated logic must lie in the minds of any rational leadership, including an anxious leadership. (Whatever else may be said about that gerontocracy, no one has yet accused it of rashness or a propensity for precipitate action.)"[4-7]

If these arguments seem all very theoretical, let us take a concrete example and see how they might apply in a real-life international crisis situation. The Korean War (1950-53) may serve as an interesting test case. For here we are presented with a non-nuclear power (China) which, in October/November 1950, attacked a major nuclear power (the United States) in a manner that significantly altered the outcome of that conflict. Did nuclear deterrence deter, as the highly sophisticated logic of game theory would suggest?

The Conflict Begins

The Korean conflict began on June 25, 1950, when more than 100,000 North Korean troops charged across the thirty-eighth parallel into South Korea.[8] There was little doubt in President Harry Truman's mind that a Soviet probing action was behind the North Korean invasion.[9] As for the

---

[4-7] Martin J. Hillenbrand, "NATO and Western Security in an Age of Transition," *International Security* (Fall, 1977), pp. 3-24.

[8] The North Korean invasion came as a surprise to the United States government, even though there had been some intelligence indicators. In retrospect, many students of the conflict have focused much attention on the speech of January 12, 1950 by Secretary of State Dean Acheson, especially his statement about the extent of the U.S. defense perimeter in the Pacific which left out Korea and Taiwan. Perhaps more important as an indicator of U.S. lack of interest in the area at the time, however, was the U.S. decision in the late 1940s to withdraw its occupation forces from South Korea. Interview with E. Allan Lightner, a career foreign service officer who was stationed in Seoul in the late 1940s, February 7, 1967, Washington, D.C.

[9] Khrushchev's memoirs throw some interesting light on Stalin's role in the initiation of the Korean War. According to Khrushchev, Kim II Sung came to Moscow in late 1949 to consult with Stalin on his intention to incite a rebellion in South Korea that would enable the North Koreans to intervene and unite the nation. Stalin reportedly cautioned prudence and "persuaded Kim II Sung that he should think it over, make some calculations, and then come back with a concrete plan." Subsequently, the North Korean leader returned with a plan and told Stalin that he was certain of its success. Stalin, however, was doubtful, thinking the Americans would intervene. As Khrushchev states: "He was worried that the Americans would jump in, but we were inclined to think that if the war were fought swiftly — and Kim II Sung was sure that it could be won swiftly — then intervention by the USA could be avoided." Stalin proceeded to consult Mao Tse-tung about Kim's

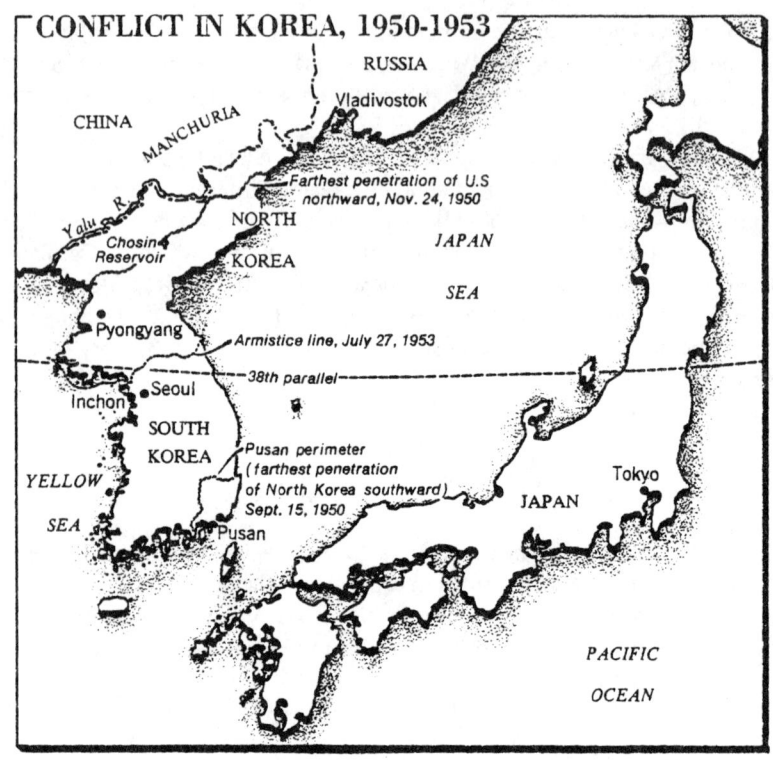

U.S. response, Truman recalled years later: "This was the toughest decision I had to make as President."[10]

The upshot of Truman's decision-making was to involve the United States in conjunction with fourteen other UN members who contributed ground troops. They acted very quickly to stave off imminent military defeat on the Korean peninsula.

The American reaction to the North Koreans' invasion of South Korea "must have been one of the greatest surprises of Stalin's life," writes Adam Ulam of Harvard University. "Having acquiesced in the loss of China, these unpredictable people now balked at the loss of a territory they themselves

plan. Mao is said to have approved, arguing that the United States would not intervene because the war would be an internal Korean matter. Khrushchev observes, however, "that the war was not Stalin's idea ... Kim was the initiator. Stalin, of course, didn't try to dissuade him ..." *Khrushchev Remembers* (Boston: Little & Brown, 1970).

10 Harry S. Truman, *Memoirs* (New York: Doubleday, 1955), Vol. II, pp. 332 ff.

had characterized as unimportant to their political and strategic interests. The Soviet Union was completely unprepared for this..."[11]

On September 15, General Douglas MacArthur executed a daring amphibious landing at Inchon, which took the North Koreans by surprise. Within a week or ten days, it became clear that the North Korean Army had been badly beaten and that only remnants would succeed in retreating across the thirty-eighth parallel. Thereafter, events moved rapidly. In October 1950, UN forces received permission to attack across the parallel because, among other things, it was impossible to achieve total defeat of the North Korean invaders if UN forces were not allowed to cross the demarcation line.

President Truman's inclination was first to let the UN make the determination on this important decision. But he apparently changed his mind, for in late September he instructed Secretary of State Dean Acheson to declare that the resolutions passed by the Security Council the previous June and July gave the Unified Command the necessary authority to cross the parallel. This was also reportedly the view held by General MacArthur and the Joint Chiefs of Staff.

U.S. Ambassador Warren R. Austin set forth the American position in the United Nations on September 30, 1950:[12]

The official barrier which has divided North and South Korea has no basis for existence in law or in reason. Neither the United Nations, its Commission on Korea, nor the Republic of Korea recognizes such a line. Now, the North Koreans, by armed attack upon the Republic of Korea, have denied the reality of such a line.

Subsequently, the UN General Assembly placed its seal of approval on the twin U.S. objectives of destroying North Korean forces and of unifying the entire country under the UN flag. The fact that the General Assembly lacked the legal authority to legislate decrees on such an important matter of peace and security, and the fact that its recommendation of October 7 had only been partially accepted, did not dissuade the United States from declaring its own military objectives to be identical with those of the UN.

---

11 See Adam Ulam, *The Rivals: America & Russia Since World War II* (England: Penguin Books, 1980), p. 171. Ulam argues that the Soviet delegate would not have boycotted the Security Council (on grounds that Communist China should be seated there) had Stalin anticipated the American reaction. According to a captured North Korean intelligence report, the North Koreans expected to conquer the South within two months of the invasion. See Lynn Montross *et al.*, *U.S. Marine Corps Operations in Korea* (Washington, D.C.: Historical Branch, USMC, 1954-57), Vol. I, p. 18.

12 United Nations General Assembly, *Official Records*, fifth Session, first Committee, September 30, 1950, p. 39.

Most importantly, General MacArthur was not restrained from crossing the parallel and initiating a rapid drive toward the Chinese border at the Yalu River, even though the Soviet Union had advisers with the North Korean Army down to the battalion level and China had issued a stern warning against such precipitate action.

South Korean troops crossed the thirty-eighth parallel on October 1. American troops followed suit on October 7. Three days later, China's Foreign Minister Chou En-lai announced that "the Chinese people [would] not stand idly by in the war of invasion."[13] These warnings, as John Stoessinger points out, "received only passing attention in Washington and Tokyo. The tendency among American government officials was to dismiss them as Chinese bombast."[14]

On October 15, however, President Truman and General MacArthur, the Supreme Commander of United Nations forces, conferred on Wake Island. The President wanted to ask the five-star general for a first-hand professional evaluation of the possibility of Chinese intervention. MacArthur considered this contingency very unlikely.[15] (At the time he was conferring with Truman, Chinese forces were already crossing the Yalu into North Korea.)

"Had [the Chinese] interfered in the first or second month, it would have been decisive. We are no longer fearful of their intervention. We no longer stand hat in hand," MacArthur stated.

Many officials in the U.S. Department of State also came to the conclusion that Chinese intervention in Korea was "unlikely." This assessment was shared by the President, the Joint Chiefs of Staff, members of the National Security Council, General Walter Bedell Smith, Director of the CIA, prominent Senators, Congressmen and political pundits of all hues.[16]

Apparently Truman and MacArthur relied on frequent pronouncements of America's non-aggressive intentions to reassure the Chinese leaders. For

13 On October 2, India's Ambassador K.M. Panikkar in Peking had announced his famous warning that if UN forces were to cross the 38th parallel, China would probably enter the war. See Panikkar, *In Two Chinas* (London: Allen & Unwin, 1955), p. 100.

14 John G. Stoessinger, *Crusaders and Pragmatists: Movers of Modern American Foreign Policy* (New York: W.W. Norton & Co., 1979), p. 85.

15 U.S. Senate, *Military Situation in the Far East*, Hearings before the Committee on Armed Services and the Committee on Foreign Relations, 82nd Congress, 1st Session, 1950, p. 3483.

16 Samuel B. Griffith, *The Chinese People's Liberation Army* (New York: McGraw-Hill, 1967), p. 124. According to one CIA "insider," the Central Intelligence Agency concluded on October 12, 1950 that Chinese full-scale intervention in Korea "was not probable in 1950".

instance, on November 16, the President had stated that the U.S. has "never at any time entertained any intention to carry hostilities into China." He added that "because of the long-standing American friendship for the people of China, the United States [would] take every honorable step to prevent any extension of the hostilities in the Far East."[17]

To the consternation of many Americans, the Chinese launched a surprise attack on South Korean and U.S. forces on October 26, 1950.[18] This attack occurred fifty miles south of the Chinese border. It was accompanied by fierce bugle calls, shrill whistles and blasts on shepherd's horns. The results were devastating. Several UN regiments were virtually decimated.[19]

PRC soldiers had moved at night in forced marches. Employing local guides and porters as direction finders, they used the barren and hostile terrain of the North Korean hills and mountains to their advantage. Then they launched their planned massive assault on MacArthur's unsuspecting army in late November 1950.

China's Decision to Enter the Korean War

The People's Republic of China, a non-nuclear power, was not deterred from attacking a nuclear power, as Pascal's Wager would suggest. Why not?

First, it seems that a Soviet *Diktat* was not needed to bring the Chinese into the war. As Allen Whiting concludes in his classic study, *China Crosses the Yalu*, "China entered the war of her own free will." To be sure, there "undoubtedly were questions of mutual responsibility, some of which may have been resolved to the dissatisfaction of one or both partners ... But the final decision to fight appears to have been basically a Chinese decision, conditioned by Russian advice and encouraged by Russian support."[20]

American reassurances failed to impress the Chinese because they had

---

17 *The New York Times*, November 17, 1950.
18 United Nations troops began reporting contact with Chinese "volunteer" forces on October 26, 1950, and such clashes occurred more frequently in early November. However, it was not until November 26, that the Chinese unleashed a full-scale attack on American and other UN forces. This massive intervention resulted in an "entirely new war," to use General Douglas MacArthur's words.
19 One day after the Chinese attack, Major General Charles A. Willoughby, MacArthur's main intelligence officer, was still voicing the opinion that "the auspicious time for Chinese intervention [had] long passed" and that "there [was] no positive evidence that Chinese Communist units, as such [had] entered Korea." See U.S. Senate, *Military Situation in the Far East*, p. 3427.
20 Allen S. Whiting, *China Crosses the Yalu* (Stanford: Stanford University Press, 1960), p. 154.

heard such rhetoric before. Had not U.S. officials declared that they would halt at the thirty-eighth parallel, and had they not crossed it? Had not the Americans wanted it believed that they would not push their offensive up to the Yalu but would stop short of the river itself, and were not U.S. troops now approaching the river? In view of such circumstances, what credence could be given to new American assertions that they would refrain from crossing the Yalu into Chinese territory?[21]

A 1977 RAND study begins its analysis with a careful assessment of the formidable problems facing the Chinese then.[22] "Examination of the military balance at that time indicates that, contrary to popular belief, PRC forces lacked even numerical superiority *vis-a-vis* the United Nations' force. United Nations soldiers numbered 440,000 while PRC ground forces totaled from 270,000 to 340,000."[23] But an even greater inequality existed in the case of UN firepower. This was "overwhelmingly superior" to PRC capabilities in terms of artillery, naval power and especially air power.[24]

Logistics and support presented another problem for Chinese military planners. Only six bridges connected China to the battlefront.[25] These transportation and communication routes "were already known to the US

---

21 See the editorial by *Jen-min Jih-pao*, November 6, 1950, quoted in Tang Tsou, *America's Failure in China, 1941-1950* (Chicago: University of Chicago Press, 1963), pp. 582-83.

22 Michael E. Brown, *Deterrence Failures and Deterrence Strategies* (Santa Monica: The RAND Corporation, 1977), pp. 13-15.

23 Allen S. Whiting, *China Crosses the Yalu: The Decision to Enter the Korean War* (Santa Monica: The RAND Corporation, 1960), p. 122. This study, was done by a former State Department intelligence analyst, and is considered the classic work on the Chinese decision.
By the end of 1952 there were over a million Chinese troops in North Korea, according to U.S. figures. See David Rees, *opus cit.*, p. 406.

24 During the Korean War, the Chinese rapidly built up their Air Force with the help of the Soviets. In June 1950 the People's Republic of China was not operating any MIG-15s in squadron service, but in July 1953 the Chinese were using about 2,000 jet fighters, nearly all of them in Manchuria. As General Vandenburg told a Pentagon press conference on November 21, 1951, "Almost overnight China has become one of the major air powers of the world." See David Rees, *opus cit.*, p. 374.

25 *Ibid.* It is important to note here that the superiority of the peasant guerrilla over the "paper tiger" of American atomic power was relentlessly drilled into new recruits of the People's Liberation Army. As Chinese General Nieh Jung-chen put it: "They [the Americans] may even drop atom bombs on us. What then? They may kill a few million people. Without sacrifice, a nation's independence cannot be upheld... After all, China lives on the farms. What can atom bombs do there?" Quoted in Samuel B. Griffith II, *The Chinese People's Liberation Army* (New York: McGraw-Hill, 1967), p. 118.

Air Force and were highly vulnerable to US air attack." Finally, the military doctrine of Mao Tse-tung proclaimed that "victory was a function of superiority of numbers, mobility of forces, and guerrilla warfare amidst a friendly population in home territory."[26] These conditions "simply did not hold for intervention in Korea."

Certainly, intervention was not an attractive proposition for Chinese leaders, the more so when the possibility of U.S. atomic retaliation on the Chinese homeland was introduced into the picture. To be sure, the possibility of an atomic attack was discussed in the Chinese press and presumably in PRC decision-making circles.[27] Furthermore, air raid drills were subsequently conducted throughout northeastern China.[28] Nonetheless, "Chinese leaders were so strongly *motivated* to intervene that they were willing to accept the risk and also the likelihood of a strong US military response, *even one including the use of atomic weapons against the mainland.*"[29] (Italics mine.)

The key factor in the Chinese decision may well have been the threat posed by MacArthur's advance toward their border. Since MacArthur had been so successful in "rolling back" communism in North Korea, the Chinese leadership might well have believed that he was not interested in stopping his crusade at the Yalu River. But there were some other important factors that went into the Chinese decision to intervene.

Under Mao, the Chinese tended to downplay the importance of nuclear weapons in affecting the outcome of a conflict. As Mao explained his stance to the American journalist Anne Louise Strong in 1946:[30]

---

26 Of particular significance to Chinese military strategy in Korea are Mao's two great studies on war which distilled from his experience fighting the Kuomintang and the Japanese, *Strategic Problems of China's Revolutionary War* (1936) and *On the Protracted War* (1938).

27 The possibility of general war was mentioned in internal Chinese press comment. A prolonged limited war in Korea was depicted as a victory for China in that it would stop the American occupation of the entire country and drain away U.S. resources. Although the Chinese public was conditioned to withstand total war if necessary, the Chinese leadership was not sure what its massive intervention in Korea would bring.

28 Rees, *opus cit.*, p. 135.

29 Alexander L. George and Richard Smoke, *Deterrence in American Foreign Policy: Theory and Practice* (New York: Columbia University Press, 1974), p. 220. See also Whiting, *opus cit.*, pp. 134-39.
Michael Linday concludes differently: "it seems quite likely that the Chinese involvement in Korea was mainly the result of confusion and not of considered policy on either side." See his *China and the Cold War*, p. 37.

30 Quoted in Alice Langley Hsieh, *Communist China's Strategy in the Nuclear Age* (Englewood Cliffs, N.J.: Prentice-Hall, 1962), p. 132.

The atom bomb is a paper tiger with which the American reactionaries try to terrify the people. It looks terrible, but in fact is not. Of course, the atom bomb is a weapon of mass annihilation: the outcome of a war is decided by the people, not by one or two new weapons.

This emphasis on the people as the ultimate determining factor of victory or defeat represented the cornerstone of Maoist military doctrine. The basic view of the limited utility of nuclear weapons was retained even after the Chinese detonated their own atomic bomb in 1964 and hydrogen bomb two and onehalf years later.[31]

The metaphor of the "paper tiger" — "outwardly strong, but inwardly feeble" — was a device seized upon by Mao to break down the "superstition" that left people intimidated by nuclear threats. According to one student of Chinese nuclear strategy, Ralph Powell, the Chinese were concerned that the destructiveness of nuclear weapons ought not to be exaggerated lest the masses be demoralized. If the basic concept of the "paper tiger" meant that in the end the U.S. imperialists could not triumph, this did not mean, however, that its real qualities could be ignored. The idea was to despise the adversary strategically, but to respect him tactically.[32]

The Chinese went to some lengths during the Korean War to show how even after nuclear attack the People's Republic of China still need not succumb to a conqueror because the basic approach of the People's War would still be applicable. As evidence, the following statement was published in November 1950, reportedly written by an "eyewitness" of Hiroshima:[33]

When you can get into a well-constructed air-raid shelter before the release of the bomb and put on a suit of white clothing and make sure to get to a place ten kilometres away immediately after the explosion, nothing shall happen to you. Look at myself. ... I have gone through the explosion of an atomic bomb and I am still growing strong as before. The atom bomb is in fact not as dreadful as American imperialism points it out to be.

When Mao Tse-tung attempted to "enlighten" Khrushchev in a visit to Moscow in the 1950s on the Chinese view of the relevance of People's War in the nuclear age, Khrushchev was shocked. As Khrushchev recounts this

31 See Jonathan D. Pollack, "Chinese Attitudes Towards Nuclear Weapons, 1964-69," *China Quarterly*, No. 50 (1972), p. 269.
32 Ralph Powell, "Great Powers and Atomic Bombs are 'Paper Tigers,'" *China Quarterly*, No. 23 (July-September, 1965).
33 Quoted in Lawrence Freedman, *The Evolution of Nuclear Strategy* (New York: St. Martin's Press, 1983), p. 277.

episode in his memoirs, he and Mao were sitting, clad only in bathing trunks, by a swimming pool in Peking:[34]

Comrade Mao Tse-tung, nowadays that sort of thinking is out of date. You can no longer calculate the alignment of forces on the basis of who has the most men. Back in the days when a dispute was settled with fists or bayonets, it made a difference who had the most men and the most bayonets on each side. Then, when the machine gun appeared, the side with more troops no longer necessarily had the advantage. And now with the atomic bomb, the number of troops on each side makes practically no difference to the alignment of real power and the outcome of a war. The more troops on a side, the more bomb fodder.

Chinese and Soviet differences over the importance of nuclear weapons notwithstanding, one can see that nuclear deterrence did not deter the Chinese. As John Stoessinger writes, "the Chinese intervention in the Korean War provides a good illustration of the practical, operational consequences of divergent perceptions in foreign policy decisions. These perceptions are, in effect, definitions of the situation in hand." Once the situation has been defined, "certain alternatives are eliminated. One does not conciliate an opponent who is perceived as implacably hostile; hence the Chinese Communists felt in the end that they had no resort but to intervene in Korea."

Continuing in this vein, Stoessinger concludes: "One does not credit the threats of an opponent whose power one feels to be negligible; hence, the American leaders perceived even specific Chinese warnings as bluff." One does not "compromise with an opponent whose ideology is perceived as antithetical to one's values; hence, the United States and China remained poised on the brink of potentially disastrous conflict, neither one accepting the other's perception of its world role as legitimate." This was "the central significance of the 'entirely new war' that was to ravage the peninsula for another two and a half years."[35]

Atomic Bombs on Manchuria?

General MacArthur wanted to respond to the Chinese attack by bombing Chinese troops and supplies in Manchuria. Truman's response was firm, although measured. He forbade MacArthur to bomb the Chinese sanctuary in Manchuria. However, he intimated that the U.S. would use all its power to contain the Chinese. At a news conference on November 30, 1950 he showed signs of losing this restraint. By not ruling out the use of atomic

---

34 Nikita Khrushchev, *Khrushchev Remembers* (Boston: Little & Brown, 1980).
35 John G. Stoessinger, *opus cit.*, p. 92.

weapons in the conflict, he implied that they might be used to contain the Chinese offensive.[36] This remark brought the British Prime Minister Clement Attlee scurrying to Washington on December 4. Subsequently, the Prime Minister received the President's private assurances that the U.S. was not planning to use the bomb. The two men then embarked on a full, candid and most revealing discussion of the Asian tinderbox.[37]

The seriousness of the situation in Korea was reflected in American polls at home. Over fifty percent of the people thought that World War III was imminent.[38] For their part, the Joint Chiefs of Staff thought the danger of war was "greatly increased." Thus, on December 6, 1950 they sent a general war warning to all unified commanders.[39] On Capitol Hill huge new defense appropriations were approved. By January, the original $ 13.5 billion defense budget for fiscal 1951 was quadrupled. Although the Administration decided against mobilization, in a short time the Korean War economic boom was under way.

36 Remarking at his press conference that the U.S. would "take whatever steps are necessary to meet the military situation," Truman was asked: "Will that include the atomic bomb?" "That includes every weapon we have," Truman replied. "Mr. President, you said 'every weapon we have.' Does that mean that there is active consideration of the use of the atomic bomb?" Truman: "There has always been active consideration of its use..." See Harry S. Truman, *Memoirs*, Vol. II, *Years of Trial and Hope* (London: Hodder & Stoughton, 1956), p. 419. According to declassified U.S. government documents, obtained through the Freedom of Information Act, the Joint Chiefs of Staff had by this time already recommended against the use of the bomb in North Korea apparently because of the lack of suitable military targets and the expected public uproar. Also, the atomic stockpile was small at this time, and many felt that it had to be kept for a clash in Central Europe. Korea was generally viewed in Washington as merely a diversion from a big Soviet push being prepared for Europe.
Paul Bracken makes this telling point: "Although there have been many studies of why the United States did not use nuclear weapons in Korea, they have overlooked what might have been a determining factor, the fact that none were there to use in the first dark days after the invasion." See his *The Command and Control of Nuclear Weapons* (New Haven: Yale University Press, 1983), p. 181.
37 See Walter LaFeber, *America, Russia and the Cold War 1945-1980* 4th ed. (New York: John Wiley and Sons, 1980), p. 119-20.
38 See David Rees, *opus cit.*, p. 172.
39 Thomas A. Donovan, a career U.S. foreign service officer stationed in The Hague at the time, writes: "When the fighting broke out in Korea, I remember that the Embassy staff went through a whole evacuation exercise, with plans for hurrying away to England if the Russians attacked West Germany..." Letter to the author, March 9, 1984.

Eisenhower Threatens Use of A-Bombs to Gain a Truce

President Dwight D. Eisenhower, who took office in 1953, has suggested that the fear of American nuclear attack eventually brought China to agree to end the war. If this indeed were the case, it would represent a significant instance of nuclear *compellance* — not deterrence.[40]

In his memoirs Eisenhower states that in the spring of 1953 he was unwilling to accept any longer the stalemate in the Korean conflict and in the armistice talks with the North Koreans and the Chinese. Thus, he seriously considered a nuclear attack upon targets in the People's Republic of China. (Previously he had supported Truman's decision not to bomb across the Yalu.) In Eisenhower's own words:[41]

One possibility was to let the Communist authorities understand that, in the absence of satisfactory progress, we intended to move decisively without inhibition in our use of weapons, and we would no longer be responsible for confining hostilities to the Korean Peninsula.

The President claims that this warning was delivered to the Chinese and that as a result they agreed to conclude the armistice agreement. Eisenhower backed up this verbal threat by ordering the moving of atomic missiles to Okinawa in early 1953. At the same time, the Administration authorized appropriations for raising additional South Korean divisions, continued to re-equip the U.S. Air Force in Korea with Sabre jets and in July dispatched another division of Marines to the Far East.[42]

The armistice talks were already well along before the Eisenhower Ad-

---

40 The distinction between *compellance* and *deterrence* is one between the active and passive use of force. Compellance or coercive diplomacy represents basically the capacity to persuade the adversary to undertake specific actions (positive influence). Whereas deterrence refers to the ability to prohibit certain policies (negative influence) on the part of the adversary. The success of a deterrent threat is usually measured by its not having to be implemented. On the other hand, the success of compellant action is measured by how closely and quickly the adversary conforms to one's stipulated wishes. According to Thomas Schelling, compellance may be easier to demonstrate than deterrence, but it is harder to achieve. Schelling maintains that compellant actions tend to be vaguer in their objectives than deterrent threat and for that reason are more difficult to attain. See Schelling, *Arms and Influence* (New Haven: Yale University Press, 1966).

41 Dwight D. Eisenhower, *Mandate for Change 1953-1956* (New York: Doubleday, 1963), p. 181.

42 For details see Robert J. Donovan, *Eisenhower: The Inside Story* (New York: Harper, 1956), p. 116. "At no time," Donovan writes, "did the President make a formal decision to enlarge the war. Some of those who were closest to him at the time are convinced that he would certainly have done so if the stalemate had dragged on. But his fervent hope was for a truce, and he would have regarded war against China as a dread step to be taken only as a last resort."

ministration delivered its admonition to the Chinese. The main outstanding issue between the two sides dealt not with territorial or political questions but simply with the repatriation of Chinese prisoners of war. The Chinese had learned that about 85,000 of 170,000 prisoners were refusing to go back to the mainland, and they wanted all their prisoners returned. Not to lose face, the Chinese demanded that the POWs, many of whom had surrendered on the strength of promised protection, be forcefully repatriated if necessary. However, United States and U.N. officials felt that they could not go back on these assurances by returning the Chinese prisoners against their will.[43]

Professor A.F. Organski is one of the few scholars to vigorously question the efficacy of the nuclear threat on the Chinese. He argues, "it is not clear why the fear of nuclear attack that failed to deter the Chinese from entering the Korean War in the first place or from driving the Americans back to the 38th parallel in the second place should suddenly have [compelled] them from insisting that their prisoners be repatriated simply because the American government made explicit a danger which had always existed." Moreover, he says, if U.S. intelligence did not even know that the Chinese were going to enter the war when they did, "it is difficult to see how they knew why the Chinese finally agreed to an armistice."[44]

Adam Ulam suggests here that the death of Joseph Stalin may have been an important factor in Chinese calculations. "If Stalin had not died in March 1953, it is quite likely that the impasse [in the negotiations] would have continued beyond the date of actual signing of the truce on July 27, 1953."[45]

43 The American decision reportedly was influenced by the activities of Dean Rusk, then Assistant Secretary of State for Far Eastern Affairs in the State Department. Rusk recalled the tragic experience of World War II when the U.S. made a secret agreement at Yalta with Stalin to return Russian POWS once the war was over. When the time came to repatriate these prisoners, many did not want to return to the U.S.S.R. because they feared harsh treatment, even death. The purges of the 1930s were still fresh in their minds, and they knew that Soviet policy was to take a very hard line toward those soldiers who had surrendered or were otherwise taken prisoner by the Germans. After some discussion in the U.S. government, it was decided to force the repatriation of all the POWs. As a result, many undertook acts of desperation such as committing suicide rather than return to the Soviet Union. During the Korean War, Rusk argued convincingly that the United States could not allow a repetition of such an unfortunate situation.
44 A.F. Organski, *World Politics* (New York: Alfred A. Knopf, 1958), p. 321.
45 Adam B. Ulam, *opus cit.*, p. 183. "It is still not clear how seriously [Eisenhower's] threat to use nuclear weapons was meant. But it is unlikely," writes Ulam, "that it scared *Stalin*. The prospect of the United States becoming more deeply involved in the Far East was far from disturbing to the equanimity of the Soviet leadership. On the other hand, the Chinese had every reason to wish for a speedy termination

At the last minute, Syngman Rhee, the 78-year-old leader of South Korea, tried to upset the armistice by suddenly freeing some 27,000 North Korean and Chinese prisoners of war. Rhee was bitterly opposed to an end to the fighting, which once again would leave Korea divided. Rhee wanted to renew hostilities in the hope of reunifying his country. But he failed in his aim.

According to David Rees, when Eisenhower was informed initially of Rhee's action by Secretary of State Dulles, "both men decided there and then that if Rhee's action meant that the projected truce was wrecked and heavy fighting broke out ... as the Communists repudiated their agreement, the U.S. would go ahead and take the war to mainland China. The targets beyond the Yalu had already been chosen."[46]

Eisenhower, his Secretary of State Dulles and others remained convinced that it was the threat to use nuclear weapons against China (i.e., *compellance*) that induced the leadership of the People's Republic of China to agree to end the fighting. In turn, this reinforced the faith of many Americans in the utility of the advanced warning coupled with the threat of heavy punishment. Thus, out of the Korean War the doctrine of "massive retaliation" was born.

New Documents on 1953 Korean Atomic Policy

As this book went to press, the U.S. State Department released hundreds of documents on the Korean War. Most of these papers were originally classified "Top Secret." They were included in the State Department's latest volume in the series called *Foreign Relations of the United States*. The volume, in two books, covers Korea from 1952 to 1954. These documents are a primary source on American foreign policy and thus are extremely important.

The 2,000 pages of documents now made public show the high level of planning and detail of discussion on possible use of nuclear weapons in Korea and China and President Eisenhower's interest in overcoming reluctance to use them. They also bear out Eisenhower's memoirs on the point that the President came into office prepared to use atomic bombs, if necessary, to end the Korean War.

At a National Security Council meeting on February 11, 1953, the record shows that the President, then in office less than a month, agreed with Secretary of State Dulles "that we could not go on the way we were

of the fighting. They had extracted maximum gains in prestige from their Korean involvement, but its continuation threatened them with disaster ..." (p. 200).

46 See Rees, *Korea*, p. 425.

indefinitely." On March 27, at a subsequent meeting, they agreed "that somehow or other the taboo which surrounds the use of atomic weapons would have to be destroyed." While Dulles was of the view that "in the present state of world opinion, we could not use an A-bomb, we should make every effort now to dissipate this feeling."

By May 13, 1953, the National Security Council was discussing a memorandum, designated NSC-147, which outlined six choices for ending military restraints. Several of these involved ending the ban on bombing raids against China and increasing air attacks on North Korea.

Several U.S. military men said they saw no particular tactical value in using atomic weapons in North Korea. General J. Lawton Collins, the Army Chief of Staff, observed: "Personally, I am very skeptical about the value of using atomic weapons tactically in Korea. The Communists are dug into positions in depth over a front of 150 miles."

President Eisenhower said he "thought it might be cheaper, dollarwise, to use atomic weapons in Korea than to continue to use conventional weapons against the dugouts which honeycombed the hills along which the enemy forces were presently deployed."

On May 21, 1953, Secretary Dulles met in New Delhi with Prime Minister Jawaharlal Nehru and told him that, if the armistice negotiations failed, "the United States would probably make a stronger, rather than a lesser military exertion, and that this might well extend the area of conflict."

Following the truce of July 1953, the Eisenhower Administration renewed consideration of the nuclear issue. According to a report of a National Security Council meeting on December 3, 1953, the "President expressed with great emphasis the opinion that if the Chinese Communists attacked us again, we should certainly respond by hitting them hard and wherever it would hurt most, including Peiping [Peking] itself." This said the President would "mean all-out war against Communist China."

At the December 1953 meeting, President Eisenhower asked Admiral Arthur W. Radford, the Chairman of the Joint Chiefs of Staff, whether he agreed that there would be a war with China if South Korea were attacked anew. Admiral Radford responded by saying that he did, adding: "We would have to strike against the Communist Chinese in the air, from Shanghai all the way north."

Interestingly, Secretary of State Dulles, who agreed that the U.S. should not shrink from using these weapons of mass destruction, nevertheless was alarmed at this recommendation. He said the State Department preferred to limit a nuclear attack to North Korea and to nearby troop concentrations. His concern, he stated, was not just that the Russians might enter the war, but that America's allies would not support the United States.

Eventually, on January 7, 1954, the State Department and the Joint

Chiefs of Staff agreed to a compromise on the use of nuclear weapons. They said that in case of a resumption of hostilities, the United States should undertake "offensive air operations employing atomic weapons against military targets in Korea, and against those military targets in Manchuria and China which are being used by the Communists in direct support of their operations in Korea."

Summary

There is no doubt that the application of game theory to the field of nuclear deterrence is a most challenging proposition. However, as the experience of the Korean War makes clear, there are some important practical problems to consider before final judgment is rendered.

In the first place, nuclear deterrence does not deter conventional attacks.[47] In Korea, the Chinese, who possessed no nuclear weapons, took on in open combat the world's leading nuclear power. They did this at extreme risk and heavy cost, but in the end they emerged with enhanced power and respect.[48]

The American decision to cross the 38th parallel and rely on its nuclear deterrent strategy to keep the Chinese at bay proved exceptionally costly to the United States. Four fifths of over 142,000 U.S. casualties in the conflict occurred *after* UN forces crossed the parallel. Moreover, the greatly widened war froze the United States into a "cold war" posture for the next twenty years, affecting particularly Sino-American relations.

Historical perspective serves only to deepen the tragic feeling held by many in 1950 that the "new war" with China was unnecessary and avoidable. As Alexander L. George and Richard Smoke state in their excellent study of the conflict: "The damaging effects of the North Korean invasion of South Korea on the subsequent course of international affairs might

---

47 Alexander L. George and Richard Smoke disagree here. They maintain that the "Korean War is less a failure of attempted deterrence than it is a failure to employ deterrence more effectively." See their *Deterrence in American Foreign Policy* (New York: Columbia University Press, 1974), p. 142. As for Chinese intervention in the war, which George and Smoke treat as a separate case, "We can speak . . . of a double failure of deterrence. Each side attempted and failed, in turn, to deter the other from moving into North Korea." (p. 187)

48 Some critics argue here that the U.S. policy for persuading the Chinese to stay out of North Korea can hardly be termed deterrence, since it relied so heavily on reassurances and made very little use of threat. However, as George and Smoke correctly point out, "the reassurances were backed by the threat implicit in the presence of American military forces, particularly air power, in Korea." *Ibid.*, p. 187.

have been substantially limited and circumscribed had it not led within five months to a new war with intervening Chinese Communist forces."[49]

To be sure, the conflict of interests anchored in the historical situation was real enough. However, it led to war only because of misperceptions, miscalculations, inept actions and an overreliance on nuclear deterrence. It is sobering to realize that the Sino-American military confrontation in Korea was one neither side wanted and both tried to avoid.

In addition, the Korean War example demonstrates that intentions and motivations *do* indeed make a difference in international relations. At no time prior to the first Sino-American clash in October 1950, did U.S. policy-makers seriously consider the possibility of Chinese intervention in the conflict. The Chinese leaders, most believed, would not be so foolhardy as to risk their meager resources against the overwhelming military forces of the world's leading atomic power.

Some critics of this analysis argue that Chinese behavior must be seen in light of the Soviet nuclear umbrella, for the U.S.S.R. was obligated by treaty to help defend the People's Republic of China if Chinese territory was attacked. However, what some of these people fail to realize is that during the years from 1950 to 1953, the Soviet Union possessed little in the way of nuclear weapons and adequate delivery systems. For his part, President Truman may well have been reluctant to attack the PRC and thus risk involving the Soviets, but his fear presumably was not of Soviet *nuclear* strength.[50]

Game theory, which is based on a purely rational objective model, does not take into account the crucial role of perception/misperception in international politics. Moreover, the theory, when applied to the complex milieu of international relations, assumes that national decision-makers see themselves as always having a choice. But this may not be true, as the Chinese decision in 1950 dramatically illustrates. Apparently, the Chinese leadership felt so threatened by the Korean action as to believe that it had no other course but to intervene in this, the "Year of the Tiger" in the Chinese calendar.[51]

---

49 Alexander L. George and Richard Smoke, *opus cit.*, p. 184.

50 It is not well known that American aircraft launched conventional bombing raids against Soviet targets during the Korean War. For instance, on October 9, 1950 two F-80 jets "beat up" a Soviet airfield sixty miles inside the border of the U.S.S.R. near Vladivostock. Official U.S. policy, however, was to avoid such incidents.

51 Ambassador Martin Hillenbrand takes issue with this analysis. "The example of the Korean War which you cite — and you could just as well have cited the example of Vietnam — doesn't seem to me to prove your point. The Chinese at that time were technically relatively unsophisticated about things nuclear. Only posses-

Some critics may argue that the Korean War is not a fair test case. While this is an example of the failure of extended deterrence, there is no indication, it is argued, that strategic deterrence has failed. However, the Soviet threat is a function of both Soviet military capabilities and the Soviet value attached to peace. The American ability to "deter" the Soviet leadership from strategic attack is thus a function of the Soviet value of peace. As the 1977 RAND study points out: "It is logically indefensible to argue that the United States has heretofore 'deterred' the Soviet Union from attacking when there is no evidence that Soviet behavior has been modified by U.S. actions."[52]

Game theory is thus not especially helpful when applied to the question of nuclear deterrence. Not only does it suffer from certain theoretical shortcomings. But it fails to take into consideration the practical reality that rationality is a function of perception. A change in our way of thinking about nuclear deterrence is overdue.

sors of nuclear weapons need to be deterred from using them against one another; they are the ones who know what the consequences would be. It is also a fact that a sort of peculiar reverse form or extension of deterrence operates in wars between nuclear and non-nuclear powers. The former are deterred because they know how awful the weapons are. "When the Chinese became a nuclear power, they did not use nuclear weapons against the Vietnamese a few years ago. This does not mean that deterrence does not work where it really matters. No one has claimed that it should work against relatively unsophisticated non-nuclear powers.
"Apart from what I might call expediential deterrence (the pure logic of Pascal's wager), there is also moral deterrence. That is the operative factor in the kinds of wars that occur between nuclear powers and non-nuclear powers; it is also frequently a component of overall deterrence as it operates in practice . . ." Letter to this writer, May 30, 1984.

52 Michael E. Brown, *opus cit.*, p. 24. John Spanier, a proponent of nuclear deterrence, writes that the limited attack in Korea "clearly demonstrated that the Soviet leaders were not deterred by the policy of massive retaliation, despite America's far greater atomic stockpile and ability to deliver it . . ." See his *American Foreign Policy*, 9th ed. (New York: Holt, Rinehart & Winston, 1983), p. 64.

> [E]veryone credited the nuclear deterrent with the victory. But if it was the nuclear deterrent that determined victory for the Americans, how can one explain the fact that the United States was herself not deterred by the Russian nuclear force...
> A.F.K. Organski

XVI. THE CUBAN MISSILE CRISIS

Serious studies challenging the conventional wisdom of nuclear deterrence are rare in the vast literature in international relations. One major exception is the rigorous investigation undertaken just a few years ago by A.F.K. Organski and Jacek Kugler.[1]

They examined fourteen major international crises from 1945 to 1975.[2] To their amazement they discovered "that the logical conditions for deterrence" were absent and by inference "that mutual deterrence" was "not taking place." They considered this "shocking" and concluded: "There is simply no way in the world . . . one can support the theory of deterrence as founded."

---

1 A.F.K. Organski and Jacek Kugler, *The War Ledger* (Chicago: The University of Chicago Press, 1980). — Professor Organski is a well respected scholar who is currently program director at the Center for Political Studies, Institute for Social Research, University of Michigan. Professor Kugler, at the time this study was done, was faculty associate at Michigan's Center for Political Studies.

2 These case studies were as follows: The Chinese Civil War in 1945-49; the Berlin Blockade in 1948-49; the Czechoslovakian coup in 1948; the Korean War in 1950-53; the Hungarian revolt in 1956; the Suez crisis in 1956; the Berlin Wall in 1961; the Cuban missile crisis in 1962; the Vietnam War in 1964-73; the Arab-Israeli War in 1967; the second Czechoslovakian coup in 1968; the Sino-Soviet dispute in 1969; the Arab-Israeli War in 1973; and the Sino-Vietnamese-Soviet dispute in 1979. — In assessing the importance of these studies one must note that the data base used by Organski and Kugler was limited. Thus, their findings must be taken with a degree of caution and compared with the findings of other scholars who have had access to more information.

Compellance Versus Deterrence

A case in point is the Cuban Missile Crisis of October 1962. Many proponents of deterrence claim that this crisis is a classic example of how the "balance of terror" served to deter nuclear conflict.[3] But as more information about this seminal event is becoming known, we can readily see that this is much too simplistic a view of the crisis.[4]

It is true, of course, that the United States enjoyed at the time an overwhelming advantage in strategic nuclear weapons *vis-a-vis* the Soviet Union. The Soviets had no more than 85 intercontinental ballistic missiles deployed and, probably because of inadequate means of communication with their missile launch crews, they did not even put them on alert. By way of contrast, the United States had nearly 300 ICBMs.[5]

This state of affairs was only too evident to Premier Nikita Khrushchev. In fact, this tremendous disparity in nuclear weaponry may well have been the crucial factor in influencing the Soviet leader to put more limited range nuclear missiles into Cuba.[6] (So far as one can judge, the decision for the Cuban venture was not Khrushchev's alone; other leaders, both civilian and military, partook in it.)[7]

---

3 See, for example, James L. Payne, *The American Threat: The Fear of War as an Instrument of Foreign Policy* (Chicago: Markham Publishing Co., 1970), p. 37. Here Payne writes: "There exists no clearer illustration of an international threat at work than the Cuban missile crisis of October, 1962 . . ."

4 In the strategic literature, the Cuban missile crisis is sometimes cited as an example of *compellance*, this being the threat of force not to *prevent* an attack but to make an adversary *do* something or *undo* something already done. According to Schelling, compellance is much harder to achieve, is more complex and is much more dangerous.
    If the missile crisis appears at its core to be technically an example of "compellance," most students of the crisis have stressed the classical elements of nuclear deterrence which they maintain were operative.

5 "Missile Gap: 1957-1960," Center for Defense Information, unpublished manuscript, 1983, p. 3. See also Department of Defense Statement on U.S. Military Strength, April 14, 1964.

6 See, for example, Michael Tatu, *Power in the Kremlin: From Khrushchev to Kosygin* (New York, 1967, p. 231. Many analysts argue that the Cuban undertaking can be attributed to politics within the Kremlin. See Arthur M. Schlesinger, Jr., *A Thousand Days: John F. Kennedy in the White House* (Boston: Houghton Mifflin, 1965), p. 796.

7 In his memoirs Khrushchev states: "When I was the head of the government and also held the highest post in the Central Committee, I never made a decision on my own, without consulting and securing the approval of my comrades in the leadership. The conditions were such that it was impossible for one man to dictate his will to the others; I was in favor of those conditions, and I did my best to

Background to the Crisis

The unprecedented Soviet decision to station nuclear weapons outside the borders of the U.S.S.R. took place against a backdrop of steadily improving Soviet-Cuban relations. Though initially reserved in its response to the Cuban revolution of January 1959, the Soviet leadership gradually became ready to exploit the political potential of the energetic and charismatic Fidel Castro. Seeing Cuba as a challenge to American influence in Latin America or, possibly, as a projection of Soviet power into the Western hemisphere, the Kremlin began to supply large amounts of military equipment to the Cuban forces. As a result of increased Soviet assistance following the fateful Bay of Pigs invasion of April 1961, Cuba was able to field one of the best equipped armies in all of Latin America.[8]

Beginning in late July 1962, Russian military shipments to Cuba suddenly increased. This was the beginning of a two-phased arms build-up involving some of the U.S.S.R.'s most advanced weaponry. The first stage concentrated on the installation of modern defensive weapons systems. These included the delivery of 24 batteries of surface-to-air missile launchers (SAMs), each of which was equipped with 24 missiles with a firing range of about 25 miles. In addition, the Soviets provided more than 100 jet planes, including Moscow's most sophisticated supersonic fighter. The second stage of this buildup started in early September 1962, with the arrival of long-range offensive weapons in Cuban ports. Among those weapons were:[9]

- 42 Ilyushin-28 (Beagle tactical) bombers, capable of delivering nuclear bombs up to a range of 600 miles;
- 6 battalions of Medium-Range Ballistic Missile (MRBM) launchers, equipped with 8 missiles each, with a range of 1,100 miles;
- 4 battalions of Intermediate-Range Missile (IRBM) launchers, equipped with 8 missiles each, with a range of 2,200 miles.

    reinforce them." See *Khrushchev Remembers: The Last Testament* (New York: Bantam Books, 1976), p. 618.

8 Morton Schwartz, "The Cuban Missile Venture," in James B. Christoph *et al.*, *Cases in Comparative Politics*, 3rd ed. (Boston: Little, Brown & Co., 1976), p. 318.

9 Most of the information regarding Soviet weapons deliveries to Cuba was taken from United States Congress, House of Representatives, Subcommittee of the Committee on Appropriations, *Department of Defense Appropriations for 1964*, Hearings, 88th Congress, 1st Session, 1963, p. 7 and United States Congress, Senate, Committee on Armed Services, Preparedness Investigating Subcommittee, *Investigation of the Preparedness Program, Interim Report on Cuban Military Buildup*, 88th Congress, 1st Session, 1963.

All of these systems were designed to achieve full operational capability by mid-December. However, according to one authoritative account, the Medium-Range Ballistic Missiles were fully operational as early as late October.[10] Significantly, these weapons were accompanied by about 20,000 Soviet personnel, including both technicians and ground troops.

The secret introduction of nuclear weapons into Cuba was occurring despite repeated and persistent warnings from highranking American officials that the United States would not tolerate the establishment of offensive bases in the area. On September 4, for instance, President Kennedy announced that the deployment of the 25-mile range SAM missiles had been detected. He said that, while the U.S. considered these weapons basically "defensive," it could not permit the installation of "offensive" missiles. Should hard evidence be obtained of the "presence of offensive ground-to-ground missiles, or of other significant offensive capability either in Cuban hands or under Soviet direction and guidance", he admonished, "the gravest issues would arise."[11]

For their part, the Soviets continued to deny any intention of putting offensive weapons into Cuba. As late as October 18, Soviet Foreign Minister Andrei Gromyko personally reassured Kennedy that no offensive missiles were being deployed in Cuba. However, at this time the Soviets had already clandestinely transferred many long-range strategic armaments and military equipment to the island. Concealed in the holds of cargo ships and in disguised crates, they were unloaded at night in order to prevent detection by American intelligence. By this time, too, U.S. intelligence officials had identified nine new missile sites.[12]

Although there was little doubt in the minds of Kennedy's foreign policy advisers that the long-range missiles were offensive in character, Khrushchev tried to argue during the crisis that this was not the case. As he told William Knox, who happened to be in Moscow at the time on behalf of Westinghouse International: "If I point a pistol at you like this in order to attack you," Khrushchev said, extending a stubby index finger across the table in Knox's direction, "the pistol is an offensive weapon. But if I am to keep you from shooting me, it is defensive, no?"[13]

There was a great deal of debate about possible Soviet motives for

---

10 By this time none of the IRBMs scheduled for delivery had actually been delivered. See Morton Schwartz, *opus cit.*, p. 325.
11 *The New York Times*, September 5, 1962.
12 For background on U.S. intelligence gathering on the missile deployment see Klaus Knorr, "Failures in National Intelligence Estimates: The Case of the Cuban Missiles," *World Politics*, (April, 1964).
13 Quoted in Elie Abel, *The Missile Crisis* (New York: Bantam Books, 1966), pp. 132-33.

undertaking this nuclear build-up on Cuba,[14] as in the past the Soviet leadership had been quite cautious in nuclear matters.

In fact, never before had the Soviets installed nuclear weapons beyond their own borders. They had not even put them in Eastern Europe where such weapons would not be considered overly provocative by the U.S. and would be relatively easy to defend. This was clearly not the case in Cuba, which was extremely close to the U.S., especially to the space and military rocket testing installations at Cape Canaveral.[15] As President Kennedy observed in his statement of October 22, "This was an area well-known to have special and historical relationship to the United States."[16]

In order to study the situation more carefully before making public the American response, the President and his closest advisers constituted themselves as an executive committee of the National Security Council (ExComm). Kennedy initially participated in these very intense deliberations. But after realizing that his presence tended to stifle opposing or critical views, he soon turned over the chairmanship of the group to his brother Robert.

The Time Element

One of the most important elements affecting the outcome of the Cuban missile crisis was not deterrence — but time. As former White House aide Arthur M. Schlesinger indicated later: "The deadline defined the strategy."[17] Had Kennedy's decision been made in a great hurry, the outcome might well have been completely different.[18]

14 Khrushchev later stated that the missiles were put in Cuba "to protect Cuba from invasion by the imperialists..." *Pravda*, January 17, 1963. According to Castro, however, the Soviet leaders "explained to us that in accepting them we would be reinforcing the socialist camp the world over ... That is why we accepted them. It was in order to insure our defense, but first of all to reinforce socialism on the international scale." *Le Monde*, March 22, 1963. In fact, the Cuban deployment was probably seen, as Allison has suggested, as "a swift, significant and comparatively inexpensive addition to the Soviet capability to strike the United States." See Graham T. Allison, *Essence of Decision: Explaining the Cuban Missile Crisis* (Boston: Little, Brown, 1971), pp. 52-53.

15 One former U.S. official says here: "I suspect that Operation Mongoose, the Kennedy program after the Bay of Pigs to 'get' Castro, may have played a role in Castro's decision to cooperate with Khrushchev on the missiles. You will find discussion of it in Schlesinger's book on Bobby Kennedy and Thomas Power's, *The Man Who Kept the Secrets*, about [CIA Director] Dick Helms. I would hope that someone one day would write a monograph on this fascinating operation and its effects on U.S., Soviet and Cuban policies."

16 *The New York Times*, October 23, 1962.

17 Arthur M. Schlesinger, Jr. *opus cit.*

18 The analysis done by Graham Allison, the foremost student of this crisis, suggests

The American leadership had hard evidence of the construction of the Soviet missile sites in Cuba on October 15. (High altitude photographs taken the day before by a U-2 reconnaissance plane, discovered the construction of nine new missile sites in Cuba with launching positions for 24 Soviet medium-range and 12 intermediate-range ballistic missiles. It was estimated by the CIA that the President would have just a little over a week before the Soviet missile emplacements might become operational. This factor was significant, for JFK had a number of important options to weigh very carefully.

Between October 16 and 22, the President and his key Cabinet and White House advisers deliberated in great secrecy.[19] They considered the following options along a kind of "escalation ladder." Six possible alternatives developed in ascending order of severity. (1) do nothing; (2) submit an American appeal to the United Nations; (3) undertake a secret approach to Castro; (4) arrange a blockade of Cuba; (5) conduct a "surgical" air strike to eliminate the missile sites; and (6) launch an invasion of Cuba.

The President made it clear at the outset that "doing nothing" was not an alternative he would accept. "That son of a bitch [Khrushchev] won't pay any attention to words. He has to see you move," he said on another occasion.[20] The ExComm therefore quickly focused on those options that involved the use of force. An immediate invasion of Cuba was rejected because it might have provoked the war Kennedy was trying to avoid. An airstrike initially recommended by some advisers would have been difficult to justify by the nation that had made Pearl Harbor a symbol of infamy. But, more importantly, it might have killed Russians who manned the sites, humiliating Khrushchev and compelling him to avenge Russian honor.[21]

> another aspect worth considering. This is the *timing of the U-2 flights over Cuba*. The U-2s were the most important source of U.S. intelligence about Cuba; their information was supplemented by refugee reports, analyses of shipping and other kinds of intelligence. According to Allison, the timing of these U-2 flights was instrumental in determining Kennedy's final decision. "Had the missiles not been discovered until two weeks later, the blockade would have been irrelevant since the Soviet missile shipments would have been completed ... An explanation of the politics of discovery is consequently a considerable piece of the explanation of the U.S. blockade." See Allison, *The Essence of Decision*.

19 On their way to one of these top secret meetings the President's advisers early on in the crisis left their cars parked outside the building. If this oversight had not been noticed shortly by an official, it would not have been long before either a reporter or a foreign intelligence agent would have wondered why so many cars possessed by toplevel members of the government were all in one place.

20 See Honoré M. Catudal, *Kennedy and the Berlin Wall Crisis: A Case Study in U.S. Decision Making* (West Berlin: Berlin Verlag Arno Spitz, 1980), p. 184.

21 One should also note that since the U.S. Air Force had classified the missiles as

The discussion was agonizing. Finally it was decided that a blockade seemed to hold out the best hope for a solution. It would entail the requisite show of strength by throwing a naval ring around the island, particularly if it were coupled with a demand that the Soviet Union dismantle its bases there. At the same time, it would halt all missiles still on their way from Russia. The major disadvantage of the blockade was that it alone would not remove those missiles already in Cuba, which were being readied for operation.

Nevertheless, the blockade would be a signal of American determination and permit the President the option of increasing the pressure on the Soviets later if the missiles were not removed.[22] Importantly, it would also give the Soviet leadership room to maneuver and to find a graceful way to withdraw. Besides allowing the Soviets to "save face," it would entail no violence — at least immediately. In the end, the blockade option was chosen by Kennedy, who tended to view the installation of Soviet missiles in Cuba as a personal challenge, with potentially damaging consequences. He chose to term it a "quarantine," since a blockade is usually considered an act of war under international law and Kennedy did not want to give the impression at first that he was seriously escalating what was already a very dangerous crisis.

In short, the major alternative courses of action were carefully sifted before a final decision was reached. However, this time-consuming process could only occur because the President and his advisers enjoyed the luxury of an entire week to decide. The very urgency of the decision and the catastrophic consequences of a wrong decision served as important incentives for policy makers to use this time wisely. As Robert Kennedy wrote after the conclusion of the crisis, "if we had had to make a decision in twenty-four hours, I believe the course we ultimately would have taken would have been quite different and filled with far greater risks."[23]

"mobile," which meant that they could be moved prior to an air strike, the commander of the Air Force would not guarantee that a surgical air strike would be completely effective. See Stephen D. Krasner, "Are Bureaucracies Important? (Or Allison in Wonderland)," *Foreign Policy*, No. 7 (Summer, 1972), p. 420. Only later did civilian experts discover that the Soviet missiles were not mobile.

22 As Stephen Krasner puts it, the missiles were removed in the end not because of what the blockade did but what it meant. *Ibid.*

23 Robert Kennedy, *Thirteen Days: A Memoir of the Cuban Missile Crisis* (New York: W.W. Norton & Co., 1969), p. 95.

The Human Factor

How important was the human factor in this crisis? Khrushchev's memoirs contain these revealing statements.[24]

And a compromise over Cuba was indeed found. The episode ended in a triumph of common sense. I'll always remember the late President with deep respect because, in the final analysis, he showed himself to be sober-minded and determined to avoid war. He didn't let himself become frightened, nor did he become reckless. He didn't overestimate America's might, and he left himself a way out of the crisis. He showed real wisdom and statesmanship when he turned his back on right-wing forces in the United States who were trying to goad him into taking military action against Cuba.

During the crisis Major Rudolf Anderson, Jr., a U-2 pilot, was shot down over Cuba by Soviet surface-to-air missiles. Under this pressure, the consensus against an airstrike in the executive committee reportedly almost broke down. In Sorenson's words:[25] "Our little group seated around the Cabinet table ... felt nuclear war to be closer on that day than at any time in the nuclear age."[26] Nevertheless, Kennedy refused to bomb the bases which would have killed Soviet soldiers who were in control of the missiles. He believed that a determined, initially nonviolent, posture by the United States would persuade Khrushchev to retreat, whereas an airstrike might well push the Soviet leader over the thermonuclear brink.[27]

Throughout this crisis President Kennedy and his close advisers were worried about the possibility of misperception by their counterparts in the Kremlin. As JFK said later in an interview with CBS, "Well now, if you look at the history of this century where World War I really came through a series of misjudgments of the intentions of others ... it's very difficult to always make judgments here about what the effect will be of our decision on other countries."[28]

Most of the published memoirs of the Kennedy era stress President

---

24 Nikita Khrushchev, *Khrushchev Remembers* (Boston: Little & Brown, 1970).

25 Theodore C. Sorensen, *Kennedy* (New York: Bantam Books, 1966), p. 714.

26 One critic would observe here: "From Sorenson's statement I gather that Kennedy *was deterred* from bombing Cuban bases because of fear of nuclear war. In this case the U.S. was deterred." Not necessarily so. While it is true that JFK (like Khrushchev) was fearful of taking a step that could lead to a nuclear war, this fear *alone* was not enough to prevent such a dreaded outcome.

27 For details see the newly released transcripts of tapes, secretly recorded by President Kennedy, at the John F. Kennedy Presidential Library in Cambridge, Massachusetts.

28 CBS News, "A Conversation with President Kennedy," December 17, 1962.

Kennedy's concern during the crisis not to back Khrushchev into a corner. As Robert F. Kennedy wrote afterwards: the President stated that "if anybody is around to write after this, they are going to understand that we made every effort to find peace and every effort to give our adversary room to move. I am not going to push the Russians an inch beyond what is necessary."[29]

The notion that "nothing succeeds like success" seems to have had a compelling influence on how proponents of deterrence tend to view the crisis. But, as those who were close to President Kennedy note, the President was convinced that his "success" was a narrow and a fortuitous one.[30] This in part, we are told, led him to lay done the firm line against his Administration's gloating over the outcome. According to Benjamin Lambeth, "By every account ... the outcome of the missile crisis was a close one, and our eventual victory was hardly foreordained ..."[31] That this was the case had something to do with the role of the President — or the human factor.

The Bureaucratic Factor

Frequently, those individuals who stress the role of deterrence in the Cuban missile crisis fail to appreciate the part played by the Washington bureaucracy. This is unfortunate for, although Kennedy went to extraordinary efforts to stay on top of things, the President still had exceptional difficulty in controlling events.[32]

"There were several random events," writes Stephen D. Krasner, "which might have changed the outcome of the crisis." The U.S. Navy "used the blockade to test its anti-submarine operations. It was forcing Soviet sub-

29 Robert F. Kennedy, *opus cit.*, p. 127.
30 Theodore C. Sorensen, *opus cit.*, pp. 808-09.
31 Benjamin Lambeth, "Deterrence in the MIRV Era," *World Politics*, Vol. 24, No. 2 (January, 1972), p. 233.
32 The Russian leadership may have been aware of this fact. The son of Soviet Foreign Minister Andrei Gromyko writes in his study of the Kennedy period that ultimate authority to make decisions was in the hands of the President. Nothing, he says, happened without the approval of Kennedy, and JFK always had to be persuaded and was never dictated to. Anatoli Gromyko does observe, however, that there was intense pressure brought to bear on the President by "militaristic" groups. For instance, he says that when an American U-2 was shot down over Cuba, "the supporters for war again demanded the implementation of an air attack on Cuba followed by an *invasion. Kennedy again* rejected their demands." See his *1036 dnei Prezidente Kennedi* (Moscow, 1968). This book appeared in English as *Through Russian Eyes: President Kennedy's 1036 Days,* translated by Philip A. Garon (Washington, D.C.: International Library, 1973).

marines to surface at a time when the President and his advisers were unaware that contact with Russian ships had been made."[33] Also during the crisis, a U-2 accidentally strayed over Siberia on October 22. "Any one of these events, and perhaps others still unknown, could have triggered escalatory actions by the Russians."[34]

On at least two occasions the bureaucracy served to frustrate important decisions made by the President, thereby bringing the U.S. and the U.S.S.R. close to the nuclear brink. In one case, this almost proved fatal.

At the onset of the crisis the President was apparently appalled to learn that his decision months earlier to remove the intermediate-range Jupiter missiles from Turkey had not been carried out.[35] JFK only discovered this failure in conversation with Adlai Stevenson, then U.S. Ambassador to the United Nations. Stevenson had suggested trading Soviet missile withdrawal from Cuba against removal of the obsolete Jupiters from Turkey. But the President had informed the Ambassador that he had already ordered those antiquated missiles removed from Turkey months before. Therefore, they were not available for a deal. As Robert Kennedy recollects: It took a brave subordinate to tell the President that his order had not been carried out and that the offending missiles were still in Turkey.[36]

The fifteen *Jupiter* missiles were installed in Turkey following the completion of an American agreement with Turkey in October 1959. Turkey owned the missiles, but the U.S. owned the warheads and placed them in the custody of its forces. They could be fired only by order of the

---

33 One former State Department official observes here: "You should look into the U.S. Navy's anti-submarine program during the crisis. After the crisis was over, the Navy proudly briefed us on its program to force Soviet submarines to surface, with which they had considerable success. We were amazed to learn that this risky operation had been going on, and I am still not sure of its purpose. I have read somewhere that Kennedy was shocked when he learned of this."

34 Stephen D. Krasner, *opus cit.*, p. 422.

35 See Robert F. Kennedy, *opus cit.*, pp. 94-95. Kenneth O'Donnell and David Powers state that JFK had given the order five times. See their *"Johnny, We Hardly Knew You"* (Boston: Little, Brown, 1972), p. 337. But these accounts may be misleading according to the new evidence unearthed by Barton J. Bernstein. He argues that "it is too simple to conclude, as have some analysts, that Kennedy ordered removal of the missiles and that the bureaucracy thwarted his instruction." A more subtle approach to understanding what actually happened may be called for. This "would acknowledge that a chief executive may often express preferences (not orders) for policies, and that he may sincerely reinterpret them as *orders* when his own inaction leaves him woefully unprepared in a crisis." See "The Cuban Missile Crisis: Trading the Jupiters in Turkey?," Political *Science Quarterly*, Vol. 95, No. 1 (Spring, 1980), p. 102-03.

36 See Robert F. Kennedy, *Thirteen Days: A Memoir of the Cuban Missile Crisis.* (New York: W.W. Norton & Co., 1969).

Supreme Allied Commander (an American) after approval by both American and Turkish governments.[37]

The main problem with the *Jupiters* was that they were liquid-fueled Intermediate-Range Ballistic Missiles. They took hours to fire; they were quite inaccurate, and they were very vulnerable. Hence, they were mainly useful in a pre-emptive strike and thus provocative. Put bluntly, one author asserts, "the Jupiters would draw, not deter, an attack."[38]

This probability was highlighted by Dean Acheson during the crisis. At one point, Truman's former Secretary of State gave a hair-raising presentation, concluding that the U.S. would have to knock out the Soviet missiles in Cuba. Someone asked what the Soviets would do in response.

"I know the Soviet Union well," Acheson replied confidently. "I know what they are required to do in the light of their history and their posture around the world. I think they will knock out our missiles in Turkey."

"Well, then what do we do?" someone else inquired. Acheson returned: "I believe under our NATO treaty, with which I was associated, we would be required to respond by knocking out a missile base inside the Soviet Union." The next question was: "Then what would we do?" Acheson stopped and thought for a moment. "That's when we hope," he answered, "that cooler heads will prevail, and they'll stop and talk."[39]

The second, more important instance of the bureaucracy frustrating a Presidential directive came in the context of Kennedy's decision to order a naval blockade of Cuba. The Navy subsequently assigned about 180 ships to the task of monitoring almost one million square miles. (The complexity of the job should not be underestimated.) Then, virtually at the last moment, the British Ambassador, who was a personal friend of Kennedy, suggested to JFK that precious time might be gained if the quarantine were modified. Orginally, it was designed to intercept Russian ships some 500 miles from Cuba. (The Navy wished to intercept Russian ships 800 miles from Cuba, so as to be out of range of the Mig fighters based on the island, but the President had reduced the distance to 500

---

37 U.S. Congress, House, Committee on Armed Services, *Hearings on the Military Posture*, 88th Congress, 1st Session (Washington, D.C.: Government Printing Office, 1963), pp. 277-81. According to Paul Bracken, "During the Cuban missile crisis President Kennedy reportedly ordered the fuses and warheads removed from American Jupiter missiles in Turkey to forestall any sort of accident in the tense environment." See his *The Command and Control of Nuclear Forces* (New Haven: Yale University Press, 1983), p. 72.

38 Barton J. Bernstein, "The Cuban Missile Crisis: Trading the Jupiters in Turkey?," *Political Science Quarterly*, Vol. 95, No. 1 (Spring, 1980), p. 99.

39 Quoted in Fred Kaplan, *The Wizards of Armageddon* (New York: Simon & Schuster, 1983), p. 305. See also Acheson's oral history at the Kennedy Library.

miles.)[40] However, if blockade procedures could now be changed so that Russian ships would not be intercepted until they reached perhaps 200 miles off Cuba, this would give the Soviet leaders a substantial amount of extra time in which, it was hoped, to change their minds. The President thought this proposal was an excellent idea, and he immediately issued an order to the Navy to contract the line of interception.

The British Ambassador's suggestion was unquestionably a rational proposal. However, high-level officers in the Navy complained loudly. Procedures, they argued, could not be changed at the last minute in such a fundamental way without causing some major foul-up which, given the circumstances of the missile crisis, could have had far-reaching repercussions. But the President and his Secretary of Defense insisted, and so the Navy gave in.

Or did it? The Navy assured Kennedy at the time that the line of interdiction had been moved closer to Cuba. But a close examination of the evidence by Dan Caldwell "confirms other suspicions... Existing accounts to the contrary, the blockade was *not* moved as the President ordered.[41] In summary, then, the Navy, even when confronted with the possibility that much of the world might be devastated in a nuclear holocaust, according to this evidence still refused to modify its standing operating procedures substantially.[42]

Although one must be cautious in drawing historical parallels, the way the Navy functioned in the Cuban missile crisis reminds one of the crisis leading to World War I. At the crucial moment in 1914, when the momentum of German mobilization was directed toward the French frontier, the Kaiser, who was fearful of a two-front war, called in the German Chief of Staff General Helmuth von Moltke. Emperor William II informed Moltke of his decision to go to war against Russia only and the need to "simply march the whole of our army to the East."[43] But General Moltke was aghast.

40 Robert F. Kennedy, *Thirteen Days: A Memoir of the Cuban Missile Crisis* (New York: Signet, 1969), p. 67.

41 Dan Caldwell, "A Research Note on the Quarantine of Cuba, October 1961," *International Studies Quarterly*, Vol. 22 (December, 1978), p. 628.

42 At one point in the crisis Robert McNamara pressed his Chief of Naval Operations George Anderson for details of the Navy's procedures for boarding Russian ships. Anderson reportedly replied by picking up the *Manual of Naval Regulations* and waving it in the face of the Secretary of Defense. He is said to have told McNamara at this time that if he wanted to know what was to be done, he should simply refer to the *Manual*. McNamara is reported to have exploded: "I don't give a damn what John Paul Jones would have done. I want to know what you are going to do, now." See Graham Allison, *Essence of Decision* Boston: Little, Brown & Co., 1971), p. 131.

43 Barton Whaley, *Codeword Barbarossa* (Cambridge, Mass.: MIT Press, 1973), p. 115.

"Your Majesty," he exclaimed, "it cannot be done." When pressed for a reason, Moltke explained:[44]

The deployment of millions cannot be improvised. If your Majesty insists on leading the whole army to the East it will not be an army ready for battle but a disorganized mob of armed men with no arrangements for supply. Those arrangements took a whole year of intricate labor to complete and once settled, [they] cannot be altered.

The vision of 11,000 trains wrenched into reverse was simply too much for Moltke to bear. So he refused the Kaiser point blank. "Your uncle would have given me a different answer," Wilhelm said bitterly.

Moltke's "it cannot be done" is, of course, hotly debated by historians, who maintain that the German General Staff had in its files an alternative plan against Russia with all the trains running eastward.[45] Be this as it may, Moltke refused to modify his prearranged response just as the U.S. Navy reportedly did in 1962, thereby narrowing the scope of the developing crisis. The fact that the Cuban missile crisis did not result in a third world war must not obscure this important fact.

Asymmetry of Motivation

Another perhaps fundamental reason — rather than deterrence — which helps explain why the United States was so successful in achieving its purpose in this particular crisis has been suggested by Alexander L. George, David K. Hall and William E. Simons. These analysts argue that in the Cuban missile crisis the American motivation to succeed was far stronger than that of the Soviet Union. Thus, the "asymmetry of motivation" favored the Kennedy Administration.[46]

In the first place, the fact that Soviet nuclear missiles were installed in Cuba was highly significant. This area was within a traditional sphere of influence of the United States. As Ronald Steel has observed, the Monroe Doctrine was really a Caribbean Doctrine.[47] To have acceded to this radical

---

44 Winston S. Churchill, *The Second World War* (London: Cassell, 1950-55), Vol. 4, p. 493.

45 Barbara Tuchman, *The Guns of August* (New York: Macmillan, 1962).

46 The concept of "asymmetry of motivation" is explored in greater detail in Alexander L. George, David K. Hall and William E. Simons, *The Limits of Coercive Diplomacy: Laos, Cuba, Vietnam* (Boston: Little, Brown, 1971), pp. 23-24.
Ambassador Hillenbrand says here: "I find the concept of 'assymetry of motivation' both useful and at the same time misleading if it implies that if one's motivation is sufficiently strong it will overrule all caution in a situation where nuclear weapons might be involved." Letter to this writer, June 1, 1984.

47 Robert McNamara stated at the time that, although the effect on the strategic balance might be small, the "potential effect on Latin America and elsewhere

change of the status quo in an area considered to be of major historical importance to the United States ("our backyard" is the phrase often used by American officials privately) the Kennedy Administration would have communicated to America's allies an indecisiveness, perhaps even a weakness or fearfulness, in defending vital interests farther away. (Kennedy had publicly declared that the U.S. would not tolerate offensive missiles on the island some 90 miles off the coast of Florida.)[48]

From the perspective of the Soviet Union, Cuba was a marginal issue — official Soviet protestations notwithstanding. To some degree, Soviet medium-range ballistic missiles in Cuba would have enhanced the Soviet capacity for a pre-emptive strike, but as Robert McNamara argued early in the ExComm deliberations, "a missile is a missile," whether launched from Cuba or the Soviet Union.[49]

President Kennedy, among others, recognized the validity of this point. However, he maintained that although the Soviet action in Cuba did not substantially alter the strategic balance of power, it nevertheless altered the *appearance* of the balance. And in matters of national will and world leadership "such appearances contribute to reality."[50]

To state this point more forcefully in the form of a question: Might not the outcome of the crisis have been quite different if the sphere of influence in which the confrontation had taken place had been Soviet rather than American? In other words, it was easier for the Soviets to back down in Cuba because they had less at stake than the U.S. It was not a vital area for them. The same was not true for the United States.[51]

The Secret Compromise

Another important factor in the successful resolution of the Cuban missile crisis that had nothing to do with deterrence was the President's willingness to compromise with Khrushchev. As we shall see, his flexibility in this regard was greater than was made public at the time.

would be large." Quoted in I.F. Stone, *In a Time of Torment* (New York, 1968), p. 18.

48 Quoted in Roger Hilsman, *To Move a Nation* (New York: Doubleday, 1967), p. 195.

49 Ronald Steel, *Pax Americana* (New York: Viking, 1967), p. 195.

50 Interview with *The Washington Post*, December 18, 1962.

51 Castro attempted to thwart the consummation of the agreement leading to the Soviet withdrawal of its missiles in Cuba by refusing to allow UN inspection. But Khrushchev and Kennedy were not to be denied. They settled for a tacit accord whereby the U.S. would verify the removal of the missiles by independent reconnaissance. See Herbert S. Dinerstein, *The Making Of A Missile Crisis: October 1962* (Baltimore: Johns Hopkins University Press, 1976), p. 229.

We know now that the traditional description of the Soviet-American tradeoff in the crisis is gravely inaccurate, thus giving almost two generations of Americans a seriously distorted view of the crisis. Traditional historical accounts tend to focus on the importance of an exchange of letters during the period between Khrushchev and Kennedy. As one student of the crisis writes, "The most crucial decision that Kennedy made ... involved the two fateful letters sent to him by Khrushchev on October 26 and October 27."[52] The "first" letter from the Soviet leader offered to remove Soviet nuclear missiles if Kennedy would give Khrushchev a personal pledge that American soldiers would not invade the island.[53] In the second, "tougher" letter, which arrived from the Soviet foreign ministry the following day, Khrushchev offered to trade Soviet missiles in Cuba for American Jupiter missiles in Turkey, a NATO ally.[54]

Many U.S. officials, academics and others apparently still believe that Kennedy, in acting to resolve the crisis without submitting to Soviet "blackmail," chose not to react specifically to the proposal put forth in the second letter.[55] As John G. Stoessinger writes, "by turning down the barter deal, Kennedy relinquished the ultimate choice between peace and war to Nikita Khrushchev." Theodore C. Sorensen, a close adviser to Kennedy, goes much further when he says that "the President had no intention of destroying the Alliance by backing down."[56]

52 John G. Stoessinger, *Crusaders and Pragmatists: Movers of Modern America Foreign Policy* (New York: W.W. Norton & Co., 1979), p. 157.

53 For an analysis of the Soviet position of the crisis see Ronald R. Pope (ed.), *Soviet Views on the Cuban Missile Crisis: Myth and Reality in Foreign Policy Analysis.* (Lanham, Md.: University Press of America, 1982). This useful book analyzes the four major Soviet commentaries on the crisis: Khrushchev's complete correspondence with Kennedy; his Supreme Soviet speech of December 1962; the relevant material from both volumes of *Khrushchev Remembers;* and a two-part article by Anatoli Gromyko, the only major Soviet academic analysis of the crisis by the son of the Soviet Foreign Minister.

54 Michael Tatu suggests that the Cuba-Turkey letter was prompted by the reaction of other Presidium (Politburo) members that Khrushchev had backed down too quickly. He advances the hypothesis that the Cuba-Turkey swap proposal constituted a middle approach between the offer contained in Khrushchev's personal letter and the demands of Soviet hardliners who insisted on an American withdrawal from all foreign bases. See his *Power in the Kremlin* (New York: Viking, 1969), p. 263.

55 See Henry M. Pachter, *Collision Course: The Cuban Missile Crisis and Coexistence* New York: Frederick A. Praeger, 1963). Publicly, the President seemed to reject the Soviet proposal. See the White House statement of 27 October 1962 in *Public Papers of the President: John F. Kennedy, 1962* (Washington, D.C.: Government Printing Office, 1963), pp. 813-14.

56 Theodore C. Sorensen, *Kennedy* (New York: Bantam Books, 1966), p. 714.

The fact of the matter is that the President, through his brother Robert, the Attorney General, entered into a secret "understanding" with Khrushchev, who later boasted that the Soviet Union had forced the "American imperial beast" to "swallow a hedgehog, quills and all." This secret agreement is described by Arthur M. Schlesinger in his book, *Robert Kennedy and His Times*,[57] but so far it has not received the attention it deserves.[58] According to the terms of this secret accord, which supplemented the President's public non-invasion pledge, it was to be cancelled at once if the Soviet government tried to claim public credit for it.[59] In the secret agreement, Khrushchev was led to believe that some time after he withdrew his missiles the *Jupiters* would be withdrawn from Turkey.[60] (RFK men-

57 Arthur M. Schlesinger, *Robert Kennedy and His Times* (New York: Ballantine Books, 1978), pp. 562-63. Schlesinger was granted permission by the Kennedy family to use the Robert F. Kennedy papers, now stored at the Kennedy Library. According to the Director of the JFK Library, the sections on the missile crisis are still classified and not organized and access is barred to independent scholars.

58 A major exception is the study by Barton J. Bernstein, "The Cuban Missile Crisis: Trading the Jupiters in Turkey?," *Political Science Quarterly*, Vol. 95, No. 1 (Spring, 1980), pp. 97-125. As Professor Bernstein writes, "New evidence — recently declassified minutes, some staff reports, key diplomatic cables, and some published parts of Robert Kennedy's still-closed papers — reopens these issues about the Turkey-Cuba missile trade and its background ... The new evidence establishes that Kennedy privately offered a hedged promise on 27 October 1962 to withdraw the *Jupiter* missiles from Turkey at a future time."
One former State Department official says here: "Re the Jupiters, you should note that this was first confirmed in the Robert Kennedy book. Many of us suspected all along that there was such a deal. And why not, since Kennedy wanted to get these missiles out of Europe anyway?"

59 Ambassador Hillenbrand would state here: "The so-called barter deal was essentially Kennedy's tossing a bone to Khrushchev which had some face-saving value for the latter but cost the former nothing since the missiles were obsolete and were scheduled for withdrawal anyway. I don't see how Kennedy's flexibility and willingness to toss Khrushchev this bone proves very much one way or the other about deterrence." Letter, June 1, 1984.
Khrushchev has this to say in his memoirs: "We knew perfectly well that this pledge was of a symbolic nature: the American rockets in Turkey and Italy were already obsolete, and the Americans would promptly replace them with more modern ones. Besides, the US was already equipping its navy with Polaris missiles. *Nevertheless, by agreeing even to symbolic measures, Kennedy was creating the impression of mutual concessions.*" (Italics mine). *Khrushchev Remembers; The Last Testament* (New York: Bantam Books, 1976), p. 584.

60 See Anatoly Gromyko, "U.S. Manipulations Leading to Cuban Missile Crisis," in *USSR International Affairs* (FBIS), September 7, 1971. Gromyko's article calls Kennedy's agreement to remove the Jupiters "a specific promise." Khrushchev makes the same claim. See his *Khrushchev Remembers: The Last Testament* (Boston: Little, Brown, 1974), p. 512.

tioned four to five months; in fact the time that elapsed was much longer. The last *Jupiter* missile was taken out of Turkey in April, 1963.)[61]

Conventional Superiority

Another important factor in the crisis which needs to be emphasized is American conventional superiority in the area around Cuba. Personally, the President credited the American success in the crisis not to nuclear deterrence but "to the presence of usable conventional forces, which left Khrushchev no choice but to withdraw his missiles or risk nuclear war."[62] As Robert McNamara later testified before Congress, the United States had assembled a "force of several hundred thousand men ready to invade Cuba" within days if the Soviet Premier had not agreed to begin withdrawing his missiles from the island.[63] In addition, the first Armored Division was dispatched from Texas to the Atlantic coast; two Marine battalions were sent to reinforce the American naval base at Guantanamo, and 1,000 aircraft were assembled in Florida. Kennedy, his Secretary of Defense reported, had taken steps to let the Soviets know indirectly what the U.S. planned, so there would be no doubt in their minds about America's intentions.[64]

In his testimony, McNamara made another significant revelation. Had a comparable situation occurred in 1961, he said, the U.S. could not have mustered a credible invasion force without first bringing home troops stationed overseas. The President drew the appropriate conclusion: "a line of destroyers in a quarantine, or a division of well-equipped men on a border, may be more useful to our real security than the multiplication of awesome weapons beyond all rational need."[65]

61 Memorandum, McNamara to President, 25 April 1963, President's Office Files 115, JFK Library. In 1963, McNamara told the House Appropriations Committee "without any qualifications whatsoever there was abolutely no deal, as it might be called, between the Soviet Union and the United States regarding the removal of the Jupiter weapons from either Italy or Turkey" See U.S. Department of Defense, *Appropriations for 1964*, 88th Congress, 1st Session (Washington, D.C.: Government Printing Office, 1963), pt. I, p. 57.

62 John L. Gaddis, *Strategy of Containment: A Critical Appraisal of Postwar American National Security Policy* (New York: Oxford University Press, 1982), p. 216.

63 McNamara testifying at *Hearings*, U.S. Congress, House of Representatives, *Department of Defense Appropriations for 1964*, 88th Congress, 1st Session, 1963.

64 It should be noted that all Soviet MRBMs were operational by October 28 and ground forces were equipped with tactical nuclear weapons. Therefore, had the U.S. decided to invade, the consequences would have been very serious. See Jerome H. Kahan and Anne K. Long, The Cuban Missile Crisis: A Study of Its Strategic Context," *Political Science Quarterly*, Vol. 88, No. 4 (December, 1972), p. 582.

65 Quoted in John L. Gaddis, *opus cit.*, p. 216.

Later, President Kennedy's National Security Adviser McGeorge Bundy emphasized the importance of American conventional superiority in resolving the crisis. "I myself would argue that what made the Soviets blink was the unfavorable conventional balance in the Cuban missile crisis, *not the prospect of a possible U.S. first use of nuclear weapons.*" (Italics mine.) As Bundy sees things, the Kremlin's decision to halt Soviet ships as they approached the blockade line "was a prudent action in the face of great conventional superiority on the spot."[66]

There is some evidence to indicate that the Soviet leadership may have agreed with this assessment. In a speech after the crisis Khrushchev suggested that he had received hard intelligence toward the end of the confrontation that an invasion of the island was imminent.[67]

One last point about alleged deterrence in the conflict needs to be addressed. Some scholars, who argue that the leaders of the Soviet Union subscribe to the U.S. doctrine of deterrence, have suggested that Khrushchev deployed his nuclear missiles in Cuba in order to deter the United States from attacking the island. Many knowledgeable students of the crisis, however, doubt whether this was indeed the case. But if deterrence of a U.S. attack on Cuba was the sole Soviet objective, the plan obviously backfired. For the Soviet nuclear weapons in Cuba seemed to provoke rather than deter.[68]

The Risk of War

It is clear from personal accounts of participants and recently declassified U.S. government documents that over the Soviet missiles in Cuba the United States was ready to go to nuclear war, if necessary. The President was almost certain that the Soviets would retaliate against the blockade by

---

It is important to note that during the Cuban Missile Crisis Robert McNamara took a much more pacific position than some of the military leaders under him who urged the use of arms.

66 Memorandum to Jason Epstein, Vice President and Editorial Director, Random House, July 7, 1982.

67 See Graham T. Allison, *opus cit.*
Peter W. Rodman, who served on the staff of the National Security Council during the Nixon and Ford Administrations, maintains: "There is no doubt that local superiority was an enormous advantage, and that it remains so in an age of nuclear parity. But dogmatic claims that conventional superiority was sufficient do not seem supportable." See his "The Missiles of October: Twenty Years Later," *Commentary*, Vol. 74, No. 4 (July-October, 1982), pp. 39-42.

68 See for example Arnold L. Horelick, "The Cuban Missile Crisis: An Analysis of Soviet Calculations and Behavior," *World Politics*, Vol. 16, No. 3 (1964), pp. 363-89.

possibly blockading West Berlin. As Martin J. Hillenbrand, who was head of the Office of German Affairs in the State Department, recalls: "I was personally involved in that tense period during the early Autumn of 1962, because it was thought, erroneously as it proved, that an obvious place where the Soviets might respond to action on our part with respect to their deployment of missiles in Cuba was in and about Berlin. Hence a Berlin emergency planning group was set up in the White House alongside that which was dealing with the Cuban missile crisis per se. I was a member of the Berlin group, the planning of which was integrated with that of the larger group."[69]

Everything was in combat readiness in the United States, and the danger of nuclear war was fully realized. For instance, Kennedy asked his wife after he imposed the blockade whether she would prefer to leave Washington and stay nearer the underground shelter to which the First Family would be taken in case of a Soviet nuclear attack. She chose to stay in Washington.[70]

Bobby Kennedy later recorded in his personal memoirs of the crisis that "We all agreed in the end that if the Russians were ready to go to nuclear war over Cuba, they were ready to go to nuclear war, and that was that. So we might as well have the show-down then as six months later."[71]

The President himself said later that the odds that the Soviets would go all the way were "somewhere between one out of three and even."[72] Officials were not sure what the effect of American determination on the Russian leadership would be, but it does seem evident that the United States was not deterred by fear of a Soviet nuclear attack.

The anxiety suffered by Khrushchev during this period is suggested in his memoirs:[73]

I remember a period of six or seven days when the danger was particularly acute. Seeking to take the heat off the situation somehow, I suggested to the other members of the government: "Comrades, let's go to the Bolshoi Theater this evening. Our own people as well as foreign eyes will notice, and perhaps, it will calm them down. They'll say to themselves if Khrushchev and our other leaders are able to go to the opera, at a time like this, then at least tonight we can sleep peacefully." We were trying to disguise our own anxiety, which was intense.

69 Letter from Ambassador Hillenbrand to this writer, April 27, 1984.
70 Theodore C. Sorensen, *opus cit.*, p. 693.
71 Arthur M. Schlesinger, *A Thousand Days*, pp. 829-30.
72 Theodore C. Sorensen, *opus cit.*, p. 705.
73 Nikita Khrushchev, *Khrushchev Remembers* (Boston: Little & Brown, 1970), p. 497

Obviously both Soviet and American leaders were alarmed by the prospect of a nuclear war over Cuba. One false step could have led them over the brink. To be sure, the Soviets avoided a direct challenge to the blockade. They slowed their ships en route to Cuba and sent through only civilian cargoes. For its part, the United States postponed boarding a Soviet ship for as long as possible, allowing some surface vessels to proceed after aerial inspection.[74]

However, despite all the mitigating circumstances that helped bring about a peaceful resolution of the conflict, we came much closer to nuclear holocaust than many people realize, guided as they are by the all too comfortable illusion of deterrent security. As Premier Khrushchev remarked after the crisis was over, the smell of burning flesh was in the air.

Summary

The Cuban missile crisis was the most dangerous and famous case in which nuclear deterrence is alleged to have played a significant role. Yet this analysis of that seminal event, however brief, reveals that the Soviet deployment of missiles to Cuba represented a major failure of United States' deterrent policy.[75] Moreover, during the crisis, nuclear deterrence was not decisive; it merely made the leadership in both the United States and the Soviet Union more cautious — which is not necessarily the same thing.[76]

---

74 According to one U.S. intelligence source, the order to delay intercepting Soviet vessels until the last possible moment was transmitted *in the clear*. Thus, the Soviets, who were certain to hear the message through their close monitoring of the situation, would learn that they had additional time to formulate a response to the blockade. This ploy revealed a sophisticated understanding of the social psychology of communication. This is that information from a distrusted source is more likely to be believed if it is obtained through the recipient's own efforts.

75 See also Alexander L. George *et al.*, *Deterrence in American Foreign Policy* (New York: Columbia University Press, 1974).

76 Ambassador Martin Hillenbrand would make the following remarks here: "I think you are too categorical in some of the statements which you make about the Cuban Missile Crisis... There is no doubt, of course, that personal leadership played an enormous role in the resolution of the crisis, as you point out, but to jump from that to the conclusion that nuclear deterrence did not deter simply does not jibe with the realities of the time. In the minds of both Khrushchev and Kennedy, the ultimate possibility of a nuclear exchange was clearly present, and I am certain that this played an important role in the way the crisis developed and in the way it was resolved.

"Perhaps the basic problem I have is that you seem to regard nuclear deterrence as something which should play a positive role in policy-making. Thus, you refer to

A.F.K. Organski puts it this way: When Russian ships carrying missiles to Cuba turned back on orders from the Kremlin, and Russian missiles already in Cuba were dismantled and sent home, "everyone credited the nuclear deterrent with the victory. But if it was the nuclear deterrent that determined victory for the Americans, how can one explain the fact that the United States was not herself deterred by the Russian nuclear force..."[77]

It is clear that President Kennedy acted with determination in persuading Khrushchev to withdraw his missiles from Cuba. But the ultimate outcome of the crisis hinged on a number of factors which were independent of deterrence. If these variables had not been present, the Soviet leadership could well have resorted to the use of nuclear weapons. Perhaps this is why President Kennedy (unlike many political commentators) was reluctant to attribute the favorable outcome of the crisis to nuclear deterrence.

For some, the central mystery of the crisis remains why Kennedy chose to risk nuclear war over missile emplacements which he knew did not dramatically alter the "balance of terror." As Robert McNamara argued early in the crisis, "a missile is a missile" no matter where it is fired. However, the answer, while unsatisfactory, appears to lie in the President's *perception* of the move.

As JFK tended to see things, Khrushchev's dangerous gambit, if left unchallenged, would be seen by many Americans — particularly his opponents — as representing a *de facto* change in the strategic balance. This perception, however false, would thus contribute to reality and have dire personal consequences for the President. As Graham Allison, the foremost student of the[78] crisis, points out in the *Essence of Decision*, failure to act

those who question the efficacy of the U.S. policy of nuclear deterrence. I prefer to put it this way: The existence of nuclear weapons in the world, particularly those in the possession of the two superpowers, is an undeniable fact. In their relations with each other, the leaders of the two superpowers are very much conscious of this fact. This conditions their behavior.

"In other words, risks are not taken which might otherwise be taken if nuclear weapons did not exist. This does not mean, of course, that the Soviet Union will not take advantage of targets of opportunity in other areas of the world when they believe they can do so with minimal risk and no nuclear involvement. However, on the Central Front, with a few exceptions during the great Berlin crisis of 1958-1963, caution has been the watchword on both sides, and even when a risk taking did occur it was always within limits. Both Soviet and American leaders were ultimately opposed to the kind of risk taking which might result in a major confrontation, despite the high level of rhetoric and verbal threat." Letter, April 27, 1984.

77 A.F.K. Organski, *opus cit.*, p. 171.
78 Kennedy indicated as much in his speech to the nation: But this secret, swift and

decisively would undermine the confidence of members of his Administration, convince the permanent government that his Administration lacked leadership, hurt the Democrats in the forthcoming election, destroy his reputation among members of Congress, create public distrust, encourage U.S. allies and enemies to question American courage, possibly invite a second Bay of Pigs, and feed his own doubts about himself. Allison quotes a statement by Kennedy that he feared impeachment, and thus concludes that the President had no choice. But, of course, he did have a choice — even if his room for action was limited.

This brings us to the real lesson of this crisis. And that is that a nation will fight — regardless of risk — if it believes that its action is legitimate. (Legitimacy is used here in a narrow sense to refer to what national decision-makers consider the right to do what they are doing no matter how repugnant the act may be.) Thus, "legitimacy" is of extreme importance in nuclear confrontations.

President Kennedy summarized the problem in the following way:[79]

I think there is a law of equity in these disputes. When one party is clearly wrong, it will eventually give way. ... They had no business in putting those missiles in and lying to me about it. They were in the wrong and knew it. So, when we stood firm, they had to back down. But this doesn't mean at all that they would back down when they felt they were in the right and had vital interests involved.

Arthur Schlesinger put it this way in his memoir of the period:[80]

The Cuban missile crisis, he [Kennedy] pointed out, had three distinctive features: it took place in an area where we enjoyed local conventional superiority, where Soviet national security was not directly engaged and where the Russians lacked a case which they could plausibly sustain before the world. Things would be different, he said, if the situation were one where they had the local superiority, where their national security was directly engaged, and where they could convince themselves and others they were in the right.

In summary, the evidence seems clear. The widely-shared belief that nuclear weapons deter confrontations or, more importantly, that they

---

extraordinary build-up of Communist missiles, *in an area well known to have a special and historical relationship to the United States* and the nations of the Western Hemisphere, in violation of Soviet assurances, and *in defiance of American and hemispheric policy* — this sudden, clandestine decision to station strategic weapons for the first time outside of Soviet soil, is a *deliberately provocative and unjustified change in the status quo which cannot be accepted by this country.* [Italics added]. Quoted in Theodore C. Sorensen, *opus cit.*, p. 703.

79 Quoted in Arthur M. Schlesinger, *A Thousand Days*, p. 831.
80 *Ibid.*

prevent them from developing into actual nuclear war is a dangerous illusion. Nuclear weapons are not the "miracle weapons" many Americans thought they were at the beginning of the nuclear era. Terror does not enhance national security. And nucelar weapons do not produce peace without being used. In short, nuclear weapons do not necessarily deter; to believe they do is to believe in magic.

> It ain't what a man don't know that makes him a fool, but what he does know that ain't so.
>
> *Josh Billings*

XVII. THE BALANCE OF TERROR: AN APPRAISAL

Nuclear deterrence is perceived in various ways by many of its proponents. Nevertheless, deterrence basically involves manipulating the behavior of an adversary by threatening him with harm. Presumably, the possession of full nuclear power will so terrify an opponent as to prevent him from undertaking action that would constitute a major military attack. In the case where two or more opposing states possess nuclear power, a "balance of terror" is said to exist that will prevent nuclear war through mutual deterrence.

The fundamental problem with this understanding of nuclear deterrence is that its adherents generally make no attempt to establish an empirical connection between fear and behavior. Indeed, many proponents tend to dismiss the whole idea of verification as hopeless because it is said that in lacking access to the relevant Soviet documents one cannot test a negative. Thus, many U.S. policymakers and others simply *assume* that nuclear deterrence works in the expected way.

However, as this study reveals, there is sufficient evidence in the public domain to raise serious questions about the effectiveness of nuclear deterrence as a primary principle in Soviet-American relations. To be sure, the paucity of information makes it impossible to render a definitive judgment at this time. But *there is a growing body of evidence that suggests that nuclear deterrence does not deter — at least not as U.S. policymakers think it does.*

Apparently, the possession of nuclear weapons by the two superpowers has made the leaders of these states more cautious over the years. But otherwise, the existence of these weapons of mass destruction does not appear to have radically changed the behavior of the United States and the

Soviet Union. Their leaders are still willing to fight if the vital interests of their countries are involved, as the Cuban missile crisis clearly demonstrated. Hardly any statesman has worried about the consequences of nuclear war more than President Kennedy. Yet he was willing to risk such a war in order to safeguard what he thought were important national interests in the established area of American influence and safety zone.

It is important to note here that misgivings about the efficacy of nuclear deterrence do not stem from any doubt about the ability of the United States and the Soviet Union to destroy each other in battle. In fact, present-day capabilities are such that they can do this many times over — even destroying the whole world in the process. Moreover, one does not doubt that the horror of nuclear war has inspired fear in the minds of the leaders of the two superpowers and their masses. However, the evidence now available does make one skeptical of claims that this fear has in turn produced dramatic changes in the behavior of these nation-states in world politics.

In case after case of conflict involving one or more of the nuclear powers (although only two have been examined in any detail here), the states affected have not acted in accordance with the dictates of the balance of terror. Why not? For a long time, we could only speculate. But with the publication of Khrushchev's memoirs in two volumes we finally have more concrete evidence to go on.[1]

Of course, these reminiscences present certain problems. For one, they are — in the words of Edward Crankshaw, who wrote the foreword, — "the apologia of a man taken from a very high plane, deposed, placed under house arrest, cut off from the world [and] consigned to oblivion." For another, they contain many inaccuracies and contradictions, although some observers have noted that this is not surprising, given the fact that Khrushchev's speech in the days of his supremacy was filled with evasions, distortions, deliberate ommissions, contradictions and even downright lies. If for these reasons and others, these memoirs have to be handled with care, there is no longer any question about their authenticity. For the tape recordings, from which the bulk of the memoirs comes, have been subjected

---

1. Khrushchev's memoirs are based on approximately 180 hours of oral dictation. These were tape-recorded, transcribed, translated into English and edited for publication in two volumes. The first volume, *Khrushchev Remembers*, was published in the U.S. in 1970. The second volume, entitled *Khrushchev Remembers: The Last Testament*, was first published in 1974. The transcript for the first volume was prepared in the U.S.S.R. It was verified against tape recordings, which in turn were authenticated by spectrographic analysis. The transcript for the second volume was prepared in the United States, and the tapes from which it was made were likewise authenticated.

to the process known as voiceprinting, which is analagous to fingerprinting, and they have passed the test.[2]

Leaders, Khrushchev says, "must be careful not to look at the world through the eyeglasses of the military." They "should keep in mind exactly what sort of destruction we're capable of today." Leaders should be aware of the losses their own countries "will suffer" even if, "God willing," they are able to destroy their enemies.[3]

"There are those," Khrushchev observes, "who don't seem to be able to get it into their heads that in the next war, the victor will be barely distinguishable from the vanquished." Thus, "a war between the Soviet Union and the United States would almost certainly end in mutual defeat."

"Can you picture what would be left after a few hydrogen bombs fell on Moscow" Khrushchev asks. "Forget about 'a few' — imagine just one. Or Washington? Or New York? Or Bonn? It staggers the mind. All the mathematical calculations made during war games, all our computers are worthless in trying to comprehend the magnitude of the destruction we would face."

Continuing in this vein, Khrushchev suggests that it is "infinitely better to prevent a war than to try to survive one. I know all about bomb shelters and command posts and emergency communications and so on. But listen here: in a single thermonuclear flash, a bunker can be turned into a burial vault for a country's leaders and military commanders."

Having outlined his case to avoid nuclear war, Khrushchev proceeds next to deal with the connection between the fear of nuclear war and state action. "I know people will say, 'Khrushchev is in a panic over the possibility of war.' [But] I am not. I've always been against war, but at the same time I've always realized full well that fear of nuclear war on the part of a country's leader can paralyze that country's defenses. And if a country's defenses are paralyzed, then war is inevitable: the enemy is sure to sense your fright and try to take advantage of it. *I've always operated on the principle that I should be clearly against war but never frightened of it...*" (Italics mine.)

2 Khrushchev's memoirs are used widely, if carefully, by scholars of Soviet affairs. The following is not atypical: "Khrushchev's account must ... be approached with great care and discretion. It is highly biased, full of inaccuracies and faulty recollections, and extremely contentious. Yet it coincides remarkably well with the accounts by Djilas and Svetlana. It should be pointed out that the memoirs of Ilya Ehrenbourg, Ivan Maisky and others confirm many of Khrushchev's characterizations, but with greater prudence and circumspection as one would suspect." See Juri Valenta *et al.*, *Soviet Decisionmaking for National Security* (London: George Allen & Unwin, 1984), p. 32.

3 Nikita Khrushchev, *Khrushchev Remembers: The Last Testament* (New York: Bantam Books, 1976), pp. 619, 561.

In another place in his memoirs Khrushchev explains what he means by not being "frightened" of war — that is, to the point of being paralyzed or deterred by this fear. "I've got no qualms about coming right out and saying we were afraid of war [during the Cuban missile crisis?]. That doesn't mean I think we should pay any price to avoid war. Certainly we shouldn't back down at the expense of our self-respect, our authority, and our prestige in the world."

Khrushchev claims that while he was head of government the Soviets were "confronted with the jealousy and aggressiveness of others toward our position, and we had to counterattack these forces." By "counterattacking when we did," the man who dominated the Soviet Union for almost ten years and held the attention of millions insists, "we won a number of significant moral victories." But these "were victories in the Cold War. We managed to avoid a hot war . . ."

If Khrushchev is to be believed here, it would seem that regardless of nuclear deterrence the Soviet Union might well fight if the Kremlin thought that its action was legitimate, or that the Soviets would lose too much face at home or abroad by backing down in a crisis. Perhaps this is why Khrushchev, among other things, appreciated Kennedy's flexibility during the Cuban missile crisis. As Khrushchev says: JFK "showed great flexibility, and together we avoided disaster."

* * *

The evidence that is available today suggests that deterrence theory, as applied to the nuclear age, is seriously deficient. For the most part, this theory has been developed in the abstract and has simply been imposed on historical circumstances. Specifically, many deterrence theorists seem to have erred in regarding deterrence as a separable, self contained phenomenon about which a useful prescriptive theory could be developed.

In applying deterrence theory, policymakers again and again have erred in several ways.

First, they have tended to take an oversimplified view of the world, particularly during the Cold War period when U.S. foreign policy came to be cast in terms of a struggle of good versus evil.

Second, American policymakers erred in relying too heavily on vaguely constructed nuclear deterrence strategies in situations more suited to conventional approaches.

Third, they made insufficient use of other means of influencing and controlling the potential for conflict in their relations with other states, such as classical diplomacy.

About midway through the nuclear age, the argument in support of deterrence was seriously modified. In view of the experience in Korea and other places around the world, many proponents now claimed that nuclear weapons were never meant to deter non-nuclear attacks; they were just supposed to prevent nuclear aggression. The result was near-catastrophe, as our study of the Cuban missile crisis has shown.

Not only did the Soviet deployment of missiles to Cuba represent a major failure of the U.S. deterrent policy, but during the crisis itself "nuclear deterrence" left a lot to be desired.[4] We came very close to the brink of disaster in 1962. Moscow's missile gambit pressed the United States to the point where, justifiably or not, the next steps could well have led inevitably to global war.

In this sense, despite his irresponsible and misguided action to install nuclear weapons in Cuba, Khrushchev must be thanked for his decision not to "doom the world" by escalating the conflict once the missile sites had been detected and President Kennedy had taken a stand. And JFK should be thanked for his willingness to compromise and his attempt to provide the Soviet leader with a face-saving way out of the confrontation.

All of this is not to say that nuclear deterrence is *never* decisive in conflict. The evidence at hand is not sufficient to warrant such a sweeping conclusion. And this is where this investigator differs most clearly from Professor A.F.K. Organski.[5] However, these findings do suggest that not only is the theory of deterrence in the nuclear age deficient, but its application over the years has contributed to a very dangerous international situation. Leaders of nations menaced by nuclear retaliation may indeed be fearful — even terrified, — but the body of evidence collected so far does not show that they have acquired the necessary respect that would prevent them from doing battle with each other, even though the conventional wisdom of nuclear deterrence assumes that they have been made inviolable by their possession of nuclear arms.

---

4 Ambassador Martin Hillenbrand disagrees. "Your conclusion that nuclear deterrence did not operate in the Cuban Missile Crisis is simply not compatible with the experience of those who participated in it . . . The reality that other factors are also operating to resolve a crisis doesn't mean deterrence is not operative as well and influencing willingness to those factors. . . . Deterrence policy does not mean you can achieve all your foreign policy and military goals simply because your deterrent is credible. Deterrence fails only if a nuclear war begins; it succeeds if a nuclear war is avoided . . ." Letter, June 1, 1984.

5 This statement may not be fair to Professor Organski, who has changed his mind about some crises over the years. In his early work he stated: "Nuclear weapons, then, do not operate as deterrents . . ." See his text on *World Politics* (New York: Knopf, 1958), p. 329. In his later very valuable study which coded crises, he was less categorical. See *The War Ledger* (Chicago: University of Chicago Press, 1980).

Traditional belief teaches that more weapons buy more security. But since the advent of nuclear weapons and the acquisition of a capacity for "overkill," the nuclear arsenals of the two superpowers have not enhanced national security. In fact, they have contributed to the decline in national and global security. The strategic insecurity of one adversary almost always means strategic insecurity for the other. Conventional pre-1945 wisdom aside, deterrence is not an adequate policy in an age of apocalyptic weapons.

At a time when there is much loose talk about war fighting strategies and nuclear deterrence, it is of utmost importance for U.S. policymakers to estimate correctly the reaction of an adversary in the escalation of any conflict. Here it is imperative for decision-makers to realize that although one can perhaps argue in the abstract that the fear of nuclear war ought to deter the leadership of a state from taking the chances it does, in fact nuclear deterrence is often not decisive.

A number of factors usually go into the making of foreign policy decisions. In the case of a decision to attack, the situation is particularly complex. But responsiveness to the manipulation of the nuclear threat by an adversary does not seem to be crucial, as previously assumed. Actually, nuclear deterrence theory tends to project as common a situation that appears rarely to exist.

In short, theory of this sort is hardly good avice to policymakers on how to confront the political reality in which they normally operate. The consequences could well be tragic if American leaders ever acted in a major crisis with the Soviet Union on the assumption that fear of nuclear war alone is decisive in determining the outcome. Failure to recognize this essential point could lead very quickly to the very war we all seek to avoid.[6]

---

6 Ambassador Hillenbrand sees the problem differently. "The problem is that rationality may not prevail in the long run. Human error, emotion and miscalculation may take over, with potentially disastrous results. Even if it is working today, deterrence may not always be effective. We need a more realistic and morally acceptable policy than one which simply relies on old slogans." Letter to this writer, May 30, 1984.

SECTION V
APPENDICES

Appendix I

Letter by Dean Rusk on the Korean War[1]

"I suppose one would have to say that nuclear weapons as a deterrent only really applies to the deterrence of a nuclear strike by someone else. Nuclear weapons do not, in the ordinary sense, deter the use of conventional weapons in lesser conflicts in various parts of the world. Nor do nuclear weapons translate into political influence in such capitals as Rangoon, Montevideo or Ouagadougou because they know that we are not going to use nuclear weapons against them. The only conventional attack which might be deterred by nuclear weapons would be a major Warsaw Pact onslaught against Western Europe.

"In any event, something has deterred the use of nuclear weapons. No such weapon has been fired in anger since Nagasaki despite many serious crises since 1945. We have had more than 400 situations of violence somewhere in the world since World War II, so one cannot say that nuclear weapons deter the use of force around the edges of the East-West relationship.

"I had the impression that your use of Korea as an example of the failure of deterrence was somewhat imcomplete. After all, Soviet nuclear weapons did not deter the United States from assisting South Korea with conventional forces even though the North Koreans were completely denied their original purpose, namely, the seizure of South Korea.[2] Something deterred North Korea, China or the Soviet Union from any bombing attacks against Japan. During the Korean War Japan was a major base for our operations

---

1 This Epilogue is taken from a personal letter from former Secretary of State Dean Rusk to this writer, dated May 22, 1984.
2 It should be noted here that the Soviet Union exploded its first experimental atom bomb in the fall of 1949, but it took some time before the Soviets would acquire a stock of the weapons and adequate means of delivery. However, at the time of the Korean War, U.S. officials, operating on a "worst-case" basis, did have to take into account the possibility that the Soviets might already have atomic weapons and a delivery capability, no matter how primitive. As David A. Rosenberg writes, "Although the JCS and the Department of Defense initiated some preparations to counter Soviet atomic capability in October and November 1949, no immediate revision of offensive war plans was undertaken." Rosenberg, "American Atomic Strategy and the Hydrogen Bomb Decision," *Journal of American History* (June, 1979), p. 80.

in Korea but a few conventional bombs dropped on Tokyo could have made a major difference in that situation.

"It was my duty as Secretary of State (1961-1969) to go through the exercise of looking fully at the total effects of a full nuclear war, both direct and indirect. That was a sobering experience and resulted in a deep respect for the consequences of nuclear war — I would not call it 'fear.'

"Since you went back to Pascal, perhaps you would like to go further back and look at Sun Tzu's *The Art of War,* dated several hundred years before the time of Christ. During World War II we were both frustrated and amused because we could not get Chinese forces in Burma completely to surround a Japanese unit. They told us that their ancient military doctrine thought that if you completely surround an enemy he will fight too hard. This ancient Chinese notion takes on new and special meaning in a nuclear age. We are not going to have a nuclear war because some nuclear government sits down and makes a calm, deliberate decision to start one — they all know that that is mutual suicide. We might have a nuclear war if a man or group of men and women find themselves driven into a corner from which they see no escape, where they lose all sense of stake in the future, and elect to play the role of Samson and pull the temple down around themselves and everyone else at the same time. It is for this reason that President Kennedy went to such pains to try to not drive Mr. Khrushchev into that kind of corner during the Cuban missile crisis."

Dean Rusk
School of Law
The University of Georgia
Athens, Georgia

Appendix II

New Documents on U.S. Nuclear Policy in the Korean War

On June 7, 1984, the U.S. Department of State issued an historical volume on relations with Korea in 1952-54. This volume, in two books, is a source of primary material on U.S. foreign policy. It contains hundreds of important papers, many of them originally classified "top secret." These documents include discussions of the possible use of American atomic weapons against North Korea and China. *Excerpts* from some of the most important discussions on their use are printed below.

Those U.S. policymakers involved in the discussions on the use of nuclear weapons include General J.S. Bradley, Staff Officer, Joint Chiefs of Staff; John Foster Dulles, Secretary of State; General John E. Hull, Deputy Chief of Staff for Operations Administration, U.S. Army; Deane W. Malott, President of Cornell University, member of special advisory committee for the President; and Admiral Arthur W. Radford, Chairman of the Joint Chiefs of Staff.

Special National Security Council Meeting

March 31, 1953

The President then raised the question of the use of atomic weapons in the Korean War. Admittedly, he said, there were not many good tactical targets, but he felt it would be worth the cost if, through use of atomic weapons, we could (1) achieve a substantial victory over the Communist forces and (2) get to a line at the waist of Korea.

Other topics were raised and then Mr. Malott brought up the question of "public hysteria with respect to atomic weapons and the danger of atomic attack." Mr. Malott argues that he nevertheless believed that we ought to use a couple of atomic weapons in Korea.

The President replied that perhaps we should, but we could not blind ourselves to the effects of such a move on our allies, which would be very serious since they feel that they will be in the battleground in an atomic war between the United States and the Soviet Union. Nevertheless, the President and Secretary Dulles were in complete agreement that somehow or other the tabu which surrounds the use of atomic weapons would have to be destroyed. While Secretary Dulles admitted that in the present state of world opinion we could not use an A-bomb, we should make every effort now to dissipate this feeling.

Special Intelligence Advisory Committee Estimate

April 8, 1953

We believe that if atomic weapons were employed by U.S./U.N. forces in any of the above alternative courses of action, the Communists would recognize the employment of these weapons as indicative of Western determination to carry the Korean war to a successful conclusion. We are unable to determine whether this recognition would by itself lead the Communists to make the concessions necessary to reach an armistice. We believe the Communist reaction would be in large part determined by the extent of damage inflicted.

National Security Council Meeting

May 13, 1953

Gen. J.S. Bradley briefed the Council on the military implications of the six possible alternative courses of action in Korea. In the course of his briefing, General Bradley stated that none of the courses of action which involved operations outside of Korea could really be effectively carried out without the use of atomic weapons.

In the event that atomic weapons were used, General Hull also warned the Council that the Joint Chiefs of Staff were convinced that they must be used in considerable numbers in order to be truly effective. While there were no good strategic targets within the confines of Korea itself, the military were most anxious to make use of atomic weapons in any of the courses of action which involved operations outside of Korea. Their use would be highly advantageous from the strictly military point of view.

The President seemed not wholly satisfied with the argument that atomic weapons could not be used effectively in dislodging the Chinese from their present positions in Korea. He inquired as to whether or not a test had been made at Bikini as to the effectiveness of a penetration type of atomic weapon. Could not such weapons be used with effect on tactical targets of the Chinese Communists?

General Hull said that the test of a penetration bomb at Bikini had been abandoned, but that tests of such weapons had been made at the Nevada Proving Grounds. The effect had been as of an earthquake, but there was some doubt as to whether use of such weapons could really be justified in terms of the large-scale destruction of enemy personnel and materiel.

The President nevertheless thought it might be cheaper, dollar-wise, to use atomic weapons in Korea than to continue to use conventional weapons against the dugouts which honeycombed the hills along which the enemy forces were presently deployed. This, the President felt, was particularly true if one took into account the logistic costs of getting conventional ammunition from this country to the front lines.

National Security Council Meeting

May 20, 1953

After further discussion of various military aspects of the problem, the President summed up the views presented by the Joint Chiefs as indicating their belief that if we went over to more positive action against the enemy in Korea, it would be necessary to expand the war outside of Korea and that it would be necessary to use the atomic bomb.

The President then indicated his anxiety lest the report by the Joint Chiefs of Staff go any further than those who were in the room, and stated that a record should be made of those who had heard the military briefing.

His only real worry, said the President, was over the possibility of intervention by the Soviets. He feared the Chinese much less, since the blow would fall so swiftly and with such force as to eliminate Chinese Communist intervention.

National Security Council Meeting

Dec. 3, 1953

Admiral Radford emphasized that the role of U.S. and U.N. ground forces would largely be limited to the actual theater of war in Korea and not spread out to Manchuria or China proper. In essence, therefore, the concept of operations called initially for a massive atomic air strike which would defeat the Chinese Communists in Korea and make them incapable of aggression there or elsewhere in the Far East for a very considerable time.

The President expressed with great emphasis the opinion that if the Chinese Communists attacked us again we should certainly respond by hitting them hard and wherever it would hurt most, including Peiping itself. This, said the President, would mean all-out war against Communist China.

The President said that he wanted an answer from Admiral Radford to a simple but very serious question. Did Admiral Radford believe that we would be at war with Communist China if they once again attacked us?

Admiral Radford replied in the affirmative, and stated that we had no option but to treat the attack in this way. We would have to strike against the Communist Chinese in the air from Shanghai all the way north. The President stated that this fitted exactly into his thinking, and he could see no other way of treating a renewed Communist attack. Admiral Radford observed that he had always thought that we had been at war with Communist China ever since the intervention of the "volunteers."

Military Implications

Secretary Dulles said it was not for him to question the military implications of the courses of action recommended by the Joint Chiefs of Staff, but he felt that he could be useful in discussing the political implications of these courses of action.

It was plain to him, continued Secretary Dulles, that Admiral Radford's course of action contemplated general war with China and probably also with the Soviet Union because of the Sino-Soviet alliance. He felt there were grave disadvantages to a course of action such as this, and the State Department believed that other steps could be taken by the U.N. and U.S. forces which would be less likely to involve the Soviet Union in the war.

The State Department felt that the first of such courses of action amounted to a full atomic strike in Korea itself. The second involved the bombing of troop concentrations in and near the area of Korea.

Memorandum

By the Joint Chiefs of Staff And the State Department
To the National Security Council

Jan. 7, 1954

1. If the Communists renew hostilities in Korea in the near future, the United States military objectives should be to:
a. Destroy effective Chinese Communist military power applied to the Korea effort.
b. Reduce Chinese Communist military capability for further aggression in the Korean area.
c. Create conditions under which R.O.K. forces can assume increasing responsibility for the defense of Korea.

2. In pursuit of these objectives in the event of Communist renewal of hostilities, the following military courses of action should be undertaken:
a. Employing atomic weapons, conduct offensive air operations against military targets in Korea and against those military targets in Manchuria and China which are being used by the Communists in direct support of their operations in Korea, or which threaten the security of U.S./U.N. forces in the Korean area.

. . .

Appendix III

What can we do: McNamara's Proposals

Writing in the December 5, 1983 edition of *Newsweek*, former Secretary of Defense Robert S. McNamara outlined eighteen concrete steps that could be taken — many of them immediately — to reduce the likelihood of a nuclear conflict. While some of these steps require agreement with the Soviet Union, many could be implemented unilaterally.

McNamara has designed these proposals with the following principle in mind: "We must recognize that nuclear weapons have no military value whatsoever other than to deter one's opponent from their use." Even though this writer disagrees with the last part of that statement, he finds much in the specific content of the proposals that he can agree with provided it is recognized from the outset that this list represents a mere beginning for tackling the problems at hand in this field.

I. Negotiate a Reduction in the Ratio of Nuclear Warheads to Missile Launchers

This proposal, which McNamara says would increase the stability of deterrent forces, would reduce the temptation to launch a pre-emptive nuclear strike. The basic idea is that the more warheads to launchers each side has, assuming a given level of accuracy, the greater the possibility that if one side launched an attack first, he could destroy the other's launchers and leave them with insufficient power to inflict unacceptable reciprocal damage. Thus, under these circumstances, the Soviets, for example, "might try to launch against us first because by doing so they could reduce the damage to themselves." If each side put only one warhead on a launcher, that kind of calculus would be impossible.[1]

> McNamara is to be commended for his emphasis on stability of forces, however, tenuous this may be in reality. But this writer believes his analysis is based on a faulty premise. Namely, that the Soviets conceivably would see utility in launching a pre-emptive strike against the U.S. Assuming rationality would prevail, it is difficult to see what the Soviets might gain from such a desperate act. As McNamara himself has pointed out, the Scowcroft Commission proved there is no window of vulnerability. Even if the Soviets could destroy all land-based missiles in the U.S. — a very, very dubious proposition — we would still have our submarines and bombers (if — only in the worst case — a portion of them). These surviving forces would be enough to inflict "unacceptable damage."

II. Renounce the Strategy of Launch-on-Warning

This step would greatly reduce the danger of the U.S. responding to an attack that did not occur — either through an accident, a human or mechanical failure or a simple misunderstanding. In McNamara's view, there is nothing to the fear that if we do not launch on warning, we cannot launch at all because a significant portion of the strategic triad is invulnerable.

III. Adopt a Strategy of "No-Second-Use Until . . ."

By this step the United States would announce that "we would not retaliate against a nuclear strike until we had ascertained the source of the attack, the size of the attack and the intentions of the attacker." This strategy would apply to any strike against the West. Its value would lie in further reducing the risk that "we might be responding to something that we misjugded — an accident or an attack by a terrorist group . . ."

IV. Strengthen Command and Control Systems

This step should be taken to "ensure that under all circumstances our retaliatory capability is assured, and that we are capable of retaining control of our forces regardless of the size of an attack upon them."[2]

V. Renounce "Decapitation" Strikes

This step would involve stating publicly that the United States would "spare the enemy's command-and-control apparatus during a nuclear exchange." It would represent "an important step in reducing Soviet incentives to strike pre-emptively." Moreover, it "would preserve the ability of the Soviets to terminate a nuclear conflict, should one start."

VI. Strengthen Conventional Forces

Even in this period of fiscal austerity, McNamara says, non-nuclear forces could be strengthened substantially. "Much could be done within the presently approved military budgets of NATO." This "would permit the NATO members to substantially raise the nuclear threshold." And it would "greatly reduce the likelihood that nuclear weapons would be used in the early hours of a military confrontation in Europe."

---

2 The author would disagree with McNamara's premise. It is an illusion to think that even after strengthening C^3I systems that we would be able to retain control of our forces "regardless of the size of an attack upon them." Certain steps in this area should be taken, particularly in centralizing command and control over nuclear forces, but one must recognize the limits of what can be accomplished.

VII. Announce No-Early-First-Use Policy

Present NATO policy, McNamara states, carries the high risk that we would use nuclear weapons in the early hours of a military conflict. Therefore, we "should publicly state that a conventional attack by the Soviet Union would be met by NATO's conventional forces." Only as a last resort should nuclear weapons be used by NATO. McNamara notes that NATO Commander General Bernhard Rogers has indicated that he would be willing to consider such a policy.

VIII. Move Toward "No-First-Use" Policy

McNamara proposes here that the NATO heads of government announce that within five years, NATO's conventional forces will have been strengthened to the point where NATO will adopt a policy of "no-first-use" of nuclear weapons. He notes that more and more military and political leaders in the West are saying this publicly. For instance, Field Marshal Lord Carver, the retired Chief of the British Defense Staff, stated in 1982 that first use of nuclear weapons by NATO would be "criminally irresponsible," because it would trigger a Soviet reaction that would destroy the West. Former Defense Secretary Melvin Laird and Admiral Noel Gaylor, former Commander in Chief of U.S. forces in the Pacific, agree with Carver, McNamara points out. And General Johannes Steinhoff, the former commander of the German Luftwaffe, said under no circumstances would he recommend first use of weapons from German soil, because it would bring a devastating nuclear strike against Germany.

IX. Withdraw Half of NATO's Nuclear Warheads

After consulting with our allies, McNamara suggests, we should begin withdrawing half the some 6,000 nuclear warheads now stockpiled in Europe. This, he says, could be done immediately. For the most part, those warheads to be withdrawn consist of old, unreliable or obsolete weapons.[3]

X. Redeploy Remainder to Rear Areas

Since many tactical nuclear warheads would still be left near the East-West German border, McNamara proposes that these be redeployed along West Germany's rear areas. This would reduce their vulnerability to an

---

3 This writer would go further than McNamara here. 3,000 nuclear warheads in Western Europe still would be dangerously excessive. Alain C. Enthoven, Assistant Secretary of Defense for International Security Affairs from 1967 to 1969, has suggested as an alternative that the number of nuclear warheads in Western Europe could be reduced to 1,000. But I agree with Paul Warnke that one could safely go further than that particularly as conventional capabilities are strengthened and serious negotiations with the Soviets were persued.

enemy attack in the early hours of a conflict and reduce the temptation to use them rather than wait and thereby lose them to the advancing enemy.

XI. Negotiate Nuclear-Free Zone

Here McNamara suggests that negotiations be undertaken with the Soviets to establish a nuclear-free zone — perhaps sixty miles wide — on both sides of West Germany's eastern border. Such a move would "build confidence on both sides that pressures for early use of nuclear weapons could be controlled."

XII. Halt Development of Destabilizing Weapons

Under this proposal the United States would halt the development of destabilizing weapons systems. Affected systems include the MX and the Pershing II missiles. The MX is destabilizing because it has a very high ratio of warheads to launchers. This means it has a very high kill capability and, since it would be easy to take out, it provides incentive for a pre-emptive strike. In a similar way, the Pershing IIs are destabilizing because the Soviets believe they could be used for a "decapitation" strike. Thus, they provide a "strong temptation for the Soviets to prevent such an attack by launching a pre-emptive strike."

XIII. Negotiate a Ban on Weapons in Space

If such a ban is not negotiated, a major new arms race will start in this area. As McNamara says, we "can gain no military advantage by crossing over it. And an attempt to do so will vastly increase our defense budget..."

XIV. Introduce "Permissive Action Links"

This idea would lead to the installation of "permissive action links" in every NATO warhead. These devices — known as "PALS" — would make it "impossible for anyone to detonate the warhead without a specific electronic or mechanical input from the President." At the same time that we apply this control to American warheads "we should endeavor to obtain the agreement of the Soviets to apply similar devices to their warheads."

XV. Negotiate a Comprehensive Test Ban

The United States would be better off today if the limited-test-ban treaty of 1963 had been expanded then to a comprehensive test ban. With the appropriate safeguards for verification, the U.S. will be more secure tomorrow if such a test ban is negotiated.

XVI. Strengthen Nuclear Nonproliferation Programs

Such a step would go far to ensure more discipline among the nations of the West that export nuclear technology to states other than the existing nuclear powers. In this context, the United States and its allies and the Soviet Union should cooperate to reduce the possibility that terrorists may obtain access to nuclear weapons.

XVII. Negotiate the Establishment of a Joint U.S.-Soviet Information and Crisis-Control Center

This proposal would establish a multinational crisis-management team of highly trained civilian and military personnel with access to top military and political leaders. It would be in operation around the clock all year long. Such a watchdog group would encourage cooperation among the superpowers and would significantly reduce the temptation of third countries or terrorist groups to use nuclear weapons. The purpose of the center would be to give political leaders quick and reliable information about the size and source of any nuclear explosion.

XVIII. Announce Policy of Lesser Retaliation

McNamara agrees with the proposal made by McGeorge Bundy "that any nuclear attack be met with a retaliatory strike at a lesser level." This "lesser-response strategy would lead to a de-escalation rather than an escalation of any nuclear conflict." The damage that even "a lighter nuclear response would inflict on the Soviets — or any potential enemy — would far outweigh any benefit they could hope to gain from launching an initial attack." Besides if a nuclear war starts, "one must try to stop it."

* * * *

McNamara is realistic about the prospects his proposals have for adoption. But he is not pessimistic. "I'll lay you odds of 10 to 1 that within five years — 10 years at the most — my idea[s] will be accepted, because of the need to reduce the risk of nuclear war."

BIBLIOGRAPHY

Books

Abel, Elie. *The Missile Crisis.* New York: Bantam Books, 1966.
Albert, Stuart et al. (eds.). *On the Endings of Wars.* Port Washington, N.Y.: Kennikat Press, 1980.
Aldridge, Robert C. *First Strike! The Pentagon's Strategy for Nuclear War.* Boston: South End Press, 1983.
Allison, Graham T. *Essence of Decision.* Boston: Little, Brown & Co., 1971.
Alperovitz, Gar. *Atomic Diplomacy: Hiroshima and Potsdam.* New York: Vintage, 1967.
Ambrose, Stephen E. *Rise to Globalism: American Foreign Policy, 1938-1980.* New York: Penguin Books, 1980.
Anderton, David A. *Strategic Air Command.* New York: Charles Scribner's, 1977.
Art, Robert et al. (eds.). *The Use of Force.* Boston: Little, Brown & Co., 1971.
Ball, Desmond J. *Deja Vu: The Return to Counterforce in the Nixon Administration.* Los Angeles: California Seminar on Arms Control and Foreign Policy, 1975.
—. *Politics and Force Levels: The Strategic Missile Program of the Kennedy Administration.* Berkeley: University of California Press, 1980.
—. *Can Nuclear War be Controlled?* London: The International Institute for Strategic Studies, 1981.
Barnet, Richard J. *Real Security: Restoring American Power in a Dangerous Decade.* New York: Touchstone Books, 1981.
—. *The Alliance.* New York: Simon & Schuster, 1983.
Beard, Edmund. *Developing the ICBM.* New York: Columbia University Press, 1976.
Beres, Louis Rene. *Mimicking Sisyphus: America's Countervailing Nuclear Strategy.* Lexington, Mass.: Lexington Books, 1983.
—. *Apocalypse.* Chicago: University of Chicago Press, 1980.
Betts, Richard K. *Surprise Attack.* Washington, D.C.: Brookings, 1982.
Biedenkopf, Kurt. *Die Atomschwelle* (Raise the Nuclear Threshold).
Blackett, M.S. *Fear, War, and the Bomb.* New York: Whittlesey House, 1948.
Blechman, Barry et al. *The Soviet Military Buildup and U.S. Defense Spending.* Washington, D.C.: Brookings Institution, 1977.
Booth, Ken. *Strategy and Ethnocentrism.* London: Croom, Helm, 1973.
Boyle, Andrew. *The Fourth Man.* New York, 1979.

Bracken, Paul. *The Command and Control of Nuclear Forces.* New Haven: Yale University Press, 1983.
Brennan, D.G. and Johan J. Holst. *Ballistic Missile Defense: Two Views.* London: The International Institute for Strategic Studies, 1967.
Brewer, Thomas L. *American Foreign Policy.* Englewood Cliffs, N.J.: Prentice-Hall, 1980.
Brodie, Bernard. *The Absolute Weapon: Atomic Power and World Order.* New York: Harcourt, Brace, 1946.
—. *Strategy in the Missile Age.* Princeton: Princeton University Press, 1959.
—. et al. *From Crossbow to H-Bomb: The Evolution of Weapons and the Tactics of Warfare.* Bloomington: Indiana University Press, 1973.
Brown, Anthony C. *Dropshot: The American Plan for World War III with Russia in 1957.* New York, 1978.
Brown, Michael E. *Deterrence Failures and Deterrence Strategies.* Santa Monica: The RAND Corporation, 1977.
Brzezinski, Zbigniew. *Power and Principle: Memoirs of National Security Adviser 1977-1981.* New York: Farrar, Straus, Giroux, 1983.
Butow, Robert J.C. *Japan's Decision to Surrender.* Stanford: Stanford University Press, 1968.

Cana, James. *War in Space.* New York: Harper & Row, 1982.
Carnesale, Albert et al. *Living With Nuclear Weapons.* New York: Bantam Books, 1983.
Carter, Ashton B. et al. (eds.). *Ballistic Missile Defense.* Washington, D.C.: Brookings, 1984.
Castelli, Jim. *The Bishops and the Bomb: Waging Peace in a Nuclear Age.* New York: Doubleday, 1983.
Catudal, Honore M. *Kennedy and the Berlin Wall Crisis: A Case Study in U.S. Decision Making.* West Berlin: Berlin Verlag A. Spitz, 1980.
—. *Soviet Nuclear Strategy.* West Berlin: Berlin Verlag A. Spitz, 1985.
Chayes, Abram and Jerome B. Weisner (eds.). *ABM: An Evaluation of the Decision to Deploy an Anti-Ballistic Missile System.* New York: Harper & Row, 1969.
Christoph, James B. et al. *Cases in Comparative Politics.* 3rd ed. Boston: Little, Brown & Co., 1976.
Churchill, Winston. *The Grand Alliance.* Boston: Houghton Mifflin, 1950.
—. *The Second World War.* London: Cassell, 1950-55, Vol. 4.
Cockburn, Andrew. *The Soviet Threat: Inside the Soviet Military Machine.* New York: Random House, 1983.
Committee for the Compilation of Materials on Damage Caused by the Atomic Bombs in Hiroshima and Nagasaki. *The Physical, Medical, and Social Effects of the Atomic Bombings.* New York: Basic Books, 1981.

Daniel, Donald C. et al. (eds.). *Strategic Military Deception.* New York: Pergamon Press, 1982.

Davis, Jacquelyn K. et al. *Soviet Theater Strategy: Implications for NATO.* Washington, D.C.: United States Strategic Institute, 1978.

Davis, Lynn E. *Limited Nuclear Options: Deterrence and the New American Doctrine.* London: The International Institute for Strategic Studies, 1975-76.

Deitchman, Seymour J. *New Technology and Military Power.* Boulder: Westview Press, 1979.

Dellums, Ronald V. *Defense Sense: The Search for a Rational Military Policy.* Cambridge: Ballinger, 1983.

Dinerstein, Herbert. *War and the Soviet Union: Nuclear Weapons and the Revolution in Soviet Military and Political Thinking.* New York: Praeger, 1959.

—. Leon Goure and Thomas Wolfe. *Soviet Military Strategy.* Rand edition. Santa Monica, Calif.: Rand Corporation, 1963.

—. *The Making Of A Missile Crisis: October 1962.* Baltimore: Johns Hopkins University Press, 1976.

Donovan, Robert J. *Eisenhower: The Inside Story.* New York: Harper, 1956.

Douglas, Joseph D. Jr. *Soviet Military Strategy in Europe.* New York: Pergamon Press, 1980.

Dyson, Freeman. *Weapons and Hope.* New York: Harper & Row, 1984.

Eisenhower, Dwight D. *Mandate for Change 1953-1956.* New York: Doubleday, 1963.

Enthoven, Alain C. et al. *How Much is Enough? Shaping the Defense Program 1961-1969.* New York: Harper & Row, 1971.

Erickson, John (ed.). *The Military-Technical Revolution: Its Impact on Strategy and Foreign Policy.* New York: Institute for the Study of the USSR, 1966.

Falk, Richard and Robert Jay Lifton. *Indefensible Weapons: The Political and Psychological Case Against Nuclearism.* New York: Basic Books, 1982.

Fallows, James. *National Defense.* New York: Random House, 1981.

Feis, Herbet. *The Atomic Bomb and the End of World War II.* Princeton: Princeton University Press, 1966.

Ferrell, Robert E. (ed.). *The Eisenhower Diaries.* New York: Norton, 1981.

Fisher, Roger (ed.). *International Conflict and Behavioral Science.* New York: Basic Books, 1964.

Fleming, D.F. *The Cold War and Its Origins.* 2 Vols. Garden City, N.Y.: Doubleday, 1961.

Frank, Jerome. *Sanity and Survival: Psychological Aspects of War and Peace.* New York: Random House, 1967.

Freedman, Lawrence. *The Evolution of Nuclear Strategy.* New York: St. Martin's Press, 1983.

Fulbright, J. William. *Old Myths and New Realities.* New York: Vintage, 1964.

Gaddis, John L. *Strategies of Containment: A Critical Appraisal of Postwar American National Security Policy.* New York: Oxford University Press, 1982.

Garner, William V. *Soviet Threat Perceptions of NATO's Eurostrategic Missiles.* Totowa, N.J.: Rowman & Allanheld, 1983.

Garthoff, Raymond. *Soviet Strategy in the Nuclear Age.* New York: Praeger, 1958.

George, Alexander L., David K. Hall and William E. Simons. *The Limits of Coercive Diplomacy: Laos, Cuba, Vietnam.* Boston: Little, Brown & Co., 1971.

—. and Richard Smoke. *Deterrence in American Foreign Policy.* New York: Columbia University Press, 1974.

Ginsburgs, George et al. (eds.). *Soviet Foreign Policy Toward Western Europe.* New York: Praeger, 1981.

Giovannitti, L. et al. *The Decision to Drop the Bomb.* London: Methuen & Co., 1967.

Glennon, Michael et al. (eds.). *The Soviet Union.* Washington, D.C.: Congressional Quarterly, inc., 1982.

Glasstone, Samuel and Philip J. Dolan. *The Effects of Nuclear War.* 3rd ed. Washington, D.C.: Department of Defense, 1977.

Goure, Leon et al. *The Role of Nuclear Forces in Current Soviet Strategy.* Coral Gables: University of Miami, 1974.

—. *War Survival in Soviet Strategy: Soviet Civil Defense.* Coral Gables, Fla.: Center for Advanced International Studies, University of Miami, 1976.

Grechko, A.A. *The Armed Forces of the Soviet Union.* Moscow: Progress Publishers, 1977.

Greene, Phillip. *Deadly Logic: The Theory of Nuclear Deterrence.* Columbus: Ohio University Press, 1966.

Greenwood, Ted. *Making the MIRV: A Study of Defense Decision Making.* Cambridge: Ballinger Publishing Co., 1975.

Griffith II, Samuel B. *The Chinese People's Liberation Army.* New York: McGraw-Hill, 1967.

Griffiths, Franklin et al. (eds.). *The Danger of Nuclear War.* Toronto: University of Toronto Press, 1979.

Gromyko, Andrei. *1036 dnei Prezidente Kennedi.* Moscow, 1968. *Through Russian Eyes: President Kennedy's 1036 Days.* Translated by Philip A. Garon. Washington, D.C.: International Library, 1973.

Groves, Leslie R. *Now It Can Be Told: The Story of the Manhattan Project.* New York: Harper, 1962.

Guhin, Michael A. *John Foster Dulles.* New York: Columbia University Press, 1972.

Gulley, Bill. *Breaking Cover.* New York: Warner Books, 1980.

Haig, Alexander. *Caveat: Realism, Reagan, and Foreign Policy.* New York: Macmillan Publishing Co., 1984.
Halle, Louis J. *The Cold War as History.* New York: Harper & Row, 1967.
Hannig, Norbert. *Abschreckung durch konventionelle Waffen: Das David-Goliath Prinzip.* West Berlin: Berlin Verlag A. Spitz, 1984.
Hanrieder, Wolfram F. et al. *The Foreign Policies of West Germany, France, and Britain.* Englewood Cliffs, N.J.: Prentice-Hall, inc., 1980.
Harvard Study Group. *Living With Nuclear Weapons.* New York: Bantam Books, 1983.
Herke, Gregg. *The Winning Weapon: The Atomic Bomb in the Cold War 1945-1950.* New York: Knopf, 1981.
Hinsley, F.H. *Power and the Pursuit of Peace.* London: Cambridge University Press, 1963.
Hook, Sidney. *The Fail-Safe Fallacy.* New York: Stein & Day, 1963.
Horelick, Arnold L. and Myron Rush. *Strategic Power and Soviet Foreign Policy.* Chicago: University of Chicago Press, 1966.
Hsieh, Alice Langley. *Communist China's Strategy in the Nuclear Age.* Englewood Cliffs, N.J.: Prentice-Hall, 1962.

Janis, Irving. *Victims of Groupthink.* Boston: Houghton Mifflin, 1972.
Jentleson, Bruce W. et al. *Perspectives 1981.* Washington, D.C., 1982

Kahan, Jerome H. *Security in the Nuclear Age: Developing U.S. Strategic Arms Policy.* Washington, D.C.: The Brookings Institution, 1975.
Kahn, Herman. *On Thermonuclear War.* Princeton, N.J.: Princeton University Press, 1960.
—. *On Escalation.* New York: Praeger, 1965.
Kaplan, Fred. *The Wizards of Armageddon.* New York: Simon & Schuster, 1983.
Kaplan, Morton A. (ed.). *SALT: Problems and Prospects.* Morristown, N.J.: General Learning Press, 1973.
Karas, Thomas. *The New High Ground.*
Kaufmann, William W. (ed.). *Military Policy and National Security.* Princeton: Princeton University Press, 1956.
—. *The McNamara Strategy.* New York: Harper & Row, 1964.
Kautsky, Karl (ed.). *Die Deutschen Dokumente zum Kriegsausbruch.* Berlin, 1919.
Kegley, Charles W. et al. *American Foreign Policy: Pattern and Process.* New York: St. Martin's Press, 1979.
Kelleher, Catharine M. *Germany and the Politics of Nuclear Weapons.* New York: Columbia University Press, 1975.
Kennan, George F. *Memoirs, 1925-1950.* Boston: Little, Brown & Co., 1976.
Koenig, Louis W. *The Chief Executive.* New York: Harcourt, Brace and World, 1968.

Kennedy, Edward M. et al. *Freeze: How You Can Help Prevent Nuclear War.* New York: Bantam Books, 1982.
Kennedy, Robert. *Thirteen Days: A Memoir of the Cuban Missile Crisis.* New York: W.W. Norton & Co., 1969.
Khrushchev, Nikita. *Khrushchev Remembers.* Vol. II. Boston: Little, Brown & Co., 1970. (Several editions).
Kissinger, Henry A. *Nuclear Weapons and Foreign Policy.* Garden City, N.Y.: Doubleday, 1958.
—. *Problems of National Strategy.* New York: Praeger, 1965.
—. *American Foreign Policy.* New York: W.W. Norton & Co., 1974.
—. *White House Years.* Boston: Little, Brown & Co., 1979.
Kolko, Gabriel. *The Politics of War: The World and United States Foreign Policy.* 1943-1946. New York: Random House, 1968.
Kruger, C.H. et al. *Causes and Effects of Stratospheric Ozone Reduction: An Update.* Washington, D.C.: National Academy of Sciences, 1982.
Kulish, V.M. *Military Force and International Relations* (Moscow: Izdatel' stvo Mezhdunarodyne Otnosheniia, 1972).

LaFeber, Walter. *America, Russia and the Cold War 1945-1980.* 4th ed. New York: John Wiley and Sons, 1980.
Laird, Melvin. *A House Devided: America's Security Gap.* New York: Henry Regnery, 1962.
Lambeth, Benjamin S. *Selective Nuclear Operations and Soviet Strategy.* Santa Monica, Calif.: Rand Corporation, 1975.
—. *Selective Nuclear Options in American and Soviet Strategic Policy.* Santa Monica, Calif.: Rand Corporation, 1976.
Leaning, Jennifer et al. (eds.). *The Counterfeit Ark: Crisis Relocation for Nuclear War.* Cambridge, Mass.: Ballinger Publishing Co., 1984.
Leebaert, Derek (ed.). *Soviet Military Thinking.* London: Allen & Unwin, 1981.
Legge, Michael J. *Theater Nuclear Weapons and the NATO Strategy of Flexible Response.* Santa Monica, Calif.: Rand Corporation, 1983.
Levine, Robert. *The Arms Debate.* Cambridge: Harvard University Press, 1963.
Lifton, Robert J. *Indefensible Weapons: The Political and Psychological Case Against Nuclearism.* New York: Basic Books, 1982.
—. et al. *Living and Dying.* New York: Praeger, 1974.
Lilienthal, David E. *The Journals of David E. Lilienthal.* Vol. II. *The Atomic Years, 1945-1950.* New York: 1964.
Linday, Michael. *China and the Cold War.*
Lockwood, Jonathan S. *The Soviet View of U.S. Strategic Doctrine.* New Brunswick, N.J.: Transaction Books, 1983.

Maddox, Robert J. *The New Left and the Origins of the Cold War.* Princeton University Press, 1973.

Mandelbaum, Michael. *The Nuclear Revolution: International Politics Before and After Hiroshima*. New York: Cambridge University Press, 1981.
Manchester, William. *Nuclear War: What's In It For You*. New York: Pocket Books, 1982.
Mao Tse-tung. *Strategic Problems of China's Revolutionary War*. 1936.
—. *On the Protracted War*. 1938.
Martin, Laurence (ed.). *Strategic Thought in the Nuclear Age*. Baltimore: The Johns Hopkins University Press, 1979.
McBrien, Richard P. *Catholicism*. Vol. I. Minneapolis: Winston Press, 1980.
McNamara, R.S. *The Essence of Security*. New York: Harper & Row, 1968.
Mearsheimer, John J. *Conventional Deterrence*. Ithaca: Cornell University Press, 1983.
Mellenthin, F.W. von et al. *NATO Under Attack: Why the Western Alliance Can Fight Outnumbered and Win in Central Europe Without Nuclear Weapons*. Durham: Duke University Press, 1984.
Montross, Lynn et al. *U.S. Marine Corps Operations in Korea*. Washington, D.C.:Historical Branch, USMC, 1954-57. Vol. I.
Moreton, Edwina et al. (eds.). *Soviet Strategy Toward Western Europe*. Winchester, Mass.: Allen & Unwin, 1984.
Morgan, Patrick M. *Deterrence: A Conceptual Analysis*. Beverly Hills: Sage Publications, 1977.
Morgenthau, Hans. *Politics Among Nations*. New York: Alfred A. Knopf. 1966.

O'Donnell, Kenneth and David Powers. *"Johnny, We Hardly Knew You"*. Boston: Little, Brown & Co., 1972.
Ogden, Suzanne P. (ed.). *World Politics 84/85*. Guilford, Ct.: Dushkin Publishing Group, 1984.
O'Heffernan, Patrick (ed.). *Defense Sense: The Search for a Rational Policy*. Cambridge, Mass.: Ballinger Publishing Co., 1983.
Olive, Marsha M. et al. *Nuclear Weapons in Europe: Modernization and Limitation*. Lexington, Mass.: Lexington Books, 1983.
Organski, A.F.K. *World Politics*. New York: Alfred A. Knopf, 1968.
—. and Jacek Kugler. *The War Ledger*. Chicago: The University of Chicago Press, 1980.
Orvik, Nils and Niels J. Haagerup. *The Scandinavian Members of NATO*. Adelphi Paper No. 23. London: The International Institute for Strategic Studies, 1965.
Osgood, Robert. *Limited War: The Challenge to American Strategy*. Chicago: University of Chicago Press, 1957.
—. *NATO: The Entangling Alliance*. Chicago: University of Chicago Press, 1962.

Pachter, Henry M. *Collision Course: The Cuban Missile Crisis and Coexistence*. New York: Frederick A. Praeger, 1963.

Panikkar, K.M. *In Two Chinas.* London: Allen & Unwin, 1955.

Paterson, Thomas G. *Soviet American Confrontation.* Baltimore: Johns Hopkins Press, 1973.

Payne, James L. *The American Threat: The Fear of War as an Instrument of Foreign Policy.* Chicago: Markham Publishing Co., 1970.

Penkovskiy, Oleg. *The Penkovskiy Papers.* New York: Doubleday, 1965.

Pennock, J. Roland et al. (eds.). *Nomos.* Vol. 14: *Coercion.* Chicago: Aldine Atherton, 1972.

Pierre, Andrew J. (ed.). *Nuclear Weapons in Europe.* New York: Council on Foreign Relations, 1984.

Pope, Ronald R. (ed.). *Soviet Views on the Cuban Missile Crisis: Myth and Reality in Foreign Policy Analysis.* Lanham, Md.: University Press of America, 1982.

Power, Thomas S. *Design for Survival.* New York: Coward-McCann, 1964.

Powers, Francis Gary. *Operation Overflight.* New York: Holt, Rinehart & Winston, 1970.

Pringle, Peter et al. *SIOP: The Secret U.S. Plan for Nuclear War.* New York: W.W. Norton, 1983.

—. and William Arkin. *SIOP: The Secret U.S. Plan for Nuclear War.* New York: W.W. Norton, 1984.

Rees, David. *Korea.*

Reischauer, Edwin O. *The United States and Japan.* Cambridge: Harvard University Press, 1957.

Riker, William H. and Peter C. Ordeshook. *An Introduction to Positive Political Theory.* Englewood Cliffs, N.J.: Prentice-Hall, 1973.

Rivlin, Alice et al. *Economic Choices 1984.* Washington, D.C.: Brookings Institution, 1984.

Rosenfeld, Stephen S. "Testing the Hard Line." *Foreign Affairs: America and the World.* New York: Pergamon Press, 1983.

Russett, Bruce M. *The Prisoners of Insecurity.* San Francisco, 1983.

—. and Harvey Starr. *World Politics: The Menu for Choice.* San Francisco: W.H. Freeman & Co., 1981.

Schall, James V. (ed.). *Out of Justice, Peace; Winning the Peace.* San Francisco: Ignatius Press, 1984.

Scheer, Robert. *With Enough Shovels: Reagan, Bush and Nuclear War.* New York: Random House, 1982.

Schell, Jonathan. *The Fate of the Earth.* New York: Knopf, 1982.

Schelling, Thomas C. *Strategy of Conflict.* New York: Oxford University Press, 1963.

—. *Arms and Influence.* New Haven: Yale University Press, 1966.

Schillin, Warner et al. (eds.). *Strategy, Politics, and Defense Budgets.* New York: Columbia University Press, 1962.

Schlesinger Jr., Arthur M. *A Thousand Days: John F. Kennedy in the White House.* Boston: Houghton Mifflin, 1965.

—. *Robert Kennedy and His Time.* New York: Ballantine Books, 1978.
Schmidt, Helmut. *Defense or Retaliation?* New York: Praeger, 1962.
Schwartz, David N. *NATO's Nuclear Dilemmas.* Washington, D.C.: The Brookings Institution, 1983.
Schwarz, Morton. *Soviet Perception of the United States.* Los Angeles: University of California Press, 1978.
—. *Soviet Perceptions of the United States.* Berkeley: University of California Press, 1978.
Scoville, Herbert. *MX: Prescription for Disaster.* Cambridge: MIT Press, 1981.
Sherwin, Martin J. *A World Destroyed: The Atomic Bomb and the Atlantic Alliance.* New York: Vintage Books, 1979.
Singer, J. David. *Deterrence, Arms Control and Disarmament.* Columbus: Ohio State University Press, 1962.
Sivachev, Nikolai V. and Nikolai N. Yakovlev. *Russia and the United States: U.S.-Soviet Relations from the Soviet Point of View.* Chicago, 1979.
Smoke, Richard. *National Security and the Nuclear Dilemma.* Reading, Ma.: Addison-Wesley Publishing Co., 1984.
Snyder, Glenn H. et al. *Deterrence and Defense: Toward a Theory of National Security.* Princeton, N.J.: Princeton University Press, 1961.
Snyder, Jack L. *The Soviet Strategic Culture: Implications for Limited Nuclear Options.* Santa Monica, Calif.: Rand Corporation, 1977.
Sorensen, Theodore. *Kennedy.* New York: Bantam Books, 1966.
Spaeth, Robert L. *No Easy Answers: Christians Debate Nuclear Arms.* Minneapolis: Winston Press, 1983.
Spanier, John. *Games Nations Play: Analyzing International Politics.* 4th ed. New York: Holt, Rinehart and Winston, 1981.
—. *American Foreign Policy Since World War II.* 9th ed. New York: Holt, Rinehart and Winston, 1983.
Speed, Roger D. *Strategic Deterrence in the 1980s.* Palo Alto, Calif.: Hoover Institution Press, 1979.
Speier, Hans. *German Rearmament and Atomic War.* Evanston, Ill.: Row, Peterson & Co., 1957.
Stahl, Walter (ed.). *The Politics of Postwar Germany.* New York: Praeger, 1963.
Stalin, Josef V. *Works* (in Russian). Stanford: 1967. Vol. III.
Steel, Ronald, *Pax Americana.* New York: Viking, 1967.
Steinbruner, John D. et al. (eds.). *Alliance Security: NATO and the No-First-Use Question.* Washington, D.C.: Brookings, 1983.
Stimson, Henry L. and McGeorge Bundy. *On Active Service in Peace and War.* London: Hutchinson, 1948.
Stoessinger, John G. *Crusaders and Pragmatists: Movers of Modern American Foreign Policy.* New York: W.W. Norton & Co., 1979.
—. *Why Nations Go To War.* 3rd ed. New York: St. Martin's Press, 1982.
Stone, I.F. *In a Time of Torment.* New York: 1968.

Suvorov, Viktor. *Inside the Soviet Army.* London: Hamish Hamilton, 1982.

Tatu, Michael. *Power in the Kremlin: From Khrushchev to Kosygin.* New York: 1967.
Trewhitt, Henry L. *McNamara: His Ordeal in the Pentagon.* New York: Harper & Row, 1971.
Triska, Jan and David Finley. *Soviet Foreign Policy.*
Truman, Harry S. *Memoirs.* New York: Doubleday, 1955. Vol. II.
Tsipis, Kosta. *Arsenal: Understanding Weapons in the Nuclear Age.* New York: Simon & Schuster, 1983.
Tsou, Tang. *America's Failure in China, 1941-1950.* Chicago: University of Chicago Press, 1963.
Tuchman, Barbara. *The Guns of August.* New York: Macmillan, 1962.
Tucker, Robert C. *The Soviet Political Mind: Studies in Stalinism and Post Stalin Change.* New York: W.W. Norton & Co., 1971.

Ulam, Adam. *Expansion and Coexistence: Soviet Foreign Policy 1917-1973.* New York: Praeger, 1974.
—. *The Rivals: America and Russia Since World War II.* New York: Penguin Books, 1980.

Vance, Cyrus. *Hard Choice: Critical Years in American Foreign Policy.* New York: Simon & Schuster, 1983.
Vandenberg Jr., Arthur H. (ed.). *The Private Papers of Senator Vandenberg.* Boston: 1952.

Weston, Burns H. (ed.). *Toward Nuclear Disarmament and Global Security: A Search for Alternatives.* Boulder, Colo.: Westview Press, 1984.
Westmoreland, William C. *A Soldier Reports.* New York: Doubleday, 1976.
Whaley, Barton. *Codeword Barbarossa.* Cambridge, Mass.: MIT Press, 1973.
Whetten, Lawrence L. (ed.). *The Future of Soviet Military Power.* New York: Crane, Russak & Co., 1976.
Whiting, Allen S. *China Crosses the Yalu.* Stanford: Stanford University Press, 1960.
—. *China Crosses the Yalu: The Decision to Enter the Korean War.* Santa Monica: The RAND Corporation, 1960.
Wieseltier, Leon. *Nuclear War, Nuclear Peace.* New York: Holt, Rinehart & Winston, 1983.
Williams, William A. *The Tragedy of American Diplomacy.* Cleveland: World, 1959.
Wise, David and Thomas B. Ross. *The U-2 Affair.* New York: Random House, 1962.
Wolfe, Thomas W. *Soviet Power and Europe, 1945-1970.* Baltimore: Johns Hopkins Press, 1970.

—. *The Soviet Union and the Sino-Soviet Dispute.* Calif.: The RAND Corporation, 1965.

Wong-Fraser, Agatha S.Y. *Symmetry and Selectivity in U.S. Defense Policy: A Grand Design or a Major Mistake?* Lanhan, Md.: University Press of America, 1983.

Wormser, Michael. *U.S. Defense Policy.* 3rd ed. Washington, D.C.: Congressional Quarterly, inc., 1983.

York, Herbert F. *Race to Oblivion.* New York: Simon & Schuster, 1970.

—. *The Advisors: Oppenheimer, Teller, and the Superbomb.* San Francisco: 1976.

Young, Oran R. *The Politics of Force: Bargaining during International Crisis.* Princeton: Princeton University Press, 1968.

Ziegler, David W. *War, Peace, and International Politics.* 2nd ed. Boston: Little, Brown & Co., 1981.

Articles

Akhromeyev, Sergei F. "Dangerous US Aspirations to Nuclear Supremacy." *Horizont* (East Germany), No. 3 (January, 1980), p. 3.

Allen, Lew. *The Bulletin of Atomic Scientists*, Vol. 40, No. 5 (May, 1984), p. 35.

Andropov, Yuri. "Interview." *Pravda*, March 27, 1983.

Barnet, Richard. "The Illusion of Security." *Foreign Policy*, No. 3 (Summer, 1973), p. 71.

Barron, John. *KGB.* New York: Reader's Digest, 1974, p. 13.

Beres, Louis René. "Nuclear Strategy and World Order: The United States Imperative." *Alternatives — A Journal of World Politics*, Vol. 8, No. 2 (Fall, 1982).

Bernstein, Barton J. "The Cuban Missile Crisis: Trading the Jupiters in Turkey?" *Political Science Quarterly*, Vol. 95, No. 1 (Spring, 1980), p. 99, pp. 102-03.

Bertram, Christoph. "The Implications of Theater Nuclear Weapons in Europe." *Foreign Affairs* (1983), pp. 305-26.

Bethe, Hans. "Interview." *The Los Angeles Times*, April 11, 1982.

Boileau, O.C. "Soviet Civil Defense Prelude to Nuclear War." *National Defense* (May-June, 1977), p. 479.

Brennan, Donald G. "Commentary." *International Security* (Winter, 1978), pp. 193-98.

Bresler, Robert J. et al. "The Bargaining Chip and SALT." *Political Science Quarterly*, Vol. 92, No. 1 (Spring, 1977), pp. 84-85.

Brodie, Bernard. "Unlimited Weapons and Limited War." *The Reporter*, Vol. II (1954), pp. 16-21.

—. "The Anatomy of Deterrence." *World Politics*, Vol. II (1959), p.173.

Bundy, McGeorge. "To Cap the Volcano." *Foreign Affairs*, Vol. 48, No. 1 (October, 1969), pp. 9-10.

—. et al. "Nuclear Weapons and the Atlantic Alliance." *Foreign Affairs*, (Spring, 1982), pp. 753-68.

Burns, John. "Russians, Too, Joke Sadly on Atom-War Survival." *The New York Times*, June 11, 1982.

Burt, Richard. "The SS-20 and the Eurostrategic Balance." *The World Today* (March, 1977).

—. "New Conventional Weapons and East-West Security: Part II." *Adelphi Papers*, No. 145 (London: International Institute for Strategic Studies, 1978).

—. "The Relevance of Arms Control in the 1980s." *Daedalus* (Winter, 1981).

Caldwell, Dan. "A Research Note on the Quarantine of Cuba, October 1961." *International Studies Quarterly*, Vol. 22 (December, 1978), p. 628.

Campbell, John C. "Soviet-American Relations: Conflict and Cooperation." *Current History*, Vol. 53 (October, 1967), p. 201.

Canby, Steven and Ingemar Dorfer. "More Troops, Fewer Missiles." *Foreign Policy*, No. 53 (Winter 1983-84), p. 9.

Churchill, Winston. "Speech in the House of Commons," March 28, 1950.

Clark, William. "High Frontier." *Newsweek*, April 4, 1983.

Clarke, Duncan L. "Arms Control and Foreign Policy under Reagan." *The Bulletin of the Atomic Scientists* (November, 1981), pp. 12-19.

Cleveland, Harland. "A Boulder in the Road." *The Christian Science Monitor*, January 18, 1984.

Cohen, Eliot A. "The Long-Term Crisis." *Foreign Affairs* (Winter, 1982-83), p. 339.

Cousins, Norman. "The Third Most Powerful Man in the World." *Saturday Review*, April 17, 1976, p.4.

Dean, Jonathan. "Beyond First Use." *Foreign Policy*, No. 48 (1982), pp. 37-53.

—. "How to Lose Germany." *Foreign Policy*, No. 55 (Summer, 1984), pp. 54-72.

Deane, Michael J. "The Soviet Assessments of the 'Correlation of World Forces': Implications for American Foreign Policy." *Orbis* (Fall, 1976), pp. 625-36.

Deudney, Daniel. "Unlocking Space." *Foreign Policy*, No. 53 (Winter, 1983-84), pp. 100-01.

Ehrlich, Paul R. "Nuclear Winter." *The Minneapolis Star and Tribune*, January 21, 1984.

—. et al. "Long-Term Biological Consequences of Nuclear War." *Science*, Vol. 222 (December 23, 1983), pp. 1293-1300.

Enthoven, Alain C. "U.S. Forces in Europe: How Many Doing What." *Foreign Affairs*, Vol. 53, No. 3 (April, 1975), p. 518.

Erickson, John. "Soviet Military Capabilities in Europe." *Journal of the Royal United States Institute*, No. 120 (March, 1975), p. 66.

—. "The Chimera of Mutual Deterrence." *Strategic Review* (Spring, 1978), p. 14.

—. "The Soviet View of Deterrence: A General Survey." *Survival*, Vol. 24, No. 6 (November-December, 1982), p. 242.

Feiveson, Harold A. "The Dilemma of Theater Nuclear Weapons." *World Politics*, 23 (January, 1981), pp. 282-98.

Gallagher, Matthew P. et al. *"The Politics of Power: Soviet Decision Making for Defense.* Washington, D.C.: Institute for Defense Analysis, 1971, p. 774.

Garthoff, Raymond L. "Negotiating with the Russians: Some Lessons from SALT." *International Security*, Vol. 1, No. 4 (Spring, 1977), pp. 3-24.

—. "SALT I: An Evaluation." *World Politics* (1978), p. 22.

Gottfried, Kurt et al. "'No First Use' of Nuclear Weapons." *Scientific American*, Vol. 250, No. 3 (March, 1984), pp. 33-41.

Gray, Colin S. et al. "Victory is Possible." *Foreign Policy*, No. 39 (Summer, 1980), pp. 14-27.

—. "NATO Defense and Arms-Reduction- Proposals." *Military Review*, Vol. 63, No. 10 (October, 1983), p. 63.

—. and Keith B. Payne. "Nuclear Policy and the Defensive Transition." *Foreign Affairs*, Vol. 62, No. 4 (Spring, 1984), pp. 820-842.

Gromyko, Anatoly A. "American Theoreticians Between 'Total War' and Peace." *Voyennava mysl'*, No. 4 (April, 1969), pp. 86-92.

—. "U.S. Manipulations Leading to Cuban Missile Crisis," in *USSR International Affairs* (FBIS), September 7, 1971.

Halperin, Morton. "The Decision to Deploy the ABM: Bureaucratic and Domestic Politics in the Johnson Administration." *World Politics* (October, 1972), pp. 62 ff.

Heymont, Irving. "The NATO Nuclear Bilateral Forces." *Orbis*, Vol. 9 (Winter, 1966), pp. 1025-41.

Hillenbrand, Martin J. "NATO and Western Security in an Age of Transition." *International Security* (Fall, 1977), pp. 3-24.

Horelick, Arnold L. "The Cuban Missile Crisis: An Analysis of Soviet Calculations and Behavior." *World Politics*, Vol. 16, No. 3 (1964), pp. 363-89.

Howard, Michael. "Reassurance and Deterrence: Western Defense in the 1980s." *Foreign Affairs* (Winter, 1982-83), p. 310.

Hyland, William. "Soviet Theater Forces and Arms Control Policy." *Survival* (September-October, 1981), pp. 194-99.

Ikle, Fred C. "Can Nuclear Deterrence Last Out The Century?" *Foreign Affairs*, Vol. 51 (January, 1973), pp. 267-85.

Jacobsen, C.G. "Soviet American Policy: New Strategic Uncertainties." *Current History*, October, 1982.

Jervis, Robert. "Deterrence and Perception." *International Security*, Vol. 7 (Winter, 1982-83), pp. 3-14 and 19-30.

Joffe, Joesf. "Europe's American Pacifier." *Foreign Policy*, No. 54 (Spring, 1984), p. 71.

Kaiser, Karl et al. "Nuclear Weapons and the Preservation of Peace." *Foreign Affairs*, Vol. 60, No. 5 (Summer, 1982), pp. 1157-70.

Kaku, Michio. "Wasting Space: Countdown to a First Strike." *The Progressive*, June 22, 1983.

Kaufmann, William W. "The Crisis in Military Affairs." *World Politics*, Vol. 10, pp. 579-603.

Keeny Jr., Spurgeon M. and Wolfgang K.H. Panofsky. "MAD Versus NUTS." *Foreign Affairs* (Winter, 1981-82), pp. 291-92.

Kelleher, Catherine M. "The Present as Prologue: Europe and Theatre Nuclear Modernization." *International Security*, Vol. 5 (Spring, 1981), p. 153.

Kennedy, Robert. "Soviet Theater Nuclear Forces." *Air Force*, March 1981, p. 78.

Kincade, William H. "Over the Technological Horizon." *Daedalus*, No. 110 (Winter, 1981), p. 110.

Kissinger, Henry A. "Strategy and the Atlantic Alliance." *Survival*, Vol. 24 (1982), p. 195.

—. "Arms Control and Europe's Nuclear Shield." *The Wall Street Journal*, January 31, 1984.

Kolkowicz, Roman. "U.S. and Soviet Approaches to Military Strategy: Theory vs Experience." *Orbis* (Summer, 1981), pp. 320-21.

Knorr, Klaus. "Failures in National Intelligence Estimates: The Case of the Cuban Missiles." *World Politics* (April, 1964).

Krasner, Stephen D. "Are Bureaucracies Important? (Or Allison in Wonderland)." *Foreign Policy*, No. 7 (Summer, 1972), p. 420.

Lambeth, Benjamin. "Deterrence in the MIRV Era." *World Politics*, Vol. 24, No. 2 (January, 1972), p. 233.

—. "The Political Potential of Soviet Equivalence." *International Security* (Fall, 1979), p. 27.

Leacacos, John P. "Kissinger's Apparat." *Foreign Policy*, No. 5 (Winter, 1971-72), pp. 3-27.

Lerner, Eric J. "Electromagnetic Pulse: Potential Crippler." *IEEE Spectrum* (May, 1981), p. 42.

Long, Anne K. and Jerome H. Kahan. "The Cuban Missile Crisis: A Study of Its Strategic Context." *Political Science Quarterly*, Vol. 88, No. 4 (December, 1972), p. 582.

McCormick, Gordon H. "Surprise, Perceptions, and Military Style." *Orbis*, Vol. 26, No. 4 (Winter, 1983), p. 834.

McDougall, Walter A. "How Not to Think about Space Lasers." *National Review*, May 13, 1983.

McNamara, Robert S. "The Military Role of Nuclear Weapons: Perceptions and Misperceptions." *Foreign Affairs*, Vol. 62, No. 1 (Fall, 1983), pp. 59-80.

—. "We Do Not Need The Pershing II." *Newsweek*, December 5, 1983.

Moore, William C. "History, Vietnam, and the Concept of Deterrence." *Air University Review*, Vol. 20, No. 6 (September-October, 1969), pp. 58-63.

Nerlich, Uwe. "Western Europe's Relations with the United States." *Daedalus* (Winter, 1979), pp. 87-111.

Nitze, Paul H. "Atoms, Strategy and Policy." *Foreign Affairs*, Vol. 34, (January, 1956), pp. 187-98.

Panofsky, Wolfgang K.H. "The Mutual-Hostage Relationship Between America and Russia." *Foreign Affairs*, Vol. 52, No. 1 (October, 1973), p. 111.

Parmentola, John et al. "Particle-Beam Weapons." *Scientific American*, Vol. 240, No. 4 (April, 1979), pp. 54-65.

Payne, Keith B. and Colin S. Gray. "Nuclear Policy and the Defensive Transition." *Foreign Affairs*, Vol. 62, No. 4 (Spring, 1984), p. 822.

Pipes, Richard. "Why the Soviet Union Thinks It Could Fight and Win a Nuclear War." *Commentary*, Vol. 64, No. 1 (July, 1977), p. 32.

Pollack, Jonathan D. "Chinese Attitudes Towards Nuclear Weapons, 1964-69." *China Quarterly*, No. 50 (1972), p. 269.

Powell, Ralph. "Great Powers and Atomic Bombs are 'Paper Tigers.'" *China Quarterly*, No. 23 (July-September, 1965).

Raloff, Janet. "EMP: A Sleeping Electronic Dragon." *Science News*, May 9, 1981.

Reagan, Ronald. "Speech." *The New York Times*, March 24, 1983.

Richardson, J.L. "Cold War Revisionism: A Critique." *World Politics*, July 1972, pp. 579 ff.

Robinson Jr., Clarence A. "Soviets Push for a Beam Weapon." *Aviation Week and Space Technology*, May 2, 1977, pp. 16-61.

Robinson, Thomas W. "Game Theory and Politics: Recent Soviet Views." *Studies in Soviet Thought*, Vol. 10 (1970), pp. 291-315.

Rodman, Peter W. "The Missiles of October: Twenty Years Later." *Commentary*, Vol. 74, No. 4 (July-October, 1982), pp. 39-42.

Rogers, Bernard W. "The Atlantic Alliance: Prescriptions for a Difficult Decade." *Foreign Affairs*, Vol. 60, No. 5 (Summer, 1982), pp. 1145-56.

Rosenberg, David A. "American Atomic Strategy and the Hydrogen Bomb Decision." *Journal of American History* (June, 1979), p. 65.

Rosenfield, Stephen S. "Testing the Hard Line." *Foreign Affairs (America and the World 1982)*, p. 505.

Sagan, Carl. "Comment and Correspondence." *Foreign Affairs*, Vol. 62, No. 4 (Spring, 1984), p. 1001.

Scheer, Robert. "Interview." *The Los Angeles Times*, January 16, 1982.

Schell, Jonathan. "The Abolition." *The New Yorker*, January 9, 1984.

Schilling, Warner R. "U.S. Strategic Nuclear Concepts in the 1970s." *International Security*, Vol. 6 (Fall, 1981), p. 69.

Schlesinger Jr., Arthur. "The Origins of the Cold War." *Foreign Affairs* (October, 1967), pp. 22-52.

Schmidt, Helmut. "The 1977 Alastair Buchan Lecture." *Survival*, Vol. 20, No. 1 (January-February, 1978), pp. 2-10.

Seignious II, George M. and Jonathan P. Yates. "Europe's Nuclear Superpowers." *Foreign Policy*, No. 55 (Summer, 1984), pp. 40-53.

Sherman, Michael E. "Nixon and Arms Control." *International Journal*, Vol. 24 (Spring, 1969), p. 335.

Singer, J. David. "Threat Perception and National Decision-Makers." *Journal of Conflict Resolution* (1958), pp. 90-105.

Slocombe, Walter. "The Countervailing Strategy." *International Security*, Vol. 5 (Spring, 1981), p. 21.

Sommer, Theo. "Europe and the American Connection." *Foreign Affairs*, Vol. 58, No. 3 (Winter, 1980), pp. 622-636.

Steinberg, Geld. "The Ultimate Battleground Weapons in Space." *Technology Review* (October, 1981).

Steinbruner, John. "Beyond Rational Deterrence: The Struggle for New Conceptions." *World Politics* (January, 1976), pp. 223-45.

—. "Nuclear Decapitation." *Foreign Policy*, No. 45 (Winter, 1981-82), p. 16.

—. "Strategic Command and Control Vulnerabilities: Dangers and Remedies." *Orbis*, Vol. 26, No. 4 (Winter, 1983), p. 953.

Tatu, Michael. "U.S.-Soviet Relations: A Turning Point?" *Foreign Affairs (America and the World 1982)*, p. 594.

Teller, Edward. "The 'Socially Responsible' Course is Civil Defense." *The Minneapolis Star and Tribune*, January 5, 1984.

Tonelson, Alan. "Nitze's World." *Foreign Policy* (Fall, 1979), pp. 78-79.

Trofimenko, Henry A. "Counterforce: Illusion of a Panacea." *International Security*, Vol. 5 (Spring, 1981), pp. 28-49.

Tsipis, Kosta. "Laser Weapons." *Scientific American*, Vol. 245, No. 6 (December, 1981), pp. 51-57.

Tucker, Jonathan B. "Strategic Command-and-Control Vulnerabilities: Dangers and Remedies." *Orbis*, Vol. 26, No. 4 (Winter, 1983), pp. 943-45.

Turco, R.P., O.B. Toon, T.P. Ackerman, J.B. Pollack and Carl Sagan. "Nuclear Winter: Global Consequences of Multiple Nuclear Explosions." *Science*, Vol. 222, No. 4630 (December 23, 1983), pp. 1283-92.

Ullman, Richard H. "Out of the Euromissile Mire." *Foreign Policy* (Spring, 1983), p. 40.

Weinberger, Caspar. "Speech before the National Press Club." *The New York Times*, May 10, 1984.
Wells, Samuel F. "The Origins of Massive Retaliation." *Political Science Quarterly*, Vol. 96 (Spring, 1981), pp. 31-52.
Wessel, Nils H. "Soviet-America Arms Control Negotiations." *Current History* (May, 1983), p. 213.
Wettig, Gerhard. "The Soviet INF Data Critically Reviewed." *Außenpolitik*, English edition Vol. 34, No. 1 (1983), pp. 30-42.
White, Ralph K. "Images in the Context of International Conflict: Soviet Perceptions of the U.S. and the U.S.S.R." in *International Behavior*, ed. by Kelman, pp. 236-76.
Wiegele, T.C. "The Origins of the MLF Concept, 1957-1960." *Orbis* (Summer, 1968).
Wit, J.S. "American SLBM: Counterforce Options and Strategic Implications." *Survival*, Vol. 24, Nos. 4-5 (July-October, 1982), pp. 163-74.
Wohlstetter, Albert. "The Delicate Balance of Terror." *Foreign Affairs*, Vol. 37, No. 2 (January, 1959), pp. 211-34.
Yanarella, Ernest J. "'Reconstructed Logic' & 'Logic-in-use' in Decisionmaking Analysis: Graham Allison." *Policy*, Vol. 8, No. 1 (Fall, 1975), pp. 156-72.
Zuckerman, Ed. "How Would the U.S. Survive a Nuclear War?" *Esquire*, March, 1982, p. 37.

Official Publications of the United States

Atomic Energy Commission. *The Effects of Nuclear Weapons*. Washington, D.C.: U.S. Government Printing Office, 1962.
Arms Control and Disarmament Agency. *Worldwide Effects of Nuclear War ... Some Perspectives*. Washington, D.C.: 1975.
—. Office of Operations Analysis. *Critique of T.K. Jones's Computation of Soviet Fatalities*. Washington, D.C.: 1979.
Congress, Senate, Committee on Armed Services, Preparedness Investigating Subcommittee. *Status of U.S. Strategic Power*. Hearings, 90th Congress, 2nd Session. Washington, D.C.: U.S. Government Printing Office, 1968, p. 138.
Congress. *Authority to Order the Use of Nuclear Weapons*. Report Prepared for the Subcommittee on International Security, House Committee on International Security, House Committee on International Relations. Washington, D.C.: U.S. Government Printing Office, 1975.
Congressional Budget Office. *Building a 600 Ship Navy: Cost, Timing and Alternative Approaches*. Washington, D.C.: U.S. Government Printing Office, 1982.

Department of Defense. *Appropriations for 1964.* 88th Congress, 1st Session. Washington, D.C.: U.S. Government Printing Office, 1963, pt. I, p. 57.
—. Directive No. 5030.15. *Safety Studies and Reviews of Nuclear Weapons Systems.* August 8, 1974, pp. 3-4.
—. *Annual Report.* 1981.
"Dulles memorandum, June 25, 1952," Dulles Papers, Box 57, "Baldwin" folder.
"Eisenhower-Dulles conversation, Juli 20, 1954," Eisenhower Papers. Whitman File: Diary Series, Box 2.
"Eisenhower to Dulles, September 8, 1953," Eisenhower Papers. Whitman File: International Series, Box 33, "Dulles/Korea/Security/Policy."
GAO *Report to Congress: The WWMCCS — Problems in Information Resource Management,* MASAD-80-2, October 19, 1981.
General Accounting Office's *Report to Congress: The Worldwide Military Command and Control System — Major Changes Needed in Its Automated Data Processing Management and Direction,* LCD-80-22, December 14, 1979.
House Armed Services Investigating Subcommittee. *Review of Defense Worldwide Communications, Phase I,* produced on May 10, 1971. *Phase II,* published on October 12, 1972, and *Phase III,* published on February 7, 1975.
House of Representatives. Subcommittee of the Committee on Government Operations, *Failures of the North American Aerospace Defense Command's (NORAD) Attack Warning System.* Washington, D.C.: U.S. Government Printing Office, 1981.
Joint Chiefs of Staff Records, "USSR" Series (3-2-46), Section 6.
Joint Chiefs of Staff. *United States Military Posture for FY 1985.* Washington, D.C.: Pentagon, 1984, p. 25.
Kennedy Papers. NSC File, Box 313, Folder 2, "NSC Meetings, 1961, Nr. 475."
Kennedy. *Public Papers of the President: John F. Kennedy, 1962.* Washington, D.C.: U.S. Government Printing Office, 1963, pp. 813-14 (White House statement of October 27, 1962).
"Nixon's press conference, January 27, 1969," *Public Papers of the Presidents: Richard M. Nixon.* Washington, D.C.: U.S. Government Printing Office, 1969, p. 19.
Office of the Historian. *Strategic Air Command, Development of Strategic Air Command, 1946-1976* (Offutt Air Force Base, Nebr.: Strategic Air Command, 1976), pp. 58-59.
Office of Technology Assessment. *The Effects of Nuclear War.* Washington, D.C.: U.S. Government Printing Office, 1979, p. 76.
Senate. Confirmation Hearings, Committee on Foreign Relations, June 22, 23, 1981.

Soviet Publications

Arbatov, G.A. "A Step in the Interests of Peace." *SShA*, No. 11 (November, 1971).

—. "Sobytie Vazhnogo mezhdunarodnogo znacheniya" ("An Event of Important International Significance"). *SShA*, No. 8 (August, 1972), pp. 3-12.

—. "The Impasses of the Policy of Force." *Problemy Mira i Sotsializma*, No. 2 (February, 1974).

Buchkarev, L. "The Question of the Sociological Aspect of the Struggle Against the Forces of Aggression and War." *Voyennaya mysl'*, No. 9 (September, 1968), pp. 8-9.

Bunkin, F.V. et al. "Specification for Pumping X-Ray Laser with Ionizing Radiation." *Soviet Journal of Quantum Electronics* (July, 1981), pp. 971-72.

Chernenko, Konstantin. "Constantly Strengthening the Ties with the Masses." *Sovetskaja Moldaviia*, February 27, 1979, pp. 1-3, in Foreign Broadcast Information Service, *Daily Report: Soviet Union*, Supplement, March 20, 1979, p. 71.

Marxism-Leninism on War and Army. Moscow: Progress Publishers, 1972, p. 100.

INDEX

ABM (antiballistic missile system), 195, 360-91, 397-98
ABM treaty (1972), 195, 366, 368, 380, 382, 389
Abrahamson, James A., 388
accuracy of missiles, 397
Acheson, Dean, 51, 447, 472
Adenauer, Konrad, 266
Afghanistan, Soviet invasion of, 231, 286, 377
Air Force, U.S., 108, 339, 380-81, 386, 390, 433
Akhromeyev, Sergei F., 206
Aldridge, Robert C., 185
Alford, Jonathan, 30
Allen, Richard, 289, 292
Allison, Graham T., 56
Ambrose, Stephen E., 97
Amory, Robert, 115-16
Anderson, Jack, 321
Andropov, Yuri, 293-95, 301, 303, 312-13, 329, 367, 377, 404
anti-satellite weapons, 376-80, 390-91
Arbatov, G.A., 171, 191, 199, 403
Army, U.S., 361, 386, 433
Aron, Raymond, 271
assured destruction, 143, 149, 179-80
Atlas ICBM, 136
atomic bomb, 96-101, 384, 399-401, 404, 433-42, 456-59, 495-97
— few in U.S. postwar stockpile, 86-89, 99
   See also Hiroshima and Nagasaki
Attlee, Clement, 454
Ausland, John C., 30

B-1 bomber, 187, 338
Backfire bomber, 280
balance of power, 199
Ball, Desmond, 351
Ballistic Missile Early Warning System (BMEWS), 134, 327
Barnet, Richard, 127, 228
Berlin, crisis, 85, 96, 127, 133
Bethe, Hans, 171, 362
Biedenkopf, Kurt, 254
bombers,
— B-1, 186-87, 338
— B-29, 85-86, 435, 437, 439
— B-52, 102, 108, 339-41, 344
— Backfire, 280
Bracken, Paul, 305, 351
Bradley, Omar, 216
Brandt, Willy, 299
Brezhnev, Leonid, 196, 199, 205, 250, 282, 285, 291, 293, 320, 403
Britain. *See* United Kingdom
Brodie, Bernard, 55, 367, 405
Brown, Harold, 139, 164, 184, 429
Bundy, McGeorge, 247, 251, 409, 479
Burt, Richard, 289
Bush, George, 333, 355

Carter, Jimmy, 164-69, 176, 184-86, 284, 286-88, 298, 318, 331, 334, 354, 358
Carver, Lord, 247, 255, 269
Chernenko, Konstantin, 199, 313
China, People's Republic of, 90, 92, 178, 194, 227, 250, 256, 267, 283, 292, 300, 329, 362, 364, 402-03, 424, 445, 449-53, 455-59, 493

523

Christian Democratic Party (Germany), 299, 315
Churchill, Winston, 436
CIA, 115-16, 382, 424-28, 448, 467
civil defense programs, 202, 412-30
Clark, William P., 292, 300, 374
Clarke, Bruce, 30, 233
Clausen, Peter A., 378
Clay, Lucius D., 96
Cleveland, Harland, 69, 221, 240, 392, 408-11
Cline, Raymond, 30
Colby, William, 168
compellance, 196
containment, doctrine of, 83-84
correlation of forces, 198-200
counterforce, doctrine of, 146, 156, 160-61, 170, 174, 181, 187, 195-97, 204
countervailing doctrine, 184-85
Cover All, 341
crisis stability, 239, 305
cruise missiles, 205-08, 215, 237, 258, 263, 276-92, 299, 301-24, 350, 370, 388,
Cuba, 127, 464-83
Cuban missile crisis, 282, 341, 402, 463-83, 486, 489, 494
Cyprus, 245
Czechoslovakia, 304, 312, 352

Dean, Jonathan, 228, 230, 248
Defense, Department of, U.S., 90, 113, 140
De Gaulle, Charles, 118, 134
Denmark, 242
deterrence by denial, 50, 201-06, 210
deterrence by punishment, 50, 54, 201, 210
Dulles, John F., 105-08, 126, 457-59, 495
Dupuy, Trevor N., 246

Dyson, Freeman, 265, 365, 392

East Germany, 242, 304-05, 312, 352
Egypt, 243
Ehrlich, Paul, 50, 392-412
Eisenhower, Dwight D., 102-10, 121-22, 134, 346, 358, 401, 418, 455-59, 495-96
Eisenhower Administration, 114
Ellsberg, Daniel, 346
EMP (Electromagnetic Pulse), 405-07
Erhard, Ludwig, 222
Erickson, John, 189-90
European Defense Community, 259

Falk, Richard, 180, 341
Ferrell, Robert E., 358
finite deterrence, 152-55
first-strike capability, 388, 396
first use. *See* no first use
Fletcher, James C., 373
flexible response, 112-20, 125-26, 219, 239, 251
France, 133, 225-26, 250, 256, 263-64, 266, 276, 286, 291-92, 294-95, 301-04, 402
Free Democratic Party (Germany), 299
Freedman, Lawrence, 76, 434
Fulbright, William J., 64

Gaddis, John L., 120, 126, 133, 151
Galosh missile system, 366
Garthoff, Raymond L., 205-06, 283
Gaylor, Noel, 377, 409
Genscher, Hans-Dietrich, 299, 315
George, Alexander, 30, 79, 193, 474
Germany. *See* East Germany and West Germany
Gonzales, Felipe, 226

Goodpaster, Andrew, 30
graduated deterrence, 110-12
Graham, Daniel O., 369, 423
Gray, Colin, 360, 384
Great Britain. *See* United Kingdom
Grechko, A., 192
Greece, 245
Greens, 300
Grenada, 176
Gromyko, Andrei, 301, 465
Groves, Leslie, 434-35, 439

Haig, Alexander, 248-50, 288-89, 292, 357
Halle, Louis J., 107
Harriman, Averell W., 39-40, 415, 419
Hatfield, Mark, 368
Herz, John H., 30
Hesburgh, Theodore M., 29
High Level Group (HLG), 24, 285
Hillenbrand, Martin J., 29, 480
Hiroshima, 43, 49, 91, 98, 404, 434-42, 452
Honecker, Erich, 312
horizontal escalation, 174, 316
Howard, Michael, 85, 216
hydrogen bomb, 90-92, 98, 100, 401, 404, 409, 412
Hyland, William, 319, 429

Ikle, Fred C., 145, 174, 284, 288
Intermediate Nuclear Force (INF), 260, 273-322
intrawar deterrence, 183, 313
Italy, 238, 262, 264, 276, 281, 334, 402

Japan, 292, 300, 338, 433-42, 493
Johnson, Lyndon B., 63, 118, 149, 244, 302, 331, 346, 355, 361-65, 383
Joint Chiefs of Staff, U.S., 114, 189, 218, 249, 292-93, 326, 333, 336, 341, 360-62, 364, 375, 377, 399, 447, 454, 458-59
Joint Strategic Target Planning Staff, 140, 346
Jones, David, 42, 248-49
Jones, T.K., 412, 419-20, 424
Jupiter IRBM, 471-72, 478

Kahn, Herman, 60, 120, 392, 417
Kaiser, Karl, 251
Kaplan, Morton A., 367
Kaysen, Carl, 376
Keegan, George, 381-82
Keeny, Spurgeon M., 372-73
Kennan, George F., 79, 83-85, 247
Kennedy, Edward, 368, 415
Kennedy, John F., 111, 131-32, 219-20, 222, 244, 321, 330-31, 346, 363, 375, 384, 418, 465-83, 486, 494
— and "flexible response," 112-20
Kennedy, Robert, 471, 477, 480
Kennedy Administration, 234
Keyworth, George A., 374
Khrushchev, Nikita, 41, 127, 133-34, 139, 218, 375, 402-03, 452-53, 463-83, 486-88, 494
Kissinger, Henry, 38, 50, 75, 95, 108, 110-11, 122-23, 151-52, 157, 181, 198, 244, 258-63, 287, 309-10, 316, 409, 429
Kohl, Helmut, 262, 299-300, 306, 315, 369
Korean War, 85, 95, 266, 445-61, 493-97
Kosygin, A., 363, 403
Kvitsinsky, Yuri, 291, 293

Laird, Melvin, 154
Lambeth, Benjamin S., 192, 200, 470
Lance missile, 237, 276
launch under attack, 174, 206, 309
launch on warning, 206, 308-09, 347-50

laser technology, 371-74
Leber, Georg, 251
Lehman, John, 65, 176
LeMay, Curtis, 139, 338-39
Lifton, Robert J., 126, 439
Lilienthal, David, 101, 400
Long, Franklin, 375-76
Long-Range Theater Nuclear Forces (LRTNF), 278, 288, 310-11

MacArthur, Douglas, 447-48, 451, 453-55
Macmillan, Harold, 134
MAD (Mutual Assured Destruction), 144-46, 180-81, 204, 361, 370, 382
Malenkov, Georgi, 401-02
Manchester, William, 331, 393
Mao Tse-tung, 89, 451-52
Marshall, George, 436
MARV (Maneuverable Reentry Vehicle), 278
massive retaliation, 105-08, 122-23, 218-19
MBFR negotiations, 251, 260, 274, 304
McCormick, Gordon H., 62
McFarlane, Robert, 292
McGovern, George, 165
McNamara, Robert S., 30, 61, 69, 111, 149, 181, 220, 240, 247, 250, 252-54, 302, 308, 310, 361-64, 409-10, 475, 478, 482, 499-502
Mertes, Alois, 251, 262
Middle East, 178, 252
Minuteman missiles, 136
— Minuteman I, 139
— Minuteman II, 342-45
— Minuteman III, 156, 342-45,
MIRV (Multiple Independently Targetable Reentry Vehicle), 156, 280, 343, 366, 391
missile gap, 131-32
missiles, 275-92

Molotov, V.M., 437
Montgomery, Bernard, 218
Multilateral Force (MLF), 221-23
MX missile, 173, 186-87, 204, 296, 343, 382, 390

Nagasaki, 91, 98, 404, 434-42, 493
National Command Authority (NCA), 166, 326, 337, 340, 343, 355, 357, 359
National Security Council, 87
NATO, 67, 94, 114-20, 124-25, 205, 215-321, 347, 350, 369, 389, 424, 472, 476
— and 1979 dual track decision, 273-91, 347
Nehru, Jawaharlal, 458
Netherlands, 277
neutron bomb, 238, 298
Nightwatch, 330, 354
Nike missile, 102, 364
Nitze, Paul, 168, 174, 289, 291-93, 304, 319
Nixon, Richard, 41, 69, 151-52, 346, 364
Nixon Administration, 156
— and no cities strategy, 180
no first use, 233, 244
NORAD, 326-27, 340, 346
Norstad, Lauris, 118, 219
Norway, 242
Novak, Michael, 30
NSC-68, 92-95, 102
nuclear winter, 50-51
Nunn, Sam, 243

Organski, A.F., 456, 462, 482, 489
ozone depletion, 408

Packard, Vance, 154
Panofsky, Wolfgang, 372-73
particle beam weapons, 372, 381, 388
Partridge, Earl, 346
Perle, Richard, 288

Pershing missiles, 205-08, 215, 237, 258, 263, 276-92, 299, 301-24, 347, 350
Persian Gulf, 178
PGMs (Precision Guided Munitions), 243
Pierre, Andrew J., 273
Pipes, Richard, 167, 316
Podgorny, Nikolai, 403
Poland, 233
Polaris submarines, 136-37, 139, 185, 222
Poseidon submarines, 137, 156, 333-36
Potsdam Conference, 434, 436, 438
Power, Thomas, 353
Presidential Directive 59, 163-69, 184-85
Presidential Review Memorandum (PRM), 284

Radford, Arthur W., 458
Reagan, Ronald, 169, 172, 186, 293, 295, 300-01, 303, 313, 319, 331, 357, 360-91
Reagan Administration, 248, 262, 286, 288, 296, 298, 304, 314-15, 333, 343, 351, 356, 358, 407, 419-24
Rhee, Syngman, 457
Rogers, Bernard, 250, 257
Roosevelt, Franklin D., 435
Rostow, Eugene, 302
Rusk, Dean, 29, 361
— and Korean War, 493-94
Russet, Bruce M., 56, 70

Safeguard, 365, 386
Sagan, Carl, 50, 392-412
SALT, 193-94, 204-05, 284
SALT I, 157, 189, 278, 282, 364, 366-68
SALT II, 282, 284
Schell, Jonathan, 393

Schelling, Thomas C., 52, 60-61, 111, 196, 443
Schlesinger, Arthur M., 271, 466, 477, 483
Schlesinger, James, 157-59, 162, 171, 182, 184
Schmidt, Helmut, 242, 263, 284, 286, 295, 299, 315
Scowcroft, Brent, 172-73, 185
Sentinel, U.S., 364-65
Shultz, George, 262
simultaneity, 176-78
SIOP (Single Integrated Operations Plan), 140-41, 182, 336
Skybolt controversy, 221-22
Slocombe, Walter, 165
Slusser, Robert M., 30
Smith, Gerard, 247, 367, 388
Smoke, Richard, 79, 193
Snyder, Jack, 195
Social Democratic Party (Germany), 299-300, 369
Sorensen, Theodore C., 469
South Korea, 292
 See also Korean War
Soviet Union, 51, 63, 74, 266-68, 300
— and civil defense, 424-28
— and Cuban missile crisis, 464-83
— and deterrence, 51, 65-66, 266
— and INF, 273, 290-93
— and Korean War, 460
— and START talks, 273
Spaeth, Robert L., 29, 37
Spain, 226, 339
Spanier, John, 47
Sputnik, 132-33, 377
SS-4, 280-82, 290, 319
SS-5, 280-82, 290, 319
SS-20, 277, 279-84, 290-95, 300-24
SS-21, 304-05, 312, 352
SS-22, 304-05, 352
Stalin, Joseph, 81, 97, 400-01, 434, 436, 442, 446, 456

527

START negotiations, 304, 343
"Stealth" technology, 186-87, 338, 341
Steinbruner, John, 165, 353, 406
Stimson, Henry L., 435-36
Stone, Jeremy, 420
Strategic Air Command (SAC), 86, 104, 108, 134, 136, 138, 140-41, 326-27, 330, 337-42, 344, 353, 357
Strategic Bombing Survey, U.S., 433-34
Strauß, Franz Josef, 313
sufficiency, strategy of, 150-51
Switzerland, 290-91
Syria, 243

Talensky, Nikolai, 191, 210, 401
Taylor, Maxwell D., 112-13, 125
Teller, Edward, 385, 398-99, 412-13
Thatcher, Margaret, 300
Titan missile, 136, 139, 342-43
Trident II missile, 185, 333-36, 383
Trident submarines, 186, 204, 333
Trofimenko, Henry, 155, 196-97
Trudeau, Pierre, 312
Truman, Harry S., 63, 86-87, 96, 164, 445-49, 453-54
— and atomic bomb, 86-87, 434-42
Tucker, Jonathan, 353, 358
Turkey, 236, 238, 245, 281, 471, 478

U-2, 133-34
Ulam, Adam, 98, 100-01, 127, 456
United Kingdom, 133, 177, 250, 262-64, 276-78, 281-82, 291-92, 294-95, 301-02, 305, 402, 439
United Nations, 250, 377, 401, 446-47, 456 459, 467
United States, 63, 65-66, 73-74, 133

Vietnam War, 127, 221
— and deterrence failure, 68, 119, 125
Voigt, Karsten, 316, 369
Vogel, Hans-Jochen, 300

"walk-in-the-woods" agreement, 291-92, 295, 300, 319
Wallop, Malcolm, 370
Warnke, Paul C., 273, 317
Warsaw Pact, 221, 224-26, 228-30, 239, 241, 246, 249-51, 255-56, 267-70, 311-12, 316, 493
Weinberger, Caspar, 65, 169, 176, 189, 231, 247, 288-89, 293, 296, 300, 357, 369, 373-74, 387
West Germany, 241, 255-56, 262-64, 266, 276-92, 301, 309, 334, 350
— and NATO, 238, 369
Western Europe. *See* specific countries
Western European Union (WEU), 264-65
Whiting, Allen, 449
Wörner, Manfred, 315, 369
World War I, 58, 473-74
World War II, 92, 95, 115, 146, 202, 277, 433, 494
Worldwide Military Command and Control System (WWMCCS), 325-91

X-ray laser, 374

York, Herbert, 382-83

zero option plan, 290-91, 295, 298, 300-02
Zhukov, Georgi, 402
Ziegler, David, 54, 154